THE DUTCH REPUBLIC
AND THE
HISPANIC WORLD
1606–1661

JONATHAN I. ISRAEL

CLARENDON PRESS · OXFORD

Oxford University Press, Walton Street, Oxford OX2 6DP

Oxford New York Toronto
Delhi Bombay Calcutta Madras Karachi
Petaling Jaya Singapore Hong Kong Tokyo
Nairobi Dar es Salaam Cape Town
Melbourne Auckland

and associated companies in
Berlin Ibadan

Published in the United States
by Oxford University Press, New York

British Library Cataloguing in Publication Data
Israel, Jonathan I.
The Dutch Republic and the Hispanic World,
1606–1661.
1. Netherlands—History—Wars of Independence,
1556–1648   2. Netherlands—History—1648–1714
I. Title
949.2'03   DH186.5
ISBN 0–19–821998–9 (pbk)

Library of Congress Cataloging in Publication Data
Israel, Jonathan Irvine.
The Dutch Republic and the Hispanic World, 1606–1661.
Bibliography: p.
Includes index.
1. Netherlands—History—Wars of Independence, 1556–1648.
2. Netherlands—History—1649–1714.
3. Netherlands—Relations—Spain.   4. Spain—Relations—Netherlands.
5. Spain—History—House of Austria, 1516–1700.
I. Title.
DH186.5.I85   949.2'03   81–22571
AACR2
ISBN 0–19–821998–9 (pbk)

Printed in Great Britain by
The Ipswich Book Co Ltd,
Suffolk

The Dutch Republic and
the Hispanic World, 1606–1661

For Jenny and My Parents

Contents

Maps, Tables, and Graphs

Abbreviations

Archives and Manuscript Collections

ACA CA	Archivo de la Corona de Aragón, section 'Consejo de Aragón', Barcelona.
AGI	Archivo General de Indias, Seville.
AGS	Archivo General de Simancas, Valladolid.
AGS EEH	Ibid. Archivo de la antigua embajada española en La Haya.
AHN	Archivo Histórico Nacional, Madrid.
ARB SEG	Algemeen Rijksarchief (Archives Générales du Royaume), Brussels, Secrétairerie d'État et de Guerre.
ARB PEA	Ibid. Papiers d'État et de l'Audience.
ARH SG	Algemeen Rijksarchief, The Hague, Archive of the States General.
ARH WIC	Ibid. Archive of the West India Company.
AWG	Archiefdienst Westfriese Gemeenten, Hoorn, North Holland.
BL	Department of Manuscripts, British Library, London.
BNM	Biblioteca Nacional, Madrid, Sala de manuscritos.
BRB	Bibliothèque Royale, Brussels, Section des Manuscrits.
BSB cod. hisp.	Bayerische Staatsbibliothek, Munich, codex hispanicus.
GA	Gemeentearchief (City Archive). This abbreviation is followed by the name of the City concerned — Amsterdam, Leiden, Haarlem, Dordrecht, Rotterdam, Delft, Gouda, Deventer, Groningen, Utrecht, Amersfoort or Vlissingen.
GAA NA	Gemeentearchief Amsterdam, Notarial Archive.

KBH	Koninklijke Bibliotheek, The Hague, Afdeling Handschriften.
PRO SP	Public Record Office, London, State Papers.
RAZ SZ	Rijksarchief in Zeeland, Middelburg, Archive of the States of Zeeland.

Other Abbreviations

ACC	*Actas de las Cortes de Castilla.*
AEA	*Anuario de Estudios Americanos.*
At.	Admiralty College.
BMGN	*Bijdragen en Mededelingen betreffende de Geschiedenis der Nederlanden.*
BMHG	*Bijdragen en Mededelingen van het Historisch Genootschap gevestigd te Utrecht.*
BVGO	*Bijdragen voor Vaderlandsche Geschiedenis en Oudheidkunde.*
CODOIN	*Colección de documentos inéditos para la historia de España.*
DPLVB	*Dokumenten voor de geschiedenis van prijzen en lonen en Vlaanderen en Brabant.*
IISEA	*Istituto Internazionale di Storia Economica 'F. Datini' Prato Pubblicazioni, serie ii, Atti della 'Prima Settimana di Studio'* (18–24 Aprile 1969), 2 vols., (Florence, 1974).
Kn.	Knuttel.
leg.	Legajo.
Res.	Resolution.
Res. Holl	Resolution of the States of Holland.
RGP	*Rijksgeschiedkundige Publicatiën*, The Hague.
Sec. Arch.	Secretarie Archief, section of the Leiden city archive.
SG	States General.
SH	States of Holland.
SRA	*Studia Rosenthaliana.*
SZ	States of Zeeland.
TvG	*Tijdschrift voor Geschiedenis.*
vroed. res.	vroedschap resolution.

Preface

While the 'new history' of structures, long-term shifts, and socio-economic trends has not ousted the 'old history' of political and military narrative, *histoire événementielle*, from its long-established place in historical studies and, indeed, present trends suggest, is never likely to, the two spheres continue to coexist in uncomfortable, and usually almost total, isolation. This is despite the fact that the evident limitations of the quantitative approach, and of economic and demographic historical determinism generally, are nowadays quite often remarked upon.[1] It is not, after all, hard to see that political and military power, historical events in other words, have frequently determined or influenced long-term patterns of social and economic development. Equally, it has been justly observed that the lack of interest on the part of most political and diplomatic historians in what their colleagues in the socio-economic sphere are saying tends to a wholly deplorable narrowness in our understanding of political and diplomatic history. It has also on occasion been pointed out, for instance by J. P. Cooper in his introduction to the fourth volume of the *New Cambridge Modern History*, that what is really needed, if we are to succeed in making better sense of history, is a determined, systematic effort to relate structures to events, to find some mode of mixing socio-economic analysis with political narrative, in short to combine into one the two predominant approaches of late twentieth-century historiography. With this latter view I, and doubtless many others, wholeheartedly concur. And yet, as Cooper noted, such a double-barrelled approach, for whatever reason, is hardly ever attempted. Despite the increasingly widespread awareness of the shortcomings of both new and old, blending the two to obtain a richer brew nevertheless occurs only very

[1] See, e.g., Lawrence Stone, 'The Revival of Narrative', *Past and Present* 85 (Nov. 1979), 7–10, 13, 21.

rarely. Thus, while it is probably true that this present mixture of political and economic history does not conform with
any of the ways that historians habitually go about their
business, I would hope that no apology is needed, at least for
the attempt. My own conviction remains unshaken that this
particular neglected path, the analysis of political events in
the light of economic trends and vice versa, offers us what is
in fact the best prospect of progressing towards a more convincing and meaningful kind of history. How far, if at all, this
particular attempt has succeeded, however, is of course
entirely for its readers to judge.

This study is about the long second struggle between the
Dutch Republic and the Spanish empire during the years
1621-48, both in Europe and the world beyond, with the
even more protracted process of Dutch–Spanish peacemaking
which continued, almost without break, from 1606 to 1650,
and finally with the new Dutch–Spanish relationship that
developed in the years 1648-61. There can no longer be any
doubt that the Spanish crown had come to accept the principle
of Dutch political and religious independence by 1606, and
that there was never subsequently any Spanish ambition or
plan for reconquering the break-away northern Netherlands.
The question as to why, despite this, a prolonged and exhausting struggle should have taken place has, however, only
very recently been posed and awaits an answer. In the past,
apart from its naval, military, and colonial aspects, the whole
subject has languished in obscurity, a truly forgotten conflict.
Yet it is obvious that the struggle was one of the most forma-
tive and decisive influences on the political and diplomatic
history of all Europe during some five decades. It is less
obvious that the second Dutch–Spanish conflict was simultaneously a basic factor in Europe's commercial, industrial,
and even agricultural development, but the latter, I believe,
is just as true as the former. Why did the struggle take place?
What were the objectives and calculations of either side?
Why did it prove so exceedingly difficult to achieve peace
despite constant heavy pressure for this on both sides? Moreover, what was the impact of this tremendous conflict on
the combatants and on neighbouring countries? These are
the principal themes and concerns of this book.

Expressed in a nutshell, the answer to these questions is that there were strong contradictory pressures towards war and peace in both the Republic and Spain, and that these contradictory tendencies derived from political and economic circumstances intimately linked to the major problems of the Republic and Spain during the early and middle decades of the century. Prominent Spaniards at this time were deeply preoccupied with the fact of their country's economic and social decline and could not do otherwise than contemplate their relationship with the Dutch in the context of that process. Equally, Dutch politicians, and indeed the Dutch public which played a prominent role in this story, were inevitably concerned by the political and economic fragility and vulnerability of their minuscule but highly successful state, wedged precariously between Europe's great powers and possessing wealth envied by all. Far from being the 'sport of kings', fought for reasons of honour, vanity, or fear of humiliation, as one historian has recently written, the conflict was rooted in the deepest needs and aspirations of the two societies principally involved.

The three scholars who have contributed most in recent years to our knowledge of Dutch–Spanish relations in this period are J. J. Poelhekke, José Alcalá-Zamora, and Geoffrey Parker. As will be evident to the reader, I have tended to differ widely from the basic conclusions and viewpoints of all three. Moreover, here and there, I have ventured to indicate this disparity with the best grace I can muster. I do hope that these authors despite my departing substantially from their views, will accept that I have also been much stimulated by, and remain greatly appreciative of, their respective contributions.

The bulk of the research on which this book is based was carried out in the Dutch national archive (*Algemeen Rijksarchief*) in The Hague, at the Archivo General, at Simancas, at the Belgian national archive in Brussels, and at a variety of Dutch and Spanish municipal and regional archives. My debt to the many archivists and librarians who assisted me, needless to say, is vast. The financial support which made this work possible came from the Social Science Research Council, in London, and for this I am deeply grateful. I have also greatly benefited from innumerable discussions, consultations, and exchanges of correspondence with a variety of historians. My greatest debt is to Professor K. W. Swart to whose advice and encouragement, from first to last, much of any merit that this book may have is undoubtedly due. I would like also to express my gratitude to Charles Boxer, Geoffrey Parker, John Elliott, José Domínguez Ortiz, J. H. Kluiver, Franz Binder, Edgar Samuel, R. A. Stradling, and I. A. A. Thompson for information, ideas, bibliographical assistance, and, above all, constructive criticism. I would like to thank also the entire Dutch History Research Seminar of the Institute of Historical Research in London, my colleagues at University College, and, above all, my family who have generously put up with being bored by me on this subject for over six years. To my wife, who not only put up with it but actively assisted in the research at The Hague, Brussels, Simancas, and Madrid, no words would suffice to express my gratitude.

Finally, a few points regarding presentation. To save space, I have given the full titles of the published works cited once only, in the bibliography. Thus all references to printed books, pamphlets, and articles in the footnotes are given in abbreviated form, though it is intended that all the abbreviations should be readily identifiable used in conjunction with the bibliography. In general, I have preferred to employ the Dutch rather than the French names for Low Countries towns where the language actually spoken is Dutch, thus Brugge for Bruges, 's-Hertogenbosch for Bois-le-Duc, Leuven for Louvain, and so forth. As a rule, I have also employed the Dutch or Spanish form in the case of personal names except where there is an obviously established English usage, as for instance Philip III, Philip IV, and the Archduke Albert. In the interests of precision, the terms Holland and Flanders are used exclusively to refer to the provinces and never either to the Republic or to the Spanish Netherlands as a whole.

JONATHAN I. ISRAEL
University College London, November 1980

1 The Low Countries, 1621–1648

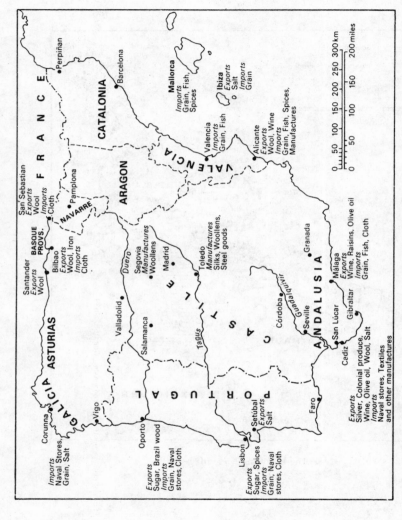

2 Spain and Portugal under Philip III and Philip IV (1600–1640), showing the main commercial and in-dustrial centres.

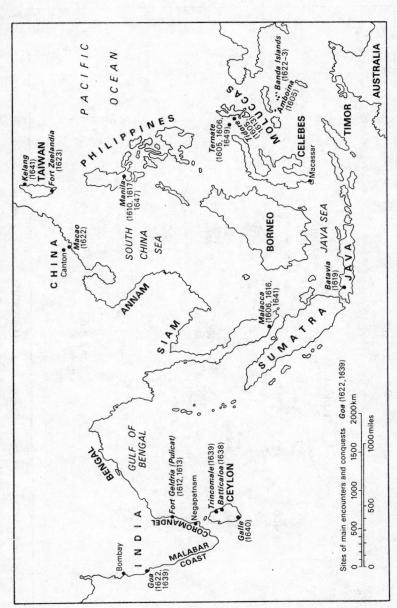

3 The Dutch–Spanish conflict in the New World (1609–1648). Sites of the main encounters and conquests are in italics.

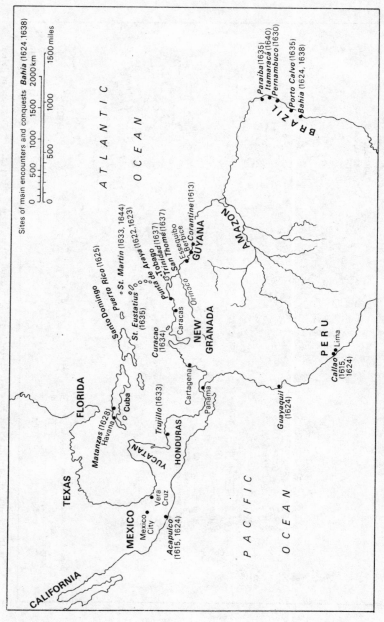

4 The Dutch–Iberian struggle in the Far East (1605–1649). Major conquests and encounters are in italics.

Chapter I

Lerma, Oldenbarnevelt, and the
Abortive Quest for Peace,
1606–1617

i TOWARDS PEACE

By the year of Philip II's death, 1598, statesmen and diplomats from London to Istanbul and from Lisbon to Stockholm, had long grown accustomed to view the long, hard, and costly struggle between the Spanish crown and its rebels in the Low Countries as a focal-point of Europe's power struggles and the Netherlands as the very heart of Europe's political, as well as financial and economic, arena. The competing monarchs of England, France, and Spain, the Sultan, Emperor, Doge, and Pope were all in their various ways absorbed in what was happening in the Low Countries. Even so, until 1598 the conflict remained of relatively limited geographical scope. Crucial for Europe, the actual fighting continued to be confined to the Netherlands alone and was thus local to one corner of Europe. The issues at stake, for all their more general significance, directly impinged only on this one area: the defiance of the Spanish Monarchy in the name of local liberties and privileges, the independence or otherwise of seven small provinces, comprising a mere 1½ million inhabitants, and the survival or not in this beleagured territory of the newly arisen Dutch Calvinist church. It was only after 1598 that the Spanish–Dutch struggle began to evolve rapidly into the first global conflict in history and the disputed issues broaden to encompass the entire world.

The new factors which thus widened the framework of the struggle, at around the turn of the seventeenth century, generated in both Spain and the Republic new pressure to end the war and, at the same time, a fresh impetus towards continuing it. Although thirty years of gruelling and costly

1

strife had taught the Spanish leadership that the rebel territory, however restricted, was also among the most defensible
and intractable of the continent and that the Dutch had
succeeded in organizing a new state of remarkable resilience
and steadily improving defences while Philip III's financial
position was gradually deteriorating, they saw also that the
winding up of Spain's other wars, with France and England,
in 1598 and 1604 respectively, enabled Spain, for the first
time since the recapture of Antwerp in 1585, to bring the
full weight of its power to bear against the Dutch. Preoccupied though they were with the financial difficulties,
they knew that the Dutch were also reeling under the cost of
the war and that they now had the best opportunity for two
decades to squeeze and weaken the Dutch, recover at least
some rebel territory, and recoup the sagging prestige of
Spanish arms. Above all, after 1598 Spanish ministers had
a much more urgent need than they had had, at any rate
since 1585, to achieve a speedy weakening of the Dutch,
owing to the sudden, unprecedented, and astounding expansion of the rebels, from that year onwards, in the Far
East, the Caribbean, and West Africa. In the vast colonial
possessions of Spain and Portugal, the latter being linked to
the Spanish crown since 1580, the Dutch had uncovered the
soft under-belly of the Spanish Monarchy and one of such
immense strategic and commercial possibilities as to promise
the rapid transformation of their minuscule, beleaguered, but
dynamic state into a world empire of great power, wealth,
and prestige. For the Republic, at the outset of the new
century, the outlook was at once distinctly more promising,
and yet simultaneously more menacing, than for very
many years.

This situation, dramatic and unpredictable, was fraught
with implications of a fundamental kind for the politics,
economies, and societies of the combatants themselves, to a
greater extent than previously for the rest of Europe and, for
the first time, for the entire globe beyond Europe. Despite,
and partly because of, the long struggle, both sectors of the
former Spanish Netherlands, the Catholic South which remained under Spanish domination, though since 1598 it
had come under the nominal rule of the Habsburg Archdukes,

Albert and Isabella, protégés of Madrid, and the breakaway officially Calvinist North, under the experienced and skilful leadership of Johan van Oldenbarnevelt, Advocate of Holland, were even more highly developed economically and militarily than the surrounding regions of Europe than they had been before 1572. By any reckoning these were wholly special territories not simply because they were the hub of Europe's commerce, shipping, and financial life or because they were the heartland of Europe's agricultural revolution or because of their leading position in the industrial sphere. Their unique networks of canals, rivers, and dykes and their dense clusters of fortifications and city-walls and defences, constructed along the most modern lines, provided a defensive, supply, and transportation infrastructure which was of unrivalled capacity and sophistication and such as the neighbouring lands of France, Britain, and Germany were largely or wholly lacking. If Philip III (1598-1621), like his father, regarded the southern Netherlands as the *place d'armes* of the Spanish Monarchy, the two Netherlands together were in a very real sense, as one contemporary described them, the 'place d'armes et escole guerrière à toute l'Europe'.[1]

In the face of the contradictory pressures impelling either side towards both war and peace, amid the utmost secrecy and with great difficulty, an intricate peace process commenced in 1606 which, after lengthy and hard negotiation, led first to the Dutch–Spanish cease-fire agreement of April 1607 and then to the complex sequence of negotiations, in which the French and English crowns played a mediatory role, and which finally resulted in the signing of the Twelve Years Truce at Antwerp in April 1609. However, the original goal, in both Madrid and The Hague, was not a truce, but a full peace. Despite the deep suspicions that either side harboured with regard to the other, the commitment to a full peace was quite strong on the part of both governments. It is true that historians have often assumed that Philip III and his principal minister, the duke of Lerma, were reluctant to countenance either peace or a truce and had to be constantly coaxed and cajoled by Albert and Isabella who, indeed, were

---

[1] Elias, 'Het oordeel', 94.

especially anxious for peace.[2] But in reality the immense step of agreeing to recognize the seven provinces as 'payses, provincias y estados libres' (free lands, provinces, and states) over which the Spanish crown had no claim, the *sine qua non* of the 1607 cease-fire and subsequent negotiations, could never have been taken in Brussels. From first to last, the initiative on the Spanish side came from Lerma.[3] In April 1606 Philip, guided by Lerma, secretly instructed Ambrogio Spinola, commander of the Spanish army of Flanders, which remained under direct royal control despite the new political arrangement at Brussels, to initiate talks with the Dutch with a view to settling the long conflict, but amid the utmost secrecy, concealing what he was doing from the international community and only after winning some further local successes against the Dutch forces which could be confidently expected that summer as a result of the prevailing military situation.[4] The Spanish intention was to strike a broad bargain with the Dutch, exchanging recognition of Dutch liberty, which Lerma now chiefly esteemed as a bargaining counter, for what he and the king most desired from them, namely complete and unconditional Dutch withdrawal from the Indies east and west, a phrase which implied the whole of Asia and the New World. The Dutch gains in the East were very recent and not yet fully secure. Why should they not be willing to barter them for a prize so hard and long fought for as their independence?

Albert had in fact on several occasions carried out peace soundings in The Hague since 1598, with the consent of Madrid, but Oldenbarnevelt, in consultation with the Stadholder, Maurits, and leading members of the States General, had always refused to respond without a prior undertaking from Spain to concede the Dutch their freedom, and this Philip and Lerma had refused to do.[5] Lerma was thus in no doubt from the outset of the new peace process, a series of soundings during 1606 beginning with the sending of Walraven van Wittenhorst from Brussels to The Hague to see

---

[2] Lefèvre, *Spinola*, 38–9; Lefèvre, 'L'intervention', 479; Trevor-Roper, 266.
[3] Bentivoglio, 528, 539.
[4] Rodríguez Villa, 124, 131.
[5] *Corresp. Alberto* ii. 27–30.

Oldenbarnevelt[6] in May as to the price that would have to be paid to secure peace. No amount of political and religious concessions short of complete independence would suffice. What determined Philip and Lerma to pay this price, with the considerable loss of prestige on the European scene that it would inevitably entail, and specifically in 1606, was the news of the major break-through achieved by the Dutch in the Far East in 1605: in that year the Dutch captured Amboina from the Portuguese and overran Ternate and Tidore, achieving virtual control of the Moluccas, the source of the most valuable spices of the East.[7] The decision to concede the Dutch their independence, referred to in Lerma's secret correspondence as the 'most difficult point' (*el punto mas dificultoso*) was, however, kept from the *Consejo de Estado* and the rest of Philip's ministers concerned with foreign affairs, and communicated to Albert and Isabella only after the resumption of talks in The Hague, again through Wittenhorst, in December 1606.[8]

The shock and indignation with which the terms of the cease-fire agreement of April 1607, negotiated by Albert and Spinola with Oldenbarnevelt, were greeted in Madrid were partly the result of the secrecy with which Lerma and the king had acted. The outcry was tinged with criticism of Lerma and the resentment of ministers who had been left in the dark.[9] But what principally threatened Lerma's position at this point, and indeed so shocked the duke and the king, was that Albert had agreed, in the king's name, to concede Dutch independence without securing anything in writing from the States General pertaining to Dutch evacuation of the Indies. In the eyes of the world, and this is what made Lerma so angry, Albert had exchanged much for virtually nothing and made it practically impossible to defend the peace policy from its outraged critics in Spain.

The reply of Albert and Spinola from Brussels to Lerma's half-pleading reprimand was that during the preliminary talks of February 1607 Oldenbarnevelt had in fact agreed to Dutch

[6] Grotius, 501–2; Meerbeeck, 1125; Kemp iii. 3; Vreede i. 145.
[7] Coolhaas, 155; Opstall, i. 5; Valentijn i. 366–7, 432, 434.
[8] *Corresp. Alberto* ii. 50, 53–4; *Corresp. Infanta*, 166, 171.
[9] Cabrera de Córdoba, 305.

withdrawal from the Indies but had refused to indicate this in the form of a written declaration prior to a mere cease-fire agreement preliminary to peace talks proper. Thus Spain's willingness to concede the Dutch their liberty had had to be affirmed seemingly without any *quid pro quo*.[10] However, the understanding was that Oldenbarnevelt would now take steps to prevent the setting up of a Dutch West India Company towards which concrete moves had been made in the States of Holland and States-General during 1606, and to dissolve the East India Company in the setting up of which, in 1602, he had been instrumental. Should the Dutch fail to keep their side of the bargain, then the king remained free to break off the talks and withhold recognition.

Oldenbarnevelt, for his part, had been left in no doubt that the price of a full peace with Spain, ensuring the permanency and security of the Republic among the states of Europe, was the sacrifice of Dutch ambitions in the Indies. Although he himself had contributed much to the early expansion of the Dutch in the East, had consistently encouraged the process and held investments in the East India Company,[11] the signs are that it was by no means a mere empty promise that he had given Albert and Spinola. He evidently believed that withdrawal from the Indies was a sacrifice well worth making for the sake of a full peace with Spain and secure, internationally recognized borders. The project to set up a Dutch West India Company which had proceeded quite far during 1606 and was strongly supported in Zeeland and at Amsterdam, was suddenly totally frozen by Oldenbarnevelt from the beginning of 1607.[12] Apparently, he was serious also about liquidating the East India Company, as his enemies within the Republic persisted in pointing out for decades after,[13] but encountered such fierce opposition

[10] *Corresp. Alberto* ii. 52; Rodríguez Villa, 156-7.
[11] Van Dillen, *Het oudste aandeelhoudersregister*, 14, 16, 18, 20; Den Tex ii. 384-406.   [12] Hoboken, 48.
[13] *Reden van dat de West-Indische Compagnie*, p. 7: 'Wij hebben noch in versche memorie dat voor ontrent 28 jaren als men metten vyandt besich was om van Trefves te tracteren onsen L. Barnevelt, om den Coning van Spangien dienst te doen, sich onderstondt d'Oost-Indische Compagnie te willen quiteren ende afdoen, maer hy siende die remonstrantien die welcke die aengaende by eenige voor-treffelycke Patriotten schrifteyck ghedaen wierden trock syne pijpen als men segdt inden Sack ende wierdt die Fluyte ofte Pijpe daer naer niet meer gehoort.'

to this that he quickly dropped the scheme, though he remained adamant that the East India Company's ambitious
plans for further expansion at Iberian expense in the East
would have to be abandoned for the sake of a settlement
with Spain.

The States General, just as convinced as the Spaniards that
it was vital to negotiate from a position of strength, and
seeing the Spaniards with the upper hand on land, had meanwhile decided, in January 1607, with the full approval of
Oldenbarnevelt, to exploit their superiority at sea and send
a powerful fleet to the Andalusian coast.[14] For the first time
the Republic was attempting to exert pressure directly on
Spain. The result, however, was further to weaken the entire
peace process. The indignation in Madrid over the cease-fire,
which at first applied only on land, was all the greater in that
the news arrived when Heemskerk, the commander of the
Dutch expeditionary fleet, was in effect blockading southwestern Spain.[15] On 25 April, after the signing of the cease-
fire but before the news reached Madrid, the Spaniards
suffered a stinging naval defeat at the battle of Gibraltar.
The outcry at this and the news from Brussels was such as
to compel Lerma and Philip to prevaricate for several months
before officially acquiescing in the cease-fire agreement. They
were also forced to go through the motions, in public, of
curbing Albert and Spinola. Diego de Ibarra, a Castilian noble
and soldier of long experience of the Low Countries, who
was one of the most outspoken critics of the cease-fire, was
dispatched to Brussels ostensibly to tighten the royal grip
over the negotiations. Ibarra typified the Castilian military
and aristocratic opposition to Lerma's policy believing that
to abandon Philip's sovereign claims over the rebel provinces
would be fundamentally detrimental to Spain's interests and
prestige (*reputación*).

But in reality the Ibarra mission was merely a stratagem on
Lerma's part to gain time. The duke had not the slightest
intention of undermining the efforts of Albert and Spinola or
of going back on his decision to concede Dutch independence,
and, to the amazement of the Spanish court, Ibarra returned

[14] Den Tex ii. 554, 567.   [15] Cabrera de Córdoba, 302, 304-5.

from Brussels after a few months with everything remaining as before in the hands of Albert and Spinola.[16] During the summer of 1607 Philip and Lerma entertained at Madrid a Hanseatic delegation financed mainly by Hamburg and these talks were used in various ways to prepare the ground for resumed negotiations with the Dutch.[17] The driving force behind Lerma's tortuous and risky policy, the factor which lent it its urgency, was the continually deteriorating position in the Indies. By 1607 the Dutch had developed a flourishing trade with the Guinea coast.[18] After their successes in the Moluccas the Dutch had launched an offensive against the key Portuguese base at Malacca. Meanwhile in the Caribbean, since 1598 the Dutch had been systematically exploiting the great salt-pan at Punta de Araya, on the coast of Venezuela, and the Zeelanders had established a network of small settlements between the estuaries of the Orinoco and Amazon in the torrid zone where neither Castilians nor Portuguese wielded more than nominal control.

The peace conference proper commenced at The Hague in February 1608. To the surprise of the Dutch, the representatives of Spain and the South Netherlands simply conceded Dutch independence at once and without any argument:[19] they offered in Philip's name to abandon his sovereign claims categorically and absolutely. The mood at the conference quickly soured, however, on 13 February, with the first session on the Indies. Jean Richardot, who together with Spinola headed the royal delegation, demanded complete evacuation by the Dutch of all the Indies. Oldenbarnevelt replied, candidly enough, that it was simply not possible politically, so intense would be the opposition, to secure agreement for such a policy in the Republic.[20] Richardot answered indignantly that the only motive which had induced Spain to countenance peace with the Republic was the king's urgent need to remove the threat to his Indies, that Dutch colonial trade concerned only a tiny élite of rich

[16] Ibid., pp. 308, 310.
[17] Ibid., p. 320; Dollinger, 351.
[18] De Jonge, *De Oorsprong*, 10–11.
[19] Meteren ix. 348; Baudius, 66–7; Den Tex ii. 602–3.
[20] Veenendaal ii. 185.

merchants, and that the interests of so few should not be permitted to obstruct so great a benefit for all, and that in any case many more Dutchmen would benefit from the revived trade with Spain than from the current traffic to the Indies. Oldenbarnevelt retorted that too many prominent personages in the Republic were involved in the East India Company for it to be disbanded and that even if this were done it would not benefit Spain, for it would simply be set up elsewhere, and while the Dutch, in return for peace, would be content to trade without seizing more territory, others would not be so readily satisfied. Here he was hinting at France. He repeated that the Dutch were ready to give up their ambitions in the Americas and halt the process of expansion in Asia, leaving either side in mutually acknowledged possession of what they then held.[21] Inevitably, this resolute rejection of what Philip and Lerma demanded as their irreducible minimum for peace spelt complete deadlock. There now followed months of fruitless and at times angry exchanges but which both the Dutch and Spanish, and the French and English delegates, did their best to prolong.[22] Finally, in August 1608 the negotiations broke down.

Yet no more than Oldenbarnevelt did Philip and Lerma wish to resume the war. Henry IV of France and James I of England, for their own reasons, likewise wanted peace in the Low Countries. On the Spanish side a key consideration was the increasingly grave financial position. Despite ending the wars with France and England, the crown's immense debts had continued to grow as a result of the heavy burden of interest payments, spreading corruption and mismanagement in high places and a trebling of the cost of the royal household since the 1590s, as well as the unavoidable increase of expenditure in the Netherlands to pay for the resumed offensive. After Spinola's advance along the eastern borders of the Republic during the summer of 1606, there was no more cash even for emergency expenditure in the Low Countries. In December 1606, when a dangerous mutiny broke out among units of the army of Flanders over arrears

---

[21] Ibid.; *Gedenkstukken* iii. 256–7.
[22] Meteren ix. 349; Den Tex ii. 595–622; Opstall i. 2–4.

of pay, Philip had been forced to cut the regular ordinary remittances from Spain to the Netherlands and, were it not for the cease-fire, would have placed the army indefinitely on a purely defensive footing.[23] As it was, the army's troop-strength was reduced with politically inadvisable haste, at the very outset of the negotiations, before anything had been settled, again simply to save money.[24] In 1607, with debts exceeding 23 million ducats, the crown had been forced, at the cost of breaking its current credit, unilaterally to re-schedule its repayments at the expense of its bankers. Besides financial pressure and his need to find a comprehensive solution to the problem of the Spanish and Portuguese Indies, Lerma also wanted to disengage in the Low Countries for internal political reasons.[25] The duke, a Valencian lacking the military expertise and outlook of his Castilian rivals, had good reason not to wish to expend the resources of the Monarchy on a struggle in the Low Countries of which he had no first-hand knowledge. To do so would have been to encourage the king to rely on advice and experience other than his own. Lerma in other words, quite apart from the pressures on him, showed a strong underlying inclination towards peace as indeed did the king himself.

When the Hague talks resumed in the autumn of 1608, the emphasis was on securing a long truce rather than a full peace. On paper Philip still offered to acknowledge Dutch independence, and the Dutch would not have agreed to the truce without this, but such a declaration in an accord which by definition was temporary was bound to be fundamentally ambiguous, the inescapable implication being that recognition would cease with the truce. Some Dutch leaders, such as François van Aerssen, the Republic's envoy at Paris, who had been prepared to support a peace agreement on the basis of a Spanish *'declaration perpétuelle de nostre souveraineté'* were strongly opposed to Oldenbarnevelt's accepting what was now proposed.[26] But even this diluted acknowledgement

---

[23] Casoni, 175-6; Elliott, *Catalans*, 187-8; Parker, *Dutch Revolt*, 238-9.
[24] BL MS Add. 14005, fo. 85ᵛ.
[25] Bentivoglio, 539; Casoni, 246; see also Th. van Rodenburg to SG, Madrid, 3 June 1612. ARH SG 4925.
[26] Barendrecht, 227.

amounted to a handsome concession on the part of Spain, and Philip and Lerma remained determined to extract some substantial *quid pro quo* for it. This time Lerma tried to barter the reduced declaration for formal toleration by the States General of Catholic religious practice within the Republic. The issue of toleration for Dutch Catholics was of course intrinsically of much less importance to the Spanish Monarchy than that of the Indies. Nevertheless, the matter was highly controversial internationally and success on this, besides placating the Pope, who was adamantly opposed to Philip's offer of peace to the Dutch heretics, would certainly have bolstered the prestige of Spain generally.

Despite strong backing for the revised Spanish offer from the French delegation led by Pierre Jeannin, Oldenbarnevelt proved as resistant to the new package as to the old. In October 1608 Philip wrote to Albert that it was his 'final, immutable resolution' that if the Dutch would concede the public practice of the Catholic religion in their territory 'only to do this service so pleasant to Our Lord will I consent to cede the sovereignty of the said provinces that belong to me . . . so that their inhabitants and subjects might enjoy it and be free.'[27] Oldenbarnevelt personally was possibly not averse to toleration for Dutch Catholics within the context of peace with Spain, having several Catholics among his own family and being of notably tolerant disposition; but again, political circumstances internally put such a step totally out of the question. Once more, the negotiations verged on collapse. Philip and Lerma, amid a mounting wave of revulsion in Spain, spent several, one imagines painful, months considering and consulting their consciences before finally consenting to what was bound to be seen at home and internationally as a humiliating setback for Spain bereft of any concession to Spanish interests.[28] The Twelve Years Truce was signed at Antwerp on the basis of Spanish acknowledgement of Dutch independence and both sides keeping what they held in the Indies east and west. Even the clause, on which the Spaniards had insisted, by which the subjects of

---

[27] Philip to Albert, 31 Oct. 1608, quoted in Rodríguez Villa, 230-1.
[28] Bentivoglio, 528, 539; Cabrera de Córdoba, 367; *Historia Malvezzi*, 122-3.

either side were excluded from entering or trading with the possessions of the other in the Indies, was so obscurely worded as to lack any real force.

Once the treaty was signed, Lerma's prime concern was to offset the loss of *reputación*, pressing on with designs which from several points of view represented a fundamentally new departure in Spanish foreign policy. Ever since 1606, and possibly before, Lerma had been preparing to engineer a major shift in the imperial ambitions, expenditure, and priorities of the Spanish crown away from northern and central Europe, away so to speak from the Habsburg connection, towards the Mediterranean and against the Islamic world. The two fundamentals of Lerma's policy in Europe after 1606 — disengagement in the Low Countries and preserving the peace with France — inevitably implied the abandonment of all schemes for advancing Spanish influence in northern Europe. In the Empire, as the Jülich–Cleves crisis of 1609-10 amply demonstrated, Spain simply could not extend its position without antagonizing France and the Republic. Throughout the sixteenth century there had persisted a constant tension in Spanish governing circles between advocates of a northern or Habsburg strategy and the proponents of orientation towards the Mediterranean. At times, such as during the early 1540s and the 1560s, Charles V and Philip II had been forced to suspend their northern ventures and concentrate against the Turks and Algerian corsairs, but only to secure their southern flank against mounting pressure, so as to be able to resume subsequently their drive in the north. By contrast, what Lerma attempted was to establish a permanent southern posture at a time when there was no significant Turkish threat but when the extension of Spanish power in the Maghreb and Levant could, in all likelihood, be achieved with less cost and effort as well as with less risk than in the north.

There was, undeniably, much logic to Lerma's thinking. The energies and aspirations of the Castilian military élite which was so vehemently against his Dutch policy had to be channelled in some direction and a resumed drive against Islam, arguably, accorded better with the underlying traditions and interests of Spain than the northern policy. If

Spain had suffered loss of prestige in the north, the Mediterranean offered abundant prospects for recouping *reputación*. The Ottoman sultan, beset with internal difficulties and locked in gruelling confrontation with the shah of Persia, was in no condition to withstand sustained pressure from Spain. Was it not shrewd politics to concentrate where gains could be made cheaply, without provoking any formidable opposition and with every prospect of arousing enthusiastic religious and national feelings among the Spanish populace? During 1607–8, as the army of Flanders was steadily reduced, Philip built up his forces in the various Castilian and Portuguese enclaves in North Africa and amassed a powerful *armada* at Gibraltar.[29] He also tightened his alliance with Muley-el-Sheikh, prince of northern Morocco and foe of his virulently anti-Spanish brother, Muley Sidan, who ruled in Marrakesh and was soon to sign a treaty with the Dutch. The first, though unsuccessful, venture, was the Spanish attempt on the Morrocan port of Larache in September 1608, made with 8,000 men and sixty-eight galleys and galleons, a display of strength which astonished those who were aware of the then wretched state of the army of Flanders.[30] Philip's decree expelling the *moriscos* from Spain, issued on the same day as the signing of the Twelve Years Truce at Antwerp, was the event which more than any other symbolized the reversal of Spanish priorities from north to south. In 1610, after extraordinarily prolonged and ostentatious preparations, the huge *armada* gathered at Gibraltar again crossed to Africa and succeeded this time in seizing Larache.[31]

To follow his expulsion of the *moriscos* and capture of Larache, Lerma planned the occupation of another Moroccan port which had been frequently used by Muslim corsairs attacking Iberian shipping, La Mámora. After several attempts this town was finally occupied in 1614. Simultaneously schemes were aired in Madrid for the occupation of Salé and still other sections of the Moroccan coast. While the Spanish

---

[29] Cabrera de Córdoba, 373, 383, 397; Israel, 'Jews of Spanish North Africa', 72–4.
[30] Cabrera de Córdoba; 345, 348.
[31] Ibid., pp. 424–5, 440, 476.

Atlantic fleet, based at Cadiz, was starved of funds and allowed to run right down, the galley fleets of Naples, Sicily, Sardinia, Valencia, and Andalusia were steadily expanded. The duke of Osuna, viceroy of Naples, and a vociferous critic of the Dutch truce, was encouraged to engage in a series of battles with Turkish fleets off the Maltese and Greek coasts. Lerma also harboured the dream of one day capturing Algiers.[32]

But effective, long-term disengagement in northern Europe necessarily required a workable and enduring solution to the Dutch–Spanish conflict and in this respect the newly signed truce was little more than a stepping-stone. The failure to induce the Dutch to disband the East India Company not only prevented a full peace in 1607-9, it virtually ensured a prompt resurgence of strife in the East. As Oldenbarnevelt must have known, his sincere desire to see the truce observed in Asian waters was scarcely more than a pious hope. In 1607, with the announcement of pending Dutch–Spanish peace talks, the Company's directors, who in any case were wholly averse to Oldenbarnevelt's policy, had agreed to mount another offensive to seize as much as possible before peace became effective. The directors had every reason to believe that the struggle in the East had now reached a decisive phase. In 1606, counter-attacking from their bases in the Philippines, a force of 3,000 Spaniards had retaken Tidore from the Dutch and established forts on neighbouring Ternate which henceforth was divided between the Dutch and Spaniards. The issue of who was to dominate the Moluccas had to be resolved and at once.[33] The Company was also anxious to weaken the hold of the Spaniards on the Philippines, partly to safeguard the neighbouring Moluccas and partly to wrest from Spain the lucrative trade in Chinese silks which at this time was routed via Manila to Mexico. As it was agreed in the treaty that in the East the truce should come into effect only a year after its inception in Europe, the war in Asia continued until 1610. The Dutch sent out powerful reinforcements. In 1609-10 Tidore was blockaded and

---

[32] De Groot, 61-5; Brightwell, 'Spanish Origins', 425-31.
[33] Meilink-Roelofsz, 183; Opstall i. 5-6, 157, 186-8.

its supply route from the Philippines cut off. On Ternate the Spaniards strove to secure at least part of the trade in cloves, but the Dutch poured in larger forces and steadily extended their control over the interior.[34] In April 1610 five Dutch warships, which for several months had been raiding shipping and harbours in the Philippines, were defeated in Manila Bay, with the loss of several ships and 170 killed, by eight Spanish galleons under Juan de Silva.[35]

While the issue of the East Indies remained unsettled and there were bloody clashes after 1609 on the coast of West Africa, where either side accused the other of violating the truce,[36] the accord also left unresolved a number of points in the Low Countries. In September 1609 a delegation from Brussels, headed by Balthasar de Robiano, arrived in The Hague to try to resolve these remaining matters.[37] In the first place, there were several disputes over border demarcation. Spanish troops had remained in control of Twenthe, the eastern part of Overijssel which Spinola had overrun in the last phase of the war, but the States General absolutely refused to recognize the Archdukes' authority in the area.[38] Neither would either side budge over the disputed Cuyk district which in the view of the States General pertained to the jurisdiction of Grave. Secondly, the Brussels delegation pressed for the lifting of the Schelde restrictions maintained by the States General on maritime traffic sailing to and from Antwerp since the early days of the Revolt, an issue of great importance, especially with regard to commerce, but over which there had been total deadlock during the truce talks. On this question neither France nor England was sympathetic to the Dutch stand, but this made no difference. Oldenbarnevelt was forced to be rigidly obdurate as he was bound by the terms of a secret undertaking by which the other six provinces had promised Zeeland, in return for the latter's reluctant acquiescence in the truce, that in no

---

[34] *Corresp. de D'Jerónimo de Silva*, 114–15.
[35] *Catálogo Filipinas* vi. lxxxiii; Opstall, 171–2.
[36] De Jonge, *De Oorsprong*, 10–12.
[37] Veenendaal ii. 347–72; Den Tex iii. 92–4.
[38] *Groot Placaet-Boeck* ii. 1170; Wagenaar x. 4; Res. SG 13 Jan. 1610 (RGP 135), p. 9.

circumstances during its duration would the restrictions be lifted or altered.[39] Moreover, there was powerful opposition to the disencumbering of the Schelde from Amsterdam, Hoorn, and Enkhuizen, towns which looked with profound distaste on proposals calculated to promote the revival of trade at Antwerp.[40] Only on the third point, compensation for private lands confiscated on either side, was there any progress.

The Robiano mission was a formal diplomatic venture on the part of the Archdukes designed to round off the truce treaty. Lerma's prime concern, however, was somehow to convert the truce into a full peace treaty and his efforts in this direction, after 1609, were shrouded in utmost secrecy. Late in 1611 he established contact with Oldenbarnevelt in a way intended to exclude France, England, and even the Archdukes completely from the proceedings. A disguised Portuguese New Christian friar, Martín del Espiritu Santo, was sent from Brussels to Rotterdam to meet an Amsterdam Jewish merchant and political agent, Duarte Fernández, who was apparently a friend and had secret access to Oldenbarnevelt.[41] Lerma's message was that in view of the constant likelihood of renewed conflict in the Far East, the truce could simply not be secure in the existing circumstances: if the Dutch would agree to withdraw from the East Indies, Spain would agree to sign a full peace, with perpetual recognition of Dutch independence. Oldenbarnevelt's response was cautious: he would react positively were he to receive a more direct and formal offer to this effect from the Spanish crown. It was subsequently decided in Madrid, among a tiny group of just three or four ministers, to send Lerma's most trusted and influential associate, Rodrigo Calderón, to Brussels to supervise further secret contacts. Calderon left for the Netherlands in April 1612, a variety of pretexts being given out to explain his journey, and amid speculation at Madrid that the king was now tired of his undoubtedly great influence on

---

[39] See p. 41 below.   [40] Res. Holl. 22 Dec. 1609.
[41] Mancicidor to Philip, Brussels 31 Dec. 1611, and 'Relacion del estado q tiene la negociacion' (Dec. 1611). AGS Estado 2294; Th. van Rodenburg to SG, 3 June 1612. ARH SG 4925.

Lerma.[42] While Calderón's instructions made clear that Dutch withdrawal from the East was the price of a full peace, this issue being, in Calderón's term, *sustancialisimo*, the matter of religious rights for Dutch Catholics was tacked on also for the sake of form, though in Calderón's words, 'little or nothing can be hoped for from this.'[43]

The chosen intermediary this time was a Maastricht notary, Paul Philip Coenvelt, who again visited Oldenbarnevelt presenting the now familiar formula. But at this point, suspicion of what was afoot began to circulate. Balthasar de Zúñiga, Philip's ambassador to the Emperor and another critic of Lerma's policy, asked Calderón point blank, when he came to Brussels, whether the latter was conducting secret negotiations; Calderón denied it. The matter then came to the ear of the French ambassador in The Hague, and the States General and Oldenbarnevelt likewise denied that talks were taking place.[44] Then, to Calderón's consternation, the Archduke Albert's officials arrested Coenvelt for discussing peace proposals secretly with Oldenbarnevelt without orders to do so from the Archduke.[45] The Calderón mission in effect foundered on this farcical episode and he returned to Spain towards the end of 1612. Lerma, however, subsequently renewed his offer of peace to Oldenbarnevelt through Theodor Rodenburg, a distinguished Dutch scholar who had been sent to Madrid in 1611, nominally on behalf of the five Dutch Guinea companies which were anxious to restore the truce on the West African coast, but who was, in effect, an unofficial representative of the States General.[46] It is not known exactly how far the 1613 contacts proceeded, almost all the relevant documentation having disappeared, but whatever progress was made was subsequently nullified by the sharp deterioration in Dutch–Spanish relations in 1614, resulting from the flaring up of the Jülich–Cleves question.

---

[42] Consulta, 20 Feb. 1612. AGS Estado 2026; Cabrera de Córdoba, 465, 473, 490–1.
[43] 'Advertencia de Ron R⁰ Calderon sobre sus despachos', AGS Estado 2294.
[44] Res. SG 8 June 1612. RGP 135, 668.
[45] Calderón to Philip, Brussels 16 and 24 July 1612. AGS Estado 2294.
[46] Consulta, 6 Aug. 1613. AGS Estado 2027.

If terminating the Dutch conflict became the lynch-pin of Lerma's foreign policy, Oldenbarnevelt showed an equally consistent and vigorous inclination towards peace, at any rate from 1606 onwards. In the first place, there was no escaping from the discomforting shift in the balance of power in the Low Countries resulting from Spain's peace treaties with France and England. Disencumbered, Philip could concentrate in the Netherlands while French and English assistance to the Dutch, though it had not ended, had tailed off rapidly. In their offensives of 1605–6 the Spaniards had taken Oldenzaal which dominated eastern Overijssel as well as Groenlo, in the east of Gelderland, Rheinberg, an important strategic crossing on the Lower Rhine, and Lingen, a key fortress town on the Ems in the extreme north-west of Germany which menaced Overijssel and Groningen. While there was little chance that the Spaniards could muster enough strength to break through the main Dutch defences which were now daunting, extensive, and highly sophisticated, there was every prospect of more and more Dutch territory being eaten away at the edges. Graver still was the financial position. In effect, it was impossible to go on with the war without either massive additional subsidies from France, as his price for which Henry IV was demanding some form of overlordship over the seven provinces or huge increases in taxation at home. The latter option hardly seemed practicable, however, as the Dutch tax burden was already by far the heaviest in Europe, not excluding that of Castile. To meet the growing Spanish pressure, the Dutch standing army had been progressively expanded since 1598, rising by 1607 to 60,000 men, costing, at 9 million guilders yearly, nearly as much as the army of Flanders.[47] This was a totally unprecedented commitment for a small country with a mere 1½ million inhabitants and one which, in the circumstances of 1606, it appeared impossible to sustain, all the more so in that the Republic could not risk reducing its large and powerful navy. With mounting debts of many millions of guilders, Oldenbarnevelt was convinced that peace or a truce was the only way out of a financial impasse of gargantuan proportions, threatening

[47] Ten Raa ii. 366–9, 377.

the Republic with wholesale mutiny and, conceivably, with total collapse.[48]

But Oldenbarnevelt, unlike the Spanish monarch, was no autocrat and needed extensive backing for a radical departure in policy. Following the first Spanish peace moves, the Advocate had convened a secret committee of the States of Holland in August 1606, to test opinion. Apart from Reynier Pauw, burgomaster of Amsterdam, a leader of the colonial interest, who from this point on stridently opposed Oldenbarnevelt's Spanish policy, the province's leadership swung in support of the peace moves.[49] At this early stage, in 1606–7 the Advocate also succeeded in winning round Prince Maurits, Stadholder and captain-general of the army and navy, in favour of peace.[50] Moreover, support for peace was widespread among the city councils which were the real seat of power in the Republic. Testing opinion in June 1607, Pierre Jeannin and his party toured Haarlem, Leiden, Amsterdam, Dordrecht, and Utrecht, conferring with burgomasters and councillors, and reported to Paris that 'leur inclination est à la Paix avec la liberté et souveraineté de leur pais, non autrement'.[51] Even Delft, the only Holland town other than Amsterdam which opposed the truce terms in 1608–9, supported the initial peace moves.[52] Leiden, a city which was to oppose peace with Spain with all the means at its disposal from the 1620s onwards, likewise welcomed the peace initiative of 1607.[53] Moreover, Oldenbarnevelt's warning that the alternative to peace was a huge increase in taxation proved highly effective in the inland provinces, not only in Overijssel and Gelderland where war-weariness and resentment at high taxes was particularly marked, but also in Friesland and Groningen. In the States General's deliberations over the 1607 cease-fire and other preliminaries to the Hague peace conference, only Zeeland posed serious objections denouncing Oldenbarnevelt's policy as 'dangereulx ende ruineulx'.[54]

---

[48] *Gedenkstukken* iii. 311.   [49] Ibid. iii. 83–7.   [50] Grotius, 509.
[51] Jeannin i. 238; Den Tex ii. 575.   [52] GA Delft vroed. res. 10 Mar. 1607.
[53] GA Leiden Sec. Arch. 445, fos. 177, 188ʳ, 188ᵛ.
[54] Res. SG 11 Apr., 20 Dec. 1607. RGP 131, pp. 47, 103; Jeannin ii. 506; Baudius, 192–3.

Politically, the advantages of peace or a truce were undoubtedly great. Recognition by Spain would at once lead to full diplomatic relations with all Europe and the Near East and the release of the Republic's unquestionable but so far constantly tied down military and naval might for actual and potential use elsewhere. In effect, the Dutch would be able to exert political influence in the world almost in the manner of a great power such as England or France. Moreover, those central institutions of the Republic which necessarily played a constantly prominent role in war-time—Stadholder, States General, and *Raad van State* (Council of State)—would undoubtedly wane in importance during peace-time, thereby reinforcing the position of the Holland regents who formed Oldenbarnevelt's power-base.

Economically, peace would unavoidably impose severe constraints on Dutch enterprise in Asia, the Americas, and Africa, plans for setting up a West India Company would have to be aborted, but, as Richardot and Spinola frequently reminded the Dutch peace delegation, would not Dutch commerce receive more than ample compensation in the revived trade with Spain, Portugal, and southern Italy? Indeed, Oldenbarnevelt evidently expected that the gains in European trade would eventually outweigh the losses and frustration of colonial trade[55] and this was a perfectly logical expectation. A resuscitated trade with the Spanish European possessions would involve much more than simply an expansion in Dutch Mediterranean trade, welcome though that would be in itself. There were close links between the Mediterranean and the Baltic commerce,[56] and the latter was, by common consent, the very foundation of Holland's wealth and prosperity. Much of the grain, timber, copper, and naval stores shipped by the Dutch from the Baltic was destined for Iberian and Italian markets. Since 1598, when the Spanish government had begun its attempts to shut the Dutch out of Iberian trade, there had been a distinct revival in the role in the Baltic of the Hanseatic towns, particularly of Hamburg.[57] At the same time Iberian salt and Spanish-American silver

---

[55] *Gedenkstukken* iii. 311.   [56] Van Dillen, 'De opstand', 32.
[57] Bang i. 190–242; Dollinger, 351.

were among the most essential items among Dutch exports to the Baltic and Russia, indeed salt and silver were the keys to dominance of the northern trade. From every angle, it seemed clear that peace with Spain would significantly reinforce Holland's hegemony over Europe's north-south carrying traffic.

When prospects for a full peace faded and attention switched to the offer of a long truce, the opposition to Oldenbarnevelt led by the Stadholder, Zeeland, the colonial interest, and the Calvinist clergy considerably stiffened, but he fought on until finally the truce was signed in April 1609. Subsequently, the Advocate persevered with no less determination to maintain the accord in the face of steadily mounting difficulties and increasing opposition. Indeed, the truce became as much the corner-stone of Oldenbarnevelt's as of Lerma's policy; undoubtedly his ultimate objective was a permanent settlement with Spain. In 1610, amidst the first Jülich–Cleves crisis, the French monarch dropped his support for the truce and prepared for a full-scale war against Spain into which he had every intention of dragging the Republic. While publicly adopting a sorrowful air on the news of Henry IV's assasination in May of that year, in reality Oldenbarnevelt was probably scarcely less relieved than was Lerma.[58] Even so, a reluctant Oldenbarnevelt, under heavy domestic pressure, had to acquiesce in the sending of Dutch troops under Maurits to join the French forces besieging Jülich which was then occupied by local Catholic nobles holding the town in the name of the Emperor's representative, the Archduke Leopold, against both the Protestant claimants to the duchies. The town fell after several weeks of siege, the Spaniards having made no move to intervene. The episode certainly demonstrated Lerma's resolve to avoid entanglements in northern Europe, but it also seriously harmed his and the king's prestige.

However peaceably inclined were Lerma and Oldenbarnevelt, Jülich–Cleves was inescapably of vital strategic concern to both Spain and the Republic because of the location of the duchies astride the main routes from the

[58] Den Tex iii. 103–4.

east to both the northern and southern Netherlands. In 1614 the fragile *status quo* established in the duchies, in 1610, collapsed as the two Protestant claimants, Johann Sigismund, Elector of Brandenburg, and Wolfgang Wilhelm, duke of Neuburg, fell to blows. The former, previously Lutheran, turned Calvinist to enhance his appeal to local Protestants; Neuburg, likewise Lutheran, turned Catholic and threw himself at the feet of Spain and the Emperor. In May 1614 Neuburg's troops expelled the Brandenburgers from Düsseldorf and a major European war seemed in the offing. This time, Oldenbarnevelt's reluctance exceeded that of Lerma. While seeing the need for the Republic to be on its guard, he believed at first that the storm would blow over without any major intervention by Spain.[59] But both sides mobilized troops and, in August, on orders from Madrid but in the Emperor's name, Spinola drove the Brandenburg garrison from Aachen and then occupied Wesel.[60] The latter, the most important Spanish acquisition in Europe during the Twelve Years Truce, was to serve, until its capture by the Dutch in 1629, as the foremost Spanish base on the Lower Rhine. This episode was even more damaging to Oldenbarnevelt than had been that of 1610 to Lerma.[61] The Dutch government had in effect permitted Spain to seize unopposed a fortress-town of crucial strategic importance which happened also to be the chief Calvinist centre of the region. There was a bitter outcry throughout the United Provinces, not least from the clergy. In belated reply to the Spaniards, the States General's forces occupied sections of Cleves and Mark, seizing Emmerich, Hamm, and Lippstadt whilst Spinola answered by taking Xanten. It is extraordinary that the Dutch and Spanish forces involved in these movements, operating in the closest proximity, did so without a single armed clash. In November 1614 the rival claimants reached a compromise at Xanten whereby Cleves and Mark were allocated to the Elector and Jülich and Berg to Neuburg. However, the Dutch and Spanish garrisons remained in most of the occupied towns.

Oldenbarnevelt was assuredly badly shaken by the events of 1614. His correspondence of 1614-15 indicates that he

---

[59] Veenendaal ii. 23.   [60] Meerbeeck, 1268.   [61] Ten Raa iii. 32-4.

was now much more suspicious of Spanish intentions than formerly and that he began systematically trying to coax both France and England into more vigorously opposing Spain's apparent ambitions. Inevitably, the dramatic shift in the balance of power in Europe following Henry's death, to the advantage of Spain, and the dismaying weakness and internal difficulties of the French regency government during these years, seemed to the Dutch to be highly detrimental to their interests. There was no greater irony in the European politics of this period than that just when Lerma had opted to disengage from northern Europe and concentrate Spanish energies in the Mediterranean, the neutralization of France immensely increased the power of Spain within Europe.[62] However pacific were Lerma's own intentions, the Spanish crown, as Oldenbarnevelt was fully aware,[63] nevertheless disposed of by far the largest military machine in Europe with over 100,000 men under arms in peace time in the Peninsula, Italy, Germany, and the Netherlands, on paper a totally overwhelming force. While Spanish spending on the army of Flanders in the years 1609–17 averaged only half the level sustained in the years 1603–6 and the reduction in actual troop-strength was even more marked,[64] this could not hide the fact that the resources of the Spanish Monarchy were still devoted essentially to maintaining a vast military apparatus, staffed by the Castilian nobility. The prospect of a combined Habsburg drive towards 'universal monarchy' was something that Oldenbarnevelt did and had to keep constantly in mind.

But despite this change in 1614, Oldenbarnevelt's Spanish policy remained one of avoiding confrontation as far as possible and preparing the ground for peace.[65] This is well illustrated by the Advocate's attitude to the power struggles in the Mediterranean, Lerma's chosen arena and one where the Dutch became an important factor politically during the truce. During 1609–10 the Republic received offers of closer political and economic ties from the Ottoman sultan, Muley Sidan, Venice, and Savoy. But eager though he was to extend

---

[62] Trevor-Roper, 268.   [63] Veenendaal ii. 94.
[64] See Parker, *Army of Flanders*, 271.   [65] Vreede ii. 260–1.

Dutch influence, Oldenbarnevelt was extremely careful not to be drawn into any alliance, pact, or co-operation against the Habsburgs. Muley Sidan wanted Dutch naval and military assistance against Spain but, apart from munitions and naval stores, received only closer diplomatic and commercial links. Following the arrival of the first Dutch ambassador in Istanbul in 1612, the anti-Habsburg faction among the sultan's ministers, led by Khalil Pasha, proposed Dutch–Turkish collaboration against both Spain and the Emperor only to find that their proposals were studiously ignored in The Hague.[66] Oldenbarnevelt greatly esteemed the new Turkish connection and unquestionably Dutch Levant trade benefited handsomely from the capitulations granted by the sultan in favour of the Dutch in 1612. The Dutch leader also wanted to see the Ottoman empire disentangle itself from Iran so that the Turks should be able, should the need arise, to act against the Habsburgs.[67] Yet he remained adamant that there should be no formal or informal Dutch–Turkish co-operation against either Spain or the Emperor.

In Italy the position was extremely intricate. Again, Oldenbarnevelt's prime concern was to minimize friction, but equally he could not help but be deeply disturbed by the collapse of French power and the increasing likelihood that Spain might now choose to eliminate the two principal obstacles to her total hegemony in Italy — Venice and Savoy. Venice, long committed to anti-Habsburg policies, hemmed in by Austrian territory on one side and Spanish (Milan) on the other, appeared to be in a particularly perilous position. After urgent pleas from the Venetian senate and again under heavy domestic pressure, Oldenbarnevelt agreed, in 1617, as Venetian-Habsburg relations further deteriorated, to the sending of 4,000 Dutch troops to enter Venetian service, but only under very strict limitations. He also refused to sign any form of defensive alliance with Venice. It is for this reason that considerable antagonism developed between Christoforo Suriano, the Venetian ambassador sent to The Hague in 1616 to procure Dutch help, and the Advocate, and that Suriano soon tended to side with Maurits and the Counter-

---

[66] De Groot, 162–81.   [67] Veenendaal ii. 95–6, 121.

Remonstrants in the growing Dutch religious crisis, against Oldenbarnevelt.

The Twelve Years Truce, then, was entered into by governments which were strongly committed to its preservation and inclined to regard it as a first step towards a full peace. Certainly, it represented a definitive end to the Dutch Revolt, as we may term the first part of the Eighty Years War, for Philip and Lerma had made abundantly clear their readiness to accept, unequivocally, Dutch political and religious independence. All considered, as Oldenbarnevelt wrote to his ambassador at Istanbul in 1614, the truce held up surprisingly well in extremely difficult circumstances, except in the volatile Far East where it lasted only about a year.[68] The Caribbean conflict had been largely defused in 1609, because the opening up of the Portuguese salt-pans to the Dutch undermined the economics of procuring salt from Punta de Araya. It is true that Iberian salt was taxed and had to be paid for whilst the latter did not, but this advantage was more than outweighed by the greater cost and risk of trans-Atlantic navigation. Almost to a man, the salt-dealers of Hoorn and Enkhuizen were content to revert to Setúbal, Aveiro, and Cadiz. In the New World it was mainly in the area of the thriving Zeelandian settlements around the mouths of Amazon and Orinoco and along the Guyana coast between that the truce was not observed. According to the Iberians, who claimed this area as their own, the Dutch presence there, and certainly any further expansion, was of itself an infringement of the truce so that they did not doubt their right to retaliate. When, in 1613, Zeelandian settlers established a new colony at the mouth of the Corantine, a Spanish raiding-party from Trinidad destroyed it soon after.[69] In 1615 a Portuguese force unsuccessfully attacked the Dutch forts on the Amazon. The Dutch for their part argued that these regions had never been under effective Spanish or Portuguese control so that their own activity there was permitted under the truce terms and that it was therefore the Iberians who were violating the treaty. In 1616 colonists from Flushing established what was to be the most thriving

[68] Veenendaal ii. 27.   [69] Goslinga, 79–80.

and important Dutch base in tropical America until the capture of Pernambuco in 1630, Fort ter Hooge (Kijkoveral), 20 miles up the river Essequibo.

On the Guinea coast the truce likewise failed to take hold. Either side read the stiplulations of the treaty differently, and the Portuguese at Elmina took to regularly attacking Dutch shipping in the area. The States General responded with its decision of August 1611 to erect a fort in West Africa, at Moree, some 5 miles from Elmina, to be garrisoned at the state's expense.[70] Neither side was ready to give up the Guinea gold trade, which was worth up to a million guilders yearly, without a hard struggle. But unquestionably the major failure of the truce was in the Far East. The *Consejo de Estado*'s hope and East India Company directors' fear that restoring access to Lisbon and its spice-market would deflect Dutch enterprise from Asia proved wholly unfounded.[71] Though the Company did briefly acquiesce in the truce, it had no intention of relaxing its grip over the spice trade or, in the long run, of giving up its ambition to break into the China trade.

In 1612, endeavouring to drive the Dutch from the important trade in South Indian cottons on the Coromandel coast, the Portuguese sacked the Dutch factory at Pulicat (established in 1610), from near-by Negapatam and São Thomé.[72] The only effect of this was that the Dutch built a new and much stronger fort at Pulicat, Fort Geldria, which was completed in 1613; from there the Dutch soon dominated the trade of south-east India and by 1619 exported 83,000 pieces of Coromandel cloth yearly to Indonesia and the Moluccas to be sold to the islanders in exchange for their spices. The Dutch, in other words, took over from the Portuguese, during the early years of the truce, one of the most vital strands in inter-Asian trade. Nevertheless, it was the Portuguese who had attacked and therefore they, in the eyes of the States General and Oldenbarnevelt, who were responsible for violating the truce in Asia.[73] In 1613, replying in

---

[70] De Jonge, *De Oorsprong*, 14–15.
[71] *Corresp. d'Esp.* i. 362–4.   [72] Raychaudhuri, 20–3.
[73] Res. SG 10 Nov. 1610, 1 Aug. 1611. RGP 135, pp. 254, 437; Veenendaal ii. 27; Terpstra, 47–8.

the Moluccas, over 1,000 Company troops and sailors, in
thirteen vessels, bombarded and stormed two of the Spanish
forts on Tidore which henceforth was divided between Dutch
and Spanish arms in the manner of Ternate.[74] The Spanish
governor on Ternate tried to retaliate by inciting against the
Dutch the natives of neighbouring Maquien and Motiel. In
1614 ten Company vessels under Laurens Reael scoured the
Philippines raiding shipping and harbours. In 1615-16 the
Spanish governor of the Philippines, Juan de Silva, amassed
a powerful force at Manila from where he planned to link
up with a Portuguese contingent from Malacca and drive the
Dutch for good from Indonesia and the Moluccas. The Portuguese squadron was destroyed by the Dutch off Malacca, but
the Manila *armada* proved its worth, in April 1617, in a fierce
battle in Manila Bay when a Company fleet under Jan Dirckszoon Lam was defeated with heavy loss.[75] Another Dutch
fleet scoured the Philippines in 1618 but achieved nothing
of note.

The East India Company was certainly responsible for the
one major violation of the truce outside Asia, the attack of
1615 on the Pacific coast of Spanish America. A force of six
East Indiamen, under Joris van Spilbergen, having sailed from
Holland and through the Straits of Magellan, attempted to
disrupt Spanish shipping off the Pacific coast of the Americas.
In July 1615 Spilbergen fought a fierce battle with the
Spanish Peru squadron off Cañete, sinking two of its vessels
and killing 450 Spaniards. From Peru the Dutch sailed to
Acapulco, where twenty Spanish prisoners were exchanged
for supplies and then northwards along the Mexican coast.[76]
A landing party fought a six-hour pitched battle with a
scratch force of Spaniards under Sebastian Vizcaino, at
Zacatula, before the fleet finally departed, crossing the Pacific
to the Far East. The raid precipitated an immediate and
massive change on the Pacific coast of the New World. A
feverish programme of strengthening old and erecting new
fortifications began which constituted for the Monarchy as

[74] *Corresp. de D. Jerónimo de Silva*, 229-33.
[75] *Catálogo Filipinas* vi. 396-7, vii, p. xxix.
[76] Viceroy Guadalcázar to Philip, Mexico City, 26 Nov. 1615. AGI Mexico
leg. 28, ramo 3. Gerhard, 117-20;

a whole a major new item of expenditure. In the years 1615–18 the viceroy of Peru spent no less than 700,000 ducats refurbishing the defences of Callao alone.[77] In 1615–18 the viceroy of Mexico built to protect the harbour of Acapulco, the entrepôt for all Iberian traffic between the Far East and the Pacific coast of Spanish America, the expensive new five-bastion stone fortress of San Diego. While the Spilbergen expedition failed to achieve anything lasting from the Dutch point of view, it certainly administered a profound and costly shock to Spain's entire American empire.

ii THE OPPONENTS OF THE TRUCE

In both the Republic and Spain, resistance to the truce was prolonged and intense, but it would be wrong to suppose that in either case was it so widespread as to threaten seriously the leadership or their policies. Lerma was certainly shaken by the generally indignant reaction in Spanish court circles to the news of the 1607 cease-fire. Nevertheless, he steadfastly pressed on, constantly urged to do so perhaps by Albert and the Brussels court, but essentially for his own reasons.[78] Again and again, Albert and Isabella denounced the opponents of the truce as a limited group representing an essentially narrow sectional interest.[79] In the end, Lerma forced the treaty through even without extracting a single substantive concession from the Dutch, but also without endangering in any way either his grip on power or his influence with the king. In the Republic too, while participants at the 1608 peace conference, such as Spinola, were surprised at the extent of anti-truce feeling among the ruling oligarchy, or rather some sections of it, they saw that the Dutch populace as a whole eagerly desired peace and relief from the many burdens of the long war.[80] Henry IV was repeatedly assured by Jeannin that most of the Dutch people favoured peace, only certain limited groups preferring war.[81] Similarly, the

---

[77] ARB SEG 183, fo. 152ᵛ; Lohman Villena, 39–44.
[78] Bentivoglio, 539.
[79] *Corresp. Alberto* ii. 50, 127; *Corresp. Infanta*, 170–1, 196–7.
[80] Spinola to Philip, The Hague, 5 Mar. 1608 quoted in Rodriguez Villa, 220.
[81] Jeannin i. 238, 249; ii. 506.

English representatives at the Hague conferences were confident that the majority of both populace and ruling élite supported Oldenbarnevelt's policy.[82] Indeed, throughout the arduous political battle of 1607–9 in the Republic, the cards were stacked heavily in Oldenbarnevelt's favour. Only briefly, during the climax of the struggle, in October and November 1608, did the final issue appear at all in doubt. In the event, the Advocate's case on finances and the need to reduce taxation won such support that not only the five inland provinces but the majority of the towns of Holland, by far the most important province, voted repeatedly in his favour.[83]

The motives of the opposition in both Spain and the Republic do indeed appear for the most part to have been essentially sectional. Albert and Isabella when referring to those who are 'for the war because of their own particular interests' had in mind those Castilian noble families whose fortunes, careers, and influence were bound up with the army, military expenditure, and the Spanish military presence in northern Europe. Commenting on the attitude of the Constable of Castile, Juan Fernández de Velasco (Duque de Frias), a leading opponent of the truce, the Infanta remarked that it caused her no surprise for 'he is advised by relatives and friends who all have an interest in the war, because they live from it and thus they are worse than the devil with all those who propose peace.'[84] Other major Castilian military figures who vigorously opposed the truce were the Duque de Osuna and the formidable Conde de Fuentes, nephew of Alva and governor of Milan. Both loudly admonished that the king should not go begging for peace, trailing his honour upon the ground.[85] According to Diego Ibarra, many South Netherlanders had also 'wept' at the disreputable content of an armistice agreement which had obtained nothing for the Catholics residing under the States General. But it is curious to see what he really meant by this.

---

[82] BL MS Add. 40837, fos. 210, 211.

[83] Ibid., fos. 70, 211, 215ᵛ, 227; Res. SG 11 Apr., 20 Dec. 1607, 15 Nov., 18 Dec. 1608. *RGP* 131, pp. 47, 100–3, 459, 468; Jeannin ii. 482, 506.

[84] *Corresp. Infanta*, 171.

[85] On Osuna, see below; on Fuentes, see Fuentes, 193–4 and Parker, *Army of Flanders*, 133–4.

He stressed that whatever Albert, Spinola, and the Brussels court might say, the senior Castilian officers in the Netherlands, Luis de Velasco, Iñigo de Borja, governor of Antwerp, and Juan de Ribas, governor of Cambrai, were convinced that so unsound an accord would undermine the security of the southern Netherlands.[86]

While in Castile, the hub of the Spanish *imperium*, the dominant class at court and in society were the nobility, a class with a strong tradition of military, imperial, and diplomatic service to the crown in the United Provinces, the nobles were on the whole much less involved in military affairs as well as being less influential politically. Indeed, much of the Dutch nobility displayed a remarkable lack of sympathy for either the military or the political ambitions of the Stadholder, Prince Maurits. On the *secreete besoigne* of the States of Holland convened by Oldenbarnevelt in September 1606 to discuss the Spanish peace offer, among the Advocate's supporters was the heer van Brederode, representing the Holland nobility, and the latter had then continued, subsequently, to vote in favour of the truce in the States of Holland.[87] The provinces of Utrecht, Gelderland, and Overijssel, where the nobility wielded great influence all solidly backed the truce against the wishes of Maurits. While there were military men among the Dutch nobles, some of whom did adhere to the prince, most of the officers of the Dutch army were in fact foreign noblemen, often French, English, or Scots, who totally lacked influence within the Dutch body politic. However Maurits himself, sincere though his warnings concerning the political and strategic dangers of the proposed truce terms undoubtedly were, did also clearly have a vested interest in continuing the war since, under the prevailing system, both his authority and his emoluments were much greater during war than in peace.

The major backing for Maurits's efforts to block the truce came from certain minority sections of the urban patriciate, particularly, though not solely, in the Zeeland towns,

---

[86] Ibarra to Philip, 24 June 1607, Rodríguez Villa, 184.
[87] *Gedenkstukken* iii. 83-7; Res. SH 27 Mar. 1607.

Amsterdam and Delft. Otherwise there was only the vociferous but not particularly effective support of a Calvinist clergy avid to liberate the South Netherlands from the 'Papist superstition' and, in some cases, capable in the service of this cause of astonishingly bellicose sentiments.[88] But despite these pressures, and particularly that of Holland's largest city which dismissed even the offer of a full peace in 1607, as tending to the 'irreparable harm and decline of these lands and their inhabitants',[89] remarkably few Holland towns were swayed by the opposition. Hoorn reportedly sided with Amsterdam on the *secreete besoigne* in 1606, and certainly Hoorn and Enkhuizen had reservations about the truce, both being keen participants in the colonial expansion, but even these towns eventually fell into line behind the majority faction supporting Oldenbarnevelt.[90] On the vote over the cease-fire agreement in March 1607, Amsterdam cast a completely isolated vote against.[91] In the crucial votes of November 1608, thirteen or fourteen of the eighteen Holland towns represented, besides the nobility, declared in favour of the truce, Amsterdam and Delft being the only major opponents, though some towns such as Rotterdam would have preferred to conclude a truce for fifteen or twenty years rather than for twelve.[92] The Delft *vroedschap* finally decided to cease its opposition in December 1608, seeing that all the provinces except Zeeland and all the Holland towns, besides Amsterdam and itself, as well as France and England, supported the truce.[93]

While the opponents of the truce in both Spain and the Republic thus consisted of coalitions of small minority groups with special interests in the war, on both sides these factions needed to present their arguments comprehensively in terms of national, strategic, and religious interest. They could not afford to appear to be narrowly based or narrowly motivated.

---

[88] De Pater, 9–13.

[89] Elias, *De Vroedschap* i. xlix; Res. Holl. 13 Sept. 1608.

[90] AWG Hoorn vroed. res. 28 Aug. and 6 Sept. 1608; AWG Enkhuizen vroed. res. 28 Aug. 1608.

[91] Res. Holl. 27 Mar. 1607.

[92] GA Rotterdam Oud Archief 2974, fo. 43. Extract vroed. res. 28 Oct. 1608; BL MS Add. 40837, fo. 215^v; Den Tex ii. 657.

[93] GA Delft vroed. res. 9 Dec. 1608.

According to the opposition, whatever the scarcity of funds, mere considerations of means had to be subordinated to strategic necessity and *raison d'état*. In Pauw's view, moreover, Oldenbarnevelt was guilty of deliberately exaggerating the gravity of the financial predicament while, on the Spanish side, Ibarra argued that the king's finances could be stretched sufficiently by placing the army of Flanders strictly on the defensive. Many of the Dutch war-party besides van Aerssen stressed that what Spain was offering was not a full concession of sovereignty, but merely a temporary recognition.[94] Prince Maurits, in his open missives to the Holland *vroedschappen* of September and October 1608 argued that the truce posed such dangers as might result in the disintegration of the state and the restoration of Spanish rule.[95] If Philip's treasury was momentarily exhausted, he maintained, the respite would simply facilitate the revival of his finances enabling the Spaniards to resume their offensive from a position of strength on its expiry. It was also uncertain whether France would continue to profer financial assistance once the war resumed after so long a pause. Furthermore, while Spain with its vast territories could safely reduce its armies considerably in order to hasten financial recovery, the Republic having so small and insecure a territory would be compelled, at continuing heavy cost, to retain most of its existing standing army. There were also, in the prince's view, grave internal dangers. Since it would be harder politically to raise the funds with which to sustain a large force in peace time, the States General's grip on Utrecht, Gelderland, Overijssel, and Groningen, provinces which had been forced into the Union of Utrecht, and adherence to the state by means of military compulsion and where much, if not most, of the populace was Catholic or Crypto-Catholic and anti-Union in sentiment, would inevitably weaken.

While the Castilian adversaries of the truce stressed the loss of *reputación* that the king would suffer in 'begging' for peace from his 'rebels', the main thrust of their arguments

---

[94] GA Leiden, Sec. Arch. 445, fos. 224ᵛ–225ᵛ, 'Consideratien van zijne Excie. ende Grave Wilhelm van Nassau'.

[95] GA Leiden, Sec. Arch. 445, fos. 201–5, 242–6; Meteren ix. 66–7; Wagenaar ix. 374–6.

was that maintaining a powerful, tried, and hardened army in the Low Countries in a constant state of preparedness constituted the very basis of the Spanish ascendancy in Europe. By making peace with the Dutch, Philip, in Osuna's view, would 'lose the best ever discipline and experience that any king has had [for his troops], for the army of Flanders not only operates in that war but is a bridle upon the neighbouring kings of France and England and all Germany, that *plaza de armas* being the training-ground from where Your Majesty should draw troops in all situations that arise.'[96] Osuna also argued, like Maurits, that peace would not greatly mitigate the financial difficulties. The cost of the southern Netherlands would, he assured his colleagues, be only marginally less in peace than in war. Another main strategic argument on the Spanish side, and one that well illustrates the interaction of events in Asia and the Americas with those in Europe, the global view that predominated in the minds of Philip's ministers, was that if left in peace at home, the Dutch would inevitably have all the greater means and opportunity to make additional gains in the Indies.[97] The outcome would be a series of colonial wars involving a still heavier outlay and more crushing burden upon Castile than the struggle sustained hitherto in the Netherlands.

After the collapse of the initial hopes in Brussels and Madrid that Dutch withdrawal from the Indies could be obtained by negotiation, the unresolved colonial question remained the most damaging hiatus in the peace party's arguments. Spinola, at one with Albert on the necessity of peace or a truce, having at first assured Philip, in the autumn of 1606, that in return for their liberty, the Dutch 'will withdraw altogether from navigation to the Indies',[98] realized full well the need to provide an alternative pro-truce argument relating to the Indies. In October 1608, after months of unproductive argument over Asia and the Americas at The Hague, Spinola wrote to Philip that in any case years of experience had shown that waging war in the Netherlands did and could not check Dutch expansion at Iberian expense

---

[96] See Osuna's 'Discurso' of Aug. 1608, BL Add. 14005, fo. 85ᵛ.
[97] See the anonymous discourse written at Madrid in Jan. 1609, ibid., fo. 98ᵛ.
[98] Quoted in Rodríguez Villa, 156.

in the Indies.[99] He maintained that by ending the enervating and inconclusive struggle in Europe, matters in the Indies would at worst be left just as they were, but that hopefully the Dutch would gradually cease their navigation to the Indies as they saw restored to them access to spices and other colonial products at Lisbon and Seville. In this connection he ventured to remind the king that the Dutch had only switched to direct trade with the Indies when cut off from the trade of Spain's European territories.

While the nobles and military commanders who dominated the politics of the Spanish Monarchy tended to assign higher priority to political and strategic than to economic considerations, they none the less appreciated that there were important economic issues that had to be faced. As has been seen, first among these was the deteriorating predicament of the Spanish and Portuguese Indies trades: the well-being of Lisbon and Seville were accepted by all as fundamental to the Monarchy as a whole. The question of the wider impact of the war, and particularly of the heavy fiscal burden that it involved, on Castile, the heartland of the Spanish Monarchy, was likewise constantly in the minds of participants to the debate. Spinola, for instance, argued the benefits that would accrue to Spain itself through release from the burdens of the Netherlands war.[1] However, on this point the advocates of war preferred to remain silent. Another issue was the impact of the war on the economy of the southern Netherlands. According to Albert, Isabella, and Spinola, the country was now exhausted, its agriculture, trade, and industry shattered, and its capacity to support a large Spanish army much reduced.[2] The pro-war party, however, retorted that on this, as on other points, Albert was misleading the king. Osuna referred to the

advantages that war brings [Flanders] which are very great. . .for it is harmful only where the army actually operates, during the summer, all the rest being enriched. And this is because all the cash that flows from Spain, sent both by Your Majesty and private individuals, remains in

[99] Spinola to Philip, 7 Oct. 1608, in Rodríguez Villa, 233-4.
[1] Spinola to Philip, 22 Dec. 1606 in Rodríguez Villa, 153.
[2] See, e.g. *Corresp. Infanta*, 196-7.

the country and because the farmer sells his produce and cattle, and the merchant his goods, at the price they ask.[3]

And indeed, the Archdukes, who kept their own chief motive, their desire to see the influence of the Castilian officers in the Netherlands reduced, well in the background, had some reason to exaggerate the economic plight of the country. In any case, the long struggle had not prevented or noticeably hindered the remarkable progress in agricultural techniques and productivity, especially in Flanders and Brabant which, together with the western half of the Republic, constituted the most advanced agricultural zone in Europe, the very heart of the agricultural revolution. Moreover, since the 1590s, the textile industries, historically of crucial importance to the prosperity of the southern Netherlands, had begun slowly to recover from the severe dislocation caused by the upheavals and turmoil of the 1570s and early 1580s.

On the Dutch side, predictably, resort to economic arguments was still more prevalent. Oldenbarnevelt's expectation that the truce would ease the fiscal pressure on the populace and benefit the European carrying trade was evidently shared by wide sections of the Dutch public and ruling élite.[4] Many Dutchmen apparently grasped that the resistance to the truce emanated predominantly from the handful of towns heavily involved in colonial enterprise, perceiving that the interests of the relatively restricted groups involved in some respects ran counter to the interests of the vast majority, including most merchants and seamen.[5] Certainly the argument that revived Dutch trade with the Peninsula would benefit the Dutch economy as a whole more than further expansion in Asia, or the setting up of a West India Company, exerted widespread appeal as can be discerned from the sensitivity of the advocates of colonial expansion on this point. Van Meteren, following Usselincx, emphatically urged his compatriots not to abandon the chance of an American empire for a renewed Iberian trade, for however tempting was the prospect of the latter it would be inherently insecure and

[3] Osuna, 'Discurso', loc. cit.

[4] GA Leiden Sec. Arch 445, fo. 252ᵛ; *Considérations d'Estat*, 26-9.

[5] Ibid. 29; Baudius, 13; Usselincx, moreover, granted that this was a prevalent view: see his *Discovrs by forme van Remonstrantye*, 7-7ᵛ.

subject to constant interference by the Spanish crown which would, anyway, reap much of the profit through rising customs revenues.[6] No less significant, the East India Company, while extremely active behind the scenes, petitioning the States General, provincial assemblies, and at least some of the *vroedschappen*,[7] refrained from intervening in the pamphlet war, sensing no doubt that to do so, given that it was not especially popular with the 'common man', would be counter-productive.

The most eloquent antagonist of the truce on economic grounds was that indefatigable advocate of the West India Company project, Willem Usselincx. Undoubtedly, he himself resented the truce chiefly because it forced the suspension of his beloved scheme. Significantly, though, the approach he adopted to attacking the truce was to concentrate on what could plausibly be predicted to be its unfavourable consequences for the Dutch economy as a whole. In the first place, he warned that the truce would partially or wholly divert the European carrying trade from Amsterdam and Rotterdam back to Spanish-controlled Antwerp. 'Business was forced, as if contrary to nature, to come here', he asserted,' by the shutting off of the oppressed lands [Flanders and Brabant]: now, in nature, what is forced remains no longer than the compelling cause continues and when this ceases everything returns to its former state.'[8] He argued that Antwerp offered unrivalled advantages for the transaction of international business, being a pre-eminent banking and insurance centre, replete with every business skill, and that once the Dutch naval blockade of the Flemish coast was removed, the Antwerp émigrés in Amsterdam would return whilst the skippers of Holland's ports would just as eagerly throng to Antwerp, Ostend, and Dunkirk to find business and sign freight-contracts as at present they came to Amsterdam. But although this contention was widely used by the Dutch war-party during 1607-8,[9] subsequently it lost much

---

[6] Meteren ix. 365, 373; Usselincx, op. cit., fos. 7-7ᵛ.

[7] See GA Delft, vroed. res. 23 Aug. 1608.

[8] Usselincx, *Naerder Bedenckingen*, fo. 4; Usselincx, *Grondich Discours*, fos. 1ᵛ, 5.

[9] See the *Copie van een Discours*, fo. 2; *Discours op den swermenden Treves*, fo. 7; Maurits too claimed, in his circular to the Holland towns, that Holland

of its force owing to Oldenbarnevelt's unyielding stand on the Schelde question. In the end, as has been seen, the truce was signed without any change in the procedure whereby cargoes conveyed between Antwerp and the sea had to be transferred onto other vessels in the Zeeland ports and pay a heavy duty to the States General. Thus Antwerp continued to languish at a considerable disadvantage *vis-à-vis* Amsterdam.

However, Usselincx's other main point proved, at least in the long run, to have much more force. He insisted that the war had in several respects acted as a crucial buttress to Holland's industries and that without the backing of the favourable wartime circumstances, manufacturing in Holland would be bound to decline.[10] In particular, the blockade of the Flemish coast had severely disadvantaged Flemish manufacturing with regard to wool supplies imported from abroad, as the German and Dutch wools which formed the bulk of Flanders's supplies had had to be imported either by river and canal from the Republic, paying the high war-time *licenten*, which were even higher for river than for maritime trade,[11] or else, via Calais, paying the French imposts. At the same time, the blockade had hampered Flemish cloth exports by forcing these to be transported either through the Republic or Calais, thereby again incurring heavy duties. However once the truce was signed, warned Usselincx, not only would Flemish woollens and linens proceed directly to their main markets, Spain, Portugal, and Italy, from Dunkirk and Ostend, but, by river and canal, Flemish manufactures would invade the Dutch market on entirely new terms, for inevitably the *licenten* would be drastically reduced in truce time, thus ending their effectiveness as a protective barrier for Dutch industry.

Moreover, in Usselincx's view, Flemish industry, once free of the hindrances of the war, would undoubtedly prove more competitive than the Dutch. Haarlem, the centre of Holland's linen industry, and Leiden, Europe's leading urban producer of woollen cloth, had achieved vigorous growth only

---

would be denuded of 'all business and prosperity' while the 'towns of Brabant and Flanders filled up'.

[10] Usselincx, *Grondich Discours*, fos. 2–4[v].
[11] Israel, 'Dutch River trade', 465–6.

comparatively recently, following the collapse of manufacturing at Hondschoote, Brugge, Ghent, and other southern
centres and the special circumstances created by the Spanish
war. In peace time, Flemish industry was bound to prove a
much more formidable rival than at any point since the
1570s because wages and costs were much lower in Flanders,
Brabant, and Liège than in Holland and because the gap in
wage costs was bound to remain since the Dutch excise taxes
were so much higher and because Flemish artisans owned
their own cottages whereas the émigré Flemish weavers of
Haarlem and Leiden rented their accommodation in a zone
of extremely high rents.[12] Nor should Dutchmen imagine,
warned Usselincx, that the Protestant loyalties of the émigrés
would keep them in Holland once the truce restored prosperity to Flanders. Many would surely revert to their original
homes attracted by the lower taxation and cheaper food
and homes.[13] And once the Flemings left, Haarlem, Leiden,
and the secondary textile industries of Delft, Gouda, and
elsewhere would collapse, for the Flemish were a highly
skilled, disciplined, and industrious work-force, moulded by
centuries of unremitting labour while the Dutch, though apt
for trade, largely lacked the proficiency for manufacturing
of their southern neighbours.

While Haarlem, Gouda, and Leiden staunchly backed
Oldenbarnevelt during the political battle of 1607-9 against
Amsterdam and Delft, opinion in the Leiden *vroedschap* as
to whether the truce would harm or benefit industry appears
to have been divided.[14] Indeed, since the 1580s the *say*
industry, at this time by far the most important textile
branch at Leiden, had been split into two distinct strands
with conflicting interests.[15] Those engaged in making Flemish-
type *says*, on the model of Hondschoote, a cloth chiefly for
export to Mediterranean markets, while profiting from the
collapse of Hondschoote, had suffered increasingly from the

---

[12] Usselincx, *Grondich Discours*, fos. 2, 6; see also De Vries, *Dutch Rural Economy*, 183.

[13] And indeed, a substantial number did; see Coornaert, 49-50.

[14] G.A. Leiden, 'Redenen voor het Bestant tegens het Oorlogh', Sec. Arch, 445, fo. 253.

[15] *Bronnen Leidsche Textielnijverheid* iii. 140, 170, 173-4, 176.

difficulties that the war placed in the way of Dutch–Iberian trade. Since the truce promised unimpeded access to the Peninsula and more trade with Europe generally, the makers of *says* for export tended to prefer peace to war. On the other hand, the makers of the heavier *herrensaaien* for the home market argued that if Holland's textile industry was to survive and prosper, the Dutch must exploit their only real advantage *vis-à-vis* Flanders, namely cheaper and more abundant wool supplies, which could be done only if the conflict continued, by means of the naval blockade and the war-time *licenten*. Continued high duties, furthermore, would have the effect of shutting Flemish textiles out of the Dutch home market. The school of thought which stressed the importance of the wool factor and the wartime protective barrier indeed lost the day in 1607–9, but their resentment at the post-1609 changes generated a powerful current of anti-truce feeling in the textile sector for many years thereafter.

There were different views also on the question of Holland's important river trade. While the truce might be expected to have stimulated both movement of goods along the Schelde, Maas, and other waterways to the South Netherlands and eastwards along the Rhine to Wesel, Cologne, and Frankfurt, by ending the insecurity that had prevailed on the rivers, and by the reduction in the *licenten*, there were also contrary arguments.[16] Oldenbarnevelt's detractors argued that with the end of the naval blockade of the Flemish coast, much of the traffic previously passing by Dordrecht and other river ports to Antwerp and the south would be diverted, by sea, to Dunkirk and Ostend, especially as the Brussels regime would be sure to use the respite to improve the canals linking the Flemish coast with Ghent, Brussels, and Antwerp. It was contended also that much of Dordrecht's presently massive and lucrative trade with Germany, including the importing of Upper Rhine timber and German wines for re-export, would be highly vulnerable to diversion, via Venlo, through the South Netherlands.

At Amsterdam, Holland's largest city but one which for

---

[16] Meteren ix. 412–13; Usselincx, *Grondich Discours*, fo. 3; Usselincx *Naerder Bedenckingen*, fo. 4.

the moment was politically isolated, while resentment at the ascendancy of the other large towns, forming Oldenbarne-velt's power-base, doubtless played a part, the *vroedschap* does appear to have been chiefly swayed in adopting its stand by colonial considerations. At Amsterdam, the clash of interest between European and extra-European trade was particularly evident. Innumerable merchants stood to gain hand-somely from the resumption of trade with the Peninsula. But it was those who were linked to colonial enterprise who at this time carried more weight in the city council.[17] Reynier Pauw, the pre-eminent figure and leader of the anti-truce faction in Holland, besides being a champion of the West India Company project, had been a founder-member of the East India Company and for many years a director of its Amsterdam chamber. He had also frequently represented the Company in audiences with the States General and figured, as did other members of his family, among the fore-most investors in its shares.[18] The *vroedschap* deployed various arguments against the truce in the States of Holland and emphasized the ambiguity of the Spanish offer of tem-porary recognition during the climax of the increasingly heated debate, from the autumn of 1608 until the signing of the truce in April 1609.[19] Observers, however, had little doubt that the city administration was chiefly motivated by its concern for the East India trade, though obviously its spokesmen were careful not to say so. The 'success of this business', reported the English delegates to London, in November 1608,

doth depend uppon the resolucon of Holland, the gentry of which pro-vince doth professe for the truce, and of nineteen towns which have voyce all declare themselves [in favour] except Amsterdam and Delft which yet make difficulty by reason that the Administration of the Indian Company doe feare that the freedom of commerce into Spayne, which is a consequent of this truce, will in a short tyme divert all their merchants and mariners from that tedious and dangerous navigacon.[20]

[17] Res. Holl. 6 Jan., 15 Feb., 6 Mar., 1607; Van Dillen, 'West-Indische Com-pagnie', 146–7.
[18] Van Dillen, *Het oudste aandeelhoudersregister*, 106.
[19] Res. Holl. 19 Mar., 27 Mar., 3 Apr., 1609.
[20] Winwood and Spencer to Cecil, 17 Nov. 1608. BL Add: MS 40837, fo. 215ᵛ.

It was no mere coincidence either, that Delft quartered one of the chambers of the East India Company and one with much more considerable funds than that of Rotterdam, or that Zeeland's contribution to the Company, in proportion to its small population, was much greater than that of Holland.[21] In the case of Delft, the city council resolutions confirm that the East India interest was consistently the major factor in determining its 'Contra-Trevist' stance.[22]

However, in the case of Zeeland, the East India interest, though important, was certainly secondary to something else as a factor behind its opposition to the truce. The Zeeland towns, led by Middelburg and Flushing, threw themselves into the debate between the provinces, and into the pamphlet literature, with furious zeal, arguing chiefly in terms of general Dutch interests and concerns. The Zeelanders insisted that the Spanish recognition was inadequate, the security of the Republic threatened, the commerce of the entire country put at risk, and the cause of the 'true Christian religion' being neglected.[23] Yet while professing alarm lest trade be diverted from the northern to the southern Netherlands, Zeeland in reality had every interest in seeing trade diverted from Holland back to the Schelde. Zeeland's concern was to sustain Antwerp but in such a way as to syphon off as much of the transit trade and profit as possible.[24] The Zeelanders' virulent antipathy to the truce derived chiefly from their fear that this would lead to the lifting or modification of the Schelde restrictions, enabling sea-borne traffic from and for Antwerp to circumvent the Zeeland ports, and to their realization that the lifting of the blockade of the Flemish coast would enable Antwerp merchants to re-route much of their trade via Ghent, Brugge, and the Flemish sea-ports which would be likewise highly detrimental to Zeeland. Indeed, the combined effect of these processes could be expected to lead to complete economic stagnation in the province. As has been seen, Oldenbarnevelt and the six peace provinces had

[21] Van Dillen, *Het oudste aandeelhoudersregister*, 35.
[22] GA Delft section 1, no. 13, iii. fos. 181, 193, 194^v.
[23] Res. SG RGP 131, pp. 103, 459, 468; *Discours op den swermenden Treves*, fo. 7.
[24] Gielens, 206–14.

only been able to blunt Zeeland's opposition during the final stages of the truce deliberations by entering into a solemn commitment that during its duration, the restrictions on the Schelde would remain unchanged.[25] But this removed only one of the two causes of the province's profound economic anxiety. After 1609 Zeeland remained by far the most hostile of the provinces to the truce, its inhabitants nurturing, as foreign diplomats there were prone to observe, hispano-phobe tendencies of extraordinary vehemence.[26]

iii THE IMPACT OF THE TRUCE

As happens so often, reality proved more complex than any of the expectations and predictions. For both Madrid and The Hague, the effects of the Twelve Years Truce, though in many ways profound and far-reaching, were such a mixture of the advantageous and disadvantageous that drawing up a balanced assessment of gain and loss was found to be extremely difficult. The Dutch pamphleteer who remarked, in 1609, that both war and peace in their different ways cause some groups in society to wax and others to wane and left it at that perhaps came closest to the mark.[27]

One undoubted benefit for both sides was the military and naval disengagement and a general reduction in forces on a very considerable scale. By the summer of 1609, the strength of the Spanish army of Flanders was down to under 20,000 men, well under one-third of the force under arms in 1606.[28] Until 1617 average annual expenditure from the Spanish treasury on the army of Flanders stood at roughly 1¾ million ducats, which was approximately half the level of spending of the years 1603–6. On the Dutch side, the States General, while retaining most of the officers and companies in its pay, so that at any time the army could be swiftly reconstituted, drastically reduced the strength of the companies. From a standing army almost as large as that of the army of Flanders in 1606, some 60,000 men, the Dutch forces were cut by half, to 30,000, by 1609 and remained with only minor

[25] *Gedenkstukken* iii. 237; Wagenaar, *Vad. Hist.* x (ii). 12–13, 123–4.
[26] *Relazione veneziane*, 73, 140.   [27] *Schuyt-Praetgens*, 1–2.
[28] Parker, *Army of Flanders*, 272.

oscillations at that level until 1620.[29] Similarly, there were massive cuts in naval expenditure and both the Dutch navy and especially the Spanish Atlantic fleet, or *armada del mar océano*, based at Cadiz, were allowed to run right down. By 1617, as a result of Lerma's policy, the *armada* was down to only thirteen vessels and 2,657 men, though after his downfall, during the years 1618-21, its strength was doubled to twenty-six vessels and some 5,000 men.[30]

However, it is remarkable that neither in the United Provinces nor in Spain did these extensive cuts result in any appreciable falling off in the burden of taxation. Despite the claims of Lerma's apologists that his truce policy made possible major savings and financial reorganization,[31] owing to the crown's accumulated deficits and Lerma's policy of increasing military expenditure in North Africa and Italy, annual royal outlay during the truce did not differ markedly from pre-1607 levels.[32] All the major taxes in Castile, inherited by Philip III from his father, including the latest addition, the *millones*, which brought in 2 million ducats yearly, remained intact. The position was only marginally better in the Republic. The cost of making up previous deficits, as well as of the new Schelde fortifications and Jülich-Cleves intervention, greatly narrowed the scope for tax reductions. Indeed, Dutch military spending from an annual level of between 8 and 9 million guilders in the years 1606-9 oscillated at a level between 6½ and 7½ million throughout the years 1611-19.[33] The result was that, apart from the major reductions in 'convoy and license' money, only a few minor tax reductions were introduced. Holland's duty on coal consumption, voted in in 1605, was removed in 1612. Holland's tax on land sown with seed (*bezaeyde landen*), introduced in 1608, was soon discarded. But most of the major excise taxes such as those on salt consumption and milling grain remained at the rates fixed before 1606 throughout the truce years.[34] It was unfortunate, especially for

[29] Ten Raa ii. 377; iii. 290-2.   [30] *ACC* xxx. 18; Dánvila, 392-3.
[31] BL MS Add. 14005, fos. 50^r-50^v.
[32] See *ACC* xxix. 35-6, xxx. 15-32; Elliott, *Revolt of the Catalans*, 187-8.
[33] Ren Raa iii. 298-301.
[34] *Groot Placaet-Boeck* i. 1782-3, 1802-10.

Oldenbarnevelt, that the fiscal rewards of the truce were seemingly so small. The real benefits lay in having avoided new taxation which otherwise would have been essential. But no populace is likely to feel gratitude for the non-implementation of projected additional taxes.

That some major sectors of the foreign trade of both the Republic and Spain expanded impressively during the truce, and in large measure on account of the truce, can be shown from a wide variety of evidence. In particular, there took place a remarkable growth in the export of raw materials from the Iberian Peninsula chiefly because the Dutch with their vast shipping resources and incomparably low freight rates made it feasible to pursue in bulk certain carrying trades which otherwise would either have been uneconomic or engaged in at a lower level. There was, however, a brief setback on the Spanish side during the years 1617–18 when the build-up of tension in Italy and the detention by royal officials of a score or so of Dutch ships in Spanish and south-Italian ports led to a temporary decline in the numbers of Dutch vessels entering ports under the Spanish crown.[35] But the main trend was one of vigorous growth. By 1619–20 total wool shipments from Castile had increased by about 30 per cent since 1612–13, and in those two years Castilian wool exports had already risen appreciably since 1610.[36] While more than half of this wool was destined for Italian ports, mainly Livorno, Genoa, and Venice, the cloth industries of Florence and Venice being heavily dependent on Spanish wools, the sacks were shipped mainly by the Dutch. Moreover, the availability of Dutch shipping on the coasts of Valencia and the Balearics also greatly stimulated exports of salt from La Mata and Ibiza to Genoa, Venice, and other Italian ports.[37]

In the west-Andalusian ports, the constant presence of more north-European shipping than in previous years resulted in a greater abundance of naval stores and Scandinavian timbers, as well as of north-European manufactures, all of which were key factors in the further expansion of Seville's

---

[35] Israel, 'Spanish wool exports', 203.
[36] Ibid., pp. 196–7.   [37] Grendi, 32, 34–5.

monopoly trade with Spanish America which took place from 1609 until 1620,[38] which was characterized especially by a growth in exports, or rather re-exports, from Spain to the Indies. Furthermore, as Seville's *procuradores* informed the Cortes of Castile, increased contact with northern Europe, and particularly with the Dutch 'rebels', stimulated a marked growth in agricultural exports from the Seville region, especially wines and olive oil.[39] Similarly, from Málaga, Alicante, and the Algarve region of southern Portugal, exports of wines, raisins, figs, almonds, and olive oil greatly increased. The return of the Dutch to Setúbal and Aveiro, the main Portuguese salt-pans, transformed the salt trade throughout Europe. Setúbal salt exports during the truce reached truly massive proportions. One of the leading dealers, Andres Lopes Pinto of Lisbon, freighted over 200 Dutch ships in the three years 1615–18 alone, by means of his Amsterdam Jewish agent, to convey salt to Holland, Flanders, Poland, and Scandinavia.[40] In all, by the end of the truce, according to the *arbitrista* Francisco de Rétama, some 820 Dutch ships were frequenting Iberian and South-Italian ports each year, these being on average larger ships with larger crews than those employed in Baltic trade.[41]

But during the first years of the truce, the overall volume of Dutch European trade contracted, owing to disruption in the Baltic caused by the Danish–Swedish war of 1611–13. The Amsterdam *vroedschap* loudly deplored the lack of trade and Oldenbarnevelt's detractors, cited the slump as evidence of the detrimental effects of the truce.[42] Yet, in reality, the enhanced position of the Dutch in the Baltic can be shown, from Danish Sound toll data, even in the case of these depression years, for the Dutch share of the total of ships entering the Baltic not only continued to increase but reached its all-time high-point, around 70 per cent of the total, precisely in the years 1609–20.[43] After 1613 an impressive expansion took place, at any rate in the European

[38] Chaunu viii, no. 2, part ii, pp. 1179, 1189, 1238, 1260–1, 1398–9.
[39] *ACC* xxviii. 168; see also Retama, 'Conssideraciones', fos. 3–5. AGS Estado 2847.   [40] Koen, 'Notarial Records', *SRA* v. 219n.
[41] Retama, loc. cit., fo. 4.
[42] Usselincx, *Waerschouwinghe*, p. 20; *Relazione veneziane*, 37; Van Dillen, 'West-Indische Comp.', 147.   [43] Christensen, graph 2; Olechnowitz, 37.

trade of Amsterdam and the North Holland ports. Much of
this growth was clearly due to the newly resumed commerce
with Spain, Portugal, and south Italy, together with a new
dynamism in sectors of Baltic trade connected with Iberian
trade, much of the Polish grain being destined for Iberian
markets and of the Iberian salt and silver for the Baltic. Not
only did Dutch shipping capture the largest slice of Baltic
commerce that it ever did during the truce years, but it was
a distinctive feature of truce-time trade that Dutch merchants
regularly freighted ships for long-haul north–south trips combining Baltic with Mediterranean trade. Typically, vessels
were freighted from Holland to Portugal to load salt, and
then direct to the Baltic to deliver and to load grain, before
returning to Holland. The reverse pattern was no less frequent, and often ships would sail direct between the Baltic
and Mediterranean twice or three times before returning
home.[44] Moreover, Dutch domination of Mediterranean
carrying between Spain and Italy and between north Italy
and south Italy during these years was scarcely less marked
and far more sudden and dramatic than in the Baltic. Almost
all the wool and salt shipped between Spain and Genoa
during the truce was carried by the Dutch.[45] Having played
scarcely any such role before 1609, Dutch shipping increasingly dominated the transfer of grains and other supplies
from Sicily, Sardinia, and Naples to Valencia during the
truce.[46] Of some thirty Dutch ships at anchor in Venice in
March 1616, at least ten had brought grain from the Spanish
viceroyalty of Sicily and several more wool and salt from
Spain itself.[47] The truce, in short, created conditions in
which Dutch shipping capacity could be utilized and developed to the fullest throughout European waters. No
wonder that in 1629 Amsterdam merchants looked back
longingly on the truce as the golden era in which they had
effectively pushed aside rivals from the trade of all Europe.[48]

[44] Bogucka, pp. 436–9.   [45] Grendi, 32, 34–5.
[46] Castillo Pintado, 78, 168–77.
[47] De Jonge, *Ned. en Venetië*, 296.
[48] 'Wij door onse mesnage ende beslepentheyt gedurende de Treves all natien
uut het waeter gevaeren, meest alle negotien uut andere landen hier getrocken en
gantsch Europa met onse schepen bedient hebben': 'Koopmansadviezen', 47.

The truce also benefitted the Dutch shipbuilding industry, provided more work for seamen, and bestowed a variety of advantages on Amsterdam and the smaller North Holland ports. The truce years, indeed, constituted one of the most dynamic phases in Amsterdam's growth as the customs returns, freight-contracts, and other evidence demonstrates. Even Willem Usselincx had to admit that there was an extraordinary amount of building activity in Amsterdam during the truce. The number of deposit accounts with the Amsterdam Exchange Bank grew much faster during these years, from 731 in 1609 to 1,202 in 1620, than at any other time in the Bank's history.[49] Attracted by the new prospects for Dutch-Iberian and Dutch-Brazilian trade, there was a sudden dramatic influx of Portuguese Jewish immigrants, the number of Jewish accounts with the Exchange Bank rising from only twenty-four in 1609 to 106, or 9 per cent of the total, by 1620.[50] The importing of Brazilian products indirectly via Portugal at this time became one of the city's major trades and also generated a valuable new industry: more than twenty sugar refineries arose in Amsterdam in the space of ten or twelve years.[51] But Amsterdam's rapid expansion during the truce was not merely untypical of developments in the country as a whole, it actually contrasted quite sharply with the position elsewhere.[52] Rotterdam, Middelburg, and Flushing entirely failed to share in Amsterdam's gains. Apart from Dordrecht, which benefitted from the revival of trade on the Rhine and Maas, the inland towns of Holland, most obviously Delft, experienced harsh economic difficulties, as also did the city of Utrecht. After duly allowing for the effects of the tariff reductions in 1609,[53] which diminished

---

[49] Van Dillen, 'Vreemdelingen', 14.   [50] Ibid.

[51] 'Deductie' (Jan. 1622) fo. 6v. ARH SH 1358.

[52] 'De Neeringhen sijn doorgaens over het gantsche Landt veel minder ghewheest als te vooren', noted one pamphleteer a decade later, 'Zeelandt is by na in decadentie ghekomen: Alle dinghen zijn met den Treves duyrder gheworden, de ghemeene lasten ende imposten sijn op de Ghemeente ghebleven': *Consideratien op den Treves*, p. 1; see also Usselincx, *Waerschouwinghe*, p. 20; *Den Compaignon vanden verre-sienden Waerschouwer*, 3–4; *Antwoordt op sekeren Brief Evlaly*, pp. 9–10.

[53] *Groot Placaet-Boeck* i. 2388/2416; Westermann, 3–30; unfortunately, no exact correlation is possible, but throughout this study I have used Westermann's estimate that the war-list resulted in approximately 25 per cent higher returns on the same volume of commerce as the truce-list.

customs returns on a given volume of trade by roughly a quarter, it emerges, as is shown on Graph 1, that in both South Holland and Zeeland customs returns, and therefore trade, stagnated throughout the truce.

Several factors determined this sectionally sluggish performance. The traffic in French wines, centred at Rotterdam and Middelburg, and crucial to their economic life, suffered appreciably both from the re-emergence of Iberian wines onto the Dutch market and, especially, from the hefty reduction, under the new tariff list, in duty on the German wines shipped by river to Dordrecht.[54] The war-list had had the side-effect of severely penalizing Rhine wines in favour of Bordeaux and Loire vintages, a *de facto* preference abruptly abolished in 1609. Dutch trade with western France was also affected by the influx of Portuguese salt which was of better quality than Brouage salt and more suitable for the preserving of fish and herring. Furthermore, while most goods from the Baltic and Scandinavia, for the South Netherlands, had, during the latter part of the war, been shipped, on the last leg of their journey, via the inland waterways of Holland and Zeeland, most of this transit trade, vital to Zeeland and to a lesser extent to Rotterdam, was diverted following the lifting of the blockade of the Flemish coast.[55] Now Dutch ships ferried merchandise such as Norwegian timber and also French wine direct by sea to Ostend and Dunkirk. Indeed, Antwerp merchants were encouraged by the Brussels regime to bypass Zeeland in their commercial arrangements. Albert, besides embarking on a programme to improve the canals linking the Flemish coast with Brugge, Ghent, and Antwerp, also astutely refused to reduce his own tariffs on river trade with the Republic in line with the Dutch reductions.[56] This significantly disadvantaged the Schelde route. Some Zeeland merchants and politicians consequently became more amenable, after 1609, to suggestions that the Schelde restrictions be lifted or modified as a means of attracting both maritime and inland water-traffic

---

[54] Israel, 'Dutch river trade', 466-7.
[55] Usselincx, *Waerschouwinghe*, 26.
[56] Kernkamp ii. 343-4; Voeten, 'Antwerpens handel'. 70-1; id 'Antwerpse reacties', 214.

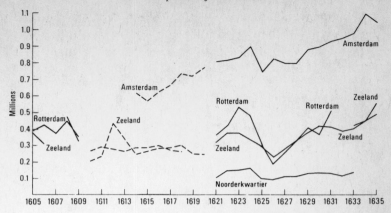

1 The 'Convoy and License' (customs) returns on all Dutch imports and exports collected by the Dutch admiralty colleges (1605–1635) (in guilders). *Source*: Becht, table no. 1.

back to the river. When the Antwerp city council endeavoured to initiate talks on this issue with the States of Zeeland in 1612–13, with the argument that lifting the ban on direct access from the sea to Antwerp would be as much in Zeeland's as Antwerp's interest, there was some favourable reaction, notably at Flushing.[57] However, Zeeland's leading town, Middelburg, decided to block any such shift in provincial policy, believing that to give in would be merely to allow direct access, permitting traffic to pass Zeeland by entirely. In effect, Middelburg preferred to wait for a possible resumption of war, seeing this as a much surer solution to the province's difficulties.

However, probably the most damaging economic development of all from the point of view of the Dutch 'common man' who figured so largely in the pamphlets, and with regard to popular attitudes towards the Oldenbarnevelt regime, was the sudden sharp escalation in food prices exacerbated by the resumption of grain supplies to the South Netherlands which had previously been forbidden and by the rapid increase in grain exports to the Peninsula and Italy. It is not

[57] Gielens, 194–7.

at all surprising that the Dutch man-in-the-street was in an ugly mood during the second decade of the seventeenth century, for food prices then rose much faster than during any other decade in the century.[58] While in general the Dutch artisan and labourer, during the late sixteenth and early seventeenth centuries, was in a unique position in Europe in that his wages kept pace or even rose faster than prices,[59] the years 1609–21 were almost certainly a marked exception to this, being a phase in which prices outstripped wages.

While important sections of Dutch and Spanish foreign trade did prosper during the truce, the effects of this selective growth were not regarded as being in the least beneficial by many contemporaries. Of course, the two economies differed markedly in type and structure, but they had in common, in contrast for example to France and Germany, an exceptionally high degree of sensitivity to shifts in foreign trade. But while European commerce was indispensable to the growth and prosperity of the Dutch economy, in the case of Spain, trade with other European countries, as many of the *arbitristas* were acutely aware, tended to work to the country's disadvantage. Because the balance of Spanish trade with Europe was fundamentally unfavourable, the more it increased in volume the worse were its ill effects.

Partly, the drawbacks of an expanded European commerce for Spain related to agriculture. While historians are prone to stress the division between arable and pastoral Spain, an often much more significant division as regards the late sixteenth and seventeenth centuries is that between farming exclusively for local markets and farming partly or wholly for export. In the Castilian interior, wool was the only agricultural product geared towards the wider European economy. But around the southern and eastern coasts wines, raisins, figs, rice, almonds, and olive oil were produced in part for export. Broadly, the latter flourished as a result of the truce while the former suffered. The Peninsula constituted a major sector of the high-price food zone of Europe, essentially the Mediterranean area, where dry conditions, low

[58] Consideratien op den Treves, p. 1; Gutmann, 117.
[59] De Vries, *Dutch Rural Economy*, 183–4.

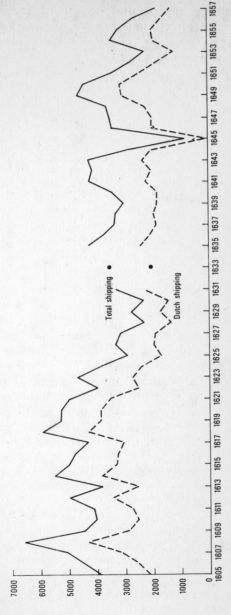

2 Shipping entering the Baltic through the Danish Sound (1605–1657). *Source:* Ellinger Bang i. 170–289.

yields, and relatively dense population enforced much higher price levels for basic foods than prevailed in northern Europe.[60] There was therefore a powerful inducement for foreign merchants to ship in cheap Baltic grain and Atlantic fish to exploit the high prices which in turn tended to undermine the position of arable farming in some parts of the Peninsula. Since the Dutch handled some two-thirds of the Baltic grain trade and at this time were greatly in advance of all competitors as regards shipping activity, Iberian agriculture was in certain respects unavoidably vulnerable to Dutch commerce.[61]

The thousands of surviving Dutch freight contracts of the truce years for the shipping of Polish wheat, rye, and other north-European foodstuffs from Holland to the Peninsula indicate that the regions most open to such penetration were Valencia, the Balearics, Catalonia, Andalusia, and, except for fish, Galicia and Portugal.[62] By 1609 grain output in the realm of Valencia was entirely inadequate, particularly to feed the large population of the city, and constant bulk importing of wheat and fish through Alicante and the city of Valencia rendered the region ever more dependent on seaborne foreign imports.[63] In Catalonia likewise, wheat prices were endemically high.[64] Eastern Spain also generated an extraordinarily strong demand for fish imports, often English or French cod, but usually shipped by the Dutch until 1621, the coastal waters of Mediterranean Spain being rather poor in fish stocks by comparison with the Atlantic zone.[65] Yet, paradoxically, the increased food imports of the truce period coincided with good harvests and rising grain yields, in Old Castile and Andalusia particularly.[66] However essential food imports were judged to be by the city corporations of Valencia, Barcelona, Lisbon, and elsewhere, the influx of cheap

[60] See Retama, 'A la Chatolica y Real Magd.' (1619), AGS Estado 634, exp. 322, fos. 23–4.

[61] See the 'Propuesta a S.M^d' (1617), BNM MS 2348, fos. 535^r–535^v.

[62] Koen, 'notarial Deeds' in the SRA series; and GA Amsterdam notarial archive index and card index.

[63] Casey, 79.   [64] Elliott, *Catalans*, 56–7.

[65] Casey, 79–80; Israel, 'Further data', 9, 10.

[66] Ruiz Martin, 'Un testimonio', p. 12.

foreign grains was bound to affect the grain-producing regions of Castile and Andalusia adversely. The Andalusian city of Jaén complained in 1612 to the Castilian Cortes of the 'disadvantages that result from allowing entry of foreign wheat when it is abundant here, as at present for the foreigners take out gold and silver of which there is great lack.'[67] Similarly, in 1621 the *arbitrista* Fernández Navarrete insisted that it was in the crown's interest to forbid cheap foreign grain imports altogether when domestic supplies were adequate.[68]

If the impact of the truce on Iberian agriculture was mixed and complaints on this score somewhat muted, the position was otherwise with regard to Spain's industries. Ever since the fifteenth century, textile manufacture in Castile had proved vulnerable to foreign competition, mainly from Flanders and France during the sixteenth century, and had suffered from the increasing demand abroad for Spanish wools which had inevitably forced up prices for the raw material at home. Yet while the various weaknesses of the Castilian cloth industries were fully evident throughout the sixteenth century, the threat of disaster had remained potential rather than real owing to circumstances abroad. Indeed, stimulated by the growth of trade with the Americas, cloth output at Toledo, Segovia, and other manufacturing centres had continued to expand until the 1590s. However uncompetitive in some respects, Spanish manufactures were cushioned until the 1590s by the severe disruption in the Low Countries, during the 1570s and 1580s, which reduced Flemish textile production to a mere fraction of its previous level, and by the marked decline in output in northern France during the French Wars of Religion.[69] The crisis for Spanish industry began only around 1600 when production began to recover in France and to a small degree in Flanders and as the output of linens and new draperies grew at Haarlem and Leiden where Flemish émigré workers had begun to produce fabrics suited to Mediterranean markets in large quantities from the early 1590s. Coinciding with the textile revival in France and Flanders and the rapid rise of a Dutch

---

[67] *ACC* xxvii. 265.   [68] Fernández Navarrete, fos. 58^V–59^r.
[69] Coornaert, 493–5; Deyon, 'Variations', 948–9.

cloth industry directed at southern markets, the growth in Castilian output ceased and decline set in.[70]

At Segovia the devastating effects of the 1598–9 epidemic caused a particularly sharp drop in production in the first years of Philip III's reign followed by a slight measure of recovery during the second decade of the century, a sequence which masks what was in fact an intensification of the long-term crisis brought on by the truce. At Toledo, however, the relatively minor setback of the first decade of the seventeenth century, was followed by an altogether steeper and more disastrous contraction coinciding exactly with the truce years.[71] At both Segovia and Toledo a new stabilization and even some recovery began from 1621 precisely. It was by no mere chance therefore, that Cortes, *arbitristas*, and crown became acutely conscious of the connection between industrial decline and increased contact with northern Europe during the years between 1609 and 1621. The situation was further aggravated by the sudden stimulus accorded by Dutch shipping to the carrying trade between Spain and Italy which caused a sharp rise in imports of Italian silks coinciding with the influx of north-European linens and woollens. Spain was swept by a wave of protectionist fervour. Various writers of the truce period accounted Spain's newly expanded commerce with northern Europe as wholly or largely prejudicial.[72] 'The damage to Spain arises from the new commerce of the foreigners', wrote Sancho de Moncada in 1619, 'for in every prosperity [i.e. trade boom] in Spain, the foreigner intervenes and sucks it forth depriving Spain of it and carrying it all to her enemies'.[73] Moncada, a Toledan, likewise deplored the parasitic prosperity of sea-ports such as Málaga, Alicante, and Bilbao to which north-European shipping was drawn, and which expanded whilst the rest of Spain declined, as being ruinous to the Castilian heartland.[74] Linked to these complaints, Moncada, Rétama, and other writers inveighed bitterly against the burgeoning exports of wool, silk, iron,

[70] Weisser, 632; Ruiz Martín, 'La empresa capitalista', 269–72, 274; id., 'Un testimonio', 9.

[71] Weisser, loc. cit.

[72] See BL MS Eg. 2078, fos. 111–13; Moncada, fos. 5–8^v; Lisón y Biedma, fo. 7; Fernández Navarrete, fos. 49^r–49^v.

[73] Monçada, fo.   [74] Ibid., fo. 16.

and other raw materials. While the represenatatives of Seville
and Madrid which were chiefly commercial centres, stood
aside in the Cortes, those of the manufacturing towns exerted
strong pressure on the crown to impose higher tariffs on imported foreign manufactures and to limit the influx especially
of woollens and silks.[75] One of the Segovian *procuradores*
maintained in the Cortes, in August 1617, that the king
'should decree that all clothing worn by his subjects, of whatever sort, should be of Spanish manufacture and from nowhere else at all.'[76] He was equally emphatic that wool
exports should be completely halted.

Indeed, possibly nothing contributed more than this industrial collapse, and the rapid decay of Castile's towns
during the second decade of the seventeenth century, to the
almost universal conviction among Spaniards of all classes
by around 1620 that the Twelve Years Truce had been a
disaster. Hence the treaty's remarkable unpopularity.[77]
Evidently, the truce was even less popular among sections of
the Spanish populace than among the politicians. But even
the most cautious of the political élite, such as the Conde de
Gondomar, who was loath to advocate renewal of the war,
was in no doubt about the disastrous economic impact of the
truce. Shortly after returning to Spain from England in 1619,
he wrote to the king of his fears for the future and the extent
of the economic disaster which he linked with the truce.
Whether or not they were inevitable effects, as he saw it, the
flood of foreign manufactures entering the country, the excessive outflow of precious metals, and the decay, poverty,
and depopulation associated with these processes had all
followed the peace treaty with England and the Dutch truce
which together had created the conditions for Spain's ruin.[78]

But if adverse economic ramifications fostered a mood
highly unconducive to renewal of the truce in Spain, precisely

---

[75] *ACC* xxx, 456, 461–2, 498–501; xxxi. 103, 158–9, 271.

[76] *ACC* xxx. 237–8; the Catalan Cortes was likewise split between 'industrial'
and 'commercial' factions, the former being fiercely protectionist: see Vázquez
de Prada, 561.

[77] Cespedes y Meneses, 97–8.

[78] Gondomar to Philip, 28 Mar. 1619, *Corresp. Gondomar* ii. 135–6, 141,
146; see also Kellenbenz, 'Spanien', 295.

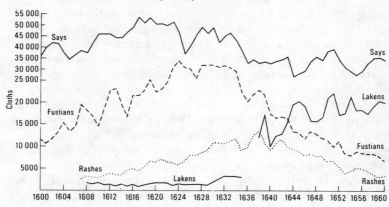

3 Leiden's output of fine woollens (*lakens*), *says*, fustians, and rashes (1600–1660). *Source*: Posthumus, *Leidsche lakinindustrie*, graphs in vols. ii and iii.

the same is true, in large measure, of the position in the Republic. The alarming predictions of the anti-truce faction in 1608–9, if exaggerated, proved to have considerable force. Besides continuing high taxation and the commercial stagnation in South Holland and Zeeland, a variety of rather ominous pressures had been brought to bear on the manufacturing towns.

Perhaps the single most important economic consequence of the truce in the Low Countries, as many Dutchmen were painfully aware, was the revival of industrial activity in the South Netherlands, or rather in Flanders and Brabant, stimulated both by the opening up of the Flemish ports, following the lifting of the Dutch naval blockade, and the Dutch tariff reductions of October 1609, which made it possible for Flemish woollens, linens, and other manufactures to compete with Dutch products on the Dutch market both for local consumption and for re-export. While linen output had begun to recover at Ghent, Kortrijk, and Oudenaarde during the 1590s, the momentum increased markedly during the truce years. At Kortrijk linen production almost doubled during the truce.[79] A high proportion of the Ghent production

[79] Sabbe, *Belgische vlasnijverheid* i. 334; Bastin, 132–3.

which was destined for Spain and the Spanish Indies reached Seville, Lisbon, and its other markets through the Dutch ports. Meanwhile at Hondschoote, after modest growth in the years 1600-9, output of *says* expanded by more than one-third.[80] However, it is significant that away from the Dutch borders, at Lille and other Walloon textile centres where the main recovery took place after the treaty of Vervins in 1598, the truce years were a period of stagnation rather than of growth.[81]

The influx of Flemish manufactures into the Republic worked decidedly to the advantage of Amsterdam whose merchants now had larger and cheaper stocks of linens and draperies for export, especially to the newly expanded Mediterranean markets. But the effect on the Dutch manufacturing towns was unavoidably adverse as regards both textiles and other sectors.[82] The brewers of Delft, then the leading brewing centre in the Republic, complained to the States of Holland as early as 1610 of the ill effects of cheap imports of South Netherlands beer.[83] By 1616, what had previously been the town's foremost industry had virtually collapsed and the town was gripped by recession. There were serious riots at Delft in August 1616, following the imposition of a new municipal tax, in which fierce resentment against the magistracy was shown and the town hall and several fiscal offices seriously damaged. In April 1618 the States of Holland granted Delft a subsidy to assist with the repairs on the town hall out of consideration for the 'decline in business and prosperity affecting the city of Delft'.[84] Meanwhile Haarlem had to cope with the rapid increase in Flemish linens appearing on the Dutch market stimulated by a reduction in the tariff on linens imported from 'enemy territory' to a mere fifth of the pre-1609 level.[85]

[80] Coornaert, 493-5.
[81] Deyon and Lottin, 31-2.
[82] Usselincx, *Waerschouwinghe*, p. 20; *Den Compaignon vanden verre-sienden Waerschouwer*, p. 4: 'want vele de Manifacturen in Brabant ende Vlaanderen om den goeden coop hebben gaen coopen ofte daer doen maecken, diese hier te lande tot profijt van onse Inwoonders hadden moghen ofte coopen ofte besteden.'
[83] Res. SH 21 Dec. 1610.
[84] Res. SH 7 Apr. 1618; Wagenaar, *Vad. Hist.* x. 96-7; van Deursen iii. 57, 59.
[85] *Groot Placaet-Boeck* i. 2404-5 and 2458-9.

With regard to the Dutch woollen-cloth industry, centred at Leiden, Delft, and Gouda, the truce brought some new opportunities but also a range of harsh new pressures. Lacking the naval blockade of the Flemish coast, it was now impossible for the States General to channel exports of German and Dutch wools to the South Netherlands via the inland waterways and this, in turn, was the essential precondition for imposing high charges on such exports. If the Dutch had attempted to persist with high tariffs on wool exports to Flanders under the new truce list, they would simply have diverted the entire trade in Baltic wools via the Flemish ports. Thus duty on Pomeranian and other German wool re-exports to 'enemy territory' fell to only one-eighth of its previous level under the 1609 list.[86] In this way Leiden for the time being lost its chief advantage over Hondschoote and Lille, namely cheaper and more abundant supplies of low- and medium-quality wools. Amsterdam, being indifferent to the duty on *heerensaaien* which were for the home market, had agreed to the impost on this product remaining at two-thirds of its previous level, but the tariffs on Hondschoote and Lille *says* which were much esteemed by Dutch exporters to the Mediterranean, as well as on English *bays* and on fustians, Tilburg *lakens*, and other imported fabrics, were drastically cut. Flemish *says* now paid only one-quarter of the duty levied in the years 1603–9.[87]

Inevitably, the greatly reduced charges on Flemish and English cloth, combined with the far lower labour costs prevailing in these neighbouring countries, provoked a fierce intensification of competition on the Dutch market. The English merchant adventurers had eagerly anticipated a boost to exports of English new draperies to Holland, from 1609, and they were not disappointed.[88] While direct English cloth exports to the Baltic sharply declined, more and more English textiles were shipped to Holland often for re-export to Germany and the Baltic in Dutch vessels.[89] It is true that the expansion in Amsterdam's European trade permitted a continued growth in total cloth output at Leiden from 72,000

[86] Ibid. i. 2482–5.   [87] Ibid. i. columns 2466–70.
[88] Merchant Adventurers to SG, Middelburg, 16 May 1609. ARH SG 4918 i.
[89] Diferee, 297; Supple. appendix A.

cloths in 1607 to 97,000 in 1620[90] and a substantial increase in the Leiden work-force, but the fierce competition of these years forced the Leiden producers to shift to some extent into cheaper, rougher fabrics so that it is possible that the actual value of Leiden's output rose very little.

Furthermore, Leiden's output only held up as well as it did because of even more serious difficulties elsewhere in Holland. Production of *say*-fustians at Gouda declined from 18,000 cloths in 1612 to 11,000 in 1621.[91] In the long run, it was in Leiden's interest to concentrate on production of high-quality fabrics where the disadvantage of Holland's high labour costs would count for least.[92] But during the truce, circumstances forced Leiden, Delft, and Gouda to move in the opposite direction. South Netherlands towns such as Tilburg and Den Bosch were more used to using high-grade Spanish wools and could produce *lakens* more cheaply than Leiden while Hondschoote *says* were of better quality than Leiden's. Moreover, English wool, if costlier, was finer than the Dutch and German varieties available in Holland, so that the English proved superior in the production of *bays* and the more expensive new draperies. Thus, there was no expansion whatever in Leiden's output of *lakens* during the truce and very little in *says*, the dominant branch.[93] The main expansion was in 'rashes' and other cheap, coarse, fabrics. Thus paradoxically, the Dutch held their own mainly in the 'coarser sorts' where it was least to their advantage to do so. Faced by this predicament, Leiden together with other Holland towns battled during 1614–15 to obtain either a return to the pre-1609 tariff list, or at least a modest 25 per cent increase in the post-1609 list, to meet only with a sharp rebuff from Amsterdam and the other commercial towns.[94] However, by way of a gesture, the States of Holland, at Leiden's request, did suspend entirely the duty on wool imports into the Republic, from 1615 onwards, indefinitely.[95]

While unrest and popular agitation against the urban

[90] Posthumus, *Lakenindustrie* ii. 129.   [91] Gezelschap, bylage 2.
[92] Wilson, 219.   [93] Posthumus, *Lakenindustrie* ii. 128–9.
[94] GA Leiden Sec. Arch. 446, fos. 164, 189, 210ᵛ, 237ᵛ; Res. Holl. 1614, p. 108; ibid. 1616, pp. 15, 30.
[95] Ibid. 1616, p. 25.

magistracies which backed Oldenbarnevelt became increasingly evident in the years after 1609, it is a remarkable fact that the phenomenon was largely limited to the industrial towns. Manifestations of artisan anger, such as the Delft riots or the unrest at Haarlem, Utrecht, and Leiden in August and September 1617, when there was prolonged agitation against the *vroedschappen* and when the Leiden burgomasters feared an attack on their town hall,[96] were menacing symptoms, but restricted to a handful of towns. In itself, such ferment could not have served the purposes of the political faction led by Maurits and Reynier Pauw which had suffered defeat at Oldenbarnevelt's hands in 1606–9. If the pro-Oldenbarnevelt Haarlem *vroedschap* claimed that a systematic campaign was afoot to set whole sections of the populace against their magistrates and undermine the authority of the *vroedschappen*, neither Stadholder nor Amsterdam burgomasters had desire or interest in openly inciting social violence or encouraging sedition for political ends. What Oldenbarnevelt's political foes had need of was a broad national cause which would unite a majority of the provinces, as the anti-truce campaign had not, and which was not socially divisive but which would facilitate the channelling of various social pressures for specific political ends. In the event, the crucial element which brought together the artisan agitation and the repulsed political faction in a truly broad national opposition to Oldenbarnevelt and the Holland regents and nobility was, of course, the spreading religious dissension within society.

The disputes between Gomarus and Arminius, professors of theology at Leiden, had since 1602 provoked steadily increasing friction between strict adherents of the doctrine of predestination and proponents of a more elastic approach to what was taken to be Calvin's teaching. Also, since the 1570s friction had persisted between those who adopted an erastian approach to ecclesiastical matters, envisaging the regents as final arbiters in church affairs, and those who demanded that the church be supreme within its own sphere. It was only

---

[96] GA Leiden Sec. Arch. 446, fo. 254, vroed. res. 6 Sept. 1617; *Ivstificatie... regeerders der stadt Haerlem*, pp. 3–4; *Letters Carleton*, 82, 117, 307; according to Carleton, Leiden was the 'fountain of these dissensions'.

after 1609 and the signing of the truce, however, that these two disputes, which had become linked, began seriously to permeate political and social life throughout the Republic. While suspension of the struggle with Spain was bound to release all kinds of pent-up pressures and resentments, Oldenbarnevelt was unfortunate indeed that what in essence was a theological disagreement of real concern to only a tiny body of men and which initially had had the States of Holland yawning with indifference, proved so apt a means of welding together and combining the various political, economic, and social grievances of the time.

The theological issues as such were of little concern to either the pro- or anti-Oldenbarnevelt factions. For some time most regents remained determined not to become involved and for many years neither Maurits nor Reynier Pauw showed any greater inclination towards strict Calvinist theology than did the Advocate himself.[97] The forging of the powerful Counter-Remonstrant party which eventually overthrew Oldenbarnevelt and the regents who backed him was the result of sheer political opportunism and the harnessing of economic grievances to an ostensibly religious cause, true though it is that theology played an indispensable part. While relatively few of the clergy inclined towards Remonstrantism and the ideas of Arminius, the Remonstrants, out of principle and a sense of self-preservation, had opposed strict regimentation of doctrine by the church authorities and asserted the ultimate supremacy of the secular authorities in church matters. The Counter-Remonstrants, in contrast, envisaged the church as 'sole judge of doctrine'.[98] Thus Oldenbarnevelt and the Holland regents, anxious as always to safeguard a more liberal approach to questions of religious belief, as well as maintain their control over the church councils which supervised the church in each district, inevitably became involved as the protectors of the Arminians. Thus gradually Counter-Remonstrantism emerged as an instrument for attacking those same protectors and eliminating the group of regents who dominated decision-making within the States of Holland.

[97] Renier, 55–7; Geyl, *Suriano*, 129, 137.   [98] Renier, 45.

While the combination of religious dissension and popular resentment against certain *vroedschappen* led to a series of disturbances and commotions, beginning at Alkmaar and Utrecht in 1610 and spreading subsequently to various towns including Leeuwarden, Rotterdam, and Schoonhoven, matters came to a head in the summer of 1617, because the regents of Haarlem, Leiden, Gouda, and other manufacturing towns, had become so fearful of social revolt and distrustful of their civic militias, that large numbers of citizenry at Haarlem, and especially at Leiden, were dismissed from the militias and it was arranged through the States of Holland that local bodies of hired professional soldiers called *waardgelders* should be raised to preserve order. These troops were raised at Haarlem, Leiden, Gouda, Utrecht, Rotterdam, and Schoonhoven. With the artisanate then further provoked, town government in the manufacturing towns became more precarious than ever. Maurits, offended by the raising of troops without either his or the States General's authority, also now had the pretext that he needed to intervene directly in the States General's name in the politics of Holland. Finally, the Stadholder launched his coup. After arresting Oldenbarnevelt, in August 1618, he toured the Holland towns at the head of troops removing from the *vroedschappen* — with particular thoroughness at Haarlem, Leiden, Gouda, and Utrecht — those regents who had supported the Advocate and Remonstrantism. At Leiden, Holland's largest industrial town, the Stadholder's intervention was greeted with a massive and noisy show of approval and enthusiasm on the part of thousands of weavers and other artisans.

The drive against Oldenbarnevelt and the pro-Remonstrant regents thus ended by removing from power the group which had negotiated the Twelve Years Truce and forced it through. Maurits's *coup d'état* was thus also an attack on the truce. During the turbulent months preceding the Advocate's downfall, both sides had sought to exploit the fact of the truce as a weapon against the other, as can be clearly seen from the torrent of pamphlets that swept the country in 1617–18. A variety of pamphleteers, including François van Aerssen who penned several angry tracts, castigated the Remonstrants as tools of Spain and maintained that the entire internal turbulence in the Republic was but a consequence of the truce which they insisted on regarding as the outcome of long and sinister scheming on the part of Philip IV and his 'Machiavellian' ministers.[99] The dissident Leiden militiamen removed in 1617 stressed, in their printed protest, that the Leiden regents had retained only those burghers who were willing to swear to a new and distinctly milder oath of civic allegiance from which had been dropped the old, stirring, clause that 'one declares the king of Spain and his adherents to be public enemies'.[1] On the other side, Oldenbarnevelt's son-in-law, Cornelis van der Mijle, indignantly refuted van Aerssen's outpourings claiming that the truce was sound and beneficial to the Republic and that the real tools of Spain were those who obstinately engaged in the 'false, Spanish, Jesuitical, practice' of fomenting ill-feeling between Prince Maurits and the regents and nobility of Holland.[2] The Haarlem *vroedschap*, in a tract which it had published before Maurits's coup to justify its conduct in purging the civic militia and confronting popular agitation, bitterly condemned the exploitation of religious controversy as a pretext and 'specieusen deckmantel' (specious cloak) for undermining established authority, at the same time defending the truce which had brought so 'burdensome and dangerous a war against so powerful an enemy to so happy, splendid, and honourable an outcome'.[3]

Elimination of the pro-Oldenbarnevelt faction in the Holland town councils in 1618, and the climate of fear and intimidation generated by Oldenbarnevelt's subsequent execution, both fatally weakened the Dutch peace party for the time being and stilled the debate over the truce. The ruthless purge also put an abrupt if only temporary stop to the Republic's internal wrangling and dissension. A wholly undisputed transition to war with Spain in 1621, however, was by no means a foregone conclusion. Argument over the truce revived to some extent in 1621, albeit in restrained and

---

[99] Aerssen, *Practycke*, 4–5, 38–9; Aerssen, *Noodtwendigh ende Levendigh discours*, 18; *Cort ende Klaer Contra-Discours*, 3, 6.

[1] *Cort verhael dienende tot justificatie*, 1, 12, 14.

[2] Van der Mijle, *Ontdeckinge*, 6–7, 10.

[3] *Iustificatie . . . regeerders der stadt Haerlem*, 3.

rather tentative terms. After Oldenbarnevelt's downfall, there remained a good many in the Republic who esteemed the truce highly enough to press discreetly in favour of renewing it. In the eastern provinces which had supported the peace moves in 1606–9, notably Gelderland and Overijssel, nobility and towns showed a marked distaste for the higher taxation that war would involve and considerable anxiety regarding the Spanish garrisons firmly entrenched along the eastern border at Groenlo, Oldenzaal, and Lingen.[4] Indeed, it seems that in March 1621 no less than five provinces — Gelderland, Overijssel, Utrecht, Friesland, and Groningen — favoured renewing the truce on the terms of 1609 and there was widespread concern in political circles lest a situation arise which would have opened anew the rift between the provinces over the question of relations with Spain.

If the downfall of Oldenbarnevelt definitively ended the quest for a full peace with Spain but without necessarily eliminating prospects for renewing the truce, much the same can be said of the downfall of Lerma, in the very same month as that of Oldenbarnevelt, August 1618. Precisely how the anti-Lerma faction at court gained in strength during 1617 and early 1618 remains to be investigated but, as the Bohemian storm clouds gathered, and the position of the Emperor temporarily deteriorated, Lerma became completely isolated among Philip's ministers in advising against Spanish intervention in Germany, in the Emperor's support. The palace revolution of 1618, engineered by Lerma's own son, the duke of Uceda, led directly to the ascendancy in the conduct of Spain's foreign affairs of Baltasar de Zúñiga, which, in turn, implied a complete reversal of Lerma's priorities in the field. The drive against Islam was forgotten. Attention focused again on the arena where Zúñiga's expertise lay — northern Europe. And yet, despite this crucial shift, despite Zúñiga's fervent belief in the need to assert Spanish power in the north more vigorously than had been done since the 1590s and his distaste for the truce terms agreed in 1609, it would be wrong to assume that the Spanish leadership was now

---

[4] See the anonymous contemporary account 'Te Noteren. Op Peckij propositie'. KBH MS 75 k 83, fo. 2; De Boer, 'De hervatting', *TvG* xxv. 48–9.

firmly set on resuming the war with the Republic. What Zúñiga was committed to was powerful Spanish intervention in Bohemia and the Palatinate and this is some respects actually enhanced prospects for a renewal of the Dutch truce by forcing Spain to divert men and funds away from the Netherlands. Zúñiga was not blind to the fact that the Dutch truce gave him a freer hand to act in Germany. Thus while it is true that the downfall of Lerma effectively disposed of the search for a full peace with the Dutch, it by no means closed the question of what policy towards the Republic Spain should adopt.

Chapter II

The Expiry of the Truce, 1618–1621

i RENEWED DELIBERATIONS

In Spain the debate over whether or not to renew the truce, and on what terms began in earnest in March 1618, some months before the downfall of Lerma. In that month Juan de Ciriza, secretary to the *Consejo de Estado*, reminded ministers that the time had come to begin formulating a policy and to consult the councils of Portugal and the Indies as to means of 'improving the truce, should it be continued'.[1]

According to our information from Flanders [he advised, summarizing recent reports] for several years the Dutch have been divided into two parties: the maritime towns want war on account of their interests while the rest press for peace so as to be free of the taxes and burdens that war brings. Also it has been seen throughout that the truce was highly favourable to the Dutch and that since it was signed, they find themselves unhindered with overflowing wealth while these realms are much diminished, since the Dutch have taken their commerce, and that this damage, if not remedied, will daily become worse.

Some weeks later the council of Portugal in Madrid submitted its views to the *Consejo de Estado* in terms highly critical of the truce. 'Conceding to the Dutch that they might freely trade outside Europe in places where Your Majesty has no forts . . . proved to be highly damaging to Your Majesty's interests.'[2] To this theme the council subsequently returned in a long *consulta* of September 1619. While only meagre reinforcements had reached the Portuguese colonies in Asia since 1609, by 1617 the Dutch establishment in the Far East had reportedly grown to about twenty forts and thirty-six

---

[1] Juan de Ciriza, 'Sobre cosas de la tregua', 2 Mar. 1618. AGS Estado 634; Brightwell, 'The Spanish System', 277.
[2] *Consulta, cons. Portugal*, 28 May 1618. AGS Estado 634.

ships.[3] The most able of Philip's Portuguese advisers on colonial affairs, Pedro Alvares Pereira, argued that since the Dutch would never agree to yield or abandon their Asian conquests, should the king decide to renew the truce, he should permit it to apply only in Europe and the New World, leaving everything 'beyond the Cape of Good Hope in a state of war'.[4] Should the Dutch refuse either to withdraw from Asia or to accept a limited truce then it would be best, he advised, to resume the war in the Netherlands but fighting defensively, by land, and offensively, only by sea. Whereas strife at sea would certainly harm the Dutch, 'war by land, on the contrary, brings them great advantages because the money that Your Majesty spends on it all ends up in their hands.' It would in any case be desirable, he added, to capture the newly flourishing Dutch factory at Pulicat so as to prevent the East India Company procuring Indian fabrics which, with much profit, were exchanged in the Moluccas and Indonesia for spices.[5] The entire Council, indeed, concurred in the importance of seizing Pulicat, arguing that this would much impede the Dutch spice trade and stimulate the rival Portuguese spice trade, based at Malacca.

The Council of Portugal was unanimous, moreover, in its view that on no account should the truce be renewed on the previous terms and several ministers, notably the Conde de Faro and the Conde de Vidigueira, afterwards viceroy of Portuguese India in the years 1622-8, expressly preferred war even to an 'improved' truce.[6] Alvares Pereira was convinced that despite the great commercial success of the East India Company, the Dutch organization remained vulnerable because the immense cost of its battle fleet, troops, and twenty forts consumed the bulk of the profit. Given the strictly commercial basis of the Company, he believed that it would prove less able than the Spanish crown to stand up to a prolonged period of increased expenditure such as a resumption of war would inevitably entail. From every angle war seemed

[3] *Consulta* cons. Portugal, 23 Sept. 1619. ARB SEG 183, fos. 138-45.
[4] Ibid., fos. 140ᵛ-142ᵛ; see also considerations of Pedro Alvares Pereira dated Lisbon, 16 July 1619. ARB *SEG* 183, fos. 162-3.
[5] See Raychaudhuri, 156-60, Glamann, 132-3.
[6] Ibid., fo. 162ᵛ.

preferable to Philip's Portuguese ministers than the existing
truce, though the war that they envisaged was decidedly not
a matter of land offensives in the Low Countries, but a maritime, colonial contest with powerful forces being dispatched
to the Portuguese Indies from Castile as well as from Portugal.
What was intended was to ruin the East India Company by
relentless joint Castilian–Portuguese action in the East.

Of course, the *Consejo de Indias* esteemed the truce no
more highly than did its Portuguese colleagues. Its ministers
urged Philip to demand compensation from the States
General for the losses incurred as a result of the Spilbergen
raid in 1615, and other incursions, as well as for the massive
expenditure on the defences of Callao, Guayaquil, Acapulco,
and Manila.

> Your Majesty has suffered in the western Indies a continuous war with
> excessive costs [complained the *Consejo*], 'even greater than those in-
> curred before the truce, for with the ceaseless infestations of the enemy
> into those seas, it has been necessary to sustain heavier expenses in the
> Caribbean islands and ports of the mainland and New Spain. . .and thus
> it is essential that it be settled that the enemy may not enter or navi-
> gate in those western seas or any adjacent routes.'[7]

This implied Dutch abandonment of the sea-lane via the
Straits of Magellan, of their settlements in Guyana and Amazonia and of Caribbean commerce. Above all, though, what
troubled the *Consejo* were the ramifications of the bitter
Dutch–Spanish confrontation that had developed since 1606
in the Moluccas and the Philippines. Maintaining the garrisons and naval forces deployed in this region, and the three
battles fought in Manila Bay during the truce, had together
entailed an intolerable drain on the king's Mexican revenues.
In 1620 the Spaniards had four forts on Ternate alone with
a total garrison of 150 soldiers and thirty-five cannon, and
maintaining these, together with the force on Tidore, had,
since 1606, cost over 1 million ducats. Total spending from
the Mexican revenues in the Philippines and Moluccas during
the twelve years 1607–19 was put at 7 million ducats.[8] As
the *Consejo* pointed out, this was equivalent to one-third of

[7] *Consulta* cons. *Indias*, 10 Aug. 1619. ARB *SEG* 183, fos. 151ʳ–156ᵛ.
[8] Ibid., fo. 156; BL MS Egerton 1131, fo. 10.

the amount spent in the same period on the army of Flanders and represented a major diminution in the remittances from Mexico to Spain for the king's use in Europe.

While the *Consejo de Indias*, like that of Portugal, categorically preferred war to a renewal of the truce on the 1609 terms, it did not, of course, yet know in which direction Philip inclined and so it also offered advice in case the king opted for a modified truce. Chiefly, what the *Consejo* wanted was that the Dutch desist from all navigation to the Americas and withdraw from the Moluccas, leaving the spice trade firmly in Iberian hands and ending the drain on the Mexican revenues. In return for such concessions, advised the *Consejo*, the king should offer to acknowledge Dutch control of the 'trade of Japan and give them spices in Lisbon or Seville at preferential prices such that they should gain some substantial benefit from giving up navigation [for spices] to the East Indies.'[9]

Philip, on the advice of the *Consejo de Estado*, also sought the views of his ministers in the Netherlands. In April 1619 Albert was asked to convene a special *junta* for the purpose to consist of Spinola, Petrus Peckius, Chancellor of Brabant, and three Spaniards, Juan de Villela, an expert in maritime and colonial affairs, the Conde de Añover, a hard-line military man, and Albert's confessor, Fray Iñigo de Brizuela. While Brizuela and Spinola as well as Albert himself were in favour of peace, the *Consejo de Estado* took account of this and imposed guide-lines for the *junta*'s deliberations. Nothing was said about either sovereignty, religion, or the reconquest of any of the United Provinces, none of these things having played any part in the Madrid deliberations, but copies of the *consultas* of the councils of Portugal and the Indies were sent and the Brussels group was told that the king had grave reservations about the truce because of its effects on the colonial empire and trade.[10] In May the Brussels *junta* replied that Philip should offer the Dutch a new truce on three conditions: the concession of the public practice of Catholicism under the States General's jurisdiction; withdrawal

[9] ARB SEG 183, fo. 159ᵛ.
[10] Philip to Albert, 23 Apr. 1619. ARB SEG 183, fo. 274.

totally from the New World and partially from Asia; and finally the lifting of the Schelde restrictions.[11] This advice was subsequently slightly modified after Philip asked the *junta* to reappraise the situation in the spring of 1620, in the light especially of the deepening crisis in Germany. Since it was clearly beyond the king's means to finance the war adequately, argued the *junta* which now included another Castilian hard-liner, the Marqués de Bedmar (afterwards Cardinal de la Cueva), he should seek to improve the truce on the basis already proposed, except — and here we discern the influence of Pedro Alvares Pereira — that since it was improbable that the Dutch would willingly leave the Moluccas, the king should leave the East Indies 'beyond the Cape of Good Hope' in a state of war. In June 1620 Philip stiffened the *junta* further with two more senior Castilian officers of the army of Flanders, Luis de Velasco, commander of the cavalry and Spinola's second-in-command, and the inspector-general of the army, Cristobal de Benavente.

The most influential of Philip's ministers in the sphere of foreign policy, after the fall of Lerma, was Don Baltasar de Zúñiga, uncle of Olivares, related by marriage to the Flemish nobility and a diplomat of great experience in European affairs. Zúñiga set down his views on the Low Countries truce in April 1619, for the edification of the king and his colleagues. As he saw it, the confrontation in the Netherlands could not be separated from the great struggle unfolding in Central Europe so that the Dutch question was inevitably a prime concern of both branches of the House of Austria. Evidently he did not believe that there was any prospect that Spain could reconquer the rebel provinces, the daunting intricacy of the Dutch defences precluding all thought of restoring either Spanish rule or the Catholic faith by force of arms.[12] Yet, at the same time he believed fervently that 'great harm has resulted from the truce now in effect owing to the terms not having been drawn up as they should have been with respect to the Indies. 'The truce, he advised the

---

[11] Albert to Philip, 30 May 1619. ARB SEG 183, fos. 318–320ᵛ.
[12] See ARB SEG 183, fos. 169–171ᵛ; and also Yáñez, 115–20, and Brightwell, 'The Spanish System', 289–92.

king, should be renewed only on 'improved' terms. If these
were not to be had without resort to arms, then war, albeit
a war without hope of final success, would be preferable to
renewing the truce on existing terms.

Though he was perfectly aware of the depleted state of the
king's finances, the demands that he proposed should be put
to the Dutch as conditions for renewing the truce were remarkably uncompromising and indeed bear a striking resemb-
lance to those insisted on during the mid 1620s by his
nephew, the Conde-Duque de Olivares, such that one can
only conclude that both Zúñiga and Olivares contemplated
even a modified truce with much distaste. Besides the public
practice of Catholicism and withdrawal from the Indies
which were both to be fully insisted upon, some form of
token acknowledgement of the king's supremacy would be
required, together with a Dutch undertaking not to ally with
any of the king's enemies and provide a fixed number of warships yearly without charge, as well as other concessions
'which should be thought up, remembering always that these
should be feasible and practicable, for in asking for impossi-
bilities we should be wasting time to no purpose.' The list of
stipulations clearly points to the basic dilemma underlying
Zúñiga's paradoxical stance toward the Dutch: while ration-
alizing his approach to some extent, like Olivares after him,
in terms of colonial, economic, and strategic interest, ultimately he was moved by his abhorrence of the humiliation,
loss of prestige, and the passivity which had resulted from the
truce.[13] He was in other words motivated essentially by considerations of *reputación*, his policy being determined by a
psychological attitude which simply could not accept the
existing *status quo* in Dutch–Spanish relations.

Philip received additional advice from a wide variety of
prominent personages. Luis de Velasco, Marqués de Beldever,
wrote in February 1619 from Flanders, categorically recommending resumption of war.[14] While he thought that
the king should offer to renew the truce for the sake of
appearances, on condition the Dutch agreed to withdraw

---

[13] As has been well observed by J. H. Elliott, see his *Conde-Duque*, 65–6, 90–2.
[14] Velasco to Philip III, 11 Feb. 1619. AGS Estado 634.

from the Indies and to reopen the Schelde, he was convinced, rightly enough, that the 'Dutch will consent to neither of these things', so that war would be inevitable. Velasco said not a word about either sovereignty or religion, nor did he believe that Spain could reconquer the rebel provinces, but, he assured the king, by waging war 'we shall force them to guard their homes and lands so that they shall not sail to do us damage in the Indies nor assist our enemies as they do now [in Germany].' Cristobal de Benavente similarly considered that it 'will be best to resume war with these rebel provinces when the truce ends, diverting them from Germany.'[15] Yet another senior officer writing from Flanders, in 1620, argued that the idleness among the troops resulting from the truce had led to a wholly deplorable decline in standards of training, discipline, and expertise to the detriment of the empire as a whole.[16] 'Idleness', he warned, 'will do us greater damage than the arms of the enemy.'

During the course of the deliberations in Madrid and Brussels remarkably little thought was given to the question of French and English reactions, an attitude encouraged by the vacillation and weakness of the French and English governments at this time. The failure of either power to make any impact on the drama unfolding in Germany strengthened the prevailing assumption that Spain could forge her Netherlands policy paying only a minimum of attention to either France or England. In fact, while professing to be willing to assist in the process of renewing the truce, both governments appear to have secretly preferred a resumption of war.[17] The Pope expressly recommended resumption of war against the heretic Dutch in the interests of Catholic Europe and the church but very little attention seems to have been paid to his views either. The one external factor which had a considerable bearing on the formation of Spain's Netherlands policy was the situation in the Empire. In August 1620, a few months before the decisive battle between the Emperor Ferdinand and the Elector Frederick for Bohemia,

---

[15] Discourse of Benavente, BL MS Add. 14005, fo. 35.
[16] Anonymous tract of 1620, BL MS. Add. 14005, fo. 48ᵛ.
[17] Elias, 'Le Renouvellement', p. 111.

Spinola, on orders from the king, marched from the Southern Netherlands with some 25,000 men, crossed Mainz, and invaded the Rhenish Palatinate, quickly occupying a large part of the territory.[18] The States General dispatched funds and troops to assist the Elector's cause and concentrated an army in Cleves. To cover the route between the Netherlands and Palatinate, a second Spanish army, of some 12,000 men, under Velasco, was concentrated at Wesel.

The scale, cost, and implications of the conflict on the middle Rhine inevitably prompted some reconsideration in Madrid. Albert, who became increasingly agitated as the expiry of the truce approached, urged Philip in December 1620 not to insist on concessions from the Dutch. To 'think at this moment of improving the truce I judge to be difficult, especially as so little time remains, and thus it would be well to consider procuring a prolongation, for as short a time as possible, in the form that it now is.'[19] The renewed deliberations of February 1621, in the *Consejo de Estado*, revealed a definite split.[20] While some ministers now considered that the German situation necessitated at least a temporary accommodation with the Dutch, the majority still maintained that despite the diversion of Spanish resources to Germany, the king could afford war with the Dutch, having so many realms and means of raising money. It was the Dutch, contended the war-party, who would crack first under the financial strain as they would need 15 million guilders yearly to fight the war but, at the most, could raise a mere 9 million through taxation. 'During the truce, the wealth of Holland has grown,' they argued, '. . .they have stirred up the wars in Germany against the Austrians. . .and have infested both Indies with their fleets for which reasons it is necessary to redeem religion, honour, and justice by means of arms, punishing the guilty and safeguarding the world from a people that would otherwise become worse every day.'

Philip's reply to Albert, of February 1621, echoed the views of his more militant advisers.[21] While the demand

---

[18] Rodríguez Villa, 354–73.
[19] Albert to Philip III, 28 Dec. 1620. ARB SEG 184, fos. 326r–326v.
[20] 'Discurrese en el consejo' (Feb. 1621). BNM MS 2352, fos. 39r–39v.
[21] Philip to Albert, 4 Feb. 1621. ARB SEG 185, fos. 24r–24v; *Corresp. d'Esp.* i. 574.

for public practice of Catholicism in the United Provinces was expressly *pro forma* rather than of substance, and could be set aside, Albert was instructed that on no account could he extend the truce, 'even though just for a short time', without securing Dutch withdrawal from the Indies and the lifting of the Schelde restrictions. Equally significant, Albert was forbidden to initiate talks with the Dutch, being empowered only to listen to Dutch proposals should there be any and settle a new truce on the basis of Dutch concessions on trade and colonies, 'for experience has shown', declared the monarch, 'how damaging and prejudicial has been [the truce] presently in effect and that were we to continue with it, it would prove the total ruin of these realms.'

The situation on the Dutch side was in some respects not dissimilar. The professed war-party or *contra-Trevisten* ostensibly had the upper hand politically, but opinion remained deeply divided as to whether war or a new truce was preferable, there being solid support for war only in Holland and Zeeland. Venetian diplomats in The Hague admitted in their reports to their Senate that it was bafflingly difficult to know whether opinion in the States General inclined more towards war or a renewed peace.[22] The English ambassador, Sir Dudley Carleton, was no less perplexed. Maurits deliberately increased the confusion by adroitly letting slip contradictory remarks in conversation with diplomats. According to the Archduke Albert, in a report to Madrid of April 1619, Maurits, upon being approached by the French ambassador, had, in secret, expressed willingness to renew the truce. Certainly Albert took at face value the assurances of the French government that it was anxious to mediate and assist in preserving the peace and that the Stadholder would respond.[23] The major risk to which the Stadholder was exposed, in 1621, was that any new truce contacts between Brussels and The Hague, particularly should the Spaniards prove moderate in their demands, were likely to provoke serious dissension in the Republic. In several respects, Maurits

[22] *Relazione Veneziane*, 139–40; Geyl, *Suriano*, 306, 307.
[23] Albert to Philip, 5 Apr. 1619. ARB SEG 182, fo. 256; Elias, 'Le renouvèllement', 108–11.

now had less motivation for opposing a truce than he had had in 1606–9. His authority, far from being threatened, was now stronger than at any stage. The developing conflict in Germany meant that the Republic was bound for the foreseeable future to maintain a large standing army and rely to a great extent upon the military and strategic expertise of the Stadholder. He also knew that there was little immediate prospect of obtaining assistance, in case of war, from either France or England. In any case, during the years 1619–21 Maurits's primary concern, inevitably, whether in war or under a renewed truce with Spain, was to maintain a sufficiently solid façade of national unity.[24]

In February 1621, with the expiry of the truce approaching, Albert informed Madrid that the French were again offering their good offices (while the French ambassador in The Hague was in fact under secret orders from Paris to encourage the war-party in breaking off the truce) and that an intermediary had come to Brussels bearing a message from the Stadholder.[25] This was Bartholde van Swieten, Mme T'Serclaes, a Catholic noblewoman acquainted with the prince, a relative of the general Tilly who commanded the army of the Catholic League in Germany, a personage who had family reasons for passing frequently between The Hague and Brussels and who became the principal link in the secret contacts between Maurits and the Brussels court during the early 1620s.[26] According to Albert's letter to the king, Mme T'Serclaes had come from The Hague to Brussels and related to his confessor, Iñigo de Brizuela, that she herself had resolved to approach the prince and that he had confided a secret message to her: if a representative of the archduke should be sent to The Hague to propose that the States General recognize the sovereignty of the Spanish king, Maurits would endeavour to secure this recognition and a lasting peace in return for certain rewards and favours from the king for himself. In fact, it was probably Albert who

[24] Carleton to Calvert, 10/20 Mar. 1621. PRO Sp 84/100, fo. 34^r-34^v.
[25] Albert to Philip, 10 Feb. 1621. ARB SEG 185, fos. 42-7; De Boer, 'De hervatting', 37.
[26] Cuvelier, 'La correspondance', 108.

initiated this contact while preferring to conceal the fact from the king. What is certain is that Maurits did respond to Mme T'Serclaes in this way having perceived the opportunity to set a political trap for the archduke which would have the effect of greatly reinforcing national unity at home and avoiding a harmful internal debate among the provinces and towns for and against the truce.

In early March 1621 Albert again assured Madrid that Maurits now showed 'inclinación y voluntad' to reduce the 'rebel provinces' to their proper obedience should a formal proposal for recognition of sovereignty be made in the king's name to the States General.[27] The Archduke urged that he be permitted to send a representative to The Hague in response to the Prince of Orange's initiative, to make the specified declaration, this being consistent with the king's previous orders. Such a step was especially timely, he argued, in view of the continuing dissension between 'Gomeristas y Armenianos', for, if lenient conditions were offered for reconciliation, on the basis indicated by the prince, many Dutchmen would be won over. 'And on the part of the Arminians', he wrote, 'they have several times and emphatically made known to us that there is advantage in making this proposition.'

Albert's assurances concerning Maurits's attitude were deliberately kept from the wider body of the king's ministers and confined to just three — Baltasar de Zúñiga, the Duque de Uceda, and the Inquisitor-General, who was also Philip's confessor. In effect, Spanish policy during these crucial months was decided by Zúñiga alone. His reaction to the news from Brussels was enthusiastic and Albert was empowered to proceed with his contacts both via the French and with Maurits directly.[28] Initially, Albert's intention was that the proposition to the States General should be made by the French ambassador in The Hague; but the sudden inexplicable unresponsiveness of the French and Maurits repeating his offer in late March, through Mme T'Serclaes, urging that the declaration be made by a representative of

[27] Albert to Philip, 2 Mar. 1621. ARB SEG 185, fo. 78; *Corresp. d'Esp.* ii. 579.
[28] Philip to Albert, 8 Mar. 1621. ARB SEG 185, fos. 88ᵛ–89; *Corresp. d'Esp.* i. 580.

the king and without further loss of time, led Albert to take the fateful step of sending Peckius to address the States General offering a full peace and reconciliation on the basis of formal submission of the seven provinces to the Spanish crown. As Albert had been repeatedly and emphatically forbidden by Philip to take the first step in initiating truce talks, Peckius was instructed to deliver his speech omitting any reference to the conditions under which the king would concurr in extending the truce.[29]

Maurits's maneouvre was brilliantly successful. As soon as it became known among the Dutch populace that Chancellor Peckius was on his way, it was assumed that he had come to ask for a renewal of the truce. This at once brought to the surface the seething, popular antipathy to the treaty prevalent in Holland and Zeeland. The *predikanten* railed against the truce from the pulpit. There were disturbances as Peckius passed through Rotterdam and he was greeted in Delft by an angry demonstration with the town's youths following his barge along a canal hurling mud and stones and chanting 'hang up the Papists!' Only with difficulty could the mob be kept back, 'from which', as one onlooker put it, 'Peckius could well see that the truce which he was thought to have come to offer renewal of, was not welcome to the common folk but went against their wishes.'[30] His reception in The Hague, if more dignified, was even more disastrous. His appeal for submission to Philip, delivered to the States General in the Dutch language in the presence of the prince on 23 March, was heard in frigid silence with much frowning and suppressed indignation. While opinions differed over the terms in which it was to be rejected, all seven provinces found the proposition itself totally unacceptable.[31] Holland and Zeeland wished to send Peckius back directly, employing uncompromising language and denying him all opportunity to negotiate further. But the inland provinces refused to

---

[29] See Philip to Albert, 29 Mar. 1621. ARB SEG 185, fo. 123.
[30] Magnus to SZ, The Hague, 24 Mar. 1621. RAZ SZ 2089; KBH MS 75k 83, fo. 1; 'Relacion', ARB SEG 185, fos. 139–41ᵛ; La Pise, 779; Aitzema, *Hist.* i. 7.
[31] Magnus to SZ, The Hague, 24 and 25 Mar. 1621. RAZ SZ 2103; ARH SG 12, 548–167, fos. 4ᵛ–5ᵛ; Wagenaar x. 420; Carleton to Calvert, 15/25 Mar. 1621. PRO SP 84–100, fo. 57.

accept this and by way of compromise it was resolved, on 25 March, that Peckius should only be admitted to a further audience after first disclosing his proposals, in secret, to the Stadholder and should the latter consider that it served the state for him to be heard.[32] In this way the provinces formally acquiesced in the prince's assuming complete and secret control over all subsequent proceedings relating to the truce.

In fact, Peckius did then confer in secret with Maurits and did disclose the three conditions under which Philip would consent to an extension of the truce, but, ironically, neither the Spanish monarch nor the States General ever knew the details of this.[33] Maurits having been empowered to keep the matter from the States General, should he so decide, subsequently told the Venetian ambassador, Suriano, that he had not made the Spanish terms known because he be-lieved that the Spanish intention was merely to sow unrest and confusion in the Republic. Albert, having disobeyed the king's orders on this point, omitted mention of the meetings in his report to Madrid.[34] During his conversations with Peckius, Maurits apologized for the tumult at Delft, explain-ing that the common folk of Holland were convinced that their whole 'well-being, advantage, and convenience' con-sisted in renewed war with Spain and therefore detested whoever sought to extend the truce.[35] Despite this, after meeting the prince, and from private contacts in The Hague, Peckius concluded, and this was strongly emphasized in Albert's report to Madrid, that if the king would agree to re-new the truce on the existing terms for a further lengthy period, there would be little difficulty in persuading either Maurits himself or the States General to agree.[36] Maurits, he believed, would dissociate himself from the real pro-war elements in Holland and Zeeland who evidently had already been sharply critical of the readiness Maurits had shown to admit Peckius to The Hague.[37] Peckius was almost certainly right. Earlier in the month Carleton had reported to London

[32] Res. SG 25 Mar. 1621. ARH SG 12548, no. 167.
[33] KBH MS 75k 83, fo. 1ᵛ; Wagenaar x. 420; Geyl, *Suriano*, 310–11.
[34] Albert to Philip, 31 Mar. 1621. ARB SEG 185; 'Relacion', ibid., fo. 148ᵛ.
[35] Ibid., fo. 145.   [36] Ibid.
[37] Carleton to Calvert, 10/20 Mar. 1621. PRO SP 84–100, fo. 34.

that if Peckius's secret proposal 'tends to the renewing of the truce in termes as it formerly stood, without new capitulation, I find that he [Maurits] will leane to the five provinces and oversway the other two [Holland and Zeeland].'[38] The French minister, Aubéry du Maurier, was of precisely the same opinion.[39] But there was no prospect, Peckius stressed, that the Dutch would make the proposal first, nor would they agree to modify the terms.

During the chancellor's return journey there were further hostile demonstrations against him at Rotterdam and Dordrecht. His discourse and the States General's reply soon appeared in pamphlet form at The Hague, Amsterdam, Leiden, and Middelburg and was certainly standard reading among the Dutch and Flemish public during the spring of 1621.[40] The Antwerp news-sheet, the *Gazette van Antwerpen*, mockingly thanked the Dutch printers for the publicity that they thereby gave to Peckius's declaration.[41] In addition, a variety of other tracts were published, almost all openly in favour of war, admitting that opinion in the Republic remained divided, castigating the *Trevisten*, and setting out once again the case for war and for the West India Company.[42] It was now allegedly proven beyond doubt that Philip persisted in challenging the independence of the Dutch state. Another truce, it was held, would, on its expiry, render Maurits too old to be an effective military leader. 'Shall we wait until our experienced officers and soldiers are dead, our foe master of Germany, as well as of Jülich and Cleves, and ourselves stripped of defences and means of resistance?'[43] And what, it was asked, were the economic fruits of the truce which some prized so highly? If various border zones in Brabant and Flanders could be farmed during the truce, and would again fall into disuse in case of war, was this not a particular rather than a common interest? 'Commerce has not increased', asserted *Den Compaignon*, 'but declined throughout the land and especially the province of

---

[38] Ibid.   [39] Ouvré, 305.
[40] Kn., nos. 3187–94.
[41] *Gazette van Antwerpen*, no. 220 (Apr. 1621), p. 6.
[42] Kn. nos. 3196–219.
[43] Den Compaignon, fo. 2.

Zeeland has suffered notable damage to her trade and navigation.'[44] The Spanish monarch had seized Dutch ships and disrupted Dutch trade with the Peninsula and Italy. The founding of the West India Company had been held up for twelve years. And of what good had resumed contact with the South Netherlands been to the Republic? Not only had the increased traffic strengthened Catholicism in the north and exacerbated internal tensions and strife, but Holland's industries had been adversely affected. 'Many have gone to buy manufactures in Brabant and Flanders, because they are cheap there, which they could have purchased here', it was asserted, 'to the profit of our people.'[45]

Whether or not Peckius was right that Maurits was ready to renew the truce on existing terms in March 1621, and almost certainly he was, it is clear that Maurits had no wish to break off contact with Brussels or rush into commencing hostilities. With most of Spain's available finance still committed to the Palatinate, the cease-fire continued in effect with virtually no violations for many months after the expiry of the truce on 9 April, to the immense confusion of the Low Countries populace and the diplomats of the entire world. It was common knowledge, even in the streets and taverns, that during the spring and summer of 1621 secret negotiations between The Hague and Brussels continued and that Maurits, working with a small group of close associates and advisers, was concealing the details of what was happening from the States General, provinces, and *vroedschappen*.[46] But even the best-informed diplomats, the papal nuncio in Brussels, the Venetian ambassador in The Hague, and Sir Dudley Carleton failed to ascertain exactly what was happening.

The great Dutch historian Aitzema, viewing the events of 1621 three decades later, had no doubt that Maurits had aborted the Peckius visit so abruptly because he was bent on war, aware that after another truce he would be too old to command and that his remaining seasoned officers would all

[44] Ibid., fo. 3; van der Capellen i. 16.
[45] *Den Compaignon*, fo. 4.
[46] Van der Capellen i. 11; *Nootwendighe ende vrypostighe Vermaninghe*, pp. 5, 14; *Corresp. Bagno* i. 28, 33.

have gone.[47] Aitzema judged also that the dramatic shift in the balance of power in Germany and the crushing of Maurits's nephew, Frederick, the winter-king, were potent additional motives for the prince to want war, so as to prevent total Austro-Spanish domination of Central Europe. But Aitzema apparently was unaware of the post-April secret truce contacts. At the time, many Dutch *contra-Trevisten* were not at all sure that the prince was still genuinely committed to resuming the conflict and with good reason.

Après que le susdit Peckius se fust retiré [noted van der Capellen some months later] on n'a laissé de continuer le traicté, mais secrèttement par une Dame et autres personnes, comme on croit. Les conditions n'ont jusques icy esté communiquées aux Provinces et ne scait on bonnement ce que l'on doit juger ny de la volonté du Roy d'Espagne, ny de celle du Prince d'Orange.[48]

Why the long delay? Was Maurits waiting, asked one pamphleteer, until the Habsburgs had completed their conquest of Germany?[49] Why the secrecy that surrounded his dealings with Brussels? Maurits, it was declared, was no longer the heroic leader that he had once been and was being misled by his confidants whom many, even of the 'good party', deemed a corrupt and self-seeking clique. It was alleged that Count Ernest Casimir van Nassau, Maurits's cousin and Stadholder of Friesland, François van Aerssen, and the seigneur de Marquette, backed by Duyvenvoorde, Bouckhorst, Voocht, Reynier Pauw, Muys, Schaffer, and Antonis Duyck were, in reality, scheming to renew the truce on terms advantageous to themselves. Despite the long-standing political alliance between the Stadholder's entourage and the Counter-Remonstrant élite in the *vroedschappen* and provincial assemblies, there was undeniably an increasing tension between these elements by 1621, resulting from the apprehensions of the

---

[47] Aitzema, *Ned. VreedeHandeling* i. 88–9.

[48] Van der Capellen i. 11; see also Carleton to Calvert, 22 June/2 July 1621. PRO SP 84/101, fos. 170ᵛ, 175; Carleton explains that until July, Maurits concealed his secret truce soundings from the States General fearing acute dissension within that body which was caught 'betwixt the hungrie appetite of some of the provinces after the continuance of the truce and the repugnance and distast of others'.

[49] *Nootwendighe ende vrypostighe Vermaninghe*, pp. 4–5, 6–7, 9, 15.

latter regarding the ever more extensive accumulation of power in the hands of the former and the secrecy amid which they wielded it.[50] At Antwerp there was mocking reference in print to Maurits's new-found eagerness for a truce whereas previously he had so loudly proclaimed for war.[51]

The death of Philip III, a few days before the end of the truce, precipitated remarkably little change in the Spanish approach to their Dutch problem. The young Philip IV, while strongly under the personal influence of his principal companion, the dynamic Gaspar de Guzmán, Conde de Olivares, who in the mid 1620s was to emerge as virtually sole arbiter of Spanish policy, during 1621–2 continued, as regarded foreign policy, to rely mainly on Zúñiga who, in any case, tended to work in harmony with Olivares, who was his nephew. While there is no reason to suppose that Olivares dissented in any way from Zúñiga's views on the Dutch, indeed all the subsequent evidence points to the contrary, the Conde's later insistence that responsibility for the resumption of war lay with Zúñiga and not with himself was at least substantially correct.[52] Knowing that Maurits was ready to renew the truce on the existing terms but persisting in their view that war was preferable to any but a substantially altered truce, neither Zúñiga nor the king was yet prepared for actual hostilities. The situation in Germany remained much too fluid. A few days after the expiry of the truce, the defeated king and queen of Bohemia were received with full royal honours in The Hague and a few days later Dutch subsidies were arranged to assist with continuing the struggle on the middle Rhine. Spanish troops now occupied most of the Rhenish Palatinate, but Protestant troops, including Dutch and English as well as Palatine and other German contingents, retained Mannheim, Frankenthal, and Heidelberg. The Spaniards had asserted themselves powerfully, but failed to win a complete victory. Since it was now essential that he return to the Netherlands to begin rebuilding the much reduced Army of Flanders, during April Spinola negotiated a

[50] Elias, 'Het oordeel', 96, 100.
[51] *Gazette van Antwerpen*, no. 272, p. 5.
[52] On the issue of Olivares's role in the resumption of war, see Casoni, 246–9; Chudoba, 254–5; Elliott, *Conde-Duque*, 86–94.

cease-fire with the German Protestant princes other than Frederick and hurriedly marched back to the Netherlands with 10,000 men, leaving the Army of the Paltinate with 20,000 under Gonzalo Fernández de Córdoba.[53] In Madrid, where it proved difficult to find enough money for the Netherlands even before the war began, urgent arrangements were made for the remission of additional funds and fiscal pressure was stepped up, particularly in Naples and Sicily,[54] the financial contribution of which provinces to the Nether-lands conflict was to be long, sustained, and heavy.

During early April, immediately following Peckius's return from Holland, on instructions from Albert and Maurits, Willem de Bye, secretary of finance at Brussels, conferred secretly in The Hague with his cousin, Joris de Bye, treasurer of the States General. According to Joris de Bye, Maurits not only desired renewal of the truce, but could be persuaded, as could the States General itself, to make certain substantial concessions to Spain, namely to lift the Schelde restrictions and undertake to launch no further attacks on Iberian possessions in the Far East.[55] Shortly after, Mme T'Serclaes journeyed from The Hague to Brussels and conveyed to Albert Maurits's apologies over the Peckius fiasco which the latter attributed vaguely to an unfortunate combination of circumstances. She also brought fresh proposals. In an un-signed note Maurits expressed readiness both to renew the truce and to try to obtain at least some modification of the terms in favour of Spain.[56] The prince later remarked to Suriano that the Brussels side had in fact initiated this ex-change, Mme T'Serclaes whom he called 'la macarella della tregua', having come to him with an unsigned note from Spinola. Be that as it may, in the aftermath of the Habsburg victories in Germany and Bohemia, and with the French crown for the moment remaining weak and unable to assert

[53] Borja to Ciriza, Brussels, 16 Apr. 1621 quoted in Rodríguez Villa, 392; *Corresp. d'Esp.* ii. 8.

[54] Philip to Albert, 22 Apr. 1621. ARB SEG 185.

[55] ARB SEG 185, fo. 193; *Corresp. d'Esp.* ii. 2, 9; Gachard, 18–19; Poelhekke, *'t Uytgaen*, 107, 176.

[56] Albert to Philip, 30 Apr. 1621. ARB SEG 185, fo. 190; Geyl, *Suriano*, 310–11; Carleton to Calvert, 22 June/2 July. PRO SP 84/101, fo. 170ᵛ.

itself in European affairs to any significant extent, Maurits was understandably anxious to deflect the full force of Spanish power from the Republic for as long as he could, had not the slightest intention of exploiting the temporary weakness of the army of Flanders to snatch a quick opening victory, and in all probability would have settled for any truce that was sufficiently palatable to be accepted by the States General and provinces. Albert, alive to the opportunity, redoubled his endeavours to coax Philip and Zúñiga into fresh negotiations, denouncing the arguments of those ministers who believed that war would halt Dutch expansion in the Indies. The Archduke maintained quite the contrary — that the Dutch had strength enough to fight an effective defensive war at home while increasing their efforts in the Indies. If the war was to resume, it must be a war of conquest in the Netherlands, he argued, knowing that this was not at all what Philip and Zúñiga had in mind, for otherwise there was every likelihood that the southern provinces would be overrun by the Dutch.

During May 1621 Zúñiga virtually alone pondered the messages conveyed by Mme T'Serclaes and Willem de Bye from The Hague.[57] Again Zúñiga and the king kept this material from the *Consejo de Estado*. Zúñiga's response, particularly to de Bye's promising report, was positive and the king authorized Albert to proceed, by whichever intermediary seemed preferable, to a renewed but modified truce.[58] However, Zúñiga's and the king's initial optimism was soon dispelled. In May and June Mme T'Serclaes conveyed fresh messages from Maurits to Albert who had wanted to arrange a meeting of either side's representatives in the neutral territory of Liège, to the effect that the prince would agree only if the Archduke committed himself and the king in advance to accepting the terms of 1609.[59] If this were done, Maurits promised to do his best subsequently to modify the terms in favour of Spain. Albert made a last try to win Philip round. He wrote in late June that the funds

[57] ARB SEG 185, fo. 234^v; *Corresp. d'Esp.* ii. 13.
[58] Philip to Albert, 16 May 1621. ARB SEG 185, fo. 237.
[59] ARB SEG 185, fos. 265^r-265^v.

received so far from Spain and Italy fell so far short of the 300,000 ducats monthly needed to take the offensive in the Low Countries that he was still totally unable to commence hostilities.[60] He warned Philip to judge well whether he was able to keep on sending over 3 million ducats yearly for 'many years, for this will be a long war, as can be seen from past experience, and unless there are adequate means it is essential that Your Majesty authorize that the truce be concluded as best it can, with our trying to improve the conditions as far as possible.'

Philip and Zúñiga, however, now made their decision for war. The drive to collect money resulted, in July, in Philip being able to remit 900,000 ducats to Antwerp. Albert was instructed that funds at the rate of 300,000 ducats monthly were available for the army of Flanders, as from August, and that he must now give the order for hostilities to commence.[61] Albert was in fact dead by the time that this missive reached Brussels, but the Archduke's demise and the resulting return of the southern Netherlands to direct Spanish rule, with the Infanta Isabella as Philip's regent, and Bedmar as her chief advisor, merely strengthened the determination not only of the king and Zúñiga but also of the *Consejo de Estado* to commence hostilities. During its discussion of the Netherlands situation of 30 July, the *Consejo* expressed full confidence that the king's earlier resolution to go to war should be put into effect, that it was now an advantageous moment to strike and that the opportunity for an offensive that year should not be lost.[62] The Dutch forces, meanwhile, remained inactive throughout July amid a continuing mood of confusion and doubt in the Republic. 'Here have been hitherto very gentil warres', wrote Carleton to the English ambassador in Madrid, 'by reason these provinces which stand only on the defensive being diversely affected, some more inclinable to peace than others.'[63]

---

[60] Albert to Philip, 24 June 1621. ARB SEG 185, fo. 264.
[61] Philip to Albert, 22 Jul. 1621. ARB SEG 185, fo. 306.
[62] Consulta 3 July 1621. AGS Estado 2035.
[63] Carleton to Aston, 26 July 1621. BL MS Add. 36445. fo. 200.

ii THE ECONOMIC WAR BEGINS

In the spring and summer of 1621, in both the Republic and Spain, the rival systems of war-time economic regulation which had evolved in the 1598–1607 period were reintroduced involving major changes in navigation, commerce, and industry. There is indeed a striking contrast between the slow, hesitant, even reluctant, resumption of armed hostilities, which began in earnest only in September 1621, and the promptness, in April, with which the combatants reverted to economic pressure. The various political and economic interest groups which had opposed the truce, or come to resent its effects, now moved hand in hand with the Spanish crown and States General to effect a sudden, violent transformation in the existing pattern of international trade. Inevitably, the consequences of this resumed economic warfare were to be felt in virtually every economic sphere right across Europe and indeed the entire world.

There were five principal elements in the Dutch programme of economic warfare against the Spanish *imperium*: the States General's resumed naval blockade of the Flemish sea-ports and the reintroduction of the 1603 wartime tariff list, both of which took effect from April 1621, the adoption of aggressive new measures designed to impede Flemish manufacturing to the benefit of Holland's industries, the strategic regulation of the Dutch river trade with the South Netherlands and north-west Germany and, finally, an officially inspired drive to effect a switch in home investment out of European and into colonial trade. For their part, Spanish ministers resolved to use their great territorial power, and their potential political control of so many of the world's important economic assets, to cut the Dutch out of major sectors of international trade and to exploit the seeming vulnerability of Dutch maritime commerce by means of systematic naval attacks on merchant shipping.

The reimposition of the Dutch naval blockade of the Flemish coast, in April 1621, took place despite the fact that the process of rebuilding the Dutch navy, which had shrunk to a mere fraction of its former self during the truce,[63] had so

---

[63] ARH SG 3180, fo. 239ᵛ; Elias, *De Vlootbouw*, 33–4.

far made only modest progress. By the summer, the admiralty colleges still disposed of only forty-six war-ships which was far too few to mount an effective blockade while at the same time providing escorts for merchant and fishing convoys and maintaining a home reserve. But by hiring and converting numbers of merchantmen, the admiralty authorities did eventually scrape together enough ships for their essential purposes. The commander of the blockade fleet, Lambrecht Hendriks, was able to station a formidable force off Dunkirk and Ostend and to position small squadrons off Nieuwpoort, Blankenberge, and Gravelingen.[64] The as yet minute *armada* of Flanders was kept tightly wedged in. But, at this point, guarding against raiders was only a minor consideration.[65] Dutch merchant vessels intercepted on departing the Flemish ports were relieved of goods belonging to enemy merchants and warned 'not again to enter any forbidden harbours in Flanders on pain of confiscation of both ships and cargoes.'[65] Foreign vessels were prevented from entering the Flemish ports.

Besides providing naval protection for Dutch shipping, the coastal blockade had several far-reaching implications. First, because Dutch merchant vessels were no longer allowed to enter Flemish ports, the handling of the carrying trade between Flanders and southern Europe by the Dutch, sustained throughout the truce, was now at an end. The imports and exports of the southern Netherlands, indeed, could, for the most part, no longer pass through the Flemish ports at all. To some extent, this led to a revival of the heavily taxed and controlled transit trade to Antwerp via the Zeeland towns. However, to a still greater extent it involved the diversion of trade through Boulogne and especially Calais. There soon developed a flourishing commerce between Calais and Dunkirk by means of small boats passing too close to the shore for the Dutch navy to intercept.[66] Other goods, especially as between the Walloon towns and Calais, passed overland. Of great significance also were the ramifications

[64] ARH Bisdom 48, fos. 42^v, 46^v, 51; Res. Holl. 1621, pp. 77–8.
[65] ARH SG 3180, fo. 187^v. Res. 29 Apr. 1621.
[66] ARH Bis. 49, fos. 31^v–32^r; Stols, *Spaanse Brabanders*, 121.

TABLE 1 Examples of increases in 'Convoy and License' (customs) duty on foreign manufactures imported into the Republic under the war-list re-imposed in April 1621

Commodity	1609		1621	
	guilders	stuivers	guilders	stuivers
Flemish linens	0	5	1	2½
Hondschoote *says*	0	8	1	11
Lille *says*	0	6	0	13½
Tilburg and other Brabant *lakens*	2	10	5	12
English unfinished *lakens*	free		free	
English bays	0	5	1	2½

TABLE 2 Examples of the 1621 increases in 'Convoy and License' money on exports of industrial raw materials by river from the Republic to the Spanish Netherlands

Commodity	1609		1621	
Baltic wool (100 lb.)	0	6	2	12
Spanish wool (100 lb.)	0	6	2	2
Baltic flax (100 lb.)	0	6	2	10
Weaving yarn (100 lb.)	3	0	21	0
Peat (per cwt.)	2	10	(forbidden)	

Source: Groot Placaet-Boeck i. cols. 2388-485.

of the closure of the Flemish ports for the inland river and canal trade between northern and southern Netherlands and between the Republic and north-west Germany. Apart from the fact that much less revenue was then needed for the navy, a major reason why the States General had maintained low import–export tariffs during the truce was that it was, in practice, impossible in truce or peace time to operate high tariffs against the southern Netherlands, as these could easily be avoided by importing and exporting – through the Flemish sea-ports. The naval blockade of the Flemish coast was, in effect, the *sine qua non* both of levying punitively high charges on the passage of supplies that the South Netherlands needed and of putting up high tariffs against South Netherlands, German, and Liège manufactures without causing a diversion of the carrying trade through Flanders.[67]

[67] Israel, 'Strategic regulation', 465.

It is no accident, therefore, that in the same month that the States General reimposed its naval blockade on the Flemish coast, it switched from the low 1609 tariff list to the (in certain cases) drastically higher 1603 list. It is sometimes stated, quite erroneously, that readoption of the latter list occurred only in July 1625, because it was in that month that the 1603 list was finally reprinted and placed on a semi-permanent footing.[68] In fact, it was on 19 April 1621, following discussion in the provincial assemblies, that the States General instructed the admiralty colleges to revert from the truce to the war list. In Zeeland the change had been eagerly anticipated and merchants alerted during the first week of April.[69] The instructions to the admiralty colleges whose officers collected 'convoy and license' money, both in the sea-ports and at the river and canal check-points on the borders of the Republic with the South Netherlands and Germany, were several times repeated so as to remove all doubt as to which rates now applied.[70] It is the introduction of the new list, in April 1621, which explains how the States General's revenue from 'convoy and license' money increased in the years 1621–5 when, in fact, the volume of Dutch trade incontestably declined.

In the case of essential or highly desirable imports into the Republic such as Baltic grain and timber, or Liège iron, which had to be shipped along the Maas through Spanish-controlled territory, the increases in the rates were minimal. The States General had no intention of impeding sea-borne commerce unnecessarily or of raising the price at home of indispensable imports. The increases in duty on major sea-borne exports and re-exports such as grain, timber, herring, salt, cheese, and butter were likewise relatively small though, owing to the immense bulk, involved a considerable increase in revenue. Because of the blockade of the Flemish coast, however, none of these sea-borne exports could reach the South Netherlands or the Spanish-occupied zones of north-west Germany except

---

[68] Sickenga, 133; Becht, table 1; Westermann, 5–6; Klompmaker, 104; Bruijn, 141; *Groot Placaet-Boeck* i. 2388–416.

[69] *Notulen Zeeland*, 1621, p. 89. Res. 5 Apr.

[70] ARH SG 3180, fos. 168ᵛ, 170ᵛ, 201. Res. 19, 21 Apr. and 7 May 1621.

via Calais and Boulogne, which meant incurring French imposts as well as additional transport costs. This made it
feasible to charge much higher rates for these commodities
when exported by river or canal or overland. Wheat, for
example, which during the truce paid only 10 guilders per
last when shipped by river to the Spanish Netherlands, paid
36 guilders, as from April 1621, for the Spanish Netherlands
and 27 guilders if conveyed up the Rhine to Germany.[71]
Herring, which had paid 4 guilders per last for the southern
Netherlands, if exported by river or overland during the
truce, paid three times as much as from 1621 and 10 guilders
for the Rhine towns. The most extreme instance was that of
salt. During the truce, many dozens of Dutch ships had each
year supplied salt direct from Portugal and the Loire estuary
to the Flemish sea-ports, bypassing the Dutch tariffs entirely.
By river South Netherlands dealers could import salt from
the Republic paying 15 guilders per hundredweight 'convoy
and license' money. From April 1621, the charge was raised
nearly seven times, to 100 guilders. The increase was so
drastic that a flourishing overland contraband trade developed
via Breda and other Brabant towns and the Dordrect *vroedschap* complained to the States General of loss of business, on
behalf of the Dordrecht skippers' guild, which handled a large
part of Dutch commerce on the Maas and Rhine.[72]

The revised tariff list was also one of several measures
introduced in the Republic during 1621 to disadvantage
Flemish and other foreign manufactures entering the Republic,
thereby aiding domestic production. The States General's
impost on imported Hondschoote *says* increased by nearly
four times under the new list, as shown on Table 1, while
that on Lille says and Tilburg *lakens* as well as most other
South Netherlands textiles more than doubled. The duty on
linen imports rose by four and a half times, thus helping
Haarlem against the cheaper linens of Ghent, Oudenaarde,
and Kortrijk. There were slight increases also in charges on
English 'new draperies', though English unfinished woollens,

---

[71] *Groot Placaet-Boeck* 1, col. 2388-416; 2415-86.
[72] Petition of Dordrecht Maas skippers to Dordrecht *vroedschap* (undated,
1621). ARH SG 12562, no. 16.

which supplied Holland's important *laken*-finishing industry, continued to be exempt. The increases in duty on industrial raw material exports from the Republic to the South Netherlands were heftier still, as is shown on Table 2. Hampered by much higher labour costs, Leiden's sole advantage in competition with Flanders and England was its readier access to supplies of cheap wools based on the Dutch commercial ascendancy in the Baltic. By steeply increasing the charges on exports of Pomeranian and Mecklenburg wools, the States General was making the most of this advantage on behalf of the Dutch textile towns and imposing an additional burden on Flemish industry which before 1621 had imported large amounts of German and Dutch wool from the Republic.

Higher protective tariffs, moreover, were not the only gains made by the Dutch cloth industries deriving from the resumption of war in 1621. When the truce expired, in April, the States of Holland initiated discussion of a whole package of economic and fiscal measures related to the war but also designed to aid home manufactures.[73] It was proposed that Holland's provincial impost on foreign woollens retailed in the province, as distinct from imported for re-export, should not only be doubled to the pre-1609 war-level, but raised another 50 per cent beyond that; this was calculated to yield additional revenue while drastically widening the price gap between foreign and domestic cloth sold in Holland. It was also proposed to raise a special duty on South Netherlands manufactures amounting to one-sixth of the value of the cloth, and in the case of Liège and other manufactures imported via enemy territory, of one-fifteenth. Amsterdam and Rotterdam were predictably cool towards these proposals, fearing diversion of trade,[74] but the province as a whole was in favour of harsh protectionist measures, and Amsterdam's delegates to the States were instructed not to persist too far in opposition to the manufacturing towns. And so, in September, the States agreed on hefty increases in the provincial duty on all foreign woollens, including the

[73] GA Leiden, Sec. Arch. 446, fos. 374-5, 378^V; GA Amsterdam vroed. res. xii, fos. 6^V, 13; Res. Holl. 1621, pp. 35, 37, 72, 74.

[74] GA Amsterdam vroed. res. xii, fos. 6^V, 56-7; Res. Holl. 1621, p. 74.

English, with particularly punitive increases on the cheaper woollens from the South Netherlands.[75] The angry reaction of the English who were in fact hardest hit by the changes was immediate.[76] The English ambassador made such insistent protests at what was seen as a blatant ploy to curb imports of English cloth to the advantage of Dutch manufacturers under pretext of needing more revenue for the war, that the States of Holland was soon deliberating whether to soothe London by exempting English woollens from the new rates or extending the charges also to home-produced *lakens* which were not yet a large part of Leiden's production. However, Leiden and other towns resisted the latter proposal[77] and the dispute with England continued until the impost on English broadcloths was partly reduced, in 1625, though not to the truce level.

The efforts of the States General and States of Holland on behalf of colonial commerce, during 1621, made much less solid progress than did those on behalf of manufacturing. Despite many months of discussion since 1619, the States of Holland were still not fully agreed on the draft West India Company charter, by April,[78] and publication of the provisionally agreed charter took place only in June. Following publication, the setting up of the Company's chambers and collecting the necessary starting capital continued to be delayed by various difficulties and disputes, the most important of which concerned the Caribbean salt trade which had revived from April, when Dutch shipping had been excluded from Portugal and Spain, and which was dominated by the North Holland ports, especially Hoorn and Enkhuizen, which possessed great numbers of ships suited to salt carrying. The controversy over whether or not to include salt in the Company's monopoly, in order to improve prospects of attracting investment, led to a bitter dispute between the majority of the Holland towns including Amsterdam, and the

[75] Res. Holl. 10 Sept. 1621; *Groot Placaet-Boeck* i. 1901, 1909.
[76] Carleton to Calvert, 15 Sept. 1621. PRO SP 84–102, fo. 171; Res. Holl. 15, 16, 18, and 20 Sept. 1621.
[77] GA Leiden, Sec. Arch. 447, fos. 42^v, 45^v, 47^v, 48.
[78] Res. Holl. 1621, pp. 2–3, 57, 72.

North Holland ports, which were understandably fearful of losing their predominance. Despite the hindrances, the authorities and the pamphleteers in their service continued to urge the public to switch its attention from European to colonial trade, to trust in a secure commerce with the Indies East and West and not to regret the losses in trade with southern Europe resulting from the Spanish embargo, Iberian trade being inherently insecure.[79]

In Spain the hub of the new economic strategy against the Dutch was to shut Dutch shipping and goods as far as possible out of the entire hispanic world, with the object of hitting at every sector of the Dutch economy. It was confidently expected, and not without reason, that such a programme would have most drastic effects. There were even some Spanish officials who envisaged keeping the army of Flanders on the defensive from the first and waging war against the Dutch only by means of a comprehensive embargo supplemented with naval harassment of Dutch merchant shipping.[80] Early in April orders were issued to the ports of Castile, Aragon, and Portugal that Dutch skippers were to conclude their business and depart by the end of the month;[81] Dutch vessels entering Iberian ports after 14 April were to be seized, as were Dutch manufactures, or other goods, belonging to Dutch subjects, discovered on board neutral shipping. A massive exodus was set in motion from the Peninsula and southern Italy. A large Dutch contingent departed San Sebastián on 14 April precisely.[82] More than thirty Dutch merchant vessels, including eleven from the salt-pans at La Mata, evacuated the ports of the realm of Valencia and sailed in convoy towards Gibraltar, escorted by Admiral Haultain's fleet then cruising off the Valencian coast.[83] A dozen or so Dutch ships which had anchored at Lisbon before 14 April

[79] See the *Missive daer in kortelijk ende grondigh werdt vertoont*, aii, bii, diii; *Levendich Discouvrs*, p. 11.

[80] See the memorandum of Hortuño de Urizar, 3 Feb. 1618. AGS Estado 2847.

[81] Philip to Fadrique de Toledo, 10 Apr. 1621. AGS Estado 2319; Labayru y Goicoechea v. 114, 654.

[82] M. de Amezquita to Philip, San Sebastián, 14 Apr. 1621. AGS Guerra 873.

[83] Haultain to SG, off Alicante, 14 Apr. 1621. ARH SG 5485 11; viceroy of Valencia to Philip, 18 Apr. 1621. ACA CA 684 86/2.

departed only at the beginning of May, but by then the
Lisbon authorities had made it clear that trade was at an end
and several Dutch ships which entered the port after 14
April had been seized.[84] Not all Dutch skippers who missed
the dead-line ventured into port, however: some skippers
turned back and one vessel from Monnikendam, laden with
Sicilian grain consigned to Lisbon, delayed by adverse winds,
simply sailed on to Holland.[85]

Of course, some Dutch trade with Spain and Portugal did
persist by various clandestine means. But as the striking
paucity of Amsterdam freight contracts for voyages to the
Peninsula from April 1621 indicates,[86] on the whole the
Dutch were in fact shut out, which, in turn, in view of the
fundamental role of Iberian trade, inevitably affected every
aspect of Dutch economic life. Dutch pamphleteers in
1621–2 were quite prepared to admit the loss of the Iberian
trade, though they pointed out that it was not entirely lost
owing to contraband activity and they claimed that what was
lost was well sacrificed for the sake of the gains to be made
in the Far East and Americas.[87] Confident reports of the
allegedly devastating impact of the Spanish embargo on
Holland were issued at Antwerp during 1621, propounding an
exaggerated notion certainly, but, as will be seen one that
was far from groundless. 'Since trade with Spain ceased',
claimed the *Gazette van Antwerpen,*[88] Amsterdam merchants
were without business, 8,000 looms stood idle in the manufacturing towns, Leiden was severely disrupted by loss of
exports to the Peninsula and thousands of Dutch seamen
out of work 'so that great distress is to be seen.'

The schemes propounded on the Spanish side during the
truce for renewed war against the Dutch had stressed not
only the desirability of a total economic embargo against
them but also for a naval force based in Flanders designed

[84] Rotterdam admiralty to SG, 22 May 1621. ARH SG 5485 i.

[85] ARH Bisdom 48, fos. 93–5.

[86] GA Amsterdam, see the box index for freight contracts for Spain and
Portugal.

[87] *Missive daer in kortelijk ende grondigh werdt vertoont,* aii, bii, diii; *Politiicq Discovrs,* 18–19.

[88] *Gazette van Antwerpen* no. 247, 6; no. 287, 3; *Levendich Discovrs,* 11.

to disrupt Dutch merchant shipping and fishing fleets. During 1620, on orders from Madrid, a programme of naval construction began in Flanders, under the direction of Juan de Villela, a former member of the Council of the Indies with long experience in maritime, commercial and American affairs. Whether the king were to resolve on peace or war, Villela envisaged the *armada* as an asset of 'all the subjects of Your Majesty. . . and especially a benefit for the Indies and its commerce' rather than merely of the South Netherlands alone.[89] And Villela's view precisely mirrored that of the *Consejo de Estado* as a whole: the new armada of Flanders was to be both the responsibility and an asset of the whole Monarchy — the means with which to curb the maritime power of Holland. A Nieuwpoort shipbuilder and contractor for naval stores, Adriaan van der Walle, was engaged, in June 1620, to build and equip at Ostend the first twelve ships of the new force. These ships, designed according to the latest naval concepts to be both fast and powerful, were to cost 323,000 ducats, a further 144,000 ducats being allocated for the guns.[90] Excepting only the guns, the work progressed rapidly and most of the vessels were ready to sail if not to fight by May 1621. While the crews were mostly Flemish, a high proportion of the officers, initially at least, were Spanish.[91] Naturally enough, this vigorous naval initiative gave rise to a measure of anxiety in the Republic, but it was to take some time before it was to be grasped just how ominous was this activity in the Flemish ports for the future of Dutch navigation and trade.

---

[89] Villela to Philip, Brussels, 22 Dec. 1620. AGS Estado 2309.

[90] See ARB SEG 184, fos. 106, 185; Villela to Philip, 13 May 1621. AGS Estado 2310.

[91] ARB SEG 185, fo. 184.

Chapter III

The Spanish Offensive
1621–1625

When hostilities commenced in late August 1621, with exchanges of artillery fire between the Dutch and Spanish forts
facing Sluis and the seizure by the Dutch of some Spanish
grain barges on the Rhine, near Wesel, the Spaniards enjoyed
a decided superiority in strength of forces. Under the States
General's war-schedule for 1621, the Dutch standing army
had been expanded from about 30,000 to 48,090 troops,
including 6,000 cavalry. Just over half of the army, 24,710,
was paid for by Holland, the next largest contingent, 7,290
men, being charged to Friesland.[1] But, while at the beginning
of the year the army of Flanders's strength had still been
much less than this, with its best troops being diverted to
the Palatinate (in January the army had numbered only
19,772 men, of whom 5,253 were Spanish and 3,850 Italian),[2]
the return of Spinola with 10,000 men in April and subsequent recruiting during the spring and summer more than
trebled Spanish troop strength to well over 60,000 men.[3]

The distinctive characteristics of the Low Countries war of
1621–48 were mostly apparent from the first. Both sides
needed a high proportion of their strength, around 30,999
men in either case, to man the thickly clustered defensive
complexes of forts, fortified towns, and dikes which had
transformed the Netherlands struggles since the 1590s into
something unlike any other in Europe's long and varied
military history. Both the United and Spanish provinces

---

[1] Ten Raa iii. 292–3.
[2] C. de Benavente to Philip, 11 Feb. 1621. AGS Estado 2310.
[3] Parker, *Army of Flanders*, 272.

constituted so daunting an array of defences that it was a foregone conclusion that despite the professionalism and relatively high standard of training of the forces involved the war would be largely static or extremely slow-moving. Indeed the conflict could not have been more unlike that waged simultaneously, nearby in Germany, not only in its lack of movement, but in its remarkably restrained, un-destructive, and civilized character. In the main, the villages, unprotected towns and prosperous, intensively farmed agricultural land on either side was kept, by mutual consent, and through fear of retaliation, safe from harm. This was a conflict which held few of the horrors for the civilian popu-lation that one normally associates with seventeenth-century warfare. Apart from one or two rare lapses, the troops were effectively disciplined, there were almost no mutinies, and during the whole length of the struggle remarkably few in-stances of the pillaging and sacking of farms and villages. Undoubtedly, the stimulatory effects of large fixed garri-sons, consuming provisions paid for in cash and readily trans-ported by river and canal over relatively large distances, far outweighed any disruptive effects of the military operations. In this extraordinarily controlled mode of warfare much power and responsibility was vested in the military governors of the garrison towns. It was here perhaps that (in the south-ern Netherlands) Castilian preponderance was most visible and most resented. Isabella was under instructions from Madrid that all those governorships which were then in the hands of Spaniards, including Antwerp, Ghent, Dunkirk, Cambrai, Ostend, and many others must remain in the hands of Spaniards while any towns captured from the Dutch must likewise be placed under Spanish officers.[4]

In August both Maurits and Spinola took the field. It was clear enough that the former, with his inferior forces, would stick to the defensive, but speculation was rife as to what strategy Spinola would adopt. Certainly, what the Dutch most dreaded was that the Spaniards would invade from the east across the IJssel into the heartland of the Republic, as had seemed imminent, in 1606. Carleton believed that Spinola would

[4] Isabella to Philip, 17 Dec. 1621. AGS Estado 2310.

now renew the warre againe at the self same place and with the same
designe where he left at the making of the truce; by attempting with a
divided army. . .to pass the Yssel: which if he can effect, he marcheth
without further impediment into the heart of these provinces and in
this time of truce he hath learned how neare he was to the accom-
plishment of his designe when he had it last in hand, and what a general
terror it struck into these provinces, but this armie is at the present in
better state than it was at that time, the places most passable putt into
better defence, and other preparations are made in that sort that it will
be worke of much difficultie.[5]

Spinola indeed marched eastwards, from Maastricht, with a
powerful force and 1,800 supply wagons in his train, while
Maurits concentrated to bar his path, between Emmerich
and Rees. On 30 August, one of the Spanish columns, under
Hendrik van den Bergh, captured the fortress of Rheidt,
cutting the supply route between the Republic and the Dutch
garrisons at Jülich and Papenmutz. But having briefly re-
connoitred the rivers which at this time were high, and perceived the strength of the Dutch defences,[6] Spinola merely
positioned his main force between Rees and Jülich so as to
block Maurits's path while Bergh, with some 8,000 men, set
siege to the town.

A few days later, the governor of Antwerp, Iñigo de Borja,
having marched 5,000 men back and forth along the Flanders
border, to confuse the Dutch, suddenly descended on the
Dutch fortifications at Watervliet, in the west of Zeeland–
Flanders, while the governor of Ostend brought up another
4,000 men from Blankenberge, threatening the Cadzand
defences from the seaward side. Hampered by heavy rain,
however, the Spaniards were too slow to prevent massive
reinforcements being shipped in from Flushing and Rotterdam, and after a fierce nocturnal battle on the dikes facing
Watervliet on 11 September, the attack was abandoned.[7]
Borja then concentrated on strengthening the Spanish forts
in the area, the programme of reconstruction continuing
over the winter months using much timber imported from

[5] Carleton to Calvert, 24 Aug./3 Sept. 1621. PRO SP 84/102, fo. 113ᵛ.
[6] Carleton to Calvert, 5/15 Sept. 1621. PRO SP 84/102, fos. 171, 173;
Gazette van Antwerpen, no. 283, p. 5 and 286, pp. 5, 7.
[7] Res. Holl. 11, 17 Sept. 1621; Isabella to Philip, 22 Sept. 1621. ARB SEG
186, fo. 102.

Zeeland and Holland until, in February 1622, the States General belatedly banned the shipment of building materials to the South Netherlands temporarily.[8] With their failure in September, the Spaniards appear to have lost a major opportunity to break through to the Schelde estuary.[9]

The Jülich campaign presents several curious features. The States General had spent a great deal on strengthening the fortifications of Jülich since 1610, and although, strategically, the town had become largely defunct since the defection of the duke of Neuburg in 1614, considerations of prestige had led to the Republic keeping there one of its largest garrisons, of between 3,000 and 4,000 men.[10] The town was so remote from the main Dutch territory as to promise a relatively easy but highly prestigious victory for the Spaniards, especially as they were probably informed that its governor had failed to provision the town adequately. On the other hand, the decision to strike the initial blow far in the south, at Jülich, however apt to enhance *reputación*, was almost totally irrelevant to the task of breaking into the territory of the Republic. It meant sacrificing the opportunity of breaching the Dutch defences while adequate funds were available. The Spanish technique was simply to blockade the town.[11] There was little fighting. In all, the siege continued for five months, the garrison surrendering, before its supplies gave out on 22 January 1622. Complying with her instructions to appoint a Castilian, Isabella named Diego Salcedo as her governor.

The remarkable inactivity of the main Dutch forces during the Jülich campaign induced much murmuring among the populace at Maurits's expense. While it is true that for the moment the Spaniards were the stronger, their troops were concentrated far in the east, in Jülich–Cleves, and far in the west, in Flanders, leaving ample scope for diversionary Dutch activity in Brabant. People wanted to know why nothing at all was done. 'Il y en a, qui s'imaginent,' noted Van der Capellan, 'que ce n'aye esté sans la volonté du Prince, que la perte du Juliers, pour rabbatre notre orgeuil, et nous faire

---

[8] ARH SG 3181, fo. 75; *Gazette van Antwerpen*, no. 315, pp. 3–4.
[9] Philip to Isabella, 6 Oct. 1621. ARB SEG 186, fo. 124; Aitzema, *Hist.* i. 118.
[10] Van der Capellen i. 13.
[11] Bergh to Isabella, 6 Oct. 1621. ARB SEG 186, fo. 124.

plus aisement condescendre a un nouvel traicté de trefves.'[12]
While some advocates of war in the Republic remained hopeful that Maurits would not in fact agree to a new truce while
the position remained so dire for the anti-Habsburg coalition
in Germany, the impression remained that more thought was
being given by those in charge of the Republic's affairs to
possibilities for a new truce than to prosecuting the war
with vigour.

However, Maurits did eventually reply to the fall of Jülich,
exploiting the gap in the Spanish dispositions, in May 1622.
Some 2,300 musketeers and a large force of cavalry, under
Frederik Hendrik, advanced from Breda beyond Herentals
to Haacht, between Mechelen and Leuven. The cavalry
ranged over the countryside, bringing some villages under
contributie, burning a number that refused to comply as well
as sacking three Catholic churches and violating some
women.[13] Certainly, the inhabitants of the region suffered a
lively shock as the States' cavalry appeared before the walls
of Brussels, Mechelen and Leuven. But Frederik Hendrik
soon had to withdraw to avoid being attacked from the
rear and, in any case, the havoc caused was very limited,
the Republic being, as Aitzema put it, always moderate in
such things. The episode provoked two scathing pamphlets,
issued at Antwerp, deriding the Dutch as godless but in-
competent barbarians.[14]

The two sides again fielded their armies in July 1622,
Maurits positioning himself on the Rhine at Schenkenschans,
while Bergh advanced upon Goch in Cleves, the town promptly
surrendering on 17 July after a brief bombardment. Bergh
also dispatched a column southwards to besiege the now
isolated Dutch garrison at Papenmutz further up the Rhine.
The Spanish moves in the east were merely a diversion, however, to facilitate Spinola's sudden descent on Bergen-op-
Zoom. So unprepared for this was Maurits that he had withdrawn 1,000 men from the town's garrison only a few days
before. But Spinola paused before encircling the town while

[12] Van der Capellen i. 14.
[13] Aitzema, *Hist.* i. 271–2; *Alder-Ghedenkwaerdichste*, fo. 4.
[14] Sabbe, *Brabant in 't verweer*, 119–30.

part of his force, under Luis de Velasco, secured his flank and occupied Steenbergen. Subsequently, this delay was seen by military cognoscenti as Spinola's principal mistake of the campaign.[15] Had he taken up siege positions on 18 July, when his troops first appeared in the vicinity, the weakness of the town's garrison would have been such that he could have easily advanced his positions close to the town walls and harbour defences. As it was, reinforcements were rushed in from Breda and Rotterdam so that the outworks beyond the main walls could be strongly defended. At Steenbergen, meanwhile, the *vroedschap* was purged, the more vocal among the Protestants expelled, and on 15 August the papal nuncio from Brussels celebrated mass there to the 'great joy of the Catholics'.

At Bergen-op-Zoom Spinola entirely failed to bring his batteries close enough to the harbour to prevent the stream of reinforcements and supplies into the town from continuing. But the Spaniards knew from the first that there was little prospect of starving the garrison out. Contrary to what has been claimed,[16] most of the sieges of the 1621–48 war were not, in fact, exercises in exhausting the defenders' supplies. Except for Jülich and Breda, all the main sieges ended long before this point was reached. The fundamental military concept of the struggle was that no matter how well provisioned and fortified a town might be, it would inevitably fall if the besiegers' emplacements, trenches, and batteries could be brought up close enough for effective mining to commence. Once powder barrels were positioned under the walls, the town had no choice but to surrender or be stormed. The crux of Spinola's defeat was that despite losing 9,000 men in casualties and desertions between 18 July and 3 October when the siege was raised, despite fierce fighting, extensive mining, and unremitting bombardment from 100 field guns, the Spaniards were unable to clear the defensive outworks and approach the main walls. On the contrary, by means of an unprecedented concentration of artillery fire, systematic counter-mining, and frequent sallies, the Dutch,

---

[15] Van der Capellen, i. 92; Aitzema, *Hist.* i. 273; Malvezzi, 123–4.
[16] Parker, *Army of Flanders*, 19.

or rather the French, English, and Scottish troops that predominated among the garrison, largely destroyed the Spanish shafts and emplacements.[17] Besides several thousand men who fled from the Spanish army to Breda and elsewhere, no less than 1,900 men deserted to Bergen-op-Zoom itself. Although the besiegers were reinforced in September by Gonzalo Fernández de Córdoba who had marched from the Palatinate in pursuit of Mansfeld's army, defeating the latter *en route* at Fleurus, Mansfeld's troops in turn reinforced Maurits who now, on 2 October, advanced upon Roosendaal. Spinola then decided to abandon a siege which in reality had already failed.

There was little on the Spanish side with which to offset this great defeat during 1622. Steenbergen was reoccupied by the Dutch soon after the withdrawal from Bergen, the former *vroedschap* restored and Catholicism again suppressed. Spinola retained only the fortress of Putte which he had constructed midway between Antwerp and Breda. An attempt in the latter part of the year by the large Spanish garrison at Lingen to raid the province of Groningen failed dismally. The Spaniards lost one of their newly built forts facing Aardenburg, in Zeeland–Flanders, to the Dutch garrison at Sluis. The only tangible success was the capture of the well-supplied and fortified fortress of Papenmutz, the 500-man garrison of which surrendered in December.[18] This at least was a blow to German Protestant morale in the Rhineland. But the overriding fact was the disastrous failure at Bergen-op-Zoom, its huge financial cost, and the loss of half of Spinola's original strike-force of 18,000 men. There now ensued at Madrid a period of renewed debate as to strategy, war-aims, and truce possibilities.

While there was no question of any overall plan of reconquest of the northern Netherlands during the years 1621–25,[19] it was the intention of the Spanish crown, whilst its Netherlands *armada* remained small, to rely on the army

[17] ARH SG 3181, fo. 457. Res. 1 Oct. 1622; Van der Capellen i. 95; *Bergues sur le Soom Assiégée*, 87, 123, 160–1, 315.
[18] Consulta 17 Feb. 1623. AGS Estado 2037; Kessel, 141–2.
[19] See my review of Geoffrey Parker's *Spain and the Netherlands* in *BMGN* vol. 96, no. 3, pp. 99–101.

of Flanders to exert pressure on the Dutch, to weaken and squeeze them, forcing them into excessive expenditure by means of limited, short-term, local offensives which so far had been left entirely to Spinola. The débâcle at Bergen-op-Zoom did not yet finally discredit this policy, but it did bring it very much into question and prepare the way for the shift over to strict *guerra defensiva* which was to determine Spanish strategy in the decade 1625–34. It also somewhat strengthened the hand of the *trêvistes* at court. One consequence of the defeat was the decision to exercise more control from Madrid over military decisions made in the Spanish Netherlands, though this proved impossible to enforce. When asked to specify the offensive plans for 1623, Isabella, on Spinola's advice, merely replied that so long as it remained unclear whether or not Mansfeld's army was to remain in the Netherlands, no plans could be formulated. This caused a split in the *Consejo de Estado*.[20] The king had not been informed of the intention to besiege Bergen-op-Zoom until the campaign had actually begun. The Duque del Infantado and some others now judged that Isabella should be required to specify which town was being considered as a target 'so that what happened last year at Bergen-op-Zoom should not again occur.' Olivares, on the other hand, held that Isabella and Spinola should not be too closely controlled from Madrid lest they feel that confidence in them was lacking, lest crucial military dispatches be intercepted by the enemy and because in a great empire there was much advantage in leaving scope for initiative in the hands of the king's local representatives.

In June 1623 the *Consejo* discussed a paper sent by Hurtado de Ugarte, a senior official in Flanders, reiterating strategic plans which he had originally proposed in 1618.[21] The army of Flanders, he urged, should be kept on the defensive and the land war made as static as possible to save money. The Monarchy should assume the offensive by sea and by means of intensified economic warfare. This approach met with a most sympathetic hearing. 'In order to capture a

[20] Consulta 10 May 1623. AGS Estado 2037.
[21] Ibid. Consulta 14 June 1623.

rebel town', considered the Marqués de Gondomar, who was now entirely disillusioned with the policy of exhausting the enemy by means of limited offensives, 'an entire summer and army is consumed without any certain success for Holland is like a water-tank that while water is taken out from one side, more enters through pipes which are her ships.' Olivares also judged more apt for 'squeezing and reducing them to what is desired, the capture of ten of their merchant ships than four towns.'

Nevertheless, despite the appeal of such reasoning, it quickly became clear that circumstances were exceptionally conducive to some form of renewed pressure by land during 1623, as a result of developments in Germany. The defeated German Protestant armies were drifting northwards, with the Catholic forces in pursuit. Maurits had to divert a large part of his army to reinforce the eastern defences of Gelderland and Overijssel, the more so as Spinola intensified the threat by conspicuously increasing the garrisons of Lingen, Olden-zaal and Grol.[22] There was a great deal of anxiety in the Republic for all could see that even with only a minimum of co-operation between the Spaniards and Tilly's forces, Spinola would be able to invade from the south whilst the Dutch would be forced to keep their army divided.[23] On 6 August, aided by a Spanish contingent, Tilly crushed the Protestant army of Christian of Brunswick at Stadtlohn, almost within sight of the Gelderland border. Shock waves spread through the Gelderland and Overijssel towns.[24]

Yet, unaccountably, Spinola made no move. He was bitterly criticized for this both in the southern Netherlands and in Spain. Luis de Velasco, complaining to Madrid of Spinola's inactivity, proposed at least a modest offensive by two armies, one from the east, attacking across the IJssel, and the other invading Dutch Brabant, bypassing Bergen-op-Zoom, both thrusts being intended to penetrate Dutch territory without besieging towns.[25] It was rumoured in

[22] ARH SG 3182, fos. 76ᵛ, 89ᵛ, 99ᵛ. Res. 22 Feb., 4 and 6 Mar.
[23] Van der Capellen i. 95.
[24] ARH SG 3182, fo. 314. Res. 14 Aug. 1623; GA Deventer, Repub. 1, no. 19; County of Zutphen to Deventer, 2/12 Aug. 1623.
[25] Consulta 14 June 1623. AGS Estado, 2037.

Brussels that Spinola had no more stomach for the war, fearing lest he further spoil his reputation.[26] The Cardinal de la Cueva, one of the staunchest advocates of war, could scarcely contain his rage at Spinola's attitude. In the wake of Velasco's missive, pressure was exerted on Isabella from Madrid to at least send an army across the IJssel, if possible assisted by Tilly. Isabella and Spinola answered that sending an army across the IJssel without first securing a viable foothold, simply in order to penetrate Dutch territory briefly, would not only be useless and costly but would actually involve loss of *reputación*, since the only result would be the capture of 'a few peasants'.[27] While acknowledging the force of this, the *Consejo* persisted in deploring the prolonged inaction.

It was not until February 1624, a month so cold that all the rivers of the Netherlands and the Zuider Zee froze solid, that Spinola gave the order for renewed activity. The frozen rivers largely removed the risk of Spanish expeditionary columns having their escape routes cut in their rear. With a sizeable force, Lucas Cayro, governor of Lingen, invaded Groningen. Owing to his not having received orders dispatched from Brussels forbidding him to sack villages,[28] he burned the Groningen villages of Winschoten, Heiligerlee, Noordbroek, Slochteren, and Scheemda, an action unique on the part of the Spaniards during the whole course of the 1621–48 war. A second and larger force under van den Bergh crossed the IJssel on 17 February near Dieren, seized the castle of Brouchorst, appeared before Arnhem firing some shots and sacked the castle of Karnem.[29] While the local peasantry crowded into the defended towns, the Spanish troops followed their orders and behaved with exemplarary restraint. After five days of singularly unproductive activity, van den Bergh pulled back from Dutch territory via Doetinchem. Velasco, meanwhile, had attempted to advance

---

[26] *Corresp. Bagno* i. 364.
[27] Consulta 26 Oct. 1623. AGS Estado 2037.
[28] Isabella to Philip, 14 Mar. 1624. ARB SEG 190, fo. 103.
[29] Consulta 31 Mar. 1624. AGS Estado 2038; *Entrada que el Exercito . . . Hizo* fos., 1–2, Ten Raa iii. 118–19.

simultaneously with the others in Brabant, but promptly withdrew owing to a sudden improvement in the weather.

The strategic debate in Brussels was resumed with new vigour in the early summer of 1624. Isabella conferred with Velasco, Fernández de Córdoba, Francisco de Medina, the then inspector-general, and van den Bergh, as well as with La Cueva and Spinola.[30] Most were agreed that a major offensive should be attempted in Brabant; van den Bergh initially preferred to invade from the east, across the IJssel, but as the river was exceptionally high that summer, he soon conformed with the rest. Eventually, van den Bergh was sent with one army eastwards, to divide the enemy, while Spinola advanced with 18,000 men northwards from Turnhout. Spinola's subsequent tactics perplexed friend and foe alike. He encamped at Gilze, some distance east of Breda, and then remained totally inactive for an entire two months. Most of his officers were decidedly against besieging Breda because the Dutch were using the ample time provided to reinforce the town massively and because its defences were among the most formidable in the Netherlands.[31] Maurits used the interval to strengthen Breda and impede the flow of supplies to the enemy army, the States General empowering his troops to confiscate wagons and horses used to try to convey provisions to Gilze.[32] Meanwhile, with Maurits concentrating in Brabant, only a small force, under Frederik Hendrik, was left in the east to cover Arnhem and Nijmegen. Somewhat lethargically, van den Bergh occupied Cleves and Gennep but, despite being reinforced by Spinola, advanced no further, offering various excuses for not assaulting Grave.[33] It is curious that even at this date, many Spanish officers in the Netherlands had their doubts about van den Bergh's reliability, but that Spinola steadfastly defended his actions to the Infanta.

At length the criticism and derision incurred by Spinola's situation forced him to act. Suddenly, on 28 August, against

[30] Isabella to Philip, 9 July 1624. ARB SEG 191, fo. 32.
[31] Ibid., fo. 88; Hugo, *Siege of Breda*, 12.
[32] ARH SG 3183, fo. 421ᵛ. Res. 7 Aug. 1624.
[33] ARB SEG 191, fos. 21–4.

the advice of his officers and with Maurits now convinced that he would not attack Breda, the Spaniards finally closed in on the town. The famous siege fortifications with which Spinola encircled Breda were built at great speed and came to be universally admired as a masterpiece of military art. Maurits, who had gradually transferred troops eastwards, at first concentrated on recovering Cleves and Gennep before transferring his forces back again, thus giving Spinola more than enough time to consolidate. When Maurits again concentrated close to Breda, there was little he could do except intensify his efforts to cut off the supply routes to the enemy army. The Spaniards flooded the countryside between their positions and those of Maurits. Almost alone among the great sieges of the 1621–48 war, Breda was simply an exercise in starving the defenders out. Hence its exceptional duration, fully nine months until the town surrendered in May 1625. There was scarcely any fighting, little bombardment, and few casualties. Spinola's technique was precisely the opposite to that which he had adopted at Bergen-op-Zoom.

Philip's ministers in Madrid were no less dismayed on hearing of Spinola's decision than his own officers had been. Even were Spinola to succeed, he would, in the view of the *Consejo de Estado*, inevitably consume a whole army and a vast sum of the king's meagre resources and all to little discernible purpose.[34] In Madrid Breda was not esteemed very highly from a strategic point of view, because it afforded no passage into the interior of the Republic. It was even suggested in the *Consejo* that it might be best to abandon the siege if Spinola could do so without excessive loss of *reputación*. Reflecting these doubts, the king asked Isabella to reconsider whether or not the siege should be continued.[35] Only after several months, and repeated assurances that Spinola was keeping his army intact, did the *Consejo* begin to warm to the enterprise. Although the Dutch tactics of blockading the besieging army were by no means ineffective, and Spinola's men suffered greatly from food shortage, there were remarkably few desertions. By March 1625 the besieging

---

[34] Consulta 18 Sept. 1624. AGS Estado 2038.
[35] Philip to Isabella, 31 Oct. 1624. ARB SEG 191, fo. 217.

army amounted to 22,840 troops facing a defending force of 3,500.[36] Apart from the success of the surprise dawn attack on Goch, launched in January, mounted by the governor of Nijmegen at the head of 5,000 men, there was little to relieve the gloom of this period in the Republic. The mood of pessimism steadily deepened as the prospects for saving Breda faded and the health of Maurits declined. On 23 April the prince died amid much foreboding for the future among populace, army, and provincial assemblies alike. His younger brother, Frederik Hendrik, was at once sworn in as Stadholder and Captain-general. In May Frederik Hendrik positioned his army close to Breda and made a last attempt to save the city. On 15 May English contingents under Colonel Vere stormed Spinola's positions at Terheijden but were then driven back by an Italian counter-charge, leaving 200 dead. On 27 May the new Stadholder withdrew, having in effect given up. A few days later, the town's governor, Justinus van Nassau, capitulated. When his well-preserved troops finally emerged, leaving behind forty-three cannon and an immense store of unused ammunition, they contrasted strikingly with the half-starved besiegers.[37]

The numerous Catholics of Breda were no doubt not adverse to the fall of the city to Philip IV. Nevertheless, many townsfolk departed, especially to Geertruidenberg which now became the major Dutch stronghold in the region. During the period of resumed Spanish rule which was to continue until 1637, the town's population remained rather low by pre-1625 standards, amounting to only 2,702 in 1631, and was substantially smaller than the military garrison of 3,000 men,[38] a striking instance of the preponderance of the soldiery in the life of many Low Countries towns of this period. The *vroedschap* was purged of Protestants and the public practice of Protestantism suppressed. Isabella nominated as governor Claude de Rye, baron de Balançon, a Burgundian noble who had distinguished himself during the siege as commander of a *tercio* of his countrymen.

[36] Consulta 3 Apr. 1625. AGS Estado 2039.
[37] Consulta 29 June 1625. AGS Estado 2039; Conde de Salazar to Philip, 5 June 1625. AGS Estado 2142.
[38] *Geschiedenis van Breda* ii. 56–7.

In terms of *reputación*, Spinola's victory at Breda undoubtedly figured as one of the major triumphs of the age. Yet the *Consejo de Estado*'s initial scepticism as to whether the enterprise served any worthwhile strategic purpose proved to be entirely justified. In no sense, not even by implication, did or could the siege form part of any wider offensive against the Dutch. Militarily, Breda was a dead end which left the way into Holland just as securely blocked by defences as before. Financially, the campaign finally exhausted the resources painstakingly accumulated by the crown in its fiscal drive since 1621. In May Isabella had written despairingly to Philip that there was now nothing left with which to pay the troops and no means of obtaining further credit at Antwerp.[39] Thus it was that in the immediate aftermath of Breda, the king, persuaded by the *Consejo de Estado*, decided that all further thought of continuing the offensive by land had to be dropped. The schedule of spending from Spain and Italy on the army of Flanders was reduced from 300,000 to 250,000 ducats monthly. Isabella and Spinola were instructed to keep the army strictly on the defensive.

ii THE MARITIME CONFLICT IN EUROPE, 1621–1625

Despite the delays experienced in 1620–1 in building up to the levels of naval strength to which either side aspired, the forces deployed by the summer of 1621 were already impressive. If, owing to lack of guns, the *armada* of Flanders was still out of the reckoning, the 1621 allocation of 480,000 ducats to the main Spanish fleet, the *armada del mar océano*, enabled its commander, Fadrique de Toledo, to muster a sizeable force: by May he disposed of twenty-six warships, including those of the Basque and Santander squadrons, manned by 3,862 seamen and 1,323 infantry.[40] In number of vessels, though not tonnage, the Dutch fleet were nearly twice as large, without counting the ships of the East India

---

[39] Rodríguez Villa, 440, 446–7; Alcalá-Zamora, 210.

[40] Consulta, Consejo de Guerra, 30 Jan. 1621, and F. de Toledo to Philip, Cadiz, 9 May 1621. AGS Guerra 873.

Company, but much more scattered. More than half of the Dutch strength, twenty-nine vessels carrying over 2,000 men and nearly 500 guns,[41] was assigned to blockade the Flemish coast. Most of the rest was committed to the protection of the Dutch merchant convoys in European waters, and of the Dutch fishing fleets and coastline.

Although a substantial proportion of the Dutch warships, no less than nine, of which seven had been built during the recent naval building programme of 1619–20, were large, powerfully armed vessels of more than 250 lasts, the so-called *schepen van force*, vessels unsuited either to blockade or to convoy duties, being intended for prolonged offensive action in distant waters, it is remarkable that the States General had no long-range offensive tasks for its fleet either at the outset or at any stage of the new conflict, at least not in European waters.[42] The Republic possessed the largest and potentially most vulnerable merchant and fishing fleets in Europe and the essential task and responsibility of the navy was to protect these. The deployment of naval forces and reorganization for war of virtually the entire body of Dutch European navigation involved a good deal of complex coordination, expense, and, for the merchant and fisherman, inconvenience. The hundreds of ships sailing each year to the Baltic and to Norway were parcelled into convoys, the rules governing which were officially published in June 1622, though they were already then in operation on a provisional basis.[43] Vessels could sail only after 1 April each year, that being the date when the naval blockade of the Flemish coast was reimposed, and not after the end of October when the blockade was lifted. Skippers had to group in convoys of not less than forty ships when a naval escort was available and, when not, in fleets of not less than fifty. There were regulations as to the total number of guns that these convoys had to have and arrangements for payments by owners of unarmed ships to a common fund to assist with the costs of those that were armed. An even stricter convoy discipline

[41] 'Lyste der schepen' (Oct. 1621). ARH SG 5458–iii.
[42] Elias, *De vlootbouw*, 32–4.
[43] ARH Bisdom, 49, fo. 29ᵛ; Aitzema, *Hist.* i. 375–6.

applied to the *straatvaart*, Dutch Mediterranean trade from the spring of 1621 onwards. After lengthy debate, these regulations were published in October 1621.[44] Again, vessels could sail only at fixed times, usually the spring, and in powerfully armed convoys, unarmed ships contributing to the cost. Additionally, regular convoys were arranged from North Holland, South Holland, and Zeeland to Bordeaux and Bayonne with which all Dutch shipping for the ports of northern France were required to sail. Similarly, there were regular convoys to London and Scotland, vessels for Hull and Newcastle being assigned to the latter. On the return voyages Dutch Baltic shipping had to form in groups of forty at the Danish Sound and ensure that they met the regulations on escorts and armaments before entering the North Sea. The Bordeaux and Mediterranean escorts waited at Bordeaux and Livorno for the time required for the return fleets to assemble.

During the first year the admiralty colleges experienced much difficulty in providing adequate escorts. The Mediterranean convoy and North Sea herring fleets were given priority as being the most vulnerable formations. The Amsterdam convoy for North Russia was allocated only one warship, the merchants being advised by the authorities that if they adhered to the regulations and provided sufficient armaments they would be safe.[45] The Maas towns' *kleyne visscherij*, the immense fleet that plied the Dogger Bank for fish other than herring, had petitioned for an escort of six warships but were provided by the Rotterdam admiralty college with only three. The Dutch were fortunate that at first, the danger in the North Sea proved to be more apparent than real.

The initial expectations on the part of Philip's ministers[46] of the newly established Gibraltar *armada* as a means of disrupting the *straatvaart* in fact went totally unfulfilled owing to the effectiveness of the Dutch convoy system. During the early 1620s Philip assigned 150,000 ducats yearly to the naval base at Gibraltar with the intention of inflicting serious

---

[44] ARH Bisdom 48, ii. fo. 164ᵛ; Res. Holl. 1621, p. 176.
[45] Res. Holl. 1621, p. 79.
[46] La Cueva to Philip, 22 Sept. and 26 Dec. 1621. AGS Estado 2310.

losses on the Dutch. Gibraltar's harbour was improved and fortified, strenuous efforts were made to overcome the chronic shortage of seamen, a large contingent of Mallorcan sailors being brought to Gibraltar and others recruited from south-west France and elsewhere.[47] Since the *armada* had ample notice of the departure of Dutch fleets for the Mediterranean, it was also in theory possible to call on reinforcements from Cadiz and elsewhere. The very first sea battle of the war indeed occurred before the new *armada* was ready for action, just beyond the Straits, on 10 August 1621, when Fadrique de Toledo with nine of his ships met a convoy of thirty-nine Dutch vessels returning from the Levant.[48] He sank five and captured two of the merchantmen, a feat which induced the Dutch to arm their subsequent Mediterranean fleets still more heavily. The forty-seven *straatvaarders* of the convoy of May 1622, laden chiefly with grain for Italy, reportedly carried, together with the four warships of their escort, 720 guns, a vast armament for the day.[49] Juan Fajardo de Guevara, in command at Gibraltar intercepted this fleet on its return, after summer trading, eighty sail having assembled to join the escorts off Livorno and Marseilles. The *armada*, reinforced by the Spanish Naples squadron, a force of twenty ships in all, attacked off Málaga on 6 October 1622. Despite six hours of continuous firing, the Dutch cleared the Straits during the night losing at most two vessels.[50] Obviously, from the Spanish point of view, so sparse a result simply did not justify the investment of men, effort, and funds. From 1623 the Spaniards discontinued patrolling the Straits with forces sufficient to tackle the Dutch convoys. From then on, the meagre and precious stocks of naval stores and seamen available in the Peninsula were concentrated increasingly at Cadiz, San Lúcar, and Lisbon.

[47] Philip to Diego de Villalobos, 4 and 14 Apr. 1621. AGS Guerra 896; Philip to Fajardo de Guevara, 2 Feb. 1623. AGS Guerra 893.

[48] *Gazette van Antwerpen*, no. 287, 27 Sept. 1621; Fernández Duro iv. 14; Dánvila, 506.

[49] ARH Bisdom 48, ii. 89, 164, 491; ARA SG 3181 fo. 97. Res. SG. 3 Mar. 1622.

[50] *Relacion del Rencventro*, fos. 1–2.

Prospects for the Flanders *armada* were in reality far better. Despite the Dutch blockade, it was easier to accumulate stocks of naval munitions and recruit suitable seamen in Flanders than Andalusia, even though the supplies had to be transported from Calais and paid a high price for. It was also impossible for the Dutch admiralty colleges to protect all the shipping using the North Sea as they protected the *straatvaart*. Early operations were restricted only because of the temporary chronic shortage of ships' guns. The first two royal warships departed Ostend only in January 1622, capturing as their first prize of the war, a Flushing vessel headed for La Rochelle laden with linen, herring, and 2,000 cheeses.[51] In February there occurred the first attack on a group of Dutch fishing vessels, twelve of the sixteen-man crew of a Vere herring *buis* being locked in the hold as it was sunk. The winter months had the advantage for the *armada* of being a time when there was no Dutch blockade, but these very months were of course bleak ones for prizes. When the Dutch blockading fleet returned to its stations off the Flemish coast in April 1622, Hendriks informed the States General that at least seven of the king's ships were lying ready for action. During the summer these took their total for captured Dutch merchantmen up to twelve. The blockade greatly hampered their actions however. On 2 October 1622 three *coningsschepen*, attempting to slip out of Ostend, were met by nine of Hendriks' ships. While two escaped, one was trapped and fought on for many hours in what was to become a legendary display of bravery.[52] Its captain, Jan Jacobsen, severely wounded and having lost most of his crew, finally blew the ship up, sinking two Dutch warships in the process. In another incident, two Ostenders were pursued by Dutch warships into the harbour at Leith in Scotland.[53] Despite the efforts of Spanish diplomats in London, hampered by counter-pressure from Dutch representatives, these ships remained blockaded at Leith for many months after.

---

[51] ARH Bisdom 49, fos. 31ᵛ–2; ARB SEG 187, fo. 27.
[52] Faulconnier i. 125.
[53] ARH Bisdom 49, fo. 124ᵛ; Alcalá-Zamora, 203–4.

The States General prepared, in March 1623, to commit twenty-seven warships to the blockade that year, five to patrol Ostend, five Dunkirk, two Gravelingen, one Blankenberge, one or two Nieuwpoort, two Leith, and the rest to cruise in the Channel.[54] Additionally, nineteen warships were allocated for the protection of the fishing fleets. Most of the rest of the navy was again assigned to convoy duties. On the whole, the blockade was again effective that year and losses reassuringly few, though the States of Zeeland expressed some dissatisfaction with the effectiveness of the blockade from the economic point of view.[55] Zeeland was keen that the maritime trade of Flanders should be thoroughly paralysed to console the citizens of the Republic for the heavy taxes and burdens that they bore. The decision reached in Madrid, in late 1623, to increase spending on the Flanders *armada* from 20,000 to 70,000 ducats monthly only began to transform the situation during 1624. In January four *coningsschepen*, on leaving Ostend, encountered nine Dutch warships, heavily damaging two in the resulting exchange of fire.[56] During the next few months several Dutch merchantmen were captured, including a yacht, carrying £5,000 in cash, seized in the Thames estuary.[57] On 15 June six of the king's ships, on attempting to leave Dunkirk for San Sebastián where they were to collect troops for Flanders, became embroiled in a twenty-hour battle with the blockade fleet, one vessel on either side being sunk. The Dunkirkers sought refuge on the English coast and were trapped there by the Dutch. On breaking out some months later, the fleet regained Mardijk though in the process either side lost another vessel.

Absorbed by the problem of defence, the States General made scarcely any effort to assert Dutch naval power around the coasts of the Peninsula. Apart from the convoys passing through the Straits and sailing to Bordeaux and Bayonne, and the activities of the Zeeland privateers, one of which in the autumn of 1624 captured a ship carrying the furniture

[54] ARH Bisdom 50, fos. 59–61.   [55] *Notulen Zeeland*, Res. 15 Sept. 1623.
[56] *Avisos muy verdaderos. . .de Flandes*, fo. 2ᵛ.
[57] Calendar of State Papers, Venetian, xviii. 263.

of the viceroy of Naples,[58] only a few small naval expeditions were sent to Iberian coasts. Haultain's fleet cruising off Spanish coasts in April and May 1621 was under orders not to open fire unless attacked[59] and was withdrawn to reinforce the home naval defences before the commencement of hostilities. In November 1622 a North Holland squadron under Hildebrant Quast scoured the Portuguese coast for three weeks, captured two Brazil ships, and then reconnoitered the Canaries.[60] In June 1623 a small Rotterdam squadron, on which the young Tromp saw his first naval voyage, likewise cruised off the Portuguese coast, though apparently without any result.[61] The Dutch authorities were well informed as to the new fortifications and the troops stationed at the major Iberian ports and bases such as Cadiz, San Lúcar, Gibraltar, Málaga, and Lisbon and knowing that landings would require large forces which were simply not available, showed no interest in such schemes. All thought of offensive action by sea in the 1620s and 1630s was reserved for the Indies.

The event which temporarily forced the States General to deviate from its otherwise fixed naval strategy and involve itself in an attack on the Peninsula, the outbreak of the Anglo-Spanish war of 1625–30, in the autumn of 1625, ironically coincided with Philip IV's decision, following the fall of Breda, to keep the army of Flanders on the defensive and take the offensive only by sea. Precisely when the naval threat from Flanders intensified, the States General, anxious not to lose the opportunity of collaboration with England, was constrained to participate in the great expedition of October 1625 against Cadiz. In early August the admiral commanding the Dutch blockade fleet, Marinus Hollaer, had warned that eleven large *coningsschepen* and eighteen privateers were now lying ready in the Flemish ports,[62] a considerably larger force than had been seen previously. Hollaer's fleet was seriously under strength, though it was subsequently

---

[58] ARH SG 3183, fo. 668.   [59] Res. Holl. 1621, pp. 35, 104.
[60] Graefe, *Kapiteinsjaren*, 17.
[61] Winkel-Rauws, 7.
[62] Hollaer to Middelburg admiralty, 6 Aug. 1625. ARH Admiraliteiten 2683.

reinforced by an English contingent. Charles I's ministers, sharing none of the Dutch reluctance to assail Iberian strong-points in full strength, at first pressed for a large Dutch con-tribution of forty ships to join the assault force. The States General, however, offered only twenty, which force com-bined with ten English warships and seventy English con-verted merchantmen and troop transports. The 100 ships of the Anglo-Dutch expeditionary force departed Plymouth in mid October, provided with remarkably elastic, not to say vague instructions.[63] Their objective was to seize and hold any Spanish naval base overlooking the sea-lanes to the Indies and, if possible, to capture the silver fleet on the return voyage. The commanders were still discussing which port to attack whilst cruising off the Portuguese coast. For various reasons, San Lúcar and Gibraltar were excluded and Cadiz decided on despite its formidable defences. The assault proved a disastrous and costly failure which virtually extin-guished altogether any lingering Dutch interest in such schemes.

Isabella herself stayed at Dunkirk for several months, from mid August 1625 onwards, marking with her presence the switch in Philip's priorities from offensive by land to offen-sive by sea.[64] Spinola was also now based at Dunkirk. Ex-perience had shown that raiding singly or in small formations yielded virtually as many losses as gains given the Dutch naval superiority. What was needed, to throw the Dutch off balance, was a massive sweep by a powerful force. Unavoid-ably, this involved a good deal of waiting until an opportunity arose to slip a large formation past the blockade fleet. Almost the entire blockade season elapsed, however, without any such occasion arising. Then on 23 October a violent storm broke, scattering Hollaer's fleet and disrupting the blockade. A flotilla of five king's ships and seven privateers, after briefly exchanging fire with five remaining Dutch vessels, escaped into the North Sea. Off the Scottish coast the Dun-kirkers encountered and attacked the Maas herring fleet. They made short work of the six warships of the escort: one

---

[63] Winkel-Rauws, 104.   [64] *Letters, Rubens*, 116–18.

was sunk, one captured, and the rest put to flight. Then, eighty-four herring *buizen* of Schiedam, Delftshaven, and Rotterdam were sunk, the crews being made prisoner and their nets and gear destroyed.[65] Throughout the North Sea the Dutch fishing fleets were overwhelmed by panic and abandoned the fishing grounds. The Dunkirk flotilla returned to base on 13 November, by which date other marauders had put to sea. The Dutch fishing ports were in uproar and there were bitter recriminations concerning the dismal performance of the naval escort. Many naval crews were alleged to be made up of mere youths without experience or courage, unfit to man warships.[66]

iii THE STRUGGLE IN THE INDIES, 1621–1625

With the ending of the truce, the Dutch–Iberian conflict in the Far East, which had continued with few interruptions since 1609, once more intensified. Under the vigorous direction of Jan Pietersz Coen, at Batavia, the East India Company forces launched an offensive in the years 1621–3 of remarkable daring and scope. The undertaking was made possible because the recent series of clashes with the English East India Company was now terminated, by an agreement between James I and the States General, and a period of active Anglo-Dutch co-operation against the Iberians in Asia initiated. Dutch strength in the East by 1623 amounted to ninety ships, an impressive body of seamen, 2,000 white troops scattered in some twenty forts among which there were four large garrisons — Batavia, Banda, Amboyna, and Ternate — and assets valued at 6 million guilders.[67]

If the series of initiatives against the Philippines, from 1617 onwards, had been largely unsuccessful from a military

[65] ARH Bisdom 52, fo. 277 and 53, fo. 87ᵛ; Consulta, Estado 25 Nov. 1625, AGS Estado 1625; Graefe, 'Marinus Hollare', 195–9; it seems from the States General's records that it was the Maas herring fleet which was decimated, though Centen Faulconnier, and Elias state that it was the Enkhuizen fleet: Centen, 48–9; Faulconnier i. 129.

[66] Frederik Hendrik to Middelburg admiralty, 14 Nov. 1625. ARH Admiral-teiten 2683; ARH Bisdom 52, fos. 266, 269–71.

[67] *Kroniek*, 2nd ser. 9, 114; Colenbrander, 312, 314.

point of view, they had certainly disrupted trade between Manila and China and caused a marked reduction in trading voyages to the Philippines by both Chinese and Japanese. Acting on the principle that breaking the Spanish trade in Chinese silks was the first step to acquiring it for the Company, Coen organized a fleet of five Dutch and five English ships which blockaded Manila Bay from January 1621 until May 1622.[68] There was virtually no fighting with the Spaniards, but, as Coen put it, 'many junks trading from China to Manila were taken and reasonably good prizes gained.'

A second fleet consisting of seven Dutch and four English vessels was dispatched to blockade Goa and disrupt the Portuguese sea-lane between the Cape of Good Hope and India.[69] The blockade was maintained for about two years until April 1623. It was part of this force which in July 1622 intercepted off the Mozambique coast the four large vessels bearing the new viceroy of Portuguese India, the Conde de Vidigueira, and most of the 200,000 *cruzados* recently voted by the Portuguese Cortes and city of Lisbon to finance the renewed war in Asia. Three of these ships ran aground and much of the silver was lost.[70] When the Conde reached Goa, he found its fortifications in disrepair, morale low, and the Dutch blockade highly effective. Indeed, so bleak was the outlook that he advised the Council of Portugal to recommend to the king that regarding the war in Asia, there was now no alternative but to make peace with the Dutch,[71] a remarkable volte-face for a minister who, only four years before, had decidedly preferred renewed war even to an 'improved truce'.

A third fleet, consisting of eight Dutch ships, was sent to blockade Malacca, the rich and varied trade of which Portuguese emporium, in spices, pepper, and Chinese wares, had long been a principal target of the Dutch.[72] But while the disruption of Malacca's commerce was deemed by the Company's governor-general at Batavia to be conducive to the

---

[68] *Kroniek*, 2nd ser. 9, 113, 114; Schurz, 348-9.
[69] *Kroniek*, 2nd ser. 9, 113-14; *Generale Missiven*, 126, 129.
[70] Consulta, Consejo de Portugal, 16 May 1623. BL MS Eg. 1131.
[71] Ibid., fo. 25.
[72] *Kroniek*, 2nd ser. no. 9, pp. 98, 113, 114; *Generale Missiven*, 138.

growth of trade at the latter, it was questionable whether the results were enough to justify the heavy cost of the blockade. 'Great damage', observed Coen, 'was done to the enemy, in his trade to China and surrounding lands, and he lost many ships . . . but little has the Company profited from this.' This indeed was the dilemma of the great Dutch Asia offensive of 1621–3 as a whole. Even during the truce, the cost of the Company's forts, garrisons, and battle fleet consumed most of the remittances sent from Holland as well as most of the profits of the Dutch inter-Asian trade. With the big offensive, the Company's costs inevitably had soared, rising in the three years 1620–2 to nearly 5 million guilders.[73] While pepper consignments from Portuguese India to Lisbon did fall off sharply during the early 1620s,[74] disrupting the navigation of the Spaniards and Portuguese in the Far East did not of itself induce a re-routing of the China trade in favour of the Dutch or that of other regions where local potentates preferred to deal with the Iberians rather than the Dutch.

Coen's appreciation that something more grandiose and decisive than merely blockading Iberian strongholds was needed, if he was to win supremacy over more of Asia's trade, lay behind the ambitious Dutch China expedition of 1622, the intention of which was nothing less than to seize control of China's foreign trade and exclude the Iberians from it by force. In April of that year, a powerful expedition of sixteen ships with some 1,300 men departed Batavia for the south China coast under the command of Cornelis Reyersen. His instructions were to try to capture the Portuguese base at Macao which Coen evidently expected would be relatively easy since the town was at that time unfortified and its inhabitants allegedly seized with fear on account of the Dutch; should this not prove possible, Reyersen was to establish a Dutch base and fortress somewhere suitable for the purposes of trade in the vicinity of 'Canton or Chincheu'. Above all the Reyersen was to secure from the Chinese authorities of Canton and Amoy, by negotiation or naked force, regular commercial access for the Dutch and an under-

[73] *Kroniek*, 2nd ser. no. 9, pp. 118; Colenbrander, 288.
[74] Disney, 51, 162.

taking that trade with the Spaniards and Portuguese would cease.[75] But while Macao was unfortified, the base had recently been reinforced with Castilian troops, artillery and supplies sent from Manila and this was to prove decisive in withstanding the attack. The Dutch tactics showed little skill. Six hundred troops advanced from the landward side while the fleet bombarded the harbour. The attackers were halted by the garrison and there was a period of heavy fire from both sides. But when the landing-party ran short of powder and shot, they were routed by a sudden charge, suffering 130 killed and a similar number of wounded. On hearing of the attack, the Chinese Emperor ordered his officials at Canton and Amoy to assist the Portuguese and Spaniards and totally exclude the Dutch.[76] In retaliation, the Dutch resorted to the most ruthless methods. The south China coast-to-coast trade was mercilessly ravaged, especially around the Chinchao estuary and Amoy, more than eighty junks being destroyed.[77] The Dutch also sacked Ku-lang-yü, a small island in front of Amoy where the Chinese merchants trading with Manila had their stores and houses. At the same time, in accordance with his orders, Reyersen began constructing a fort on the nearby Pescadores islands.

Despite the humiliating repulse of the Dutch from Macao and the fury of the Chinese court, Coen's China expedition in the end achieved some part of its purpose. However, this took some time to become evident. On learning of the episode, Philip IV issued instructions for the permanent fortification of Macao, work carried out during the next years with the assistance of the Chinese Emperor. In 1624, Chinese counter-attacks forced the Dutch to transfer their base in the Pescadores to the island of Taiwan where it became known as Fort Zeelandia.[78] In response to the Dutch challenge on

[75] BL MS Eg. 1131, fos. 237–9; 'Relacion verdadera de la India Oriental' (Goa, 1624), BL MS Add. 13976; *Kroniek*, 2nd ser. no. 9, pp. 113–14, 119; Groenevelt, 87–90; Colenbrander, 270–3; Blussé, 32–4.

[76] *Relacion en que se da aviso*, pp. 2–3.

[77] Ibid.; *Journalen Bontekoe*, 59, 63, 65, 69; Groenevelt, 90–106; Blussé, 35–6.

[78] Mac Leod i. 501–2, Blussé, 41–3.

Taiwan, the Spaniards landed a force in 1626 which seized and fortified Kelang on the north-east coast. For some years, the island remained divided into Dutch and Spanish zones. But Fort Zeelandia soon proved an immense success commercially. During the 1630s over a million pounds of sugar yearly was imported from the mainland and shipped to Europe, taking advantage of the temporary devastation of the Brazilian sugar plantations and the falling off of Brazilian sugar supplies to Europe.[79] A lucrative trade developed also in silks, porcelains, and Japanese goods. But not until 1642 were the Dutch able to capture the Spanish forts on Taiwan and complete their domination of the island.

Dutch progress in the China trade, however, came too late to justify prolongation of the offensive on anything like the scale sustained during 1621–3. Furthermore, Anglo-Dutch co-operation collapsed following the so-called Amboina massacre in February 1623, and this likewise weakened the Dutch resolve to continue with the blockades.[80] While fighting between Dutch and Iberians continued in the Philippines, Moluccas, Taiwan, and elsewhere during the mid 1620s, the momentum of conflict considerably slackened. But if the Dutch as yet had relatively little to show for their efforts, the mood of the Portuguese was decidedly the more pessimistic. The Council of Portugal was thoroughly disheartened both by the power of the Dutch offensive and by Philip's response. In recommending war in their *consultas* of 1618–21, Philip's Portuguese ministers had not so much envisaged a mobilization of Iberian resources to fight in the Netherlands, but a chance for securing large-scale Castilian aid for waging the war in Asia. This initially obscured difference in intentions became manifest within months of resumed hostilities. One leading Portuguese minister, the count-bishop Nuno Alvares, while still advocating war, in January 1622 strongly criticized the *Consejo de Estado* for its attitude to the Far Eastern Theatre. 'War waged on the rebels in the East', he argued, 'will have more useful effects than that waged now in the Netherlands, for four or five millions are expended

---

[79] Glamann, 153, 156, 157, Blussé, 42–3.   [80] *Generale Missiven,* 121.

there yearly besieging one town while with one-fifth of this, properly managed, they can be ejected from the East which would inflict greater damage on them than taking four Netherlands towns, for from Asia they extract the wealth with which they maintain their armies.'[81] After the loss of Vidigueira's ships and cash, the Council of Portugal advised Philip that whilst a new effort was needed, Portugal itself could remit no more funds during 1623, suggesting that a large contribution should be made from Castile and its possessions, in addition to that already being sent from Mexico City to the Philippines and Moluccas.

The *Consejo de Estado* did recommend the dispatch of more men and money to the Far East, but also expressed some displeasure at the Portuguese attitude, one or two ministers remarking that the Portuguese seemed desirous of reducing Castile to being their tributary.[82] By September 1623 the Council of Portugal had turned a complete volte-face in its strategic thinking, advising Philip to seek 'some accord with Holland, for prospects for the war become daily more impossible.'[83] This was too much for the *Consejo de Estado*. 'The heaviest pressure to end the truce with Holland', complained Pedro de Toledo, 'came from the Council of Portugal which insisted that if the Dutch were not diverted at home they would continue to expand in the East.'

The time for seeing the benefit of this war can not yet, in its begin-nings, have arrived [the incorrigible Diego de Ibarra advised the king], for the enemy must have mounted the utmost effort of which he is capable and if Your Majesty persists with the war that he wages, clearly they will not be able to keep it up, and under pressure from Your Majesty's armies, the finance that they have for both undertakings [ie. the European and colonial wars] must decline, so that it will lack for the one or the other. And since their principal object then will be their own conservation, they must weaken in such distant and costly conquests, and thus, even as regards Portugal's interests, Your Majesty can order nothing so useful as continuing the war, as Your Majesty has so prudently decided.[84]

In the New World there was no prospect of any large-scale

---

[81] BL MS Eg. 1131, fo. 145.
[82] Consulta Estado, 22 May 1623. BL MS Eg. 1131, fos. 162-4.
[83] Ibid., fo. 25.
[84] Consulta Estado, 23 Oct. 1623. BL MS Eg. 1131, fos. 263-5.

Dutch offensive in the early 1620s to compare with that in the Far East. Indeed, the only important undertaking before 1624 was the sustained attempt, during 1621–3, before incorporation of the Caribbean salt trade into the West India Company's monopoly, on the part of the North Holland towns, headed by Hoorn and Enkhuizen, to resume the carrying of Caribbean salt on a large scale and particularly that of Punta de Araya. For the supporters and advocates of the West India interest in the Republic, the early 1620s were a period of disarray and bitter frustration,[85] following the issuing of the Company's charter on 3 June 1621. For the Spanish crown it was an opportunity to consolidate its hold over the New World, tighten Seville's trading monopoly, and crack down on North European attempts at commercial infiltration.

In the Republic, besides the controversial issue of the salt trade, several other points relating to the complex organization of the proposed Company, the raising of its starting capital, election of directors, and the absorption of the Zeeland settlements in Amazonia into the Company, delayed matters for month after month. But salt was the principal problem. The more that advocates of the Company became convinced that without the salt trade there would be no chance of securing sufficient investment,[86] the more the North Holland towns dug in their heels. It was not that Hoorn, Enkhuizen, Edam, and Medemblik opposed the West India Company as such. On the contrary, in many ways they figured among its most ardent supporters. No less than four directors of the Noorderkwartier chamber of the Company, during the years 1623–36 were simultaneously burgomasters of Hoorn. The problem was that while representatives of the projected Company assured these towns that a large number of ships, 100 to 200 yearly, would be sent to the Caribbean for salt and that the Company would ensure an adequate supply for the local herring and salt-refining industries, these towns continued to fear loss of dominance of this trade and consequent harm to their shipping

---

[85] Res. Holl. 1621, pp. 2–3, 72, 205, 222.
[86] Res. Hol. 30 Sept. 1621.

industry.[87] The States of Holland resolved by majority vote to include the salt trade in the Company's monopoly in March 1622, but it took until June before this decision was finally confirmed and the Company's charter amplified by the States General.[88]

Ironically, just as the dispute over the Caribbean salt trade was finally settled, Punta de Araya, envisaged in Amsterdam as a key magnet for investment,[89] effectively ceased to be a viable proposition at all. For the Dutch excluded from the salt deposits of Portugal and Andalusia from April 1621, access to alternative supplies had quickly become an urgent necessity. A number of Hoorn and Enkhuizen ships took salt from the Punta during the spring and summer of 1621.[90] But the crucial importance of Punta de Araya being as well appreciated in Madrid as in Holland, a garrison and makeshift fort were in position by September 1621 when a first batch of North Holland ships were repulsed and sailed back empty to Holland.[91] With provisional defences in place, the Council of the Indies sent expert military engineers to the site, work on stone fortifications commenced and additional troops and artillery were brought in. In January 1622 twenty-seven Hoorn and Enkhuizen salt-ships landed 1,500 men in an attempt to overrun the Spanish positions, but were beaten off by the governor of Cumaná.[92] In November 1622 a fleet of forty Noorderkwartier salt-ships exchanged fire with the Spanish fort for two days and landed a second sizeable force which, however, was again repulsed.[93] Three of the Dutch ships were sunk. In January 1623 yet another large fleet appeared, unsuccessfully attacked the fort, and was eventually forced to return to Holland devoid of salt.[94] The losses suffered by Hoorn's citizenry at this time long lingered in the local memory as a gloomy landmark in the town's history.[95]

[87] Res. Holl. 13 Oct. 1621, 10 Jan. and 19 Apr. 1622; Velius, 328–9.
[88] Res. Holl. 23 Mar. 1622; Goslinga, 125.
[89] GA Amsterdam vroed. res. xii, fo. 109.   [90] Velius, 327.
[91] ARH SG 3180, fo. 571ᵛ; ARH Bisdom 48, ii. 170; Goslinga, 126–7.
[92] ARH Bisdom 48, ii. 174–5; Cardot, 352.
[93] GA Amsterdam NA 747, fos. 843, 844; *Nederlandsche zeevaarders* i. 23.
[94] Cardot, 354; Goslinga, 128.   [95] Velius, 328.

Amplification of the Company's charter in June 1622 did not yet mean the commencement of active operations. There now ensued a long delay during 1622-3 while efforts were made across the length and breadth of the country, especially by the *vroedschappen*,[96] to raise the necessary starting capital. The generally unpromising outlook, during the first months of this drive, especially whilst the siege of Bergen-op-Zoom was in progress, did nothing to alleviate the Company's problem, though supporters became more hopeful that investment in the Company would pick up, following the lifting of the siege.[97] With the active assistance of the States General and provinces, a vigorous campaign of advertising and propaganda was launched. While it is perhaps doubtful whether the general war-related recession in Dutch European trade, during the early 1620s, was really very conducive to a shift of investment patterns from European into colonial trade, the Company's advocates strove to encourage such a transfer of resources, openly attempting to exploit the damage to European commerce caused by the war.

These lands [held one West India propagandist] following the expiry of the truce with. . .Spain have completely lost their trade and navigation with all the king's lands, all Spain, much of Italy, Sicily, and other islands both Mediterranean and Atlantic. Navigation through the Straits to Italy and the Levant owing to this cause, and still more to the increase in the numbers of Algerian pirates. . .has become very dangerous and virtually fruitless, thus we must necessarily seek trade elsewhere.[98]

Tracts issued at Amsterdam, Leiden, and Middelburg assailed the public with glittering visions of the Guinea gold trade, Brazilian sugar plantations, Mexican and Peruvian silver mines, and Venezuelan salt.[99] Naturally, the risks and difficulties were obscured while much was made of various presumed potential allies in the New World — the Portuguese Jews and black slaves in Brazil and the Chilean and Amazonian

---

[96] Bijlsma, 105; Acquoy, 1-9.
[97] Van der Capellen i. 99.
[98] *Korte onderrichtinghe ende vermaeninge*, fos. 3-4; see also *Voorganck vande West-Indische Compaignie,* p. 7.
[99] See the foregoing and *Levendich Discours*, pp. 11-12; and Ruyters, pp. 10, 29-30, 36.

Indians who were reportedly eager to assist with despoiling the Spaniards and Portuguese.

One element in the clash of interests between the Company and the European carrying trade, which was much discussed during 1621–3, was the question of sugar imports to the Republic from Portugal which, as has been seen, had developed into a major activity during the truce and stimulated a rapid growth in Amsterdam's sugar-refining industry.[1] From April 1621 a group of merchants trading with Porto, Viana, Aveiro, and Lisbon, mainly Amsterdam Sephardi Jews, petitioned the States of Holland to be allowed to continue shipping Brazilian sugar to Portugal in 'enemy' ships, prior to importing the sugar to Holland, and for assurances that such sugar, handled on their account, and captured by the navy, Company, or Zeeland privateers would not be subject to confiscation.[2] In January 1622 what became a famous test case arose over a consignment of captured Brazilian sugar, brought into Rotterdam, but claimed by Thomas Nunes da Pina, an Amsterdam Jewish merchant. The matter was hotly debated in the States General, States of Holland and Zeeland, various *vroedschappen*, and the admiralty colleges. Amsterdam vigorously opposed the request arguing that the Amsterdam merchants concerned were seeking their own 'particular' interest and not, as they claimed that of the city and nation, in 'notable contempt of the West India Company' with the interests of which theirs so obviously clashed.[3] Predictably, Middelburg likewise opposed the petition of the Jewish merchants trading with Portugal.[4] After hearing recommendations from the admiralty colleges, the States General finally resolved in October 1623 neither to permit Dutch subjects to freight enemy ships nor to exempt such cargoes from confiscation.[5]

---

[1] See the 'Deductie', ARH SH 1358, fos. 1–7.

[2] ARH Bisdom 49i, fos. 8–9, 50, 113^V–114, 172^V–173; Res. Holl. 1622, pp. 6, 12, 16, 56; Israel, 'Dutch Sephardim', pp. 25–6.

[3] GA Amsterdam vroed. res., vol. xii, fos. 90, 93^V–94, 106^V. Res. i, 10 Mar. and 18 Apr. 1622.

[4] *Notulen Zeeland* Res. 26 Feb. 1622.

[5] ARH Bisdom 50, fos. 198^V–199^V.

Despite the advertising drive, the bleak prospect for European trade, the favourable attitude of the Venetian and French authorities who facilitated the selling of the Company's shares on their territory, the response of investors on the whole was disappointing.[6] The one major exception was the province of Groningen, where investment targets were not only met but considerably exceeded.[7] Curiously, in neighbouring Friesland the response was sparser than almost anywhere else. The Amsterdam Sephardi Jews who had dominated dealings in Brazilian sugar before 1621 and whose general commercial position now markedly deteriorated, contributed a mere half of 1 per cent of the Company's starting capital.[8] Of Holland's leading merchants, scarcely any followed the example of Baltasar Coymans, who invested 20,000 guilders, in committing large sums.[9] But for the historian, no less significant than the difficulty in procuring funds is the actual structure of investment in the Company. As is shown in Table 3, the contribution of the maritime towns, except Middelburg and Flushing, was much smaller than one might expect. A remarkably high proportion of the funds of the Amsterdam and South Holland chambers in fact derived from outside Amsterdam and Rotterdam, the contribution of the latter being especially meagre. The backbone of investment in the Company came rather from the inland towns such as Leiden, Delft, Dordrecht, Gouda, Utrecht, Deventer, and Groningen. Leiden alone contributed almost one-tenth of the capital of the Amsterdam chamber. Thus, it would seem that the funds that the Company did succeed in attracting was not so much capital diverted from the European carrying trade as wealth accumulated inland which had previously found little outlet in maritime commerce. The size of the Company and the States General's backing evidently inspired a confidence in inland investors which small trading ventures in the ports could not, thus unlocking new resources for commerce.

The first major Dutch venture in the New World after 1621,

---

[6] *Voortganck vande West-Indische Compaignie*, pp. 3, 5, 7. Wassenaer v. 102–3.
[7] Van Winter, 8, 12–13, 18.
[8] Van Dillen, 'Vreemdelingen', 00.
[9] ARH WIC 18, Kapitaalboek van de kamer Amsterdam.

Table 3 Some Sources of the West India Company's starting capital of 7,108,161 guilders*

Chamber	Capital	Lodged At	Some sources of Investment	
Amsterdam	f2,846,520	Amsterdam	Leiden	f269,800
			Haarlem	f134,150
			Utrecht	f214,775
			Deventer	f110,000
			Nijmegsekwartier	f100,000
			County of Zutphen	70,000
			German States	76,450
			Amsterdam Sephardim	33,900
			Friesland	±10,000
			Capital raised in France	121,200
			Danish Court	4,000
Zeeland	f1,379,775	Middelburg	Middelburg	f897,475
			Flushing	f199,600
			Veere	f132,700
			Tholen	f100,000
Maas	f1,039,202	Rotterdam (f250,660)	Arnhem	f35,000
			Deventer	f10,000
			Zwolle	f10,000
			François van Aerrsen	f25,000
		Delft (f336,165)	Delft	?
			The Hague	?
		Dordrecht (f468,377)	Dordrecht	?
			Gelderland	f80,000
Groningen	f836,975	Groningen	Friesland	±f50,000
			Drenthe	f50,000
			City of Groningen	±f400,000
Noorderkwartier	f505,627	Hoorn and Enkhuizen	Enkhuizen	f123,235
			Hoorn	?
			Friesland	?

*Derived from ARH WIC 18, Kapitaalboek van de kamer Amsterdam; Luzac i. 318; Bijlsma, 105-9; Capellen i. 305; van Winter, 17; Schneeloch, 6; Centen, 39.

other than the attempts on Punta de Araya, was the sailing of the Nassau fleet in April 1623, bound for the Pacific coast of Spanish America and then for the Far East. The sending of a more powerful force to follow up the Spilbergen expedition of 1614–15 in the expectation either of intercepting the Peruvian silver convoy, before it reached Panama, or, failing that, the Manila galleons *en route* to Acapulco, had been planned jointly by the States General and the East India Company since at least 1619.[10] Maurits himself had initially shown much interest in the scheme, then cooled somewhat during the period 1620–1 when his Spanish policy became uncertain, and then, from 1622, showed renewed ardour. The West India Company directors, though invited at a late stage to participate in the expedition, declined, preferring to concentrate on their own projects. The fleet, composed of eleven large warships, including two of the heaviest *schepen van force* in the States' navy, the *Amsterdam* and the *Delft*, both of 400 lasts, had 1,637 men, including 600 troops, on board.

From the first, the costly Nassau venture proved ill fated. Jacques l'Hermite, who commanded until his death in June 1624, knew precisely when he needed to reach Arica on the Peruvian coast, to encounter the silver consignment being transported from Potosí to Callao, but hampered by contrary winds in rounding the Straits of Magellan, missed the silver by a few days.[11] From late April to mid August 1624 the fleet blockaded the Peruvian coast, destroying more than thirty ships in Callao harbour and burning the port of Guayaquil, but, despite this, capturing virtually no booty. Under its vice-admiral Schapenham, the force subsequently proceeded to Acapulco but failed to intercept the Manila galleons and, apart from spreading alarm throughout Mexico, achieved nothing of note.[12] Eventually Schapenham crossed the Pacific but was forced to disregard his instructions to blockade Manila Bay, in the expectation of catching the fleet of junks laden with silks from China which arrived each April, owing to the now dreadful condition of his men and ships. A rump of the fleet finally returned to Holland via the Cape of Good Hope in 1626. An undoubted epic of human endurance, the enterprise yielded its promoters virtually no gain whatever.

[10] Voorbeijtel Cannenburg, xi.
[11] Ibid. xxiv, lxxvii, 67–8, 69.
[12] Israel, *Colonial Mexico*, 167–8.

The first official gathering of the West India Company directors, the Heren XIX, commenced at Amsterdam on 3 August 1623. Several days were devoted to considering the Company's opening strategy.[13] Some directors argued for sending an auxiliary fleet to follow the Nassau expedition round the Straits of Magellan to pillage the Pacific coast of the Americas. Others preferred to resume the attack on Punta de Araya in overwhelming force. Some wished, above all, to try to capture a major Spanish base in the Caribbean such as Havana or Panamá, despite the formidable fortifications.[14] Those who gained the upper hand at first were those who pressed for a modest expedition to West Africa, to consolidate the Company's inherited and thriving gold trade in that region and thus demonstrate the profitability of the Company for the benefit of actual and potential investors. By October 1623, however, the Heren XIX had finally switched to the more ambitious course of planning a large-scale attack on Brazil.[15] The lure of Brazil's sugar output, the value of which was estimated by the Company to be around 5 million guilders yearly, and the country's relatively weak defences cast an irresistible spell.

The Company's first large-scale venture, the expedition under Jacob Willekens a former Amsterdam fishmonger, composed of twenty-six ships and 3,300 men, left Holland in January 1624 and appeared off Bahia, the chief town of the colony on 8 May. After a brief bombardment the Dutch entered the town almost unopposed.[16] It was deserted except for a few blacks and New Christians. The news of this setback, which reached the Peninsula a month before it did Holland, caused an electric reaction in Lisbon and Madrid. At a joint meeting of Philip's *consejos* of Portugal and State on 2 August, his Portuguese ministers admonished their Castilian colleagues that recapturing Bahia concerned 'Castile and the rest of the Monarchy as much as Portugal, for it is

[13] Ratelband, pp. l–li.
[14] *Kroniek* xxii (1872), 238; in 1622 Havana fortress was stocked with fifty guns and a permanent garrison of 200 troops besides the town militia, Wright, *Historia documentada*, 110.
[15] Ratelband, lix–lx; Boxer, *Dutch in Brazil*, 14–15.
[16] Aitzema, *Hist.*, i. 858, 1095; Boxer, *Dutch in Brazil*, 21–3.

beyond question that from Bahia, the Dutch, by way of the Rio de la Plata and Buenos Aires, can infest the realm of Peru.[17] It was also proposed that if the reports that the New Christians were aiding the Dutch proved correct, the commander of the expedition to be sent out should be instructed to deport the New Christians to Portugal. Philip's Spanish ministers needed little persuading. It was provisionally agreed to dispatch a powerful force, the greater part of which should be Castilian and paid for by Castile. Nevertheless, Portugal as well as Andalusia was alive with preparations for months. The Portuguese contribution eventually amounted to twenty-two ships, 1,263 seamen, and 2,345 seasoned troops, to procure which the Council of Portugal had removed the men from the Portuguese North African garrisons of Tangiers, Ceuta, and Mazagán and replaced them with raw recruits.[18] In communicating the position to Brussels, Philip urged Isabella, just as Spinola was commencing the Breda campaign, to step up the pressure in the Netherlands in aid of Brazil 'for the chief reason why we decided to renew the war with the Dutch on the expiry of the Truce, was that our army should engage them on land so that they should not have the forces to attempt ventures such as this by sea.'[19]

The Heren XIX, delighted by their success, set to work preparing a follow-up fleet knowing full well that Philip's response would be as swift as he could manage. The Company indeed was unfortunate that its second fleet for Brazil was long held up in Holland by adverse winds.[20] A huge Iberian *armada*, under Fadrique de Toledo, thus far easily the largest force to have crossed from Europe to the New World, costing in all 2 million ducats,[21] comprising fifty-two ships and 12,500 men, of which 8,900 were Spanish, appeared off Bahia on Easter Eve 1625. Even so, all need not have been lost for the Dutch, had their demoralized garrison not given

---

[17] BL MS Eg. 1131, fo. 296.
[18] Ibid., fo. 306.
[19] Philip to Isabella, 17 Aug. 1624. ARB SEG 191, fo. 119; Boxer, *Dutch in Brazil*, 24.
[20] Van der Capellen i. 330, 335, 338; De Laet i. 32–5, 79, 85–6.
[21] ACC xlix, 39.

in so promptly. The main Dutch relief force of thirty-four ships, under Boudewijn Hendricks, burgomaster of Edam, reached Bahia a month after its capitulation. Against the overwhelming Iberian force, there was nothing they could do. When eventually the disastrous news reached Holland, a wave of pessimism as to the future prospects of the Company swept the country, one seasoned observer concluding that it was now virtually done for.[22]

Having given up hope of Bahia, Hendricks sailed north into the Caribbean. Provided with a powerful force, representing a major investment, he was determined to accomplish something of significance for the Company. On 24 September 1625 he entered the harbour of San Juan at Puerto Rico and opened fire on its fortress, San Felipe del Moro. The Spanish governor, Juan de Haro, a tough veteran of the Netherlands wars, withdrew into the fortress with 300 men. The Dutch pillaged the town and cathedral while their officers destroyed wine stocks to preclude a collapse of discipline. Their efforts to reduce the fort by cutting off supplies, however, were much hampered by the terrain which made it impossible to encircle the Spaniards closely enough to prevent provisions seeping through both from the hinterland and Santo Domingo.[23] After five frustrating weeks, Hendricks admitted defeat and abandoned the siege. He embarked his entire force, engaged in a final fierce exchange of fire with the fort, and put to sea. In Holland, where premature news of the capture of Puerto Rico had caused intense excitement,[24] word of the failure plunged the public anew in gloom. Subsequently, Hendricks cruised for many months in the Caribbean, capturing in all twenty-four Spanish ships and sacking the fort on Margarita, near Punta de Araya. Following his death in July 1626, his depleted and demoralized force finally departed for Holland.

To add to the damaging and costly defeats at Bahia and Puerto Rico, a third and fourth major setback cast their shadow over the Company's early record and future

[22] *Brieven Reigersberch*, 56.
[23] Wassenaer xii. 54–6; De Laet i. 104–8; Boxer, *Dutch in Brazil*, 27–8.
[24] RES SG 22, 24 Jan. 1626. ARH SG 3185, fos. 23, 24.

prospects. Since the only really convincing commercial asset at the Company's disposal was the Guinea gold trade, from the outset the directors desired to secure this trade by eliminating Portuguese competition and interference in the area. This meant capturing the great Portuguese fortress at Elmina. Following the unsuccessful attempt to relieve Bahia, part of the relief force, under Andries Veron, joined forces with another squadron under Jan Dirckszoon Lam off Sierra Leone and appeared off Elmina in late October. The Dutch numbered thirteen sail and 1,200 men. The outlook for the Portuguese looked decidedly grim until the Dutch landing force was ambushed by local Africans in alliance with the Portuguese, and 442 Dutch sailors and soldiers were ingloriously massacred, bringing the whole enterprise to a premature end.[25]

While the Holland and Groningen chambers of the West India Company concentrated, as far as the New World was concerned, on schemes of conquest and attacking Iberian shipping, giving little thought to the planting of colonies, the position was otherwise in the case of the Zeeland chamber. While no less zealous than the rest for conquest and pillage, the Zeelanders, and especially certain prominent merchant houses of Flushing, notably those of Jan de Moor and Abraham van Pere,[26] had striven for more than two decades to foster trading and tobacco-growing settlements in the Guianas and Amazonia. Where these colonies had taken root and established friendly relations with the local Indians, as on the Essequibo and Berbice, a profitable trade in dyewoods and tobacco throve. From 1621 the Zeeland chamber of the Company was envisaged as having a special responsibility for protecting the settlements and extending their scope. Once again, though, the Company was unfortunate. In 1622–3, even before the Company was yet in a position to intervene, the Portuguese, under the ruthless Bento Maciel Parente, launched an offensive in Amazonia which largely cleared the network of Dutch forts on the Para, Xingú, and neighbouring tributaries.[27] A Company

---

[25] De Jonge, *De Oorsprong*, 18–19.
[26] Goslinga, 410–12.
[27] Netscher, 55; Edmundson, 652–3, 658, 662; Goslinga, 411–12.

force subsequently succeeded in destroying the Portuguese outpost established by Maciel at Mariocay in 1625, and in briefly establishing a Dutch presence on the Amazon, but a second Portuguese offensive in the same year led to the final expulsion of the Dutch from Corupá and virtually the whole Amazon basin. Even the frequenting of the mouth of the Amazon by Dutch shipping was largely abandoned after 1625.

In many ways, it is remarkable that the Company weathered the sequence of early disasters as well as it did. Certainly, even its most ardent adherents, taking stock of its position by 1626, could discern few if any grounds for optimism. 'Though we lose our capital,' sighed van der Capellen, 'yet the king of Spain suffers thereby.'[28] Yet plainly such compensation hardly sufficed for the majority of the Company's investors.

iv THE ECONOMIC CONFLICT DURING THE EARLY 1620s

Despite various lacunae in the enforcement of the ban against Dutch shipping and goods imposed by Philip IV in April 1621, in general the embargo proved highly effective[29] and had profound consequences for both Dutch and Iberian economic life. The crown's chief difficulty in this sphere was the lack of an adequate administrative and judicial machinery in the ports. In the harbours of Castile, the *corregidores* had but limited means for searching neutral and allegedly neutral shipping and checking commercial procedures. Prosecutions at this stage went through the ordinary courts which left ample scope for local obstruction of royal policy; thus, for instance, in May 1622 a French ship seized by the *corregidor* of Málaga for carrying Dutch merchandise was simply released again by the Chancillería of Granada.[30] The system of certificates insisted on for consignments of foreign goods entering Iberian ports, which were required to figure oaths that nothing

---

[28] Van der Capellen i. 393–4.
[29] Though several historians have denied this, see Alcalá-Zamora, 183–4; Casey, 96–8.
[30] Corregidor of Málaga to Philip, 17 May 1622. AGS Guerra 877.

of Dutch origin or owned by Dutch subjects was included, oaths attested in the port of embarcation, was as yet rudimentary. Moreover, the *corregidores* found, as in the case of an English ship detained at San Sebastián in April 1622, that it was no simple matter distinguishing Leiden fabrics from similar Flemish and English varieties.[31]

Undoubtedly, various loopholes remained. But to exploit these tenuous opportunities, Dutch merchants and skippers had to go to increasing lengths. Many merchants, including a number of Amsterdam Jews, migrated to Hamburg, Bremen, Glückstadt, Calais, and London from where they could more easily continue their business with the Peninsula and this to some extent was bound to involve loss of trade for the Republic. The number of Amsterdam Sephardim, a group particularly involved in Iberian trade, banking with the Amsterdam Exchange Bank, fell from 106 in 1620 to only seventy-six by 1625, a loss of more than a quarter;[32] profiting from this, the Hamburg Bank increased the number of its Sephardi depositors between 1619 and 1623 from twenty-eight to forty-three. Other merchants preferred to persevere with their Peninsula business, from Holland, surmounting the new obstructions as best they could. In the main, Dutch shipping and seamen could no longer be employed for either Spain or Portugal. But even commissioning English, German, or French ships, and accepting the higher costs involved, by no means assured success. The *Margaret* of London was seized at Cadiz in April 1622, having sailed with its cargo of timber from Holland to London to fetch the necessary documents and having attempted to sell the consignment in Cadiz in the name of London merchants.[33] While London, Hamburg, and Calais magistrates were frequently disposed, for suitable fees or on other grounds, to attest fraudulent oaths and certificates, Dutch merchants were inevitably involved in loss of time, much higher costs, and extra risk. A Lisbon New Christian who was arrested and

[31] Consulta, cons. Guerra, 5 June 1622. AGS Estado 2139.
[32] Van Dillen, 'Vreemdelingen', p. 14; Kellenbenz, *Sephardim*, 225, 258.
[33] BL MS. Add. 36446, fos. 51–4.

had his assets seized, in 1622, for violating the ban on trade with the Dutch, was found with a letter from an Amsterdam Sephardi merchant who had migrated to Hamburg, confiding that he had an order from the Hamburg Senate to local magistrates requiring them to attest his certificates for Portugal without his in fact taking any oath.[34]

A clear example of how drastically the embargo transformed Dutch trade with the Peninsula, even while to some extent such activity persisted, is that of the salt trade to Setúbal. Each year between 1609 and 1621 hundreds of Dutch ships had loaded Setúbal salt and shipped it to Holland, Flanders and the Baltic. Owing to the great volume of traffic, freight rates and insurance charges had been low and this had been reflected in the prevailing low price of Iberian salt in northern Europe. From April 1621 the picture is totally different. Besides the fact that Amsterdam merchants now freighted far fewer ships to Setúbal than previously, a high proportion of those they did send were foreign, or Dutch provided with foreign crews and papers,[35] and, as is shown in Table 4, the merchants paid charges three, four, and even six times as high.

Table 4 The rise in the freight price of shipping Setúbal salt to the Netherlands, 1615-1624*

Date of Contract	Salt Consignment		Freight Price Per Last of Salt (guilders)
25 May 1615	Setúbal–Amsterdam	(Dutch ship)	11½
22 June 1615	Setúbal–Amsterdam	"	11½
23 Oct. 1618	Setúbal–Dunkirk	"	9¼
31 May 1619	Setúbal–Zeeland	"	9
27 Aug. 1620	Setúbal–Ostend	"	12
14 Nov. 1620	Setúbal–Ostend	"	11½
1 Apr. 1623	Setúbal–Amsterdam	(French ship)	60
22 Apr. 1623	Setúbal–Amsterdam	(Dutch ship)	54
11 Apr. 1624	Setúbal–Amsterdam	"	34

*GA Amsterdam Box index, freight-contracts, *Soutvaart.*

[34] Fernando Alvia de Castro to Philip, 19 Nov. 1622. AGS Estado 2847.
[35] *Sources inédites de l'histoire du Maroc*, ser. ii (i). 261-2.

The Amsterdam freight-contracts also demonstrate a decided shift from using Dutch to hiring foreign ships in the case of Amsterdam merchants who persisted in trading with Spain after April 1621. A notable instance is that of the Portuguese Jewish firm of Jerónimo and Duarte Rodríguez Méndez who had traded from Amsterdam with Málaga, whence they had migrated, since 1616, invariably employing, until 1621, Dutch ships. They were, with their intimate knowledge of Málaga and its merchant community, particularly well qualified to continue trading with the town after 1621. But to do so, they switched to freighting Scottish, English, and French ships and paying drastically higher freight charges than formerly. In August 1622 they consigned timber to Málaga in the ship of Robert Hill of Queensferry. A month later they sent another cargo to Málaga from Holland in the *Gráce of Hull*. In November 1623, during the *embargo general* of neutral shipping imposed by the Spanish crown in Andalusia, one Glasgow and two St. Malo vessels were found to be containing timber, cloth, and other merchandise belonging to the Rodríguez Méndez of Amsterdam.[36] Another significant example concerning Málaga is that of Cornelis Michielsz. Blauw, an Amsterdam merchant who shipped several consignments of Norwegian timber to the town during the 1620s, but mainly engaging French ships and crews based at Calais.

The continuing Dutch commercial infiltration was contemplated with evident disquiet by the *Consejo de Estado*. Spanish ministers knew that their measures had had a profound effect, but were determined to make them yet more effective. 'Since the truce ended', held Agustín Messia, at the meeting of 6 July 1622, 'all information received from informants in Holland, and from the Infanta, confirm both the present distress of the Dutch and that the way to squeeze them is to strip them entirely of their commerce.'[37] The Duque del Infantado agreed that the 'greatest hostility that can be shown the Dutch is to deprive them completely and totally

[36] GA Amsterdam NA 628, pp. 503-4, 513-17; P. de Arze to Olivares, Málaga, 2 Nov. 1623. AGS Guerra 890.
[37] Consulta 6 July 1622. Estado, voto A. Mexía. AGS Estado 2036.

of their trade.' Moreover, it was clearly perceived that to tighten the embargo further far-reaching administrative changes were needed. Enforcement would have to be entrusted to a new body of officials and 'in no way left to the ordinary justices, for it has been seen how weakly they proceed where such great rigour is required.'[38] It was realized also that if the loopholes through Portugal and Navarre, from both of which came reports of flourishing contraband trade with the Dutch were to be closed, the king would have to ignore various constitutional privileges of those realms. In September 1622 the *Consejo* advised Philip that 'in order that the frauds perpetrated concerning contraband goods entering these realms be promptly and effectively remedied, Your Majesty should form a special *junta* at Madrid, composed of councillors of State, War, Portugal, Indies and Finance to deal only with the question of contraband and correspond with the officials in the ports.'[39] This was the origin of Philip IV's *Junta de Comercio*, set up in December 1622 under the Marqués de Montesclaros, a former viceroy of both Mexico and Peru and a fervent advocate of economic warfare against the Dutch in the interests particularly of Spain's ascendancy in the Indies.

During 1623 the *Junta* began to employ special commissioners, *veedores de comercio*, to work in conjunction with the *corregidores* in the ports. The captain-general of Galicia, on orders from Madrid, introduced new and more exacting boarding and inspection procedures in the ports of the north-west.[40] In Portugal, where the local administration was considered by the *Consejo de Estado* to be particularly unreliable as regarded implementing the ban against the Dutch, Castilian officials were brought in and placed, not under the supervision of the Council of Portugal, but under that of War. Diego López de Haro, who was entrusted with imposing the new boarding procedures at Lisbon and Setúbal, reported to Madrid in May 1623 that he had

---

[38] Ibid. and Consulta 12 Aug. 1622. AGS Estado 2036.
[39] Consulta 28 Sept. 1622. AGS Estado 2036.
[40] Cerralvo to Philip, 26 May 1623. AGS Guerra 898; Cerralvo to Philip, 19 Feb. 1623. AGS Guerra 901.

seized five or six Dutch ships attempting to trade under the
guise of being neutrals and arrested several Lisbon merchants.[41] A Scots vessel which had brought wheat to Lisbon
from Rotterdam escaped after threatening Castilian officials
with a volley of musket fire. At Setúbal, Lopez de Haro
seized several more Dutch vessels manned by Scots and
German crews and provided with false documents. While he
judged that the Dutch had by then been largely forced out
of the trade with central Portugal, he complained that the
ban was being imposed much less stringently at Porto and
Viana in the north, and at Faro in the Algarve. Other reports
confirm that these three ports and Aveiro were indeed the
centres of the contraband trade with Holland. Yet one should
not suppose that Dutch merchants were able to continue
trading, even with these ports, with impunity. The Amsterdam
freight-contracts again show that very high charges had to be
paid and either foreign ships employed or Dutch ships pur-
porting to be foreign which, especially in the latter case,
involved considerable risk. An Enkhuizen vessel whose crew
claimed to be Flemings from Calais, was seized at Faro in the
spring of 1624 despite having sailed first from Holland to
London to obtain English papers.[42]

In the eastern realms of Spain the *Junta*'s efforts were inevitably hampered by the strength of the local privileges and
constitutions. Relying on the existing administrative machinery was bound to be a highly imperfect procedure. But the
matter was deemed urgent, for before 1621 large numbers
of Dutch ships had frequented the ports particularly of the
viceroyalties of Valencia and Mallorca. In April 1621 the
viceroys of the eastern realms had been ordered to search all
foreign ships entering port, for Dutch goods.[43] In Catalonia
and Aragon officials were required also to check imports
entering overland from France. The primary objective of the
crown in eastern Spain was to force the Dutch to relinquish
the salt-pans of La Mata, Ibiza, and others which between

[41] López de Haro to Philip, 7 Jan. 1623. AGS Guerra 895; Lopez de Haro to
Philip, 19 May 1623. AGS Guerra 988.
[42] GA Amsterdam NA 747, fos. 897-9.
[43] AGS Estado 2847, 'Para la prohibicion del comercio de los rebeldes',
sections on Catalonia, Valencia, and Aragon.

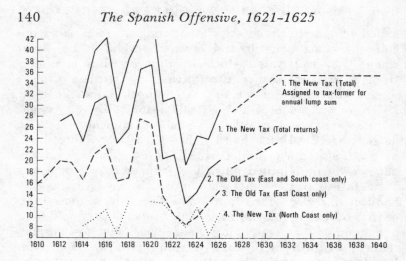

4 Spanish wool exports (1610–1640). Returns from the Castilian Wool Export Duties, quoted in millions of maravidíes. *Source*: Israel, 'Spanish wool exports', 200.

1609 and 1621 had played so essential a part in Dutch carrying activity between Spain and Italy.

As in Castile and Portugal, the royal embargo in eastern Spain undoubtedly had far-reaching effects. At a time of sharply rising salt prices in Italy, as well as in northern Europe, the salt-pans of La Mata fell into virtual disuse, no salt being loaded there in 1622 'owing to the wars of Flanders.'[44] The non-availability of Dutch ships to carry wool from Alicante to Livorno and Genoa, from April 1621, caused a massive fall during the early 1620s in the amount of Castilian wool shipped to Italy.[45] Following a decision by the *Junta de Comercio*, the viceroy of Valencia also put a stop to the importing of East India spices, a major item in the trade of Alicante, unless the bales had been sealed in Lisbon, a measure intended to exclude both Dutch and English spices; judging from the anguished outcry of the Alicante city

[44] ACA CA 603, doc. 6. Pedro Martínez de Vera to N. Mensa, 9 Mar. 1623; ibid., doc. 5, viceroy of Valencia to Philip, 11 Feb. 1623.
[45] Israel, 'Spanish Wool Exports', 200, 201, 204.

council, this too was effective.[46] Moreover, the loss of trade
by the Dutch in eastern Spain inevitably also impeded Dutch
commerce with North Italy. Since Spanish wool and salt had
been two of the chief commodities supplied by the Dutch to
Livorno, Genoa, and Venice, the loss of contact with eastern
Spain appreciably reduced the number of Dutch vessels
visiting Italian ports.[47] Correspondingly, the frequency of
Hamburg and other Hanseatic ships docking at Genoa and
other ports, perceptibly increased as German shipping began
delivering more wool and salt from eastern Spain.

One lesser realm of Spain which received special attention
from the *Consejo de Estado* and *Junta de Comercio* in connection with the embargo against the Dutch was Navarre. As
early as May 1621 officials on the Basque coast had reported
that Dutch cloth, unloaded at the neighbouring port of
Bayonne, in France, was being conveyed overland, across
the Pyrenees, evading the customs authorities at Irun and
San Sebastián, via Pamplona and the dry ports on the
Castile-Navarre border.[48] This was confirmed by the viceroy
of Navarre who repeatedly complained of the attitude of
Navarrese Cortes which asserted that the prohibition violated
the privileges of the realm. Montesclaros impatiently dismissed Navarre's objections as 'of little substance'; but the
problem of the flourishing contraband route remained.[49]
An official sent from Madrid to investigate reported that
between August 1621 and September 1622 thirty Dutch
ships had unloaded cargoes at Bayonne and St. Jean de Luz
consigned for Castile, via Navarre, and taken on wool and
silver remitted to Bayonne, from Madrid, by the same
route.[50] This particular contraband route was regarded as a
speciality of the Amsterdam Jews who had close links with
both the large Sephardi community of Bayonne and the
Portuguese New Christian merchants of Madrid.

To check the infiltration through Navarre, customs officials
from the Basque coast were assigned to the Castile-Navarre

[46] ACA CA 603 12–16 and 12–28.   [47] Grendi, 34.
[48] Miguel de Manchola to Philip, 24 Sept. and 29 Oct. 1621, 22 Apr. 1622,
and viceroy of Navarre to Philip, 15 Sept. 1621. AGS Estado 2139.
[49] Consulta 6 July 1622. AGS Estado 2036.
[50] Consulta 31 Oct. 1622. AGS Hacienda 592.

dry ports 'with which', it was reported in October 1622, 'contraband merchandise is no longer transported by that route with such ease and disorder as previously.'[51] The viceroy also endeavoured to tighten the ban in Navarre itself. But undoubtedly a sizeable loophole remained. In January, and again in December 1624, the viceroy of Navarre reported that the flow of Dutch goods from Bayonne persisted, 'particularly of all sorts of spices'.[52] Such was the growth in Dutch shipping and trade to Bayonne and St. Jean since 1621, that in August 1624 a group of Amsterdam merchants, seconded by the burgomasters of Amsterdam, Dordrecht, Delft, and Rotterdam, petitioned the States General for the establishment of a permanent Dutch consulate at Bayonne and approaches were soon made to the French crown.[53] The Spanish crown intensified its efforts. In April and July 1625 the *Junta* reviewed representations from the Navarrese Cortes demanding the lifting of the embargo in Navarre and particularly of the ruling that no East India spices were to be admitted unless in bales sealed at Lisbon. The Cortes maintained that the ban contravened Navarre's *fueros*, that Dutch goods that did not enter Navarre seeped through the more easterly Pyrenean passes into Aragon, and that Navarre's trade 'had completely ceased because the spices which formerly reached Aragon through Navarre, since the prohibition pass via Béarn.'[54] Philip's answer was that the interests of Spain as a whole required that the embargo in Navarre remain in force, but that steps would be taken to enforce it more effectively in Aragon.

In addition to shutting the Dutch out of the carrying of Spanish wool and salt to Italy and confiscating Dutch goods and moneys in his Italian realms, it was in Philip's power to damage Dutch interests in the Italian Peninsula in other ways.[55] The Spanish viceroys of Naples, Sicily, Sardinia, and

[51] Ibid.

[52] Viceroy of Navarre to Philip, 24 Jan. 1624. AGS Estado 2645.

[53] ARH SG 3183, fos. 445ᵛ–446. Res. 17 Aug. 1624.

[54] Consultas, *Junta de Comercio*, 17 Apr. 1625. AGS Estado 2847, and 6 July 1625. AGS Estado 2645.

[55] Philip III to the Italian viceroys, 27 Mar. 1621. AGS Estado 1883; Conde de Castro to Philip, Palermo, 26 July 1621; AGS Estado 1893; Marques de Castañeda to Philip, Genoa, 14 Oct. 1624. AGS Estado 2038.

Milan, who together ruled over half of Italy, together with the powerful Spanish ambassadors at Genoa and Rome, were expected to assist with the economic war against the Dutch and help combat the dealings of Dutch representatives, such as Hendrik Muilman of Deventer, Dutch consul at Genoa, who during 1624 arranged for several Dutch vessels, bearing Hanseatic papers, to load salt at Ibiza for Venice and Nice. The single most important commodity imported to Genoa and Venice during the early seventeenth century was grain. While there was assuredly little that Madrid could do to disturb the transport of Baltic grain to Venice in Dutch ships, the ban on employing Dutch vessels to ship wheat from Sicily, the other major source of supply for North Italy, undoubtedly had some impact, enabling the English and other maritime nations to acquire more of the Italian coast-to-coast trade. In the case of Genoa, with which the Spanish crown traditionally had close political and economic links, heavy diplomatic pressure was brought to bear to dissuade the Genoese senate from purchasing grain from the Dutch.[56] When the viceroy of Naples temporarily suspended the ban against Dutch shipping during the winter of 1621-2, a period of famine throughout the Italian mainland, so as to facilitate the procurement of emergency food supplies, he received a stern rebuke from the king who ordered him to confront popular unrest rather than again resort to the Dutch.

In the Netherlands and north-west Germany the initiative in the economic battle inevitably lay chiefly with the Republic. Dutch ships were banned by the Spanish crown from the Flemish sea-ports, but the States General itself prohibited such traffic and enforced its ban through its blockade of the Flemish coast. The Dutch also had the advantage when it came to manipulating the inland river and canal trade, a major dimension in the commerce of the Low Countries and Germany. The *Consejo de Estado* originally proposed extending the Spanish ban on trade with the Dutch to the inland waterways in 1622, but encountered considerable reluctance on the part of the Brussels administration, owing

---

[56] Philip to viceroy of Naples, 22 Jan. 1622. AGS Estado 1884.

to the large revenues from the *licenten* that would be lost if the rivers were closed and because of the reliance of the army, and to some extent of the entire population of the Spanish Netherlands, on foodstuffs and other supplies imported from the Republic. In January 1623 Philip reminded Isabella that she had not yet responded to the *Consejo*'s proposal. Soon after, Luis de Velasco urged the king to force Brussels to embark on a total river blockade, 'deeming that it would be possible for us to occupy some towns on the river Weser with which the Dutch would remain without any commerce except what they have by sea.'[57] The *Consejo* warmly approved, only the Marqués de Gondomar expressing doubt owing to the resentment against Spain such action would provoke among the Catholic Rhine principalities.

In December 1623 Isabella took the step of prohibiting the entry of any English cloth to the Spanish Netherlands from the Republic or up the Rhine beyond Wesel, with the intention of diverting at least part of the distribution of English textile shipments to the continent away from the Republic via Calais and Dunkirk and some of the finishing of English cloth from Holland back to Antwerp, the original home of this industry.[58] According to subsequent Spanish reports from London, at least some English unfinished cloth that would otherwise have been shipped to Holland was in fact in this way diverted to the Spanish Netherlands.[59]

In the spring of 1624 Isabella reluctantly agreed to impose a total river blockade, provided that the king made good the loss of revenue, sending a list of the returns from the *licenten* as well as several additional river tolls, amounting in the year 1623 to over 800,000 florins, or some 270,000 ducats.[60] The break-down for the *licenten* on the Spanish side for 1623 is given in Table 5. The *Consejo de Estado* was in no mood to abandon further economic action against the Republic simply for the sake of Brussels's finances and Isabella was ordered to implement the blockade, mortgaging 400,000 florins of royal lands in the southern Netherlands to soften the

[57] Consulta 24 June 1623. AGS Estado 2037.
[58] Consulta, Junta de Comercio, 28 Feb. 1624. AGS Estado 2847.
[59] Carlos Coloma to Philip, London, 2 July 1624. AGS Estado 2847.
[60] Isabella to Philip, 21 Mar. and 18 Apr. 1624. ARB SEG 190, fos. 122, 135.

Table 5 Philip IV's revenue from the *licenten* on river trade with the Republic
in 1623

Licenten paid at	Amount (fl.)
Antwerp	105,585
Ghent	29,000
Brugge	6,000
's Hertogenbosch	17,032
Venlo	150,000
Roermond	56,000
Maastricht	59,000
Grol	3,400
Oldenzaal	2,300
Lingen (River Eems)	25,000
Rhine and Lippe	170,000
Total	622,917

impact.[61] Even so, it was not to be until July 1625 that the
Brussels regime finally embarked upon this drastic course
of action.

In the meantime, the Dutch had already imposed a series
of temporary river blockades mainly intended for the strategic end of weakening the army of Flanders at crucial stages
in the fighting by cutting off the supply of those provisions
otherwise normally permitted to the enemy under the war-
list readopted in April 1621. Under this list it was forbidden
at all times to export certain items, notably arms, ammunition, copper, and naval stores, either to the Spanish Netherlands, Spain, Portugal, or Spanish Italy. These, particularly
copper and naval stores, were the supplies the Spanish
Monarchy was most urgently in need of from 1621, and the
States General had no intention of facilitating their supply,
despite the determination of the Spanish crown to avoid
buying them from Dutch sources and the handsome profits
that Dutch merchants thus to some extent had to forgo.
The prohibition against shipping munitions to the enemy was
published in April 1622, listing all arms, ammunition, salt-
peter, copper and copper goods, sails, ships' masts larger than
a certain width, and other naval stores as well as in the case
of the South Netherlands, grain.[62] This prohibition was

[61] Philip to Isabella, 29 May 1624. ARB SEG 190, fo. 225.
[62] ARH Bisdom 49, i. fo. 64; Aitzema i. 375-6.

backed up by the army at the border posts, on the inland waterways and routes of the Netherlands, and by the blockade fleet in the Channel which regularly searched neutral shipping *en route* for Spain or Portugal, removing contraband goods from their cargoes.[63] The temporary strategic blockades in the Netherlands applied to all foodstuffs, a number of non-contraband materials, especially timber, and at certain times, horses, horse-fodder, and other items; herring, other fish, sugar, butter, cheese, salt, and wine were the commodities most affected.

It has been noted that during the siege of Jülich Maurits campaigned with rather less than his customary energy. During October 1621 the States General debated whether to close the Rhine and Maas to the passage of provisions so as to hamper the besieging army. Though Holland was somewhat reluctant, the province consented on 23 October, provided that herring, fish, and salt were exempted.[64] The ban was imposed, but Maurits curiously did not favour this action and it was rescinded after only a few days. During the siege of Bergen-op-Zoom, however, the situation was quite otherwise. When the siege began, the States General promptly closed all routes to Flanders and Brabant to every sort of foodstuff, including salt and wine. Though in most respects Zeeland, which felt itself to be particularly threatened by the siege, wholeheartedly supported the ban, the inclusion of wines, at Holland's insistence, was much resented at Middelburg where French wines were the chief item of commerce and Antwerp one of the town's largest markets.[65] The States General ordered the military governors of Breda, Heusden, and Geertruidenburg to employ their troops to stop the passage of supplies overland to the Spanish army, to the point even of confiscating the axles from the village wind-mills of north Brabant. Despite some evasion, it would seem that such action was highly effective. A huge diversion of trade began, with shipments of provisions by sea particularly from Zeeland and Rotterdam to Calais and Boulogne, from

[63] Journal, ARH SG 5502, i.
[64] ARH SG 3180, fos. 501ᵛ, 512, 513ᵛ, 553, 577ᵛ.
[65] ARH SG 3181, fos. 350ᵛ–351ʳ.

where, having paid the French imposts, and at considerable cost and difficulty, the Spaniards transported the supplies to Dunkirk and from there by canal and overland to their encampments around Bergen. To reduce the flow reaching Spínola by this means, the States General raised the *licenten* for Calais for the interim to the higher level that applied normally to the Schelde, and raised to the previous Calais level the charges for all French ports beyond Calais as far as the Somme estuary. The 1622 blockade remained in force for nearly three months in all being lifted only on 19 October.[66] Though Middelburg certainly profited from the brisk trade in foodstuffs with north-east France that developed during the blockade, its merchants were also left with large stocks of unsold French wine.

During 1623 the major military threat to the Republic emanated from the east and the main pressure for economic counter-action from Overijssel and Gelderland. Fearing that the Spanish forces on the Ems and Lippe might besiege one of the Overijssel towns, that province began pressing early in the year for the closure of the Rhine, Maas, IJssel (beyond Deventer), Ems, and Weser.[67] In early April the maritime provinces consented and the rivers were closed. Soon after, the States General also closed the Schelde and routes to Flanders and dispatched warships to block the Ems and Weser estuaries.[68] Ignoring protests from Bremen and the Danish crown over the shutting of the Weser, the States General persisted with this policy for many months. By July, however, the Amsterdam and Rotterdam herring interest and the town of Dordrecht, which suffered particularly from any disruption of river trade, were so aroused by the stoppage on the Rhine, that the States of Holland began pressing for herring and fish to be exempted.[69] Deadlock was reached when Friesland and Groningen retorted that if herring and fish were to be excepted then so should butter and cheese; the eastern provinces and Zeeland then reluctantly

[66] Ibid., fos. 466, 472ᵛ, 474ᵛ, 478.
[67] ARH SG 3182, fos. 76ᵛ, 89ᵛ, 90ᵛ.
[68] Res. Holl. 31 Mar. 1623; ARH SG 3182, fo. 132ᵛ.
[69] ARH SG 3182, fos. 276, 277ᵛ, 283ᵛ284; GA Deventer, Republiek i. no. 19. J. Lulof to Deventer vroedschap, 26 July 1623.

agreed to a general reopening of the rivers. No sooner did this happen, though, than the destruction of Christian of Brunswick's Protestant army at Stadtlohn, close to the Gelderland border, by Tilly's forces assisted by a Spanish contingent, led to an immediate reimposition of the blockade at the insistence of Deventer, Zwolle, and other eastern towns.[70] Intelligence from Wesel and elsewhere confirmed that both the Spanish and Catholic League troops spread along the Overijssel and Gelderland borders were suffering severely from lack of provisions[71] and at the insistence of Maurits and the inland provinces, the action was prolonged until early October, despite mounting protests in Holland. A week before the blockade was finally lifted, representatives of the South Holland herring fishery appeared before the States General representing the losses they had suffered through the blockade and demanding a speedy resumption of sales to Cologne, the main entrepôt for Dutch herring on the Rhine.[72]

In July 1624, shortly after Spinola again took the field, the States General once more halted the passage of provisions including wine, beer, and horse fodder into Brabant 'so that the enemy who has an exceptional dearth in his army should not be supplied.'[73] The ban was soon extended to the Schelde and Flanders. While Gelderland was anxious to extend the prohibition further, to all the eastern routes from the Republic into Germany, Holland was again worried as to the impact on herring sales to Westphalia, and the Rhine remained open, even though it was obvious that much of the food shipped up the Rhine was being unloaded at the Spanish garrison-towns of Wesel and Rheinberg and conveyed over-land via Venlo to Spinola's army.[74] Just as in 1622, there was also a massive diversion of foodstuffs through Middel-burg and Rotterdam to north-east France. Again the charges on provisions shipped to Calais, and several ports beyond, were temporarily raised.

In January 1625, on advice from the Rotterdam admiralty

[70] Ibid., Lulof to Deventer, 41. 14 Aug. 1623.
[71] ARH SG 3182, fo. 357^v.
[72] Res. Holl. 26 Sept. 1623; ARH SG 3182 fo. 388^v.
[73] ARH SG 3183, fos. 390, 399. Res. 25, 29 July 1624.
[74] ARH SG 3183, fos. 625^v, 665, 745^v.

college, which was responsible for the Rhine, that so much and such a variety of food was being shipped up the river that even grain was now passing by that route, something almost unheard of, Holland at last consented to closure of the Rhine also.[75] As usual the blockade had a marked effect. When Breda finally surrendered, it was starkly obvious that the besiegers wanted far more for supplies than the besieged. After the fall of the town, disregarding the pleas of the admiralty colleges, now chronically short of funds for the navy,[76] the States General decided to maintain the blockade for a further period which, as always, suited some but inconvenienced others. After some weeks, on 12 June the Amsterdam herring dealers, backed by the city's burgomasters, pressed for immediate reopening of the rivers to prevent disaster to the herring industry. Herring and other fish exports were quickly exempted from the ban. Shortly afterwards, having consulted the new Stadholder, the States General finally consented to reopen the rivers and inland routes, as from 30 June 1625, except for the routes to Breda and 's-Hertogenbosch which both remained under a special local blockade.[77] The Maas, Schelde, and Brabant routes had by then been closed for all foodstuffs, timber, and some other supplies for little short of a year.

If the series of river blockades combined with the naval blockade of the Flemish coast undoubtedly significantly interrupted Dutch exports to Flanders, Brabant, Liège, and Westphalia, and caused major diversions of trade from the inland routes to the sea-lanes to north-east France, the war in all its ramifications had a wide range of effects on the life and economy of the Dutch people. But perhaps more than anything else, what most impinged on the ordinary man was the inevitable heavy increase in taxation, a phenomenon most marked during the 1620s when the army was growing rapidly. Spending on the army oscillated at between 11 and 13½ million guilders in the years 1621–5, before rising much higher thereafter. The demands of the state were thus roughly

[75] ARH SG 3184, fos. 29, 31.
[76] Ibid., fos. 224, 232, 243V, 248V.
[77] Ibid., fo. 248V. Res. 23 June 1625.

half as much again during the early 1620s as they had been either during the truce or during the closing years of the previous war.[78] The even more dramatic increase in naval spending was partly paid for from the increased returns on customs duties, but these did not suffice and regular supplementary subsidies from the States General were necessary.

Apart from the new provincial sales tax on cloth, so resented by the English, Holland adopted few major new taxes during 1621, owing to disagreement over what to tax. In October Maurits rebuked the States for the delay, urging Holland not to allow the state to fall victim to its enemies for lack of money.[79] Imposts on tobacco and cooking oils were agreed but relatively meagre progress had been made by December when Leiden, Enkhuizen, and the nobility protested to the other towns at their dilatoriliness in stepping up taxation. But during 1622 the picture rapidly changed. The province's consumption tax on herring and salt fish was increased by a guilder per barrel, the duty on beer consumed increased, and from April 1622 a heavy impost placed on consumption of English, Scottish, and Liège coal, another Dutch measure of the early 1620s which significantly damaged English exports.[80] Early in 1623 Holland was pressed by the States General to find an extra 1,200,000 guilders immediately, to pay troops who had been left unpaid for months. The province debated a 100th penny or 1 per cent levy on assessed wealth, but failed to agree. Wine duty was blocked by Dordrecht for German wines, by Rotterdam for French, and by Amsterdam for both with the argument that it would cause 'diversion of trade'.[81] On 15 March Maurits again reproached the province for the delays in paying the soldiery and warned of the danger of mutinies. Three days later Holland voted a 200th penny or ½ per cent on wealth and doubled its tax on soap.[82]

Early in 1624 Holland introduced the novel impost of stamp duty, *'t kleyn zegel*, on all legal transactions, an

[78] Ten Raa iii. 298–302.
[79] Res. Holl. 13 Oct. 1621.
[80] *Groot Placaet-Boeck* i. 1750/3, 1856/9.
[81] Res. Holl. 1623, p. 21.
[82] Ibid., 30 Mar. 1623; *Groot Placaet-Boeck* i. 1836/7.

example emulated the following year by Utrecht and Zeeland
and eventually, in many other parts of Europe, including
Castile, where stamp duty (*papel sellado*) was introduced
in 1636.[83] A proposal to tax foot-wear was discarded on the
ground that it would weigh excessively upon the poor.[84]
Amsterdam, anxious as always to deflect as much of the
burden as possible away from trade onto consumption, urged
another rise in beer duty, a new butter tax, and increases
in the important imposts on milling and storing grain which,
inevitably, raised the price of bread. The milling duty was
increased at this time by 25 per cent; later, after further increases in 1627 and 1636, it was collected at double the rate
that had applied during the years 1605-24.[85] Despite the
care of the States to avoid imposts apt to provoke the less
well off, trouble erupted in various towns, early in June 1624,
with the imposition of 4 guilders on every barrel of butter
sold. An immense and not entirely peaceful demonstration
took place at Amsterdam and there were riots at Delft,
Hoorn, Enkhuizen, and The Hague.[86] However, the worst
violence occurred at Haarlem. Unable to quiet the mob with
powder alone, the town militia fired shot, killing five and
wounding a considerable number. The news caused jubilation
at Brussels and word was sent to Spain that the Dutch populace were now on the verge of revolt against those who had
usurped authority.[87]

To meet the emergency of the siege of Breda, beer duty
was increased again, in October 1624, and another 200th
penny levy imposed. Meanwhile, in the other provinces,
despite considerable resistance in many quarters, fiscal pressure mounted roughly *pari passu*. In 1624-5, Utrecht introduced besides stamp duty a heavy tax on tobacco, increased
its impost on salt, and, following Holland, doubled its duty
on soap, an important item in a country so devoted to the

[83] *Actas* xvi. 229.
[84] GA Amsterdam, vroed. res. xiii. fo. 165.
[85] *Groot Placaet-Boeck* i. 1780/1.
[86] GA Amsterdam vroed. res. xiii, fo. 186; Leiden to Pieter Deyman, 5 June
1624, Leiden Sec. Arch. 963; Wagenaar, *Amsterdam* i. 486; van der Capellen i.
276; Schrevelius, 198-200.
[87] La Cueva to Philip, 15 June 1624. AGS Estado 2314.

cult of cleanliness.[88] The States of Zeeland, in 1624–5, adopted the impost Holland had earlier imposed on herring and fish consumption and voted in a 100th penny levy.[89] Yet all this was far from enough. 'Leur ruyne ne fuit jamais si proche d'eux qu'à cette heure', commented the French ambassador, Aubéry du Maurier, in April 1624.[90] By September 1625 many of the troops were reportedly three or four months behind in pay. The admiralty colleges were chronically short of funds for the navy. The outlook appeared unrelentingly ominous. 'The costs are too great,' lamented Reigersberch, 'Revenue is wholly insufficient and there is little room for more taxation; here, there is nothing but gloom for the present and fear for the future.'[91]

That the Spanish embargo, exclusion from Spain's European territories, and the resulting adverse effects on Baltic trade produced a general commercial recession of some severity in the United Provinces is incontestable. The reports circulated by the *Gazette van Antwerpen* and sent by Spanish ministers in Brussels to Madrid were doubtless overdrawn,[92] but the irreducible fact is that there was a slump in shipping and trade. The rise in returns on 'convoy and license money' from April 1621 was appreciably less than the 25 per cent or so, that would easily have been achieved under the new tariff list, had the overall volume of Holland's commerce even remained stagnant. As is shown in Graph 2, a depression, which was most marked in Zeeland, persisted throughout the maritime zone until the year 1628.

The initial impact of the conflict on Dutch manufacturing was more mixed, but again not particularly favourable, as is shown in Graph 3. Output of *say*-fustians at Gouda continued the steady downward trend evident since the early years of the truce. At Leiden developments in the textile industry during these years are remarkable in that output of moderately good-quality fabrics, such as *says* and bays, fell,

[88] *Groot Utrechts Placaet-Boeck* ii. 564–5, 726, 767, 797, 812.
[89] *Notulen Zeeland*, Placaet, 30 Oct. 1624 and Res. SZ 18 Mar. 1625.
[90] Aubéry du Maurier, 399.
[91] *Brieven Reigersberch*, 23.
[92] Consulta 28 Sept. 1625. AGS Estado 2039, fo. 2; *Gazette van Antwerpen* 247, p. 6, and 309, p. 8.

albeit only slightly, while production of cheap, coarse fustians and rashes considerably increased.[93] In view of the problem of high labour costs besetting Dutch industry, it would have been more advantageous for Leiden to develop in the opposite direction, producing more, not fewer, quality textiles. But war with Spain, steadfastly advocated by the Leiden *vroedschap*, and the policy of seeking increased protection against Flemish and English competition, inevitably involved sacrificing foreign markets, particularly in the Mediterranean, for the sake of cornering a larger slice of the domestic market. Whether or not it was a conscious strategy, the Leiden city council was in effect moulding the town's industry around the home market and cheap supplies of Baltic and home-produced wool. In the spring of 1623, following protests from groups of Leiden wool-combers over continuing sales of wool to Flanders, the Leiden *vroedschap* persuaded Amsterdam and the rest of the States of Holland to agree to a total ban on the export of home-produced wool.[94]

The early consequences of the war on the industries of the Spanish Netherlands were marginally unfavourable only so far as they slowed the rate of growth that had been achieved during the truce. Output at Hondschoote and Ghent continued to grow, only more slowly than previously while Lille actually did much better than during the truce.[95] The adverse effects of the Dutch naval blockade of the Flemish coast, the increased cost and difficulty in procuring supplies of Baltic, Scottish, and Spanish wools, which now had to be imported via Calais, and the inconvenience of consigning exports from Calais and Boulogne, rather than from the Flemish ports, were largely offset by the removal of Dutch and reduction in other foreign competition in the Iberian and Ibero-American markets.[96] In effect, the loss of sales in Holland and Zeeland strengthened the direct trading links between the Spanish Netherlands, and especially Antwerp, and the Iberian ports.

[93] Posthumus, *Lakenindustrie* iii. 930–1, 932, 941.
[94] GA Amsterdam, vroed. res. xii, fos. 195^v–197^r; *Groot Placaet-Boeck* i. 1172–3. Res. 22 Apr. 1623.
[95] Coornaert, 50, 53, 57; Bastin, 134; Deyon and Lottin, 31–2.
[96] Bastin, 135.

If Flemish manufacturing weathered the early 1620s with fair success, the renewal of hostilities with the Dutch can also be said to have saved Castile's industries from subsiding into a state of total collapse. The decline suffered during the truce years by the Spanish textile towns had been disastrous and proved irreversible; but the sudden curbing of the influx of foreign fabrics other than the Flemish, arising from the exclusion of Dutch shipping, created the conditions for a modest but definite process of recovery at Toledo, Segovia, and elsewhere which, indeed, would seem to have continued until around the end of the Dutch war.[97] The sharp slump in exports of wool from Castile during the 1620s, again caused by the absence of Dutch shipping,[98] for some time assured abundant supplies of cheap wool, a phenomenon almost unprecedented in early modern times, and from this, Castile's industries, gravely weakened though they were, could not fail to profit. The 1620s were the decade in which the urgent appeals of the *arbitristas* for some measure of protection for Spain's manufactures, against foreign competition, were at last answered in some measure as a result of the crown's Dutch policy and shown to be well founded.

v TRUCE TALKS, 1621–1625

A remarkable feature of the Dutch–Spanish conflict of 1621–48 is that while Philip's order to Isabella of July 1621, that armed hostilities should now begin, did seemingly diminish the prevailing confusion and uncertainty over the Low Countries situation, active belligerency did not in fact put an end to the talks between the antagonists regarding possible renewal of the truce. Indeed, truce soundings continued uninterruptedly over the next few years in parallel with the fighting. Awareness of these contacts eventually permeated not only Europe's diplomatic circles but also Low Countries public opinion to such an extent that doubts as to the reality of the war were soon voiced on all sides and continued for a considerable time.

[97] Ruiz Martin, 'Un testimonio', p. 9n; Weisser, 632; Le Flem, 535, 536.
[98] Israel, 'Spanish wool exports', 198, 200.

Mme T'Serclaes returned to Brussels from The Hague in July 1621 and confided to Iñigo de Brizuela that Maurits still favoured renewal of the truce and that should Isabella indicate, by an unsigned note that the prince could show to certain leading personages of the States General, that she was willing to accept the terms of 1609, in the name of the king, he would devise means of inducing concessions to Spain during the ensuing formal negotiations.[99] Isabella chose to reply by word of mouth only, however, asking Maurits to send a representative to confer with hers at Liège or some other neutral place. Isabella was firmly guided in her responses to The Hague by her council of state, consisting of Peckius, Spinola, Brizuela, and La Cueva, on the basis of written instructions from Madrid. It was the friar Brizeula, apparently, who divulged what was afoot to the papal nuncio at Brussels. The latter responded by repeatedly reminding Isabella and Spinola that the Pope opposed peace between Spain and the Dutch and that the interests of religion required continuation of the war.[1] However, remarkably little attention was paid to these papal interventions in either Brussels or Spain. Philip's ministers at Madrid, impatient though they were for hostilities to commence, remained hopeful that the Dutch would prove sufficiently pliable on questions of colonies and commerce, these being the issues that mattered, for a new truce to be agreed upon within a matter of months.[2]

Mme T'Serclaes returned from The Hague in September with the message that if Isabella would secretly apprise the prince, again in an unsigned note, of the king's minimum conditions for a truce, Maurits would endeavour to persuade the States General to comply, promising that he would not, in any case, divulge that he had such a message from the Infanta.[3] Mme T'Serclaes added that it appeared that the re-opening of the Schelde was attainable because on this the interests of Zeeland significantly diverged from those of

---

[99] Isabella to Philip, 16 Aug. 1621. ARB SEG 186, fos. 40-1, and copies of unsigned notes of Isabella and Maurits to each other.

[1] *Corresp. Bagno* i. 32-4, 42, 44.

[2] Consulta, Guerra, 23 July 1621. AGS Estado 2139.

[3] Isabella to Philip, 22 Sept. 1621. ARB SEG 186, fo. 99; *Corresp. d'Esp.* ii. 31.

Amsterdam. She was also of the opinion that the Dutch could be brought to renouncing their navigation to the New World and would agree to at least stabilizing the *status quo* in Asia. While the States General would immovably oppose granting the public practice of Catholicism on its territory, the Dutch could be induced to give a secret undertaking to tolerate private practice in Catholic homes. In reply, Isabella thanked the prince for his 'goodwill', but declared that she could not state the minimum conditions without first consulting the king.

Philip and his advisers were much pleased to learn that the Dutch were disposed to yield over the Schelde and enter into a secret undertaking on Catholic toleration.[4] Maurits's move was seen in Madrid as a 'certain sign that the [Dutch] greatly desire the truce.' Philip authorized the Infanta that provided the Dutch would additionally agree to yield a few places in the Far East, she could now enter into formal truce talks, but that she was to negotiate in such a way that the Dutch should not suppose that there was any real eagerness for the truce on the Spanish side. Furthermore, she was instructed to demand more, initially, than the king was actually prepared to settle for, namely, total withdrawal from the Indies besides the lifting of the Schelde restrictions and the public practice of Catholicism. During the course of these soundings, Maurits gave Isabella to understand that he was acting thus far entirely independently of the States General without the latter knowing what was afoot.[5] Whilst in Brussels, Mme T'Serclaes added that the prince's way of conducting policy was causing mounting discontent and suspicion in Holland and that Amsterdam's deputies had bluntly asked the prince whether he was engaged in secret dealings with Brussels which he had denied. In Madrid it was taken for granted that Mme T'Serclaes's comings and goings could not be kept secret and that the prince must be acting in close conjunction with the States General. In fact, as van der Capellen and other Dutch contemporaries relate, whilst it was common knowledge that secret talks were in

---

[4] Philip to Isabella, 20 Oct. 1621. ARB SEG 186, fo. 136.
[5] ARB SEG 186, fos. 99, 238ᵛ.

progress, the details were scrupulously reserved to the tiny entourage of politicians surrounding the prince to the exclusion of the main body of the States General and provincial assemblies.[6] The situation was evidently causing mounting annoyance to the Holland regents in Amsterdam and elsewhere.

Philip's apparently uncompromising response to Maurits's peace feelers inevitably discouraged the prince from continuing in his efforts to revive the terms of 1609 or to secure terms substantially similar. A final attempt was made by the prince to terminate the conflict before it really took hold by seeking the intercession of a third party, the Danish crown. Early in November 1621 Christian IV sent word to Madrid, offering Philip Danish mediation towards securing renewal of the terms of 1609, his intervention being considered by the *Consejo de Estado* in January 1622.[7] Once again the *Consejo* reiterated its previous position: the point of the war was not reconquest of 'rebel' territory but to force the Dutch to concede better terms than those obtained in 1609; for the king to agree to what had already proved disastrous to Spanish interests was simply out of the question. The king's negative reply to Copenhagen in effect ended the initial phase of wartime truce negotiations. Contact between Brussels and The Hague lapsed throughout the period of the siege of Bergen-op-Zoom.

Talks resumed, on Maurits's initiative, during the winter of 1622–3 when the States General's treasurer-general, Joris de Bye, again communicated truce proposals on behalf of the prince to his relative, Willem de Bye, at Brussels. Once again, confidence restored by the Spanish failure at Bergen-op-Zoom, the Dutch offered only the terms of 1609.[8] Discreet approaches were also made on Maurits's behalf to the Infanta through the prince's Catholic relatives, Jan van Nassau and the baron van Merode. At Madrid deliberation of this new Dutch initiative was entrusted by the king to a small

[6] Capellen i. 11; *Briefwisseling Grotius*, 112.
[7] Christian to Philip, Copenhagen, 3 Nov. 1621; Consulta, Estado 19 Jan. 1622. AGS Estado 2036.
[8] Isabella to Philip, 7 Apr. 1623. AGS Estado 2147; Gachard, 19.

junta headed by Brizuela who was now back in Spain having been preferred to the bishopric of Segovia. La Cueva advised from Brussels that, in view of the mounting financial distress of the Dutch, Philip should simply prevaricate in the expectation of time working to his advantage. The *junta* totally disagreed. Although Brizuela's fellow members, Agustín Messía and Fernando Girón, had earlier expressed themselves in favour of the war, it was now considered that the royal financial predicament had become so grave that unless truce talks were promptly entered into there was every risk of mutiny and unrest leading to a collapse of royal authority in the Spanish Netherlands.[9] These recommendations inevitably only widened the existing rift among Philip's ministers over the issue of the Dutch war. Considered misconceived by Olivares, Montesclaros, and other hard-liners who had the ear of the king, Brizuela's findings were in the end simply ignored.

During the spring of 1623 Mme T'Serclaes once more emerged as the principal go-between.[10] She assured Isabella that Maurits was still disposed to negotiate an early end to the conflict but that he was forced to tread with great caution because both the States General and the provinces remained deeply divided over the issue of the war, while the common folk were 'fort contre la trêve'. The impulse towards peace was particularly strong among the regents and nobles of Holland and the inland provinces, and in March Holland secretly proposed to the States General that in view of the increasing and ruinous burden of the war on the provinces' finances, truce talks with Spain should now be entered into.[11] Maurits proposed to Isabella that if she would now formally indicate her acceptance of the 1609 terms to the States General, he would arrange for a subsequent official clarification of the notoriously imprecise fourth article ensuring that in future it would be strictly observed on the Dutch side. Over a period of months, the Brussels peace-party

---

[9] Consulta, Brizuela's junta, 19 Jan. 1623. AGS Estado 2147.

[10] ARB PEA 1379, 'Lettres et mémoires touchant ce qui se traitait en matière de trêve par voie de la veuve de Tserclas qui correspondait avec le chanoine Danckart' (Feb. 1623–Oct. 1627).

[11] Van der Capellen i. 165.

headed by Peckius and Spinola remained hopeful that an end
to the conflict was now in sight. But there followed only a
sequence of further trips by Mme T'Serclaes between the two
Netherlands capitals and exchanges of messages which ultimately led nowhere. Opinion at Brussels was just as bitterly
divided as at Madrid and in The Hague. Writing to Urban
VIII, Bagno observed that the higher Castilian officers and
officials in the Netherlands remained implacably hostile to
the truce, but that Isabella herself and Spinola were so
determined that the war should be brought to an end that
he feared that it could not be long continued.[12] Spinola, he
judged, was at bottom merely fearful of further spoiling his
military reputation following the disaster at Bergen-op-Zoom.

At Madrid disagreement deepened as the months passed.
Brizuela persevered in pressing for the truce, dismissing La
Cueva's assertions that the Dutch were reeling under the
financial pressure of the conflict (though indubitably they
were) by observing that the alleged crisis of funds did not
seem to prevent the States General from continually assemb-
ling fresh armies and fleets. It was Philip, argued the *junta*,
who lacked the means to wage war effectively and that this
excessive and infinite burden was 'consuming and ruining
Spain'.[13] If the king could obtain tangible improvements in
the 1609 terms regarding colonies or the Schelde then a new
truce should be promptly agreed to. One pro-truce memorial
put to the *Consejo de Estado* at this time argued that the
Dutch were actually financing the conflict with the funds
that Philip remitted to the Netherlands to pay his troops,
and which gradually seeped into 'rebel' hands, and that by
opting for peace the king would both damage the Republic
financially and save Spain from being utterly drained of resources; the same author dealt scathingly with the strategic
argument that Flanders was Spain's best *plaza de armas*,
asking what sense it really made to concentrate resources at
one extremity of the empire leaving the rest devoid of funds
and defences.[14] In November 1623, after learning from

---

[12] *Corresp. Bagno* i. 330.
[13] Consultas of Brizuela's *junta*, 5 Mar., 4 and 14 July, 10 Aug. 1623. AGS
Estado 2147.
[14] BRA MS 16136, fos. 223ᵛ–226ᵛ.

Brussels that the Dutch were immovably determined to stick at the terms of 1609,[15] Brizuela and his sympathizers asserted that the king must now cut his losses and recognize that to fight on without the necessary means was to court disastrous setbacks in the southern Netherlands. To this Montesclaros grimly retorted that if asked which he judged worse for Spain, losing towns in Flanders or submitting again to the terms of 1609, he had no doubt that it would be the latter, the 'truce being so harmful and prejudicial'.[16] Inevitably, with Olivares at their head,[17] the hard-liners won through. The king solemnly confirmed his earlier resolution to make no truce until the Dutch were ready to make substantial concessions, news of which was greeted with some satisfaction by the papal nuncio as well as the Spanish officers in the Netherlands.

Endeavours to end the conflict continued through 1624 on much the same lines as in the previous year through Mme T'Serclaes, the painter Rubens, and the latter's brother-in-law, Jan Brant, as well as other intermediaries. Maurits offered once again to ensure clarification and stricter enforcement of the articles concerning the Indies if Spain would aquiesce in the terms of 1609.[18] Isabella strove to shift Philip from his adamant refusal to countenance such a truce, employing a variety of arguments, to which the king replied that the earlier agreement had worked entirely against the interests of Spain and that as far as he was concerned his funds sufficed to persevere with the war for another twelve years.[19] Accordingly, once Breda was firmly encircled, in August 1624 Isabella informed Maurits, through Mme T'Serclaes, that she could agree to enter into formal truce negotiations only if she received a prior commitment that the States General would agree to lift the Schelde restrictions and at least agree to stricter enforcement of the 1609 clause

[15] Rubens wrote to Peckius from Antwerp, in September, advising that his contact in The Hague confirmed that the Dutch insisted on 'una semplice accettatione della tregua, o niente', see Gachard, 267–9.

[16] Consulta, Brizuela's *junta*, 14 Nov. 1623. AGS Estado 2147.

[17] Elliott, *Conde-Duque*, 92.

[18] Peckius to Isabella, 1 Mar. 1624. ARB PEA 1379.

[19] *Corresp. d'Esp.* ii. 138.

concerning the Indies.[20] As in previous years, the communications between Brussels and The Hague of 1624 mainly concerned the Indies and the Schelde. The question of sovereignty was not raised and Bagno was appalled by the scant attention paid to matters of religion.[21] A polite deadlock ensued which continued throughout the Breda campaign and its aftermath much to the discontent of pro-war elements in the Republic which remained highly suspicious of Maurits's role and not without reason.[22]

[20] Isabella to Maurits (unsigned), 8 Aug. 1624. ARB PEA 1379.
[21] *Corresp. Bagno* i. 513.
[22] *Basuyne des Ooreloghs*, 15–17.

Chapter IV

The Dutch Counter-Offensive,
1626–1633

i THE STRUGGLE FOR THE LOW COUNTRIES

If the Spaniards had enjoyed the advantage of larger forces during the early years of the struggle, until the fall of Breda, the balance shifted dramatically during the period 1626-8. Even as she toured Breda in triumph, Isabella was in the midst of implementing Philip's instructions of June 1625, placing the army of Flanders on an exclusively defensive footing and cutting its mobile strike force from over 30,000 to only 24,000 men. Together with reductions in the garrisons, the total cuts brought the army down to just over 50,000 men.[1] The architect of this far-reaching reorganization, Olivares, was, like most of his colleagues, quite convinced that pressing the land offensive was now pointless and that different forms of pressure were needed if the Dutch were to be forced to acquiesce in a truce on Spanish terms. While Olivares was one of the most determined of Philip's ministers that the war should go on until this was achieved (as he put it, if necessary for another dozen years or more) he was at the same time adamant that the war must be fought as economically as possible, enabling the king to maintain sufficient forces in Italy and Germany, support the Emperor, and keep the French in check. The Conde-Duque's policy, in other words, was a remarkable mixture of intractable resolve to fight on and insistence on the slimming down of the army of Flanders to save money. Paradoxically, some of his colleagues who were most disposed towards ending the war, notably Spinola, were at the same time the most opposed to Olivares's plans for army cuts. Spinola insisted that much larger forces

[1] Isabella to Philip, Breda, 5 July 1625. AGS Estado 2315.

than the Conde-Duque envisaged would be needed in the Low Countries for as long as the conflict dragged on.

Part of the dispute over troop-levels on the Spanish side concerned the mobile field-force. During 1625–7, the transition period following the fall of Breda, when the Spanish offensive was definitively ended, the Conde-Duque urged a mobile force of only 20,000 infantry and 4,000 cavalry, though by 1628, after several years of argument with Spinola, he was ready to countenance a slightly higher figure.[2] In Spinola's view, given the size and dispositions of the Dutch forces, the minimum mobile force required to defend the southern Netherlands and the Spanish enclaves in north-west Germany was 30,000 infantry and 5,000 cavalry. There was dispute also over the size and number of fixed garrisons that were needed, the only point of agreement being that the fixed force should comprise half of the army. Where Olivares originally pressed for a total of 20,000, or at most 24,000, garrison troops,[3] Spinola judged that the minimum required, given the number of essential fortified strong-points, was 35,000. The actual size of the Spanish garrison-force in February 1626 was 31,046 troops, 6,000 distributed in twenty garrisons in Flanders, 3,962 manning twenty-four fortified positions in Brabant, and 21,084 garrisoning the strongholds on the Maas, Lower Rhine, and Eems.[4] Despite the setbacks of 1626–7, in 1627–8 this force was further reduced to around 29,000 men. The actual distribution of the Spanish garrisons in the Low Countries early in 1628, after the loss of Oldenzaal and Grol, is shown in Table 6.

Thus the Spanish army of Flanders during the later 1620s was considerably smaller than during the years 1621–5. Though one historian has suggested that it was as large as 69,000 in 1627,[5] or only marginally less than during the

[2] Olivares, 'Sobre la forma en que se podria encaminar en Flandes lo de la union' (24 June 1626). AGS Estado 2040; 'Parecer de su ex el conde duque' (16 Dec. 1626). AGS Estado 2040; Olivares, 'Primer Papel' (April 1628). AGS Estado 2320.

[3] Olivares, 'Sobre la forma' fo. iv.

[4] Consulta 30 Mar. 1626. AGS Estado 2040.

[5] Parker, *Army of Flanders*, 271; see, however, Philip to Isabella, 15 June 1627. ARB SEG 197, fo. 51 and Table 7 above.

Table 6 The fixed garrisons of the army of Flanders, March 1628*

	Officers	Men	Total
Flanders			
Hulst and neighbouring forts	68	776	844
Dunkirk	45	659	704
Damme	85	461	546
Land van Waas	109	391	500
Brugge–Gent canal	95	386	481
Dendermonde	48	307	355
Blankenberge canal	21	297	318
Mardijk	38	279	317
Nieuwpoort	39	280	319
Cadzant forts	c37	243	c280
Aalst	42	178	220
Blankenberge	10	162	172
Ostend	36	130	166
Passendale	11	123	134
Veurne	15	98	113
Brugge	11	88	99
Minor garrisons	26	156	182
Total Flanders	736	5014	5750
Brabant			
Breda and outlying forts	420	3647	4067
's-Hertogenbosch	212	2518	2730
Zandvliet–Antwerp	483	3035	3518
Total Brabant	1115	9200	10315
Maas			
Maastricht	?	?	c1000
Roermond	46	460	506
Venlo	10	84	94
Wallonia			
Cambrai	46	512	558
Rhine–Eems–Lippe			
Wesel	358	2719	3077
Rheinberg	222	1473	1695
Lingen	194	1159	1353
Orsoy	50	384	434
Lippstadt	54	642	696
Düsseldorf	51	530	581
Geldern	c50	c350	c400
Jülich	59	338	397
Papenmutz	18	252	270
Düren	17	169	186
Minor fortresses	251	1765	2016
Total for north-west Germany	1274	9781	11105
Grand Total			29328

*Relacion de los officiales y soldados (March 1628). AGS Estado 2321.

years of the offensive until 1625, in fact this figure is misleading as is indicated on Table 7 and from 1626 the army's
strength consistently stood at between 48,000 and 55,000
men, implying a shrinkage by around one-third. The figures
submitted to Madrid by the army paymasters-general in this
period usually included the troops stationed in the Rhenish
Palatinate, a force counted in with the army of Flanders for
financial purposes but which otherwise had little direct
bearing on the Netherlands conflict. The army of the Palatinate was some 13,000 men strong. On the other hand, the
official figures omit the troops raised and paid for locally by
the South Netherlands provinces which amounted to roughly
one quarter of the army. In July 1627, when the Palatinate
troops are discounted, the total forces in the Low Countries
under Spinola's command amounted to about 54,000 men.[6]
In March 1628 the king was paying altogether for 51,968
troops of which 13,195 were quartered on the Middle Rhine;
allowing for the locally raised troops, this again implies a
total in the Netherlands and north-west Germany barely
exceeding 50,000.[7] In his missive of June 1627 Philip instructed Isabella that her army of 54,000 men sufficed for
guerra defensiva and that she should neither increase it nor
attempt any offensive action.

In the very years that the Spanish forces in the Low Countries were reduced and kept to a level some 30 per cent
lower than that of the early 1620s, the States General considerably expanded its army. Coinciding with this decisive
shift in the balance of forces, there began in the United
Provinces a much more active debate than previously over
objectives and strategy. Until late in 1625 the Spanish
offensive, inferiority of numbers and the successive defeats
of the Protestant forces in Germany had combined to con-
fine the Dutch to a static, defensive posture and largely
confined strategic debate to the question of the distribution
of the fixed garrisons. Philip IV, by taking the decision to
fight only *guerra defensiva* by land and *guerra offensiva* by sea,
in effect abandoned the military initiative to the Dutch who

---

[6] 'Relacion' (July 1627). AGS Estado 2319.
[7] 'Ron de los officiales y soldados' (Mar. 1628). AGS Estado 2041.

Table 7 The strength of the army of Flanders, 1607–1647*

	Spaniards	Total Infantry	Cavalry	Grand Total
Mar. 1607	6,545	37,307	4,164	41,471
Mar. 1609	6,528	13,759	1,500	15,259
May 1619	6,310	25,832	3,378	29,210
Dec. 1619[1]	5,758	–	–	21,950
June 1620[2]	–	–	–	22,040
Jan. 1621[3]	5,253	–	–	19,772
Mar. 1622[4]	6,332	–	–	38,152
Mar. 1623[5]				46,689
Apr. 1624[6]				(55,000)
Mar. 1626[7]				54,003
June 1627[8]				35,906
Oct. 1627[9]				34,761
Feb. 1628[10]				34,762
Sept. 1633	5,693	45,067	7,648	52,715
Mar. 1636[11]				69,703
Feb. 1637[12]	–	65,000	(7,000)	(72,000)
Oct. 1639[13]		70,000	10,000	80,000
Jan. 1640	17,262	76,933	11,347	88,280
Dec. 1643	10,438	63,422	14,095	77,517
Feb. 1647	9,685	53,724	11,734	53,724

*These are the forces maintained in the Low Countries by the Spanish crown but excluding the troops paid for locally by the South Netherlands 'Finances'. The latter amounted in 1623 to 15,722 men and generally constituted about one quarter of the army. Thus when comparing the Army of Flanders with the Dutch army during this period, the figures in the last column must be increased by roughly 25 per cent. Where no source is indicated, the figures follow Parker, *Army of Flanders*, 271–2. The figures in brackets are my approximations.

[1] 'Relacion' (Dec. 1619) AGS Estado 2309.
[2] 'Relacion' (June 1620) AGS Estado 2309; the figure given in Parker includes 22,000 troops then with Spinola in the Palatinate.
[3] C. de Benavente to Philip, 11 Feb. 1621. AGS Estado 2310.
[4] 'Relacion' (26 Mar. 1622). AGS Estado 2139, doc. 110.
[5] The figure of 62,606 given in Parker, includes the troops in the Palatinate; the above figure is from both Consulta 14 Apr. 1623. AGS Estado 2037 and BL Add. 14007, fo. 385.
[6] The figure given in Parker includes the army of the Palatinate.
[7] Casuso Maeda to Philip, 22 Mar. 1626. AGS Estado 2316.
[8] 'Relacion' (July 1627). AGS Estado 2319.
[9] Ruiz de Pereda to Philip, 20 Oct. 1627. AGS Estado 2321.
[10] 'Relacion' (Mar. 1628) AGS Estado 2321.
[11] Consulta, 12 Apr. 1636. AGS Estado 2051.
[12] M. de Salamanca to Philip, 8 Feb. 1637. AGS Estado 2051; of these, no fewer than 44,000 were required for the fixed garrisons.
[13] Consulta 25 July 1640. AGS Estado 2055.

now had to decide how to use it. Despite the changed circumstances, Holland in general preferred to stick to the static,
defensive posture to which army and state had become
accustomed, partly because this would require fewer troops
and less expenditure than any offensive, and partly because
the province had no real designs on Spanish-controlled
territory.[8] Frederik Hendrik, however, and following his
lead, the *Raad van State*, together with Zeeland and the
inland provinces, pressed both for a more active policy and,
to support it, increases in expenditure and forces.

Remarkably, it was not only Amsterdam, Rotterdam,
Delft, and Dordrecht, towns which were soon to back the
1629 truce initiative, that favoured a purely defensive posture. Haarlem and Leiden, the core of the Holland war-
party, for all their unwavering commitment to the struggle
showed not the slightest interest in schemes of conquest in
the Netherlands.[9] On 5 March 1626 Frederik Hendrik
appeared, together with the *Raad*, before the States of
Holland to urge adoption of a supplementary military budget
to raise expenditure so that an additional 7,000 French and
German infantry could be added to the standing army of
48,153 troops maintained since 1621.[10] The prince argued
that for the moment the Spaniards were obviously exhausted,
following their effort at Breda, and that the chance had
therefore arisen to seize the initiative and boost the sagging
morale of the Republic's populace. Privately, he was anxious
also to shake off the dismal influence on his reputation of
the loss of Breda during the opening months of his stad-
holderate. While several provinces were keen to back the
prince's martial aspirations, the designs of the inland provinces widely diverged from those of Zeeland. Groningen,
Overijssel, and Gelderland were chiefly interested in launching local attacks against the Spanish garrisons at Lingen,
Oldenzaal, and Grol to clear the Spaniards from the Republic's
eastern border, secure themselves against the threat of

[8] Aitzema ii. 119.
[9] Res. Holl. 24 Feb., 5 and 10 Mar., 6 Apr. 1626; Poelhekke, *Frederik Hendrik*, 127.
[10] Res. Holl. 5 Mar. 1626; Ten Raa iv. 355.

Spanish raids, and create a buffer zone between themselves and the adjoining German lands increasingly dominated by the armies of the Emperor and the Catholic League. Zeeland displayed meagre interest in the eastern border but a powerful inclination for the conquest of more territory along the Schelde and in Flanders. With immaculate skill Frederik Hendrik satisfied the provinces that he was nurturing offensive plans for all fronts. In the case of Holland, the prince eventually overcame the obstruction on the part of Leiden and Delft.

Positioning the bulk of his field army near Rees, to deter the Spaniards from sending reinforcements north of the Rhine, the prince dispatched 7,000 men under his trusted cousin, Ernst Casimir van Nassau, to besiege Oldenzaal. The town capitulated on 1 August after a mere ten days' bombardment, a surprisingly easy success for the Dutch given that the town had long rated as one of the three bastions of Spanish and Catholic power north of the Rhine. The swift break-through at so strategic a point later prompted the chronicler Aitzema to ask how different history would have been had the Spaniards employed the great resources of men and cash so ineffectively and wastefully expended at Bergen-op-Zoom and Breda to strike instead, as the Dutch had feared and foreign diplomats expected, from Oldenzaal, Grol and Lingen westwards, across the IJssel.[11] Hampered by lack of funds, Spinola made no move to cross the Rhine fearing that if he did so the Dutch army at Rees would board its fleet of river-ships and descend, much faster than his troops could march back, on Flanders.[12] Ernst Casimir, to the surprise of many Dutchmen, merely dismantled Oldenzaal's fortifications and then left the town which Isabella then cited as evidence, in her report to Madrid, that indeed the Dutch objective had been to lure Spinola away from Flanders. The entire situation reflected the sudden new weakness of the Spanish situation, though this did not prevent scathing criticism of Spinola on the part of Olivares.[13]

[11] Aitzema, *Hist.* ii. 126.
[12] Isabella to Philip, 27 Aug. 1626. AGS Estado 2317.
[13] 'Parecer de su excelencia el conde duque' (16 Dec. 1626). AGS Estado 2040.

As had been the case under Maurits, during the early 1620s, strategic decisions on the Dutch side under Frederik Hendrik continued to be confined to a tiny, entrenched, group of men. During the later 1620s and early 1630s, with only slight variations in personnel, a handful of specially favoured politicians, notably Noordwijck (Holland nobility), Schaffer (Groningen), Haersolte (Overijssel), Ploos (Utrecht), Beaumont (Zeeland), and Holland's provincial pensionaries, first Antonis Duyck, and after his death in 1629, Jacob Cats, largely monopolized the role of advising the Stadholder and were entrusted by him with managing, organizing, and, on occasion, manipulating the States General and the provincial assemblies.[14] The same men invariably dominated the States General's 'secret committee on the employment of the army' and the committees delegated to the army during campaigns even though these committees were in theory elected afresh by the States General each year. In reality, these key personages were not genuinely elected at all but were regularly nominated by Frederik Hendrik: they were his adherents and managers rather than the representatives of their provinces. They together with the Stadholder made all the real decisions, often with the States General and the provincial assemblies having only the vaguest notion as to what was happening. In late August, the prince embarked his army at Rees, descended the Waal and sailed through Zeeland, disembarking at the eastern end of Dutch Flanders. But having tested the strength of the Spanish defences around Hulst, he re-embarked and returned to Rees. At this point, on 11 September, the States General did try to influence the proceedings and secretly resolved that in view of the recent disastrous defeats of the Danish king, Christian IV, by the Habsburgs, in north Germany, Frederik Hendrik should undertake some further offensive action that year in order to bolster morale at home and give at least some comfort to the Republic's allies.[15] A majority of the assembly envisaged

[14] Res. SG. 28 Aug. 1626. ARH SG 3185, fo. 349; Res. Holl. 2 July 1627; Aitzema, *Hist.* ii. 147; A. Duyck to Ernst Casimir, The Hague, 5 Aug. 1626. Archives iii. 7--8.

[15] SG secret res. 11 Sept. 1626. ARH SG 4562, fos. 125–6; Res. Holl. 23 and 24 Sept. 1626.

either an attack on Lingen, as Groningen and Overijssel preferred, or, as Gelderland desired, on Grol, but the final decision as to whether, where, and when to attack was expressly left to the prince and the usual small secret committee of the States made up of Duyck, for Holland, and representatives from each of the other provinces. The States General laid down only that Frederik Hendrik must avoid a pitched battle.[16] In the end, the prince and his advisors agreed that the Spaniards were too well prepared for the moment, at Grol and Lingen as well as at Geldern, for anything further to be attempted that year. During October, both armies were disbanded for the winter.

Eager to exploit the enemy's growing weakness, the States General adopted a second supplementary army budget early in 1627, which added a further 3,000 infantry and brought the army's total up to 58,000 men.[17] For the first time in the history of the Spanish–Dutch struggle, the States' army was now appreciably larger than the king's. In March the States General debated in secret which offensive strategy to adopt: the inland provinces, except Gelderland, urged an attack on Lingen, Holland on Breda, and Zeeland, predictably, an offensive in Flanders.[18] However, after a feigned advance on Wesel, Frederik Hendrik suddenly descended, in July, as Gelderland had wished, on Grol, before the town could be reinforced.[19] In this town, which dominated the eastern fringe of Gelderland, was a major Catholic centre, and more strongly fortified than Oldenzaal, was invested considerable Spanish prestige. A column of relief, under van den Bergh, approached, but hampered by cash shortage and a squabble between Castilian and Italian officers over which national contingents should head the column, this force was too slow to prevent Frederik Hendrik encircling Grol with his formidable siege-fortifications. There were several skirmishes, and on the night of 15 August the

---

[16] Secret res. SG. 23 spet. 1626. ARH SG 4562, fo. 126.
[17] Ten Raa iv. 356.
[18] Pedro de San Juan to Juan de Villela, 19 Mar. 1627. AGS Estado 2318.
[19] La Cueva to Philip, 1 and 25 Aug. 1627, and Spinola to Philip, 20 Oct. 1627. AGS Estado 2319; van der Capellen i. 429.

Spaniards mounted a head-on assault which cost them sixty dead; but nevertheless, van den Bergh managed to give the impression to friend and foe alike that his efforts were essentially *pro forma*, lacking any real bite. Before long, the walls of Grol had been mined and breached by English contingents of the besieging army. After repulsing the first charge, the 900-strong garrison capitulated, on honourable terms, on 19 August. There had been no question of their being starved out. Jubilation swept the seven provinces and a corresponding gloom the Catholic Netherlands.

But whilst this was happening, Spinola had not been totally inactive. Indeed, he managed to rub much of the shine off the prince's second victory by sending a sizeable force, with building materials, by barge, past the Dutch fortifications at Lillo, on the Schelde, below Antwerp.[20] In and around Zandvliet, the Spaniards erected a daunting complex of fortifications, behind the main Dutch defences on the east bank. Apart from extending Antwerp's defences, this opened a yawning gap in the Dutch dispositions, for there was no barrier to prevent Spanish river craft from Zandvliet raiding Tholen, Goes and the region of Bergen-op-Zoom. To the evident discomforture of the States General, by December 1627 the Spanish garrison at Zandvliet was the largest in the whole of the Low Countries after Breda.

Despite the *Consejo de Estado*'s anger at the perfunctoriness of the army of Flanders during 1627, and in particular at Spinola's not having marched in person to the relief of Grol, at Madrid the marquis continued to be deemed indispensable. The fact was that none of the Castilian *tercio* or garrison commanders was thought to have either the skill or the tact with the different national contingents that the position of commander-in-chief demanded.[21] In granting Spinola permission, in January 1628, to return temporarily to Spain, Philip's ministers assumed that his absence from the Netherlands would be brief. In fact, the campaign of 1627 proved to be Spinola's last in the Low Countries and

[20] *Mémoires*, 41; Wassenaer xiv. fo. 60.
[21] Consulta 6 Nov. 1627. AGS Estado 2041.

he was never to return. The army of Flanders thus now faced a prolonged crisis of command in addition to its many other difficulties.

Nevertheless, at the beginning of 1628 the position again became grave for the Dutch. At the request and instigation of Philip IV, and with the specific purpose of putting pressure on the Dutch, a large part of the army of the Catholic League, under Tilly, together with some Imperialist contingents, during December 1627 entered East Friesland, seizing several towns and strong-points in close proximity to the Groningen border and the Dutch garrisons at Emden and Leerort.[22] Much to the anxiety of the States General, these forces then took up winter quarters and there ensued a series of complaints, from Tilly to the Dutch authorities, over the activities of the Dutch soldiery in the area and the ban on the passage of foodstuffs from Dutch territory overland or by sea to East Friesland, with which the States General sought to inconvenience his troops and force them to withdraw. There was no actual fighting, but considerable tension. There was also widespread apprehension throughout the Republic throughout the first half of 1628, lest the Emperor and the Catholic League might be on the point of attacking in conjunction with the Spaniards.[23] Olivares and Philip indeed hoped to launch a two-pronged attack on the Republic from the east, in conjunction with Wallenstein, with the intention of striking such a blow at Dutch public morale as to induce the States General to agree to immediate talks and to modify the 1609 truce terms in favour of Spain.[24] Though some thought was given at Madrid to besieging Rees, Olivares and his colleagues believed that the strategy most likely to bring about a favourable truce quickly was a two-pronged deep-penetration raid in massive force, one column of Spanish and German troops to push across the Veluwe towards the heart of the Republic, and the other, Imperialist troops

---

[22] Van der Capellen i. 443; Aitzema, *Hist.* ii. 430–1; Philip to Aytona, 4 Nov. 1627. AGS Estado 2235.

[23] Van der Capellen i. 444, 451, 452, 465; La Cueva to Philip, 25 Jan. 1628. AGS Estado 2321; *Briefwisseling Grotius* iii. 236.

[24] Olivares to Spinola, Aranjuez, 30 Apr. 1628, Spinola to Isabella, Madrid, 1 May 1628. ARB SEG 126.

backed by the Spanish garrison at Lingen, to enter Groningen and Friesland. Isabella gave the order for preparations in the Spanish Netherlands whilst heavy diplomatic pressure was brought to bear on Vienna to co-operate with Philip's plans. However, Isabella's chronic shortage of cash and the Emperor's reluctance to be drawn further into the Low Countries conflict effectively aborted the scheme.[25]

Besides the inauspicious general situation, the States General was greatly worried by the necessity of diverting large forces to Groningen and Emden, by the possibility that the East Frisian ports of Norden and Grietzyl might be turned into naval bases for attacks on Dutch shipping in the North Sea and by the continuing Spanish build-up at Zandvliet.[26] On the Stadholder's advice, the States General readily opted for a further increase in the size of the Dutch forces, a static defensive posture for the time being, and a programme of new fortifications on the extreme north-eastern frontier and in western Brabant, facing Zandvliet.[27] As in previous years, the key decisions rested with the Stadholder and a tiny inner committee of the States General, though the views and aspirations of the different provinces were regularly taken into account.[28] Late in the campaign season, with the progress of the new defences and the easing of tension in East Friesland, there was again talk of resuming the offensive against the Spaniards. Frederik Hendrik concentrated a powerful force in Brabant to draw the Spaniards to that front, hoping to create an opportunity for Ernst Casimir to descend upon Lingen.[29] At the same time, there was continuing strong pressure from Zeeland for the prince to besiege either Hulst or Sas van Gent. On this occasion, Isabella's ministers at Brussels received accurate intelligence from The Hague, through Dutch informers recruited by Manuel Sueyro, the Portuguese New Christian spy-master

[25] Isabella to Spinola, 31 May 1628. ARB SEG 126; *Letters, Rubens*, 244–5.
[26] Res. SG 11 and 23 Mar. 1628. ARH SG 3187, fos. 117, 140; Van der Capellen i. 444; Wassenaer xiv, fos. 69, 76ᵛ, 96ᵛ.
[27] SG to SZ, 4 Oct. 1628. RAZ SZ, vol. 934; Ten Raa iv. 22–4; *Mémoires de Frederic*, p. 50.
[28] Aitzema, *Hist.* ii. 443.
[29] Van der Capellen i. 480.

who operated from Antwerp.[30] In the event, no more came of the Dutch than of the Spanish schemes for the year.

During the winter of 1628–9, despite the continuing ascendancy of Wallenstein's forces in north Germany, the advantage swung back emphatically in favour of the Dutch. While the States' army had continued to grow, the position of the army of Flanders had rapidly deteriorated as a result of the onset of the Mantuan Succession crisis in Italy, which diverted Spanish troops and funds away from the Low Countries, and the loss of the Mexican silver fleet in September 1628 to the Dutch West India Company fleet under Piet Heyn, off the north coast of Cuba, which had utterly dislocated Philip's financial schedules. The fall of La Rochelle to Louis XIII and the mobilization of the French army for intervention in northern Italy against Spain further strengthened the position of the Dutch. The lack of money and supplies in the Spanish Netherlands was now critical. Isabella and her advisers were filled with foreboding lest the Dutch should attack. 'And should they besiege Breda or 's-Hertogenbosch', she wrote despairingly to Philip in February 1629, 'we see no way of saving either, for there are no supplies for their defence. . .and the troops are in such a state that I know not how they have suffered such misery, for most have not been paid for four months.'[31]

Frederik Hendrik was thus well aware, by February 1629, that despite the risk of Imperialist intervention, he now had a unique opportunity to attack from a position of overwhelming strength and shake Spain to the core.[32] In The Hague, the talk was of besieging Lingen, Wesel, or 's-Hertogenbosch though all sorts of confusing information reached Brussels where it was reported that Friesland was anxious for the offensive to be directed against Lingen, Zeeland wanted the attack to be against Hulst and Holland against Zandvliet.[33] But to launch a major offensive while safeguarding the

---

[30] 'Avisos de Olanda', The Hague, 22 Sept. 1628. AGS Estado 2320.

[31] Isabella to Philip, 13 Feb. 1629. ARB SEG 200, fo. 57.

[32] GA Leiden Sec. Arch. 447, fo. 99; *Res. Holl. 16 Feb. 1629;* Mémoires, 51–2.

[33] Corresp. *Lagorissa*, p. 128.

Republic against a possible Imperialist intervention, the Dutch army had to be still further expanded, and to achieve this the prince had first to overcome the growing resistance in Holland to further rises in military expenditure. The States of Holland debated whether to vote the additional money for a major offensive during the second half of February, but remained thoroughly split.[34] Eventually, in voting on 28 February and 1 March, a majority emerged in favour of granting the means for the offensive, but certain towns persisted in obstructing the Stadholder's plans. It was not Amsterdam, though, which led this opposition. At Amsterdam, where a political contest, during the mid 1620s had resulted in the emergence of a new dominant clique, at odds with Pauw and his adherents and the policies for which they stood,[35] there prevailed at this time a definite willingness to co-operate with the prince whose support was needed against the hard-line Counter-Remonstrant towns which were pressing for a renewed drive against the Arminians whose fortunes in the province had latterly somewhat revived. The towns which obstructed the prince's offensive, Haarlem, Enkhuizen, Edam, and Schoonhoven,[36] were all foci of strong Counter-Remonstrant feeling, solidly anti-Spanish and dedicated to the war. But the *vroedschappen* of these towns were angry at the gradual collapse at Amsterdam and Rotterdam of the men of 1618 and the re-emergence of members of the old oligarchy together with some new elements which were unwilling to enforce strictly the edicts against the Arminians. Expressing their annoyance at the prince's sympathetic attitude to the new rival leadership in Holland, several strongly Counter-Remonstrant towns asserted that no offensive against the Spanish forces should be launched until 'religion and regime' within the Republic had been properly secured. However, Frederik Hendrik showed his political adroitness by winning Leiden, the largest of the Counter-Remonstrant towns to his side through direct contact with the burgomasters.[37]

[34] Res. Holl. 16, 17, 21, 22 Feb. 1629, *Mémoires*, 53.
[35] Elias, *vroedsch. van Amst.* i. pp. lxxii, lxxiv, lxxvii–lxxviii.
[36] Res. Holl. 10 and 21 Mar. 1629.
[37] Vroed. Res. 2 Feb. 1629. GA Leiden Sec. Arch. 447, fos. 99ʳ–99ᵛ.

Between February and April 1629 the Dutch army expanded from 71,443 to 77,193 men,[38] so that it was now approximately half as large again as the army of Flanders. At Madrid, where Olivares and Philip had finally yielded to the arguments of the truce party and brought themselves to agree to a truce on the terms of 1609,[39] it was now expected that despite the all too obvious danger, the war would in fact cease before the blow fell.[40] Philip and his ministers concentrated their attention on the intense diplomatic activity in progress rather than on strengthening the defences of Spanish Netherlands. While distinctly lacking enthusiasm for van den Bergh as commander-in-chief, he was thought preferable to Juan Bravo, governor of Antwerp, who was old and sick, or the experienced *tercio* commander, Francisco de Medina, or any of the available Castilian officers. In any case, it was hoped that the whole question of the army's command was now superfluous. But the truce talks simply dragged on. Frederik Hendrik, having amassed a strike force of 28,000 men on the Rhine border, during late April and arranged for some intense cavalry activity around Wesel and Lingen to confuse the Spaniards suddenly swept towards 's-Hertogenbosch and set siege to the town. Isabella, her ministers and the army commander, van de Bergh, frantically began mustering forces with which to try to relieve the city before the Dutch forces had completed their siege fortifications, sending for reinforcements to the Palatinate and beseeching the Emperor for assistance.[41] But as almost nothing had been done beforehand, it took almost two months before van den Bergh was able to march towards the encircled town with a substantial force. The Spaniards, considerably weaker in numbers, encamped close to the Dutch positions for several weeks until 17 July, searching in vain for a weak point to attack.[42] Eventually, van den Bergh set off towards Wesel hoping to save 's-Hertogenbosch by means of a powerful diversionary thrust. From Wesel, the Spaniards advanced

---

[38] Bordes, 23.
[39] See pp. 226–7 below.
[40] Philip to Isabella, 5 Apr. 1629. ARB SEG 200, fo. 138.
[41] Isabella to Philip, 3 May 1629. ARB SEG 200, fo. 203.
[42] 'Brieven s'hertogenbosch', pp. 9–25.

north of the Rhine towards the IJssel which was crossed by
the vanguard, under Lucas Cayro, at Westervoort, during the
night of 22 July.[43]

Consulting with his regular advisors, Noordwijk, Schaffer,
Haersolte, and others Frederik Hendrik determined not to
raise the siege of 's-Hertogenbosch, but instead to raise yet
additional forces to counter the invasion from the east. More
troops were enlisted on a temporary basis and, on 26 July,
the States of Holland arranged for the dispatch of urban
militia units to various Brabant fortress towns, to relieve the
professional garrison troops who were then switched to the
eastern front, the garrisons of Heusden and Steenbergen, for
instance, being replaced by 500 Amsterdam *schutters*. In all,
the force under the Stadholder's command, including 5,000
militiamen, 1,200 West India Company troops hastily brought
up from the fleet being prepared against Brazil, and detach-
ments of armed sailors, amounted to the wholly unprecedented figure of 128,877 men.[44] It soon emerged that the
Spanish counter-operation was much more than a mere raid.
Van den Bergh crossed the IJssel with the bulk of his strike
force and then moved his make-shift bridge of boats northwards to Dieren, to secure it against the Dutch troops at
Arnhem. The Emperor's aid, 16,000 men, under Count von
Montecuculi, now arrived. Inevitably, the latter shared none
of the reluctance of the Spaniards to devastate the Dutch
countryside and van den Bergh came under considerable
pressure from his Austro-German allies to condone the
burning of Gelderland crops and villages as a means of in-
timidating the Dutch public and compelling the Stadholder
to lift the siege of 's-Hertogenbosch.

In early August two Habsburg columns penetrated further
into Dutch territory, Montecuculi with 10,000 men towards
Amersfoort, via Ede, burning villages as he went, and a
Spanish force northwards towards Deventer. The States
General and the Dutch public undoubtedly were severely
shaken, though the Stadholder remained remarkably cool.
On 13 August the Imperialists approached Amersfoort, which

[43] *Victoria Famosa*, pp. 1–4.
[44] Aitzema, *Hist.* ii. 883–4.

surrendered with a promptness which shocked the entire Republic; its *vroedschap* was purged and Catholic worship restored. Montecuculi later claimed that he could easily have captured Utrecht also had he received even a minimum of support from van den Bergh. The Spanish column meanwhile bypassed Deventer, failed to take Hattem, near Zwolle, and then swerved south-westwards towards Harderwijk, inflicting only slight damage as it went. Then suddenly the picture was totally transformed. Aware that Wesel was but lightly held and that a section of its walls had partly collapsed, the energetic Dutch governor of Emmerich, Otto van Gent, had prepared a surprise attack on the town. In a dawn assault on 19 August van Gent stormed into Wesel with 1,000 infantry, killing a hundred or so Spaniards and Italians who resisted; the German troops who constituted the bulk of the garrison, merely looked on, shouting for their pay, and then surrendered or escaped.[45] Fifty field guns were captured together with a vast store of supplies and beer. Van den Bergh seized upon the pretext to pull back. Amersfoort was abandoned within four days. He even wished to abandon the IJssel crossing-point, but at Isabella's insistence Spanish troops, under Jan van Nassau, held the position at Dieren for several more weeks. Not surprisingly, the astounding news of the loss of Wesel and withdrawal from the Veluwe had a totally shattering effect on both Philip and Olivares.[46]

Meanwhile, at 's-Hertogenbosch Frederik Hendrik made steady progress against the town's curtain of outer forts, employing over 100 field guns besides numerous mortars. Slowly the Dutch entrenchments and underground shafts edged nearer Fort Isabella, a key position in the defences, despite determined sallies from the defenders, heavy fire, and counter-mining. In mid July, after ten weeks of siege, Fort Isabella and most of the satellite forts capitulated, enabling the Dutch to approach the town walls proper. The prince subjected 's-Hertogenbosch to a merciless cudgelling

---

[45] Isabella to Philip, 9 Sept. 1629. ARB SEG 201, fo. 196; Wassenaer xvii, f101ᵛ.

[46] Philip to *Consejo*, undated Sept. 1629. BNM MS 2361. fo. 501.

in which most of its houses were demolished by mortar-propelled grenades. But the besiegers lost many men, including the commander of the English regiments, Colonel Edward Vere, from the heavy return fire. On 9 September the English troops successfully mined and stormed the last remaining sector of the outer defences. Then after another week of bombardment and the threat of further mining, the town's 3,000-strong garrison finally capitulated.[47] Amid the dismay and anguish at Madrid, blame was heaped by Olivares on those of his colleagues who had put their faith in the early conclusion of a truce and on the lack of suitable commanders.[48] His own choice for command at this juncture, Gonzalo Fernández de Córdoba, simply refused to serve in the Low Countries.

Despite Isabella's yielding to secret pressure from the States General and withdrawing her troops from the IJssel crossing-point, so as to further the truce negotiations which resumed in that month,[49] a retreat which totally bewildered the populace of the eastern Netherlands, the Dutch for their part renewed their offensive in December. The opportunity was simply too good to miss, with the army of Flanders a broken reed, its supplies and munitions exhausted, its morale depleted, and mutinous symptoms spreading. According to Aytona, only the dregs were left in the German and Walloon *tercios*, most of the usable troops having departed for where the pay was better.[50] Fanning out over Westphalia during the winter of 1629–30, Dutch columns from Wesel, Rees, and Emmerich ejected the Spanish garrisons from Steel, Weerle, Ratingen, Angeroort, and other small towns and strongholds.[51] However, an attempt to dislodge the Spaniards from Düsseldorf, in January 1630, failed. The Spanish commanders desperately strove to pull their defences together and suppress the mutinous agitation. In April the governor of Ghent hanged fourteen of his garrison.[52]

[47] 'Brieven 's-Hertogenbosch', 26–37.

[48] Olivares's *voto* on Low Countries affairs, undated Oct. 1629. AHN Estado leg. 727.

[49] Sec. Res. SG 2 Oct. 1629. GA Amsterdam, Algemeen Bestuur no. 11, fo. 184; GA Deventer, Rep. 1, no. 19, Zutphen to Deventer, 10 Oct. 1629 (os.).

[50] Aytona to Philip, 24 Nov. 1629. BRB MS 16149, fo. 2^v.

[51] Wassenaer xviii, fos. 53, 74^v.   [52] Ibid., xix, fo. 19; BRB MS 16149, fo. 16.

But the winter push in Westphalia was followed, to the relief of Aytona, by a total lull. The Spaniards remained invitingly weak but Frederik Hendrik acquiesced in the disbanding of the additional troops raised in 1629, at Holland's insistence, and the cut in strength by one-third of the fifty companies raised in 1628.[53] While both the Holland peace towns, led by Amsterdam, and the *contra-Trevisten*, led by Haarlem and Leiden, were against resuming the offensive in the summer of 1630, it would seem that the Stadholder also was content to go along with this for, as is shown below, he was discreetly supporting the truce moves. Thus apart from some cavalry skirmishes around Wesel, during July, there was little fighting of note during 1630. Frederik Hendrik devoted himself to improving the fortifications of Wesel, 's-Hertogenbosch, and other strong-points.[54] The Spaniards profited from the respite to reorganize, engage in much painstaking reassessment of defensive strategy, and ponder the problem of command. With Fernández de Córdoba refusing to take over the army of Flanders, Isabella tried to obtain the transfer of Tilly from the army of the Catholic League, but neither he nor his chief employer, the duke of Bavaria, proved willing.[55] While the issue of command remained unresolved, the authority of Hendrik van den Bergh, in whom the king now had scant confidence, was gradually whittled down. Meanwhile, at Madrid an extremely important and difficult decision was reached by Philip, Olivares, and the *Consejo* during early 1630, on the advice of Aytona and ministers at Brussels, which was unavoidably damaging to Spain's prestige: despite their reluctance to remove the Spanish pressure from the borders of Groningen and Overijssel, it was agreed that the remaining Spanish *plazas fuertes* north of the Rhine — at Lingen, Lippstadt, and Hamm — together with Papenmutz and Sparemberg would have to be evacuated and the troops used to bolster the garrisons south of the Rhine and in Brabant and Flanders.[56]

[53] Res. SG. 8 June 1630. ARH SG 3189; Poelhekke, *Fred. Hend.* 334–5.
[54] Wassenaer xix, fo. 111.
[55] Aytona to Philip, 26 Apr. 1630. BRB MS 16149, fo. 16.
[56] Isabella to Philip, 30 June 1630 and Consulta, 5 Jul. 1630. AGS Estado 2044; 'esto es cosa de harta consideracion', Olivares observed gloomily with

The strong-points were offered to both the Catholic League and the Emperor. Although neither party was eager, when the Spaniards finally evacuated Lingen, to the utter amazement and bafflement of the Dutch,[57] in July 1630, the Imperialists moved in. On the Rhine itself, having lost Wesel, previously their principal base, the Spaniards concentrated their attention at the near-by river-port of Rheinberg which soon became, together with Breda and Zandvliet, one of the three largest and most lavishly provisioned Spanish garrisons in the Low Countries.

Following the break-down of the 1629–30 truce-talks, the year 1631 was intended by Olivares to be a year of Spanish recovery in which the balance of strength in the Netherlands would once again be tilted against the Dutch. His scheme was to hold a reduced front in increased force but also to launch some local offensives not as part of any broad strategic plan but simply to inflict some punishing local reverses on the Dutch, to rub the shine off their victories, and to weary and discourage them.[58] The ending of the Mantuan war and the peace with France signed at Cherasco, in June 1631, made it again possible to bolster the army of Flanders with a massive transfer of men and money from both Italy and Spain. In the spring, 2,300 Castilians arrived by sea from Corunna, the first such troop-ferrying operation of the war, while 9,782 Spanish and Italian infantry marched from Milan across Germany to the Netherlands under the newly chosen commander of the army of Flanders the Marques de Santa Cruz. By the summer, the marquis had over 14,000 Iberian and Italian troops with which to spear-head his now rapidly improving army. In July, Aytona judged the army of Flanders to be qualitatively better than at virtually any time since the beginning of the war.[59]

---

reference to the evacuation of Lingen, 'porque no es negable la reputacion grande que se pierde en entregar plaza tan importante, confessando en esta entrega la imposibilidad de defendella. . .'

[57] Wassenaer xix, fo. 89.

[58] Consulta 11 July 1631, voto de Olivares. AGS Estado 2045.

[59] Aytona to Philip, 2 Apr. and 23 July 1631. BRB MS 16149, fos. 53ᵛ–64.

But Frederik Hendrik and the States General simultaneously resolved to re-expand their own forces, following the respite and reductions of 1630, and to launch a new, major, offensive to follow their triumphs of 1629. However, having to deal with a suddenly more assertive attitude on the part of Holland (caused by the temporary co-operation of both the Amsterdam and Leiden factions), the Stadholder was forced to present strategic matters for discussion on a somewhat broader basis than usual. His initial attempt to obtain routine approval for 8,000 or 9,000 more troops for that year without yielding any say in the formulation of strategy ran into immediate difficulty in the States of Holland, particularly from Haarlem and Leiden, the most steadfast war-towns.[60] In April, in the midst of a political dead-lock, the prince disclosed in a secret session of the States General that he was planning a thrust deep into Flanders, to besiege either Brugge or Dunkirk, and that to do this he needed two field armies, the second being required to protect the Dutch provinces.[61] Hence the unavoidable need for additional troops. Eventually the prince and his adherents had their way except that in 1631 Frederik Hendrik was apparently saddled with several States General delegates to the army who, for once, were not entirely of his choosing. His other problem was how to keep his designs secret and, indeed, in May he complained several times to the States General about the persistent rumours in the country that he was planning to march deep into Flanders,[62] though this did not deflect him from his plan.

Having gathered 30,000 troops and eighty field guns at Emmerich, the prince embarked this massive force on an imposing *armada* consisting of 3,000 river craft with which he sailed to IJzendijke, in Zeeland–Flanders. From there he penetrated, via Maldeghem, to the strategic Brugge–Ghent canal, spreading panic through Flanders. Part of the Dutch army crossed the canal by pontoon bridge on the night of 2 June, the Spaniards in the vicinity having mostly abandoned

---

[60] Res. Holl. 13, 19, 22, 25, 29 Mar. 1631.
[61] Sec. Res. SG 8 and 30 Apr. 1631. ARH SG 4562, fos. 199, 200ᵛ.
[62] Sec. Res. SG 12 May 1631. ARH SG 4562, fo. 201.

their posts. But just as the Dutch seemed poised for a tremendous victory, the rapid approach of Santa Cruz with a powerful force, to their rear, provoked a fierce split between Frederik Hendrik and several of the States General's deputies to the army over how to react. The States of Holland, for the moment, was in an assertive mood. The prince, his officers, and some of the deputies wished to press on with the siege of Brugge, arguing that Santa Cruz would not be able to cut all their supply routes. Several of the deputies, however, rigidly opposed what they claimed was a dubious and risky enterprise which would jeopardize both army and state, exerting such pressure on the prince, that he felt obliged to withdraw.[63] Not surprisingly, this fiasco had a temporarily disastrous effect on the army's morale. After the heavy expenditure and elaborate preparations of the spring, it was a humiliating setback which eloquently testified to the drawbacks of what for once was a genuinely dual system of control of the army. The papal nuncio in Brussels, much relieved, reported to Rome that only the slowness and hesitation of the Dutch had saved the Spaniards from catastrophe, for if Frederik Hendrik had struck two months before with Santa Cruz still far from the Netherlands nothing could have prevented him from traversing Flanders and capturing Dunkirk.[64] The prince now encamped at Drunen in North Brabant, while Santa Cruz positioned his forces at Lier and Herentals.

During the late summer, the Spaniards in turn amassed an imposing amphibious force, at Antwerp, and, in early September, in line with Olivares's policy of local offensives, not to besiege towns but to secure local advantage, attempted a bold, if limited, thrust. Ninety large, flat-bottomed barges, bearing 5,600 troops and seamen, plentiful artillery, and large quantities of construction materials, under Jan van Nassau, sailed with impunity past the Dutch battle-fleet on the Schelde, by keeping to shallow water. Proceeding past Bergen-op-Zoom, this *armada* rounded Tholen, spreading panic throughout Zeeland and South Holland. Simultaneously, Santa Cruz brought up a second powerful force, via

---

[63] *Verdadera relacion*, pp. 2-3; *Mémoires*, 125-6; van der Capellen i. 625-6; *Kroniek* (1866), p. 408.

[64] *Corresp. Lagonissa*, 269, 272.

Roosendaal, to the Prinseland district, facing Tholen. The objective was to erect strongly defended forts either side of the Channel between Tholen and the mainland which could then be supplied from Breda.[65] This venture, had it succeeded, would certainly have represented a major setback for the Republic. The Dutch were fortunate that twenty of Nassau's craft, loaded with building materials, ran aground on the north side of Tholen, at low tide. Waiting for these barges, the Spaniards gave the Dutch navy time to bring up sufficient strength to trap them. There ensued a three-hour, mist-enveloped night-battle, clearly heard from Zierikzee, known as the battle of the Slaak. Nassau and a few barges escaped, but most, and the bulk of the provisions and guns, were captured or sunk. The Dutch took 4,000 prisoners in this famous victory.

If the Dutch had failed to make any headway against the improved army of Flanders in 1631, despite the additional forces made available to Frederik Hendrik, in the next year diversion of part of the Spanish forces away from the Netherlands gave the prince another opportunity for a massive break-through. Following the newly worked-out procedure, reflecting the temporarily resurgent influence of Holland, Frederik Hendrik repeatedly conferred with the deputies of the States General itself, and eventually obtained authorization to recruit extra troops for a major offensive against Antwerp.[66] However, during May, following further consultations as well as advice from several South Netherlands nobles, including Hendrik van den Bergh, who was now actively plotting against Spain, the prince switched objectives from Antwerp, thought too heavily defended, to the Maas valley.[67] On 22 May the States General issued a public manifesto to the southern provinces calling on the people to revolt and throw off the 'heavy and intolerable yoke of the Spaniards'. The manifesto promised not only military

---

[65] ARH SG 3190, fos. 488ʳ–488ᵛ; Aytona to Philip, 23 Sept. 1631. BRB MS 16, 149, fo. 64; Consulta 26 Oct. 1631. AGS Estado 2045; van der Capellen i. 640–1, 645; Aitzema, *Hist.* iii (i). 434–6.

[66] Sec. Res. SG 5 Feb. and 21 Mar. 1632. ARH SG 4562, fos. 207, 209.

[67] Sec. Res. SG 19 May 1632. GA Amsterdam, Algemeen Bestuur 11; ARH SG 4562, fo. 210.

assistance but in a significant reversal of previous Dutch policy, assurances that the public practice of Catholicism in the south would be tolerated. This last greatly alarmed Isabella and her ministers who were only too aware of the unpopularity of the Habsburg cause and regarded popular anxiety for the preservation of Catholicism as the principal bulwark of the regime.

The rapid advance of the Swedish forces in Germany, in the spring of 1632, to Frankfurt and the Rhine, induced Isabella and Santa Cruz to send urgently needed reinforcements from the Netherlands to the army of the Palatinate.[68] Spanish intelligence in Holland, the weakness of which was a frequent theme with Isabella's ministers, had failed to reveal the extent of the Dutch preparations, and the tapping of the army of Flanders at this crucial moment in effect sealed Frederik Hendrik's victory. By late May the prince had overwhelming forces at his disposal, 30,000 men massed in the east and a strike force of 8,000 under Count Willem van Nassau at Rammekens, threatening Flanders and Antwerp. Santa Cruz was forced to divide his reduced field force, leaving 5,000 men under the Conde de Feria to cover Antwerp, and concentrated the rest, a mere 9,000, at Diest. With less than a third as many men, Santa Cruz dared not try block the prince's path. In early June Venlo fell to the Dutch after two days' siege, swiftly followed by Roermond and Straelen. The prompt surrender of these towns was partly due to the hostile attitude of the populace towards the Spanish soldiery.[69] On 8 June Dutch forces took Sittard and proceeded to take up siege positions around the great fortress city of Maastricht. Santa Cruz kept his distance awaiting the arrival of Fernández de Córdoba and the army of the Palatinate now marching at top speed on Maastricht. At this point Count Willem forced the surrender of two key Spanish forts below Antwerp, and Hendrik van den Bergh openly revolted against Spain, fleeing to Liège from where he issued manifestos calling on the people to revolt, lambasting the

---

[68] Consulta 6 Apr. 1632. AGS Estado 2046; Aytoria to Philip, 9 June and 22 Oct. 1632. BRB MS 16, 149, fos. 76, 85.
[69] Ibid.

despotic rule of the Spaniards, their small regard for the
Catholic nobility of the Netherlands and oppression of the
people.[70]

Having fortified his siege positions front and rear, Frederik
Hendrik commenced the work of edging his trenches closer
to the walls of Maastricht. Their defenders were to be reduced by the now familiar combination of relentless cudgelling from his field batteries and the driving of shafts
underground for blasting. Following the arrival of Fernández
de Córdoba, the combined Spanish force, constrained to
take some action, moved up and encamped close to the
Dutch dispositions where it remained fruitlessly for the next
six weeks, searching for a weak point. On the Spanish side
there was little movement or firing. Count Willem meanwhile
landed near Hulst and succeeded in capturing several ela-
borately constructed and well-supplied fortresses in the
vicinity. To the south of Maastricht, on 15 July, units of the
French contingent of the Dutch army took the important
fortress of Argenteau. By early August Frederik Hendrik had
succeeded in driving his *approches* close enough to begin
digging shafts under the walls of Maastricht proper. At this
juncture, the Imperial general Papenheim crossed the Rhine
with 15,000 men and joined forces with the Spaniards though
the three Habsburg armies together only slightly surpassed
the Dutch in numbers. On 17 August, knowing that little
time remained the Imperialists flung themselves in vain
against the Dutch positions. Three days later Frederik Hendrik
sprang his mines successfully blasting great gaps in the city
walls and, though several Dutch assaults were repelled by the
1,400 surviving defenders, they opened negotiations soon
after and finally surrendered on 23 August. The joy of the
Dutch was restrained, however, by the danger of their situation. It was now widely expected in the capitals of Europe
that the three Habsburg armies would proceed to blockade
the somewhat weakened Dutch force in Maastricht, besieging
the former besiegers. But owing to the critical position in
Germany, Papenheim was compelled to depart and Santa
Cruz so desperately short of cash that he had to fall back

[70] Aitzema, *Hist.* iii (ii). 16–20.

and place his army on the defensive.[71] On 5 September, Dutch troops under Stakenbroeck, penetrated still further south, taking the town of Limburg.

The discrediting of Spanish arms could not have been more complete. The defeat was one of the most serious that Spain ever suffered, for the loss of Maastricht and Limburg left the garrisons of Rheinberg, Jülich, Geldern, Orsoy, and Düsseldorf almost totally cut off from the Spanish Netherlands. Never had Spain's hold on the now sullen populace of the 'obedient provinces' appeared more precarious. In desperation, Philip instructed Isabella to seize and fortify as many towns and strong points in the Maas valley, either side of Maastricht, as possible, and, if feasible, contrive the murder of van den Bergh.[72] The powers of Olivares's confidant, Petrus Roose, were further enhanced and this official was entrusted with investigating every aspect both of the military disaster and of the treason of van den Bergh and his noble adherents. The disaster faced Philip and Olivares with the stark choice of either conceding a truce on Dutch terms which they again refused to consider, or of somehow enlarging the remittances to the Netherlands, rebuilding the army of Flanders and launching a counter-offensive to swing the balance back against the Dutch. For if this was not done, further catastrophic setbacks seemed inevitable. Early in November 1632, the Dutch mounted a surprise attack on Orsoy which momentarily succeeded though it was finally beaten off by Spanish reinforcements from Rheinberg after several hours of bitter fighting, leaving 250 Dutch dead in the town.[74] But any scheme to shift the balance inevitably required time. Olivares had already given a good deal of thought to the project of sending the king's younger brother Ferdinand, the Cardinal-Infante, as governor of the Netherlands and providing him with powerful reinforcements, but if the latter were to be strong enough to serve their purpose there was no prospect that this could be done before 1634

[71] Aytona to Philip, 27 Aug. 1632. BRB MS 16149, fos. 81ʳ–81ᵛ; *Mémoires*, 155–8.

[72] Philip to Isabella, 4 Oct. 1632. AGS Estado 2239.

[73] Philip to Roose, 11 Dec. 1632. AGS Estado 2239; Delplanche, 52, 72.

[74] Isabella to Philip, 8 Nov. 1632. ARB SEG 205, fos. 261ʳ–261ᵛ.

at the earliest. For the moment it was evident that the army of Flanders would have to hold its own in difficult circumstances against the superior Dutch forces.

Yet despite the humiliation of Spanish arms, the withdrawal of Papenheim, the profound impact on the population of the southern provinces of the States General's proclamation guaranteeing freedom of Catholic worship, (and the fleeting, but none the less real, prospect, in the aftermath of Frederik Hendrik's lightning advance on Maastricht, that Spanish power in the Netherlands might collapse altogether, and some form of reunification of Flanders and Brabant with the northern provinces take place), in reality Spain's military position had improved by the time that Maastricht fell to the point that any such possibility had vanished. All considered, the emphasis that the renowned Dutch historian Pieter Geyl laid on what he called the 'missed opportunity of 1632' was largely misplaced.[75] As has been seen, the prince's forces had been considerably weakened by the protracted and hard-fought siege of Maastricht and were now further reduced by a serious outbreak of sickness. Even without Pepenheim, the Spanish reinforcements from the Palatinate, together with the frantic but intelligent activity of Santa Cruz, Aytona, Carlos Coloma, and Fernández de Córdoba, probably the four best and most experienced Castilian commanders in the entire Spanish Monarchy at the time, had, by September, succeeded in turning the military balance right around, at least for the moment.[76] While a majority of the States General urged the prince to invade Brabant and to exploit the dramatic effect of his recent successes, Frederik Hendrik with good reason refused, arguing that he was now simply too weak and the Spaniards too strong.[77] The prince's alternative proposal, that be besiege Geldern instead, was coolly received by the States General which regarded the latter enterprise as too meagre a followup to Maastricht. Reunification was, indeed, a fleeting possibility in the minds of both northerners and southerners during

[75] Geyl, 'Een verzuimde kans', pp. 42–3; Geyl, *Geschiedenis* i. 415–16.
[76] *Corresp. Lagonissa*, 368; Capellen i. 657.
[77] Ibid.; *Mémoires*, 156–8.

the late summer and autumn of 1632, but, by the time that Maastricht actually fell, no such outcome could, from a military point of view, be realistically expected.

The Dutch resumed their offensive, having restored their superiority in forces,[78] in the spring of 1633. With Count Willem posing a threat to Flanders from Zeeland with a force of 5,000 men, Frederik Hendrik massed the bulk of his field force at Schenkenschans. On 11 May he appeared before Rheinberg, now the foremost Spanish base in the east, and besieged the town, using river gun-boats and armed barges to prevent supplies being brought down river from Düsseldorf.[79] Meanwhile, Aytona, with an army of 14,000, advanced eastwards to the Maas which was only lightly covered by a Dutch cavalry force under Stakenbroeck. Aytona occupied Maaseik, Montfoort, Weert, and the highly strategic Stevensweert, where, taking advantage of the Stadholder's being occupied elsewhere, he erected powerful fortifications commanding the Maas between the Dutch garrisons at Roermond and Maastricht. Simultaneously, Rheinberg was subjected to the usual furious bombardment and sapping, its battered garrison surrendering after a mere three weeks, on 4 June.

Having left Stevensweert in the capable hands of the young duke of Lerma, Aytona encamped during June, July, and August, in various parts of Brabant, skilfully evading Frederik Hendrik but at the same time remaining close enough to both Stevensweert and Antwerp which was covered by 3,500 men, under Carlos Coloma, to prevent the Stadholder from attacking either.[80] It was the prince's intention to bring the Spanish army to a pitched battle, but in this, despite repeated attempts to engage Aytona, he was unsuccessful. On 3 September Count Willem suddenly shipped from Zeeland to Sluis and descended on the neighbouring Spanish fortress known as the *Sterre Schans*. He captured this within two days and then returned to Flushing. Shortly after, he swooped again on Flanders and captured the key fortress of Philippine.

[78] Aytona to Philip, 12 May 1633. BRB MS 16149, fo. 99.
[79] Aitzema, *Hist.* iii (ii). 136.
[80] Aytona to Philip, 4 Aug. 1633. BRB MS 16,149, fo. 103; Sec. Res. SG, 22 Sept. 1633. ARH SG 4562, fo. 224.

Spanish troops from Brugge retook the *Sterre Schans*, but the Dutch held the more crucial Philippine. Meanwhile, Frederik Hendrik himself was in a state of perplexity. There were long conferences between the prince and the States General's deputies to the army over how best to proceed and periodic consultations with the States General itself. Frederik Hendrik made it plain that as he saw it the Spanish dispositions were such that it was impossible for him to attempt Stevensweert, Antwerp, or Breda with any real prospect of success. He hesitantly suggested that he should penetrate enemy territory without besieging any major town and winter there in several small towns with the object of undertaking some major venture the following spring. The States General, as so often during the brief period 1631–3, when the prince's power was relatively weak *vis à vis* the provinces, reacted coldly to his plan and directed him instead to attempt the siege of Breda, against his judgement.[81] In fact, the prince declined to do so and the plan was deferred to the following year. Nevertheless the episode clearly illustrates the reduced state of the prince's authority at this time when he was still at odds with the Counter-Remonstrant factions in the city councils but no longer able fully to rely on the co-operation of Amsterdam and the Arminian faction of the States of Holland.

ii THE MARITIME CONFLICT, 1626–1633

The punishing break-out of the *armada de Flandes* during the autumn of 1625, and growth in the number of Flemish privateers, induced the States General almost to double its blockade force during 1626 despite continuing assistance from the English. Officially, the fleet for the Flemish coast increased from eighteen to thirty warships, each of a minimum of 120 lasts and twenty guns.[82] There was also more pressure on the assembly to provide larger naval escorts. Deputies of the Maas herring fishery petitioned in April for more adequate protection so as to prevent losses such as

[81] Sec. Res. SG, 22 Sept. 1633. ARH SG 4562, fo. 224^v.
[82] ARH Bisdom 53, fo. 33.

those of the previous year. There was also much concern among the other herring fleets, based at Enkhuizen and in Zeeland.[83] By July 1626 fifteen royal ships were ready for action at Dunkirk and Ostend besides a similar number of smaller privateers.[84] During most of the year this force was effectively wedged in, only the occasional raider breaking out and inflicting damage, though, as before, a ceaseless stream of small boats plied between Calais, Dunkirk, and Ostend carrying goods of all kinds, including large amounts of Baltic naval stores.[85] Even so, in September five Dunkirkers slipped past the Dutch and struck again at the Maas herring fleet, sinking eighteen *buizen*, reportedly after throwing the crews overboard.[86]

From the Spanish viewpoint, the Dutch blockade at this stage undoubtedly seemed effective. The *armada* was also much hindered by the chronic lack of cash which generally bedevilled the Brussels regime in the aftermath of the fall of Breda, so that in fact some of the royal fleet could not be adequately armed or manned.[87] Inevitably, the situation produced some doubt in the *Consejo* as to whether the strategic decision to wage *guerra defensiva* by land and *offensiva* by sea was really viable. Pedro de Toledo, for instance, deemed Spanish naval potential in the North Sea to be very limited and questioned whether reducing the whole burden of the war to an offensive by sea, where the enemy preponderated, might not mean loss of the initiative on both fronts.[88] Olivares together with Montesclaros and other ministers, remained entirely convinced, however, that they were right to reduce the army to a minimum and concentrate on the maritime conflict. Meanwhile the States General, faced with increased commitments in the North Sea, would probably have preferred to attempt nothing in Iberian waters during 1626–7. But continuing English pressure

[83] Res. At. Middelburg, 19 Aug. and 1 Dec. 1626. ARH Admiraliteiten 2456.
[84] ARH Bisdom 53, fo. 140.
[85] At Amsterdam to SG, 23 July 1626. ARH SG 5944.
[86] ARH Bisdom 53, fo. 198ᵛ.
[87] Consulta, 13 Jan. 1627. AGS Estado 2041.
[88] Consulta, 24 June 1626, fo. 2. AGS Estado 2040.

for joint action led to the fitting out of another fleet of twenty ships to sail with the English, though in the end, owing to delays on the Dutch side, it sailed alone. This force, under Laurens Reael, left Holland in November 1626 and cruised for several months off Portugal, Morocco and Madeira. Apart from bottling up numerous Brazil ships at Porto and Lisbon, this voyage, which lasted until June 1627, was singularly unproductive.[89]

While the Dutch blockade of Flanders had worked reasonably well in the face of the increased Spanish pressure during 1625-6, in 1627 the deterioration in the finances of the Dutch admiralty colleges, partly due to the suspension of 'convoy and licence money' from October 1625,[90] caused a marked decline in effectiveness. The Amsterdam and Noorderkwartier colleges were very late in getting some of their warships to sea and unable to meet their full quotas. The Maas herring fleet was seriously delayed in getting to sea because its escort ships were long held up owing to cash shortage.[91] During the months January to March 1627, before the blockade commenced, the *armada* and privateers captured thirty-eight Dutch and English vessels and sank eighteen.[92] Losses continued despite the blockade and, in late August, fourteen Dunkirkers returning to Flanders from northern Spain, sailing round Ireland and Scotland, descended on the Enkhuizen herring fleet off the Shetlands. Of the seven escorting warships, one was sunk, two captured, and four fled.[93] Once again, a substantial number of *buizen* were sunk. The indignation in the Holland herring towns was the greater in that the admiralty authorities had received several warnings from Dutch shipping in the Bay of Biscay that such an attack was being prepared in the Basque ports. Enkhuizen protested in the States of Holland at the escort's feeble resistance, blaming low morale on the irregularity of naval pay. In all, over 150 Dutch and English ships and

[89] *Kroniek* (1866), pp. 530–8, Winkel-Rauws, 178–89.
[90] See pp. 218–21 below.
[91] ARH Bisdom 54, fo. 163ᵛ.
[92] La Cueva to Philip, 23 Apr. 1627. AGS Estado 2318.
[93] J. Liefhebber to SG, off Newcastle, 8 Sept. 1627. ARH SG 5496 i. ARH Bisdom 54, fos. 249ᵛ-250; Res. Holl. 9, 13, and 27 Sept. 1627.

fishing craft were taken or sunk by the *armada* and privateers in 1627, bringing over half a million guilders in revenue to the Flemish admiralty board.[94]

In 1628 the initiative shifted further in favour of the *armada*, and the Dutch blockade continued to deteriorate, while the income of the Flemish admiralty board sharply increased and marine insurance rates at Amsterdam soared to new heights.[95] In the first two months the *armada* took thirty-six prizes worth 400,000 ducats and sank three. All this was despite the States General's resolution of November 1627 to strengthen the blockade fleet further to a total of forty-five sail, twenty-six to seal off the Flemish coast and nineteen to be divided into four supplementary squadrons to patrol the North Sea and the Channel.[96] A fifth squadron of four ships, in addition to the forty-five, was assigned to the Bay of Biscay. The Dutch proved increasingly unable, however, to contain the Dunkirkers. Losses steadily mounted even among the inshore fishermen using small boats close to the Dutch coastline. In May 1628 the *drossaart* of Terschelling advised the States General that the island's economy was being severely disrupted.[97] Once again, the navy's performance gave cause for complaint. In June 1628 200 herring *buizen* were held up in port for several weeks owing to the unpreparedness of their escorts. There were minor attacks on the *buizen* during August which cost some fifteen craft.[98] The Noorderkwartier college blamed its difficulties in protecting the Enkhuizen herring fleet adequately on a growing shortage of naval seamen caused by low and irregular pay.[99] In all, during 1628 the *armada* and privateers sank or captured 245 Dutch and English ships and fishing craft, considerably more than in any previous year.[1] The receipts of the Flemish admiralty board, at 1,776,887 guilders, amounted to well over twice as much as in 1627, the previous best year since the beginning of the war.

[94] Baetens, 'Flemish Privateering', 62, 75.
[95] La Cueva to Philip, 6 Mar., and Isabella to Philip, 11 Mar. 1628. AGS Estado 2321.
[96] ARH Bisdom 54, fo. 305ᵛ.   [97] ARH Bisdom 55, fo. 99; Malo i. 333.
[98] ARH Bisdom 55, fo. 198ᵛ.
[99] At. Noorderkwartier to SG, 29 June 1628. ARH SG 5498, i.
[1] Baetens, 'Flemish Privateering', 62, 75.

Despite the inevitably weakening effect on the *armada* of the severe financial crisis of 1629 in the South Netherlands and the emergency on land which compelled Isabella to divert resources from the Flemish ports, the contraction in the *armada*'s activity was offset by a continuing growth in privateering so that in value, at least, total Dutch losses were actually up on those of the previous year. Although the States General had now found a bold new commander for its blockade fleet, in the person of Piet Heyn, the victor of Matanzas, his competent management of the fleet was, unfortunately for the Dutch, of only very brief duration. He was killed in a fierce battle off Cape Gris Nez, on 18 June 1629, in which ships from the blockade fleet eventually captured three which had slipped out from Ostend.[2] Heyn's funeral at Delft was a memorable state occasion attended by numerous members of the States General and provincial assemblies as well as directors of the West India Company. His death only added to the mounting anxiety in Holland and Zeeland at the trend of affairs in the North Sea. In September the Brouwershaven section of the Zeeland herring fleet was raided by privateers and forced to take refuge in Scottish harbours.[3] A particularly disturbing development for the States General was that one captured privateer proved to have a number of Dutchmen among its crew, including the captain; this was but an early symptom of what later developed into a sizeable drift of sailors from Holland and Zeeland to Dunkirk and Ostend.[4] In all, the *armada* sank or captured sixty-eight Dutch and English vessels in 1629, whilst the privateers accounted for 176; total receipts of the Flemish admiralty board amounted to 1,844,881 guilders.[5] Meanwhile, during the summer of 1629, a small Dutch naval squadron cruised off the coasts of Portugal and Galicia and effected a landing at the fishing village of Buarcos which was plundered and burnt, an occurrence quite unique during the entire war.[6]

---

[2] Graefe, 29.
[3] Res. At. Middelburg, 8 Sept. 1629. ARH Admiraliteiten 2457.
[4] ARH Bisdom 56, fo. 125v.
[5] missing footnote.
[6] At. Rotterdam to SG, 14 July 1629. ARH SG 5500, i.

During 1630, with spending on the *armada* far below the planned level of 20,000 ducats monthly, the royal fleet was virtually paralysed. Aytona, a firm believer in the view that naval and economic pressure was the way to bring the Dutch to the truce-table on acceptable terms, greatly regretted this unavoidable by-product of the Mantuan war.[7] He was encouraged, though, by the uninterrupted expansion in privateering which benefited from the disarray of the Dutch blockade fleet, which was seriously under strength during that year, as well as from the indifferent leadership of its new commander, Hildebrant Quast.[8] In all, 196 Dutch vessels were captured by the privateers in 1630, and a further twenty-four sunk; this compared with twenty-seven taken and fifteen sunk by the *armada*.[9] The Flemish admiralty board's receipts broke another record at 1,910,984 guilders. Privateering at Dunkirk was now established as a major international business. The most successful firm, van de Walle, in which evidently Spinola himself had a tenth share, captured, within a few days, during July 1630, six Dutch Rouen ships and a returning Guinea vessel carrying gold bullion and ivory; these seven prizes alone were worth 200,000 ducats.[10]

Dunkirk privateering continued to flourish during 1631, if slightly less spectacularly than in 1630. The private firms took 161 Dutch prizes and sank a further twenty-two.[11] At the same time, in the aftermath of the Mantuan war, the *armada* somewhat revived. With a total financial provision of 350,000 ducats during 1631, the *armada* again represented an imposing force. After the troop-ferrying voyage of March 1631, eleven of the *armada*, together with a group of Hanseatic troop-transports, returned to Corunna during the summer. Eleven more royal ships lay ready to emerge at Dunkirk while yet another powerful *armada* was being prepared at Lisbon. While the Dutch admiralty colleges knew that this last was probably for a planned counter-offensive

---

[7] Aytona to Philip, 8 Sept. 1630. BRB 16, 149, fo. 37; Consultas 23 and 28 Feb. 1630. AGS Estado 2044.
[8] Res. At. Middelburg. 17 June 1630. ARH At. 2458.
[9] Baetens, 'Flemish Privateering', 62, 75.
[10] See again Aytona to Philip, 8 Sept. 1630.
[11] Baetens, 'Fleming Privateering', 62, 75.

in Brazil, they could not exclude the possibility that the Lisbon force was intended to join the Dunkirkers at Corunna and sail for the Netherlands. After consulting the Stadholder, the States General decided that Quast should remain with the blockade fleet off the Flemish coast but be reinforced so that he should be strong enough to meet head on a possible combined Hispanic–Flemish *armada* sailing up the Channel. To this end, the colleges were instructed to strip the merchant convoys of their escorts.[12] Quast, however, as surely missed the second troop transport which arrived at Mardijk with 4,000 Spanish infantry in late October as he had the first, most of his fleet then being in port for revictualling. The removal of the escorts meanwhile had inevitably eased the work of the Dunkirkers. At one point, in October, a whole convoy of twenty-nine grain ships was captured.[13]

The year 1632 was a record one for prizes from the Dutch, if not for total receipts, and Madrid could justly claim a telling victory in the North Sea.[14] Again, the impact of the privateers greatly eclipsed that of the fleet. In all, twenty-seven craft were sunk and 278 captured, a high proportion being *hoekers* of the Maassluis North Sea fishing fleet.[15] The Zierikzee section of the Zeeland herring fleet was attacked in Scottish waters by six privateers and lost several *buizen*.[16] Representatives of the islanders of Terschelling, Texel, and Vlieland again protested to the States General that their coasts were infested with Dunkirkers whose raids were ruining the islands.[17] Privateers also scoured the Jutland coast which occasioned a protest from the Danish court to Madrid. [18] The Flemish admiralty board's receipts were a little lower though, in 1632, than during the three record years 1628–30, amounting to 1,618,556 guilders.

[12] Van der Capellen i. 650; Aitzema, *Hist.* iii (i), 456–60.
[13] Malo i. 331.
[14] *Relacion verdadera y nueva*, p. 2.
[15] In the four years 1632–5 Maassluis alone lost some 200 fishing craft to the Dunkirkers: see ARH SG Bisdom 57, fo. 59.
[16] Res. At. Middelburg, 29 July 1632. ARH SG 2458.
[17] ARH Bisdom 59, fos. 227v–228.
[18] Consulta 26 Aug. 1632. AGS Estado 2333.

iii THE WAR IN THE INDIES, 1626–1633

While confidence in the West India Company, domestic and foreign, had been severely shaken by the dismal failure of the Company's expensive initial projects, the position had been somewhat mitigated by the success of several minor pillaging expeditions to the Caribbean and Brazilian waters dispatched during the early 1620s. By 1626 the Company's directors found themselves compelled to change course and to set aside for the moment grandiose schemes of conquest, in order to recoup by making the most of the opportunities at sea. This more restrained, but more profitable, phase was to continue until 1630. In one of the most successful of these plundering expeditions, Piet Heyn ravaged the shipping in Bahia harbour in March 1627, seizing 2,565 chests of sugar as well as much other booty. Four months later, a small squadron in the Caribbean intercepted a Honduras galleon sailing to Havana, capturing silver, indigo, cacao, and other cargo valued at over a million guilders. In all, the Company captured fifty-five Portuguese and Spanish ships in 1627,[19] a success which somewhat revived the public's faith in the organization and its shares.

The high-point of the raiding activity of the late 1620s was of course Piet Heyn's sensational capture of the Mexican silver fleet at Matanzas Bay, in Cuba. As the Company's directors judged Veracruz, Havana, Porto Bello, and Cartagena, the four main entrepôts of Spain's American trade in the Caribbean to be too strong to permit the treasure fleets to be attacked in port, the location which proffered the best chance of a successful interception were the straits between Cuba and the tip of Florida through which the treasure fleets passed *en route* to Spain. Even so, interception was rendered difficult because any Dutch fleet in the area was bound to be spotted by the Spaniards at near-by Havana from where warnings would be relayed to the treasure fleets. Indeed, Heyn was detected by the Spaniards but, owing to various mishaps, the yachts sent out failed to find the treasure fleet which had already left Veracruz. On 8 September the silver

---

[19] De Laet iv. 283.

galleons found themselves trapped fore and aft by Heyn's force close to the Cuban shore. The Spanish commander, Juan de Benavides, sought refuge in Matanzas Bay, hoping to land the treasure safely. The Spaniards were seized by panic, however, and the Dutch captured both ships and treasure virtually unopposed. Heyn's richly laden fleet eventually arrived back in Holland in January 1629. The treasure and goods were valued at over 11 million guilders, some two-thirds of the annual cost of the Dutch army; the admiral was fêted in Haarlem, Leiden, and Amsterdam and presented before the States General.

This coup, which stunned Spain and all Europe, touched off a fierce debate among the Company's directors as to how the handsome proceeds should be employed.[20] The more dedicated proposed ploughing the entire profit back into the Company. Greed and a desire to impress the public, however, led to the paying out of a handsome dividend to the Company's investors. The seamen who had actually captured the silver though were, much to their discontent, but poorly rewarded. Heyn's own share was a modest 7,000 guilders, which prompted him to leave the Company's service forthwith. While the price of the Company's shares shot far above the previous high-point briefly, the improvement was not sustained. Indeed, a number of prominent investors, notably Cornelis Bicker, a leading figure in both political and business circles in Amsterdam, were astute enough to pocket the dividend and sell out almost at once. Within a year, the Company's shares had lost nearly half their value.[21]

The combination of skill and exceptionally good luck which had made possible Piet Heyn's triumph in 1628, could hardly be relied on to recur and, in a way, the significance of Matanzas was that it demonstrated to discerning minds just how unreliable and unlikely a basis for the Company's future such plunder really was. The point was underlined the following year when the directors attempted to repeat their success, sending a fleet of twenty-six sail to the Caribbean under Adriaen Janszoon Pater. The Spaniards

---

[20] Aitzema, *Hist.* ii. 518.
[21] Van Dillen, 'Effectenkoersen', 9–10.

countered by simply holding their treasure fleets in port until Pater having exhausted his supplies, eventually withdrew empty-handed from the area.[22] In order to recoup the Company's outlay before returning to Holland, Pater had scoured the Caribbean for many months but despite his competence took only five prizes.[23] Off the New Granada coast, in February 1630, Pater dismantled the fort and sacked the township of Santa Marta, but again the booty was meagre.[24]

With the sudden improvement in their finances, during 1629, the Company's directors again discussed mounting a major offensive in the New World with the aim of overrunning an important Iberian possession. While, as before, some directors would have preferred to attempt Cuba, Panamá, or Punta de Araya, the majority was set on Brazil. 'Various places in America were considered,' recalled de Laet in 1636, 'but when all had been thoroughly pondered, our eye fell once again upon Brazil. What other places were considered, we shall not mention here so as not to warn the enemy. It may be that God may still one day grant the Company the chance to conquer these.'[25] While the final decision was to try to establish a secure foothold in Brazil, it included an element of compromise with those who aspired to conquest in the Caribbean. The instructions issued to Hendrick Corneliszoon Loncq who had been Heyn's second-in-command at Matanzas and who commanded the Brazil expedition of 1630, required him, once Pernambuco had fallen, to sail northwards to join forces with Pater and try to occupy Santiago de Cuba, one of the few key strategic positions in the Spanish Caribbean which was weakly defended. As well as being potentially an excellent base for Caribbean operations generally, the Dutch hoped that from Santiago they would secure control of the Cuban copper mines.

---

[22] However, Pater's mission was not simply one of pillage: he briefly captured and built a fort at the Spanish township of San Tomé, on the Orinoco estuary, but after some fierce fighting, decided to withdraw, Cardot, 355–6.

[23] De Laet iv. 283.

[24] Restrepo Tirado, 250–1, *Ned. Zeevaarders* i. 114, 118.

[25] De Laet ii. 102.

The resolution to attack Brazil was reached before the opening of formal truce negotiations with Spain, in October 1629, but during, or after, the secret talks of February–May 1629, of which the Company's directors doubtless had at least some inkling. Although it is true that the inner logic of the Company's position dictated a shift from pillage to conquest at around this time, it is nevertheless highly probable that the planned occupation of north-east Brazil was, from the first, intended to influence the States General's negotiations with Spain by boosting the Company's visible assets in the New World. In August 1629, in the midst of the Spanish-Imperialist invasion across the Veluwe, the Company postponed its Brazilian expedition and at the request of the States General temporarily diverted its troops and supplies to Utrecht and Gelderland. With the commencement of the formal truce negotiations, the Company had every reason to resume its preparations swiftly and throw all it had into the attack.

During the internal Dutch debate of 1629–30 over the Spanish truce offer, the West India Company campaigned vigorously in opposition to any accord. An end to the war would have drastically curtailed the scope of the latter, effectively leaving it with just the Guinea trade and the Guianas. The directors had to admit that the profits of their organization were insignificant, but argued that the benefit that the nation at large derived from its operations was the real point, not the position of its investors who were said to have 'invested their cash more out of love than thirst for profit'.[26] It was pointed out that the Company was a leading employer, maintaining over 100 ships and many thousands of seamen, troops, and other employees.[27] As a purchaser of weapons, munitions, foodstuffs, and cloth, the Company came second only to the state itself. Furthermore, the Company had unquestionably dealt heavy blows to Iberian

---

[26] *Consideratien ende Redenen der E. Heeren Bewindhebberen*; Aitzema, *Hist.* ii. 912–17.

[27] An estimate of 1633 gives the total of the Company's employees at between 6,000 and 8,000, see *BMHG* xxi (1900), 367; in 1644, after a decade of expansion in Brazil, the figure was estimated at 10,000, see the *Aenwysinge datmen van de Oost ende West-Indische compagnien*, p. 6.

power both directly, and by forcing Philip IV to increase his spending on his American defences and suffer heavier debts and interest charges as a result of the long delays in departure of several of the New World treasure fleets. Undeniably, the holding up of the Peru fleets, over the winters of 1625-6, and 1628-9, had greatly contributed to the Dutch victories in the Low Countries.

The 1629-30 truce negotiations split the Holland town councils in a way fraught with disturbing implications for the colonial companies. Preoccupied with the problems of the domestic situation, Amsterdam, Rotterdam, Delft, and Dordrecht had now turned entirely against the war and were pressing for an early truce. While Rotterdam had traditionally stood aside from the colonial cause, Amsterdam and Delft in 1606-9 had constituted the main bulwark of the colonial interest in Holland and the turning of these towns against the war inevitably greatly weakened the companies' position. The Delft *vroedschap* was in something of a dilemma, being still a strong supporter of both colonial companies, but never-theless considering that the first priority was to achieve peace or a truce.[28] At Amsterdam the West India Company, which was more directly threatened by the prospect of peace than the older company, had recently lost much ground politically as a result of being closely tied to the men of 1618, the strict Counter-Remonstrant faction who had been the chief advo-cates of the Spanish war. This had led to the Company be-coming involved in the contest for power of this faction, whose appeal to Amsterdam's wealthy classes was evidently waning during the 1620s, and the increasingly powerful ele-ment in the *vroedschap*, headed by Andries and Cornelis Bicker. If the Company's ill-advised public support for the Counter-Remonstrant opposition to the burgomasters, on church matters, made the position worse,[29] neither was Cornelis Bicker's selling off of his large holding of the Company's shares calculated to improve the atmosphere. But probably, given that the leading opponents of the Spanish

[28] GA Delft vroed. res. 11 Oct. 1629.
[29] *Copie vande Requesten van de goede gehoorsame Burgeren*, 11-13; van Hoboken, 53; van Dillen, 'West. Ind. Comp.', 154.

truce at Amsterdam, men such as Reynier Reael and Simon van der Does were also West India Company directors, and at the same time leaders of the *vroedschap* opposition to the Bickers, there was no way that the Company could have avoided succumbing to the changing mood and posture of Amsterdam's merchant body. Ultimately, it seems likely that the underlying conflict of interest between the colonial and European carrying trades ensured the early collapse of the West India Company's influence at Amsterdam. Paradoxically, the chief bulwarks of the Company in Holland, by 1629, were the non-maritime towns, especially Haarlem, Leiden, and Gouda, together with the Noorderkwartier towns, Enkhuizen and Hoorn.

The Brazil fleet under Admiral Loncq, in all sixty-seven ships bearing 7,000 men and 1,170 guns, attacked in February 1630, swiftly overrunning Olinda and Pernambuco. The Portuguese in north-east Brazil soon rallied, however, under the skilful leadership of Mathias de Alburquerque and wedged the Dutch tightly in to their coastal foothold so that they could be supplied only by sea. When word reached Lisbon and Madrid, Olivares and his colleagues threw themselves into frantic activity, intending to mount an overwhelming counter-attack on the model of that of 1624. The ruinous situation in the Spanish Netherlands and Italy, however, meant that this could be done only if a large subsidy were promptly obtained from Portugal.[30] The response of the Lisbon city council and other Portuguese bodies was somewhat grudging. Portugal, they claimed, was now completely impoverished having submitted to several rounds of emergency taxation, including the drive since 1628 to provide reinforcements for the Far East. Though they voted some additional money, they considered that Castile should supply the bulk of what was needed.

The Castilian–Portuguese *armada* that sailed from Lisbon under Antonio de Oquendo in May 1631 was in fact altogether weaker than that of 1624. The king's intentions had had to be modified in the light of the critical situation in Europe and Oquendo's task was merely to convey 2,000

---

[30] Philip to Lisbon city council, 30 Apr. 1630. *Elem. Hist. Lis.* iii. 374.

Spanish, Portuguese and Neapolitan troops to assist the forces already opposing the Dutch but without tackling the latter head on. Roughly three-quarters of the finance for the expedition derived from Castile and only one quarter from Portugal. On its approach, the Iberian force was engaged by a Company squadron under the brave but luckless Pater: both Spaniards and Dutch suffered heavy damage, the Dutch flagship being sunk and Pater drowned. In the end, a mere 700 troops reached the Portuguese lines facing Pernambuco, including 300 Neapolitans under the conte di Bagnuoli. The Dutch forces on land remained hemmed in throughout 1631-2. Only after the arrival of substantial reinforcements in the winter of 1632-3, was the Company able significantly to enlarge its Brazilian bridge-head.[31]

Meanwhile, the bitter struggle in the Caribbean continued, the Dutch unwavering and remarkably steadfast in the face of repeated setbacks at Spanish hands. In all, three Company fleets scoured the Caribbean in 1630, but extracted little profit. During 1631-2 several more costly expeditions likewise yielded meagre results. In 1633 a Company squadron under Jan Janszoon van Hoorn pillaged Trujillo in Honduras, and in August attacked San Francisco in Campeche Bay, where he captured nine ships and a large store of Campeche wood and cacao, and sacked the township.[32] At the same time, some progress was made during these years in procuring salt from sources other than Punta de Araya.[33] For five or six years two pans especially were used by the Company's ships, one at Tortuga, off Venezuela, and the other on the island of San Martín. At both of these the Company erected forts. Although the formidable governor of Cumaná, Benito Arias Montano, nephew of the renowned hebraist of that name, attacked and destroyed the fort and installations on Tortuga in 1632, the Dutch soon returned. But the Spaniards landed again the following year, this time bringing the famous engineer, Antoneli, who devised a means of flooding the pan and rendering it useless. Meanwhile, a much

[31] Boxer, *Dutch in Brazil*, 51-2; Cabral de Mello, 45-6.
[32] De Laet iii. 187-95.
[33] At. Amsterdam to SG, 6 Oct. 1628, and Amsterdam burgomasters to SG, 11 Oct. 1628. ARH SG 5498, ii.

larger assault was being planned by the special *junta* that met
in Madrid under Olivares's chairmanship to determine war-
strategy in the Indies, for San Martín where the Dutch had a
more powerful fort.[34] In June 1633 1,300 Spaniards under
Lope de Hoces, one of the best Spanish naval commanders,
landed from the regular Peru fleet, bound for Panamá, and
after a short siege forced the surrender of the eighty defenders
on terms. The fort was then manned on a permanent basis
by 250 Spanish troops. Four months later Arias Montano
surprised and captured another Dutch fort recently erected
this time on the mainland, at the salt-pan at the estuary of
the Unare river.[35] By the autumn of 1633 the Dutch had
been finally and decisively defeated in the battle for
Caribbean salt.[36]

Surveying the scene in the Indies east and west at the time
of the renewed Dutch–Spanish truce talks of 1632–3, Dutch
observers could scarcely avoid concluding that the struggle
for the Spanish Indies was as good as lost, the outlook in
Brazil bleak, and the East India Company's resolve and
capacity to sustain the conflict against the Iberians in Asia
exhausted. Further investment in the colonial war hardly
seemed very tempting. Despite twelve years of expenditure
and effort, Formosa and a thus far barren foothold in Brazil
were the only gains. Little wonder that early in 1633 the
West India Company's shares hit a record low on the Amsterdam exchange at less than one-third of the level attained
after the capture of the silver fleet.[37]

iv ECONOMIC CONFLICT, 1625–1633

Despite substantial modifications in the administration of
trade in the Peninsula during 1621–4 and the exclusion of
the Dutch for the most part from Iberian trade, *Consejo* and
king remained dissatisfied owing to persistent reports of continued, if much reduced, Dutch economic infiltration. In
January 1624 Philip entrusted to a new committee composed

[34] *Ned. Zeevaarders* i. 166–9.
[35] *Relacion cierta . . . Benito Arias Montano*, pp. 1–3.
[36] *Ned. Zeevaarders* i. 136–40.
[37] Van Dillen, 'Effectenkoersen', 9–10.

of Juan de Pedroso, president of the *Consejo de Indias*, Hurtuño de Urizar, Jan Wouwer (Juan Boberio), a leading Flemish financial official, and Gabriel de Roy, former Spanish agent at Cologne, the task of finding remedies for the 'excesses with which the rebels trade in Spain'.[38] As a result, in October 1624 Philip established the subsequently famous Seville Admiralty Board or *Almirantazgo*. This body had essentially two objectives: to organize a regular convoy system between Flanders and Spain, modelled on the Spanish Indies trade, and to head a new system of checks and controls on foreign ships, merchants and cargoes in Spanish ports which was to supersede previous arrangements.[39] To ensure the zeal and efficiency of its officers, an important working principle was borrowed from the Inquisition: most (nine-tenths) of whatever the *Almirantazgo* confiscated, it kept for its own uses and organization. The *Almirantazgo* in fact entirely transformed commercial administration in Spain and stands as one of the principal innovations of the Olivares's era.

Despite the efforts of the *Almirantazgo* to mobilize the merchants of Flemish and German background in the Peninsula into an effective organization, it failed in the event to progress as a trading body.[40] While it did dispatch a few ships to Flanders and North Germany, it proved unable to overcome the merchants' abhorrence of its strict procedures, heavy taxation, and insurance charges, not to mention the prospect of pitched battles with the Dutch blockade-fleet off the Flemish coast. Its original objective of operating a heavily armed convoy of twenty-four ships,[41] on the model of the Indies trade, was fairly soon abandoned. In its second capacity though, the new institution flourished and soon developed a large inspectorate as well a judicial machinery, the powers of which, like those of the Inquisition, cut right

---

[38] Cédula 8 Jan. 1624. AGS Estado 2847.
[39] Cédula 4 Oct. 1624. AGS Estado 2847; Domínguez Ortiz, 'Guerra económica', 78–9.
[40] *Cavsas por donde crecio el comercio de Olanda,* fo. 1.
[41] Cédula, 4 Oct. 1624. AGS Estado 2847, fo. 7ᵛ. the crews of two of the ships mutinied and took the vessels to Holland, 'Aviso de Olanda', 4 July 1626. AGS Estado 2316; Stols, 128–9.

across the boundaries of Castile, Aragon, Valencia, and
Navarre. To collaborate with the Spanish body, a new Flemish
admiralty office was set up in 1625 at St. Winoxbergen, near
Dunkirk. The *Almirantazgo* was directed by a central court
at Madrid, known as the *tribunal mayor del Almirantazgo*.
By 1626 the organization had sixty officers in Andalusia alone.

The *Almirantazgo* injected an entirely new rigour into the
processes of boarding neutral ships in Spanish ports, in-
specting certificates and seals, checking warehouses, employing agents in foreign ports and in speeding up the prosecution
of commercial offences which were taken out of the hands
of the ordinary courts. Since the remuneration of *Almirantazgo* officers was linked to confiscations, it is scarcely surprising that they tended to err on the side of stringency.
Complaint abounded. *Almirantazgo* officers 'act in such a
way towards both foreigners and natives', protested the
Málaga city council in 1626, 'that they are depopulating
the town.'[42] The *Almirantazgo*, complained Seville in August
1627, were abusing their powers to 'make themselves powerful with all merchandise'. 'The *Almirantazgo*', wrote one
observer some years later 'closed the door to all commerce,
of friends and enemies alike, with their certificates, inspections, condemnations and confiscations such that within a
short time, Spain was without trade, ships or foodstuffs,
customs revenue fell and the country's produce had no means
of exit.' While it would be an exaggeration to suggest that
the dexterity of the Dutch contrabandists was ever totally
defeated, evasion of the Spanish embargo against the Dutch
undoubtedly became extremely difficult. For instance, late
in 1624 the Dutch merchant Baltasar de Moucheron, descen-
dant of the renowned personage of that name, freighted a
Glückstadt vessel, through an agent at Hamburg, to sail to
Archangel from where it was to ship Russian products to San
Lúcar, the *Almirantazgo* officers, searching the entire ship,
uncovered a letter revealing Moucheron's ownership of the
cargo and confiscated the lot.[43] And many another elabo-
rately camouflaged consignment was similarly detected.

[42] Consulta, 30 June 1625. AGS Estado 2645.
[43] GA Amsterdam NA 697, fo. 129 and 636, fo. 176.

In the case of cargoes from England and France, the *Almirantazgo* had little choice but to accept the certificates signed by local authorities, though they searched English and French ships and cargoes none the less thoroughly for that and employed various informers, such as Diego de Castro Cortazar, a detector of frauds in London, on behalf of the Spanish embassy during the mid 1620s.[44] In Flanders, on the other hand, the rigorous procedures concerning certificates for cargoes to Spain became a considerable burden on merchants already encumbered with the problem of circumventing the Dutch naval blockade and with the highest freight and insurance rates in Europe.[45] Owing to the political weakness of the Hanseatic towns, the *Almirantazgo* also advanced its cause with considerable success in North Germany. Aided by the Danish crown which, following its defeats at Habsburg hands, embarked on a policy of cultivating good relations with Spain, the *Almirantazgo* was able by 1628 to impose its stringent requirements on Hamburg, Lübeck, and Bremen with respect to their Iberian trade. Gabriel de Roy, sent from Spain to Germany for this purpose, established offices at Hamburg, Glückstadt, and Friedrichstadt from which all Hanseatic merchants trading with the Peninsula had to obtain their certificates.[46] When the *Almirantazago* began confiscating cargoes accompanied by affidavits from local authorities only, Hamburg and its sister towns complained bitterly to Madrid that their merchants should thus be subjected to an exacting procedure from which English and French merchants remained exempt. However, Philip and his *Consejo* remained adamant.

Essentially, the *Almirantazgo*'s endeavours were directed towards imports. Whilst it was taken for granted that it was in this sphere that the Dutch could most readily be injured, it was also of course from imports that Spain's own manufactures had in the past suffered damage. Even so, the *Almirantazgo* was empowered by a royal *cédula* of January 1627,

---

[44] *Consulta*, junta de comercio, 21 Apr. 1624, fo. 1. AGS Estado 2847.
[45] Consulta 20 May 1631. AGS Estado 2045.
[46] Consulta 1 Sept. 1629. AGS Estado 2329; Consultas 6 June and 12 Aug. 1630. AGS Estado 2331; *Cavsas por donde cracio el comercio de Olanda*, fos. 1ᵛ–2ᵛ.

to exact deposits from exporters, repayable upon presentation of documents certifying that cargoes had been unloaded elsewhere than in the United Provinces. During the year or so that this measure remained in force, Seville complained to the king that re-exports of colonial produce to northern Europe were suffering as did the farmer of the wool-duties regarding wool exports.[47] This led to a clash between the *Almirantazgo* and the Council of Finance which pressed for removal of the deposits to assist the customs returns. Eventually, following protests also from the Hanseatic towns, king and *Consejo*, affirming that the real objective of the embargo was to shut out Dutch imports, agreed that the procedure should lapse.[48]

The changes in the regulation of commerce in Spain, from 1624, provided a most disagreeable surprise for the English when they returned to Peninsula trade, following the Anglo-Spanish peace of 1630. The English envoy to Madrid, Arthur Hopton, found 'many alterations [in trade] since the last peace, principally by occasion of the *Almirantazgo*';[49] the English were especially discontented, he reported to London, because Philip had 'sett soe many oversiers uppon the trade of merchants'. In April 1631 a London-owned but Dutch-built vessel, sailing from London with an English cargo, was seized by the *Almirantazgo* at Bilbao, its confiscation being promptly confirmed by the tribunal at Madrid.[50] Other English ships built in Holland were confiscated during the early 1630s, at Lisbon, Cadiz, San Lúcar, and Málaga. In September 1633 a London merchant suffered seizure at Málaga of a consignment of Silesian linens for which he lacked papers signed by the Spanish agent at Hamburg. 'The Spanish king had ordained', commented the English envoy, 'that no forraine commodity shall be brought into his kingdoms, but with certificate that they come from a contry that is a friend, and to that purpose he placed an officer in Hamburgh to give certificates without which no trade is

---

[47] Seville to Philip, 7 Sept. 1627. AGS Estado 2646; consulta 24 Oct. 1627. AGS Hacienda 632.
[48] Consultas 14 May, 14 June 1628. AGS Estado 2328.
[49] BL MS Eg. 1820, fos. 13ᵛ, 24.
[50] BL MS Add. 36448, fo. 13.

admitted from the said city.' The same diplomat thought it best that since the 'articles of peace being not so cleare in this case of certificates', English traders should simply comply with the *Almirantazgo'* requirements.[51]

Evidently the most acute friction between *Almirantazgo* and neutrals did arise from confiscation of ships 'in part or wholy of Holland fabrick'. All the neutral nations were equally affected and both Hamburg and London were for the most part compelled to remove vessels of Dutch manufacture from the Iberian routes. The Polish monarch repeatedly requested permission for Danzig to use Dutch-built ships in its rapidly expanding trade with the Peninsula, but Philip steadfastly refused: during the 1630–1 Polish–Spanish negotiations over emergency grain shipments to the Peninsula, the Spanish representative in Warsaw was instructed to 'exclude totally from the transaction ships built in Holland'.[52] In April 1633 four Dutch-manufactured ships of a convoy bringing wheat from Livorno to Lisbon were seized, prompting a long dispute in Spanish–Tuscan relations.[53] In cases where English, French, or Hanseatic merchants wished to use, for Iberian trade, originally Dutch vessels which had been taken by the Dunkirkers, and which they had purchased in Flanders, it was essential to obtain a special licence from the *Almirantazgo*.

With the Dutch effectively excluded from Iberian trade, the shipping of Spain's vital imports and exports fell principally into the hands of the English — except during the years 1625–30 — and Hanseatics. Christian IV of Denmark also endeavoured to exploit the opportunity, but the company that he set up in 1621 to handle trade between the Peninsula and the Danish realms was largely unsuccessful.[54] The Hamburg convoys for the Peninsula, bearing Swedish copper, Norwegian masts, Polish pitch, and other much needed supplies, as well as grain became for a quarter of a century a characteristic feature of the European economy,[55] to the

[51] Ibid.
[52] Consulta, Junta del Almirantazgo, 13 Jan. 1631. AGS Estado 2648.
[53] Consulta, Junta del Almirantazgo, 11 July 1634, AGS Estado 2653.
[54] Bering Liisberg i. 334–40.
[55] ARH Bisdom 53, fos. 76ᵛ, 111; no. 54, fos. 96ᵛ–239, 253ᵛ; Kellenbenz, *Unternehmerkräfte*, 61, 63; Kellenbenz, *Sephardim*, 144; Koopmansadviezen', 47.

obvious annoyance of the Dutch and Danes. In 1625 over fifty vessels sailed in the Hamburg convoy for the Peninsula, chiefly to Lisbon, San Lúcar, and Cadiz. The Hamburg convoys of 1627 and 1629 likewise both exceeded fifty vessels, while that of 1633 totalled forty-three vessels. Despite Dutch disapproval, Lübeck was also very successful in expanding its trade with the Peninsula, organizing its own convoys and sending two and a half times as many ships to Spain and Portugal in the decade 1630–9, as during the decade 1610–19 when such business had been virtually monopolized by the Dutch.[56] The Lübeck convoy of 1626, for instance, consisted of seventeen ships. Like Hamburg, Lübeck sent its convoys the long way to the Peninsula, round Scotland and Ireland, so as to minimize what was in any case a high degree of interference with the copper, masts, and munitions from the Dutch and English navies and privateers.[57] The organization of the new Hanseatic trade with Spain was inevitably slow, clumsy, and expensive, but, with the exclusion of the Dutch and the formidable backing of the *Almirantazgo*, it did prosper. Besides Hamburg and Lübeck, Glückstadt and some other towns, including Danzig itself, greatly expanded their own direct contacts with the Peninsula.[58]

Despite the expansion of trade with England and North Germany, the Spanish authorities were unable to procure enough naval stores to supply the Castilian and Portuguese *armadas* and trans-Atlantic convoys adequately, or find enough non-Dutch shipping capacity to sustain previous levels of salt and wool exports. Thus the question of possibly employing some Dutch ships temporarily for particular purposes which were deemed indispensable, was regularly put to the *Consejo de Estado*. Until 1626 the crown proved totally inflexible on this issue, but from that year it became more selective. Following the damage caused by storms to the armada which returned to the Peninsula from Brazil in

[56] ARH Bisdom 53, fo. 111; Vogel, 135–41.

[57] See the official reports of Jaspar Liefhebber of 1629 and 1630 in ARH SG 5500, ii, and 5502, i.

[58] Consultas, Junta de Estado, 28 Sept. 1627, and 3 Jan. 1628. AGS Estado 2328; Jurgens, 197, 203–7.

1626, for instance, permission was given for a limited period for merchants to buy naval stores from the Dutch.[59] In January 1626, however, the *Consejo* refused permission to use Dutch vessels to a contractor who was finding difficulty in finding suitable ships to convey Dalmatian mercury, urgently needed for the American silver-mines, from Venice to Seville.[60] Various requests for permission to import Swedish copper from Holland were refused, despite the desperate shortage of this commodity. However, in October 1627 the Consejo accepted an offer from a Rotterdam merchant, Jan Jansen, made via Brussels, to send, in violation of the States General's edict, a cargo of masts from Norway to Corunna, in return for filling his vessel with Spanish products to be shipped to a neutral destination.[61] In 1628, when the desperate financial position forced the crown to try to profit from the effects of the embargo, in a way which had not been envisaged previous to the onset of the Mantuan Succession crisis, a Flemish merchant resident at Málaga, Adrian Paez, was licensed to import 1 million *escudos*' worth of prohibited Dutch and English goods, mainly Baltic stores, fish, and textiles, paying a 6-per-cent levy, 60,000 *escudos*, on top of the regular duties;[62] even so the transaction was rigorously scrutinized by the *Almirantazgo*, and Paez was eventually arrested for violating the terms and his stock seized. Moreover, this type of relaxation of the embargo, designed purely to secure a windfall profit for the crown, was apparently not resorted to again.

If shortage of copper and naval stores was acute in Spain and Portugal throughout the 1620s, the relatively good harvests of these years obviated any serious problem as regards grain supplies, except, as has been noted, at Naples in 1622. The picture changed dramatically, however, in 1630, when one of the worst famines of the century struck Portugal and the whole of northern and eastern Spain.[63] The desperate emergency temporarily wrecked the grain-supply

[59] Boxer, 'War and Trade', fn. 20.
[60] Consulta 5 Jan. 1626. AGS Estado 2328.
[61] Consulta 6 Oct. 1627. AGS Estado 2041.
[62] 'Los condiciones. . .Adrian Paez'. AGS Estado 2042.
[63] Consultas 12 and 17 Sept. 1630. AGS Estado 2648; Elliot, *Catalens*, 558.

aspect of the embargo. In August 1630 Philip reluctantly authorized the local authorities in Vizcaya, Asturias, and Galicia to arrange grain shipments from northern Europe, resorting to Dutch supplies and shipping if necessary.[64] In October Navarre petitioned the king for permission to use Dutch ships temporarily for emergency grain imports, since no supplies were available in western France; as the north coast and Mallorca had already obtained such authorization, Philip consented provided the 'viceroy and *audiencia* deem it necessary'.[65] In Portugal, great efforts were made to procure supplies from Germany before the king finally authorized the 'bringing of what is necessary in contraband ships, as long as these are not of the rebels, though they may be of their manufacture, and the purchasing of the grain anywhere, even in enemy lands.'[66]

Despite the concessions of 1630, and similar temporary measures in 1632, it should not be supposed that this development signalled the revival of the Dutch grain trade to the Peninsula. In 1630 the Dutch themselves had no grain to spare, as a result of the disruption in the Baltic, and the States General was forced to impose a temporary ban on grain exports which remained in force until August 1631.[67] When the Dutch Baltic trade began to recover from the long depression that had begun in 1621, the Iberian markets indeed exerted a powerful influence on the process, but only indirectly. The sustained boom in Dutch grain-carrying from the Baltic to the west, beginning in 1631, consisted primarily of shipping Polish grains to the ports of western France,[68] mainly Nantes, Bordeaux, and Bayonne, from where the consignments were shipped on to Lisbon, Seville, Alicante, Valencia, and Naples by the English, French, and Hanseatics. The only restraint on neutral shippers was that they had to forgo using Dutch-built craft except during brief intervals of particularly severe food shortage in Spain and Portugal. After a relaxation during the Portuguese famine of 1632, the

[64] Philip to Consejo, 11 Aug. 1630. AGS Estado 2331.
[65] Consulta 10 Oct. 1630. AGS Estado 2648.
[66] 10 Dec. 1630. AGS Estado 2648.
[67] ARH Bisdom 58, fos. 136, 226.   [68] Bogucka, 438–9.

Spanish crown suddenly reimposed the prohibition on the use of Dutch-built ships by neutrals which led to the seizure of several English and Hanseatic ships which had not had advance warning.[69] Remarkably, the English envoy to Madrid commented only that this would at least serve to increase English merchants' respect for the Spanish regulations.

For Dutch Baltic trade, the most vital strand in Dutch European commerce, the second Spanish war thus involved a whole decade of severe recession, besides a reduction of more than 10 per cent in the Dutch share of Baltic traffic, and a drastically new pattern of carrying, the route between Poland and western France becoming the main axis, superseding the pre-1621 longer voyages to Portugal, Spain, and Italy. For a quarter of a century Dutch activity in southwestern France was intense, with Amsterdam, Rotterdam, Noorderkwartier, and Middelburg naval escorts constantly in the area. While the Dutch virtually ceased shipping Iberian wines to northern Europe, they further enhanced their preponderance in the shipping of French wines. It is also true that Dutch manufactures continued to seep from Bayonne, via Navarre and Aragon, to Madrid, while sizeable amounts of registered and unregistered Castilian wool was transported from the Basque coast or overland to Bayonne to be shipped by the Dutch to Brittany, Normandy, and Calais (for Flanders); but this tortuous procedure was in reality more symptomatic of what the Dutch lost than of anything gained. Until the autumn of 1625, when the Anglo-Spanish war began, and again after its conclusion in 1630, the great bulk of wool from northern Spain destined for northern France and Flanders was shipped by the English.[70] During the years 1625–30, when the English were likewise shut out, exporters chiefly relied on small French craft to convey the wool the few miles from Bilbao and San Sebastián to St. Jean de Luz, the first port across the French frontier, from where the Dutch shipped the wool to its north-European markets.

[69] BL Eg. MS 1820, fos. 323–4.
[70] See the lists of wool consignments from Bilbao in 1625–6, AGS Tribunal Mayor de Cuentas 815 and Israel, 'Spanish Wool Exports', 204–5.

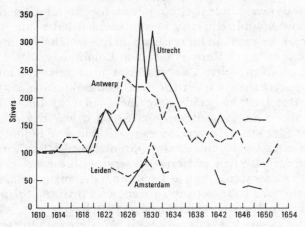

5. The price of salt at Utrecht, Antwerp, Leiden, and Amsterdam (1610–1650) (Stuivers per sack). NB The weight of the sacks in each of the four series is unspecified, and obviously different. *Sources*: Posthumus, Inquiry ii. 290–2; *DPLVB* ii. 828–31.

While the Spanish embargo substantially affected almost every sector of Holland and Zeeland's European commerce, the most acute problem that arose concerned salt supplies. While the States General had known that exclusion from the Iberian salt-pans potentially posed a major threat both to the herring and fish industries and to Dutch exports to the Baltic, among which salt, together with herring, was the most important, it had been expected that supplies from Punta de Araya would solve the difficulty. The defeat in the battle for Caribbean salt was fraught with serious consequences for the entire Republic. As is shown on graph 5, the price of salt rose steadily during the 1620s, but this alone is not the whole story. In the later 1620s, in an effort to conserve dwindling salt stocks, the States General was forced to ban the export of salt from Dutch ports.[71] Moreover, the problem was not only one of quantity but of quality. With the arrival of large amounts of Tortuga salt from the West Indies in the years 1628–32[72] the quantitative difficulty was apparently

[71] See graph 5.   [72] See pp. 203–4 above.

somewhat eased, but Tortuga salt was found to be relatively unsuitable for salting either fish or meat. Amsterdam tried to use the opportunity to secure a lifting of the ban on salt exports both to stimulate the Tortuga salt trade and to boost exports to the Baltic.[73] Enkhuizen and the herring interest, however, were fearful that suspending the ban would further push up the price of all types of salt at home.[74] Amsterdam failed to get its way, and the salt ban remained in force. Furthermore, if Tortuga salt was useless for the fisheries, French salt was little better, at any rate for herring. In 1629, lacking Setubal salt or an equivalent, the bumper herring-catch of that year had to be salted with the Brouage variety. The result was a disastrous rotting of the herring stocks involving numerous merchants in heavy losses.[75]

But if salt became a pressing issue in Holland, so it did likewise in Spain. Since 1621, the salt-pans of Cádiz and La Mata had fallen into virtual disuse while the traffic at Setúbal was much contracted.[76] While Spanish manufacturing and inland agriculture undoubtedly profited from the embargo against the Dutch, Iberian salt, like wool, wine, and olive oil exports had slumped catastrophically since 1621. The *Almirantazgo* was besieged by critics who were ever eager to remind the crown that it was losing considerable revenue from the shrinkage in trade with northern Europe. One opponent of the *Almirantazgo* considered that because of its 'excesses and abuses, more than the might of the Dutch, the navigation and trade of Spain falters, the vineyards cease to be cultivated, the salt-pans are no longer worked and His Majesty's revenues diminish whilst those of the French king grow and French wines and salt are shipped to the Baltic where previously they were unknown.'[77] The predicament induced Philip to set up a special *junta* to ponder the question of salt and, as a result, the crown switched, in 1630, from a total embargo on the

---

[73] Amsterdam burgomasters to SG, 11 Oct. 1628 and At. Amsterdam to SG, 6 Oct. 1628. ARH SG 5498, ii.

[74] At. Enkhuizen to SG, 11 Oct. 1628 and At. Dokkum to SG, 28 Sept. 1628. ARH SG 5498, ii.

[75] Amsterdam vroed. to SG, 9 Apr. 1630. ARH SG 5501, ii; Velius, 333.

[76] Consulta 8 Mar. 1626. AGS Hacienda 621.

[77] 'Sobre las propuestas del Almirante Jacques Collart', (Madrid, 1637). BRB MS 12832 fo. 136.

carrying of Iberian salt by the Dutch to an attempt to cream off a windfall profit by selling Dutch merchants licences for Iberian salt in Brussels. The scheme was both to sell licences to Dutch merchants allowing them to take on salt at any of six ports, Setúbal, Aveiro, San Lúcar, Cadiz, Lisbon, or Puerto de Santa de María, but not Ibiza or La Mata or Alicante, and at the same time impose much heavier export duties than previously on all salt exports.[78] The *Almirantazgo* was charged with ensuring that the Dutch imported only grains, munitions, naval stores, or fish; any Dutch manufactures, spices or other goods were subject to automatic confiscation. The Spanish king's new price for salt sent shock waves throughout European commerce. When the English returned to Setúbal in March 1631, numbering forty sail, they were appalled by both the price and the troops stationed aboard for the duration of their stay.[79] Protests from Lisbon and Ibiza that the new price would ruin what remained of their trade left the crown unmoved.

Isabella advertised the offer through commercial channels in the Republic and after selling the first fifty licences, in the spring of 1630, reported jubilantly that the new price, 10 ducats for every *moya* of salt, would fetch 400 ducats for every 100 last ship.[80] The States General was caught in a dilemma. The need for Iberian salt was urgent, but to condone Philip's selling of salt licences to Dutch merchants would undermine the West India Company's interests in the Caribbean, buttress the finances of the enemy, and involve loss of prestige. As so often, opinion among the towns was divided. Amsterdam urged that the licences be tolerated so that supplies of Iberian salt could be procured, reminding the States of Holland of how French salt had ruined the 1629 herring-catch.[81] Middelburg, on the other hand, deeply involved in the trade to the Loire estuary as well as in the West India Company, was vehemently against.[82] As usual during

---

[78] Consulta 14 May 1630. AGS Estado 2044; 'Condiciones. . .para venir por sal a Espana', AGS Estado 2239; *Discurse sobre. . .la Guerra Maritima*, 44–6.

[79] BL MS Eg. 1820, fos. 14ᵛ–15ᵛ.

[80] Consulta 30 Apr. 1631. AGS Estado 2044.

[81] GA Amsterdam vroed. res. xv, fo. 149ᵛ, 29 May 1630, Amsterdam to SG, 9 Apr. 1630. ARH SG 5501, ii.

[82] *Notulen Zeeland*, 17 Apr. 1630.

this period, the decision went against Amsterdam, and purchase of the Spanish salt-licences was officially forbidden.[83] Even so, the Amsterdam freight-contracts show that throughout the 1630s a number of Dutch merchants did in fact obtain these licences from Brussels.[84]

While the Dutch struggled to maintain their ascendancy in Europe's carrying trade, the economic war on the waterways of the Low Countries and north-west Germany took a distinctly new turn. In the summer of 1625, shortly after the Dutch had lifted their 1624–5 blockade, the Infanta, complying at last with Philip's instructions, suspended the *licenten* on the routes between southern and northern Netherlands, prohibiting all trade with the 'rebels' by water or overland.[85] Spanish troops closed the Rhine to the Dutch at Wesel and the Ems at Lingen. At once, urgent discussion commenced among the Dutch towns and provinces on how best to respond.[86] At Dordrecht, the hub of Holland's river trade, local businessmen were extensively consulted before the *vroedschap* recommended to the States of Holland that the most effective way of forcing the Spaniards to abandon so damaging an initiative would be to retaliate in kind prohibiting trade both with enemy territory and neighbouring neutral lands such as Liège, Munster, and Cologne so as to prevent provisions reaching the South Netherlands through these areas.[87] Amsterdam similarly thought it best to 'follow the example of the enemy' and suspend all river and overland trade.[88] On 16 October, after two and a half months of stoppage on the rivers, amid plunging butter, herring, and cheese prices in Holland,[89] the States General issued its sweeping edict of retaliation, the so-called *placaet van retorsie*,

[83] ARH Admiraliteiten Res. At. Middelburg 17 Sept. 1630; *Notulen Zeeland*, 7 Sept. 1630.

[84] GA Amsterdam, box index of freight-contracts, Setúbal.

[85] *Ordinantie ons Heeren des Conincx (Brussels, 29 July 1625)*; Israel, 'A Conflict', 56.

[86] SG Res; 12 Aug. 1625. ARH SG 3184, fo. 320ᵛ; Res. Holl. 23 Sept., 2, 3 Oct. 1625.

[87] GA Dordrecht, vroed. res. 27 Sept. 1625.

[88] GA Amsterdam, vroed. res. xiv, fo. 123.

[89] La Cueva to Philip, 17 Sept. and 2 Oct. 1625. AGS Estado 2315; *Analecta Vaticano-Belgica*, 2nd ser., vi. 661.

prohibiting all commerce either with enemy territory or neutral lands by river or canal or overland.[90] The admiralties' gunboats on the rivers and the garrison troops set to work stopping the traffic that was now flourishing on the routes to neutral territory. To back up its measure, the States General imposed the Schelde *licent* for the interim on trade to Calais and Boulogne and the still higher Bosch *licent* on trade to Dutch border areas such as the Prinsenland district. Applications for exemption for consignments arranged before 16 October were rejected, affecting, among others, Louis de Geer, who was unable to take delivery of a stock of pistol and musket parts due to be shipped down the Maas from Sittard.

As usual, the impact of these Low Countries river blockades was drastic. While food prices plunged in Holland, they soared in Flanders and Brabant.[91] The blocking of the routes to Munster, Osnabrück, and Cologne completely disrupted the business life of Deventer, Zwolle, Nijmegen, and other towns in the eastern Dutch provinces but proved a windfall for Holland, except for Dordrecht which suffered severely during these years as imports of German wines into the Republic and German wine re-exports from Holland to the Baltic all but collapsed. Much of the trade diverted from Overijssel and Gelderland flowed via Amsterdam,[92] Hoorn, and Enkhuizen to Bremen and Hamburg whence the cargoes were shipped up the Weser and Elbe and then overland to Munster, Lingen, and the Rhine.[93] Bremen, previously the victim of Dutch economic warfare, now reaped a handsome profit. There was also a predictable boom in traffic between South Holland and Zeeland and the ports of north-east France. Attempts by the Rotterdam and Middelburg admiralty colleges to have the sea-trade to north-west Germany brought under the Schelde *licent*, on the same basis as that to north-east France, were blocked by Amsterdam.

Such was the disruption to the normal patterns of trade that The Hague, Brussels, and Madrid soon all came under heavy pres-

---

[90] Res. SG 16, 18 Oct. 1625. ARH SG 3184, fos. 405ᵛ, 408ᵛ.
[91] *DPLVB* i. 63, 85, 104–5, iii. 712, 720, 734–5.
[92] Usselinex, *Waerschouwinghe*, p. 20; Bang ii. 8, pp. 340, 361, 376, 380.
[93] Advys, Raad van State to SG, 24 July 1626. ARH SG 5494, i.

sure to dilute the measures. In May 1626, pressured by Overijssel and Gelderland, the two eastern provinces which suffered
most, the States General delegated a committee to consider
whether inland trade with neutrals might be restored on the
basis of a higher than usual *licent*. Besides the Stadholder and
Raad van State, however, Amsterdam, Middelburg, Leiden,
Haarlem and other towns continued to insist on strict adherence to the *placaet*.[94] By January 1627 Overijssel and
Gelderland were so indignant over the situation that they
were threatening to withold their regular payments to the
States General's treasury and even to restore the *licenten*
on their rivers without the agreement of the States General.
Holland's attempt to secure a compromise on the basis of
merchandise to neutral territory paying the Bosch *licent*
was rejected by the inland provinces which were prepared
to countenance such charges only if they were imposed also
on merchandise sent by sea to Bremen and Hamburg. Higher
charges for Bremen and Hamburg, while acceptable to most
Holland towns, were resolutely blocked by Amsterdam.[95]
Meanwhile, Holland's desire to compromise was viewed with
dismay by Zeeland where there was widespread anxiety that
if commerce to neutral territory were restored, the increased
traffic through Zeeland to north-east France would be diverted
inland along the Rhine and Maas. The diversion by sea was
certainly spectacular. Great quantities of herring, cheese, and
salt-fish, ultimately destined for Flanders, was shipped from
Flushing, Middelburg, and Rotterdam to Calais indirectly,
via Dover, so as to evade the extra duty.[96]

In February 1627 the Middelburg *vroedschap*, aroused by
accusations that its policy was motivated by local self-interest
alone, drew up a reasoned defence of the Dutch blockade in
its existing form.[97] Claims that the blockade was not really
denying provisions to the enemy, but only diverting trade
into unnatural channels and stripping the admiralty colleges
of sorely needed funds were categorically rejected: Middelburg

[94] GA Amsterdam vroed. res. xiv, fos. 159^V, 182^V; GA Leiden, Sec. Arch. 447,
fos. 303, 332.
[95] Res. Holl. 18, 19 Jan. 1627.
[96] *Notulen Zeeland*, 18 Mar. 1626.
[97] 'Consideratien' (5 Feb. 1627), RAZ SZ 933.

insisted that great damage was being inflicted on the southern Netherlands. If provisions were reaching Flanders, via Calais, these were extremely costly due to the high *licenten*, the French imposts, and inflated transport charges. Salt was reportedly selling at Liège at five times the price prevailing in Holland.[98] Rye was then selling at Ghent for substantially more than was wheat at Middelburg. The Zeeland towns could claim with some justice that their policy served both the local and the national interest.

In March 1627, with the States of Zeeland being specially convened to defend the river blockade, Overijssel and Gelderland declared that they would not advance one penny of their contributions to naval expenses until inland trade with neutrals was restored. According to the Deventer *vroedschap*, Overijssel's trade with Hanover and Brunswick, via Munster and Osnabrück, had now been wholly diverted to Holland, Bremen, Hamburg, and the rivers Weser and Elbe.[99] There was also much discontent within Holland, especially at Dordrecht and among the agricultural interest, which complained of the lack of imports from Liège of lime, iron, and mill-stones for windmills.[1] On the other hand, the manufacturing towns, Haarlem and Leiden, eager to continue the shutting out of South Netherlands and Westphalian manufactures and the shutting in of wool supplies, inclined to a 'general closure', designed to placate the inland provinces by halting sea-borne trade to north-east France and northwest Germany, as well as inland commerce with Germany and Liège.[2] But Amsterdam remained unmovable. Although the general discontent was eased by the States General's decision of 17 July 1627 to allow imports of necessary materials, notably lime, iron, and coal, from neutral territory, but not of enemy goods or manufactures, the basic deadlock continued. Finally, it was recognized by the Holland leadership that the only way to reconcile the conflicting interests was to restore inland trade to its regular basis, with

---

[98] Ibid., fos. 9–13.
[99] Res. SG. 30 Jan. 1627. ARH SG 3186, fo. 46.
[1] *Notulen Zeeland*, 1627, p. 108.
[2] Res. Holl. 10, 20 Mar. 1627

neutral and enemy territory alike.[3] Thus, despite continued resistance from Haarlem, Leiden, Hoorn, and Enkhuizen, this was finally agreed to in October.

Meanwhile the Spaniards had initiated a fresh project with which to enhance the impact of their river blockade. It was planned to construct a new canal which was ingeniously designed to permit shipping to pass uphill, by means of several locks, which would link the Rhine, at Rheinberg, with the Maas, at Venlo, via Geldern. Work had begun in August 1626 and much of it was completed a year later. In theory, the canal would have enabled the Brussels regime to divert much of the Republic's Rhine trade through the South Netherlands. The Dutch displayed considerable anxiety over this grandiose undertaking which was inspected by Isabella in person in July 1627, and evidently excited great interest among the population of the loyal provinces. The painter Rubens was among the enthusiasts for the *Fossa Eugeniana*, as the projected waterway was known, envisaging it as an apt device with which to abate the pride of the Hollanders.[4] In the end, however, despite immense effort and expense, the technical difficulties proved insuperable.

The rivers remained open on the Dutch side for a mere three months before the States General again decided to regulate trade for strategic purposes. In January 1628, following the incursion of Imperialist and Catholic League troops into East-Friesland,[5] the States General tried to induce these forces to withdraw by banning exports of foodstuffs either up the Ems or overland to East-Friesland, under pretext that it was necessary to conserve supplies in the Republic during the Polish–Swedish conflict in the Baltic. The Spanish Netherlands had meanwhile suffered high prices,[6] shortages, and disruption of trade uninterruptedly since the summer of 1625. If loss of the *licenten* had cut royal revenues and scarcity of provisions contributed to reducing the army to

[3] Res. SG. 9 Oct. 1627. ARH SG 3186, fo. 426; GA Dordrecht, vroed. res. 11 Oct. 1627; Res. Holl. 9 Oct. 1627.

[4] Isabella to Philip, 27 Aug. and 12 Nov. 1626. AGS Estado 2317; La Cueva to Philip, 28 Feb. and 3 July 1627. AGS Estado 2317; *Letters, Rubens*, 95, 142–3, 172.

[5] Aitzema *Hist.* ii. 431.

[6] *DPLVB* i. 63, 85, 104–5, 112.

its now pitiful condition, the hardship caused to the population generally made it far more difficult for the regime to extract additional subsidies from the provincial assemblies just when these were most urgently required. According to Rubens, Antwerp was now languishing 'like a consumptive body which is gradually wasting away. Every day we see the number of inhabitants decreasing for these wretched people have no means of supporting themselves either by manufacture or by trade.'[7]

As a consequence of the Italian crisis, the collapse of the royal finances and the obviously impending Dutch offensive, by early 1629 Philip and Olivares were in desperate need of additional subsidies from the southern provinces and, for this reason, they finally heeded the pleas from Brussels and consented to the lifting of the Spanish blockade. The rivers were reopened on the Spanish side, after nearly four years, in April 1629.[8] The crown soon received its recompense. Flanders voted an unprecedented extraordinary subsidy in 1629, bringing its total payment to the crown in that year to 1,680,000 florins, compared with 960,000 florins in 1624 and 660,000 in 1619.[9] The contribution of the States of Artois reached half a million florins in 1630, two and a half times what the province had paid the crown in 1620.[10]

The States General imposed its next river and overland blockade on the Spanish Netherlands on 17 May 1629, immediately following Frederik Hendrik's descent on 's Hertogenbosch. The stoppage applied at first only to the routes to Brabant and Flanders, the Rhine, Eems, and Weser remaining open.[11] There were then the usual pronounced differences among the Dutch over the form of the blockade. Zeeland wanted the Rhine closed 'lest business should be diverted there to the great prejudice of the inhabitants of Zeeland'.[12] Many Holland towns wanted both the Rhine and the sea-lanes to Calais and Bremen closed.[13] Amsterdam

---

[7] Quoted in Parker, *Europe in Crisis*, 191.

[8] Isabella to Philip, 3 Mar. 1629. AGS Estado 2322; see the *Nieuwe Lüste van't recht.*

[9] *Tafels* i. 40, 68, 69, 77, 84.   [10] Hirschauer i. 345; ii. 122–39.

[11] Res. SG 13, 14 May 1629. ARH SG 3188.

[12] Notulen Zeeland, 11 July 1629.   [13] Res. Holl. 7 July 1629.

wanted both to remain open but eventually, in July, agreed to closure of the Rhine.[14] When the threat of a joint Spanish-Imperialist invasion from the east developed later in July, the States General extended the blockade also to the Ems while the inland provinces and manufacturing towns stepped up the pressure for closure of the sea-lanes. As enemy troops poured across the IJssel, the States General dispatched warships to the German coast and blockaded Bremen, the Weser, and the Jade, though not the Elbe.[15] The tension eased only with the withdrawal of the Habsburg forces during October. When the States General finally lifted its river blockade on 1 November, it had been in force for five and a half months.

Following the 1629 campaign, there was no significant action on the Low Countries waterways for several years apart from a continuing Spanish ban on the movement of timber down the Rhine to the United Provinces.[16] The massing of Spanish forces at Antwerp in August 1631 in preparation for Jan van Nassau's assault on Tholen evoked only a short ban on the export to the South Netherlands of various materials. Nor did the States General use the river-blockade weapon during the triumphant offensive of 1632. While the States of Zeeland was apparently eager to initiate another blockade during the siege of Maastricht, neither the Stadholder nor *Raad van State* saw any need for such action from a military point of view. The lull in the strategic regulation of the river and overland trade was to continue until 1635.

v CONTINUED TRUCE AND PEACE TALKS

By the autumn of 1625 the Spanish crown was revising its approach to negotiations with the Dutch at the same time that it was changing its military strategy in the Low Countries and reducing its forces. All these processes were essentially shaped by Olivares himself. The Spanish war with the Dutch

[14] Res. SG 7 July 1629. ARH SG 3188, fo. 393.
[15] Res. SG 25 Aug., 1 Sept. ARH SG 3188, fos. 486ᵛ, 503; Res. Coll. Middelburg, 1 Sept. 1629. ARH Admiraliteiten 2457.
[16] Kessel, 237–8; Israel, 'Dutch River Trade', 485.

had, by late 1625, become essentially the Conde-Duque's war and the negotiations his negotiations. Despite the crown's financial exhaustion, Olivares considered that Spain should adjust to a long, defensive war, involving a minimum of effort and expense, designed to weary and inconvenience the Dutch for as long as it took to induce them to sign terms advantageous to Spain. Keeping the Dutch in check, in this way, was also a means of minimizing Dutch intervention in Germany, confining the Republic to the role of passive spectator of the steady growth of Habsburg power in the Empire.

In the autumn of 1625, reflecting the marked increase in Olivares's influence over Low Countries affairs, following the fall of Breda, there took place an important shift in the demands of the Spanish negotiators. Under fresh instructions, sent to Isabella in November, the concessions now required of the Dutch included, besides withdrawal from the Indies and reopening the Schelde, some token acknowledgement of Spanish overlordship and the public practice of Catholicism. Notably greater stress was now laid upon the latter than had previously been the case at any stage in the period 1606–24, Philip declaring that in his Dutch policy he was motivated exclusively by the interests of religion.[17] Inevitably, Olivares's maximalist position, with its wholly spurious stress on religious motivation, immediately widened the gulf between Spain and the Dutch as, presumably, it was intended to do. As a result of this and also of the commencement of French aid to the Dutch in the form of the subsidies paid to the States General during the mid 1620s, under the treaty of Compiègne of 1624, there was a pronounced falling off in truce contacts during 1625–7. Olivares had apparently lost patience with the labyrinthine procedure which had thus far led nowhere and it was probably on his authorization that a pamphlet appeared at Seville in 1625, informing the Spanish public of the truce talks, though in rather distorted form for propaganda purposes: it was announced simply that the prince of Orange and his adherents were so downcast in the aftermath of the loss of Breda that they had made overtures to Spain.[18]

---

[17] *Corresp. d'Esp.* ii. 236–7.
[18] *Relacion verdadera de las treguas y paces*, pp. 1–4.

Nevertheless, after a pause, contact resumed during 1626, under cover of prisoner-exchange talks being conducted at the small Flemish town of Middelburg. Isabella's representative, Johan Kesselaer, raised the issue of a truce with the Dutch delegates, Daniel Slachmulder and Gerard van Berckel, burgomaster of Rotterdam. There was a flurry of new activity in which the painter Peter Paul Rubens was again active, visiting Holland in July 1627, and on other occasions. It was reported to the States General that Spain would acquiesce in a new truce if the Republic would acknowledge token Spanish sovereignty, accept at least one Catholic church in each town, reopen the Schelde, and withdraw from the Indies.[19] Naturally, the Dutch flatly refused these terms, but proposed an unconditional cease-fire, of several months, on land only (so as not to prejudice the position of the colonial companies) during which terms could be hammered out. Apparently, most of Philip's ministers were ready to agree, but Olivares, and hence the king, were not.[20]

The impasse was broken a year later owing to a sudden softening in the Dutch position resulting partly from the deterioration in Franco–Dutch relations of the late 1620s, which included the temporary suspension of French subsidies,[21] and doubtless still more from the unbroken string of Habsburg successes in Germany. Berckel told Kesselaer that the States General now no longer insisted, as a precondition for talks, on Spanish acceptance of the first article of the 1609 treaty styling the Dutch provinces as 'free provinces'. This seemingly opened the way to some sort of acknowledgement of Philip IV.[22] Olivares's critics in Spain who had been inhibited from questioning his stance on sovereignty were suddenly released from their constraint by this manoeuvre and exerted heavy pressure on the Conde-Duque to agree to new truce talks. As from April 1628, a series of stormy

[19] Aitzema, *Ned. Vreedehandeling* i. 118–19.

[20] Consulta, Junta de Estado, 6 Feb. 1627. AGS Estado 2041; Olivares argued that by agreeing to a cease-fire, Spain would be allowing the Dutch to intensify their effort and step up their strength overseas and in the Indies.

[21] Waddington, 77, 124–5; Corresp. Lagonissa, 75; *Vrede-vaen voor all Liefhebbers vant Vaderland*, pp. 4–5, 14, 16.

[22] Consulta, Junta de Estado, 23 Apr. 1628. AGS Estado 2042.

meetings of the *Consejo* left Olivares's authority temporarily somewhat battered.[23] A group of at least seven ministers, headed by Spinola and Brizuela, urged prompt acceptance of the Dutch offer of talks without further delay.

Since Olivares had professed to place such importance on the cause of religion, Bishop Brizuela and also the king's confessor and other ministers insisted that in reality the church would be best served by a truce. For such a war as the Conde-Duque was proposing would certainly result in the loss of more Catholic territory to the Dutch while, with the truce, a resurgence of Arminian–Gomarist controversy was to be hoped for as well as increased infiltration of Catholic priests into the northern Netherlands. In any case, Gelves and others stressed there was not the slightest prospect of breaking through the Dutch defences. One minister, the Marqués de Santa Cruz, added that the unremitting recruiting for Flanders was also simply hastening the depopulation of Spain. Only Olivares, Montesclaros, the Duke of Feria, and the Marqués of Leganés persisted in arguing for rejection of the Dutch offer. Olivares demands were strikingly reminiscent of those of his uncle, Balthasar de Zúñiga, in 1621: recognition of Philip as 'perpetual protector and sovereign' of the seven provinces, expressed through yearly tribute payments, the stamping of the king's profile on Dutch coinage, and admission of royal representatives to meetings of the States General and other bodies, besides a Catholic church in each Dutch town, reopening of the Schelde, withdrawal from the Indies, and indeed several other conditions.[24]

Olivares had his way at first, but the onset of the Mantuan Succession Crisis, the unavoidable diversion of Spanish forces from the Netherlands, and the loss of the Mexican silver fleet, all combined to undermine his stand. In September 1628, with both the royal finances and armies in pitiable state, a committee of ministers which included the Conde-Duque advised the king that he must shift his ground at once and dispatch *pleins pouvoirs* enabling Isabella to resume talks

---

[23] See the series of consultas in AGS Estado 2042; *Corresp. Lagonissa,* pp. 99–100.

[24] Cuvelier, 'Les Negociations', 73–5; Alcala-Zamora, 300.

with a largely free hand.[25] In January 1629 Philip authorized Isabella to conclude a truce on terms similar to those of 1609, that is, on condition that the Dutch disbanded, or at least restricted the scope of the West India Company.[26] Olivares, for his part, continued to criticize the policy of moderation forced on him by his colleagues, arguing that the apparent Dutch response was merely an elaborate deception.[27]

Isabella, having received her *pleins pouvoirs* in February 1629, at once renewed contact with Frederik Hendrik. But now it was the turn of the Dutch to prevaricate.[28] The delay was not the result of any intention to prevent truce talks on the prince's part, but because, having finally obtained his subsidies from Holland and with the Spaniards so weak, the Stadholder understandably had no wish to miss the chance of a major military break-through. However, no sooner had the siege of 's-Hertogenbosch begun than Berckel was dispatched to Roosendaal where he met Kesselaer on 18 May, to examine Philip's authorization and to hear the details of the thirty-four truce that Isabella was offering.[29] Frederik Hendrik's response, through Berckel, raised high hopes, both at Brussels and Madrid, of an early end to the war, and by late July Philip was already joyfully assuming that the truce was all but concluded.[30] It thus caused a considerable shock on the Spanish side when the prince declared that the proposed terms would first have to be agreed upon by the individual provinces. Isabella tried to threaten that if 's Hertogenbosch fell, the truce offer would be withdrawn. In August the *Consejo* advised Philip to send Isabella 'an even freer authorization than has been sent hitherto, if such be possible, to conclude the truce'.[31] Finally, in desperation Isabella launched her forces in the massive thrust across the Veluwe.

After Frederik Hendrik and his close advisers informed the full States General of the truce moves afoot, the assembly

[25] Consulta 28 Sept. 1628, *Corresp. d'Esp.* ii. 410.
[26] Philip to Isabella, 14 Feb. 1629. ARB SEG 200, fo. 62.
[27] 'Voto del Conde-Duque' (2 Jun. 1629). AHN Estado leg. 727.
[28] Isabella to Philip, 3 Mar. 1629. ARB SEG 200, fo. 82ᵛ; Straub, 320-4.
[29] Isabella to Philip, 18 May 1629. ARB SEG 200, fo. 251; Aitzema, *Hist.* ii. 908.
[30] Philip to Isabella, 26 July 1629. ARB SEG 201, fo. 119.
[31] Consulta 16 Aug. 1629. AGS Estado 2043.

resolved to keep the matter secret for the moment and, further, not to proceed with the process whilst Habsburg troops remained in the Veluwe and on the IJssel.[32] On 21 September the States-General directed Berckel to inform Kesselaer that there could be further progress only after the unconditional withdrawal of both the Spanish and Imperialist forces. In her eagerness, Isabella sent a messenger post-haste to Roosendaal to inform Berckel that all the troops would be promptly evacuated.[33] In response, the States General voted on 2 October to submit the momentous issue of the Spanish truce offer to the provinces and city councils. The gradual divulging of the truce moves to the Dutch political élite as a whole was looked on with the greatest unease and distaste at Brussels and Madrid. La Cueva wrote to Olivares of his fears that the public debate in the Republic would make matters even more difficult than they already were by enabling the French and Venetians to interfere.[34]

The public controversy over the truce, beginning in October 1629, soon came to be known in Dutch political circles as the 'groote saecke' or 'groote werck', that is, the 'great affair', to distinguish it from the mass of lesser business. Without doubt the 1629–30 debate was the most complicated and acrimonious dispute in the United Provinces since 1618. Only in the east of the country was the issue relatively quickly resolved. In Overijssel and Gelderland, as in 1606–9, the widespread dislike of the heavy taxation and other burdens of war and the traditional predilection for peace among both nobility and towns swept the board. The war party in the east, led in the Zutphen area by the noble diarist Alexander van der Capellen, was everywhere defeated within a few days. The Deventer *vroedschap*, while expressing some anxiety that the Emperor should be included in the truce, and by no means unmindful of the West India

[32] Secr. res. SG. 5 Sept. 1629. GA Amsterdam, Algemeen Bestuur no. 11, fo. 181ᵛ.
[33] Ibid., fos. 182ᵛ–183ʳ. AWG OAH 110, fo. 62. Isabella to Philip, 30 Sept, 1629. ARB SEG 201, fo. 233.
[34] La Cueva to Olivares, 9 July 1629, AGS Estado 2043.

Company's interests, was emphatically in favour,[35] and the position differed little among the other towns and the leading nobles. There was prompt agreement to support the truce in both the States of Overijssel and Gelderland.[36] There was more of a fight in Utrecht where the chief towns, Utrecht and Amersfoort, partisans of the Counter-Remonstrant cause, rejected the truce proposals outright. But there too a pro-truce resolution was forced through within a few days, at the insistence of the nobility and clergy, the whole procedure being skilfully orchestrated by the Stadholder's principal manager in Utrecht, Adraan Ploos.[37]

But if war-weariness prevailed in the east, it soon emerged that the position was quite otherwise elsewhere. While Friesland and Groningen prevaricated for some weeks before declaring themselves, it was immediately apparent that the Spanish truce offer met with little favour in the north.[38] Both provinces were eager to clear the Spaniards from Lingen and both were deeply apprehensive concerning the mounting Habsburg victories in north Germany;[39] but then these considerations applied equally to Overijssel and Gelderland. The large local investment in the West India Company was certainly an important factor in Groningen, but, as has been seen, in Friesland such investment was minimal. But however this perplexing phenomenon is to be explained what is certain is that the negative attitude of these provinces was in no way inspired by Frederik Hendrik and his entourage. On the contrary, Groningen's chief deputy to the States General, Goosen Schaffer, who, as has been seen, was a regular member of the prince's inner circle, did his best to steer the proceedings in the same direction as had Ploos and Haersolte in

[35] GA Deventer vroed. res. 1 Oct. 1629 (os).

[36] Res. Overijssel, 2 Oct. (os). ARH Provinciale Resoluties 486; Res. Gelderland, 7 Oct. 1629 (os). ARH Provinciale Resoluties vol. 9; Van der Capellen i. 551–2, 555–6.

[37] GA Utrecht vroed. res. 3 and 16 Oct. 1629; GA Amersfoort, vroed. res. 15 Oct. 1629; *Kroniek* (1867), pp. 300–1; Van der Capellen i. 555, 569.

[38] GA Groningen, vroed. res. 9 Oct. 1629; Zeeland deputies to SZ, 28 Dec. 1629. RAZ 2113; W. Marienburg to Deventer, The Hague, 6 and 10 Oct. (os). GA Deventer i, no. 19.

[39] Marienburg to Deventer, 15 Oct. 1629. (os). GA Deventer i. 19.

Utrecht and Overijssel.[40] The pressure for continued war against Spain in the north unquestionably derived exclusively from local causes. The city of Groningen rejected talk of a truce outright but stated that it would welcome a full peace (which was not then feasible) once the finances of the Republic were again in order, when the kings of France and England had been duly consulted and provided that the interests of the West India Company were fully secured.[41]

Meanwhile, it was plain enough that Zeeland too would uncompromisingly reject the Spanish offer in view of the particular interests of Middelburg and Flushing and the preponderance of these towns in the politics of the province.[42] There was little that the Stadholder's friends, notably Simon van Beaumont who was sent from The Hague to explain the Spanish offer to the States of Zeeland, could do to mitigate the province's attitude. The Flushing deputies even ventured to criticize, in discreet terms, the prince's conduct in having promoted and facilitated the truce moves. Middelburg's deputies insisted that a truce would ruin the province because it would inevitably cause a severe and prolonged slump in naval, privateering and West India Company activity and spending which would mean loss of work for thousands of seamen and deprive Zeeland's merchants of their business while the revival of the Flemish sea-ports which would unavoidably follow would divert Zeeland's transit trade with Antwerp which, indeed, as has been seen, had considerably increased since 1621 as a consequence of the war. The other voting maritime towns of Zeeland, Zierikzee and Vere, were less involved in the transit trade with the Spanish Netherlands but like Middelburg and Flushing were heavily committed to the West India Company. The Zeeland agricultural towns, Goes and Tholen, had no choice but to go along with the maritime towns of their province but were distinctly less uncompromising in their tone.

---

[40] GA Groningen, vroed. res. 3 and 5 Oct 1629 (os).

[41] Ibid. vroed. res. 15 Oct. 1629 (os); the *Discovrs over den Nederlandschen Vrede-handel*, published at Leeuwarden, likewise argued that the Republic should reject all talk of a truce but agree to sign a full peace.

[42] *Notulen Zeeland,* 1629, 363–70; Zeeland deputies to SZ, The Hague, 28 Dec. 1629. RAZ 2113.

With six of the Republic's provinces divided three against three, the resolution of Holland, had the province been able to reach one, would certainly have been decisive. But in Holland, as in Groningen and Friesland, the position differed strikingly from what it had been in 1606-9 and there was a good deal of entrenched opposition to the truce offer despite the best efforts of Noordwijck and Cats, Frederik Hendrik's managers of the States of Holland, who, as Carleton reported to London, did their best to get the truce accepted. The only real parallel with 1609 is that once again Amsterdam totally failed to get its way even though its policy accorded with that of the Stadholder. The Amsterdam *vroedschap*, dominated by a group that was liberal on church matters and put the interests of the European carrying trade before that of the colonial companies, voted on 9 October categorically in favour of the truce.[43] Amsterdam judged that the burdens, heavy taxation, and financial difficulties occasioned by the war had continued long enough. Rotterdam and Dordrecht, the latter having suffered severely from the recent disruptions of the river trade, also declared strongly in favour, while Delft and Alkmaar were sympathetic.[44] Initially, only Haarlem and Gorinchem rejected the truce offer outright,[45] but the *vroedschappen* of Leiden and several other towns were also decidedly cool. Leiden's deputies to the States of Holland were instructed to block the truce moves until the States agreed to establish a stricter ordering of religion and regime within the Republic.[46] Since the victory of the liberal opponents of the Counter-Remonstrants at Amsterdam and Rotterdam in the mid 1620s, Haarlem and Leiden had become ever more embittered at the progressive crumbling of the coalition of 1618. The faction consisting of Haarlem, Leiden, Gouda, Enkhuizen, and some other towns had for several years endeavoured to secure stricter imposition of the States General's edicts against Arminians and Catholics

---

[43] GA Amsterdam vroed. res. xvi, fo. 109, 9 Oct. 1629.
[44] GA Rotterdam, vroed. res. 11 Oct. 1629; GA Delft vroed. res. 11 Oct. 1629; Israel, 'Holland Towns', 44-5.
[45] GA Haarlem vroed. res. 9 Oct. 1629; GA Gorinchem vroed. res. 9 Oct. 1629.
[46] GA Leiden, Sec. Arch. 448, fo. 139^v.

and the exclusion from public office of persons refusing to swear to uphold the Reformed Faith as defined by the synod of 1618–19 at Dordrecht. Of course, in several ways, the church controversy in Holland had, from early on, been linked to the question of relations with Spain. Just as Oldenbarnevelt had been liberal in religion and sought peace with Spain, so Andries Bicker, Gerard van Berckel, and other liberal Holland burgomasters of the late 1620s, proved eager supporters of the truce moves. By its resolution of 11 October, the Leiden city council tied together, even more closely than they had been joined before, the chief issue in the Republic's external relations with what remained the principal internal issue, the feuding over theology and church government. Leiden subsequently was to persist together with Haarlem, Gouda, Hoorn, and Enkhuizen, forming the core of a formidable Holland war-party.

Weeks of furious activity in the States of Holland produced no result whatever. On 10 November the deputies voted in the presence of the Stadholder:[47] the nobility, Dordrecht, Amsterdam, Rotterdam, Delft, and Alkmaar declared for the truce; Haarlem and Gorinchem were totally opposed, while the rest, including Leiden, Gouda, Hoorn, and Enkhuizen, insisted that the securing of church and regime internally, prior guarantees for the West India Company, assurances of peaceful intentions from the Emperor, and consultation with the Republic's allies must precede further truce talks. Hoorn did not take up the religious issue but otherwise shared the reservations of the latter towns.[48] In December Frederik Hendrik intervened in the States of Holland trying to break the deadlock. While pretending, as he had in September, to be entirely neutral on the main issue, wishing only to defer to the decision of the States General, in fact, as various observers noted and Aitzema subsequently recorded, he undoubtedly spoke in favour rather than against the truce.[49] His intervention took the form of suggesting

---

[47] Ibid., fo. 144ᵛ; Zeeland deputies to SZ, The Hague, 10 Nov. 1629. RAZ 82 2099.

[48] AWG Hoora vroed. Res. 15 Oct. 1629.

[49] Aitzema, *Ned. Vreedehandeling* i. 127; 'Aviso de Holanda (6 Nov. 1629). AGS Estado 2322; Carleton to Dorchester, 15 Oct. 1629. PRO SP 84, 140, fos. 71–2.

means to make the negotiations securer for the Republic: he recommended that the States General of the southern provinces should be required to ratify any settlement signed by Philip and Isabella and that it be required that key Spanish fortresses, considered strategically threatening to the Republic, notably Lingen and Zandvliet, should be dismantled.[50] To this intervention on the part of the Stadholder, the Contra-Trevist towns responded coolly. Leiden deemed 'with reverence that His Excellency's proposal would not assure the security of the negotiation'. The response of the Hoorn *vroedschap* was similarly negative.[51] On 13 December the States of Holland voted once again: there were still only five votes for; five were against — Haarlem, Gorinchem, Schoonhoven, Purmerend, and Den Briel — while the rest persisted with their stringent preconditions which Amsterdam refused to countenance.[52]

As the deliberations continued in the States of Holland during January and February 1630, heavy pressure was brought to bear on the war-towns, particularly on Haarlem. The *vroedschap* reacted by drawing up a lengthy defence of its position, which, contrary to accepted procedure, was then published, on the pretext that a distorted, pirated version was already in circulation.[53] Like Leiden, Haarlem reasoned that the truce would occasion a resurgence in both Arminian and Catholic activity, spreading religious dissension throughout the land. The *vroedschap* also held that the truce would prove detrimental economically, though the printed resolution scrupulously avoids any reference to Haarlem's own interests.[54] Every town was anxious to put its arguments in terms of the national interest and to avoid seeming to be motivated by its own particular concerns. Thus Haarlem argued that during the former truce 'business had diminished', that the province of Zeeland had suffered especially and that the Spanish crown had seized Dutch ships in Iberian ports.

[50] GA Rotterdam, vroed. res. 10 Dec. 1629; GA Leiden Sec. Arch. 448, fo. 169^v.
[51] AWG Hoorn, vroed. res. 11 Dec. 1629.
[52] GA Leiden Sec. Arch. 448, fos. 169^v–170^v.
[53] See the foreword to the *Resolutie der Stadt Haerlem*.
[54] *Resolutie der Stadt Haerlem*, 11–12.

The appeal to public opinion in Holland by the war-party had in fact begun as soon as the Spanish truce offer had been divulged. Virtually all the pamphlets published in the Republic in 1629-30 stridently denounced the truce, which suggests that popular support for the war, at least in the maritime provinces and in the north, remained very strong, a most remarkable phenomenon after a decade of steeply rising taxation and increased food prices. Most of these tracts were published in towns where the *vroedschappen* were against the truce, confirming that the propaganda war was largely controlled by elements among the political élite. The supposedly secret protest of the West India Company directors to the States General, of October 1629, for instance, was published at Haarlem by the regular printer to the *vroedschap*.[55] Another tract issued at Haarlem was the hard-hitting *Discovrs Aengaende Treves*. Several Contra-Trevist pamphlets appeared at Leeuwarden.[56] Usselincx's *Waerschouwinghe*, of 1630, was not the only fiercely anti-truce publication which appeared at Flushing. The strategy of the truce towns on the other hand was to try to avoid the recourse to the public. Rotterdam moved in the States of Holland that it should be forbidden to publish tracts of any kind dealing with the truce negotiations and that the clergy who, once again, were particularly vehement adversaries of the truce, should be compelled to cease their pronouncements on the subject from the pulpit.[57] In Rotterdam itself, the *predikanten* received a strong warning from the burgomasters.

Frequently, the pamphlets are highly revealing as to the reasoning and motives that influenced the attitudes of the Dutch public to the Spanish truce offer. The pamphleteers knew where to put the emphasis. The old charge that, whatever he pretended, Philip was implacably resolved on reconquest of the seven provinces, constantly recurred.[58] The public was reminded of the dangers posed by the Habsburg

[55] *Consideratien ende redenen.*
[56] See the *Remonstrantie, van weghen den Coninck van Bohemen*; and *Discovrs over den Nederlandschen Vrede-handel.*
[57] GA Rotterdam vroed. res. 26 Nov. 1629.
[58] *Missive Inhoudende den Aërdt vanden Treves*, pp. 8, 9, 36 *Discovrs over den Nederlandschen Vrede-handel*, D3ᵛ.

advances in North Germany. The arrogance, cruelty, blood-lust, and sheer untrustworthiness of the Spaniards, venerable themes of the original anti-Spanish propaganda of the 1570s and 1580s, were unceasingly played on.[59] The populace were warned that the real aim of Spain was simply to promote dis-cord and disunity, just as during the last truce, and to attack once the Republic was sufficiently weakened. Fear of a re-surgence of both Catholicism and Arminianism and renewed religious strife was exploited, though it is perfectly under-standable that ordinary folk should have been apprehensive on all these grounds and, in some cases, had good reason for being so. Several pamphlets also dealt with the economic implications of the truce, and the widespread fears that trade and industry might be diverted from the country somewhat more freely than the official resolutions of the towns and provinces. Middelburg and Flushing could give undisguised priority to their commercial interests in the debate in the States of Zeeland because their needs largely coincided with those of the province as a whole. It was impossible, though, for Zeeland to lay much stress on the precariousness of its transit trade to Flanders and Brabant in the national debate, because, apart from Rotterdam, the rest of the country was uninvolved. In Holland, on the other hand, interests were so disparate and liable to conflict that however prominent economic concerns were in the minds of the province's politicians, these could be referred to only obliquely, as in the case of the published resolution of the Haarlem *vroedschap*.

It was readily admitted in the pamphlets that the Republic had lost its Iberian trade, but it was held that the establish-ment of the West India Company more than compensated for the loss.[60] Where only 5,000 or 6,000 seamen had been em-ployed in Iberian trade during the truce, the Company, by 1629, employed 18,000 or 20,000 people. It was argued that manufactures had suffered during the truce but were now,

---

[59] *Klaere Aenwijsinge,* pp. 7-8, 26-7; Usselincx, *Waerschouwinghe,* pp. 1-5; Swart, 44-6.

[60] *Klare Aenwijsinge*; Usselincx, *Waerschouwinghe,* p. 20; *Antwoordt op sekeren Brief Evlaly,* pp. 9-10; *Consideratien op den Treves,* p. 1; *Redenen waeromme,* fo. 31.

despite the difficult economic circumstances of the late 1620s, prospering, as readers were encouraged to ascertain by consulting the good weavers of Leiden and Haarlem.[61] The *Klaere Aenwijsinge* admitted that agriculture in Dutch Brabant and other border areas would profit from the truce, but dismissed this as a 'particular' interest irrelevant to the needs of the people as a whole; the general interest, it was maintained, would be better served by a continuation of the war. Usselincx conceded that the Dunkirkers were causing considerable damage to Dutch navigation and trade, and that Dordrecht particularly had suffered from the river blockades, but nevertheless insisted that both Dutch European trade and manufacturing would be best assisted by a continuation of the war, even without taking into account the added bonus of the West India Company. It was argued also that wages, rents, and agricultural profits were all keeping up better during the war than they had during the truce.

These intricate public proceedings in the Republic were viewed with undisguised dismay in Brussels and Madrid.[62] Spanish ministers were gratified that Frederik Hendrik was backing the truce moves but were perplexed by the strength of the opposition among the public and sections of the political establishment. In December 1629 Philip wrote to Brussels that while it would be neither wise nor dignified to press any harder, should the Dutch finally respond positively, Isabella might sign in the king's name without needing to refer back to Madrid.[63] The Spaniards, however, were not entirely passive spectators of the wrangling in the Republic: Isabella apparently promoted efforts in Zeeland to influence opinion in favour of reopening the Schelde, a proposal which had found at least some support in the province, in 1612–13.[64] In addition to the chronically difficult financial situation and the impact of the loss of 's-Hertogenbosch, she also had to face mounting tension in Flanders and Brabant. People

---

[61] *Klare Aenwijsinge.*
[62] Pedro de San Juan to Olivares, 30 Oct. 1629. AGS Estado 2322; *Corresp. d'Esp.* ii. 491, 494.
[63] Philip to Isabella, 13 Dec. 1629. ARB SEG 201, fo. 294.
[64] Jan Wouwer to Olivares, Brussels, 13 Nov. 1629. AGS Estado 2322.

were now openly disparaging Spanish rule and particularly the much detested Cardinal de la Cueva. The nobility too was restless and in December 1629, meeting in secret session, the nobles and clergy of Flanders petitioned Isabella to reduce the influence of the Spaniards in the civil and military establishment and assign more positions and offices to local nobles.[65]

Contact between Frederik Hendrik and Isabella continued, during 1630, through Berckel and Kesselaer. At the same time the English crown, recently allied to the Dutch but now at peace with Spain, was asked by Philip to intervene as mediator. Isabella and Aytona repeatedly assured the king that the Dutch were not trying to deceive, but were simply paralysed by internal dissension and the 'insolence' of the Gomarist towns.[66] Berckel, who was close to Frederik Hendrik and an active supporter of the truce, assured Kesselaer that, besides the prince, many leading Dutch politicians were keen to conclude the truce and, certainly the prince himself continued to favour the truce,[67] though he was distinctly unenthusiastic regarding the English offer of mediation as he wished to adhere to the policy which had been followed, since 1621, of excluding the English and French from the proceedings. The efforts of the English ambassador, Sir Henry Vane, to inject new life into the negotiations did prompt further discussion in the provincial assemblies and city councils, but otherwise made no significant impact. Enkhuizen's response was simply to reiterate its previous resolution not to agree to truce talks until religion and regime had been secured internally.[68] The Dutch want to 'make their peace by themselves their owne way' concluded Vane, in October.

While the Spanish crown persevered, through 1630 and 1631, in trying to reach agreement with the Dutch on the basis of the 1609 terms, partly through direct contact, supervised by Aytona,[69] and in which Rubens was again active,

[65] BL MS Add. 14007, fo. 427.

[66] Aytona to Philip, 9 June 1630. BRB MS 16, 149.

[67] 'He hath bin and is still affected to the Truce': see Vane to Dorchester, 10/20 Aug. 1620. PRO SP 84/142, fo. 15.

[68] AWG Enkhuizen vroed. res. 17 Sept. and 2 Dec. 1630.

[69] BRB MS 16, 149, fo. 70ᵛ.

and partly via London, in reality the picture was totally transformed by the Dutch conquest of Pernambuco in February 1630. For Spain now had a rigid condition, failing satisfaction of which there would be no truce, which had previously been lacking. Philip and Olivares now insisted that the Dutch must surrender their Brazilian foothold in exchange for Breda, Lingen, or some other compensation.[70] Restating his position in January 1632, the Conde-Duque assured his colleagues that he desired a truce but again insisted that first the Dutch must give up their Brazilian gains for Breda or another town together with financial compensation.[71] When Isabella reported, following word from Rubens in May 1632, that the States General would agree only to the terms of 1609, retaining Pernambuco, Philip retorted that such terms were wholly unacceptable and would threaten the very ascendancy of the Iberians in the New World.[72] On this point, the *consejos* of the Indies, Portugal, and State were unshakable. Philip declared that rather than settle for so disadvantageous an arrangement, it would be preferable, despite the absolute necessity of diverting troops from the Netherlands to the Palatinate to face the Swedes, to risk losing more territory and towns in the Netherlands to the Dutch, postponing further negotiation until circumstances became more favourable.

When it came, the Dutch offensive of 1632 shook Spanish power in the South Netherlands to the core. So precarious was the king's authority after Frederik Hendrik's breakthrough and the humiliation of his forces, that it seemed for a time that there was indeed a chance of a general revolt in the southern provinces against Spanish rule. Even as her agent, Rubens, negotiated with Dutch representatives at Liège, Isabella, distraught by the defeats, gave way to the irresistible pressure for a convening of the southern States General, even though she had no authority for this from

[70] Philip to Isabella, 2 Nov. 1631. AGS Estado 2238.
[71] Voto del Conde-Duque, 14 Jan. 1632. AGS Estado 2046.
[72] Philip to Isabella, 24 Jan. 1632. ARB SEG 205: 'dexandoles con aquella plaza ninguna tregua es buena porque podran levantarse estando en paz con el comercio de las Indias Occidentales enflaqueciendo el absoluto dominio que yo tengo en ellas.'

Spain.[73] Aware of the pressure, the *Consejo* in Madrid had
indeed advised Philip that the States General should not in
fact be convened and the king had already written forbidding
the Infanta to do so, but his missive arrived too late. The
assembly met, for the first time since 1600 and the last in its
history, at Brussels in September 1632.[74] Aytona afterwards
justified the panic measure to the king, arguing that it had
become essential to show the populace that it was not Spain
but the Dutch who were blocking the peace moves;[75] moreover, he considered that there would be little likelihood of
obtaining further war subsidies from the 'obedient provinces'
without first allowing the States General to meet. The fact
that the king had forbidden the assembly was of course
kept secret.

Despite the steep increases in taxation since 1621, the
southern Netherlands was still relatively lightly taxed compared with the United Provinces. Nor had the country suffered
any serious damage from Dutch attacks or Spanish troop
movements. Those statements of the period which do refer
to the extreme misery of the region, such as Rubens's description of Antwerp in 1627, invariably refer to the effects
of the 1625–9 river blockade and not to the war as such.
While it is true that there was a good deal of revulsion against
the war in the south, such reactions were by no means so
pervasive as one might suppose. In their provincial remon-
strances to the Infanta, while some provinces, notably
Flanders, Brabant, and Luxemburg, requested immediate
peace talks with the Dutch, others such as Hainault, Tournai,
and Walloon Flanders, did not. Wallonia had its grievances.
It was demanded that the Spanish soldiery should be better
disciplined and that more Walloon officers should receive
senior commands, but these provinces did not press for an
early end to the war.[76] Indeed, it would appear that the
Dutch–Spanish struggle with its drastic impact on Europe's
patterns of trade had its uses for parts of the southern

---

[73] *Actes* i. 3–6; Aitzema, *Ned. Vreedehandeling* i. 180.
[74] *Actes* i. 3–6; Aitzema, *Ned. Vreedehandeling* i. 180.
[75] Aytona to Philip, 12 Oct. 1632. BRB MS 16, 149, fos. 84–5.
[76] *Actes* i. 21, 27, 33, 40–5, 53–4, 59.

Netherlands much as it did for various localities in the north. Walloon Flanders, dominated by industrial Lille and Douai, expressed fears that the granting of salt-licences to Dutch merchants, enabling the latter to send ships to the Peninsula, would undermine the thriving export of textiles from the 'obedient' provinces to the Peninsula and Ibero-America by providing a loophole for Dutch manufactures. Thus, the Spanish embargo against the Dutch was regarded in the Walloon provinces as one of the conditions of local industrial prosperity.

However, in the southern States General Flanders and Brabant dominated and, in mid September, with Aytona's approval, Isabella yielded to the pressure for negotiations. A States' delegation headed by the duke of Aerschot and archbishop of Mechelen met the northern States General's delegates to the army who included Haersolte, Beaumont, and a pro-truce burgomaster of Dordrecht, at Maastricht. The southern delegates pronounced their willingness to conclude a full peace with the United Provinces in the name of the southern States General and the Infanta who was acting for the king of Spain, in accordance with the authorization of 1629. The Dutch representatives replied with a list of nine demands which they insisted would have to be agreed to before any peace negotiations proper could commence. These included a demand for the total withdrawal of Spanish troops from all the Netherlands provinces, for the future allegiance of troops in the South Netherlands to the southern States General only and not to the king of Spain, and the temporary occupation of various southern towns by Dutch forces.[77] The sweeping nature of these demands came as something of a shock to the southern delegates and the Infanta's only response was to ignore them, but she nevertheless went ahead with the plans for sending a peace delegation to The Hague. Her principal adviser at this time, Aytona, believed that if 'condiciones tolerables' were obtainable, a truce was now vital, for it seemed to him that by tying down and exhausting the king's forces as it was, the struggle was merely enabling France to exploit Spanish weakness as she chose throughout Europe.[78] But, with his practised eye, he grasped after a few weeks that in fact there was virtually no chance of a settlement.

At The Hague, the States General duly consulted the seven provinces as to whether peace talks should be entered into. Instantly, the rift among the public was opened anew whilst the French, Swedish, and Venetian ambassadors plunged into fervent activity arousing the opposition so that, as a pro-peace politician put it, 'they themselves might be free of the plague of Europe [Spain] and through our efforts and taxation maintain their rest, security, and interests'.[79] But, as always, it was not foreign pressure but domestic interests which mattered most: the same observer, a burgomaster of Deventer, complained bitterly of the pernicious influence of local economic pressures on the course of the proceedings. The peace party, just as in 1629, swept the board in Overijssel and Gelderland where Frederik Hendrik's confidants secured a quick decision in favour of peace.[80] They won also in Utrecht, though there was a sharp tussle between the pro-peace nobility and the anti-peace towns of Utrecht and Amersfoort. The Utrecht *vroedschap* had insisted that religion, regime, and colonial companies should all first be reformed and secured before any negotiations with the 'other side'.[81] Even Gelderland which was strongly in favour of peace did have its conditions: it wanted a secure future for the colonial companies and full toleration for Protestants in the South Netherlands.

The three hard-line, anti-peace, provinces — Zeeland, Friesland, and Groningen — chose to await Holland's decision before declaring their own. In Holland, the controversy over religion had now largely subsided, removing what on the surface had been the chief point of dissension in 1629. Despite this, however, it at once emerged that the province was now

[78] Aytona to Philip, 12 Oct. and 7 Nov. 1632. BRB MS 16149, fos. 84–5, 87ᵛ.

[79] W. Marienburg to Deventer, 2 and 30 Oct. 1632. GA Deventer, Rep. 1, no. 19.

[80] Secret resolutions of Overijssel, Gelderland, and Utrecht, 21 Oct. 1632. ARH SG Loketkas 198.

[81] GA Utrecht, vroed. res. 26 Oct. 1632; Zeeland deputies to SZ, 19 Oct. 1632. RAZ SZ 2102; Van der Capellen i. 658.

just as deeply split as before. The Amsterdam *vroedschap*,[82] voting on 5 October, again pronounced in favour of peace. The next day, Dordrecht resolved to employ every means to terminate the war.[83] Likewise, the nobility, Delft, Rotterdam, and Alkmaar supported the peace moves, as did the formerly strongly Counter-Remonstrant towns of Gorinchem and Purmerend.[84] Religion was now patently a broken reed in the hands of the Contra-Trevisten. But the opposition to peace remained formidable: Enkhuizen was prepared to resume peace talks only if these were to be with the southern provinces only, excluding the Spanish king.[85] Hoorn similarly advanced impossible conditions such as the indefinite garrisoning of various key southern towns with Dutch troops.[86] Once again, Leiden, Haarlem, and Gouda were hostile. Leiden refused to agree to anything more than simply hearing the proposals of the southern side.[87] Haarlem's stringent conditions were subsequently adopted by Zeeland, Friesland, and Groningen as the platform of the war-party:[88] exclusion of Spain from the peace, withdrawal of all non-Netherlands troops from the South Netherlands, indefinite Dutch occupation of Dunkirk, Ostend, Antwerp, Rheinberg, Breda, Orsoy, and Lingen and, finally, toleration for Protestantism in the south.

Holland voted to agree to talks on 15 October, Leiden alone rejecting the proposal outright. Shortly after, Groningen consented to talks on the conditions mentioned above.[89] Zeeland followed suit but insisting that the talks must be with the southern provinces as 'free States with the exclusion of the king of Spain and Infanta', that the Reformed Faith be tolerated in the south and on several economic conditions which were distinctively Zeeland's own:[90] first, that the Schelde restrictions should remain in force; secondly, to prevent diversion of trade from Zeeland, that the southern

---

[82] GA Amsterdam vroed. res. xv, fo. 265.
[83] GA Dordrecht vroed. res. 6 Oct. 1632.
[84] GA Delft vroed. res. 8 Oct. 1632.
[85] AWG Enkhuizen vroed. res. 6 Oct. 1632.
[86] AWG Hoorn vroed. res. 6 Oct. 1632.
[87] GA Leiden Sec. Arch. 449, fos. 1–8.
[88] GA Haarlem vroed. res. 5, 9 Oct. 1632.
[89] Sec. Res. SG 23, 27 Oct. 1632. ARH SG Loketkas 198.
[90] Ibid., Sec. Res. 2 Nov. 1632.

States General be forbidden to lower its imposts in the Flemish ports below those pertaining on the Schelde; and thirdly, chiefly at Zierikzee's request, that there should be no tariff preference for salt refined in the southern provinces as against salt refined in the North. Finally, Friesland also gave its consent.[91]

The next battle was over the issue of excluding Spain. While some towns, including Gouda, Enkhuizen, and Hoorn,[92] fought hard over this, neither Leiden, Haarlem, nor Zeeland appear to have felt any enthusiasm for the prospect of being at peace with the South Netherlands while remaining at war with Spain. While the Enkhuizen, Hoorn, and Groningen *vroedschappen* were motivated chiefly by considerations relating to colonial trade, Leiden, Haarlem, and Zeeland were even more concerned about economic competition from the South Netherlands. Amsterdam thus easily had its way in the States of Holland. 'Those of Holland', commented Aitzema, 'were more moderate [than the war provinces], considering that if Spain were excluded they would not then enjoy freedom of commerce in Spain, Italy, and other lands of the king'.[93] In late November Zeeland, though not Friesland and Groningen, agreed to talks with or without Spain.

The representatives of the Brussels States General arrived in The Hague on 4 December and, on 23 December, the Dutch delegation, headed by Adriaan Pauw, presented the Dutch States General's conditions for peace. The main demands were for recognition of the Dutch colonial companies and the scope of their charters, the Schelde restrictions, together with agreed controls on imposts in the Flemish ports, guarantees for Zeeland's salt exports to Flanders, the withdrawal of all Spanish troops from the Netherlands, mixed administration for a period in several South Netherlands towns, the ceding to the Dutch of Breda, Geldern, and the whole of the populous region known as the Meierij of 's-Hertogenbosch, including Helmond and Eindhoven, situated to south of the town of 's-Hertogenbosch, the toleration of Protestantism in the southern Netherlands, and assurances

[91] Ibid., Sec. Res. SG 12 Nov. 1632.
[92] GA Gouda, Oud-Archief, vol. 50, fo. 48[v]; AWG Hoorn vroed. res. 8 Oct., 3 and 14 Dec., 1632.　　　　[93] Aitzema, *Hed. Vreedehandeling* i. 194.

that Dutch Jews would receive the same rights and privileges in Spain and Portugal as other Dutch subjects. There were also various other Dutch conditions such as the neutralization of Rheinberg and its reversion to the archbishop of Cologne.[94] While most Dutch politicians were willing to abandon notions of actually conquering or absorbing the southern Netherlands, the majority were still determined to break Spanish power in the region and reduce the south to the status of a client state of the Republic. Frederik Hendrik was clearly in favour of adopting a harsh opening position.

Meanwhile, at Brussels, Philip's ministers were reinforced by the return from Madrid, in December, of the Flemish official Petrus Roose, a passionate royalist who enjoyed the full confidence of both king and Conde-Duque and who was now raised to the presidency of the royal council at Brussels. Roose, Aytona, and Fernández de Córdoba persevered to keep the Brussels States General in check. In particular, they endeavoured to continue separate negotiations, through their agent Rubens, who had last been sent directly to Holland in December 1631, with Frederik Hendrik.[95] The Dutch provinces voted four to three in favour of granting Rubens another pass-port, but the indignation of the duke of Aerschot and other leaders of the Brussels States General led to the scheme being dropped. Roose certainly succeeded, however, in tightening the reins on Aerschot and his colleagues and steadfastly refused to sign any new *pouvoirs* for the southern delegation to replace Philip's 1629 authorization. The Dutch delegates were more than justified in their suspicion of the documents that the southern side brought to The Hague, for in fact Philip had secretly repudiated his earlier authorization, by missive of November 1632, and this Roose concealed from both the Dutch and the southern States General.[96] With the king's approval, Roose also sought to exploit the differences among the southern provinces.[97] In effect, he skilfully and unscrupulously implemented Olivares's scheme of both playing for time and undermining the peace talks so as to

[94] Aitzema, *Ned. Vreedehandeling* i. 213–20; Israel, 'Holland towns', 58–9.
[95] *Original Unpublished Papers*, 166–7, 171.
[96] De Boer, *Friedensunterhandlungen*, 54.
[97] *Corresp. d'Esp.* ii. 681.

enable the king to proceed with his preparations for sending a powerful new army to the Netherlands in order to stifle popular unrest, restore royal authority, and make it possible to bargain with the Dutch from a position of strength. Olivares's unyielding position was that the king should on no account settle with the Dutch until the States General was ready to acquiesce in returning Pernambuco as well as Limburg, Maastricht, and Venlo, but with the rather unprincipled addendum that Isabella might sign an interim truce without such concessions, provided that the Emperor was omitted from the terms 'for if the Emperor is not included in the truce or peace, we shall be able, under that pretext, to improve it afterwards.'[98]

The delegations reassembled at The Hague on 18 February 1633 to hear the southern response to the Dutch terms. After both sides had reasserted their dissatisfaction with the *pouvoirs* of the other, the southern delegation rejected one by one all the major items among the Dutch conditions. The articles concerning withdrawal of Spanish troops, mixed administration in the southern ports, and several others were declared fundamentally incompatible with the sovereignty of the Spanish monarch.[99] Pauw and his colleagues replied that Philip's sovereignty would be no more prejudiced than was Charles I's by his being unable to use English troops in Scotland; the southern side answered that they were not informed about England and Scotland but well knew their obligations to the Spanish crown. On the Meijerij, the Brussels delegation denied that the region was legally tied to the former seat of the bishopric and proposed that the matter be referred to a mixed commission that would arbitrate following the signing of the peace. Following the Infanta's instructions, the southern side also demanded that Pernambuco be returned to the Portuguese crown offering Breda together with a cash payment in exchange. The gulf between the two sides over the Indies was found to be even wider than with regard to the rest.

During the ensuing weeks, the Dutch peace party made

---

[98] Consulta 9 Jan. 1633, voto de Olivares. AGS Estado 2334.
[99] *Actes*, i. 85–6, 95, 105–6.

every effort on two separate fronts, pressing their Dutch
opponents to demand less and the southern representatives
into conceding more.[1] When Holland's delegates in the
States General tried to have the demand for mixed administration in the Flemish ports dropped, Zeeland's deputies
answered that they had only agreed to negotiate with Spain
on condition that continued closure of the Schelde was
linked to regulation of the duties in the Flemish ports, to
avoid diversion of trade from Zeeland, which in turn, in their
view, necessitated a measure of Dutch control in the Flemish
ports.[2] The States General eventually voted by four provinces
to three, after some angry exchanges, to drop the demand
for mixed administration and to draw up new *pouvoirs*
acknowledging the position of the Spanish crown in the
South Netherlands. On 1 April 1633 Pauw and his colleagues
presented the States General's revised demands to the southern delegation, revealing significant modifications in the
Dutch stand. What the Republic now demanded was the
whole Meierij plus Breda and Geldern, neutralization of
Rheinberg, guarantees on the Flemish imposts, and, in view
of the seemingly insuperable deadlock over Brazil, limitation
of the truce to Europe only, leaving the war in the Indies to
continue;[3] the Republic dropped its demands for evacuation
of the Spanish soldiery and shared administration in the
Flemish ports and on the issue of the Dutch Jews, which
aroused strong feelings in the *Consejo* at Madrid,[4] now asked
only that the goods and assets of Dutch Jews in Spanish territories should be safeguarded. At this point the truce party
was clearly in the ascendant.

Frederik Hendrik who had been instrumental in securing
some softening in Zeeland's position, and whose policy it still
was, early in 1633, to manage the Dutch assemblies by
collaborating on essential matters with Amsterdam continued
to work discreetly for the truce. In a tense meeting at The

---

[1] De Boer, *Friedensunterhandlungen*, 80–2, 83–4.
[2] Among the Holland towns, Hoorn fought hardest against Amsterdam on this
point, AWG Hoorn vroed. res. 13 Jun. 1633.
[3] *Actes* i. 143, 146.
[4] Philip to Roose, 6 Mar. 1633. AGS Estado 2026; Israel, 'Dutch Sephardim',
27–8.

Hague with Johan de Knuyt and other Zeeland deputies, the prince admitted that he favoured a peace or truce with Spain, provided that it was secure and reputable and safeguarded Zeeland's interests.[5] Meanwhile, at Brussels the friction between Philip's ministers and the southern States General was becoming more intense and Roose advised the king that the moment had come to formally revoke Isabella's authority to conclude a truce. The extent of the trust that king and Conde-Duque now held in Roose is shown by their extraordinary step of sending Roose deeds cancelling Isabella's authority to conclude a truce without informing the Infanta and leaving it to Roose to judge when and how to use the deeds.[6] Aerschot and his colleagues, despite unremitting effort, were quite unable to persuade Roose and his Spanish colleagues to agree to any new concessions.[7] When talks resumed at The Hague during May, the southern side stood their ground on the Meierij, rejected the demands for Geldern and concerning the Jews, and offered Breda only in return for Pernambuco; the sole new concessions were to agree to the neutralization of Rheinberg and to raise the offer of financial compensation to the West India Company from 300,000 to 500,000 ducats.[8]

The negotiations were now close to collapse. When the position was reviewed in the States General, the war provinces urged that the talks now be broken off; the best that the peace party could do was to have the whole matter referred back to the provinces and *vroedschappen*. Aerschot returned to Brussels to plead with the king's ministers for some new concession which would save the negotiations. The way to peace in the Netherlands, he and his colleagues believed, was to find some compromise formula for the Indies.[9] Their proposal was that in return for restituting Pernambuco, the Dutch should be permitted by the king to trade on agreed terms with Pernambuco and two or three other ports, in the Moluccas, Philippines, and Guinea where

[5] De Boer, *Friedensunterhandlungen*, 141–2, *Kroniek* (1867), pp. 299–300:
[6] *Corresp. d'Esp.* ii. 690–1.
[7] ARB SEG 206, fos. 188^r–188^v.
[8] *Actes*, i. 148–52.
[9] *Actes*, i. 416.

Dutch and Iberians were neighbours. Isabella consulted Madrid, but the king replied, by letter of July 1633, that he would agree neither to a truce limited to Europe nor to the Dutch enjoying commercial access to any part of the Spanish or Portuguese Indies. Philip insisted that any peace or truce agreed on must conclusively end the conflict between Spain and the Dutch and that therefore the unqualified restitution of Pernambuco was essential.[10]

Frederik Hendrik's recommendation to the States General, at this juncture, was that the truce should be accepted if the king would yield on three crucial points: transfer of the Meierij in its entirety, guarantees on the Flemish imposts, as desired by Zeeland, and retention by the Dutch of what they then held in the Indies.[11] The exchanges between the rival factions in the Republic were growing increasingly acrimonious. Once again, the first and second chambers of the States of Utrecht endeavoured to sweep aside the objections of the towns of Utrecht and Amersfoort; so incensed at this was the Utrecht *vroedschap* that, disregarding accepted procedure, the town protested direct to the States General at the overweening and unconstitutional conduct of the Utrecht nobles with whom the town had long been at odds for dominance of the province.[12] In Holland, where some small towns, such as Schiedam, adopted no position and were prepared to follow whichever side offered the more persuasive arguments,[13] the peace towns exerted every kind of pressure at their disposal. So far had the split between Amsterdam and the West India Company now proceeded that the *vroedschap* authorized its deputies in the States of Holland to agree, if need be, to Dutch withdrawal from Brazil.[14] Rotterdam likewise instructed its representatives to concede whatever was necessary to end 'this sorrowful and burdensome war'.[15] Dordrecht urged its deputies to strive by every available

[10] Philip to Isabella, 19 July 1633. AGS Estado 2240.
[11] Frederik Hendrik to SG, 1 June 1633, in *Actes* i. 425–6.
[12] GA Utrecht, vroed. res. 20, 21, 23 May 1633.
[13] GA Schiedam, vroed. res. 9 June, 9 Aug. 1633.
[14] GA Amsterdam vroed. res. vol. xvi, fos. 1r–1v; De Boer, *Friedensunterhandlungen*, 104.
[15] GA Rotterdam vroed. res. 9 June 1633.

means to achieve peace.[16] But with no less vigour, Haarlem and Leiden mobilized their side to bring the peace process finally to a halt. As before, Gouda, Hoorn, and Enkhuizen wished the war to continue beyond Europe;[17] for these towns, the question of the colonial companies' future was clearly paramount. To command a majority in their province, Amsterdam, Rotterdam, and Dordrecht had to settle for harder terms than they themselves were inclined to for there was no chance of persuading even all the moderate towns to accept withdrawal from Brazil.[18] Once again, the result was deadlock with no further concessions being offered to Spain but with agreement (opposed by Haarlem) that the talks should not yet be broken off. The States General finally resolved, on 7 July, by four provinces to three, and amid mounting acrimony, to continue negotiations for the time being.[19] But it was clear that at this juncture the basic deadlock in the Republic was unbreakable.

[16] GA Dordrecht vroed. res. 6 June 1633.
[17] Gouda vroed res. 7 June 1633; AWG Hoorn vroed. res. 13, 29 June 1633.
[18] Res. Holl. 1, 9, 10 June 1633.
[19] Ibid., 7, 8 July, 1633.

Chapter V

Stalemate, 1634–1640

i AN AGEING LAND WAR

During 1634 the balance of power in the Netherlands shifted back, after eight years of clear Dutch supremacy, far enough in favour of Spain to result in total military deadlock. Frederik Hendrik was greatly delayed in 1634 in taking the field owing to the reluctance of Holland to vote the extra funds needed[1] and a serious outbreak of unrest at Leeuwarden which necessitated the sending of troops to Friesland to help restore order.[2] Through assiduous endeavour and an improved provision from Spain, Aytona succeeded in fielding an army of 30,000, including three Castilian *tercios*.[3] In late June Aytona suddenly marched on Maastricht, first recapturing the outlying fortresses of Leut and Argenteau and then besieging the city itself. Meanwhile Jan van Nassau was dispatched with a secondary force to attempt a surprise night-attack on Rheinberg, from Geldern; the Spaniards succeeded in scaling the walls of 'the whore' and would probably have taken the town had not heavy rain ruined their powder and led to the assault being called off. With its field army now too weak to risk a direct attack on Aytona, the States General assumed responsibility for saving Maastricht, directing the prince, by secret resolution of late August, to try to dislodge Aytona by besieging Breda, the garrison of which was then down to about 2,000 men.[4] Should the Spaniards then choose to persevere at Maastricht, at least Breda would probably fall first. Frederik Hendrik descended upon Breda with just 15,000 men. As the Dutch had hoped, Aytona at once raised the siege of Maastricht and marched on Breda. As States General

---

[1] Res. Holl. 14, 20 July 1634.   [2] See pp. 303–4 below.
[3] Aitzema, *His.* iii (ii). 557.
[4] Sec. Res. SG 28 Aug. 1634. ARH SG 4563.

and prince had previously agreed must be done in this eventuality,[5] the Dutch promptly withdrew, after just two days of trench-digging, 'assez desplaisants', according to Huygens, 'de n'avoir peu caresser ceste belle maistresse à nostre aise'. Both the Stadholder and Aytona displayed consummate skill.

The arrival in the Netherlands in late 1634 of the Cardinal-Infante, Ferdinand, accompanied by 11,000 Spanish and Italian troops with whom he had marched from Italy and, jointly with the Emperor's forces, crushed the Swedes at Nördlingen, heralded what would have been a major and prolonged Spanish offensive to retake the initiative in the Low Countries had not France, a few months later, in May 1635, declared war on Spain and the Empire. Even so, as is shown by Table 7, the effort by Spain in the next five years was by far the most massive in terms of outlay and manpower of the entire Dutch–Spanish war. This formidable build-up was made possible by the extremely high level of financial provision from Spain and Italy maintained during the years 1634–40 resulting from the Conde-Duque's determined fiscal drive of these years launched throughout the empire. Although in the end much of this strength had to be expended defending the south and west of the Spanish Netherlands from the French, it is nevertheless true that the original, and to some extent the continuing, primary purpose of the endeavour was to throw the Dutch off balance and inflict on them enough local defeats to produce a truce on terms satisfactory to Philip IV. To modern minds the position of the Spanish Netherlands wedged between France and the Republic appears quite hopeless, but in terms of the realities of the early seventeenth century when the defences of this area were still much superior to those of France itself, it was plausible that Philip and Olivares could reckon on holding the French at arm's length with only a modicum of effort, especially with some Imperial aid while exerting real pressure on the Dutch. The essence of the Spanish strategy was to hit the Dutch principally in the Rhine and Maas valleys to recover the strategic crossing-points which had been lost.[6] In this

[5] *Briefwiss. Huygens* ii. 16–17; Aitzema, *Hist.* iii (ii). 549; Vincart, *Relations Militaires*, 63.

[6] Consulta, 'Junta particular', 22 Feb. 1635. AGS Estado 2050; Ferdinand to Philip, 18 Mar. 1635. ARB SEG 212, fo. 269.

way, maximum use could be made by Spain of the sporadic Imperial assistance available, the sense of security that the Dutch had achieved be severely shaken, and bargaining counters acquired with which to induce the Dutch to relinquish Pernambuco.

The Cardinal-Infante's attempt to strike a swift initial blow at the Dutch before the Dutch and French armies could combine against him, and whilst the Stadholder's demands for extra troops and money were being obstructed by Holland,[7] failed dismally. The Spanish troops badly bungled an attack on Philippine. While Ferdinand blamed subordinates, the Papal nuncio blamed the Cardinal-Infante himself for having gone hunting whilst prayers for the success of the operation were being recited in the churches.[8] With a French army of 30,000 sweeping into the country through Luxemburg, Ferdinand next sent 15,000 men under his second-in-command, Prince Thomas of Savoy to block their path. The Spaniards were caught in the open and routed with the loss of 4,000 men, both the governors of Ostend and Antwerp, Alonso Ladrón and the Conde de Feria respectively, being captured. During the first week of June 1635 the French and Dutch armies simultaneously crossed the Maas, either side of Maastricht, and advanced jointly towards Brussels, approaching Tienen with 60,000 men, one of the largest field armies ever seen in Europe. Tienen fell after a brief resistance and was brutally pillaged, the Dutch and especially the French commanders losing control of their men who, reportedly, committed numerous rapes, something virtually unheard of in the Low Countries wars since 1621. But unintentionally, by their sacking of Tienen, the invaders markedly enhanced the willingness of the populace to co-operate with the Spaniards. The strategy of the invasion was largely determined by the relatively inexperienced French commanders. Frederik Hendrik evidently saw little point in besieging Leuven as it was surrounded by fortified towns and could not subsequently be held;[9] however, the French insisted.

[7] Res. Holl. 14 Feb. 26, 28 Apr., 2 and 5 May 1635.
[8] *Corresp. Stravius*, 65.
[9] Aitzema, *Hist.* iv (i). 207.

During the third week in June Franco-Dutch forces occupied Diest, Aerschot, and Tervuren and then encircled
Leuven where Ferdinand had left 4,000 Irish and Walloon
troops under Grabendonk before retiring on Brussels. However, despite appearances, the massive invading army was by
now the more vulnerable, owing to mounting difficulty in
procuring provisions, continuing disorder among the French,
and the arrival across the Rhine of an Imperial army under
Piccolomini.[10] With some reluctance, the French eventually
agreed to abandon the siege of Leuven and on 4 July there
began a head-long retreat north-eastwards towards Weert. A
garrison was left at Diest to impede pursuit, though the town
was soon captured by Aytona in his last success before his
sudden death, in August, which was universally recognized as
a great loss to a Monarchy in dire need of all the political and
military talent it could muster. To justify the immense but so
far sterile invasion, Frederik Hendrik, who now assumed
charge of the joint Franco-Dutch forces, marched on Geldern,
a long-standing Dutch objective; but at this point, the whole
Low Countries were suddenly astounded by the news of the
successful night attack, on 26 July, by 1,300 troops from
Geldern, on the great Dutch fortress at Schenkenschans, on
the Gelderland-Cleves border.[11] As the Spanish public were
soon informed, this invincible fortress 'the key to Holland',
where both Maurits and Frederik Hendrik had regularly
martialled their armies before taking the field, dominated the
strategic fork where the Rhine divided into Rhine and Waal.
Besides commanding a major trade route, the fortress yielded
direct access to the heartland of the Dutch state. Powerful
shock waves spread through the Republic.[12] The prince at
once departed Geldern for Schenkenschans.

Frederik Hendrik dared not risk a battle, though the States
of Gelderland evidently urged him to, or try to blockade
Schenkenschans from all sides,[13] for the Cardinal-Infante
who was now the stronger, with 40,000 men, had already
crossed the Maas at Stevensweert, occupied Erkelens and

[10] Ferdinand to Philip, 11 July 1635. ARB SEG 213, fo. 1.
[11] Ibid., fo. 54ᵛ; Luna y Mora, 398; *Mémoires*, 196; Aitzema, *Hist.* iv (i). 207.
[12] Lois, *Cronijcke*, 138; *Breve y verdadera relacion*, 1–4.
[13] *Brieven Reigersberch*, 195; Wagenaar xi. 205.

Stralen, and was advancing rapidly, while the French force was decimated by desertions and epidemic. To begin with, the Dutch were content to seal off Schenkenschans to the north and west, enabling Ferdinand to reinforce the fortress and to erect a connecting fortress, Fort Ferdinandus, between Schenkenschans and Cleves.[14] At the same time Spanish and Imperialist troops occupied Cleves, Goch, and other neighbouring towns. Requiring a secure passage between Cleves and Spanish Brabant, Ferdinand also subsequently heavily fortified the stronghold of Gennep where he stationed 1,500 men under the Irish colonel, Preston. During October 1635 a subsidiary Spanish column stormed the town of Limburg. To secure the passage to Cleves, cutting off the Dutch garrisons at Venlo and Maastricht, the Spaniards next needed to strengthen their hold on the Meierij and especially to fortify Helmond and Eindhoven. Indeed this strategic theme dominated Olivares's hard-worked mind during the winter of 1635–6 when he and the king repeatedly urged Ferdinand to hasten the work, assuring him that he could win no greater glory were he to take Paris or The Hague than in securing Schenkenschans.[15] 'So that from there,' in Philip's words, 'we can make war in the heart of Holland, and I hope that if it happens thus, with this fort and, as you say, clearing the Maas valley, they will have to make peace or a truce as we would wish.'[16] 'The opinion of all the soldiers here', asserted the Conde-Duque, 'is that the conservation [of Schenkenschans and the passage to the Veluwe] matters more than that of Antwerp; this they feel emphatically, Leganes and Felipe de Silva adding that it matters more even than Antwerp and Brasil together.[17]

Originally, the strategy envisaged for 1636, in both Madrid and Brussels was *guerra defensiva* against France and again *offensiva* against the Dutch. Olivares in fact wanted Ferdinand to occupy positions beyond Schenkenschans, in the Veluwe and 'Overisse', both to secure the stronghold and widen the

[14] Ferdinand to Philip, 20 Aug. and 11 Oct. 1635. ARB SEG 213, fos. 89, 166.
[15] Philip to Ferdinand, 11 Dec. 1635. ARB SEG 213, fo. 396; 'voto del conde duque', 16 Nov. 1635. AGS Estado 2153.
[16] Philip to Ferdinand, 25 Oct. 1635. BL MS. Add. 14007, fo. 53.
[17] Olivares to Ferdinand, 14 Mar. 1636. BSB cod. hisp. 22, fos. 10–12.

gap in the Dutch defences. Ferdinand was still giving priority to the Dutch front as late as May 1636, planning to invade Dutch territory through Cleves.[18] Even if Schenkenschans were to fall, and as early as October 1635 Ferdinand personally had doubted whether it could be held,[19] he would have penetrated Gelderland, provided the Emperor did as he was proposing in the way of invading French territory, through Alsace. Partly because the Emperor's enterprise failed to materialize, and partly due to the rapid Dutch advances in Cleves, Ferdinand finally abandoned his offensive. On 16 March Dutch troops had captured Griethausen from the Imperialists and shortly after had occupied the town of Cleves as well as Fort Ferdinandus. Jan van Nassau and Piccolomini had advanced with 16,000 Spanish-Imperial troops trying to reopen the route to Schenkenschans but were forced to withdraw owing to critical shortage of provisions. By all accounts, the territory of Cleves was by now stripped bare whilst the renewed Dutch river blockade was highly effective.[20] Schenkenschans itself was subjected to an unremitting bombardment from the Rhine banks and the navy's river gunships as was eloquently depicted in a painting by Gerrit van Santen which hangs today in the Rijksmuseum. Battered beyond endurance, on 30 April 1636 the 600 survivors of the original garrison of 1,500 surrendered to Count Willem van Nassau. On the news, there were heart-felt thanksgiving services and celebrations throughout the Republic while at Madrid, at the loss of the 'finest jewel that the king had possessed in those states with which to accommodate his affairs', this 'great blow for all Spain' in his own words, the Conde-Duque flew into one of the most desperate rages and bouts of distress of his entire career.[21]

The States General had poured men and money in such profusion into its counter-offensive of the spring of 1636 that all available funds for the rest of the year were now exhausted.[22] The Dutch had no alternative but to keep to

[18] Ferdinand to Philip, 26 May 1636. ARB SEG 214, fos. 449–461[V].
[19] Ferdinand to Philip, 11 Oct. 1635. ARB SEG 213, fo. 166.
[20] Res. SG 19 Feb. 1636. ARH SG 3195, fo. 121; *Brieven Reigersberch*, 271.
[21] Olivares to Ferdinand 25 May 1636. BSB cod. hisp. 22; 'Voto del conde-duque', 17 June 1636. AGS Estado 2051.
[22] Wagenaar xi. 235.

the defensive, despite repeated urging by Louis XIII that they should take the field. At the last moment, the Cardinal-Infante had resolved to invade France, rather than the Republic, being fearful of leaving the French free to invade Italy which lay temptingly open, knowing through Roose's intelligence services that the Dutch were for the moment unable to attack him in the rear.[23] In a famous episode, the Spaniards swiftly penetrated as far as Corbie, spreading panic throughout northern France. To ease the pressure on the French, Frederik Hendrik belatedly took the field, in September, with a mere 13,000 men, remaining inactive, at Langstraat, content with compelling the Spaniards to detach part of their army, under Feria, to encamp opposite him, around Mol.

Strategy was again intensively discussed during the early months of 1637 at The Hague just as at Madrid and Brussels. The marked slackening in the Dutch war-effort discernible since 1634 continued over the winter of 1636-7 with Holland insisting on reductions in troop levels which considerably diminished the means at the Stadholder's disposal: the additional companies raised in 1629 and subsequently were now dissolved while the fifty companies added in 1628 were reduced, by one-fifth of their strength, to 120 men each.[24] On the other hand, much assisted by the French pressure on the Spaniards, the prince could safely thin down his more northerly garrisons and concentrate enough troops to secure further gains, even though he had no choice but to field armies considerably smaller than he had commanded during the 1629-33 period. Certainly, there were sanguine expectations in The Hague during the spring of 1637 when Geldern, Breda, Antwerp, Hulst, and Dunkirk were all seriously considered as possible targets.[25] With lavish promises of French help, the prince eventually determined to attempt Dunkirk in a combined operation with the fleet. In May the army was concentrated at Rammekens to await a favourable wind. Meanwhile at Madrid and Brussels, despite the danger of

---

[23] Vincart, *Camapaña de 1636*, 81-2; Delplanche, 100.
[24] Res. Holl. 15, 16, 21 Dec. 1636.
[25] *Mémoires*, 200-2.

French incursions into Italy and Spain, and whilst it was plainly easier to invade the exposed north-east of France than to penetrate Dutch territory, most ministers continued to prefer concentrating against the Dutch: if the Republic were to be detached from its French alliance, if there was to be an acceptable truce, it was essential to allow the Dutch no respite from the pressures of the long war and to extract additional bargaining counters with which to bring the Dutch to terms.[26] Ferdinand himself decidedly preferred *guerra offensiva* against the Dutch. Olivares believed that the army would be forced to concentrate against the French, as in 1636, though in the event, when the opportunity arose, he too backed the policy of attacking the Dutch.

After three weeks of being held up at Rammekens by contrary winds, the prince abandoned his attack on Dunkirk and switched his attention to Breda. Having disembarked at Bergen-op-Zoom, the prince marched on the town with 18,000 men which were soon supplemented with some 5,000 South Holland villagers to assist with the digging. Ferdinand, his troops scattered across Flanders and Artois, reacted too slowly to prevent Frederik Hendrik from completing his fortifications.[27] After spending two weeks ineffectually, close to the Dutch lines, encamped with 17,000 men, the Cardinal-Infante marched eastwards on Venlo. The States General had spent a good deal strengthening its fortifications and the town was now garrisoned by 1,200 men;[28] nevertheless, in three days of bombardment, Ferdinand set fire to much of the town, provoked uproar among its inhabitants, and forced the surrender of the garrison. Roermond surrendered a week later after a similar battering. Ferdinand and his officers next deliberated whether to besiege Grave or Nijmegen or turn south to face the invading French. They opted for the latter course. Olivares, however, subsequently criticized the Cardinal-Infante for not having disregarded the French threat and continued his thrust into Dutch territory.[29]

[26] Consultas 8, 25, and 26 Feb. 1637. AGS Estado 2051.
[27] Consulta, Junta de Estado, 7 Mar. 1638. AGS Estado 2053; Aitzema, *Hist.* iv (i). 542.
[28] *Mémoires*, 209.
[29] 'Voto del conde duque', 7 Oct. 1637. AGS Estado 2051.

Frederik Hendrik meanwhile reduced Breda in his habitually methodical manner, clearing the town's outer defences, working gradually towards the walls, mining systematically when this became possible and saturating walls and town with cannon and mortar fire. When Breda eventually capitulated, on 7 October, only 1,600 of the original 3,500 man garrison survived, while Dutch losses totalled 850 killed and 1,300 wounded. According to the official tally, the Dutch batteries fired a total of 23,130 canon balls at the town without counting mortar grenades and 'fire-balls'.[30] The news inspired the usual celebrations in the Republic, including a good deal of drinking among the garrisons. Ferdinand chose this moment to order another surprise attack on Rheinberg, this time from Geldern, Venlo, and Roermond, hoping to find the town's defenders 'sumno vinoque sepulti'.[31] The attackers again managed to scale the walls, and held one gate for two hours such that Rheinberg would assuredly have fallen had supporting troops arrived in time.

During the winter of 1637–8, Spanish ministers were once again inclined to expend their main effort on the Dutch rather than the French front. There were plans to hasten the fortification of Helmond and Eindhoven and resume the blockade of Maastricht as well as renewed talk of accosting Rheinberg.[32] To finance these ambitions, Philip and Olivares were preparing to spend 4,774,000 ducats in the Netherlands during 1638 and maintain 80,000 troops. To bolster the Spaniards, Imperial troops under Piccolomini wintered in Jülich, Cleves, and the Aachen area. The scale of the French preparations during the spring of 1638 eventually led to a reluctant change of priorities: in March 1638 the *Consejo* agreed that, despite the overriding need to exert pressure on the Dutch, the main thrust would have to be directed against the French, to save Italy or Spain from a major invasion.[33] Meanwhile, on the Dutch side, prince and States General deliberated whether to strike at Hulst, Damme,

[30] Aitzema, *Hist.* iv, 582.
[31] *Brieven Reigersberch*, 403; Vincart, *Campaña de 1637*, 66.
[32] ARB SEG 217, fos. 353ᵛ, 452.
[33] Consulta, Junta de Estado, 7 Mar. 1638. AGS Estado 2053.

or Antwerp. Frederik Hendrik, apparently, was at this stage keen to attack the first of these and reluctant to tackle the last. It was pressure from the States General that led him to switch to an attack on Antwerp.[34] Amsterdam had suffered one defeat after another in her attempts to influence Dutch strategic and foreign policy during the mid 1630s and with this decision to attack Antwerp, her opponents in the States of Holland and States General once again firmly steered the state on a course which ran flatly against the interests of the Republic's greatest city.

In June 1638 the Stadholder massed his army at Voorne and sent 6,000 Scots, German, and Dutch troops ahead, under Count Willem, to seize Kallo and two other key forts on the left bank of the Schelde below Antwerp. The Spaniards, under the new governor of Antwerp, Felipe de Silva, reacted vigorously and, after several days fighting, forced their way through the dykes, around the Dutch positions, overwhelming their enemy in a bloody and confused night-long battle. For the loss of 284 killed and 822 wounded, the Spaniards shattered the Dutch force at Kallo, killing hundreds, taking 2,500 prisoners, including two colonels and numerous sailors, as well as eighty-one river craft and dozens of guns.[35] 'The greatest victory that Your Majesty's arms have had since the Netherlands war began' was how Ferdinand styled this success and, certainly, 'ce grand désastre', as van Aerssen called it, the only pitched battle of the entire war, was a stinging setback for the Dutch which severely curtailed Frederik Hendrik's efforts in 1638. The position of the allies in the Low Countries was further weakened, in July, when the Spaniards defeated the French, at St. Omer, and in subsequent weeks with the halting of the French invasion of the Spanish Basque country, at Fuenterrabia. In an effort to recoup prestige, in mid August, Frederik Hendrik marched across Brabant and descended upon Geldern, with 16,000 men, rapidly encircling the town with his entrenchments. But again fortune favoured the Cardinal-Infante who, with the

---

[34] *Mémoires*, 222-3.

[35] ARB SEG 219, fos. 254^V-55^V; Aitzema iv (ii), 35; *Breve y Ajustada Relacion*, fo. 5^V; *Efetos de las Armas Españolas*, fos. 6-8.

help of near-by Imperialist forces, concentrated enough strength to attack the besiegers head on, forcing the Dutch into a disorderly and humiliating withdrawal which cost them 1,000 men.[36] During September, Frederik Hendrik, chastened by two serious setbacks in one season, encamped without venturing anything further, near Grave. All considered, the year 1638 was one on which Philip and Olivares had every reason to congratulate themselves.

Throughout 1638 the Conde-Duque had insisted that the overriding aim of Spanish arms, by land and sea, in the Low Countries, was to achieve 'buenos sucesos contra holandeses', this being, as he saw it, the only feasible way to achieve an acceptable truce.[37] The reckoning with the French was to be put off in effect until after the Dutch war was ended. It is in this context that the historian must place the great Spanish naval offensive of 1639 against the Dutch, the climax of the prolonged effort to shift the balance in the Netherlands which had begun in 1634, and a most remarkable deployment of scarce resources, at a time when Spain was at war with its arch-enemy, France. On land, however, wedged tightly between the French and Dutch, the Spaniards were unable to undertake a new initiative during 1639. It was quite otherwise, though, with the Dutch who still had four or five major objectives in the land war.[38] As has been seen, the aspirations of Zeeland lay chiefly in Flanders where the conquest of such densely populated, heavily fortified, and economically highly developed districts as Hulst, Brugge, Damme, Sas van Gent, and Ghent would handsomely add to the security, vitality, and influence of Zeeland. Despite the coolness of the Holland maritime towns and lukewarmness of the Stadholder, many inland towns were also eager to acquire Antwerp which they doubtless envisaged as a jewel with which to offset the preponderance of Amsterdam. In the east the most important remaining objective, especially for Gelderland, was the Overkwartier (Geldern) which it was intended to reincorporate into the province of Gelderland despite the overwhelmingly

---

[36] *Famosa vitoria que ha tenido el señor Infante Cardenal,* pp. 1-4; Nettesheim, 214-15.

[37] Consulta 11 May 1638, and undated, Oct. 1638. AGS Estado 2053.

[38] *Mémoires,* 229-30; Wagenaar xi. 89 (notes).

Catholic character of the district. Additionally, there was a widespread desire to retake Venlo and Roermond so as to connect Maastricht once more with the rest of Dutch territory, as well as to enforce the Republic's claim to the Meierij, by seizing Helmond and Eindhoven.

However, during the winter of 1638-9 the Dutch were increasingly apprehensive lest the Emperor's forces might again begin playing a more active role in the Low Countries, as Piccolomini's troops successively occupied Cleves, Goch, Xanten, Kranenburg, and other towns on the eastern Dutch border.[39] During the spring, Frederik Hendrik was planning to devote the summer campaign to the capture of the heavily defended fortress town of Hulst, in Flanders, and in June he duly disembarked his army at Philippine while leaving a second force in the east, to cover the Maas and Rhine. The crushing defeat of the French at Thionville, by Piccolomini and the duke of Lorraine, however, persuaded both Stadholder and States General that the situation was too dangerous to permit involvement in a major siege in Flanders. The Dutch forces concentrated at Philippine from where they could both draw off some of the Spanish pressure on the French besieging Hesdin and remain in readiness to ascend swiftly to the Maas or Rhine. After the fall of Hesdin, Frederik Hendrik sailed to Bergen-op-Zoom and from there, in nine days during early August, marched across Brabant to Rheinberg. But with the French now inactive and formidable Imperial as well as Spanish forces close by, the prince decided that it would be useless attempting to besiege Geldern.[40] In early September the Dutch army sailed from Rheinberg back to Flanders and encamped near Hulst. It was from here, with his attention fastened on the great conflict unfolding in the Channel, that the prince issued his secret instructions to Tromp to disregard Charles I's objections should the chance arise to destroy Oquendo's *armada* in English waters where the Spaniards had sought refuge.

In the next year, 1640, the twentieth of the war, Frederik Hendrik took the field early, disembarking at Philippine on

---

[39] *Brieven Reigersberch*, 511, 514, 526.
[40] *Mémoires*, 252-4; *Briefwiss. Huygens* ii. 461-2.

17 May. With the French now besieging Arras and the Cardinal-Infante's army tied down in Artois, circumstances favoured a Dutch break-through in Flanders and the prince's inclination was to attempt Brugge.[41] So as to encircle the town, part of the army, under Count Hendrik Casimir the young Stadholder of Friesland, endeavoured to cross the Brugge–Ghent canal at Fort Steenschans, but after a sporadic twelve-hour action, on 21 May, was repulsed by the defending Spanish forces. The prince's design on Brugge now appeared hopeless, as, in Huygens's words, all the defences in the area were 'occupez, guettez et gardez à merveille'. The prince therefore advanced northwards from Maldegem towards Sluis, hoping to take St. Donaes, and the other Spanish forts facing Sluis, from the rear. Again, the Dutch forces found their path blocked.[42] In late June the prince suddenly advanced via Philippine on Hulst, but, despite the swift capture of a key fort, he was unable to take other positions without which the town could not be encircled. In a skirmish on a redoubt near Hulst during the night of 3 July, Hendrik Casimir, Stadholder of Friesland, received severe wounds from which he died a week later. Abandoning Hulst, the prince sailed to Bergen-op-Zoom and then marched overland, via 's-Hertogenbosch, on Geldern. Here, however, heavy rain had reduced the environs to impassable mire[43] and there seemed no chance of any progress. By early September Holland was once again pressing for early wintering of the army, in order to save money; but, out of courtesy to the French king, the prince persuaded the States General to keep the army in camp, though inactive, for another month.

While Amsterdam had repeatedly failed to sway the States of Holland as a whole, either on the issue of war or peace, or on basic strategy; there remained one question on which most of the province was united in opposing prince and *Raad van State* — that of troop levels and army expenditure. It is for this reason that military spending was the sole area in which the Stadholder found himself constantly at odds with a largely united Holland during the later 1630s. In the autumn

---

[41] *Mémoires*, 261, 264; *Briefwiss. Huygens* iii. 28–9, 31–2, 41.

[42] Aitzema, *Hist.* v (i). 16, 87.

[43] Aitzema, *Hist.* v (i). 89.

of 1640 a major clash occurred in the States General when Holland, except for Leiden and one or two other war towns which disassociated themselves from his policy,[44] urged the dissolution of the fifty companies raised in 1628, on top of the cuts that had already been voted. This trial of strength led in turn to an extensive reappraising of both objectives and strategy.[45] With the Catalan Revolt in progress, but before that of Portugal, Holland, headed by Amsterdam, insisted that the Spanish crown was now so weakened that the army of Flanders was incapable of taking the offensive and that the Dutch army should keep to the defensive likewise, so as to minimize costs. The Stadholder was held to be exaggerating the risk of a combined Spanish–Imperial invasion of the Republic. Retaining more troops than could be paid, Holland argued, was simply a recipe for mutiny. With every additional conquest since 1629, the bill for garrisons and fortifications had been further swollen and was now so immense that maintaining a large field army, as well, was totally out of the question, particularly at a time of increasing losses at sea when more energetic action against the Dunkirkers was required. Holland's answer to the prince's suggestion that taxes should be further increased was that the province did not consider it prudent or feasible to comply. The prince's case, much reinforced in the aftermath of the Portuguese secession, in December, was that the Spanish Monarchy was now visibly on the verge of disintegration and that consequently the opportunity existed for major territorial gains to the honour, benefit and strengthening of the Republic and the further humiliation of Spain. Eventually, a compromise was devised whereby the fifty companies were retained, but no longer paid by the provinces but solely from Generality funds, an arrangement which unavoidably meant reducing resources available for other military expenditure.

ii THE STRUGGLE AT SEA, 1634–1640

During the mid 1630s the pattern of the sea-war changed

---

[44] GA Leiden Sec. Arch. 450, vroed. res. 23 Oct. 1640.
[45] Res. Holl. 10, 13, 30 Oct., 22 Dec. 1640, and 24 Jan., 2 Feb., and 9 Mar. 1641; *Corresp. d'Estrades,* 103.

discernibly as compared with the 1626-32 period when the Dunkirkers had enjoyed the initiative and the Dutch convoys and fishing fleets seemed almost defenceless.[46] After 1632 the forays of the *armada* were less frequent, the damage done by the Dunkirkers significantly less, and the confidence of the Dutch to some extent restored. As the Flemish admiralty authorities acknowledged,[47] the Dutch navy now showed greater skill in protecting the Republic's shipping, even though the overall direction of operations which, until 1638, remained in the hands of Van Dorp, Jaspar Liefhebber, and Hildebrand Quast, continued to be distinctly mediocre. Total receipts of the Flemish admiralty declined to under 1.8 million guilders in 1633-4, as compared with 3.2 million in 1631-2,[48] while Dutch shipping losses in the five years 1633-7 were cut to about half the level of losses of the 1628-32 period.

In 1635 the activity of the Flemish privateers was particularly slack, though this was largely compensated for by a spectacularly successful raid by the *armada* on the herring fleets. The Flemish admiral, Jacques Colaert, set sail with fourteen ships on 14 August, joined six more at sea, and, on 17 August, encountered the Enkhuizen herring fleet, 160 busses, *en route* to the fishing grounds. The fleet was accompanied by only one warship which was swiftly put to flight. In all, Colaert caught and sank eighty-five busses, taking the crews prisoner.[49] The tradition of civilized restraint towards Dutch fishermen made prisoner, which had prevailed since 1625, and in which Rubens for one took much pride,[50] was maintained in exemplary fashion. Three days later, Colaert intercepted the Maas herring fleet, scattering its escort and disposing of twenty more busses.[51] After a brief encounter with a poorly led Dutch force of twenty-two warships, under Quast, the raiders reached Dunkirk totally unscathed, carrying

[46] Malo i. 333-4.
[47] ARB SEG 213, fo. 114; Stradling, *Spanish Dunkirkers*, 547, 549-50.
[48] Baetens, 'Flemish Privateering', 62.
[49] Enkhuizen to SG, 22 Sept. 1635. ARH SG 5515, ii; ARH Bisdom 62, fos. 190-1; Luna y Mora, 401; *Mem. Hist. Esp.* xiii. 247-8; Centen, 76-7; De Boer, 'Nogmaals', 339-40.
[50] *Letters, Rubens*, 69, 128.
[51] Res. SG 5 Sept. 1635. ARH SG 3194, fo. 443.

975 captured fishermen and having dealt the Dutch herring industry some 2 million guilders' worth of damage. The loss of shipping amounted to over 8,000 tons. The news provoked uproar in Holland. At Enkhuizen, where virtually every inhabitant suffered financial loss, the populace rioted against the navy, throwing two naval captains into the sea and ransacking the house of Admiral Quast.[52] There were also lesser disturbances at Rotterdam and Goes. Colaert conducted a second impressive sweep, in October, when he captured a variety of prizes including the ship and person of Cornelis Corneliszoon Jol, one of the West India Company's most remarkable commanders who, having safely braved every danger in the Caribbean, was then *en route* for Holland: Jol's famous ship, the *Otter*, was towed into Dunkirk on 2 October, and Jol himself imprisoned with many another Dutch sailor at St. Winoxbergen. In the aftermath of Colaert's raids, the Dutch navy was for several months in a state of complete disarray. In mid November, the pensionary of Rotterdam complained that a merchant convoy for Nantes and Bordeaux had by then been held up, waiting for their naval escort, at Rotterdam, for no less than fourteen weeks.[53]

The States General did at least have the satisfaction of prompt revenge on Colaert. In February 1636 commanding three royal warships, the Flemish admiral was encountered off Dieppe by a Zeeland squadron under Jan Evertsen. In the ensuing five-hour battle forty-eight Dutch sailors were killed, but two of the king's ships were sunk and 200 Flemings, including Colaert, pulled from the sea.[54] For the Dutch the year was also a relatively good one with respect to shipping losses which were the lowest recorded since 1625, though assuredly still far from negligible. In September, however, the States General had less cause for satisfaction when the Spaniards successfully accomplished their largest troopferrying operation from Corunna thus far. Thirty-eight ships,

[52] *Brieven Reigersberch*, 203-4, 207-8; Centen, 77; Faulconnier, 139; De Boer, 'Nogmaals', 341.

[53] Res. SG 15 Nov. 1635. ARH SG 3194, fo. 537.

[54] At. Middelburg to SG, 26 Feb. 1636. ARH SG 5516, i; *Brieven Reigersberch*, 250-1.

[55] Vincart, *Campaña de 1636*, 60-1; Alcalá-Zamora, 390.

consisting of the *armada* and transports, slipped past Van Dorp's blockade fleet and into Dunkirk, by night, carrying 4,000 Spanish infantry and 1½ million ducats in silver.[55]

Although during 1637 Dutch shipping losses declined still further, they remained substantial and, in fact, the Spaniards achieved some noteworthy feats. In May 1637 there was a two-day battle in the Mediterranean when twenty galleys from Naples and Sicily fought ten becalmed *straatvaerders* off the coast of Corsica. Nine of this Genoa-bound convoy were captured together with their cargoes of grain.[56] In July the Flanders *armada*, now commanded by the Navarrese, Miguel de Horna, sank two Dutch warships and captured, in the Channel, an entire convoy of twelve vessels bearing munitions to France. Also in July thirteen Dunkirkers again attacked the herring grounds, sinking another warship and at least thirty-six *buizen*.[57] Finally, in December, assisted by exceptionally favourable winds, the *armada* shipped 5,000 Castilian infantry from Corunna to Dunkirk in only five days.[58] However, in late 1637 the Dutch navy at last acquired commanders worthy of its calibre when Van Dorp and Liefhebber were replaced respectively as lieutenant-admiral and vice-admiral of Holland by the less select socially but immeasurably more competent Tromp and Witte de With. Amsterdam was reportedly as pleased with this news as with that of the simultaneous capitulation of Breda to the Stadholder: share prices leapt.[59]

Tromp succeeded in rendering the 1638 blockade of the Flemish coast somewhat more effective than those of previous years, at least as regards shutting the Dunkirkers in, despite a setback during the spring when two separate Dutch merchant convoys, returning from western France, were attacked at the mouth of the Channel resulting in the sinking of two Dutch warships and capture of twenty-six merchantmen. In all, the number of Dutch vessels lost to the Dunkirkers in 1638 was possibly as low as forty-eight.[60] In its

[55] Vincart, *Campaña de 1636*, 60–1; Alcalá-Zamora, 390.
[56] Fernández Duro iv. 162.
[57] ARH Bisdom 64, pp. 236–7; *Mem. Hist. Esp.* xiv. 201–2.
[58] Boxer, *The Journal*, 3; Alcalá-Zamora, 390–1.
[59] Briefwiss. Huygens ii. 328.
[60] *Col. Nav.* vii. 1–5; Malo i. 346.

economic aspect, however, the Dutch blockade of the Flemish coast undoubtedly deteriorated at this time.[61] Unable, since May 1635, to use Calais as an entrepôt for English re-exports destined for Dunkirk, the English were now becoming increasingly restless at the Dutch ban on direct trade between the English and Flemish ports. By 1638 Charles I's increasingly pro-Spanish policy included the escorting by the English navy of convoys of English shipping from Dover to the Flemish ports and with these Tromp was forbidden by the States General to interfere. Besides munitions, large amounts of Spanish wool and French wine reached Flanders from Dover in this way.

The year 1639 marked the end of Philip IV's sustained drive of the 1634–9 period to force the Dutch to what he regarded as acceptable terms, with the most shattering defeat suffered by Spain at sea since 1588. The year began auspiciously for the Dutch when a fleet of twenty-seven ships attempted to depart Dunkirk on 18 February, bearing 2,000 Walloon infantry for the Spanish Pyrennean front. After a fierce battle in which both sides suffered heavy damage, Tromp's fire forced the fleet back into port with the loss of three vessels;[62] for this success, the admiral was received by the States General and presented with a gold chain, though in fact the Dunkirkers effected their departure unmolested only a few days later. During the spring it became clear that the huge *armada* being prepared in Galicia represented far more than the now familiar Spanish troop-ferrying operation to Flanders. Spain, seemingly, was about to challenge Dutch sea-power in northern Europe in an unprecedented manner. As to some extent in 1637, the States General was now caught in a strategic dilemma at sea. While Holland continually pressed for stronger escorts for the convoys and fishing fleets as well as for a tight blockade of the Flemish coast, the latter had been shown to be almost useless as a means of preventing powerful fleets reaching the Flemish ports from Spain. The Stadholder and inland provinces had argued that the overriding priority should be

---

[61] De Boer, *Het Proefjaar*, 62–3; Res. Coll. Middelburg, 21 June 1638. ARH At. 2461.

[62] De Boer, *Het Proefjaar*, 92–3.

to try to prevent reinforcements reaching the army of Flanders and that to do this Dutch naval strength should be concentrated in the west of the Channel, even if this meant weakening the protection afforded to merchant shipping. Tromp, supported by the prince and inland provinces, insisted on meeting the Spanish *armada* head on and, as early as May concentrated his main strength in the straights between Portland Bill and Cap de la Hague.[63] The shield against the privateers having thus been lowered, it was, paradoxically, in this very year, when the main Spanish naval power was eventually shattered, that the Dunkirkers regained much of the initiative in the wider struggle at sea.[64] In June first an entire Rouen convoy of thirteen Zeelanders was captured by a fleet of eleven privateers, and then a second Zeeland convoy, returning from London, was taken likewise. There were bitter cries of protest from Flushing and Middelburg and, under heavy pressure from the maritime provinces, the States General reluctantly ordered Tromp to abandon his station in the west of the Channel and return to the Flemish coast. For a time the blockade of the Flemish coast was resumed. In September, once there was definite word that the *armada* had sailed, Tromp split what remained of his fleet, after a number of ships had had to return to port for repairs and refitting, leaving De With with ten ships off Dunkirk, while he himself cruised in the Channel with a mere thirteen.

The Spanish *armada* of 1639 numbered roughly 100 ships, including its English and Hanseatic transports.[65] The sixty-eight warships comprised most of the Flemish *armada*, totalling twenty-one vessels, and squadrons from Cadiz, Lisbon, Naples, Galicia, and Vizcaya. The largest ship was the *Santa Teresa*, a 1,200 ton Portuguese galleon carrying sixty guns. Philip's ministers were still debating the exact purpose of this massive show of force as late as July. In the aftermath of the closure of the Rhine route to Spanish forces, following the fall of Breisach in 1638, the objective was to ship an

---

[63] De Boer, *Armada van 1639*, 40-2.
[64] *Breve y Ajustada Relacion*, fo. 6.
[65] De Boer, *Armada van 1639*, 54; Boxer, *The Journal*, 12, 36; Alcalá-Zamora, 429-30, 438.

exceptionally large troop force to Flanders while, at the same time, challenging the Dutch fleet, at a point in the season when usually it was somewhat run down, to a decisive battle for naval supremacy. Antonio de Oquendo who commanded the *armada* had orders to destroy Tromp's fleet, if he had the chance, even if the Dutch sought refuge in an English port and at the risk of an open rupture with England.[66] The decision to sail straight up the Channel rather than around Ireland and Scotland was determined partly by fear of adverse autumn weather in northern seas and partly by the desire positively to seek a head-on clash. In all, the *armada* carried over 20,000 men, more than two-thirds being Spanish and Italian troops.

The *armada* reached the mouth of the Channel on 10 September, and sighted Tromp's fleet, now slightly extended to eighteen sail on the 15th off Beachy Head. The next day, the great battle commenced with a prodigious expending of powder that could be clearly heard from Dover, Calais, and Dunkirk. Tromp repeatedly cut across the front of the *armada* in line formation, subjecting it section by section to local Dutch superiority of fire-power. However, the north-westerly wind favoured the Spaniards, blowing the two fleets, the Dutch first, inexorably towards the Somme estuary. Tromp in fact was trapped and would probably have been swept to destruction on the French coast had not Oquendo disengaged at totally the wrong moment. The next day, after a change in wind direction, the firing resumed though with less ferocity as the two fleets drifted back northwards towards the English coast. Tromp, his strength increased to nearly thirty sail, renewed his attack in line formation, off Folkestone, raking the disorderly Spanish mass front and rear. Eventually, compelled to disengage to replenish his exhausted powder stocks, the Dutch fleet drifted into Calais while the *armada*, its supplies likewise depleted, sought English protection and provisions at the Downs. Tromp returned swiftly to the scene, however, and blockaded the Spaniards for over a month whilst the Dutch admiralty colleges spent every available penny in fitting out every

[66] Alcalá-Zamora, 425–6.

available ship. The rapid build-up that followed was by any reckoning a most impressive demonstration of the young Republic's power and resources:[67] within two to three weeks, Tromp had ninety-six warships manned by 9,784 seamen and troops off the English coast. The position for the Spaniards looked increasingly desperate. There was intense diplomatic activity in London. Charles again warned the Dutch not to affront him in 'his own chamber' by attacking, though in fact Tromp now received secret instructions from States General and Stadholder to disregard English objections, should the chance arise to liquidate the Spanish fleet. Finally, on 21 October, the Dutch suddenly swept in, firing salvo upon salvo. Most of what remained of the *armada* (many of the Dunkirkers had succeeded in escaping) was beached and then destroyed by the Dutch without resistance being offered. The bulk of the troops escaped ashore and were subsequently shipped to Flanders, by the English. The defeat was overwhelming: of the original forty-seven Spanish, Portuguese, and Neapolitan warships, some two-thirds had been destroyed.[68]

Spain's sea-power was now shattered, except at Dunkirk, and the Dutch had incontestably won one of the great victories of the age. Yet this famous battle had a most surprising result on the course of the conflict in the North Sea and Channel. The finances of the Dutch admiralty colleges were totally exhausted by the vast effort of 1639. Lack of pay in turn exacerbated the increasing shortage of seamen from which the Dutch navy suffered and increased the seepage of sailors to Flanders to serve with the privateers who were able to pay better.[69] Early in March 1640 Tromp advised the States of Holland that while twenty Dunkirk fregates were already at sea, and seven or eight more ready to follow, such were the shortages of men and finance that the annual blockade of the Flemish coast would have to be delayed.[70] In the end, so bad was the position that the States General, despite pressure from Holland, decided not to impose a

[67] Res. At. Middelburg, 7 June 1640. ARH Admiraliteiten 1462; *Mémoires*, 259–60.

[68] *Alcalá-Zamora*, 455–6.

[69] ARH Bisdom 63, fo. 327; Res. Holl. 12 Sept. 1640 and 22 Jan. 1641.

[70] Res. Holl. 6, 13 Mar. 1640.

blockade during 1640 at all.[71] Armada and privateers exploited the opportunity to the full. Business confidence in Holland reached one of its lowest points of the entire war. The Dutch suffered punishing losses. In June, apprehensive on account of its return fleet sailing from the Far East, the East India Company dispatched five warships to the Shetlands to escort the fleet on the last leg of its journey; the squadron was attacked by Dunkirkers flying Dutch flags, two being destroyed and two captured.[72] Holland now arranged for the dispatch of Tromp with twenty-two sail to the Shetlands which somewhat reassured the Company, but left Dutch home waters still more exposed.

The success of the Dunkirkers during 1640, while not cheap, was considerable. On 9 July De With intercepted eleven Dunkirkers in the Channel, under Miguel de Horna; they had with them two prizes, including a *straatvaarder* belonging to the Rotterdam burgomaster, Coulster. In the fierce battle which followed both sides suffered heavy damage, two of the Dunkirkers being captured. Tromp himself, after returning from the Shetlands, retrieved at least a dozen Dutch ships from the enemy and sank or captured three *coningsschepen* and seven privateers.[73] One privateer was burned under the guns of an English fort near Plymouth, its governor being afterwards mollified with meats and cheeses. But none of this assuaged the anxiety in the Dutch maritime towns and States of Holland and Zeeland. On 16 January 1641 Holland presented the States General with a protest signed by 159 leading Amsterdam merchants, bewailing their exceptional losses during 1640.[74] Thus, paradoxically, the great victory at the Downs actually heralded a period of increasing Dutch losses at sea and savagely high insurance and freight rates.

ii COLONIAL CONFLICT, 1634–1640

By 1634, despite the recent breakdown in truce negotiations

[71] ARH Bisdom 62, fos. 146–7.
[72] De Boer, *Tromp en de Duinkerkers*, 6.
[73] De Boer, *Tromp en de Duinkerkers*, 6.
[74] ARH Bisdom 68, fos. 11–12, 56.

with the Brussels States General, the precariousness of the Dutch colonial companies' schemes for further expansion at Iberian expense was manifest. During its offensive of the early 1620s, the East India Company had made significant headway only in Taiwan; during the years 1626–34 the Company had made scarcely any effort to renew its attacks. The conquest of Pernambuco had certainly enhanced the prestige of the West India Company, but whilst the Dutch forces in north-east Brazil remained tightly wedged in by the joint Portuguese–Spanish forces, there was only the heavy cost of maintaining the foothold without any profit. The companies' vigorous efforts to rally support in Holland during the great political battle of 1633, over the Brussels peace offer, had only served to highlight the deepening uncertainty as to the companies' future. Amsterdam, Rotterdam, and Dordrecht had clearly shown their willingness to sacrifice the companies' prospects for further gains from the Iberians and even to surrender Pernambuco for peace.[75] Similarly Delft, once a pillar of the colonial interest, now unequivocably put peace before the needs of the companies. By 1634 it was starkly obvious that the prolific claims that had been made for years that the Spanish war served the fundamental interests of the Republic better than peace would either have to be speedily substantiated or otherwise become thoroughly discredited.

Everything was rightly seen to hinge on the debate among the Holland towns. 'There are persons in our country,' complained one pamphleteer, in 1636, 'even of standing and quality, who disparage the West India Company and belittle it, such that one listens with wonder and grief; but however wise they account themselves, yet they see no further than their noses reach.'[76] The trade and navigation of a great maritime power such as the Dutch Republic, argued the companies' apologists, would necessarily always be vulnerable to arbitrary interference, embargoes, and other hostile measures on the part of envious and grasping foreign states. Holland's European trade was not merely encountering

[75] See pp. 248–9 above.
[76] *Reden van dat de West-Indische Compagnie* etc. (n. p. 1636),p. 5.

unwelcome hardship at this particular juncture; in fact it was inherently unstable and insecure, inviting interference from every quarter. Colonies and colonies alone could provide Holland's merchants with safe, stable, and enduring commerce.

While the renewed Dutch drive for colonies was evident across the entire globe during the mid and later 1630s, the focal point of the contest came to be centred increasingly in Brazil. For both sides the stakes were immense. The West India Company had in effect risked its entire future prospects and all that remained of its prestige and resources on the venture. Should the failure to break through to profitable colonial exploitation continue much longer, it would become impossible to stave off Amsterdam's efforts to terminate the war. Meanwhile, Philip and Olivares were determined not to make peace without recovering, by force or negotiation, all of Brazil. Since 1630 this had been the first of their war-aims. Despite the massive and continuing draining of resources from Spain and Spanish Italy for the Netherlands, additional large sums and contingents were repeatedly made available for the increasingly bitter struggle in Brazil. Nor were men, money, and commercial prospects the only stakes: the unremitting pressure exerted from Madrid on the Portuguese to provide more for the defence of their own colonies exacted a heavy price in anti-Castilian resentment and political obstruction in Portugal. By 1634 the Lisbon city council was protesting that the realm was totally unable to contribute more being wholly impoverished 'by the subsidies paid to reinforce India and Brazil and because commerce which used to be the principal resource of this realm, has ceased entirely.'[77] Both the fiscal pressure and Castile's interference with Portugal's trade continued unabated until the secession movement began, in December 1640.

The resumed Dutch offensive in the Indies in the end met with an appreciable measure though by no means complete success. In April 1634 the West India Company directors decided, on the basis of what proved to be misleading information, to seize and hold the Caribbean island of Curaçao, 'a suitable place where we can procure salt, hard-wood and

---

[77] Lisbon to Philip, 1 Aug. 1634. *Elem. Hist. Lisb.* iv. 76.

other items and from where we can infest the enemy in the West Indies.'[78] An expedition, consisting of six ships and 400 men, overran the island in July 1634, and began building forts. Though the salt lagoons proved to be useless, the Company and its supporters contrived to secure Holland's agreement to a 264,000-guilder subsidy to help finance the permanent fortification and garrisoning of the island.[79] Only subsequently did it emerge that, so long as the Dutch-Spanish war continued, Curaçao in reality had no commercial possibilities.

In Madrid the loss of Curaçao which was regarded as readily defensible and dangerously close to the main sea-lane between Seville and Panamá, was considered a major set-back. A special *junta de Curaçao* was set up under the chairmanship of Olivares himself to consider ways of recovering the island.[80] Initially, it was hoped to repeat the success achieved at San Martín in 1633 and to land 3,000 men from the 1635 outward-bound *flota* for Panamá. The Conde-Duque, in fierce temper, advocated the systematic slaughter of the Dutch defenders, once defeated, maintaining that the overruning of Curaçao was partly attributable to the excessive leniency shown to the Dutch earlier at San Martín and elsewhere. Though his colleagues strove to dissuade him, pointing out that this would be to invite the Dutch to retaliate in kind with captured Spanish seamen and soldiers, Olivares appears to have remained adamant at least for a time. As it happened, owing to the outbreak of the war with France, and the intensification of the fighting in Brazil, no troops could be spared for Curaçao and the project of reconquest was suspended indefinitely. However, the small Zeelandian colony on the island of Tobago, which had been established in the late 1620s, was eliminated by Spaniards from near-by Venezuela and, almost unique in the history of the Dutch–Spanish conflict in the Caribbean, the defenders were massacred, presumably on orders from Madrid. The news provoked furious anger in the Republic and it was in

[78] Res. Heren XIX, 6 Apr. 1634. *Nederlanders* i. 18–22.

[79] Res. Holl. 19, 23, 27 Feb., 9 Mar. 1635; Wagenaar xi. 246.

[80] Consultas, *Junta de Curaçao*, 22 Jan. and 8 Mar. 1635, in *Ned. Zeevaarders* i. 76–9, 205–10.

retaliation for this atrocity that the Dutch troops stationed at Essequibo, under Aert Gronnewegen, acting on orders from Holland, sacked the township of San Tomé, on the Orinoco estuary and raided Trinidad in 1637.[81] Meanwhile, in 1635 another Zeelandian expedition had successfully seized and colonized the island of St. Eustatius which henceforward was the main Dutch stronghold in the Leeward group. In 1640 the neighbouring island of Saba was colonized from St. Eustatius.

In Brazil the Dutch continued to be confined during 1633–4 to a narrow strip which was useless commercially, though their forces did make some progress in the north, taking the island of Itamaracá in June 1633. Slowly, though, the Company's troops gained the upper hand around Pernambuco also, finding in their colonels, von Schoppe and Arciszewski, German and Polish respectively, brilliant commanders who showed remarkable skill in negotiating the unfamiliar tropical terrain. It was in the year 1635 that the Dutch made their break-through.[82] In January, their forces seized Paraíba. In March a hispano-Neapolitan column, under Bagnuoli, was routed at Porto Calvo. Finally, after a three-month siege the *arraial*, the main Portuguese defensive complex in the Pernambuco region, fell to Arciszewski. With this success, a start could be made at reviving the region's now derelict sugar plantations. But at first progress was slow. In January 1636 an enemy column retook Porto Calvo and, although this force, after advancing further, was defeated by Arciszewski, at Mata Redonda, for more than a year the Iberians were able to launch guerrilla raids from Porto Calvo, ravaging the whole Dutch-occupied zone. To hasten consolidation of Dutch Brazil into a viable, defensible and, above all, profitable colony, the West India Company directors decided to appoint a governor-general for the territory, with virtually full control over the now considerable forces amassed there. The personage selected for this post was the imposing Count Johan Maurits van Nassau-Siegen, cousin of the Stadholder, cultured patron of scholarship and the arts, and a skilful

[81] Kesler, 530-1; Goslinga, 414, 436-7; Menkman, *West-Ind. Comp.* 91.
[82] Boxer, *Dutch in Brazil*, 54, 58-60; Cabral de Mello, 46-7.

soldier who had distinguished himself at the sieges of Maastricht and Schenkenschans.

Shortly after taking up his post, commanding some 4,000 men, Johan Maurits routed the Iberians under Bagnuoli again at Porto Calvo in February 1637. At that stage, he made no attempt to pursue the enemy south of the broad São Francisco river, assuming that the latter would serve as a reliable barrier between Dutch and Portuguese Brazil. During the rest of 1637, he concentrated on improving conditions throughout the subjugated zone and endeavouring to revive the shattered economy. Abandoned sugar mills were auctioned off, various inducements offered, and gradually sugar output began to recover. Freedom of worship was granted to both those Catholics who had opted to remain under Protestant masters and to the Sephardi Jews who soon formed a major element among the territory's small but multifarious population and played a prominent role in both the production of and trade in sugar.[83] There was also some further territorial expansion. In December 1637 Dutch troops occupied the Ceará region of northern Brazil.

By this time it had become fully evident to both the governor-general and the Company directors that the new colony would yield worthwhile profits only if adequately primed with black slaves to work the plantations and mills.[84] Early steps to procure shipments of slaves from the Guinea coast had been taken in 1635. Immediately after his victory at Porto Calvo, Johan Maurits dispatched a powerful expedition from Pernambuco to West Africa which succeeded in August 1637, in capturing the great Portuguese fortress-base at Elmina;[85] almost at once, there was a boost in slave shipments to Dutch Brazil. The other major impediment to the colony's progress was the resurgence of Portuguese raids into the Dutch zone from across the São Francisco river. Only now was it fully appreciated, both in Dutch Brazil and in Holland, that the territory would never be secure until the neighbouring Portuguese base at Bahia was overrun.[86] Despite

[83] Wiznitzer, 128-42.   [84] Boxer, *Dutch in Brazil*, 82-4.
[85] Ibid. 84; De Jonge, *De Oorsprong*, 19.
[86] Barlaeus, 226-7; Perez de Tudela, 24-5, 63.

the lack of promised reinforcements from home, the Count prepared his fateful attack early in 1638, sailing from Pernambuco in April, with 3,600 European and 1,000 Indian troops. After landing unopposed near Bahia, he encircled the strongly-defended town only to find that his forces were insufficient to mount a regular siege of any length.[87] He thus staked everything on a furious night assault which the Portuguese only just succeeded in repulsing. Having lost several hundred of his best men, Johan Maurits withdrew and sailed back to Pernambuco.

Meanwhile, the East India Company's forces likewise resumed the offensive during the mid 1630s, principally under the direction of the vigorous Antonie van Diemen who served as governor-general at Batavia in the years 1636–45. Van Diemen who, by 1639, had no less than eighty-five warships at his disposal in Asian waters, believed fervently in the concerted use of Dutch sea-power right across the East with a view to choking off the remaining trade of the Iberians and further expanding that of the Dutch. His strategy was to hold in check the more resilient Spaniards in the Philippines and Moluccas and concentrate his offensive against the Portuguese. Accordingly, he intensified the seasonal blockades of Malacca, which had been resumed in 1633, and mounted a similar blockade, with usually around ten ships, for long periods annually during the years 1636–44, of Goa.[88] Two naval battles were fought off Goa in January 1638 and September 1639, in which four Portuguese galleons were destroyed for the loss of two Dutch vessels; in the second of these encounters, fifty Dutchmen died as against 400 Portuguese. As regards Malacca, the town was likewise cut off from the sea for long periods. 'Our blockade', noted van Diemen in December 1636, 'causes very slack trade at Malacca and consequently we find commerce here, at Batavia, growing daily.'[89] In 1640 Van Diemen mounted a full-scale siege of Malacca, with the help of native allies, from land and sea. After a heroic resistance and heavy loss, being still under allegiance to the Spanish crown, the Portuguese finally

[87] Aitzema, *Hist.* iv (ii). 57–8.
[88] Mac Leod ii. 98–9, 111–13, 119–23, 133–5.
[89] Quoted in Colenbrander i. 149.

surrendered the base to the Dutch in January 1641.[90]

Linked to the offensive against Malacca and Goa was the Dutch invasion of Ceylon. Although the Dutch had been invited on several occasions in the past by the native rulers of Kandy to assist them in their struggle against the Portuguese who controlled most of Ceylon's coastline from their six great forts, but not the interior, it was only after van Diemen's arrival in 1636 that the authorities in Batavia resolved on intervening in Ceylon with the aim of securing control of the cinnamon trade.[91] In May 1638 a combined Dutch–Sinhalese force captured Batticaloa, one of the six Portuguese strongholds which commanded Ceylon's coastline. The Dutch promptly took over the fortress, with the agreement of their allies, and soon commenced their dealings in cinnamon. In May 1639, after a brief bombardment, the Dutch took the other Portuguese east-coast fortress, Trinconomalee. In March 1640, following up their previous successes, the Dutch captured one of the west-coast fortresses, Galle. By 1641, the year in which the Portuguese possessions in the Far East cast off their allegiance to Spain, while half of coastal Ceylon remained under the Portuguese, the Dutch securely dominated the rest and controlled a large part of the island's cinnamon exports.

While, from the mid 1630s onwards, the emphasis in both Indies was on conquest, pillaging the Iberian sea-lanes continued to be a constant pre-occupation of both colonial companies. West India Company squadrons continued to infest South Brazilian, West African, and Caribbean waters in search of booty. In the Caribbean there were a series of incursions linked particularly with the name of Cornelis Jol, though, despite the latter's skill and prowess, the proceeds were remarkably meagre. Without question, however, the entire Caribbean remained extremely hazardous for Spanish shipping and huge sums from the various royal treasuries in Spanish America were spent on strengthening the fortresses and garrisons of the region. Among several such programmes, during the years 1634–40, new fortifications were constructed

[90] MacLeod ii. 205–6, 216–19.
[91] Montanus, 495; Goonewardena, 9, 11–20, 28, 37.

around the town of San Juan, in Puerto Rico, at a cost of 110,000 ducats, raised mainly in Mexico, though 20,000 ducats were collected in Puerto Rico itself by means of additional taxation.[92] After the famous exploit, in March 1635, when Jol tried to capture the weakly defended port of Santiago in Cuba, with only two ships, the *Consejo de Indias*, reacting in its habitual manner, drew up plans for yet another formidable Caribbean fortress, to be financed from Mexico City.[93]

After commanding another arduous, but minor, Caribbean expedition in 1636–7, Jol was appointed to lead a much more powerful force fitted out by the Company in 1638, with the aim of attacking one of the treasure fleets. In August 1638 the Spanish mainland convoy, consisting of fifteen ships, sailed from Cartagena for Havana, loaded with bullion, despite warnings that Jol was in the vicinity, being misled by the Dutch stratagem of scattering their fleet to conceal its size. Three sporadic battles were fought off north-west Cuba,[94] but hampered by the reluctance of many of his captains to tackle the towering galleons, Jol failed to press home his attack. Despite the failure of this venture, the Company decided to make a similar attempt two years later. Jol entered the Caribbean in July 1640, in command of twenty-four sail and 3,700 men, in what was to be the last of the major Dutch incursions into the region. Once again, for many weeks the Dutch blockaded the north coast of Cuba. However, the Spaniards, amply warned, simply held their galleons in port. Weakened by a series of misfortunes, including a violent tempest which engulfed several of his ships, Jol finally withdrew in defeat to Pernambuco, in October.

The response of the Spanish crown to the relentless Dutch pressure in the Indies was by no means confined to erecting new fortresses and strengthening garrisons. Despite the great burden of these defensive measures, Philip and Olivares were ready to assign large additional resources to challenging the Dutch naval ascendancy, at any rate in the New World. The

[92] Vila Vilar, 17–18, 40–1.   [93] Wright, *Santiago de Cuba,* 62–3.
[94] Aitzema, *Hist.* iv (ii). 58.

long-mooted scheme to base a permanent naval task force in the Caribbean which would be strong enough to deal on its own with the lesser Dutch fleets and, in combination with one or other of the *flotas*, with even the largest, began to be implemented by the viceroy of New Spain, the Marqués de Cadereita, during the later 1630s. It was intended to raise an extra half a million or more ducats yearly from Mexico and the Caribbean possessions with which to maintain a fixed battle force of fifteen sail.[95] In December 1636, after intensive bargaining, the Mexico City council finally agreed to contribute another 200,000 pesos annually to the war effort and the other Mexican towns quickly followed suit. A programme of naval construction was launched at Campeche and Havana and 100 heavy guns were ordered from the foundries at Manila. But the *armada* of Barlovento was destined to take shape much more slowly than had been hoped. Despite the further intensification of fiscal pressure in Mexico, tax yields failed to rise, owing to the economic depression which was affecting most of Spanish America during these years.[96] Most of the galleons were still unfinished towards the end of 1639. Simultaneously, fiscal pressure was stepped up throughout Central America.

At the same time, king and Conde-Duque were planning a supreme effort to break the Dutch naval primacy in Brazilian waters and retake Pernambuco in the process by means of a massive new Castilian-Portuguese *armada*, being gathered at Lisbon. The proceeds of the relentless tax drive in Portugal, combined with Castilian subsidies, ships and men were slowly collected, during 1637–8, into a powerful force, amounting, when the *armada* eventually sailed in the autumn of 1638, to forty-six sail. The Dutch, not unnaturally, were in some confusion as to the purpose of this force and its connection, if any, with the simultaneous intense activity at Corunna and the French invasion forces, at Fuenterrabía. The West India Company directors, in any case, made the mistake, despite Johan Maurits's apprehensions, of assuming that the Spaniards,

---

[95] Palafox, 41–3. Israel, *Colonial Mexico*, 193–4.

[96] On the failure of the Mexican tax drive and the economic situation in New Spain, see Palafox, 42–3; Israel, 'Mexico and the "General Crisis"' 40–1; and pp. 295–6 below.

while under such heavy pressure from the French, could not be thinking of diverting so huge a force to Brazil. Hence the lack of any urgent reaction. Fortunately for the Dutch, the *armada*, under the Conde da Torre, lost much time and, through disease, many men at the Cape Verde Islands. Even so, the Iberians succeeded, in January 1639, in catching the Dutch Brazil forces at a time when their strength was relatively low. Only the incompetence of da Torre saved the Dutch from a direct assault on Pernambuco, in overwhelming strength. Instead, unaware of his advantage, da Torre insisted, against the advice of his officers, in sailing down the Brazilian coast to Bahia, hoping that there he would be able to replenish his manpower and supplies.

Prospects for the Dutch remained ominous, however, as the Conde succeeded in accumulating considerable additional forces while only modest reinforcements arrived from the Republic. The *armada* finally sailed from Bahia for Pernambuco in November 1639 with no less than eighty-seven sail, including eighteen Castilian and twelve Portuguese galleons. To face this immense force the West India Company's admiral off Brazil, Willem Loos, disposed of forty-one ships carrying 2,800 men, roughly one-third of the *armada*'s manpower.[97] Having been blown back and forth for many weeks by adverse winds, da Torre finally encountered the Dutch off Itamaracá. A sporadic five-day battle ensued, in which, despite the at times furious firing, losses on either side were singularly light. While Loos himself was killed at the outset, many of his subordinates clung back, refusing to move in close to the towering galleons. Though the battle itself was indecisive, its aftermath was an unmitigated disaster for Spain. Da Torre, drifting northwards, again became embroiled in bad weather. Eventually he simply allowed his fleet to disperse in all directions, towards the Azores, the Caribbean, and Bahia. This was the last of the combined Castilian–Portuguese offensives in Brazil.

---

[97] *Kroniek* xxv. 515–29; Boxer, *Salvador de Sá, 116–20; id., Dutch in Brazil*, 93–4.

iv THE ECONOMIC CONFLICT, 1634–1640

During the mid and later 1630s both the United Provinces and Spain continued to employ economic means to influence the wider conflict while, at the same time, the struggle continued, as before, to exert a pervasive influence on the economic life of all Europe and the European Indies.

The States General reverted to the use of river blockades as a strategic weapon during the campaigns of 1635-6, in an episode which is particularly revealing regarding the links between military strategy and economic interest in the Dutch politics of the period.[98] The fall of Schenkenschans to the Spaniards, and the ensuing concentration of both Spanish and Imperialist troops in Cleves and adjoining areas, posed, as has been seen, the most serious threat that the Republic had faced since 1629. As the Dutch army moved to block the path of the Spanish–Imperialist forces, the States General, in mid August, temporarily banned the passage of provisions and materials along the Rhine and Maas beyond the Dutch border.[99] Soon after, the *Raad van State* advised extending the blockade also to the routes to Brabant and Flanders and to the Ems and Weser. While the inland provinces at once agreed, Holland vacillated, while Zeeland, having altogether discarded its earlier zeal for river blockades against the Spanish Netherlands, simply refused.[1] On 30 August the States General instructed the Middelburg admiralty college to halt the flow of supplies into Flanders and its sector of Brabant without waiting for Zeeland's consent. The States of Zeeland reacted angrily, appealing to Amsterdam and the Holland maritime towns which were clearly sympathetic to Zeeland's new point of view.[2] As a result, the blockade remained limited to just the Maas and Rhine and the routes between, for several months, despite the urgent need to weaken the Cardinal-Infante's army and clear evidence that the Habsburg forces were critically short of supplies.[3]

---

[98] Israel, 'Strategic Regulation', 486-90.

[99] Res. SG 18 Aug. 1635. ARH SG 3194, fo. 410v.

[1] Res. SG 25 Aug. 1635. ARH SG 3194, fo. 425.

[2] GA Amsterdam vroed. res. xvi, fos. 97r, 97v; *Notulen Zeeland*, 15 Sept. 1635.

[3] Res. Holl. 11 Sept. and 12 Oct. 1635.

During January 1636 the provinces' delegates conferred with Frederik Hendrik on the issue of the river blockade on several occasions. Both prince and inland provinces persisted in pressing for closure of the Brabant routes, Schelde, Ems, and Weser. Holland and Zeeland objected that in the newly transformed circumstances of the war, with Calais and the other ports of north-east France closed to the Spaniards, the inevitable effect would be to divert Dutch provisions to Dover from where the English would convoy the edibles direct to Ostend and Dunkirk.[4] And any such loss of trade to the English, it was added, was decidedly to be avoided. The Stadholder answered that the blockade would be brief and that should Dutch supplies reach Flanders from England, it would be a costly and laborious matter to transport them to the enemy forces on the Maas and Rhine. Late in January the Amsterdam *vroedschap* reluctantly yielded, so that Holland consented to closure of the Schelde, Ems, and Weser and all routes between, though, at Amsterdam's insistence, the Elbe remained open.[5] In March bitter protests reached The Hague from Bremen and Emden and the Count of East Friesland.[6] Bremen also wrote directly to the Amsterdam city council maintaining that the States General's prohibition would inevitably fail in its strategic purpose while, lamentably, depriving the Swedish forces in Germany of their provisions, all to the advantage of the Emperor.

Predictably, the ban instigated massive diversions in trade and, before long, the argument was resumed as to whether the blockade ought to be extended further. While the admiralty colleges confirmed that great quantities of provisions were being shipped from North Holland, via Hamburg, to the Spanish forces in Cleves and from South Holland and Zeeland, via Dover, and in English ships, to Dunkirk,[7] Amsterdam refused to countenance closure of

[4] Res. SG 19, 21, 23 Jan. 1636. ARH SG 3195, fos. 57ᵛ–58, 66ᵛ–67; Res. Holl. 24 Jan. 1636.
[5] GA Amsterdam vroed. res. xvi, fo. 114; SG Res. 1 Feb. 1636. ARH SG 3195, fo. 87ᵛ.
[6] *Quellen und Forschungen*, 9–10, 36–7.
[7] GA Rotterdam vroed. res. 19 May 1636; Res. SG 29 Mar. 7 Apr. 1636. ARH SG 3195, fos. 200ᵛ, 216ᵛ; Res. Holl. 20 Feb. 1636.

the sea-lane to Hamburg and this, in turn, involved keeping open the route to Dover. However, as to the latter there was now mounting alarm at Rotterdam, Middelburg, and Flushing as vast stocks of salt fish, herring and wine were bought up by English dealers and imported to Dover for re-export to Flanders, activity which continued unimpeded throughout April and May owing to the delay that year in imposing the Dutch naval blockade on the Flemish coast.

Although Schenkenschans was recovered on the last day of April, for some weeks afterwards the threat from the Spanish–Imperialist forces on the Gelderland border remained and, at the insistence of the Stadholder and inland provinces, the blockade was continued until the end of June. This two-month prolongation produced a bitter clash between Zeeland and the other provinces.[8] By the time the blockade was finally lifted, the maritime towns had acquired so strong an aversion to the river blockade weapon that for the rest of the Spanish war there was no possibility of using the technique again.[9] Despite the recurrence of situations in which he would like to have reimposed a river blockade on the Spanish Netherlands, such as during the 1637 siege of Breda, when there occurred a huge transport of Dutch supplies to the Cardinal-Infante's army, via Bergen-op-Zoom,[10] the Stadholder had simply to swallow his anger. In effect, the 1635–6 river blockade was the only one imposed by the States General after the outbreak of the Franco–Spanish conflict closed the ports of north-east France to the Spaniards thereby denying the Dutch ports the opportunity for profit which passed instead into the hands of the English. Because of the changed circumstances, Holland and Zeeland adamantly refused to tolerate such measures again. This is why late 1635 and early 1636 constituted the one and only occasion in Dover's history when foodstuffs and French wines imported from the United Provinces were re-exported to Flanders on a large scale.[11] At other times, Dover's role as

---

[8] *Notulen Zeeland,* 28 May, 8, 13, and 20 June 1636.
[9] Aitzema, *Hist.* iv (i), 301.   [10] *Briefwiss. Huygens* ii. 226.
[11] While no French wine was re-exported from Dover in 1634, from December 1635 to November 1636 3,666 tuns were re-exported, chiefly to Flanders; see Kepler, 55.

an entrepôt, during the period that both France and the Republic were at war with Spain, was largely confined to supplying Flanders with silver, wool, and colonial products from the Peninsula, and the Peninsula with Flemish linens, woollens, and other manufactures.

The prohibition against Dutch shipping and merchandise in the Peninsula remained in force during these years with little fundamental change. While the Spanish crown continued to issue some passes permitting Dutch ships to come for salt and, from time to time, would permit entry of Dutch vessels carrying grain or munitions, Dutch trade to the Peninsula remained very restricted while that of the Hanseatic towns and English continued to flourish. Thus throughout north Germany, during the later 1630s, there continued to be considerable investment and ship-building tailored to the needs of the booming *Spanienfahrt*.[12] Even the Polish king became interested and had a hand in the sending of at least one convoy of eight vessels direct from Danzig to the Peninsula in the autumn of 1636. The city of Lübeck alone sent an average of thirty-seven ships yearly to the Peninsula during the six years 1634-9, the peak years being 1634-5. The total number of Hansa vessels on the Iberian run approached 200. As regarded munitions and naval stores, besides the Spanish crown's preference for dealing with neutrals rather than the Dutch, those Dutch merchants who did enter the field, such as the Amsterdam Jew, Lopo Ramírez, who sent munitions and grain to Cadiz and Naples during the late 1630s,[13] ran the constant risk of detection and penalties in Holland. Despite the frequent laxness of the Dutch admiralty colleges, their officers were perfectly capable, on occasion, of uncovering such contraventions of the States General's ban on munitions exports to hispanic lands, as is shown by the seizure at Enkhuizen, in February 1640, of the ship *Breda* which was found to be sailing for Portugal with war supplies registered for Marseilles.[14] But, unquestionably, the main deterrent continued to be the *Almirantazgo*. By and large,

[12] Vogel, 141; 'Brieven Blommaert', 113-14; Olechnowitz, 37-8.
[13] SRA viii. 301n.
[14] ARH Bisdom 67, pp. 63, 67.

during these years Dutch merchants only ventured to send vessels to the Peninsula when they had obtained salt-passes from Brussels and this necessarily involved close supervision and tight regulation. Trade by subterfuge and false papers remained risky, not only owing to the ruthless thoroughness of the *Almirantazgo*, but because the now numerous Hanseatic and English seamen thronging Iberian ports had a vested interest in assisting the Spanish authorities. In this way, in 1637 the *St. Paulus* of Amsterdam, denounced by Lübeck skippers to the *Almirantazgo*, was forced to depart hurriedly from Málaga.[15]

In southern Italy, however, where the *Almirantazgo* did not operate, the position was, by the 1630s, quite otherwise. Naples, Sardinia, and Sicily were in fact the only parts of the hispanic world where something like a regular maritime commerce with Amsterdam was possible. Prominent Amsterdam merchants such as Lopo Ramirez, Willem Muilman and Hendrik and Dirk Dommer remitted grain and other cargoes to southern Italy, using at least some Dutch ships and, apparently experiencing little difficulty.[16] The Neapolitan merchant Stefano Tierri posted a brother, Jacoppo Tierri, in Amsterdam during the 1630s as well as another brother in London. Importing olive oil from Puglia to Amsterdam, the Tierris sent various cargoes to southern Italy, on one occasion chartering a Dutch vessel to load pilchards at Plymouth for Cività Vecchia and Naples. Lopo Ramirez several times shipped Sicilian grain to Naples in Dutch vessels. Willem Muilman had important connections in Venice and, above all, in Genoa, and part of his business consisted in shipping salt and grain from Sicily to the north-Italian ports. Doubtless, had it been possible, he would also regularly have sent ships to La Mata and Alicante to convey the more expensive but superior Spanish salt, as well as wool, to northern Italy, but this he could not do. While it has been assumed that the *Almirantazgo*'s efforts in the Valencian ports were largely ineffective during these years,[17] the evidence of the Amsterdam

---

[15] GA Amsterdam NA 1056, fo. 38.

[16] GA Amsterdam NA 694 B, doc. 60 and box-index of freight-contracts, Naples.

[17] Casey, 97–8.

freight-contracts definitely points to the contrary. One aspect of Amsterdam's war-time connections with Naples became notorious throughout the Republic during 1637: several leading Amsterdam personages, allegedly including the Bickers themselves, had been involved in hiring ships to the Spanish viceroy for royal use in the Mediterranean; the revelation provoked a furious and prolonged row in the States General and States of Holland, which was eagerly exploited by those towns antagonistic to Amsterdam, and which led to the setting up of a commission of inquiry, under François van Aerssen, one of the chief opponents of the Amsterdam leadership which, however, was barred by the Amsterdam *vroedschap* from carrying out its task.[18]

While the main strand in Dutch European trade, the carrying of Baltic products to the west, undoubtedly recovered somewhat from the severe depression of the 1620s, from 1631 onwards, it did so to a slightly lesser extent than did such carrying by non-Dutch merchants. Thus the Dutch share of shipping passing through the Danish Sound having fallen from a truce-time level of 80 per cent to around 70 per cent during the 1620s, fell further by several per cent during the later 1630s.[19] As it happens, the mid and later 1630s were a period in which grain prices rose exceptionally high in both northern Spain and Portugal,[20] but the English and Hanseatic towns, evidently, were better placed to exploit the opportunity than the Dutch. Fear of the *Almirantazgo* continued to pervade the international merchant community at Lisbon owing, in the words of the Lisbon municipality, to the 'condemnations, losses and interference that they suffer every day from the contraband officers'.[21] The Lisbon city council ventured to tell the king that the *Almirantazgo* and the economic embargo were 'not the remedy for reducing the rebels to obedience. . .for at present there is not one foreign ship in this city, while before the prohibition of contraband, they overflowed our ports.' After repeatedly urging Lisbon to make do with supplies shipped by the Hanseatics and English,

---

[18] *Briefwiss. Huygens*, 255, 275; *Brieven Reigersberch*, 510, 517.
[19] Christensen, 88, 104, 316; Unger, 273.
[20] *Elem. Hist. Lisb.* iv. 152; Labayru y Goicoechea, v. 714.
[21] *Elem. Hist. Lisb.* iv. 137, 145.

as well as by the Genoese from Sicily, Philip reluctantly renewed permission to use Dutch vessels for the period until
the reaping of the 1636 harvest, in November 1635. But this
resurgent Dutch grain trade to Portugal was strictly limited
and controlled. The Dutch could bring only grain and, until
September 1636, when the limit was raised to 150 lasts,
exclusively in small vessels of up to seventy-five lasts; they
could sail only to Lisbon and, on leaving, could load only
with heavily taxed salt.[22] Elsewhere in Portugal, as well as
throughout Spain, the Dutch continued to be shut out. Of
thirty foreign ships entering the port of Faro, in the Algarve,
during the five years 1636–40, no less than twenty-one, or
more than two-thirds, were English, most of the rest being
Hanseatic.[23] Evidently, no difficulties were placed by the
French authorities, after May 1635, in the path of English
skippers sailing to the ports of western France to collect
cargoes of grain (shipped from the Baltic by the Dutch) for
the Peninsula.

The adverse impact of the Spanish war on Dutch European
trade continued to show also in other ways, notably in ab-
normally high freight-rates, soaring insurance charges, and the
recession in the vital herring industry. The cost of shipping
Setúbal salt to Holland, using the royal salt-passes, oscillated
during the years 1634–40 at around 30 guilders per last,
sometimes rising as high as 40 guilders;[24] prevailing rates, in
other words, remained nearly three times as high as during
the truce period. The pressures and losses to which the
herring industry were subjected likewise constituted a substantial setback to Dutch European commerce as a whole.
The destruction of several hundred busses by the Dunkirkers
represented many millions of guilders of damage. The direct
result was a marked and sustained contraction in the size of
the herring fleets of Enkhuizen, Schiedam, Delftshaven, and
other ports,[25] which, in effect, marked the beginning of the
long decline of the Dutch herring industry, though there was

[22] *Elem. Hist. Lisb.* iv. 155-7, 201-2, 205.
[23] Rau, 'Subsidios', 219-27.
[24] GA Amsterdam, box-index freight-contracts, Soutvaart.
[25] Kranenburg, 33-4, 217-18; Wätjen, 'Zur Statistik', 159; Centen, 58-9,
88, 95.

some temporary recovery at the end of the Spanish war.
Schiedam's total herring catch during the decade 1621–30
was almost exactly one-third less than in the decade 1611–20;
but even this reduced figure was cut by another third in the
decade 1631–40, the 1630s being the worst decade for
Schiedam until after 1720.[26] Despite sharp reductions in
sales to the South Netherlands, traditionally one of the
chief markets for Dutch herring, exports of the commodity
to other parts of Europe inevitably were cut. Thus average
annual Dutch herring exports to the Baltic during the decade
1630–9 were running at 12½ per cent less than the level
maintained during the period 1600–19,[27] despite the fact
that herring consistently fetched much higher prices in
Poland during the decades 1621–40 than either previously
or subsequently.[28]

By contrast, manufacturing output in both Holland and
Spain benefited from the war. During the years 1621–35
Haarlem, Leiden, Gouda, and Utrecht had adhered to a
steadfastly Contra-Trevist stand which tallied with their
preference for high tariffs on foreign cloth imports and
restrictions on wool and flax exports. Imports of English
and Liège, as well as of Flemish, textiles into the Republic
had been massively reduced during the 1620s, while the
disruptions of war had also served to stunt the not incon-
siderable textile potential of Westphalia.[29] In theory, and to
a large extent in practice, the war-policy ensured an abundance of cheaply priced medium- and low-quality wools from
Pomerania, other parts of Germany, and the United Provinces
themselves, enforced the dominance of Holland cloth on the
home market, and boosted Dutch exports to the Baltic, to
the detriment of English and Flemish cloth, that had formerly
been shipped there from Holland.[30] In one of the most

---

[26] Feijst, 104–6.
[27] Van der Woude ii. 406; Unger, fig. i.   [28] Unger, 271.
[29] De la Court, *Welvaren van Leiden*, 29–30, 100–2.
[30] While J. D. Gould arguably underrated the contribution of Dutch policy to
the English trade and industrial depression of the 1620s, he did admit that the
'protectionist policy of the Low Countries was a major cause of the general weakness of the broadcloth industry throughout the early seventeenth century':
Gould, 85; see also Supple's remarks.

drastic setbacks in English textile history English textile
exports to the Baltic were drastically pruned back during
the 1620s just when there occurred a remarkable growth in
the importance of cloth as a proportion of total exports
shipped by the Dutch to the Baltic: from a mere 2 per cent
in 1615, boosted by the depression in shipments of salt and
herring, the figure for textiles jumped to 8 per cent in 1625
and remained at 7 per cent in 1635.[31] Of course, the picture
was not wholly one of gain for the Dutch. To weigh against
their progress at home and in the Baltic, the Holland cloth
towns had been stripped of their former Iberian markets
and, indeed, by backing the war, helped reinforce the already
marked orientation of the Flemish linen and woollen industries towards the hispanic world. On balance though, we
learn, the weavers and clothiers of Haarlem and Leiden,
despite the high taxation that it involved, were well satisfied
with the Spanish war.[32]

Taking together all branches of Leiden's woollen industry,
overall production, in contrast to England's but like that of
Flanders, had definitely expanded since 1621, Leiden's total
output during the quinquennium 1630–4 being over 8 per
cent higher than in the quinquennium 1620–4 which in turn
was several per cent higher than production in the previous
quinquennium.[33] A striking feature of this phenomenon is
that the most dynamic sectors were fustians and rashes,
Leiden's cheapest and coarsest fabrics. In some ways, this was
illogical, since, as has been pointed out,[34] in the long run
Leiden's only hope of surmounting the challenge posed by
the much lower wage-rates that prevailed in England and
Flanders was to specialize in high-quality fabrics where the
disadvantage of high labour costs would weigh least. But, in
fact, given the policy of the Leiden *vroedschap*, the initial
effect was bound to be to stimulate growth in quite the
opposite direction, since, at least until 1635, the Spanish
war encouraged, even compelled, concentration on the home
market and reliance on relatively cheap wools.

However during the decade or so from 1635 Leiden's total

---

³¹ Christensen, 465–6.   ³² See the *Klare Aenwijsinge* (1630).
³³ Posthumus iii. 930, 932.   ³⁴ Wilson, 216–19.

output fell markedly, more than wiping out the gains of the 1621-35 period; all the cheap branches, *says*, rashes, and fustians, contracted appreciably.[35] But measuring by quantity alone is deceptive: the actual value of Leiden's production not only continued to increase but increased much more rapidly than before 1635. This remarkable phenomenon was due to a sudden transformation in the structure of the Dutch textile industry which deserves a good deal more emphasis from historians than it has yet received. The fundamental restructuring in Holland coincided with the outbreak of the Franco-Spanish war which, paradoxically, forged new links between the Holland cloth towns and Spain while at the same time strengthening the resolve, at any rate of Leiden, to prolong the Dutch-Spanish war. Leiden's output of fine *lakens*, worked from expensive Castilian and Andalusian wools, more than quadrupled in the four years 1635-8,[36] making the United Provinces, for the first time, a major importer and consumer of Spanish wool, a larger consumer indeed than Venice, then still one of the principal markets for this commodity.[37] In 1635 France and Spain had closed their ports to each other's products and this had halted the movement of Spanish wools to northern France, traditionally an important market, and no less importantly closed the door (Calais) by which Spanish wools had since 1621 reached the Spanish Netherlands and Liège.[38] The English who, in the years 1630-4 had shipped almost all the wool, leaving the Spanish north coast for northern France, now conveyed virtually all of it to Dover and London or direct to Amsterdam. While some of this wool was undoubtedly shipped from Dover to Dunkirk, there remained a massive surplus in northern Europe in need of new markets and outlets. The Franco-Dutch alliance against Spain was thus literally a windfall for Leiden. Certainly more Spanish wool was put to use in England itself at this time, but the bulk was shipped on to Holland.[39] Together with the new material came new skills. During the decade 1635-44, with the boom in output of

[35] Posthumus iii. 930, 932.   [36] Posthumus iii. 930, 932.
[37] Israel, 'Spanish Wool Exports', 201.   [38] Ibid., pp. 208-9.
[39] *A Brief Narration*, 9.

high-quality woollens, 706 Flemish, French, and German artisans settled in the city of Leiden, compared with only 330 during the decade 1625–34.[40]

The blow to production of cloth from Spanish wools in the southern Netherlands was particularly serious in that Dutch policy, since 1621, had created a shortage of the cheaper German wools and virutally eliminated Dutch wools from the Flemish market. The result was an overall shortage of wool. It is true that the decline at Hondschoote, from 1635 onwards, was partly compensated for by increased production of *says* at Brugge and that as a result of the wool shortage, there was now an increasing emphasis in Flanders on linen production from home-produced flax, notably at Ghent.[41] But despite the near elimination of French manufactures from the Peninsula and Ibero-America, potentially a huge gain for Flanders,[42] the loss of the route through Calais, combined with the continuing Dutch naval blockade of the Flemish coast, inevitably hampered the export of Flemish manufactures which had now only the precarious outlet via Dover.[43] Daunted by the punitively high Dutch tariffs, Antwerp and other South Netherlands merchants sent very little through the Republic.[44] At Lille, another leading woollen centre of the Spanish Netherlands, a definite decline in production was evident, as from 1635.[45]

The virtual elimination of French as well as Dutch products from the Peninsula, enforced by an *Almirantazgo* with jurisdiction from Lisbon to Valencia and from Navarre to Gibraltar, undoubtedly further improved prospects for Castile's own industries in the short and medium term. In this respect Castile also benefited from the Dutch naval blockade of the Flemish coast. Despite the continued decline in the overall level of Seville's monopoly trade with Spanish America during these years, exports of Toledo, Segovia, and Catalan cloth to the Indies at this time must certainly have increased. This demonstrates that the historian should not be too ready to assume that the gradual falling off in the official transAtlantic traffic which, in any case, until 1640 was much less

---

[40] Posthumus iii. 883–4.   [41] Coomaert, 53, 57; Bastin, 135.
[42] Bastin, 136.   [43] *Discurso sobre. . .la Gverra Maritima,* 35.
[44] Ibid., p. 35 Bastin, 135.   [45] Deyon and Lottin, 32.

marked than the depression in trade between the Peninsula and northern Europe,[46] necessarily constituted an economic setback for Spain as a whole.

The wider question of the impact of the Dutch–Spanish struggle, after 1621, on European-American trade generally, and on the overall economic development of the Spanish New World possessions, leads into controversial territory. Historians of colonial Spanish America agree that while silver remittances from the Indies to Spain had fallen off sharply since 1600, there was no very significant reduction in actual silver output from the American mines until the late 1630s and no severe down-turn until the late seventeenth century. A number of historians have explained the growing discrepancy between American production and the official trans-Atlantic remittances in terms of what they see as the increasing self-sufficiency of the Spanish New World colonies. It is argued that the decline in imports from Spain reflects a diminishing need for European products and a tendency to invest more funds in the Indies, producing a more diversified and independent productive structure, especially in Mexico and Peru, the main economic and population centres of the Spanish New World.[49] Others have explained the discrepancy differently, arguing that Spain's loss was northern Europe's gain, in other words that the surplus silver was being diverted to northern Europe in payment for illegally imported French, English, and Dutch merchandise.[48] But in fact neither of these explanations fits very well with the evidence. As regards contraband trade, all the signs are that such activity was choked to a minimum during the years 1621–48 when the war situation, the spread of garrisons and officials and the special measures taken at Buenos Aires and Córdoba to check illicit activity in southern South America rendered the ban on direct trade with foreigners generally effective.[49] This can be

---

[46] Chaunu viii, no. 2, part ii. 1404, 1507-8, 1590, and vii. 50-1.

[47] Lynch ii. 195, 209, 212; Bakewell, 227-30, 242-3; see also Elliott, 'América y el problema', p. 16 where doubt is expressed concerning this view.

[48] Brading and Cross, 175-6, 579.

[49] Canabrava, 143-9; Elliott, 'América y el problema', 19; Israel, *Colonial Mexico*, 138.

demonstrated not only from the fact that reports of commercial infringements and frauds circulating in Mexico in this period invariably concern contraband activity on the official trans-Atlantic convoys, rather than trade with illicit entrepôts in the Caribbean, but from the situation that arose on the island of Curaçao, newly conquered by the Dutch. Curaçao was ideally situated for contraband activity and for a long period during the latter half of the seventeenth century it was to be the most important such entrepôt in the entire New World. But during the barren years before 1648, there was not the slightest hint of its future prosperity. On the contrary, the island was so isolated from the mainland, so totally devoid of possibilities for profit, that the West India Company's directors seriously considered abandoning the outpost in order to save the expense of holding it.[50]

As for the bullion retained in the Indies, it would be easier to accept that it was put to productive use in Mexico and Peru, if there was not so much evidence that the surplus was in fact diverted to the periphery of the Indies for non-productive military ends.[51] The growing discrepancy between American output and remittances to Spain was essentially caused by the crown's increasing need to spend more on imperial defence against the Dutch, both in the New World and the Far East. The new fortresses, garrisons, and fleets absorbed enormous sums. Even so, such expenditure might arguably have had a stimulatory effect, had most of it taken place in Mexico and Peru; but in fact the bulk of the subsidies remitted from Mexico City and Lima were sent to isolated and beleaguered outposts where there was next to no economic activity and from where communications were hopelessly disrupted by the West India Company fleets — Havana, Punta de Araya, Puerto Rico, Trinidad, and, above all, Manila and the Moluccas. Fortification of the town of San Juan, in Puerto Rico, during the years 1634–8, cost 110,000 ducats, most of which was provided from Mexico, though 20,000 ducats was raised in Puerto Rico itself, by means of additional taxation; meanwhile the economy of

---

[50] *Nederlanders* i. 50–1; Van Brakel, 49–50; Menkman, *Nederlanders*, 44–5.
[51] Dánvila, 4–99; Arcila Farías, 196–8.

Puerto Rico was completely paralysed by Dutch action.[52]
The garrison at Havana consisted of 200 infantry in 1621 and
was subsequently increased substantially; the royal fortress
had fifty guns and walls, the strength of which were renowned world-wide. Among the treasure captured by Piet
Heyn in 1628 was the Mexican subsidy for that year for
Havana amounting to 100,000 pesos; in the event, the
Dutch again captured the Mexican Havana subsidy in 1634,
amounting now to 137,000 ducats.[53] The total cost of the
king's defences in the Indies, noted a Dutch pamphleteer
with pride in 1630, was running at the equivalent of 5 million
guilders yearly.[54]

The increase in taxation in Mexico and Peru between 1621
and 1648 as a direct result of the Dutch war was unquestionably heavy. The total package, including 350,000 ducats
from Peru and 250,000 ducats yearly from Mexico, under
Olivares's 'Union of Arms', introduced in 1628, and the
400,000 ducats yearly imposed in 1637 on Mexico, Central
America, and the Spanish Caribbean islands for the *Armada
de Barlovento*,[55] in theory by far exceeded 1 million ducats
yearly. The Spanish American Creoles resisted so far as they
could, insisting that they simply could not meet such an
additional burden at a time of deep economic depression.
This may be dismissed as a stock reply to royal demands for
more cash, but substantial evidence supports the claim that
after 1621 Mexico, Peru, and virtually the whole of Spanish
America moved into a deep and prolonged depression. Output at most of the Mexican mines kept up less well than at
Zacatecas, the most productive and efficient, but even there
production declined after 1636.[56] Output at Potosí, by far
the most important mining centre in South America, continued to decline steadily, as it had done since the 1590s.[57]
The expansion of the Spanish-owned *haciendas* slowed down
or ceased, impeded both by slackness of demand and, in

[52] Vila Vilar, 17–18, 40–1.
[53] Wright, *Hist. Havana* i. 180–1, ii. 48, 55, 72–3.
[54] *Redenen waeromme* (1630), p. 13.
[55] Israel, 'Mexico and the "General Crisis"', 41–2.
[56] Ibid., pp. 38–9; Bakewell, 242, 246.
[57] Brading and Cross, 575.

plantation areas, by the soaring cost of black slaves which indeed the West India Company reckoned to be one of the most damaging effects of its offensive on the Spanish American economy.[58] Despite more rigorous collection of the customs duties, in Peru, and increases in the charges on a number of products, total customs returns in the vice-royalty inexorably declined after 1621.[59] Similarly, in Mexico, despite the relentless intensification of fiscal pressure, tax yields ceased to rise after 1636 and actually fell, reflecting not just the slump in silver production, but a general contraction in the volume of trade and production.[60] Mexico's trade with Peru and neighbouring Central America, according to the Mexico City council, withered almost to nothing.[61] Central America itself was likewise gripped by depression.[62] Indigo culture, the dominant activity in Guatemala, Honduras, and Nicaragua, stagnated as a large part of the European market was captured by Dutch indigo shipped to Amsterdam by the East India Company from south-east India and other parts of Asia.[63] For the duration of the Dutch–Spanish war, but not before or after, purchasing indigo from the Indian hinterland was one of the prime activities of the Dutch factories on the Coromandel coast.

Of course, as is undeniable, mercury shortage played a crucial role in cutting Spanish American silver output after 1636, and this in turn must have exacerbated the American depression.[64] But since levels of silver production remained relatively high until the late seventeenth century, and less and less of this silver was being shipped to Spain, mercury shortage in itself obviously does not explain the general stagnation in the commerce and plantation agriculture of Spain's New World possessions. In any case, an essential part of the explanation must surely lie in the various pressures arising from the Dutch war: heavier taxation, diversion of

---

[58] *Consideratien ende Redenen* (1629), p. 7; on the sharp decline in slave imports to the Spanish Indies by the 1630s, see Palmer, 15–18.

[59] Rodríguez Vicente, 173–6.   [60] Palafox, 42–3.

[61] Israel, *Colonial Mexico*, 196–7.

[62] MacLeod, *Spanish Central America*, 264, 267, 268–9.

[63] Ibid., pp. 182–4; Raychaudhuri, 163–4.

[64] Bakewell, 227–30, 242–3.

resources to remote military outposts, disruption of Caribbean and Atlantic sea-lanes, shortages of slaves, naval stores for the Spanish trans-Atlantic fleets and of north European merchandise for re-export to the Indies, and, finally, the influx of East India Company indigo onto the European market.

Philip and Olivares not only substantially stepped up fiscal pressure in Spanish America, they also relentlessly increased taxation throughout the European empire. It is often imagined that Castile shouldered the crushing burden virtually alone. In fact, this is far from the truth. In Flanders and Artois, as has been seen,[65] taxation roughly trebled in the decade 1620-9 and it remained at an exceptionally high level through the 1630s.[66] The demands on Portugal were likewise extremely heavy and emerge as by far the principal grievance of the Lisbon city council and other representative bodies during the 1630s. Still more exacting were the demands on the Milanese, Naples, Sicily, and Sardinia which regularly dispatched large sums to Antwerp and where, once again, the government paid a heavy price in popular discontent, preparing the ground for the risings of 1647.[67] Even in the realms of eastern Spain, sizeable subsidies were granted under the 'Union of Arms', from the late 1620s onwards, at least by Aragon and Valencia, and much of this money also was sent to the Low Countries. But it is true that Castile did not escape the general intensification in fiscal pressure even though it would seem that Olivares consciously sought to push as much of the mounting burden as possible onto America, the South Netherlands, Portugal, and Spanish Italy. In Castile, crown and Cortes also at least professed to try to devise taxes which would 'not burden the poor, but come upon the rich'.[68] In Castile, it was not just a matter of more taxation but of a new fiscal approach.

By far the largest increase in Castile had been introduced in 1626, arising from the financial emergency following the costly Brazilian expedition of 1625 and the siege of Breda, the regular subsidies paid by Castile to the crown known as

---

[65] See p. 000 above.
[67] Villari, 123–46.
[66] *Tafels* ii. 41, 58, 67, 71, 90.
[68] *ACC* xlix, 56–7.

the *millones* being doubled from 2 to 4 million ducats yearly.[69] As the excises on basic items such as wine, oil, meat, and vinegar were already dangerously heavy, the money was raised by additional imposts on paper and salt consumption, on shipping anchoring in Castilian ports and by a 1 per cent increase in the general tax on sales. As regards other new taxation the introduction of a swingeing additional levy on salt in January 1631 caused bitter resentment especially among the populace of Galicia, Asturias, and the Basque country where there was widespread rioting.[70] In 1631 also the crown introduced two new taxes on the Castilian nobility, a commutation of feudal military obligations, known as *lanzas*, and a levy on pensions and honours.[71] Doubtless much of the antipathy towards the Conde-Duque evinced by Castilian nobles during the 1630s derived from these measures. Yet another subsidy, imposing a further 400,000 ducats yearly on Castile, was voted in 1632 and raised through new duties on sugar, chocolate, tobacco, paper, and fish. In 1634 tobacco was encumbered with yet another duty. In 1636 came a new excise on playing cards and, in the same year, following the Dutch example, stamp duty on legal transactions. Finally, in 1638, yet another 400,000 ducat annual subsidy was introduced and raised by increasing the excises on wine and meat.

Cortes and royal ministers had often stated in the past that excessive taxation had been, and was, a principal cause of Castile's continuing decline and depopulation. This had been argued by Spinola and the Spanish *trèvistes* in 1606-9 and had been a not infrequent theme ever since. Thus, modern historians incline towards one view expressed at the time when they attribute a leading role to the Dutch war in hastening the process of Spain's decline.[72] But while, undeniably, there is some force in this, the harm caused to the country's social and economic fabric by extra taxes to pay

---

[69] *ACC* xliv. ii. 14-15, 16, 235; Danvila, 500.
[70] *ACC* xliv. 92-3, 100-19.
[71] Domínguez Ortiz, *Política y Hacienda*, 227.
[72] e.g. J.H. Elliot, referring to the Dutch war, asked '¿Como hemos de explicar esta larga y agnizante persistencia que contribujó probablemente mas que nada a la gran derrota de la España del Conde-Duque?', (El Conde-Duque, 90-1).

for the war is only part of its impact on Spain and, arguably, the less important part. If the Castilian Cortes had long complained of heavy taxation, it had, since the truce years, insisted still more emphatically that 'permitting entry from abroad of all kinds of goods of silk and wool. . .and linens, with which the foreigner has totally drained the realm of money and depleted its trade and commerce' was destroying Spain's industries, depriving the poor of work, and turning them into vagabonds.[73] However costly, the war brought a measure of protection which significantly reduced cloth imports, diminished wool exports, and hampered the importing of cheap grain which had undercut the Spanish product. Industrial production at Toledo, Segovia, and other centres was stabilized for a quarter of a century. As regards protection for agriculture, this was written into the very terms of the grant by which the Cortes agreed to double the *millones*, in 1626. Complying with the pressure from the Castilian towns that 'wheat should not be imported from abroad by sea so that agriculture can be restored to its former state', Philip, by decree of February 1626, banned all imports by sea except when and where expressly permitted, of wheat, barley and rye, a ban which was renewed in 1632, after the 1630–1 harvest failures.[74]

v FURTHER CONTINUED TRUCE TALKS, 1634–1640

Following the vote in the States General, of July 1633, by four provinces to three in favour of persevering with the peace negotiations with the Brussels States General, Frederik Hendrik moved rapidly away from the pro-peace stance which he had adopted in 1629–30 and in late 1632 and early 1633. During August, the provinces discussed new advice from the Stadholder that if Spain would not yield over the Meierij and the Indies by the end of the month, these being the essential points, then the talks should be broken off.[75]

[73] *ACC* xxx. 456.
[74] Ibid. xliv. 73, 243; Larraz, 85.
[75] ARH SG 12548, sec. res. 11 June 1633; GA Haarlem, vroed. res. 4 Aug. 1633; GA Leiden Sec. Arch. 449, fos. 49ᵛ–50; GA Rotterdam, vroed. res. 10 Aug. 1633; De Pange, 75–6; De Boer, *Friedensunterhandlungen*, 121.

Frederik Hendrik had now finally concluded that his policy of collaboration with Amsterdam and the political Arminians in seeking an accommodation with Spain to which he had clearly been 'inclinable', as one English diplomat put it, ever since 1625, was a political strategy which simply could not be made to work. He simply had to face the fact that his previous pro-truce policy was not a viable means of managing the provinces or maintaining his grip on the decision-making process. His volte-face, after several months of characteristic-ally cautious political manœuvering, moreover, had little or nothing to do with French pressure or allurements. The Stad-holder's ingrained dislike of being politically dependent on other powers and his rather suspicious attitude concerning Richelieu's real intentions, both of which had been much intensified following the Anglo-Spanish peace of 1630 which Charles I had negotiated without consulting the States General, and the Franco–Spanish treaty of Cherasco, in 1631, remained as great as ever. The French envoy to The Hague, Hercule de Charnacé, had found, during the spring of 1633, that the prince was then totally unresponsive to French appeals to him to desist from supporting the moves towards a truce with Spain.[76] At bottom, the matter had nothing to do with Richelieu's diplomacy. The prince changed his mind, and with it his entire approach to managing the States General and provincial assemblies, only because he became convinced, during the summer of 1633, that the Amsterdam faction in the States of Holland, even with his own full support, was just not strong enough to overcome the oppo-sition among the provinces and the Dutch populace to peace or a truce with Spain. Among Frederik Hendrik's managers, Schaffer in Groningen, Beaumont in Zeeland, and, above all, Noordwijck in Holland had, for all their efforts, been unable to deliver the votes of those provinces in favour of the truce. No sooner had the prince proposed breaking off the truce talks if the Dutch conditions were not promptly complied with than Groningen, Zeeland, and Friesland moved enthu-siastically to support his stand as did the Holland faction that opposed Amsterdam — Haarlem, Leiden, Gouda, Hoorn,

[76] *Archives* iii. 36–7.

Enkhuizen, and others. The Holland nobility, under the lead of François van Aerssen who was now restored to the prince's favour, switched sides from a pro-truce to a pro-war stand as also did the province of Utrecht adroitly manipulated by the prince's manager, Ploos.[77] However, the four or five leading pro-truce towns strongly resisted, trusting that somehow a means of breaking the deadlock could be found.[78] The French stepped up their efforts to derail the proceedings. On 11 August the States General debated a new French offer of financial and military assistance, amounting to a formal alliance against Spain, but was unable to reach a decision. Charnacé, was informed that for pressing reasons a decision on the matter would have to be postponed. But the French ambassador was much heartened by the unmistakable shift in the Stadholder's policy. He reported to Paris that the prince was now apparently willing to drop both his truce efforts and the peace party, though he still feared the influence of the prince's wife, Amalia van Solms 'qui a un infiny pouvoir sur luy, et qui par de petits interetz de femme est passionément pour la trêve'.[79] In November, in the face of French protests at the delay in replying to the offer of alliance, a third dead-line was fixed by the States General by which Brussels must concede the basic Dutch demands.

The Holland peace towns fought on. The Delft *vroedschap* resolved, on 30 November, that the Brussels delegates 'should not be dismissed before it is seen what outcome the Almighty in this most important matter shall be pleased to grant.'[80] On 2 December the States of Holland voted once again on whether or not to break off the negotiations. There were just four votes in favour of an immediate rupture — Haarlem, Leiden, Gouda, and the nobility which, until the autumn of 1633, had always supported the peace moves; seven towns demanded the unconditional continuation of talks — Amsterdam, Rotterdam, Delft, Edam, Monnikendam, Medemblik, and Purmerend; the rest, including Dordrecht, Hoorn, and Enkhuizen, favoured a compromise position, sending the Brussels representatives back, for the time being, without

[77] De Pange, 62; Poelhekke, *Frederik Hendrik*, 404.
[78] GA Rotterdam vroed. res. 10 Aug. 1633.
[79] *Archives* iii. 38–41.   [80] GA Delft vroed. res. 30 Nov. 1633.

any definite break.[81] Yet while the peace party, led by Pauw, had undoubtedly gained some ground in the States of Holland, the defection of the Stadholder with whom he clashed bitterly at this time and the dramatic switch at this stage in Utrecht, where the towns of Utrecht and Amersfoort and the pro-war faction among the nobility now took control of the province's policy, strengthened the hand of the war-party elsewhere. On 9 December 1633 the States General voted, in the prince's presence, by five provinces to two, for an immediate, total break and, by implication, in favour of the French alliance.[82] Only Holland and Overijssel voted against.

Meanwhile Roose, backed by Olivares, manoeuvred deftly to choke off the peace movement in the South Netherlands.[83] The eloquent plea for peace by Professor Puteanus of Leuven, dedicated to Aytona, but published at The Hague, which re-marked that the wise Prince of Orange favoured peace (as indeed he still did when the pamphlet was written during the spring of 1633), was banned by Roose from circulation in the southern provinces as being an undesirable influence.[84] To counter its impact, Roose, with Machiavellian subtlety, permitted circulation in the southern provinces of the *Anti-Puteanus*, by the virulently pro-war Dutch Calvinist aca-demician Barlaeus. In vain the Brussels assembly besought Roose and the more flexible Aytona, for suppression of the *Anti-Puteanus* and another war-tract circulating, in French, in the Walloon provinces. In October the Brussels States General decided, as a last resort, to try a direct appeal to the king: Aerschot was dispatched to Madrid. In Spain, however, the duke was arrested and investigations were subsequently begun into his suspected links with Bergh, Warfusée, and other insurgent nobles. Finally, a few weeks after Isabella's death, following special instructions from Madrid drawn up on the advice of Roose, the Brussels assembly was dissolved by Aytona, Roose, and their colleagues.

At Madrid, during the spring of 1634, there was little

---

[81] Private Notulen, Nic. Stellingwerff, cited Poelhekke, *Fred. Hend.*, 404–5.
[82] *Actes* i. 468; De Pange, 83.
[83] Delplanche, 72, 76.
[84] See Eric Puteanus, *Des Oorlogs ende Vredes Waeg-schale.*

sense of an opportunity having been lost, or of the dis-
appointment of 1629–30. Rather the mood was of a potentially disastrous crisis successfully surmounted, in Olivares's
view chiefly owing to the steadfastness of his right-hand man
in the Netherlands, Roose.[85] Aytona was empowered to
conclude a new truce should acceptable terms be forthcoming,[86] but, at meetings during March 1634, the *consejos*
of State, Portugal, and the Indies all wholeheartedly concurred in the Conde-Duque's judgement that during 1632–3
the Dutch demands had been completely unacceptable.[87]
Juan de Solórzano, the renowned jurist, Juan de Palafox, and
other experienced members of the *Consejo de Indias* were
totally convinced that to grant the Dutch any commercial
opening in the Indies, as Aerschot and his colleagues had
urged, would be to destroy Seville's commerce, for the Dutch
with their profusion of shipping and low freight-rates, once
given the opportunity, would easily thrust aside Spain's
highly taxed, monopoly-orientated Indies merchants. In the
Consejo de Estado Olivares's assertion that any settlement
along the lines of the 1633 terms would be more disadvantageous, for Spain, than persevering with the burdensome
war, was endorsed by virtually every member, the duke of
Alva, marquises of Leganés, Gelves, and Santa Cruz, Cardinal
Zapata, and the Inquisitor-General. The most experienced
soldiers, Leganés and Santa Cruz, also seconded the Conde-
Duque's stricture that no settlement would be acceptable
unless Maastricht were regained, for strategically that 'door'
left the Spanish Netherlands wide open to the Dutch.

The Dutch–Spanish negotiations broken off, the States
General proceeded to reach its decision on the French offer
of alliance. Frederik Hendrik took the matter vigorously in
hand and was supported eventually by six of the provinces
and at least nine of the eighteen voting towns of Holland.[88]
In mid January, the Stadholder conferred with each province's

---

[85] Delplanche, 52.

[86] Consulta 16 Mar. 1634. AGS Estado 2048.

[87] Consulta, Consejo de Indias, 4 Mar. 1634, Consulta, Consejo de Portugal,
undated, Mar. 1634. AGS Estado 2152.

[88] See the letters of Charnace to Richelieu of Jan. 1634, *Archives* iii. 46–7,
49; Montanus, 594; De Pange, 95–6.

delegates to the States General and endeavoured to talk Pauw, Holland's pensionary, and other leading pro-truce figures in the States of Holland out of 'leur aveuglée passion à la trêve'. Amsterdam and its allies concentrated their resistance to the proposed alliance around the clause that would bind France and the Republic not to negotiate a truce or peace with Spain 'que conjoinctement et d'un commun consentement', arguing that this undertaking infringed the sovereign rights of the States General. On 24 February 1634 Amsterdam protested in the States of Holland that if the province endorsed this clause, the city would have no part in it or consider the committment binding, demanding that its protest be inscribed in the province's public resolutions.[89] Rotterdam, Dordrecht, and Alkmaar followed Amsterdam's lead but the peace towns were outvoted in the provincial assembly by the rival block headed by Haarlem, Leiden, Gouda, Hoorn, and Enkhuizen. If previously, until the summer of 1633, the *Trevisten* had failed to get their way with the Stadholder's support, with the prince's switching to the other side, Amsterdam was totally defeated.[90] The alliance with France was finally signed by the States General on 15 April 1634.

Despite the terms of the treaty, and the subsequent French declaration of war against the Habsburgs, the Stadholder and States General's delegates to the army resumed separate, secret negotiations with Spain in the autumn of 1635, following the loss of Schenkenschans and the overrunning of Cleves by Spanish and Imperialist forces. The fact that the prince delayed many weeks before providing Louis XIII with an account of the proceedings may owe something to the annoyance that he felt towards his French allies following the fiasco of the 1635 campaign. In any case, on 27 September 1635 Cornelis Musch, griffier or secretary of the States General, and one of the prince's close confidants, met

[89] GA Dordrecht vroed. res. 7 Feb. 1634; Aitzema, *Ned. Vreedehandeling* i. 287.

[90] Aerssen to Richelieu, The Hague, 2 Apr. 1634, in *Archives* iii. 56: the prince claimed Aerssen, had made the provinces 'perdre la volonté de traicter avec l'Espagne, laquelle avoit sy bien prins ses racines qu'elle n'a peu estre arrachée sans grande contestation'.

the Cardinal-Infante's political secretary, Martin de Axpe, together with Cristobal de Benavente, at Kranenburg in Cleves. The emissaries argued for seven hours, apparently in the harshest terms.[91] Spain insisted on Dutch withdrawal from the New World, extension of the truce to both Indies, and the exchange of Maastricht, Limburg (which fell to the Spaniards a few weeks later), the Over-Maas region, Venlo, Roermond, Rheinberg, and Orsoy all for Schenkenschans, Breda, and its region, Zandvliet, and financial compensation for the West India Company. Musch angrily rejected these 'excessive' demands, but intimated that the States General would agree to exchange Maastricht and Limburg for Schenkenschans and Geldern and might consider surrendering its American conquests for Breda and 6 million guilders compensation. The Far East, however, according to Musch, would have to remain outside any truce owing to the alliances which the Republic had formed with eastern potentates at war with Spain. It is surely significant that this hardening in what was probably the East India Company's attitude to renewed peace talks with Spain exactly coincided with the Company's resumed offensive against the Iberian colonies in Asia, a policy which was evidently very popular with investors in Holland: the opening of Van Diemen's expansionist drive at this time coincided with the most dramatic increase in the price of the Company's shares of virtually the entire seventeenth century.[92] Musch insisted also that the Emperor must be encompassed in any settlement. Much of the argument was about the East Indies, Axpe contending that omission of the East from the truce would inevitably perpetuate the friction and conflict between Spain and the Dutch. On the compensation for the West India Company, Axpe offered a mere 1 million guilders. The conference ended with Musch wagering 100 ducats that the Dutch would retake Schenkenschans before the Spaniards would Limburg; Axpe answered with a wager of 1,000 ducats

[91] Reports of Axpe to Ferdinand and Ferdinand to Philip, ARB SEG 213, fos. 216-19; Axpe to Ferdinand, Gennep, 1 Oct. 1635. AGS Estado 2050; Montanus, 599-60; Wagenaar xi. 214-15.

[92] Van Dillen, 'Effectenkoersen', 10-11.

that Limburg would fall first; Musch adhered to his original bet, remarking: 'We are not so rich.'

The Kranenburg conference was the work of Frederik Hendrik, his confidants and the States General's delegates to the army. The matter was put before the States General in secret session on 19 October, when the Stadholder advised that in view of the 'exorbitantie' of the Spanish demands there was little point in proceeding.[93] When the issue then came before the provincial assemblies, there was ill-concealed annoyance in certain quarters, notably at Leiden and Middelburg, at the way the meeting had been arranged, without the knowledge of the provinces, which was taken to infringe the fundamental procedures of the state.[94] The rest of the Zeeland towns, however, refrained from criticizing the prince and endorsed the conduct of Johan de Knuyt, the province's delegate in the Stadholder's camp who had been party to his dealings.[95] In secret session on 5 November, in the prince's presence, the States General resolved that Musch should resume his deliberations with Axpe at the proposed meeting-place, Turnhout, to determine whether the Spaniards would modify their demands and cede at least Geldern as well as Breda, Zandvliet, and Schenkenschans.[96] In the conference in the town-hall of Turnhout on 3 and 4 December there was again considerable wrangling over the East Indies. When Musch asserted that the extension of the truce to Asia would deprive 28,000 Dutch seamen of work, Axpe retorted that these sailors would find better employment in the revived trade between the Republic and Spain and that in any case no truce would be stable which was not general. Musch then demanded that if the East was to be included, Spain must give up Geldern and Stevensweert, modifying this subsequently to just Geldern. The meetings broke up in deadlock.[97]

In Holland, there was intensive debate on the renewed

---

[93] Sec. Res. SG 19 Oct. 1635. ARH SG 4563, fos. 359ᵛ, 367.

[94] GA Leiden, Sec. Arch. 449, fo. 182ᵛ; *Notulen Zeeland*, 2 Nov. 1635; *Brieven Reigersberch*, 235.

[95] *Notulen Zeeland*, 12 Nov. 1635.

[96] Sec. Res. SG 5 Nov. 1635. ARH SG 4563, fos. 356, 367.

[97] Report of Musch to SG, 15 Dec. 1635. ARH SG 4853; 'Copia de la ultima sesion que se tuvo en Tornaut', ARB SEG 213, fos. 477–81; Ferdinand to Philip, 22 Dec. 1635. ARB SEG 213, fo. 475.

Spanish truce offer during November and December 1635 resulting in the now habitual division of opinion.[98] Once again, the Amsterdam *vroedschap* was eager that the talks be brought to a fruitful conclusion to conserve the Republic's finances and to halt the 'increase of many pressures' that the Spanish struggle involved. Frederik Hendrik's adherents, Aerssen, Musch, Noordwijck and others manoeuvred, with the assistance of Haarlem, Leiden, and Gouda, to stem Amsterdam's influence, one of their strategems being to secure prolongation of the posting of Adriaan Pauw in Paris on a supposedly essential displomatic mission.[99] The French envoy at The Hague, meanwhile, had formally protested at the separate Dutch-Spanish talks on 14 December and only at this stage were the French belatedly informed. Despite the disapproval in various quarters, the States General proceeded to arrange another meeting at Turnhout, with only Friesland voting to block the proceedings.[1] Anxious to allay the suspicions at Paris, Charnacé was assured that Musch's fresh mission to Turnhout was solely 'pour apprendre les intentions de l'ennemy touchant un traicté general de paix'.

Angered by what was deemed in Brussels a distinct hardening in the Dutch stance, as between the September and December conferences, Axpe delayed and then postponed the January meeting prompting a considerable show of irritation on the Dutch side.[2] In February the talks were broken off amid mutual recriminations which, however, on the Dutch side may have been in part a manouevre to throw the French off the scent. In any case, during April a Dutch nobleman, Nicholas van der Duyen, heer van Rijswijk, was sent to Brussels with a letter from Musch to Axpe. Rijswijk took the opportunity to remind Ferdinand's ministers of the strength of peace feeling in the Republic, asserting that Holland, Overijssel, Gelderland, and Utrecht (he was being somewhat misleading only as regards the last) all favoured peace. He

---

[98] GA Leiden, Sec. Arch. 449, fo. 188; GA Delft, vroed. res. 17 Dec. 1635; GA Amsterdam vroed. res. xvi, fos. 99^v-101; *Brieven Reigersberch*, 217, 225.

[99] Archives iii. 88-9.

[1] Sec. Res. SG 3, 9 Jan. 1636. ARH SG 4853.

[2] Sec. Res. SG 10 Feb. 1636. ARH SG 4853; Aitzema, *Ned. Vreede-handeling* i. 341.

urged that the Cardinal-Infante send an emissary to The Hague to continue the negotiations. As he lacked any written authorization to make this proposal, the Cardinal-Infante declined to do so but was nevertheless encouraged that for the first time a Dutch personage of standing had been sent from The Hague to Brussels.[3] He was further heartened by the interception of a letter from Charnacé at The Hague, revealing that the Dutch were indeed, as they professed, leaving their French allies in the dark as to what was afoot. Several more notes followed.

Undoubtedly many of Philip's ministers were eager to make the most of the temporarily favourable military situation in the winter of 1635–6 and press hard for a separate Dutch truce. The young duke of Lerma advised the Cardinal-Infante, then encamped at Gennep, that such a truce was now a necessity for Spain, that Spanish arms would not be able to gain any decisive advantage over the Dutch, and that to recover what was indispensable, namely Dutch Brazil and Maastricht, the king should agree to cede Breda and Schenkenschans and make a large payment to the West India Company.[4] Benavente urged a somewhat harder line, maintaining that Spain must recover all the Republic's American acquisitions and Venlo, Roermond, and Limburg as well as Maastricht, in return for Breda, Schenkenschans, a payment to the West India Company, and Spanish recognition of the *status quo* in the Far East. Roose, predictably, adopted a still harder line, mirroring the steely resolution of his master, Olivares: the Conde-Duque's view was that the Dutch offer was simply inadequate, particularly as regarded the Far East, and that Ferdinand should be ordered to step up his offensive, Spanish military successes against the 'rebels' being the surest path to better terms.[5] As advised by his *valido*, Philip duly instructed his brother to intensify the pressure on the Dutch while simultaneously continuing talks.[6]

[3] Axpe to Olivares, 9 Apr. 1636. ARB SEG 302; Ferdinand to Philip, 30 Apr. 1636. ARB SEG 214, fos. 346–52; 'Recado q el sr de Riswiq truxo a D. Martin de Axpe', ARB SEG 214, fos. 353–5.

[4] 'Voto del duque de Lerma' (2 Oct. 1635). AGS Estado 2050.

[5] 'Voto del presidente Roose sobre la tregua', 'El Conde Duque sobre los ultimos despachos de Flandes' (7 Dec. 1635). AGS Estado 2050.

[6] Philip to Ferdinand, 11 Dec. 1635. ARB SEG 213, fos. 393–402.

Whilst the secret 1635-6 Dutch-Spanish contacts were in progress, moves preliminary to the convening of a general European peace congress were afoot in several capitals. The origin of what eventually developed into the Munster and Osnabrück peace conferences of the 1640s lay in the efforts of Pope Urban VIII, in 1635-6, to halt the spreading conflict between France and the Habsburgs, the principal Catholic powers, which threatened to plunge all Catholic Europe in unprecedented political and social turmoil from which only the Protestants would gain. From the outset, the Pope received the assistance of the Emperor but met with a subtle blend of seeming co-operation and actual obstruction from both France and Spain. In Madrid the Pope was accounted pro-French and, following a *Consejo de Estado* resolution of November 1635,[7] the crown pursued a policy of resisting the papal moves behind the scenes. In Paris there was inevitably little enthusiasm for an initiative which would leave intact the very Habsburg preponderance which Louis and Richelieu aspired to break.

But Richelieu, with his customary adroitness, nevertheless discerned advantages for France in appearing to back the peace moves and particularly in drawing the Dutch Republic into the papal proceedings, his objective being to minimize the now obvious risk of a separate Dutch-Spanish settlement. Richelieu knew that the steadily increasing pressure for peace evident in Holland would somehow have to be headed off. In the Republic moves began towards arranging for Dutch participation in the 'general peace of all Christendom'.[8] On 30 April 1630, the same day that Ferdinand wrote to Philip that he would try to cultivate further secret Dutch-Spanish talks, Charnacé advised the States General that France had accepted the Pope's invitation to send delegates to negotiate peace with Spain and the Empire at a European congress, on condition that its ally, the United Provinces, should be represented also and should negotiate jointly with France as stipulated in the Franco-Dutch treaty of alliance.[9] The States General responded favourably.

[7] Leman, 374-6.
[8] GA Haarlem vroed. res. 24 Apr. 1636.
[9] Aitzema, *Ned. Vreede-handeling* i. 343.

From May 1636 onwards the policy of the Dutch war-party was to seek to deflect the pressure for peace by insisting that all efforts should be directed to the general congress which, by agreement among the European powers, was scheduled to meet at Cologne, and that the sequence of separate, secret talks with Spain should cease. To strengthen their hand, Amsterdam and the peace towns strove to effect the recall of Adriaan Pauw, from Paris, so that he would be on hand to battle for renomination as Pensionary of Holland, his term being due to expire during the summer of 1636. However, Musch, Aersen, and Noordwijck, Amsterdam's opponents in the States of Holland once again carried the day, prevented Pauw's recall, and secured the election of the pliable Jacob Cats, pensionary of Dordrecht and a virtual pawn in the hands of the Stadholder's party.[10] Frederik Hendrik was now managing the States of Holland, as far as he could, by relying on the combination of Haarlem, Leiden, and Gouda.

While Louis XIII nominated his delegates, he refused to send them to Cologne until Philip issued appropriate *sauf-conduits* for the delegates of France's allies, the Dutch, and this seemingly trivial matter in effect paralysed the entire peace process during the years 1636-8, for the Dutch likewise refused to attend at Cologne until appropriate passports were delivered by Spain, and these were not forthcoming. When, finally, in October 1638, Spanish *sauf-conduits* were delivered to The Hague through the Venetian ambassador, the States General refused them, since Roose, whom Philip had entrusted with drawing up the wording along lines specified by Olivares, had referred to the Dutch provinces simply as allies of France.[11] In December 1638 the Cardinal-Infante advised Madrid that the Imperial agent at Brussels was now adding his weight to the international pressure on Spain to issue papers acceptable to the Dutch and asked whether he should not now acquiesce so as to avoid the Spanish crown appearing as the sole obstacle to peace. The reply from Madrid was that he most certainly should not.

[10] Wagenaar xi. 242-3.
[11] *Corresp. d'Esp.* iii. 175; *Corresp. Stravius,* 259; Aitzema, *Ned. Vreede-handeling* i. 370, 373.

But while obstructing a general peace, behind the scenes the Spaniards were more active. What Philip and his ministers wanted was to extract a separate settlement with the Dutch on what they termed 'condiciones razonables' which, in turn, would enable Spain to conclude a much more favourable settlement with France or, at least, enable Spain to subject France to much heavier military pressure than otherwise. In May 1637 Olivares reaffirmed that what was indispensable to Spain was the recovery of Maastricht and the Maas valley as far as Gennep, one crossing over the Rhine and restitution of the Dutch gains in the New World for which Spain was prepared to offer Breda and at least 1 million ducats compensation.[12] In March 1638 Philip reiterated his basic stand to his brother in terms which were clearly the Conde-Duque's: first, Spain's position on Maas and Rhine must be restored by restitution of Maastricht, Rheinberg, and Orsoy; second, the Dutch zone of Brazil must be recovered in exchange for Breda and 3 or 4 million guilders.[13] On these terms Ferdinand was again empowered to conclude a truce.

Early in 1638 secret Dutch–Spanish talks resumed through Benedict van Ressel, curate of Loon-op-Zand who was sent to The Hague to meet Aerssen and Noordwijck, ostensibly to discuss the issue of the passports for Cologne, but in fact to make proposals for a separate Dutch–Spanish truce. Ferdinand was keen to exploit the growing pressure for peace in the Republic which was now obvious to ministers in Brussels, not only in the hope of securing a satisfactory separate settlement with the Dutch, but to embarrass the war-party and encourage Holland's evident reluctance to vote additional funds for the war.[14] Olivares endorsed this initiative but held out little hope of real headway until the Dutch should suffer further military and naval reverses at Spanish hands. And without such victories, asserted the Conde-Duque, it would be 'impossible' to secure the truce 'without great damage to ourselves and advantages to our enemy'. Ressel made several

[12] 'Voto del conde duque' (24 May 1637). AGS Estado 2052.
[13] Philip to Ferdinand, 17 Mar. 1638. ARB SEG 219, fos. 454–5.
[14] Ferdinand to Philip, 20 May 1638. ARB SEG 219, fo. 49; Consulta 11 May 1638, fos. 11ᵛ–12. AGS Estado 2053.

trips to The Hague, but apparently made little or no progress and eventually his purpose became known to Richelieu who delivered brusque warnings to the States General through the new French ambassador, D'Estrades.[15]

Intent on finding means to establish secret links with The Hague, while throwing the French off the scent, the Cardinal-Infante also sought to employ two other intermediaries during 1638. In May he attempted to send one of the Antwerp burgomasters, again ostensibly to discuss quite different matters, but the latter was refused a passport. In August he dispatched Friar Josèphe de Bergaine, bishop-elect of 's-Hertogenbosch, purportedly to discuss ecclesiastical organization in his diocese, but in fact to propose a separate truce on the basis of the Dutch giving up their Brazilian conquests, Maastricht, and one of the Rhine crossings.[16] On the issue of whether it was now best to openly demonstrate Spain's eagerness to conclude a truce or outwardly simulate lack of concern, there was sharp disagreement between the Cardinal-Infante and Roose of whose immense influence at Madrid the king's brother was now heartily tired. Olivares steadfastly backed his underling in advocating the harder line, while beseeching Ferdinand to respect Roose's wise advice.[17]

Reviewing the position early in 1639, the Cardinal-Infante admitted that he had made no progress towards a separate settlement with the Dutch, but continued to draw comfort from the now powerful desire for peace in the Republic.[18] Although secret contacts between Brussels and The Hague continued, through Ressel and the bishop, it was during the spring of 1639 that papal and French diplomats learnt the purpose of their trips and from that time, the Dutch no longer made any effort to treat Ferdinand's initiatives confidentially.[19] Frederik Hendrik himself took to sending Richelieu details of the Spanish proposals. In Madrid the *Consejo* concluded that since the Dutch refused to concede Spain's

---

[15] *Corresp. d'Estrades*, 36.

[16] Ferdinand to Philip, 2 Aug. 1638. ARB SEG 219, fos. 460-469[v].

[17] 'El Conde Duque sobre el punto de la tregua' (Sept. 1638). AGS Estado 2053.

[18] Ferdinand to Philip, 15 Feb. 1639. AGS Estado 3980.

[19] *Corresp. Stravius* 359, 360; *Corresp. D'Estrades*, 37-8, 61-2.

minimum requirements through negotiation, these would have to be extracted by force: northern Brazil was to be reconquered by the *armada* then being prepared at Lisbon, while the Dutch navy was to be swept to destruction in its home waters by the vast *armada* being assembled at Corunna. The result was the twin naval offensives of 1639. The humiliation and catastrophic losses suffered by Spain at the Downs, at the hands of the Dutch fleet, under Tromp, certainly extinguished all remaining hopes of wresting concessions from The Hague by *force majeure*. What remained unaltered, for the time being, was the Spanish policy of blocking the general peace while secretly pursuing a separate settlement with the States General.

What finally shattered the Conde-Duque's Dutch policy were the disastrous reverses suffered by Spain during 1640. Shock waves from the Catalan insurrection and the loss of Artois to the French during the summer, followed by the still more devastating secession of Portugal in December, soon traversed the entire hispanic world. Within a few tumultuous months, the Spanish Monarchy ceased to be the formidable force and imposing entity that it had been in Europe and the wider world for so long. Following the disasters of the summer, Philip instructed Brussels that the prompt conclusion of a truce with the Dutch provinces was now vital, that every conceivable means should be employed to this end, including the immediate provision of *sauf-conduits* for Cologne satisfactory to the Dutch.[20] The Spanish objective during the latter part of 1640, before the impact of Portuguese events, was to try to secure an immediate settlement with the Dutch by postponing any solution of the most intractable issue, Brazil, either for subsequent agreement at the Cologne conference, which would mean several years after the main Dutch-Spanish truce or else by excluding Brazil from the truce altogether.[21] At the same time, Ferdinand offered Frederik Hendrik a full peace to follow the cease-fire should such be preferred by the States General to

[20] Consulta 17 Nov. 1640. AGS Estado 2055; 'propongo paz y mas paz', exclaimed Olivares, 'y para esto se han embiado poderes a todas partes.'

[21] Ibid.; Ferdinand to Philip, 11 Dec. 1640. AGS Estado 3860; Ferdinand to Frederik Hendrik, Brussels, 6 Dec. 1640. AGS Estado 3860.

a truce. Coming on top of everything else, the shattering news of the revolt of Portugal reduced king and *Consejo* to a state of complete panic. Ferdinand received new orders to conclude truce arrangements, if possible, with both the Dutch and the French, on the basis of all sides holding what they then held, both in Europe and in the Indies. Thus, during the final months of Habsburg rule in southern Brazil (which followed Portugal in seceding from Spain in February 1641) Philip IV was in effect willing to partition the country with the Dutch under a formal treaty.[22] For the first time a Spanish monarch offered a share not only of the New World, but of his own American possessions, to another power. The only condition for which Ferdinand was to press, with both Dutch and French, was that these powers should undertake to refrain from assisting the king's Catalan and Portuguese rebels for a year or eighteen months. Even this proviso was to be dropped, however, should it threaten to hinder the proceedings. Should Ferdinand find that he could settle on these terms with the Dutch, but not the French, he was empowered to conclude without further reference to Madrid.

[22] Consulta 16 Jan. 1641. AGS Estado 3860; *Corresp. d'Esp.* iii. 391–2.

Chapter VI

The Final Struggle, 1641–1648

i THE LAST LAND CAMPAIGNS, 1641–1646

After months of argument in the States General and provincial assemblies over the Republic's aims and strategy in
the aftermath of the near crumbling of Spanish power during
1640, Frederik Hendrik had devised a compromise with
Holland assuring him enough troops to exploit Spain's weakness in at least a limited way. On 3 June 1641 the prince reviewed his 19,500-man field force, at Lith, before marching,
via Grave, on the powerful Spanish fortress commanding the
Maas valley at Gennep. Two small Spanish armies were formed
at Diest and Venlo and although they were too slow to prevent the Stadholder completing his siege fortifications, the
near by Spanish forces threatened his communications and
considerably complicated the operation. Conducted in an
exceptional heat-wave, a notable feature of the campaign
was the defection from the Cardinal-Infante's forces of large
numbers of Portuguese soldiers who, inspired by the news
from Portugal, went over to the Dutch hoping to return to
their homeland as indeed many of them did, via Amsterdam.
The garrison of Gennep, numbering 1,500 men under the
Irish colonel Thomas Preston, fought valiantly, mounting
numerous sallies and a furious counter-fire.[1] Among the
Dutch dead was the engineer Jakob van Aitzema, brother of
the historian Lieuwe. As usual during the second Dutch–
Spanish war, the remaining defenders (300 having been killed)
surrendered after relentless sapping and mining had rendered
their main walls untenable. The fall of Gennep in late July
was followed by several cavalry skirmishes and lesser engage-
ments at Tienen, Zandvliet, and elsewhere, while the Stadholder, now in increasingly ill health, and the bulk of the

---

[1] *Briefwiss. Huygens* iii. 175, 177–8, 184–5, 194; *Mémoires*, 283–92.

army remained encamped inactively, through August, near Gennep. After conferring with the States General's deputies to the army who came to his bedside, on 5 September, the prince resolved to ship the army to Flanders in order to help the French by diverting Spanish forces.[2] After encamping for some weeks at Assenede, the army transferred to near Bergen-op-Zoom, during the first half of October, before disbanding for the winter.

Conferring among themselves and with the French crown early in 1642, the Dutch provinces agreed to attempt, in combination with French forces, to overrun Geldern and the Overkwartier, this being one of the major remaining Dutch objectives. However, on 26 May the new governor of the Spanish Netherlands, Don Francisco de Melo (the Cardinal-Infante had died in November 1641), succeeded in defeating the French near Honnecourt, killing 1,200 and capturing 2,000. Owing to this and the approach of sizeable Imperialist forces, prince and States General agreed to abandon their plans for Geldern and remain on the defensive, shadowing the Spanish troops. The army encamped for a period in Brabant and then marched to the Rhine to shield Rheinberg and Orsoy; the tedium was relieved only by an occasional minor skirmish. Principally, the 1642 campaign contributed to the gradual recovery of Spanish prestige in Europe: the world was shown that despite the disasters of 1640-1, the Spanish Netherlands remained a defensive complex so formidable that its governor was able, with a modicum of Imperial help, to hold at bay the armies of both France and the Republic.

Following the fruitless 1642 campaign, the feuding between the States of Holland the the prince's supporters resumed with new intensity. The essential weakness in the Stadholder's post-1633 political strategy was laid bare whenever attention focused on finance. While, within the context of his wider aims and strategy, the prince could still count on the particular interests of Haarlem and Leiden and the jealousy of these and other towns of Amsterdam's greatness to split the province, the Holland war-party had quite different motives

---

[2] *Briefwiss. Huygens* iii. 228.

for wanting the war to continue from those of the prince, and were not opposing Amsterdam in order to secure more funds for the army or subsidize new conquests. It is for this reason that Amsterdam was much more successful at rallying support for its policies in the field of finance than for either determining military strategy according to its likes or bringing the war to an end. On the issue of war-finance alone could Amsterdam's politicians break out of their isolation and turn the tables on the Stadholder. In January 1642 proposals to reduce the permanent standing army, by cutting the number of men in each company, were agreed on almost unanimously by the States of Holland, only the nobility voting against.[3] The prince's objections, and delaying action by Zeeland and Utrecht, held up the decision in the States General for some months, but in December the provinces agreed unanimously on the reductions and a new *staat van oorlog* was prepared for 1643,[4] reducing the total size of the army from over 70,000 to 60,000 men. This episode was widely recognized as a turning-point in the history of the struggle for dominance in the Republic between prince and Amsterdam to the advantage of the latter. 'Son authoritté se diminue beaucoup' noted D'Estrades of the prince, referring to the 'jalousies que les peubles ont de luy, et principallement la province de Hollande qui attire à elle, autant qu'elle peust, les autres provinces.'[5]

As a result of the 1642 *reductie*, the field force mustered by Frederik Hendrik, in May 1643, was extremely modest.[6] This was a major factor in Melo's confidence that he could penetrate French territory in maximum force without fearing a Dutch attack in the rear. His initiative led only to the most crushing defeat in the history of the army of Flanders, at Rocroy on 19 May. The Dutch army was shipped to Flanders in mid June but was able to pose no serious threat, partly because of its small numbers, and partly because the French, after their costly victory, largely withdrew from the scene, allowing Melo to concentrate what remained of his army in

[3] Res. Holl. 22, 27 Jan. 1642.
[4] Res. Holl. 2, 11, 14 Apr., 1 Aug., 8 Oct., 19 Dec. 1642, Aitzema, *Hist.* v. 356; Ten Raa, iv. 131-4.
[5] *Corresp. d'Estrades*, 149, 156.   [6] Aitzema *Hist.* v. 529.

Flanders. During July and August, the Stadholder encamped near Philippine, facing the Spaniards quartered around Sas van Gent. During this period the French took the opportunity to capture Thionville while Melo sent a force under his best commander, the Neapolitan, Andrea Cantelmo, to reoccupy Eindhoven and reinforce Spanish claims even over the northern part of the Meierij where the Spaniards seized the fortress of Heeswijk, close to 's-Hertogenbosch.[7] In late August the prince transferred, via Bergen-op-Zoom, to Noortgeest where he encamped facing the main Spanish force, quartered to the north-east of Antwerp. In this area, on 3 September the prince's son, Prince Willem, ambushed an enemy column, capturing 600 Spaniards, including a senior cavalry commander, Don Juan de Borja.

The year 1644 was one of resumed success for Dutch arms though it began inauspiciously, in May, far away from the Netherlands, at the battle fought between the Portuguese and Spaniards near Alburquerque, in Extremadura. While the invading Portuguese column had the best of the action, its Dutch contingent, under Colonel Eustatius Pijk, part of the Dutch military aid which had been sent to assist the Portuguese revolt suffered the impact of the initial Spanish attack, sixty-eight Dutch soldiers being killed and Pijk and other officers captured.[8] In early June Frederik Hendrik once again shipped to Flanders, encamping near Philippine. Spanish troops likewise concentrated in the area, letting off a tremendous salvo on 14 June, to mark the news of Philip IV's victory at Lérida. In late June the prince transferred his camp to Eeckeloo and then, in July, to Maldegem. The French meanwhile profited from the concentration of the Spanish forces against the Dutch by capturing Gravelingen. On the night of 27 July the Dutch forced the canal running from Ghent and swiftly occupied Zelzate and the network of forts around Sas van Gent. Having cleared the path with unexpected speed, the Dutch began their siege of the latter town. The Spaniards under Melo (Marqués de Tor de Laguna) and Count van IJssemburg, aided by troops of the duke of

[7] *CODOIN* lxxv. 451; Aitzema, *Hist.* v. 529.
[8] Consul Pieter Cornelis to SG, Lisbon, 4 June 1644. RAZ SZ 2114.

Lorraine, kept up their pressure on the prince but decided not to risk an all-out assault. Instead, Tor de Laguna hastily constructed a new canal, linking Meerdonk, Moerbeke, and points further west, providing a reserve defence-line for Antwerp and Ghent, in case Sas van Gent should fall. Once again, there was no question of starving the garrison or exhausting its supplies. The bombardment was relentless. When the town governor, Andrés de Prada y Múxica, eventually surrendered on 5 September, after six weeks of siege and some fierce hand-to-hand fighting, with heavy losses on both sides, with Dutch trenches, shafts, and mines all around and much of the town demolished by exploding grenades, the battered defenders still had ample food and munitions.[9] The satisfying spectacle of the surrender was reportedly observed by 'une foule incroyable de Zélandois'. The army remained encamped near by until mid October.

After a quiet phase on the home political front during 1644, in which the Stadholder's friends in the States of Holland managed to block further proposed force reductions, this time in the cavalry,[10] Frederik Hendrik suffered another setback in his struggle with Amsterdam early in 1645. The French crown was anxious that the Dutch should resume their offensive in Flanders and Frederik Hendrik was keen to comply.[11] Accordingly, he tried to prevent the diversion of Dutch resources to the naval action against Denmark in conjunction with Sweden, on which Amsterdam and the maritime towns insisted as a consequence of the passionately resented decision of the Danish monarch to drastically increase the Sound dues charged on foreign shipping. The prince went so far as to arrange, through D'Estrades, for Mazarin to impress on the Dutch ambassador at Paris that he, the Cardinal, and the queen-mother, the French regent were 'mal satisfaits de MM. les Estats d'entreprendre une nouvelle guerre contre le Roy de Danemarc et négliger celle qui est contre le Roy d'Espagne'.[12] The outcome was a compromise: Holland having refused to vote the funds needed for the 1645

---

[9] Vincart, *Campaña de 1644*, 13–6; Aitzema *Hist.* v. 771.
[10] Res. Holl. 26 July 1644.
[11] Res. Holl. 28 Feb. 1645.   [12] *Corresp. d'Estrades*, 238–9.

campaign in Flanders until the States General agreed to the expedition against Denmark, both offensives were resolved upon. This in turn led to a renewal of the argument over Dutch strategic objectives in the South Netherlands. While historians have traditionally made much of Amsterdam's distaste for plans to attack Antwerp, Amsterdam fearing that were Antwerp to be liberated from the Spaniards, its trade would revive at the expense of Amsterdam, in fact Antwerp was a highly popular objective in the Republic, particularly with the inland provinces, and Frederik Hendrik came under considerable pressure to direct his attention towards the city on the Schelde.[13] The prince, however, felt no particular enthusiasm for so daunting an operation which the Spaniards could be expected to oppose with every man — and their troops in the Netherlands now amounted to 77,200[14] — at the cost of leaving the rest of the country totally exposed to the French, and preferred to concentrate on east Flanders, 'ce cher pais de Waes auquel on a faict d'amour tant d' années de suitte', as Huygens expressed it.

In mid June 1645 Frederik Hendrik shipped his army to Philippine and advanced again on Zelzate. After more than two months of inactivity at Zelzate, Eekloo, and Maldegem, on 29 September the army moved on Ghent. There was a desultory exchange of fire with the city walls in which two or three men were killed. Then, in early October, after being lulled into a false sense of security, the Spaniards were caught off guard when the prince moved swiftly against Hulst, an objective less difficult, assuredly, than Antwerp, but nevertheless formidable enough. Intricate fighting ensued for five key outlying forts — Spinola, St. André, Kieldrecht, Moervaert, and Ferdinand. In the main, these formidably protected complexes, manned by hundreds of men, surrendered one by one after only token resistance. After a fortnight Frederik Hendrik was able to close in on the town itself and begin the usual furious cudgelling with mortars and artillery. The town buildings having suffered extensive damage from exploding missiles, the 1,200 man garrison surrendered

[13] Aitzema, *Hist.* vi 237.
[14] Consulta 28 Mar. 1645. AGS Estado 2063.

on 4 November, with their supplies largely intact.[15]

By early 1646 the political battle over the Munster peace negotiations was reaching its dramatic climax, the mood of Holland had turned decidedly against the war, and it was only with considerable difficulty that Stadholder and war-party could keep the land war in progress. While the prince received backing for a further offensive against the Spaniards from Zeeland and the inland provinces (including Gelderland, which, though basically inclined to peace was anxious for some last territorial gains, particularly Geldern and Venlo[16]), Holland held up the preparations in March and April 1646, resisting insistent demands from States General and *Raad van State,* as well as heavy pressure from the French.[17] In effect, Holland used its weight at this crucial juncture to speed up the peace negotiations, refusing to vote the necessary funds for the 1646 campaign until delaying tactics on the part of other provinces with regard to Munster were dropped, which duly happened during May.

Having secured his army, Frederik Hendrik first remained encamped inactively for some weeks at Breda. It was there that he signed a secret agreement with the young Louis XIV and Mazarin, accepting a French contingent of 6,000 men to strengthen his army for an attempt on Antwerp, on con-dition that should the town fall the public practice of Catho-licism would continue to be tolerated. This accord was signed in the name of the States General, though neither that body nor the provinces had discussed the matter, and both Holland and Zeeland subsequently repudiated the undertaking, though not the actual design on Antwerp.[18] Indeed, the in-land provinces, Zeeland, and even some Holland towns, jealous of Amsterdam's greatness, remained keen on the project to the end. In July, as French forces entered Flanders from the west, Frederik Hendrik advanced from Zeeland. On 2 August Dutch troops attacked Fort Molensteeg, near

---

[15] *Briefwiss. Huygens* iv. 228-31; Brand, 236-7.
[16] Van der Capellen ii. 172, 174.
[17] Res. Holl. 20, 23 Mar., 17, 25 Apr., 3 May 1646.
[18] RAZ SZ 3236, copies of draft resolutions of 12, 14, 15 Sept. 1646; Ait-zema, *Hist.* vi. 230-2.

Ghent. Anticipating a combined Franco-Dutch attack on Ghent or Brugge, the Marqués de Castel-Rodrigo, the new governor of the Spanish Netherlands, concentrated his men in Flanders. Then suddenly, in the second week of August, the Stadholder swerved right around, seizing Temse and approaching Antwerp along the Schelde, from the south-west. With frantic haste, the Spaniards rushed every available man to the defence of Antwerp, leaving the whole of Flanders open to the main French force. The French units attached to the prince reportedly pillaged systematically and raped scores of women in the approaches to Antwerp, incensing the South Netherlands population the more in that such conduct had continued to be almost unknown on the part of either the Dutch or Spanish soldiery.[19] To the last, the second Dutch-Spanish war had remained the most restrained of conflicts. As a result of Castel-Rodrigo's efforts, the prince's advance on Antwerp was successfully blocked at Rupel-monde. Seeing no chance of breaking through from the west, Frederik Hendrik then ordered vice-admiral Johan Evertsen and the force on the river-fleet at Lillo, to attempt a surprise assault on the labyrinth of defences from below Antwerp.[20] On 11 August several hundred troops and sailors stormed and briefly held the key fort at Bouregat but were driven back by withering counter-fire. Frederik Hendrik subsequently withdrew to St. Gilles but remained encamped close to the Schelde.

During mid September, the secret debate over strategic priorities in the Stadholder's camp reached a new climax. Holland's delegates to the army urged, despite French pressure to the contrary, early disbandment of the army, ostensibly to save money.[21] However, most of the other provinces were anxious to renew the attempt on Antwerp, the pros-pects for which had improved again when the French set siege to Dunkirk on 13 September, forcing Castel-Rodrigo to divide his forces in a bid to save Flanders's chief port.

[19] Vincart, *Campaña de 1646*, 126.
[20] Ibid. 174; Frederik Hendrik to Evertsen, 11 Aug. 1646, and Evertsen to SZ, 12 Aug. 1646. RAZ SZ 1261; De Jonge, *Levensbeschrijving*, 45-7.
[21] Aitzema, *Hist.* vi. 237.

But Gelderland and probably the prince too preferred an attack on Venlo and by switching Holland's support to Gelderland, during this final offensive, Amsterdam did indeed engineer Dutch efforts away from Antwerp, aided by the other Holland maritime towns. Frederik Hendrik, who in any case needed little persuading, duly shipped to Bergen-op-Zoom, marched via 's-Hertogenbosch to the Maas and descended upon Venlo, showering the town with exploding missiles, hoping to force a prompt surrender as the Cardinal-Infante had done in 1637.[22] But Castel-Rodrigo had managed to reinforce the garrison and it soon became clear that the town would fall only after a prolonged siege. In October the French, triumphant at last in Flanders, took Dunkirk, but the Dutch, deeply divided, failed to agree on whether or not to persist with the siege of Venlo and the attack was abandoned. Indeed, there was considerable doubt in the Republic, where it was now an open secret that Frederik Hendrik had suddenly switched to supporting the truce moves, whether the prince was at all serious in his advance on Venlo, the impression being widespread that his manouevres were purely *pro forma.* At Munster the pro-truce Dutch plenipotentiaries actually went so far as to assure their Spanish counterparts that the operation against Venlo was not meant in earnest.[23]

During early 1647 the French once again urged the States General to field an army and the Stadholder, in the last weeks of his life, went through some ambiguous motions, ostensibly in preparation for doing so. But the Holland peace-party was now overwhelmingly in the ascendant in the States General and their position was further strengthened by the distaste and fear aroused among wide sections of the Dutch public by the recent French advances in Flanders as well as by the solid progress that had now been achieved in the peace talks at Munster. Holland simply refused to vote the funds and, thus, during 1647 the States General found itself with no alternative but not to take the field.

---

[22] Vincart, *Campaña de 1646*, 223.
[23] *Corresp. Diplomática* i. 430.

ii THE END OF THE WAR AT SEA, 1641–1647

The final phase of the war at sea was one of the most dramatic of the entire struggle. The revival and re-expansion of both Flemish *armada* and privateers, already foreshadowed in the years 1639–40, was sustained with remarkable success until 1646. Despite twenty years of striving to contain the threat and the great improvement in the command and tactics of the Republic's navy, the level of Dutch losses rose appreciably during the early 1640s, driving freight and insurance rates to a new peak.[24]

In February 1641 the admiralty colleges warned the States General that the combined strength of *armada* and privateers, totalling seventy sail, was now more formidable than had ever been seen previously.[25] But while the maritime towns, increasingly agitated, sought to pressure the States General into further strengthening naval defence in the North Sea, the Stadholder, inland provinces, and Holland inland towns were equally determined to reduce the forces in home waters so as to exploit the 'schoone occasie', the golden opportunity to profit from the revolts of Catalonia and Portugal which had all but paralysed the once powerful Spanish Monarchy. These groups now strongly urged the use of Dutch sea-power for more grandiose purposes than mere defence. Already, in January, the States General had debated Richelieu's request that the Republic send fifteen warships to join the French fleet being prepared for Catalonia, but Holland had blocked the proposal. The pressure that built up in the States General for sending a powerful fleet in support of insurgent Portugal, however, was not so easily resisted. On 8 March the States of Holland split over proposals to dispatch twenty sail that summer to disrupt Spanish sea-power off the Portuguese coast.[26] It was reported in the Republic that the Spaniards were already blockading Lisbon to prevent essential munitions reaching the country from the Republic and France,[27] but though the maritime towns accepted that it was advantageous for the Dutch to support the Portuguese insurgents, they

[24] Schreiner, 324; Baetens, *Nazomer* i. 384–5.
[25] ARH Bisdom, vol. 68, fo. 45; Centen, 96–7.
[26] Res. Holl. 8 Mar. 1641.   [27] *Brieven Reigersberch*, 661.

insisted that the mounting threat from Flanders and the
navy's chronic shortage of seamen precluded the sending of
a strong fleet to Portugal, as well as to Flanders. The argument continued through March and April ending in victory
for the inland provinces and the decision to prepare the
expedition to Portugal.[28] In July Admiral Gijsels, appointed
to command the force, was instructed by the States General
to clear the Portuguese coast of Castilian shipping, to try to
intercept the Spanish treasure-fleet returning from the
Caribbean to Seville, and to seize Dutch merchant vessels
illegally attempting to convey munitions or naval stores to
Spanish ports.[29] Gijsels's fleet cruised off the Portuguese
coast for several months, the major incident being an inconclusive but bitterly fought battle with twenty-four
Spanish and Flemish ships off Cape St. Vincent.[30]

The inevitable consequence of the expedition to Iberian
waters was that Tromp was seriously hampered in his efforts
to seal off the Flemish ports by shortage of ships, supplies,
men, and funds. Among other danger signs the accelerating
defection of Dutch sailors to Flanders, where wages were
better and employment prospects expanding, naturally
caused great anxiety in the Republic.[31] Although exact
figures for the year are wanting, there can be no doubt that
Dutch losses of both merchantmen and fishing vessels, during
1641, were amongst the highest of the war.[32] They included
a richly laden East Indiaman, the *Delft*, a convoy of eight
fluits that had been *en route* for Koenigsberg with salt from
La Rochelle and at least thirteen *fluits* carrying salt from
Portugal *en route* to Amsterdam. The Dutch fishing commu-
nities, disrupted more than ever by the Dunkirkers, brought
such pressure to bear on the States General that in July
instructions were issued to Tromp and the admiralty colleges
to retaliate in future against Flemish fishermen, bringing all
those encountered together with their nets and boats into
Dutch ports.[33]

[28] Res. Holl. 9, 12, 16, 19 Mar., 18, 23 Apr. 1641.
[29] ARH Bisdom vol. 68. fos. 299-301.
[30] De Jonge, *Ned. Zeew.* i. 332, 380.
[31] Res. Holl. 23 Apr. 1641; De Boer, *Tromp en de Duinkerkers*, 25.
[32] Res. Col. Middelburg, 4 Nov. 1641. ARH Admiraliteiten 2463.
[33] Res. Col. Middelburg, 1 July 1641. ARH Admiraliteiten 2463.

The year 1642 was again one of the most successful for the Dunkirkers. In all, as can be seen on Table 8, 118 Dutch vessels were captured without counting those prizes brought by Dunkirkers into Spanish ports which were certainly far from a negligible number.[34] The receipts of the Flemish admiralty board from Dutch prizes, during 1642, totalled 1½ million guilders. Once again, Tromp suffered from both lack of funds and men.[35] In October the admiral gloomily calculated that a total of between forty and fifty Flemish privateers were infesting the seas, manned in part by former Dutch navy men. The heaviest losses were suffered late in the year, after October, when, as usual, the Dutch naval blockade was lifted. Indeed, during November 1642 occurred one of the most memorable incidents of the entire Dutch–Spanish war in the North Sea when five *coningsschepen* met the Muscovy convoy returning to Amsterdam from Archangel: the eighteen richly laden vessels were escorted by two warships; in the ensuing fight one of the latter and eight *Moscowvaerders* were captured involving heavy losses for many among the élite of Amsterdam's business community.[36] In December, six *fluits* from a Zeeland Bordeaux convoy were taken. Consternation reigned at Middelburg and Flushing as at Amsterdam 'at the excessive and intolerable damage suffered by the inhabitants of these lands as a result of which great anxiety has arisen among both merchants and common folk'.[37]

During 1643 the Dunkirkers continued to take their toll of Dutch shipping in the Channel, the North Sea, and, on occasion, the Atlantic. Tromp estimated in October that the privateers numbered at least sixty sail or more than twice the strength of *armada* and privateers combined in 1627 when the level of forces for the blockade of the Flemish coast had last been raised (to forty-five sail).[38] Not only did the foe

---

[34] Baetens, 'Flemish Privateering', 63.

[35] Res. Holl. 8 May, 13 Sept., 27 Nov. 1642; Res. At. Middelburg, 29 Oct. 1642. ARH At. 2464.

[36] ARB Admirauté 581, doc. 40. 9 Nov. 1642; Res. At. Middelburg, 17 Nov. 1642. ARH Admiralteiten 2464; *Corresp. d'Estrades*, 147-8; Malo i. 368.

[37] Res. Col. Middelburg, 1 Dec. 1642. ARH Admiraliteiten 2462.

[38] Tromp to SG, 20 Oct. 1643. RAZ 2113; Witte de With to Col. Middelburg, off Dunkirk, 18 June 1643. RAZ 2113; Res. At. Middelburg, 20 June 1643. ARH Admiraliteiten 2464.

Table 8 Dutch Shipping Losses to the Dunkirkers, 1642-1644*

Types of vessel captured or sunk	1642	1643	1644
Warships	1 (28 guns)	1 (26 guns)	1 (200 lasts; 32 guns)
Muscovy ships (*Moscowvaerders*)	8	–	–
Straatvaarders	2a	–	1e
East and West India ships	2b	1d	–
Fluits (over 150 lasts)	11	18	10
Fluits (100–150 lasts)	26	15	10
Fluits (under 100 lasts)	12	4	1
Smacks and boats (under 50 lasts)	18	12	37
Herring busses	5c	6	12
Other fishing craft	33	41	66
Total	118	98	138

*ARB Admirauté 581.

a The 240-last *St. Joris* (20 guns), sailing from Gallipoli with silks, fine glass, and other luxuries; and a 130-last vessel sailing from Livorno for Amsterdam with almonds, syrop, damasks, and olive oil.

b Den Harinck, a 160-last Guineavaarder (16 guns), sailing from Amsterdam to Elmina with timber, stone, and manufactures, and a 150-last vessel from Dutch Brazil carrying sugar and tobacco.

c All from Zierikzee.

d *Den Snouk* (200 lasts, 18 guns) sailing from Brazil with sugar, tobacco, Brazil wood.

e A 160-last, 20-gun vessel, sailing from Xanto and Livorno with silks, currants, and other Levantine products.

now dispose of two to three times as many ships as during the late 1620s, but there had been a dramatic increase in the level of fire-power. Meanwhile lack of seamen and funds reduced Tromp's effective blockade force, at times, as low as seventeen and even only twelve ships. Under such conditions it was clearly impossible to prevent periodic break-outs from Dunkirk and Ostend the most dramatic such instance occurring in September when a pack of twelve privateers, under Admiral Boudewijn Smeecart, slipped away subsequently sweeping the Norwegian coast and North Sea taking twenty-eight prizes in all.[39] To add to the Dutch navy's troubles, the economic blockade of Flanders was increasingly circumvented, following the outbreak of the English civil war and

[39] ARB Admirauté 581, doc. 33.

the uncompromising policy of Parliament's navy of escorting English convoys regularly in and out of Dunkirk. Even so, it would be mistaken to suppose that the Dutch naval blockade of Flanders was now totally ineffective.[40] Apart from the twenty-eight vessels lost in the September break-out, two-thirds of the year's remaining losses occurred during the four winter months — January, February, November, and December — when the blockade was not in force and one third during the blockade months.

Under the Franco–Dutch agreement of February 1644 by which the allies had agreed to concentrate their land operations that year in Flanders, the Dutch undertook to deploy their usual blockade force and also collaborate with the French army should it besiege one of the Flemish ports. In March it was reported that enemy naval strength in the Flemish ports now stood at sixteen royal warships and sixty privateers.[41] When the French forces duly besieged Gravelingen, Tromp positioned five warships to seal off the harbour, but, as in previous years, the main Dutch effort was concentrated on Dunkirk and Ostend. Such were the forces available to the enemy that heavy losses were again inevitable, but though on paper the number of Dutch vessels taken in 1644 exceeded the figures for 1642 and 1643, the proportion of merchant vessels was appreciably lower, the great bulk of the losses being fishing craft. The most notable incident occurred in late November 1644, after the lifting of the Dutch blockade, when eleven privateers attacked a Rouen convoy returning to Zeeland capturing a 200-last thirty-two-gun warship and seven *Rouenvaarders* for the loss of one Ostender.[42] The Flemish admiralty board's receipts for Dutch prizes during 1644 totalled a round million guilders.

With the fall of Gravelingen and the increasingly precarious position of Dunkirk itself, there was some tendency during 1645 for both wealthy citizens and privateering firms and vessels to depart, though in many cases this meant simply a transfer of activity to Ostend. Total receipts of the Flemish

[40] *Mem. Hist. Esp.* xvii. 202.
[41] Res. Holl. 18 Mar. 1644; Baetens, 'Flemish Privateering', 54.
[42] Res. Col. Middelburg, 23, 30 Nov. 1644. ARH Admiraliteiten 2465; Centen, 105.

admiralty board in 1645 wore down to only about half the level for 1644, though the number of Dutch prizes was still impressive at eighty-four.[43] These included a 180 last *straatvaarder, Den Keiser,* sailing from Xanto to Amsterdam with coral, currants and other Levantine wares as well as various *fluits* mostly carrying French or Portuguese salt northwards and Baltic timber or grain westwards. During 1646 there took place a marked decline in the number of privateers operating, down from sixty in 1644 and forty-four in 1645 to thirty-six in 1646,[44] but those that remained enjoyed relatively easy pickings despite the besieging of Dunkirk, by the French army and Dutch navy, in September, owing to the fact that that year the Dutch mounted a mere skeleton blockade along most of the Flemish coast, because lack of funds greatly reduced the number of blockade ships available.[45] Total Dutch shipping losses again amounted to eighty-six and the Flemish admiralty board's receipts from Dutch prizes were up on those of 1645 at 728,326 guilders. The fall of Dunkirk certainly further disrupted Flemish privateering to some extent but owing to the lack of figures for the first half of 1647, the final months of Dutch–Spanish hostilities in Europe, it is hard to know how complete or effective was the transfer to Ostend and Nieuwpoort.

iii THE LAST OFFENSIVES IN THE INDIES, 1641–1648

For the Dutch West India Company, the period from the disarming of the Castilian and Neapolitan troops in southern Brazil by the Portuguese insurgents against Philip IV, during the spring of 1641, until the ratification of the treaty of Munster in April 1648, falls into two distinct transitional phases: the Company's position in the western hemisphere was changing rapidly in ways which exerted a profound influence on the general evolution of Dutch policies towards the hispanic world. The first phase, from early 1641 until the insurrection of the Portuguese planters against the Company's rule in Dutch Brazil in June 1645, was a period in

[43] Baetens, loc. cit. 63.   [44] Baetens, loc. cit. 54.
[45] SG to SZ, 3 Aug. 1646. RAZ SZ 952; De Boer, *Tromp en de Duinkerkers,* 95–6.

which the Company felt sufficiently assured of its position in Brazil to reduce its forces there appreciably, in which its standing and the price of shares in Holland, if not high, were at a tolerable level,[46] and during which it sustained active ambitions for conquest in Spanish America.[47] From June 1645 the Company's prospects and attitude were fundamentally transformed, above all by the rapid deterioration of its position in Brazil, to the point that it can be said to have defected for practical purposes from the ranks of the Dutch war-party.

The combined influence of the Dutch colonial companies had failed either to prevent or seriously delay the Dutch–Portuguese treaty of reconciliation and alliance signed by the States General in June 1641 shortly before the sending of Dutch naval and military forces to assist the Portuguese rebels against Spain. If the colonial interest had discerned the opportunity to exploit Portuguese weakness to seize additional Portuguese territories and trade in the Indies for the Republic, the combined pressure of the Stadholder's party, anxious to support Portugal so as to further weaken Spain in Europe and facilitate conquest in the Spanish Netherlands, together with that of the Holland maritime towns anxious to resume trade with Portugal, especially to secure salt, proved overwhelming, even without the added weight of Richelieu who was little disposed to allow the needs of Dutch colonial trade interfere with his schemes for demolishing Habsburg predominance in Europe. Even so, until 1645 the Dutch–Portuguese accord offered the West India Company one seemingly solid advantage: just as Philip IV had now for some months been willing to do, the Portuguese crown, in effect, recognized the Company's rule in north-east Brazil and dropped its claims to the territory, thus releasing the Company's military might for use elsewhere.[48] While the Company's mounting financial difficulties

---

[46] At least until early 1644, Van Dillen, 'Effectenkoersen', 9–10; it is true, however, that the real collapse of the Company's shares occured in 1644, that is before the revolt in Brazil, and seems to have been essentially due to a sharp fall in sugar prices, see Cabral de Mello, 44, 273–5, 301.

[47] 'Brieven Blommaert', 193–4.

[48] *Kroniek*, 1869, 397–9, Palafox, 39.

precluded any large-scale offensive in Spanish America, enough could be, and was, undertaken to confirm the vigorous continuance of the Company's former ambitions.

During the early 1640s the fortifications and naval forces at Curaçao were steadily strengthened and a policy of sporadic aggression against the Spanish settlements on the Venezuelan, Colombian, Cuban, and Puerto Rican coasts initiated in combination with systematic harassment at sea.[49] In October 1641 a fleet of six Dutch vessels scoured the gulf and lagoon of Maracaibo, plundering and pillaging settlements and seizing stocks of tobacco and cacao.[50] The Spaniards replied in October 1642 when a force from Venezuela temporarily ejected the Dutch from Bonaire, the island next to Curaçao, but decided against risking an attack on the main Dutch base. From 1642, when Pieter Stuyvesant became governor, the Company's spending on Curaçao which, as the Zeeland chamber noted, 'costs the Company a great deal each year without yielding any profit or return cargo'[51] was considerably stepped up. In November 1642 Stuyvesant attacked Puerto Cabelo on the Venezuela coast, sinking four ships in the harbour. In 1644 Stuyvesant launched a major attack with twelve ships and over 1,000 men on the Spanish garrison of San Martín, the scene of the Dutch defeat in 1633; but despite overwhelming advantage in numbers, the Dutch were unable to reduce the small Spanish force and after a four-week siege withdrew in defeat.[52] But the most remarkable West India Company thrust in the Spanish New World during the 1640s was the expedition of five ships and several hundred men, under Hendrik Brouwer, which rounded Cape Horn in April 1643 and operated for several months in southern Chile.[53] Though this force managed to burn one of the Spanish forts at Chiloe and establish a temporary Dutch base at Valdivia, as well as initiate friendly contact with Indians hostile to Spain, hopes of establishing a permanent base and an effective alliance with the Araucanians against

[49] Menkman, 'Van de verovering', 169.
[50] *Ned. Zeevaarders* (Wright) ii. 96, 98.
[51] De Nederlanders i. 49, 50, 51; van Brakel, 48–9.
[52] Menkman, *De Nederlanders*, 53; Goslinga, 135.
[53] Barlaeus, *Bras. Geschichte*, 770–4; Barros Arana iv. 376- 88; Gerhard, 131.

Spain were soon disappointed. After several months, disillusioned with their Indian allies and their supplies exhausted, the remnant of the expedition abandoned Valdivia and sailed back to Dutch Brazil.

When the Company was consulted by the States General with respect to the Munster truce negotiations, in June 1644, the directors, then reeling from the 1643–4 collapse of the Company's shares,[54] due to a sharp fall in sugar prices in Europe which, ironically, derived in large measure from the resumption of Dutch trade with Portugal and Portuguese Brazil, following the Dutch-Portuguese truce of 1641, were anxious to advance their position in Spanish America, and in particular to secure fresh gains in the Caribbean and exploit their alliance with the Chilean Indians. They still definitely preferred a continuation of war with Spain in the Americas, even if a new truce were to be agreed on in Europe.[55] The directors were especially eager to press on with the conflict should the proposed merger of the West and East India Companies, a project intensively discussed in the provincial assemblies and States General during the spring and summer of 1644, come about, as the leadership of the former hoped. Were Philip to enjoy peace in his Indies, the directors warned, his power in Europe, which derived chiefly from his Peruvian and Mexican riches, would quickly revive to the dire cost of the Republic and its allies. In the event that the merger should not take place, and should the States General resolve on peace in the Indies as well as in Europe, then the Company's interests could best be secured by securing full commercial access to the American possessions of Spain. Modifying its position somewhat in April 1645, the directors declared that 'if the merging of the companies takes place, continuation of the war would be the more profitable [course] in both the east and west Indies.'[56] Should the companies remain separate and a comprehensive

---

[54] Van Dillen, 'Effectenkoersen', 9–10; Cabral de Mello, 44, 273–5, 301.

[55] 'Consideratien vande Westindische Compe deser Landen' (Amsterdam, 18 June 1644). ARH SG 4854; Tor de Laguna to Philip, Antwerp, 6 May 1644. AGS Estado 2062; *Kroniek, 1869*, pp. 397–9; *Aenwysinge datmen van de Oost en Westindische Compagnien*, pp. 33–5.

[56] 'Consideratien vande Westindische Compagnie' (April 1645). ARH SG 4854.

truce with Spain be agreed on, the Company would need acknowledgement by Spain of all its conquests in Brazil, the Caribbean, and West Africa, and Philip's recognition of the Company's right to trade with all parts of the New World not under direct Spanish administration and control and, preferably, with those regions which were so controlled.

By the autumn of 1646, following a sequence of unmitigated misfortune since the summer of 1643, the Company had been compelled to modify its stance significantly. Expectations of merging with the East India Company having receded, and in view of the 'excessive costs' which the Company now faced on account of the rising of the Portuguese in Dutch Brazil, the directors of the now fatally weakened company were principally anxious to avoid any risk of being left alone at war with Spain, in the New World, should there be peace in Europe. Since 1644 there had been a rapid decline in Dutch naval power in the Caribbean[57] and the unavoidable need to deploy what remained of the Company's depleted resources in Brazil finally removed, as the directors now recognized, any prospect of the Company being able to resume the offensive against the Spanish colonies. The directors were also now ready to face the fact that there was scant likelihood that Philip would concede full access to his American possessions. They lodged their hopes of placing the Company's future on a securer basis in seeking more limited commercial concessions, proposing that the Dutch plenipotentiaries at Munster be instructed to represent to the Spanish delegates the chronic shortage of black slaves that had arisen in the Spanish American possessions, since the secession of Portugal had cut them off from their traditional sources of supply, and that the 'Company is now virtually master, or has every prospect of becoming so, of the trade in slaves of which the American lands under the king of Spain have such need.'[58] This constituted a remarkable departure from the Company's traditional style of thinking and one which accurately identified the single most urgent economic problem of the Spanish Indies at that juncture. From

---

[57] Cabral de Mello, 43–4.
[58] WIC directors to SG, 14 Nov. 1646. ARH SG 4856.

November 1646 onwards the Company evolved, in both its ideas and curtailed investment programme, towards becoming an essentially peaceful trading organization content to act as agent or supplier to the colonies of foreign powers.[59]

The East India Company meanwhile remained consistently cool towards the prospect of peace with Spain while at the same time being eager, in the event of peace, to secure assurances that would serve to contain Spanish power and influence in the Far East, for it would be quite wrong to suppose that the secession of the Portuguese colonies from Spain, in 1641, had put an end to the conflict of Dutch and Spanish interests in the area. In one key locality, Taiwan, the Dutch did in fact succeed in eliminating Spanish power when, in 1641 the governor of Fort Zeelandia mounted an expedition of eight vessels and 800 men which captured the main Spanish base on the island at Kelang, on 25 August, and the subsidiary fort at Tamsoei, a few days later.[60] But the Spaniards remained entrenched on Ternate and Tidore as well as in the Philippines, posed a continuing threat to the Dutch spice trade as well as controlling, from Manila, much of the China trade, and, of course, retained their claims to the insurgent Portuguese colonies.

Should peace be resolved on, the East India Company directors advised the States General in June 1644, the Company's interests required that two fundamental concessions be wrested from Spain in the Far East:[61] first, that the Spanish crown commit itself not to extend its forts and trade beyond the limits that then applied, for were the Spaniards to do so, particularly in the Moluccas, they could easily interfere with the Company's commerce; secondly, were Spain to recover any of the Portuguese territories in the East, on the pretext that they had rebelled against the king's authority, this likewise would be extremely prejudicial to the Company so that under either a truce or peace agreement, in the directors' view, the States General should extract an undertaking that these possessions would remain out

[59] Van der Capellen ii. 192; *Kroniek* (1869), pp. 446–50.
[60] *Generale Missiven* ii. 173–5; Mac Leod ii. 309–10.
[61] 'Consideratien vande Oost Indische Compe deser Landen' (23 June 1644). ARH SG 4854.

of the power of Spain. In April 1645 the Heren XVII re-iterated that 'while the East India Company judges it preferable that the war with the Castilians in the East Indies should continue', a truce would be acceptable provided the 'Castilians continue with their navigation just as it now is without being able to extend it' and that they should 'remain out of Portugal's Indies without being able to trade there'.[62] Additionally, the Company pressed to be admitted to the trade of the Philippines.[63]

The East India Company's considerable efforts against the Spaniards in the Far East, following the successful conclusion of the struggle for Formosa in 1641, were, from a military point of view singularly fruitless. In 1645 a Dutch force under Martin Gerritszoon de Vries scoured the Philippines, but accomplished almost nothing.[64] In March 1646 the governor-general at Batavia sent de Vries back to the Philippines, with seven ships and 748 men, to blockade Manila Bay, disrupt Chinese trade with the islands, and try to intercept the silver galleon sailing from Mexico. After an inconclusive four-hour battle on 17 March with two large Spanish galleons and four junks, and after five months of blockading the Spaniards, de Vries was definitely worsted in another action on 1 August in which he lost two ships. In April 1647 de Vries returned yet again to the Philippines with no less than fourteen sail and 1,810 men, but apart from pillaging some lesser Spanish forts and settlements, again failed to inflict any significant reverse on the enemy, though he did seal off Manila Bay for several months.[65] During 1648 another Dutch expedition from Batavia, consisting of eight ships under Abel Tasman, scoured the Philippines, plundering coastal settlements and junks, but once again without any solid result. Yet these costly and seemingly wasteful expeditions directed by the Company's new governor-general, Cornelis van der Lijn (1645–50), were in fact partly motivated by sound commercial sense. By thus disrupting Chinese

[62] 'Consideratien vande Oostindische Negotianten' (24 Apr. 1645). ARH SG 4854.
[63] Sec. Res. SG 21 Jan. 1645. ARH SG 4854.
[64] *Dagh-Register*, 1644–5, pp. 174–5; Mac Leod, 360.
[65] Mac Leod ii. 360.

trade with Manila, the Dutch swelled their own commerce at Formosa; apparently a hefty profit was obtained during these years from the diversion of and drastic price-movements in Chinese pepper.[66]

In the Moluccas, while the Dutch continued to hem in the Spanish forts on Ternate and Tidore and virtually monopolized the lucrative spice trade, little or no progress was made towards eliminating the unwelcome Spanish presence.[67] Indeed, Dutch–Spanish friction in the Moluccas continued longer than in any other region of the world. The very last battle of the Eighty Years War was fought on Ternate on 18 July 1649, more than a year after ratification of the treaty of Munster, but before official publication of the news in parts of the East, after 250 Spaniards and 600 native troops had landed from Tidore on part of Dutch-held Ternate and began destroying spice plantations; a smaller Dutch force sent to repel the invaders was driven back with heavy loss.

iv THE DISMANTLING OF THE EMBARGOES, 1641–1648

Immediately before the secession of Portugal, an event which more than any other undermined Spanish power, while Philip IV's economic measures against the Dutch had been weakened in several ways, the Dutch nevertheless remained excluded from most sectors of Iberian trade and the embargoes a most effective instrument of pressure on Dutch maritime and commercial interests. Some licences were being sold to Dutch merchants enabling them to ship foodstuffs and munitions, but not manufactures or spices, to certain specified Portuguese and Andalusian ports and depart with heavily taxed salt and a maximum of one pipe of wine or 3,000 oranges and lemons; they were unable to load with wool, colonial products, or wine and fruit in commercial quantities.[68] The process was strictly controlled and restricted by Castilian bureaucracy such that until 1641 the shipping of Iberian salt to Scandinavia and the Baltic as well as to Flanders remained largely in Hanseatic, English, and to

[66] Ibid. ii. 360; *Generale Missiven* ii. 328; Mac Leod ii. 363.
[67] Mac Leod ii. 290, 421.
[68] ARB SEG 222, fo. 164, memorandum May 1639.

a lesser, but increasingly important extent, Danish hands.[69]
While temporary permission had on occasion been granted
for the use of Dutch ships in conveying grain to the Basque
provinces, Galicia, Valencia, and Mallorca, Dutch shipping
had not been admitted to the most crucial sector, Andalusia,
and access to the other regions had been promptly terminated
as soon as the worst 'crises de subsistance' had passed. Thus
while the Dutch clearly did increase their trade with Naples
and Sicily during the 1640s,[70] the *Almirantazgo* continued
to assert itself stringently throughout Spain, in Valencia and
Navarre as well as in Castile.

Internal pressure for a further relaxation of the embargoes
against the Dutch of course remained strong and there continued to be a good deal of debate on the matter among the
royal councils at Madrid.[71] Powerful interests, mercantile
and bureaucratic, urged increased contact with the Dutch to
stimulate salt, wine, and other exports, to swell customs
revenues, to assist grain imports, and, above all, to improve
the flow of copper, timber, pitch, and other naval stores
from Scandinavia and the Baltic. It was also pointed out,
rightly enough, that one effect of Philip's measures against
the Dutch was to inflate Louis XIII's revenues from French
salt and wine exports.[72] But, on the other hand, powerful
pressure continued to be exerted in favour of retention of
the embargoes, especially from the *Almirantazgo* itself,
anxious as ever to preserve its *raison d'être*, but also from
foreign, and especially Hanseatic, merchants with a vested
interest in the system. There was strong support for the
embargoes also from both Castilian and Flemish textile
manufacturers and their adherents who were keen to continue to benefit from the exclusion of Dutch and French
cloth from the Spanish realms and the Indies. Above all,
there was eager support from several of the king's ministers,
after as before the fall of Olivares in 1643, who still regarded economic pressure as an effective, indeed one of the
few remaining effective means, by which the Spanish crown
could bring the Dutch to acceptable terms.

[69] Pieter Meyers to G. de Roy, Lübeck, 5 Dec. 1644. ARB SEG 232, fo. 232.
[70] Baetens, *Nazomer* i. 356–7, 370–1.
[71] See BRB MS 12832, fos. 126–37.   [72] Ibid., fos. 136v–137v.

A notable example of such forthright mercantilist thinking was the paper drawn up in Brussels for the Cardinal-Infante, in May 1639, by García de Yllan, a leading Antwerp business-man of Portuguese New Christian extraction who, among other activities was then importing gunpowder and other munitions from Denmark to Flanders (often via England) through his Jewish correspondent, Duarte Nunes da Costa at Hamburg. García de Yllan was one of the most influential merchants in the Spanish Netherlands and one of those who most obviously profited not only from the war against the Dutch but from their exclusion from trading with the his-panic world.[73] His submission was a rebuttal of a paper by Willem Willemsz. Coninck, a Dutch salt merchant from Hoorn who had advised Petrus Roose of various frauds practiced by Dutch businessmen using salt-licences issued by the Spanish authorities and who had suggested a relaxa-tion of the restrictions on Dutch shipping.[74] Yllan not only argued against Coninck's proposals, but maintained that the restrictions should be tightened and the flow of Iberian salt to the Dutch reduced, for the Iberian product was not only much superior to the French, and that of the West Indies, but was indispensable to the Dutch fishing and herring indus-tries which he regarded as an essential pillar of the Dutch carrying trade in Europe and beyond; the salt consignments, he observed, were also being used to smuggle silver to Holland, 'the silver which they dispatch to the East Indies to buy pepper . . . to Aleppo and Alexandria and elsewhere in the Levant . . . and also to Muscovy and elsewhere in the North, the principal foundations of all this trade being the fisheries which they conserve with Iberian salt and the silver which they ship to the ports with which they deal and thus it is that they obtain from Spain the means with which to defy and attack Spain.'[75]

The Portuguese Revolt, without doubt, drastically curtailed

[73] ARB SEG 222, fo. 379v; Christian IV to Cardinal-Infante, 20 Sept. 1639. ARB Sec. d'Etat Allemande 558, fos. 100–1; Denuce, 31–4.

[74] Cardinal-Infante to Philip, Brussels, 27 May 1639. ARB SEG 222, fo. 156.

[75] 'siendo los principales fundamentos deste comercio las pesquerias que con-servan con la sal de España y la plata que navegan a los puertos adonde trafican, y ansi se puede decir que de España sacan las fuercas y armas con que la offen-den y ponen en mayores aprietos', ARB SEG 222, fos. 160v–161v.

the scope of the Spanish embargo against the Dutch, especially by breaking Madrid's grip on the European salt-trade. The new monarch of Portugal, John IV, necessarily dependent on Dutch aid, shipping, munitions and grain, promptly threw open his ports to the Hollanders and their salt-carriers and, indeed, appointed an official Portuguese agent in Amsterdam to assist with the flow of aid in the person of the remarkable Lopo Ramirez or, as he was known in the synagogue, David Curiel.[76] Within months of the December revolution, the Dutch had largely recovered their former control of the international salt trade. By April 1641 Amsterdam merchants were sending large amounts of Setúbal salt to Stockholm, Danzig, and Koenigsberg as well as importing a great deal to Holland. As an inevitable result of this shift, the carrying of Iberian salt to northern Europe in Hanseatic ships virtually ceased. Hamburg and Lübeck dealers in salt switched to freighting Dutch ships to Portugal, and the specialized ship-building for the *Spanienfahrt* at Lübeck came to a halt.[77]

The States General actively encouraged the resumption of trade with Portugal as with rebel Catalonia and, in particular, facilitated the supply of strategic wares — arms, munitions, and grain — to both of these territories while at the same time continuing its ban on the supplying of such stores to the rest of Spain and its empire. From 1641 regular naval escorts were provided for merchant convoys sailing to Portugal from Holland and Zeeland, the admiralty colleges issuing licences for arms and ammunition exports on payment of cautionary deposits, redeemable within six months, on presenting certification that the supplies had been delivered either in Portugal or Catalonia. Huge quantities of munitions were dispatched from Amsterdam, Rotterdam, and Middelburg. In July 1641 Lopo Ramirez signed a contract with the first Portuguese ambassador to The Hague for 100,000 *cruzados*' worth of gunpowder, shot, and weapons to be delivered in Portugal.[78] Jan van der Straeten shipped a large stock of gunpowder to Barcelona, during 1641, for use against

[76] GA Amsterdam, box-index, freight contracts, 'Zouvaart', 1641–8.
[77] ARB SEG 232, fo. 232; Vogel, 36, 141.
[78] GA Amsterdam NA 1555 B, pp. 1103–4.

the 'general enemy'; the same merchant dispatched at least 4,000 muskets, 2,000 pikes, fifty large guns, and 50,000 musket shot to Lisbon that same year.[79] Gerrit Trip and Pieter Outgers of Amsterdam likewise shipped large consignments. The fact is that the initial and subsequent success of the Portuguese revolt was only made possible by the massive transfusion from Holland, for the French crown simply could not fulfill this role. In February 1641, when this huge operation had hardly begun, the States General calculated that it had already licensed the dispatch of 12,200 muskets, 3,000 pikes, seventy-four large guns, and a vast quantity of ammunition to the insurgent areas of the Peninsula.[80] It is true that a certain amount of munitions were sent also from Hamburg, notably by Duarte Nunes da Costa (Jacob Curiel) brother of Lopo Ramirez, and directly from Sweden, but undoubtedly the main supply came from Holland. Zeelanders also apparently participated to a significant extent. Wouter Abrahamsen of Flushing, for instance, was licensed, in February 1642, to ship 2,000 muskets, 1,000 pikes, and a large quantity of pistols and other arms and ammunition to Portugal.[81]

The collapse of the Spanish embargo against the Dutch in Portugal in turn forced some further relaxation in the embargoes in Galicia and Asturias. Ever since the 1620s the important Galician fishing industry had suffered increasingly from declining provision of salt from Portugal, due to the post-1621 chronic shortage of coast-to-coast shipping.[82] The Portuguese secession precipitated a full-scale crisis for the Galician economy, however, for the royal authorities would no longer permit the importing of supplies from rebel Portugal. Although a number of English ships were freighted to carry salt from Cadiz to Pontevedra, it proved impossible to provide anything like sufficient stocks in this way. For this reason, Fernando Montezinos, the New Christian financier who then held the royal contract for provisioning Galicia

[79] ARH Bisdom vol. 68, pp. 44, 55, 68.
[80] Ibid., p. 59.
[81] Res. Col. Middelburg, 17 Feb. 1642. ARH Admiraltieiten 2463.
[82] Consulta 30 July 1630. AGS Hacienda 664.

with salt, was given permission in Madrid to import French salt from La Rochelle to Pontevedra and Betanzos using Dutch vessels;[83] at least one of the vessels supplied to Montezino's La Rochelle agent for this purpose was freighted in Amsterdam by the renowned Jewish physician, Dr Ephraim Bueno, who had formerly lived and studied in south-west France.[84] In the same period Montezinos obtained permission to employ Dutch vessels in conveying grain to Ceuta, a former Portuguese enclave in North Africa which was retained by the Spaniards and in this way further increased his contacts with Amsterdam.

At the same time, during the early 1640s the Spanish crown continued to issue numbers of passes to the Dutch to ship grain to various parts of the Spanish mainland, particularly the north. In July 1643, for instance, the eighty-last Dutch ship, the *St. Laurens*, which had been captured by the Dunkirkers, was restored to its owners because it had delivered grain to San Sebastián with an *Almirantazgo* pass and was returning to Rotterdam with an *Almirantazgo*-registered cargo of Castilian wool and Basque iron.[85] Similarly, during 1644 two small Flushing vessels were released intact by the Flemish admiralty board as they were *en route* to Bilbao and San Sebastián with timber and provisions and were holding Spanish passes. Understandably, the Hanseatic interest in Spain was extremely scathing about this practice,[86] and there was likewise strong opposition in Flanders where merchants pressed for a return to total exclusion of the Dutch.

And yet, despite the drastically reduced scope and diminished effect of the Spanish embargoes against the Dutch during the early 1640s, it would be wrong to suppose that these were now scarcely more than a dead letter. On the contrary, at any rate until 1645, the Spanish economic campaign against the Dutch remained a powerful factor in European commerce, chiefly owing to the continued exclusion of the Dutch from Andalusia which, in one way was actually

[83] Cedulas 20 Oct. 1642 and 7 Oct. 1646. AGS Hacienda 906.
[84] GA Amsterdam, Box-index, soutvaert.
[85] ARB Admirauté 581, doc. 22.
[86] *Cavsas por donde crecio el comercio de Olanda*, fos. 2ʳ–2ᵛ; *Discurso sobre. . .la Gverra Maritima*, 44, 49.

strengthened rather than weakened by the Portuguese Revolt by removing any reason for Dutch merchants to seek salt-passes for Cadiz and San Lúcar. The Amsterdam freight-contracts confirm that Dutch merchants were unable to freight Dutch ships to Andalusia. The movement of Spanish American colonial products from Cadiz and San Lúcar to northern Europe unquestionably remained firmly in the hands of the English, Hanseatics, and Danes.[87] For this reason, virtually all the ships sailing from southern Spain to northern Europe brought in by the Dunkirkers during the early 1640s on suspicion of being Dutch turned out to be genuinely non-Dutch. In January 1643 a large vessel captured *en route* from Málaga to Amsterdam, laden with wool, wine, and raisins, proved, as the skipper claimed, to be from Danzig and to have been freighted in Hamburg.[88] Two valuable prizes taken *en route* from San Lúcar to Amsterdam during 1644, carrying silver, cochineal, American hides, Campeche wood, wool, figs, and olive oil, were restored by the Dunkirkers intact on attesting that they were Hanseatic owned, in Lübeck and Danzig respectively, and manned by Hanseatic crews. Moreover, the Hanseatics at least continued to play a prominent role in the official trade between Seville and the Spanish Indies, consigning manufactures, buying up return cargoes in Mexico, Peru, and the Caribbean, and freighting Hanseatic ships to join the trans-Atlantic convoys. Lübeck alone reportedly lost twenty vessels in six years during the 1640s in the service of Seville and the Spanish crown in the Indies.[89]

One factor which somewhat reinforced the Spanish embargoes against the Dutch during the last phase of the struggle was the treaty signed in March 1641 between Spain and Denmark. During the early 1640s relations between Denmark and the Republic as well as Sweden steadily worsened as Copenhagen drew closer to the Habsburgs and adopted a more abrasive attitude to Dutch navigation passing through the Sound, all of which was to have far-reaching implications

[87] Baetens, *Nazomer* i. 354–5, 372–4, 375–6.
[88] ARB Admirauté 581, Jan. 1643.
[89] *Causas por donde crecio el comercio de Olanda*, fo. 6.

for European commerce. Under the treaty the Danes received extensive new privileges in Spain, established a resident at Madrid and a consul at San Lúcar, and undertook not only to ship timber, naval stores, and other supplies both to Spain and Flanders but to obtain their vital salt supplies not from Portugal but from Andalusia. The Danes also agreed to exclude Dutch goods from their cargoes to Spain and also ships of Dutch manufacture, even when Danish-owned.[90] Thus while during the 1640s Amsterdam merchants freighted Dutch ships in great abundance to deliver Portuguese salt to Swedish, Polish, and Prussian ports, there are scarcely any instances of Dutch merchants shipping salt to the various Danish realms. On the other hand, a ship sailing from Andalusia and taken by the Dunkirkers in 1643 on suspicion that it was Dutch, which was carrying salt from Cadiz to Copenhagen, proved to be owned in Glückstadt, which port was under the Danish crown.[91] Remarkably, just when investment and shipbuilding for the *Spanienfahrt* was drying up in the Hansa towns, there was a flurry of such activity not only in Schleswig-Holstein and Denmark proper but also at Oslo, Bergen, and Trondheim.[92]

The debate in the Spanish lands over whether to tighten or to relax the embargoes against the Dutch went on after the Portuguese secession as it had before.[93] It is true that the best means of pressuring the Dutch, control of Portugal's salt supplies, had now gone, that Barcelona was in rebel hands, and that the embargoes had all but collapsed in Naples and Sicily. Moreover, the fall of Olivares, in January 1643, presented an obvious opportunity for changing course with respect to many long-standing policies while, only recently, the crown had had to admit the indispensability of Dutch shipping in supplying salt to Galicia and Asturias. Yet, on the other hand, the Hanseatic interest, even though this was now waning, the new Danish involvement, pressure from the *Almirantazgo* and textile manufacturers, and above all the

[90] BL MS Add. 14010, fo. 268.
[91] ARB Admirauté 581, doc. 36.
[92] Johnson, 80.
[93] *Discurso sobre. . .la Gvuerra Maritima*, 44, 49.

fact that the embargoes were denying the Dutch the fruits of Spain's American commerce counteracted all the pressures working in favour of an end to economic confrontation with the Republic. After the *Consejo* had considered, but rejected, new proposals for establishing contact with Dutch financiers and merchants late in 1643, Philip reminded his governor in the Spanish Netherlands that 'allowing the Dutch to enjoy trade with Spain during the war could well be the way to perpetuate it, for only owing to lack of such trade have they desired the truce.'[94] Nor was the crown insensitive to the fact that a volte-face on the economic front would inevitably undermine the position of the Flemish privateers which it rightly recognized as one of its few other remaining means of exerting effective pressure on the Republic. One noted test case which aroused the interest of merchants in the Peninsula and reflected the conflict of views among the king's ministers arose in 1645 over an English ship of Dutch manufacture which was seized in the Bay of Biscay by Basque privateers;[95] the vessel was laden with French salt and vinagre. Despite vigorous protests from the English ambassador, with whom the crown was anxious to remain on good terms, the *Almirantazgo* and then the *Consejo de Guerra* declared the ship forfeit. Subsequently the matter caused a split in the *Consejo de Estado*; finally Philip himself decided that the ship should be restored to its owners.

A major step towards the dismantling of the embargoes occurred in October 1644 when, apparently for the first time, the crown gave permission for Dutch vessels to be used in transporting grain to parts of Andalusia, notably Málaga.[96] In the view of Hanseatic merchants in Spain who bitterly resented this shift in policy, the concession soon enabled the Dutch to 'make themselves once again masters of the merchandise of Spain and the Indies'. This was a gross exaggeration, but it was certainly true that a marked revival of Dutch trade with east Andalusia began in the autumn of 1644. In November 1644 the Dunkirkers released a 130-last

[94] Philip to Tor de Laguna, 28 Jan. 1644. ARB SEG 219, fo. 103.
[95] Consulta 9 Sept. 1645. AGS Estado 2064.
[96] *Cavsas por donde crecio el comercio de Olanda,* fos. 2ʳᵛ.

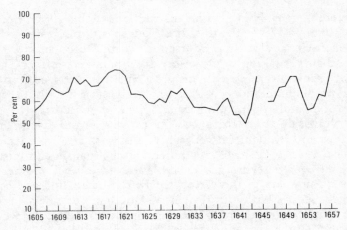

6 The proportion of Dutch vessels among total shipping entering the Baltic through the Danish Sound (1605–1657). *Source*: Ellinger Bang i, tables.

fluit sailing from Málaga to Amsterdam, bearing wine, raisins, and an *Almirantazgo* pass.[97] During 1645–6 a totally novel phenomenon since 1621, dozens of Dutch vessels delivered grain and loaded wines and fruit at Málaga.[98]

The economic conflict between the Republic and Spain finally ended in the summer of 1647, by which date Dutch ships and goods had officially been shut out of Spain for twenty-six years. In February 1647, following agreement on peace terms at Munster, The Hague, and Madrid, the Dutch plenipotentiaries at Munster informed the Conde de Peñaranda, who headed the Spanish delegation, that the blockade of the Flemish coast had now been officially terminated, the ban on shipment of grain from the United Provinces, copper, naval stores, and munitions lifted, and the first ships belonging to the king's subjects admitted to Dutch ports; the Spanish authorities were asked now to open the ports of Spain, Flanders, and southern Italy to Dutch shipping, on the same basis.[99] In Madrid the *Consejo* promptly concurred in ending

---

[97] ARB Admirauté 581, Nov. 1644.
[98] Wätjen, 224–5, 262, 406–14.
[99] Consulta 5 Aug. 1647. AGS Estado 2067; *Corresp. diplomatica* i. 492–3.

the embargoes, Philip issuing instructions to the *Almirantazgo*, in June 1647, both to admit Dutch shipping and goods henceforth and to deal courteously with Dutch seamen and merchants, making every effort to minimize friction. These instructions were issued anew to Spanish ports authorities and naval commanders in August, though this did not prevent the odd final confiscation taking place. A vessel from Hoorn carrying salt from Ibiza to Venice was seized by Spanish galleys and brought into Alicante in August 1647 and it took over a year of intricate, combined Dutch-Spanish administrative effort to secure its release.[1] But from the summer of 1647 a new era in the history of Dutch navigation and commerce began. With the revival of Dutch trade to Spain and the Dutch carrying trade between Spain and Italy, the whole of the Dutch carrying trade in Europe received a boost which, despite the temporary interruption caused by the first Anglo-Dutch war of 1652-4, and the second of 1665-7, continued until the 1670s. The proportion of Dutch among total shipping entering the Baltic rose from 1648, as can be seen from Graph 6, to levels comparable with those of the Twelve Years Truce period.

Unauthorized interference by *Almirantazgo* officials with Dutch ships and merchandise did not of course totally cease in a day or a month and there were, in any case, numerous difficulties relating to trade between the Republic and Spain which remained to be settled, but from the summer of the 1647 it was emphatically the policy of king and *Consejo* to minimize in every way the hindrances to Dutch trade with Spanish lands. Precisely to reduce friction and improve the still delicate relations prevailing between Dutch crews and Spanish local officialdom in the ports, the *Consejo* decided, in March 1648, that from then on, the *Almirantazgo, corregidores*, and Inquisition should, with regard to the Dutch, combine their boarding and inspections so that each vessel was boarded only once instead of three times, as had been the case hitherto.[2] In September 1648 Philip agreed to admit the first Dutch consuls to Spain, Jacome van den Hove,

[1] Leopold to Philip, 8 Jan. 1648. AGS Estado 2169; Hoorn to SG, 10 Dec. 1648. ARH SG 5543, ii.
[2] Consulta 10 Mar. 1648. AGS Estado 2668.

consul for Cadiz and Puerto de Santa María, and Isaac van
Swanenburg for Seville and San Lúcar. Both were courteously
received and their co-operation sought in the working out of
new procedures for the inspection and checking of Dutch
ships and cargoes in Andalusian ports. In December 1648,
after various complaints from the Dutch about the treatment
that they were receiving in the north coast ports, the Marqués
de Velada, to whom Philip increasingly entrusted supervision
of Dutch affairs in the Peninsula, and his colleagues of the
Consejo, sent a high-ranking official to tour the Cantabrian
ports and to curb the continued heavy-handedness of some
local officials.[4]

v THE DUTCH–SPANISH NEGOTIATIONS AT MUNSTER AND THE DRIVE FOR PEACE, 1641–1648

One direct consequence of the Portuguese Revolt was the
most searching reappraisal at Madrid of Dutch–Spanish relations for many years, certainly since 1629. While most of
Philip's ministers agreed, in January 1641 and in subsequent
months, that no effort should be spared to conclude either a
full peace, or a truce, or a simple cease-fire with the Dutch
by means of secret approaches to Frederik Hendrik, and
while full authority to do this was conferred first on the
Cardinal-Infante and, following his death in November, on
his successor, Don Francisco de Melo, Philip's advisers remained extremely doubtful as to the chances of reaching any
sort of settlement.[5] Besides some differences of opinion as
to how to proceed, the entire Spanish leadership was convinced that the 'accidente de Portugal', as they termed the
Revolt, made it harder, not easier, to conclude peace with
the Dutch, even though the king's sudden willingness to
recognize Dutch Brazil removed what had been the most
difficult stumbling-block in the negotiations of the 1630s;

[3] Consulta 17 Sept. 1648. AGS Estado 2168; Van den Hove to SG, 24, 30
Aug. 1648. ARH SG 5543, ii.

[4] Consulta, Junta de Estado, 2 Dec. 1648. AGS Estado 2168.

[5] Consulta 16 Jan. 1641. AGS Estado 3860; 'Poder a Don Francisco de Melo
para qualquiera Paz, Tregua, Suspension de armas, o otra capitulacion' (23 Dec.
1641). AGS Estado 2305.

all were convinced, and in the short and medium term they were right, that with such an unprecedented opportunity to exploit Spanish weakness and conquer more territory both in Europe and the Indies, there was little inducement for the States General to come to the peace table. The Conde-Duque and his adherents not only emphasized that the Dutch could now expect handsome gains from remaining at war with Spain, but continued to entertain doubts as to the wisdom of rushing into a settlement with the Dutch on almost any terms.[6] One member of the *Consejo*, the Marqués de Mirabel, even argued that it would be actually disadvantageous for Spain to settle quickly with the Republic given that the most urgent priority now was to suppress the Portuguese insurgents; for by tying the Dutch down in the Netherlands, he held, 'they will not be able to offer assistance to Portugal and without this the duke of Braganza's venture will not succeed.'[7] He was right at least in that Dutch help to the Portuguese was vital to their cause.

In any case, the outcome of the secret approaches arranged by the Cardinal-Infante to Frederik Hendrik, in December 1640 and early 1641, both directly and by means of Imperial intercession, were far from encouraging. In February both the prince and his close associate, Cornelis Musch, sent back negative answers to Ferdinand's new political secretary, Miguel de Salamanca.[8] In March Ferdinand admitted to the king that he saw little prospect of a favourable Dutch response as long as the prince remained stubbornly inclined to continue the war and the alliance with the French. The Austrian emissary, the count von Auersperg who arrived in The Hague during the spring together with Jean Friquet, a Burgundian confidant of the Cardinal-Infante, ostensibly on other business, but in fact to endeavour to mediate between Madrid and the Stadholder, soon arrived at the same conclusion, leaving Holland empty-handed, in June.[9] Nevertheless, according to Friquet's analysis, Spanish diplomacy was

[6] *Corresp. d'Esp.* iii. 403; see Olivares's memorandum of Jan. 1641, appendix to Poelhekke, *Vrede van Munster*.
[7] Consulta 16 Jan. 1641. AGS Estado 3860.
[8] BNM MS 2372, fos. 707, 711.
[9] *Corresp. d'Esp.* iii. 409, 423, 441.

perfectly right to concentrate its efforts continually on the prince since the latter effectively held all the keys to Dutch policy and because, despite his current apparent leaning towards the Dutch war-party, in fact he was not at all firm in his resolve to prolong the war. His advanced age, increasingly poor health, and fear of hazarding his brilliant military reputation based on exploits of long ago, all pointed, in the Burgundian's view, to an underlying inclination towards peace. The Dutch provinces, in contrast, were and would remain profoundly split owing to the wide disparity of their interests. Friquet's view was undoubtedly astute.

Ferdinand persevered with his efforts until his death in November 1641. His successor as governor of the Spanish Netherlands, Don Francisco de Melo, continued in the same vein.[10] The Spanish leadership were in a desperate position and were now clearly ready to try virtually anything to coax the Dutch into separate negotiations. Austrian mediation having failed, Danish intercession was tried but with equally little success. Most remarkable of all, in March 1642 Jean Friquet, who, under Melo, remained the principal Spanish intermediary in the secret contacts with The Hague, was instructed by Melo, presumably on orders from Madrid, to promise Frederik Hendrik that not only would Philip concur in all the territorial and commercial concessions made with regard to Brazil by the upstart Portuguese king, but that in return for peace Spain would also concede to the Dutch freedom of commerce with the entire Spanish empire in Europe and the Indies.[11] While it is hard to know how seriously this offer was meant, it certainly points to a state of extreme frustration at Brussels and Madrid. In any case, Friquet's mission failed. But it was soon followed by others. In April 1643 Melo received a seemingly more encouraging reply from the prince, but once again it led to nothing definite.[12]

Meanwhile, the international moves prior to the Munster Congress continued, albeit exceedingly slowly and with scant enthusiasm on the part of Spain. In December 1641, after

[10] Consulta 24 Sept. 1641. AGS Estado 2056; *Corresp. d'Esp.* iii. 450, 457.
[11] See Melo's instructions to Friquet of May 1642, *Corresp. diplomática* i. 314-15.
[12] Philip to Melo, 5 June 1643. AGS Estado 2250.

talks in Hamburg, the monarchs of France, Sweden, and
Spain, and the Emperor agreed to commence the peace congress proper in simultaneous gatherings at Munster and
Osnabrück.[13] In January 1642 Frederik Hendrik advised the
States General of the agreement, asking for a decision as to
whether the Republic should participate and, if so, to nomi-
nate plenipotentiaries and begin formulating the Dutch terms
for a truce or peace with Spain.[14] The States General then
referred the *groote saecke* back to the provinces in the usual
way, and the provinces to the towns and nobles. With the
prince recommending participation, agreement to do so was
reached readily enough, but an ominous note was sounded in
various quarters, including Leiden, where it was insisted
that any truce with Spain must be on 'godly and secure
terms', meaning that the Spanish king must surrender all
claims and pretension over the seven provinces, that nothing
be done to the detriment of the Reformed Church, that the
East and West India Companies be fully maintained, in
accordance with their charters, and that the Dutch plenipotentiaries to Munster be subjected to oaths not to give or
receive gifts of any kind. There was no further progress,
however, for many months owing to differences over procedure both among the rival powers and the Dutch provinces
and towns. Months of delay ensued before international
assent was obtained fixing the opening of the conferences
for July 1643. The Dutch provinces only began to hammer
out their recommendations to the States General as to the
Dutch peace terms in the spring of 1643 and, as late as May,
the provinces were still arguing over whether to send a small
delegation to Munster of three or four representatives, as
Holland wanted, or a larger body with a plenipotentiary for
each province, as the others preferred and as was eventually
decided.[15] When the States General reviewed the situation in
secret session on 25 May, only Holland, Overijssel, Utrecht,
and Groningen had so far nominated their plenipotentiaries.[16]

---

[13] Aitzema, *Ned. Vreedehandeling*, i. 416.
[14] GA Leiden. Sec. Arch. 450, fos. 110^r-110^v.
[15] GA Leiden, Sec. Arch. 450, fos. 110^r-110^v; GA Haarlem, vroed. res. 22
May 1643; Aitzema, *Ned. Vreedehandeling,* i. 449.
[16] Sec. Res. SG 25 May 1643. ARH SG 4853.

Quite reasonably, the Spanish crown was not yet willing, during the years 1642–3, to invest its hopes of terminating the Dutch conflict on tolerable terms in a projected international peace conference which might or might not convene and which in any case it viewed with suspicion as essentially a device of Richelieu. Following the departure from power of the Conde-Duque, in January 1643, and partly inspired by the increasing antagonism between Holland and the Stadholder, Philip and his ministers accordingly resolved, amid great secrecy, on a bold, if somewhat bizarre, new endeavour once again essentially intended to dislodge Frederik Hendrik.[17] A Spanish official, Francisco de Galarreta, was dispatched to Brussels with orders to confide the real object of his mission to no one but the governor and the personage selected to go to The Hague. Philip's offer was to recognize Frederik Hendrik and his heirs as legitimate rulers of a rump northern Netherlands based on Holland by way of some form of perpetually valid enfeoffment, 'infeudación, subinfuedación, o en otra forma si se hallase mas apropósito', with the choice of receiving his new lands from either the Spanish crown or the Emperor. In return, the prince was to arrange for both Zeeland and the Dutch-conquered zone of Flanders to be transferred to the Spanish Netherlands to assure 'security of free navigation to Antwerp', together with 's-Hertogenbosch, the Maas towns, Nijmegen, and one or two crossings over the Rhine to 'secure [Spanish] communications with Germany'. The prince was also to restore Dutch Brazil to Spain and agree on at least some concessions in the Far East. Finally, the prince was conceded liberty of Catholic worship in his new territory, though Galarretta was instructed not to press this last point if it seemed likely to endanger the negotiation. The plan was certainly imaginative.

Melo's first choice of intermediary was Willem de Bye, secretary of finance at Brussels, who was 'usually employed on such missions owing to his wife being a relative of Huygens, the secretary and confidant of the prince'.[18] Subsequently, it was decided to employ instead Josephe Bergaine,

---

[17] See the royal instructions to secretary Galarreta, in 'Negociacion secreta', CODOIN lix. 207–13.
[18] Ibid., p. 229.

bishop of 's-Hertogenbosch, who was likewise much experienced in such dealings. But the bishop's application for a passport was also delayed by the Dutch and he resorted to an intermediary, a disguised Franciscan friar who met the Stadholder secretly in The Hague in December 1643 and on several subsequent occasions. In February 1644 it was the turn of a Walloon nobleman, Philippe le Roy, who was conceded a passport to enter Dutch territory on private but not public business. Before being ejected, Le Roy met Frederik Hendrik in secret and also managed, on orders from Madrid, to deliver a sensational proposal to the States General: he indicated that Spain would be willing in future to transport the silver used to pay the Army of Flanders from Spain in Dutch ships and via Holland, paying the Dutch customs duties, instead of in English ships and via England.[19] Although this remarkable attempt to obtain separate negotiation by appealing to their presumed greed likewise failed, it undoubtedly aroused great interest at Amsterdam and was a talking-point for some time among the Dutch. Later in 1644 a variety of emissaries from Brussels met secretly with the Stadholder, a process which Frederik Hendrik deliberately span out, subtly arousing expectations by means of politely ambiguous answers.[20] While it does not seem, from D'Estrades' dispatches, that the prince revealed any of the Spanish secret propositions of 1643-4 to the French, suggesting that he was now less completely at one with them than he had been earlier, probably his main motive for thus protracting his contacts with Brussels was to prevent or delay a shift in Spanish tactics towards concentrating on the States General.

But eventually the Stadholder's courteous but impenetrable replies, combined with the unmistakable waning of his authority within the Republic at this time, led Philip and his advisors to reconsider their entire approach. In March 1644 Philip thanked Melo for his untiring efforts with the prince thus far but also dwelt on the problem arising from the 'differences which the Dutch have with the Prince' and the difficulty of knowing to which approach to assign priority:

[19] Philip to Tordelaguna, 28 Jan. 1644. ARB SEG 231, fo. 103; Aitzema, *Hist.* v. 672-4; van Dillen, 'De Opstand', 33-8.
[20] 'Negociacion Secreta', CODOIN lix, 349-50, 384-5.

such that great skill and adroitness is needed to handle matters in such a way that the one [approach] should not hinder or ruin the other. . . and from here it is difficult to determine precisely to which negotiation preference should be given for while, should it succeed, that with the Prince would be best, we must not spoil the negotiation with the States General without having the other at a point where it is virtually certain to succeed.[21]

In May a special *junta* at Madrid again pondered whether it was really in Spain's interest to concentrate on accommodating the Dutch rather than France and whether it was really best to persevere with the prince rather than with the States General. While at least one minister, the Marqués de Santa Cruz, dissented from the now long-prevailing preference for a settlement with the Dutch, arguing that it was far more urgent to make peace with France, and while all Philip's advisors admitted that there remained 'great and considerable drawbacks and damage' for Spain in making peace with the Dutch with respect to colonies and commerce, king and *junta* nevertheless agreed that their first objective had to be peace with the Dutch and that this should be pursued by both routes.[22]

In effect, everything was left to the discretion of Melo and the Marqués de Castel-Rodrigo who at this juncture had special responsibility for the Munster negotiations. At this stage, and even as late as October 1644, Bergaine, Melo, and Castel-Rodrigo remained deeply perplexed by the prince's answers but willing to give his sincerity the benefit of the doubt. By December 1644, however, Castel-Rodrigo had made up his mind: 'now I fear more than ever that the Prince mocks the king's authority and is deceiving those who are there on the part of His Majesty, diverting them with ceremonious and polite words to gain time and dispose of matters to his advantage.'[23]

Meanwhile the formal Dutch–Spanish truce negotiations, scheduled for Munster, were trapped in the intricate maze of the disparate interests of the Dutch provinces and towns.

[21] Consulta 13 May 1644. AGS Estado 3860.
[22] CODOIN lix. 339–40.
[23] CODOIN lix. 413; Consulta, Junta de Estado, 4 Jan. 1645. AGS Estado 2063.

The July 1643 deadline came and went without the provinces yet agreeing on the composition of their delegation let alone on its instructions.[24] In secret session of the States General in September, the Zeeland deputies declared that they would only agree to the dispatch of the plenipotentiaries to Munster if the provinces were given full 'contentement ende satisfactie' over the Instructions to the delegates and the 'points to be negotiated with the enemy'.[25] In October the States General agreed that each province should choose its own commissioners to confer with the Stadholder on the drawing up of the instructions.[26] Soon after, Zeeland raised the fundamental issue which had always been its primary concern throughout the long series of negotiations with Spain since the 1590s, demanding that the 'enemy' must concede that the same imposts and fiscal regime should be maintained in the Flemish harbours as on the Schelde, Zwijn, and Sas.[27] Zeeland appealed for a prior commitment from the other provinces that if the 'enemy' did not concede this point, which it accounted vital for the Republic as a whole, not merely for Zeeland, the peace talks would be broken off at once; the other provinces declined to enter into any such undertaking but agreed to accept this demand as among the 'chief and most important' in the instructions. During October the provincial commissioners, Prince and *Raad van State* both hammered out draft instructions and reviewed the delicate question of the troop levels and military expenditure to be maintained during the projected truce. The prince and his adherents proposed a fixed truce-time standing army of 39,980 infantry and 5,580 cavalry, a total of 45,650 men, which would have meant a reduction of the existing standing force by one quarter.[28] For the moment this issue was left undecided.

---

[24] GA Haarlem vroed. res. 21 July 1643.

[25] Sec. Res. SG, 2 Sept. 1643. ARH SG 4853.

[26] Sec. Res. SG, 3 Oct. 1643. ARH SG 4853; Aitzema, *Ned. Vreedehandeling* i. 452-3; the commissioners included Meinertswijck and Aernem for Gelderland, Mathenesse, Stevelshouck, Schaep, Kessel, and Cats for Holland, Knuyt and Stavenisse for Zeeland, Nederhorst and Hoolck for Utrecht, Crack and Veldriel for Friesland, and Aldringa and Clant for Groningen.

[27] Sec. Res. SG 7 Oct. 1643. ARH SG 4853.

[28] 'Staet sommier vant Chrijchsvolk' (Oct. 1643). ARH SG 4853.

During November 1643 and several subsequent months the provinces concentrated on detailed examination of the proposed instructions and discussing whether to fix the term of the projected truce with Spain at twelve years, a longer term, or leave the matter open.[29] Apart from the demand for unqualified recognition by Spain of Dutch independence and sovereignty, and the issue of the Indies which was thought to require a good deal of further debate, as well as consultation with the colonial companies, the major draft demands were these: the ceding of the Meierij in its entirety, that the Schelde remain closed on the part of the States General; that subjects of the Republic trading in the lands of the king should not be subjected to higher imposts or more restrictive stipulations than his own subjects or those of any other state; that imposts in the Flemish harbours must be as high as those levied on the Schelde, Zwijn, and Sas; that Dutch seaman and other subjects in Spanish lands should not be subjected on any pretext to harassment, arrest, or detention; and that Spain accept unaltered the religious *status quo* in the Republic, meaning that the States General would reject any Spanish proposal intended to improve the position of Dutch Catholics; the provinces also agreed that there should be no cessation of hostilities until agreed truce terms were ratified by the Spanish monarch.

In March 1644 six provinces concurred that not all the principal demands would necessarily need to be met by Spain for the talks to continue. Zeeland, on the other hand, insisted that the provinces should undertake beforehand to break off the negotiations should Spain reject certain key items, notably those relating to the Indies and the Flemish harbours.[30] The Zeeland deputies argued that it was notorious that during the 1609–21 truce the Spaniards had introduced special duties on the Schelde, Zwijn, and Sas to render 'fruitless' trade by these routes from the Republic, and to benefit

[29] GA Leiden, Sec. Arch. 450, fo. 179ᵛ. vroed. res. 7 Dec. 1643; Sec. Res. SG, 2 Nov. 1643. ARH SG 4853.

[30] 'dat de bovenstaende poincten in soodanige voegen absoluelijcke vast ende onbewandelick souden moeten werden gestelt, datmen op souden breecken ende de handelinge affsnijden ingevalle de voornoemden poincten vanden vijant niet en souden connen worden geobtineert'. Sec. Res. SG, 10 Mar. 1644. ARH SG 4853.

trade and navigation to the Flemish harbours, so that 'from the beginning of the previous Truce, Brabant, Flanders, and other provinces were supplied with various goods, even salt-fish and herring from these lands, through the Flemish ports.'[31] To make the matter even more urgent, the 'enemy' had now improved his harbours at Dunkirk and Ostend since the last truce and, given a further respite, would assuredly further improve the canals dug then, linking the Flemish ports with the inland towns of the South Netherlands, all of which, if not guarded against, would severely damage the commerce of the Republic.

At this same juncture the States of Friesland reminded the States General of its concern for the interests of the East India Company, the issue which appears to have been upper-most in Frisian minds during the Munster negotiations with Spain.[32] Friesland was anxious both for the Company's navigation and trade to be secured on the most advantageous basis and for the Company's charter to be renewed, with provision for a separate Frisian chamber to look after the substantial investment of the province's inhabitants in Asian commerce, 'for from the advantageous terms to be made with the enemy and from the profits to be secured, no provinces can or should be excluded, any more than they are from the taxes [for the war] to which Friesland contributes the most after Holland.'

By May 1644 the bulk of the States General's instructions were ready, but a few items remained to be finalized and these were to hold up the dispatch of the Dutch plenipoten-tiaries to Munster for many more months. In particular, six provinces still maintained that if Spain refused to yield over the Flemish harbours the matter should be reconsidered by the States General before the talks were broken off, while Zeeland refused to accept this.[33] Furthermore, there re-mained the delicate task of drawing up instructions on the Indies in consultation with the East and West India Com-panies. Indeed, apart from the fixing of expenses and other

---

[31] 'Tot justificatie van het gesustineerde vande Heeren Staten van Zeelandt' (Mar. 1644). ARH SG 4853.

[32] Res. S. Friesland, Leeuwarden 1 Dec. 1643. ARH SG 4853; Hallema, 81.

[33] Sec. Res. SG, 5, 10, 12 May 1644. ARH SG 4853.

minor details relating to the organization of the Munster deputation, most of the States General's attention for the rest of 1644 and early 1645 was taken up as far as the projected peace negotiations were concerned, with thrashing out the instructions relating to the Indies.[34] Undoubtedly, there was a marked loss of momentum in Holland's peace drive during this crucial period, the most probable reason for which is that Amsterdam, Rotterdam, and the Noorderk-wartier towns at this juncture devoted their whole energies and attention to rallying support for intervention in the northern war on the side of Sweden against Denmark.

Only in April 1645 did Holland's deputies to the States General begin to press for the dispatch of the Dutch pleni-potentiaries to Munster without further delay, despite some unsettled points relating to the Indies and the disagreement over the Flemish harbours. Predictably, Zeeland refused to agree to the sending of the plenipotentiaries 'before and until the preliminary points are firmly settled'.[35] In July Holland stepped up the pressure sending an extraordinary delegation of five, as well as its ordinary delegates, to the States General where they demanded 'seer instantelijck' that a firm departure date be fixed.[36] On 14 July six provinces duly voted for dispatch of the plenipotentiaries on 10 August, but adamant objections from Zeeland led to further delay. Finally, despite the failure of attempts to persuade the States of Zeeland to conform with the vote of the other provinces following re-sumed heavy pressure from Holland during the autumn, the States General delivered its instructions to its plenipotentiaries on 28 October by six votes to one. On 3 November Zeeland solemnly protested that the procedure was in violation of the articles of the Union of Utrecht and the 'fondamentele maxi-men' of the state.[37] After some final months of obstruction and prevarication the Dutch delegates left for Munster early in January 1646.

Despite the increasing disenchantment of Philip's ministers with Frederik Hendrik's replies, in late 1644 the discouragingly

---

[34] Sec. Res. SG, 20 June 1644, 10 Jan. 1645, 24 Apr. 1645. ARH SG 4854.
[35] Sec. Res. SG, 29 Apr. 1645. ARH SG 4854.
[36] Sec. Res. SG, 12, 13 July 1645. ARH SG 4854.
[37] Sec. Res. SG, 3 Nov. 1644. ARH SG 4854.

long delay in the dispatch of the Dutch plenipotentiaries to Munster left Philip with no choice but to persist in his secret approaches to the Stadholder. During the winter of 1644–5 a hispano-Walloon nobleman, Antonio Galla de Salamanca, seigneur de Noirmont, who had several times before been used on such missions during the early 1640s, had a series of interviews at The Hague with Frederik Hendrik, Cornelis Musch, and Zeeland's plenipotentiary, Johan de Knuyt, under instructions from the Marqués de Castel-Rodrigo.[38] Noirmont stressed the dangers to the Dutch of continued French expansion in the Netherlands, a consideration which the Spaniards well knew was causing some discomfort among the Dutch; he proposed secret talks at The Hague to circumvent the elaborate inaction at Munster. The prince refused on account of the Republic's treaty obligations to France and because, so he said, such a move would give the Dutch provinces still greater scope for disrupting the proceedings; even so, he succeeded in convincing Noirmont and Castel-Rodrigo that he now sincerely favoured peace and that the campaign of obstruction was essentially the work of the Zeelanders and other particular groups within the Republic. In a meeting of February 1645 Noirmont also laid before the prince a fresh offer from the Spanish king:[39] in return for the Prince's assistance in speeding up the truce process, Philip would cede to him and his heirs in perpetuity the district of Geldern. The prince expressed polite astonishment and made only an evasive answer.

The Spanish leadership now found itself in a deepening quandary. Added to the other pressures, the desire for peace with the Dutch in the southern provinces now reached a new pitch of intensity. In October 1645 the States of Brabant petitioned Castel-Rodrigo for permission to negotiate once again on a states to states basis with the Dutch.[40] Castel-Rodrigo himself and most of his advisors at Brussels, except,

[38] Castel-Rodrigo to Philip, 17 Dec. 1644. AGS Estado 2063; 'Relacion de lo que ha negociado el señor de Normont' (6 Jan. – 1 Feb. 1645), AGS Estado 2063; *Corresp. d'Esp.* iii. 675–9; Consulta, Junta de Estado, Zaragoza, 26 July 1645. AGS Estado 2062.

[39] 'Relacion del viaje hecho por el señor de Normont a la Haya' (18 Feb. – 3 Mar. 1645). AGS Estado 2063; Poelhekke, *Vrede van Munster*, annex no. viii.

[40] *Corresp. d'Esp.* iii. 542–3, 546, 549.

predictably, Petrus Roose, inclined in favour of this approach. Also in favour was the Conde de Peñaranda[41] whom Philip had named to head his delegation at Munster and who, in this capacity, had travelled across France and the South Netherlands to the episcopal city during the summer of 1645. Peñaranda, henceforward a figure increasingly influential among Philip's advisers, was totally convinced that Spain's interests lay in an accommodation with the Dutch rather than with France, first, because, as he put it, 'I hold the Dutch more scrupulous and reliable than the French in carrying out the undertaking and commitment to peace, so that we can rest more secure with whatever is negotiated with the Dutch';[42] secondly, 'because their power can never be so formidable to his Majesty's monarchy as that of the French'; thirdly, 'because the Dutch do not have such hatred for us nor such sense of national rivalry as do the French'; fourthly, because Dutch territory did not immediately adjoin Spain as did France; and lastly because 'if we cede territory to the French, in the Low Countries, we give them the arms and means to make themselves masters of all seventeen provinces . . . but if we cede territory to the Dutch in the Netherlands we make them formidable to the French whose rebels, malcontents and Huguenots they shall have at their disposal' whenever changed circumstances should provide an opportunity for a combination of Dutch, Swedes, and other Protestants against France on behalf of their religion.

In Peñaranda's view, prospects for progress, via The Hague, were better than at Munster where the French could more easily interfere, though for the moment he remained pessimistic regarding both approaches.[43] Even so, he favoured the plan for an initiative promoting talks between the two States General which would at least serve as a gesture to South Netherlands opinion. However, when Castel-Rodrigo contacted the States General in The Hague, its response was negative:

[41] *CODOIN* lxxxii. 155, 185.

[42] Peñaranda to Castel-Rodrigo, Munster, 28 Aug. 1645. AGS Estado 2063: 'porque tengo a los holandeses por mas religiosos y seguros en observar la promesa y juramento de la Paz que a los franceses, y assi se pudiera quedar con mas seguridad en lo que con holandeses se asentase.'

[43] Peñaranda to Castel-Rodrigo, 21 Oct. 1645. AGS Estado 2063.

it would countenance negotiations at Munster only. Philip's response was likewise negative and the whole proposal was accordingly dropped. For the time being, it seemed that there was no way forward.

The gloom enveloping the Spanish delegation at Munster finally lifted with the long-awaited appearance of the Dutch plenipotentiaries in January 1646. In the first Dutch-Spanish conference, on 16 January 1646, Peñaranda delivered a stirring Latin peroration appealing to the delegates to lay aside the animosities of the past and strive nobly together towards an enduring peace. Without more ado the conde and his colleagues, the bishop of Cambrai and the Burgundian official, Antoine Brun, indicated Philip's willingness to acknowledge categorically Dutch independence and sovereignty. However, on the pretext of finding fault with the Spanish *pouvoirs*, the Dutch suspended the negotiation almost at once and a further period of delay ensued. Seeing that the Dutch army was preparing to take the field, in April Castel-Rodrigo wrote direct to the States General complaining about the prevarication and requesting an immediate cessation of hostilities to facilitate the talks.[44] The States General refused. However, behind the scenes the *Trevisten* were now rapidly gaining ground assisted by the disclosure some weeks earlier, arranged by Peñaranda, that the French had secretly proposed to the Spanish plenipotentiaries a Franco-Spanish *accommodement* whereby the Dauphin, Louis, would marry the Spanish Infanta, with the entire Spanish Netherlands being ceded to France as the dowry; the sudden prospect of acquiring the French as immediate neighbours and the duplicity revealed by this episode evidently caused a profound shock at The Hague and considerably weakened the position of the pro-French party at a crucial moment.[45] In the States General and provincial assemblies work now resumed on drafting the instructions concerning the Indies.[46]

The two sides' plenipotentiaries reconvened at Munster in

[44] Castel-Rodrigo to SG, 25 Apr., and SG to Castel-Rodrigo, 1 May 1646. ARH SG 4855.
[45] *Corresp. diplomática* i. 285–6; Van der Capellen ii. 141–5.
[46] Sec. Res. SG 25, 26 Apr. 1646. ARH SG 4855.

May 1646 and this time there was rapid progress. That month, incontestably, was the great turning-point in the drive for a Dutch-Spanish settlement. Peñaranda was soon heartened to realize that Zeeland's Knuyt who, at the same time, was Frederik Hendrik's own personal representative was co-operating with Pauw, who for so long had been the foremost antagonist of the prince, and that this could only mean that Frederik Hendrik himself was now discreetly supporting the truce moves.[47] On 13 May the Spanish side renewed its proposals of 28 January for a truce of twelve or twenty years. The Dutch answered with their list of seventy-one conditions. On 17 May Peñaranda's team formally agreed to most of these, including permanent closure of the Schelde on the part of the States General, on the understanding that trade would be allowed, as previously, on the basis of trans-shipment in Zeeland. But in reply to the demand for the whole Meierij, the Spanish side proposed the setting up of a *Chambre mi-partie*, a board of equal numbers of Dutch and Spanish representatives to study the details and determine precisely which districts did adhere to the jurisdiction of 's-Hertogenbosch. The demand relating to the Flemish harbours[48] (which was debated in the royal council and strongly objected to at Brussels on the grounds that such an arrangement would be highly damaging to Flanders) and one or two lesser points were at first rejected as incompatible with the king's sovereign rights. However, as the Dutch remained adamant, Peñaranda and his colleagues agreed a few days later to cede the entire Meierij 'à condition qu'au regard du spirituel de la dite Mairie et plat pais sera trouvé quelque expédient et tempérament pour la satisfaction de l'une et l'autre partie' and reluctantly yielded over the question of imposts in the Flemish harbours.[49] On 30 May the Dutch formally accepted the Spanish concessions and gave the requested assurance on Catholic rights in the Meierij. Apart from the issue of the Indies which by mutual agreement had been left to afterwards being the most difficult and some matters of border demarcation in the Low Countries,

[47] *Corresp. diplomatica* i. 312, 321–2.
[48] *Corresp. diplomática* i. 321–2, 331–2.
[49] Aitzema, *Ned. Vreedehandling*, ii. 87.

everything now appeared to be settled and the main section of the negotiation completed.

The break-through at Munster, during May, and the subsequent agreement of July 1646 between Castel-Rodrigo and the States General on a general return and exchange of prisoners, ratified and implemented in Madrid during August,[50] provoked the opponents of a Spanish settlement within the Republic, backed by French diplomacy, to mobilize every means to recover the initiative and block the truce. Discussion of the *groote saecke* throughout the Netherlands and at every social level rose to fever pitch in a torrent of pamphlets, tavern-orations, and disquisitions from the pulpit. Resistance to the truce remained formidable, particularly in Zeeland, but also in Friesland and Groningen, in the industrial towns of Holland, and among certain towns and nobles in Utrecht and Gelderland. Even so, one striking difference between the popular tracts of 1646–7 and those of 1629–30 and 1632–3 is that for the first time, pro-peace propaganda was in evidence in comparable quantity to the material advocating continued war and evinced just as much élan and determination. The frequently repeated argument that Dutch taxation in truce time was necessarily almost as heavy as during the war, so that the common man should not expect the truce or peace to be substantially less burdensome, was firmly rebutted: the truce would incontestably and considerably diminish the burden on the common man, as well as the taxes on shipping and trade.[51] Those numerous spokesmen who persisted in arguing that the war benefited business were dismissed as devoid of judgement: the continued pressure of the Spanish war would prevent the Republic safeguarding its commercial, colonial, and fishery interests effectively from the encroachments of the English, Danes, and Portuguese; once at peace with Spain, it was held, the Republic would easily be able to put the Portuguese in their place both in Brazil and the Far East.[52] While both the war

[50] Philip to Juan de Santelizas, 30 July 1646. AGS Estado 2257; Philip to Castel-Rodrigo, 12 Aug. 1646. AHN Estado leg. 1411.

[51] *Munsters Praetje*, fos. 2ʳ–2ᵛ; *Tuba Pacis*, fo. 5ᵛ; *Montstopping aende Vrede-haters*, fos. 6ʳ–6ᵛ.

[52] 'Portugal sal so in Brasil als Oost-Indien beter koop gheven' was a favourite refrain of the peace faction: see *Munsters Praetje*, fo. 2ᵛ; *Montstopping aende Vrede-haters*, fos. 4ʳ–4ᵛ; *Verscheyde stvcken*, fo. 3.

and peace factions feared diversion of population, trade, and industry to Flanders and Brabant, the latter insisted that there was much less danger of seriously damaging diversion whilst these territories remained under Spain than were they to come under the now more powerful monarch of France.[53] To console industrialists for the expected losses in northern Europe, one pamphleteer endeavoured to whet their appetite for the Spanish market which he believed would bring more profit than exports elsewhere.[54] Of course, there were also numerous warnings as to the dangers of having France as the immediate neighbour of the Republic, in the South Netherlands. Nevertheless, it is clear that the arguments of the opposition still exerted considerable persuasive force.

It is everywhere known [riposted one author] that by peace or truce the common man in the enemy's provinces will greatly increase his prosperity and business, while the common man here will largely be stripped of his trade and manufactures, since many store-keepers who during the war have their goods manufactured here, will then have them manufactured in Flanders and Brabant to obtain them cheaper. . . and that when the Flemish sea-ports are opened not only will consumption of our manufactures greatly decline in all lands but so will price-levels because their goods are manufactured more cheaply than ours. . .and that the inhabitants of Brabant and Flanders will no longer obtain their foodstuffs and French, Spanish, Italian, Irish, Scandinavian, and Baltic wares through these lands but directly by sea, all to the detriment of the ordinary man here.[55]

To the widespread pro-peace argument that Dutch shipping

---

[53] 'Maer wertet Treves, blyvende consequentelijck Vlaanderen onder den lammen Spagniaert, sijt verseeckert dat niemandt, hy sy Catholyck of Ghereformeerdt, lichtelijk sal verhuysen uyt Hollandt nae Brabant of Vlaenderen', *Munsters Praetje*, fos. 4ʳ-4ᵛ; see also *Hollandsche Sybille*, p. 20, *Missive ivt Middelburgh*, pp. 7, 10.

[54] 'Vier jaren vrye Commercie in de Landen des Conincks van Spagnien, alleen voor onse Manifacturen, sullen ons aenbrengen meer proffijt, als hondert jaer in alle andere gedeelten Europe', *Verscheyde stvcken*, fo. 2ᵛ.

[55] 'Want 't is immers notoir dat. . .door de Vrede of Treves de gemeene Man van d'andere Provintien onser Vyanden grootelijcx in welvaert en Neringe sal toenemen en die van dese Landen hare Neeringen en Hantwercken voor een groot deel onttrecken: door dien dat veel Winckel-houders haer manufacturen diese by d'Oorloge hier te Lande laten maken, Als dan om de goede koops wille in Vlaenderen en Brabant sullen laten maken,' *Antwoordt Op't Mvnsters Praetie*, fo. 2ᵛ-3ʳ; *Suchtich, en Trouwhertich Discours*, p. E3; *Nederlants Beroerde Ingewanden*, fos. 3ʳ-3ᵛ.

and seaman would benefit by the removal of the threat of the Dunkirkers, the author of the counter-blast to the *Munsters Praetje* held that 'what unquestionably outweighs this is the fact that all freight rates and seamen's wages will fall, so that skippers and crews will surely earn less than they do now.'[56] The proponents of peace were urged to consider the experience of the last truce when, allegedly, 'there was neither business nor prosperity'.[57] Inevitably, it was pointed out that the interests of the East and West India Companies would suffer, but it is not surprising, particularly in view of the much changed circumstances of the latter, that far less emphasis was placed on this aspect than had been the case in 1629–30 and 1632–3;[58] not very convincingly, the advocates of war maintained that it would be easier to exert pressure on Portugal and bolster the Company's position in Brazil whilst the Republic remained at war with Castile. In any case, in view of what were the preponderant anxieties of the public, the pro-war pamphleteers concentrated their fire on the expected prejudicial effects of the truce on manufactures and home trade rather than colonial issues. Weakest and least emphasized of all was the war-faction's obviously dubious claim that the French, the traditional friends of the Republic, whatever their detractors might say, would make most acceptable neighbours.

The appeal of the pamphleteers was emphatically to the 'gemeene man' (the common man) marked by occasional willingness to exploit popular prejudices against nobles, élite merchants, and, in some cases, heads of city government. What counted essentially were the interests of the small man, the artisan, shop-keeper, seaman, farmer, and

---

[56] 'Dat alle scheeps vrachten en maent gelden daer tegens weder sullen affslaen dat de schippers en Bootsluyden dan minder sullen winnen als nu twelcke van ongelijck grooter consideratie is, '*Antwoordt Op't Mvnsters Praetie*, fo. 3.

[57] The truce shall 'de Ingesetene doen vergaen of verloopen, de stijlen, de neeringen, handtwercken vervoeren, wegh brengen, verplanten, gelijck in de voorgaenden Treves ghebeurt is, wanneerder noch neeringhe noch welvaren was. Doch alle memorien, voorgaende ervarentheydt, waerschouwingen mogen niet helpen. Het Troansche Paert, het groote Munsters Monster moet ingehaelt op den throon gestelt worden', *Nederlants Beroerde Ingewanden*, fo. 3ᵛ.

[58] Ibid., fo. 4; *Suchtich, en Trouwhertich Discours*, fo. E3.

small investor, not the requirements of the great merchants against whom there was widespread ill feeling and envy. Leaders of the so-called Spanish faction, the *gespagnoliseer-den*, such as Adraan Pauw and Andries Bicker, were denounced as having been bribed by the Spaniards and blinded by the lure of Spanish silver and restored trade with Spain, in which they themselves would benefit to the detriment of the populace as a whole.[59] Against the 'Spanish wantonness' of the Beverens and de Witts, the leading families of Dordrecht, many among the Dordrecht textile workers, retailers, and other small men felt bitter anger and resentment.[60] The common notion that the nobility uniformly opposed the truce on account of their own 'profit, interest, and well-being' likewise played a part, though it was not difficult to show that in fact the interests of the nobles were very varied and that they figured on both sides of the argument.[61]

As the pamphlet war continued, the manoeuvering in the provincial capitals and at The Hague proceeded without pause. In May 1646, following a vote in the States of Gelderland, at Arnhem, the province proposed in the States General that a fresh demand should be added to those thus far put to the Spaniards at Munster, namely the ceding of the Geldern district, the so-called *Overkwartier*, to be incorporated into Gelderland.[62] There was general agreement among the provinces and the plenipotentiaries at Munster were instructed to present this additional desideratum but, at Holland's insistence, neither to threaten nor actually to break off negotiations should the Spaniards prove unwilling. Whether or not this proviso was actually divulged to the Spanish side, which in the increasingly convivial atmosphere prevailing at Munster is by no means unlikely, the Spaniards certainly rejected this new demand outright and obdurately continued to do so throughout the subsequent negotiations.[63] Geldern in fact was never to be incorporated into the Dutch state.

[59] *Des Druckers Belydenisse*, fo. 4.
[60] *Magasyn van meyneedige ontucht*, pp. 4–5, 8, 11.
[61] *Het ghelichte Munstersche Mom-Aensicht*, p. C9ᵛ.
[62] Sec. Res. 18, 22 May, 1646. ARH SG 4855.
[63] Plenipotentiaries to SG, Munster. 6 July 1646. ARH SG 4855; Aitzema, *Ned. Vreede-handeling* ii. 89–90.

During July and August 1646 the provinces reviewed what had so far been settled at Munster and deliberated whether the proposed truce should be for twenty or thirty years.[64] In the States of Holland there was also consideration of whether the negotiation for a truce might not now be converted into one for a full peace, as had first been suggested in that assembly in the debates of August 1643. In September there was a short, sharp, tussle in the States of Holland in which the majority (including Haarlem which at this dramatic juncture switched sides, joining the peace party) overruled Leiden and Gouda. The latter towns insisted that the Dutch-Spanish negotiation should continue to be for a truce of twelve or fifteen years only and which, in any case, should not be signed until Spain conceded better terms than had been extracted thus far.[65] Leiden and Gouda were overwhelmingly outvoted, however, and the Holland majority put before the States General its famous proposal to convert the truce talks with Spain into a full peace negotiation.[66] This aroused yet another bout of furious discussion throughout the Republic. Pauw, the Bickers, and their allies, subtly aided from the sidelines by an aged and ailing Stadholder, now clearly had the upper hand, but all was not over yet. Overijssel and Gelderland readily consented Holland's proposal on 13 October.[67] Utrecht soon followed suit, though there persisted a strong feeling in the States of that province that better terms could be extracted from Spain, that there should be no concessions on church matters in the Meierij and that a Spanish peace should be negotiated hand in hand with France, as stipulated in the treaties of alliance.[68] Zeeland predictably rejected Holland's proposal outright, maintaining that behind Philip IV's temporary mask, the result merely of prevailing adverse circumstances, lurked an undying hostility that would never be satisfied until all the seven provinces were

[64] Res. SG 27 July, 15, 17, 18 Aug. 1646. ARH SG 4855; van der Capellen ii. 155–9.
[65] GA Haarlem vroed. res. 15 Sept. 1646; GA Leiden Sec. Arch. 450, vroed. res. 16 Sept. 1646.
[66] Sec. Res. SG 18 Sept. 1646. ARH SG 4855.
[67] Sec. Res. SG 13 Oct. 1646. ARH SG 4855.
[68] see, e.g., GA Amersfoort MS no. 35, vroed. res. 13 Sept. 1646.

overrun and subjected again to the 'Spanish yoke'.[69] But this was thread-bare rhetoric. Zeeland specifically objected that the army would fall into decay and lose all experience and expertise in war,[70] that both Dutch trade and industry would inevitably decline from the moment the peace took effect and be diverted elsewhere,[71] that the interests of the East and West India Companies were being foolishly sacrificed, that the South Netherlands would be left to languish perennially under the 'Spanish yoke', and, finally, that the peace would assuredly work to the advantage of the Papists throughout the Netherlands provinces.

Meanwhile special meetings of the States of Friesland and Groningen had been convened to consider the proposal for a full peace. Harangued by two delegates from Holland, the pensionary of Alkmaar, and, significantly, Albert Ruyl, pensionary of Haarlem, who seems to have been the key figure behind the defection of that town from the war party (as a result, it was rumoured, of various bribes emanating from Amsterdam)[72] Groningen consented and on 23 October Groningen and Friesland declared in favour in the States General. Holland, over the objections of Leiden, now mounted heavy pressure by means of a 'notable and great number of extraordinary deputies' on Zeeland;[73] finally, in the face of Zeeland's obduracy, the States General voted by six provinces to one on 27 October to work for the conclusion of a full peace. Once again, Zeeland's delegates angrily deplored what they regarded as a blatant infringement of the articles of the Union of Utrecht.

In November the main focus of attention reverted to colonial matters and the intricate business of border demarcation as the towns and provinces sought to hammer out their instructions for the crucial last phase of the Munster talks. The provinces agreed to press for commercial access

---

[69] Sec. Res. SG 17, 18, 20 Oct. 1646. ARH SG 4856.

[70] 'Dat de Militie sal comen te vervallen ende datmen t'eenmael buyten de experientie van Oorloge sal geraecken.'

[71] 'Dat de Neringen ende commercien perijcul loopen merckelijck te verminderen ende oock gediverteert ende elders getransporteert worden.'

[72] *'T Hollands Rommelzootje*, 2.

[73] GA Haarlem vroed res. 8 Nov. 1646; GA Leiden Sec. Arch. 450, fo. 266ᵛ; Sec. Res. SG 27 Oct. 1646. ARH SG 4856.

for the companies to the Spanish Indies east and west to begin with but that their delegates should accept mutual exclusion by each power from trade and navigation to the colonies of the other if the Spaniards proved immovable and to insist on full Spanish recognition of all Dutch conquests from Spain, including the territory subsequently lost to the Portuguese in Brazil, since the summer of 1645, or which might be lost in future in Brazil or Africa.[74] This implied Spanish acceptance of the Dutch gains in Ceylon, Taiwan, the Maluccas, Malacca, Angola, and Guinea as well as in Brazil and the Caribbean. The Spaniards were also specifically to undertake, in the interests of the East India Company, not to try to extend their presence or trade either in the Moluccas — which was tantamount to conceding the Dutch a monopoly of the spices of the Moluccas despite the presence of Spanish forts there — or in any of the Portuguese Asian colonies that the Dutch had not conquered. As regarded border demarcation the main unresolved issues concerned the so-called *landen van Overmaas*, the districts of Valkenburg, Dalem, and 's-Hertogenrade to the north and east of Maastricht which Frederik Hendrik had overrun in 1632 but which in 1635 and subsequent years had been partially reoccupied by Spanish troops. The *Raad van State* was urging that undisputed possession of these localities was essential for the security and maintenance of Maastricht.[75] The States General had agreed to demand full possession of these districts but had also decided that if the Spaniards should stubbornly refuse that the talks should not be broken off but that the Dutch delegation should concede the setting up of a *Chambre Mi-partie* to adjudicate both the Overmaas dispute and other demaracation problems in the Hulst district and other border zones of Flanders. The Dutch plenipotentiaries were instructed also to continue their efforts to obtain Geldern and to resist Spanish demands on religious matters in the Meierij.

The Dutch and Spanish delegations reconvened at Munster to settle these final points in December 1646. All the cards

---

[74] Sec. Res. SG 18, 23 Nov. 1646. ARH SG 4856.
[75] Raad to SG, 18 Nov. 1646. ARH SG 4856; Haas, 1–4.

were now in Peñaranda's hands as the States General's secret
instructions had been leaked to Brussels and the Spaniards
were therefore aware that neither over the Indies, nor the
Overkwartier, nor Geldern, would the Dutch go to the point
of breaking off the talks.[76] Whether or not Philip IV would
have reconsidered his rigid determination (as he appears to
have done in 1641-2) to at all costs exclude the Dutch from
trading with Spanish America had the Dutch been prepared
to break off we shall probably never know. Peñaranda and
Brun had been carefully briefed by the *consejos* of State and
of the Indies as to how to handle the issue of the Indies in
the first instance.[77] While, to begin with, they were to demand Dutch withdrawal from the Caribbean and Brazil, but
not their conquests in Asia, should the Dutch refuse, as inevitably they would, Peñaranda was to concede Spanish
recognition of all the Dutch conquests in the Indies east and
west including the maximum limits of Dutch Brazil as of the
year 1641. However, he was to insist on total exclusion of
the Dutch from trade and navigation to the Spanish possessions in clear, categorical terms and not the impenetrable
formula which had been resorted to in 1609. Brun parried
the opening Dutch demand for access with a closely reasoned
speech, pointing out that even the king's own non-Castilian
subjects were excluded, that the English had accepted this
exclusion in the treaty of 1630, that it in no way implied
unfriendly intentions on the part of King Philip but that the
matter was of such vital importance to Spain that the king
was ready to break off entirely rather than yield to this
demand.[78] Although this was not necessarily true and, if
driven to the point, Philip would at least have reconsidered
whether he would concede anything to the Dutch in the
Indies,[79] Peñaranda knew that he could safely be intractable. The Dutch had to be content with Spanish recognition
of the Dutch conquests in the Indies east and west, including
Dutch Brazil at its greatest extent, as of 1641, together with

---

[76] *Corresp. diplomática* i. 477-8.
[77] Consultas, Junta de Estado, 23 Jan. 1645, 10 Sept. and 24 Nov. 1646.
AGS Estado 2255.
[78] Aitzema, *Ned. Vreedehandeling* ii. 175-7.
[79] *Corresp. diplomática* i. 312-13.

an undertaking that the king's subjects in the Far East would not seek to extend their trade beyond the limits that then applied, guaranteeing Dutch control of the Moluccan spice trade, though the Spanish forts on Ternate and Tidore were to remain.[80] The Spaniards agreed to the compromise proposals for the Overmaas and Flemish border localities, rejected the demand for Geldern, and insisted on guarantees for the public practice of Catholicism in the Meierij.

The points agreed in December 1646, together with those settled the previous May, were drawn up and provisionally signed at Munster on 8 January 1647, by all the plenipotentiaries, including Knuyt for Zeeland (who, besides being Frederik Hendrik's creature, had also been bribed by the Spaniards[81]), but excluding Utrecht's representative, Nederhorst.[82] The news signalled the start of the final great political battle over the peace in the Republic. The burning controversy evidently absorbed every community and district . in the seven provinces. Late in January Antoine Brun, journeying from Munster, and Philippe le Roy, from Brussels, entered the Republic to negotiate various subsidiary points with the Stadholder, who was now openly associated with the peace terms, and generally to promote the peace process among the provinces and towns, a procedure which included a further distribution of personal gifts from the Spanish monarch.[83] The violent objections of the French ambassador, Zeeland, and Utrecht deflected the States General from according the visitors any official recognition, but they were none the less cordially received at Deventer and various other peace towns. Brun also visited Leiden where, however, he was presumably less cordially received. Joining the rising wave of peace propaganda, Brun's eloquent missive to the States General from Deventer, affirming Spain's sincere desire for peace with the Dutch, was published in several editions at Dordrecht and elsewhere.[84]

---

[80] 'Articulen provisionelick overcomen den 27 Decembris 1646', ARH SG 4856; Aitzema, *Ned. Vreedehandeling* ii. 188.

[81] See p. 000 below.

[82] Aitzema, *Ned. Vreedehandeling* ii. 188.

[83] *Corresp. diplomática* i. 494-5; Van der Capellen ii. 165; Truchis de Varennes, 351-2.

[84] *Vertoogh van Antoine de Brun.*

However, the opposition to peace was far from defeated yet, as the concerted and at times, vitriolic campaign against the provisional terms during early 1647, both before and after the death of Frederik Hendrik on 14 March, amply demonstrates.[85] Nederhorst's refusal to sign the draft treaty on the ground that his colleagues had, in effect, infringed the States General's instructions, having scarcely tried to compel the concession of Geldern and 'absolute sovereignty' in the Meierij, received the full backing of the States of Utrecht and the Utrecht and Amersfoort *vroedschappen*.[86] Utrecht, together with the rest of the opposition, also protested that not enough had been secured for the West India Company and that to proceed further towards peace with Spain, without moving conjointly with France, was tantamount to breaking the solemn treaty obligations entered into with the French crown in 1635 and renewed in 1644.[87] Zeeland indignantly repudiated Knuyt's action, demanded that the clause concerning the Flemish sea-ports be strengthened, and objected that the draft formula on the Indies conflicted with the agreed instructions in that they contained no Spanish undertaking with respect to Portuguese Brazil and West Africa.[88] Friesland demanded adjustment of the wording on the Meierij and the unqualified acquisition of both Geldern and the Overmaas.[89] Groningen made the same demands, insisting also, like Zeeland, on an undertaking from the Spanish crown to remain outside all the territory in Brazil and Africa occupied by the Portuguese, beyond the limits held by the Dutch in 1641, as regarded forts, troops, and trade.[90] In Gelderland, where there was a series of special meetings of the Landsdag to debate the negotiated terms, opinion was

[85] *Corresp. Sousa Coutinho* ii. 31–2, 41, 59, 69.

[86] Sec. Res. SG, 22 Jan. 1647. ARH SG 4856.

[87] GA Amersfoort MS 1013. vroed. res. 21 Feb. 1647; GA Amersfoort MS 1016, 'Bedenckingen vande Regeerders der stad Amersfoort'.

[88] Zeeland insisted that 'de Spaensche gheneralijck sullen moeten blyven uyt alle de plaetsen die de Portugysen in Brasilien ende andersints onder het Octroy vande West-Indische Compagnie behoorende zijn besittende'; see also *Kroniek* (1869), pp. 446–50.

[89] Van der Capellen ii. 178; Aitzema, *Ned. Vreedehandeling* ii. 317–19; Haas, 20–1.

[90] Aitzema, *Ned. Vreedehandeling* ii. 275–8.

divided:[91] the Nijmegen quarter adhered closest to Holland's stance, looking on the prospect of the incorporation of Geldern with mixed feelings, as the new quarter would be certain to assume a prominent role in the politics of the Landsdag, and would greatly reinforce the Catholic presence within the province; the Zutphen quarter aligned closest to the opposition, insisting strongly on incorporation; in the Veluwe views wavered between the other two. Meanwhile virtually all the objections of the other provinces were echoed by Holland's second city, Leiden,[92] which was now virtually isolated within the province.

Holland approved the draft treaty as it stood and, over Leiden's objections, took steps to pressure the other provinces into accepting it likewise, but the opposition remained too formidable to be elbowed aside speedily or easily.[93] The beginnings of the long economic recession of 1647–51 which was felt in the Low Countries, as well as the rest of western Europe, at this time, featuring scarcity of grain, high food prices, diminution of trade, falling rents and wages were blamed by a great many ordinary Dutchmen on the peace with Spain.[94] To stiffen the resistance, the French ambassador, Servient, issued missives to Zeeland and the inland provinces, recalling the age-old treachery of the Spaniards, and denouncing 'ceux qui pour favoriser les intentions de l'ennemy, voudroient rompre la constante union qui a duré si longs temps entre vostre nation et la nostre'. Forced to compromise, Holland agreed in May that a last effort should be made to acquire Geldern and the Overmaas, together with changes in the wording relating to the Meierij, to remove any question as to the absoluteness of Dutch sovereignty there; but Holland also insisted that there be no change in the clauses concerning the Indies and the Flemish harbours. While this proved enough to swing Gelderland, Friesland, and Groningen, securing a majority vote, Zeeland and Utrecht were able to delay the return of the Dutch plenipotentiaries

[91] Sec. Res. SG 12, 28 Jan. 1647. ARH SG 4856; Capellen ii. 172–4, 179, 182.
[92] GA Leiden, Sec. Arch. 450, fos. 274ᵛ–276ʳ. vroed. res. 18 Feb. 1647; GA Haarlem, vroed. res. 8, 20 Apr. 1647.
[93] Aitzema, *Ned. Vreedehandeling* ii. 335.
[94] Van der Capellen ii. 184; Gutmann, 233.

to Munster for several more months, until Holland forced compliance by delaying its contribution to the States General's assistance to the hard-pressed West India Company.[95]

Talks resumed at Munster on 17 September 1647, much to the annoyance of the Spanish side, who had supposed that the actual negotiations were now completed.[96] Over the question of religion in the Meierij, there were prolonged and angry exchanges, but the Spaniards refused to budge. Nor were they at all compliant on the other questions. The only substantive change was an agreement to exchange Geldern for an equivalent Dutch territory within six months of ratification, any disagreement as to what was 'equivalent' to be submitted together with the Overmaas question to the projected *Chambre mi-partie*. But this clause was never implemented.

In November 1647 the seventy-nine articles of the draft treaty were once again referred back to the provinces for approval. Though Utrecht refused to countenance finalization until solid progress had been made in the Franco-Spanish negotiations, and Zeeland remained adamantly opposed, four provinces — Friesland, Groningen, Overijssel, and Gelderland — voted with Holland, approving the terms and the return of the plenipotentiaries to Munster, to conclude. The formal signing of the articles, on behalf of States General and king, took place in the Munster town hall on 30 January 1648. Knuyt again signed for Zeeland, but Utrecht's representative, Nederhorst 'dont la probité et sincère affection envers la France ne se peut estimer', as was reported to Paris, refused.[97]

The final dramatic phase of the political battle in the Republic, over the Spanish peace, was that from February to May 1648, over ratification. The pamphlets of either side were avidly consumed. The vehemence of the debate at this late hour amazed Peñaranda and his colleagues.[98] In Gelderland, at a special meeting of the Landsdag during February at Zutphen, the lingering objections of the Zutphen quarter

[95] Sec. Res. SG 8, 10, 13 Aug. 1647.
[96] *Négociations secrètes* iv. 161.
[97] S. Utrecht to Amersfoort, 9 Feb. 1648. GA Amersfoort MS 35; *Négociations secrètes* iv. 205.   [98] *Corresp. diplomática* iii. 172–4.

were submerged by Nijmegen and the Veluwe.[99] At the special gathering of the States of Utrecht heavy pressure was brought to bear from outside, leading to a weakening of the opposition and the defection of Amersfoort, which was loath to promote discord among the provinces,[1] but even so the war-party succeeded in preventing the province ratifying during February and March. Holland tried to secure ratification in the States General by majority vote on Sunday 29 March, but while four provinces voted for, and the Frisian delegates were yet to receive instructions, Groningen and Overijssel refused to allow a mere majority to settle so fundamental a matter. Friesland ratified the very next day, but Zeeland now held the chair in the States General and blocked any further move during the following week. On 4 April, against the advice of the young Stadholder, Prince Willem, five provinces voted for ratification, with Zeeland and Utrecht against. However, within a few days, Utrecht faltered and switched to the majority, leaving Zeeland isolated. On 28 April a States General delegation came before the States of Zeeland, in Middelburg, in a last effort to persuade the province to conform with the rest. When Zeeland refused, the other six provinces went ahead and ratified the treaty. The famous and moving ceremony of exchanging notices of ratification and taking of oaths, at Munster town hall, depicted in masterly fashion by Gerard Terborch, who was present at the proceedings,[2] took place on 15 May, in the absence of any representative of Zeeland. But Zeeland finally acquiesced and agreed to publish the peace, to prevent discord within the Republic, on 30 May. The peace was published throughout the Republic amid widespread rejoicing on 5 June, though neither the Zeeland towns nor Leiden complied with the States General's request to the town councils for public festivities and thanksgiving to mark the event.[3]

[99] Van der Capellen, ii. 210–11.
    [1] GA Amersfoort MS 35, vroed. res. 12, 13, 14, 16 Mar. 1648; Wicquefort i. 112.
    [2] Terborch's masterpiece hangs today in the National Gallery, London.
    [3] GA Leiden Sec. Arch. 963, fo. 237. vroed. res. 4 June 1648; Kernkamp, *Prins Willem*, 60.

Chapter VII

The Aftermath, 1648–1661

It is perhaps tempting to assume that the seventy-nine articles of the treaty of Munster, so long and arduously argued over, marked a definitive break in the long history of Dutch–Spanish strife and that the peace was joyfully received by the populations concerned. Certainly, it appears to us in retrospect as something firm and final. To contemporaries, however, the peace treaty seemed highly fragile and problematic as well as in several respects inconclusive. A settlement which had encountered such deeply entrenched opposition among sections of Dutch society, in Holland as well as elsewhere, was in any case, even in more normal circumstances, scarcely likely to be immediately fully secure. In the difficult constitutional and economic conditions of the years 1648–51 its very survival was, for some time, in serious doubt. Peñaranda, after the first glow of satisfaction in 1648, observed the subsequent deterioration in relations with mounting anxiety and, by March 1649 and for two years after that considered a resumption of the war between Spain and the Republic to be a distinct possibility.[1]

If there were mixed feelings about peace in the Republic, there were certainly no doubts at Madrid. Spain had sacrificed economic and colonial interests to gain a political objective which, to Philip's ministers, continued to seem of overriding importance. Although the years 1647–52 were a time of mounting crisis in Spain, as in many other parts of Europe, of severe economic dislocation and serious disturbances in Naples, Sicily, and Andalusia, the concurrence of prolonged civil war and political turmoil in France, with the onset of the Frondes, enabled Philip IV to gradually reconquer

---

[1] *Corresp. diplomática* iii. 353–4.

Catalonia and regain ground from the French in Flanders. The European balance of power, delicately poised, seemed for the moment to be shifting back in favour of Spain. But Spanish hopes of resuming the upper hand in the struggle with France, as the *Consejo de Estado* was acutely aware, depended, among other things, on preserving the peace with the Dutch which, in turn, meant resolving, or at least easing, the various problems in Dutch-Spanish relations bequeathed by Munster. Again and again, at this time, Spanish ministers made it crystal clear that they regarded the minimization of friction with the Dutch as one of Spain's most vital political interests, but as the Dutch political and economic crisis of 1647-51 deepened, the prospects for a further *rapprochement* receded and the likelihood of a new rupture steadily increased.

Even before the ratification of the peace treaty, Philip and the *Consejo* were more than willing to follow up the accord with new agreements designed to forge closer links with the Republic. The king and his advisers were keen to post an ambassador to The Hague and, in particular, to exploit the coolness in Franco-Dutch relations which had developed since 1646 when the Dutch had first begun to deal in earnest with Spain, separately from France.[2] Essentially, the Spanish objective was to procure some kind of defensive pact with the Republic which would assert the integrity of the Spanish Netherlands, or failing that at least of Flanders and Brabant, against France, establish a common Dutch-Spanish policy of maintaining the *status quo* in Westphalia, and strengthening the military potential of the Flemish *plaza de armas* by providing provisions, arms, munitions, and recruits for the Spanish army and *armada* as well as Amsterdam's financial services. Philip also had a second key objective: in view of the steadily deteriorating relations between the Republic and Portugal, following the Portuguese gains at Dutch expense, in Brazil, and the Portuguese recovery of Angola from the Dutch during the summer of 1648, Spanish ministers were keen to find some way of exploiting the

---

[2] Brun to Peñaranda, 2, 7, and 10 July 1648. ARB SEG 602; *Corresp. diplomática* iii. 295-8; Truchis de Varennes, 377.

tension to the advantage of Spain and even hoped to achieve a Dutch-Spanish offensive league or at least some form of Dutch-Spanish co-operation intended to accomplish the reconquest of Portugal by Spain and of Brazil and West Africa by the Dutch and Spaniards jointly.[3]

But the projected Spanish diplomatic drive of 1648 in the Republic quickly foundered on the rock of mounting Dutch-Spanish friction over the various unsettled issues left over by the peace treaty, friction exacerbated by the persistently strong anti-Spanish sentiment in the Republic. In January 1648, after some Dutch officials had been taken prisoner by Spanish troops garrisoned at Navagne, the States General, under heavy pressure to secure the whole of the Overmaas for the Republic, and following the advice of Prince Willem, had dispatched troops to occupy and garrison Valkenburg, Dalhem and 's-Hertogenrade which in turn led to several minor clashes with the Spanish soldiery garrisoned at Limburg, Navagne and Leut, and the taking of further prisoners by both sides.[4] Despite the determination of Holland's delegates to exert a restraining pressure, and their insistence that the status of the disputed territory remained 'questieus', which certainly kept matters from deteriorating further than they otherwise would have done, the situation in the Overmaas remained very tense until the autumn of 1649 when Antoine Brun, having taken up his post as Spanish ambassador at The Hague was able to arrange a rough interim compromise pending the convening of the *Chambre Mi-partie* as well as a general return of prisoners. During that time, the unfortunate inhabitants of the Overmaas were showered with placards and counter-placards from Brussels and The Hague, caught between rival jurisdictions and subject to two sets of fiscal officials and soldiery. Even more alarming was the bitter religious controversy which flared up in May and June 1648 and continued throughout the crisis period until 1651, particularly in the Meierij, but also in the regions of Breda, Bergen-op-Zoom,

---

[3] Consulta 15 Sept. 1650. AGS Estado 2072; *Corresp. diplomática* ii. 297–8; Truchis de Varennes, 376.

[4] Res. Holl. 15, 21 Jan. 1648; Wicquefort i. 172, 281; Wagenaar xii. 21; Haas, 46–54.

and Dutch Flanders. With ratification of the peace, numerous Catholic clergy, regular, secular and Jesuits, returned from the Spanish Netherlands to these Generality Lands, as they were known, to resume charge of their parishioners who in their great majority had remained loyal to Rome, as well as to reclaim the hundreds of former ecclesiastical buildings and properties in these areas.[5] The undisguised display of Catholic feeling accompanying this sudden influx in turn provoked an angry backlash in the Protestant parts of the country, particularly Zeeland, Utrecht, and the northern provinces. As a consequence, during May and June, measures designed to impose the reformed faith more stringently on the newly acquired districts were pushed through in the States General against the wishes of the dominant Holland faction but with the eager support of Haarlem, Leiden and some other Holland towns.[6] A lapsed edict of December 1636, expelling Catholic clergy from the Meierij, was reissued and extended to apply to the whole of the Generality Lands, a decree which in the view of Spanish ministers flatly contradicted the articles of the peace treaty guaranteeing freedom of movement to the subjects of either power in the European lands of the other.[7] Troops were used to close monasteries, eject priests, remove Catholic images from churches, schools, and hospitals, and, rather patchily, to enforce public practice of reformed worship. Naturally, such procedures soon elicited loud protests from Brussels where the new governor, the Austrian Archduke Leopold, was urging that the various unsettled points relating to religious life and church properties in the Generality Lands be deferred until the meeting of the projected *Chambre Mi-partie*.[8] An official sent by the Arch-

[5] Brun to Philip, The Hague, 26 Dec. 1649. AGS Estado 2070; Heurn iii. 1.
[6] *Groot Placaetboek* i. 257; Wagenaar xii. 20-1; Hubert, 115; *Geschiedenis van Breda* ii. 185-6; Rogier ii. 575-6, 608-10; in May 1649 there was also discussion as to whether to strip Catholic officials in the Meierij of their offices, the States of Holland, over the protests of Haarlem and Leiden, insisted that such functionaries should be left at their posts, provided of course that they discharged their duties satisfactorily, Res. Holl. 18 May 1649.
[7] Res. Holl. 8 Mar. 1650; this was one of the arguments used by Spanish officials in 1649-50 to evade the Dutch contention that Spain was violating the same articles by refusing entry to Dutch Jews to Spain and Spanish Italy.
[8] Res. Holl. 16 July 1648; Hubert, 115.

duke to The Hague to negotiate, Petrus Stockmans, was rather rudely received. As regards the setting up of the *Chambre Mi-partie*, to which the States of Holland proved favourable during discussions in December 1648, there were such strong objections from Zeeland, Utrecht, and other provinces, as well as Leiden, that the whole matter was postponed indefinitely.[9]

There was also a good deal of recrimination over matters of trade regulations and tolls as between the North and South Netherlands. The States of Zeeland repeatedly complained, in 1648 and subsequently, that the Spanish undertaking in the peace treaty to raise the tolls in the Flemish sea-ports to the Schelde level was not being observed and that in consequence 'all trade and commerce on the Schelde, Sas and Zwijn is daily diminishing more and more and being diverted to the Flemish harbours'.[10] Partly this diversion involved goods being shipped by sea from Holland to Ostend and along the Flemish *binnenstromen* to Brugge, Ghent, and Antwerp, and therefore caused no loss to Holland, but in part also it involved the shipping of merchandise directly from the Baltic, Scandinavia, and elsewhere to Ostend bypassing Holland as well as Zeeland. If most of the anger provoked by this shift was nevertheless confined to Zeeland, considerable ire was aroused in Holland by the seizure by Ostend privateers of various Dutch vessels carrying arms and munitions to French ports.[11] The States General sent a representative, Jan Copes, to confer with Peñaranda and other Spanish officials, at Antwerp, but while the Conde arranged for restitution of the ships to their Dutch owners in August 1648, the Spanish authorities continued to claim that under the commercial capitulations agreed at Munster in February 1648, as a supplement to the main treaty,[12] they were entitled to seize munitions, though not other Dutch

[9] Res. Holl. 9 Dec. 1648; Haas, 49-50.
[10] SZ to SG, 1 Oct. 1648. GA Dordrecht, section 115 (Maashandel), doc. 336; GA Vlissingen inventaris no. 195, 'Corte deductie op de gelegentheyt vande havenen van Oostende ende Brugge int stuck van negotie'; Brun to Philip, The Hague, 25 Mar. 1650. AGS Estado 2170.
[11] Aitzema, *Hist.* vii. 165; Wagenaar xii. 23-4; Wicquefort i. 174-5.
[12] For these articles, see *Corresp. diplomática* iii. 205-7.

cargoes, *en route* to enemies of Spain. This and other unsettled points relating to commerce were deferred for subsequent negotiation.

Yet another complication relating to trade, which caused
widespread exasperation in the Republic, was the continuance
of tolls levied by the Spaniards on Maas traffic either side of
the Dutch enclave at Maastricht, at Roermond and Navagne
respectively, which were accounted a major hindrance to
the river trade to Maastricht and Liège.[13] The town of Dordrecht, the centre of Holland's river trade, was particularly
anxious that this matter be resolved quickly. 'Une ville', in
the words of the French Resident, Brasset, 'qui, dans la
négotiation de la paix avec l'Espagne, a pris hautement
l'affirmative contre la France,'[14] Dordrecht remained the
town which, after Amsterdam, was most resolutely committed to the Spanish peace; but a major reason was that the
town stood to gain greatly from the planned post-war lowering of tolls and removal of restrictions on north-south river
traffic. What the Dordrecht *vroedschap* and powerful Dordrecht Maas-skippers guild wanted was reciprocal removal of
the Dutch toll, or *passagie-gelt*, levied at Maastricht, together
with the Spanish tolls which were supposed to be in retaliation for the Dutch toll. On 6 August 1648 a petition from
the 'merchants and skippers' trading on the Maas was read to
the States of Holland, requesting reciprocal removal of the
Dutch and Spanish tolls, a petition strongly supported by
Dordrecht.[15] Holland agreed to take up the matter in the
States General, but no progress was made and all the Maas
tolls remained in force. Neither the States General nor
Brussels seemed willing to take the first step in dismantling
the obstructions.

Traditionally, historians have stressed the role of the
young Stadholder, Willem II, in the reintensification of
Dutch–Spanish friction, at least from the summer of 1649
onwards. As Stadholder and captain-general, the prince's
authority was undeniably diminished as a result of the peace,
and the first post-Munster round of army reductions, which

---

[13] Wicquefort i. 173-4.
[14] *Archives* iv. 276.   [15] Res. Holl. 6 Aug. 1648.

took place during the summer of 1648, and risked being much further diminished as a result of the additional army cuts which were urged by the dominant Holland faction during 1649–50, and which became the core-issue of the great constitutional crisis of those years. Nor can it be denied that whatever the various motives of the parties concerned, the chief pretext for maintaining a substantial standing army, in 1649–50, was the alleged danger from Spain and Spain's uncontrollable ally, the duke of Lorraine, whose undisciplined troops made various incursions into the Meierij during 1649. Willem, moreover, detested both the Spanish peace and those responsible for it: 'je voudrois', he wrote in August 1649, 'rompre le col à tous les coquins qui ont fait la paix, et. . .je ne perdray pas un moment de temps de faire ma capable pour les ruiner. . .'[16] He had been marked out by Peñaranda as a foe of Spain from the moment that he had assumed the Stadholdership.[17] But care must be taken not to overemphasize Willem's part. Owing to his youth and inexperience, he inevitably lacked much of the political weight that his father had had, though, as has been seen, even Frederik Hendrik's authority had been much reduced since 1643. During the winter and spring of 1648, Willem's role in supporting Utrecht, Zeeland, and the rest of the opposition against the peace had been minimal, while he did not even try to obstruct the 1648 army reductions, though this did not prevent Haarlem, Leiden, and Alkmaar from vigorously opposing them in the States of Holland, Leiden proclaiming the 'dangers which in this conjuncture of time and circumstance are likely to arise from the projected reduction of the army.'[18] Evidently, Willem's stance only assumed the significance that it did owing to the popular pressures arising on all sides in opposition to the policies of the dominant Holland faction.

The widespread grievances which moulded the Dutch political and economic crisis of 1648–51 arguably derived mainly from the temporarily severe economic circumstances of these years, exacerbated by certain specific economic

---

[16] *Archives* iv. 314; Groenveld, 10; see also Muller, 142.
[17] *Corresp. diplomática* ii. 264, iii. 353.
[18] Res. Holl. 27 June, 8, 13 July, 1648.

frustrations connected with the Spanish peace, though it is true that the generally sombre mood was also tinged with anger at the Catholic resurgence in the Generality Lands. Amsterdam, Dordrecht, and the rest of the leading group in Holland were indeed unfortunate that just when they had finally overcome the bitter opposition to the Munster treaty, the Republic, together with the rest of western Europe, was caught up in one of the severest recessions of the century. Of course, the main cause of the relative economic deterioration — several years of almost continuous bad weather leading to the disastrous harvests of 1647–51 which, despite the boom in the Baltic grain trade which brought a handsome profit to the merchants of Amsterdam, imposed soaring grain and other food prices on Holland[19] — had little directly to do with Dutch–Spanish relations. But as so often in times of economic distress, the depression served to aggravate already entrenched economic resentments and complaints. In this way it became a favourite theme of the Dutch anti-peace pamphleteers of 1649–50 that the Spanish peace was the cause of the slump and the high food prices, that the 'peace consumes and removes what the [Spanish] war gave us'.[20]

The detractors of the dominant Holland faction mocked the expectations of a new golden age, of glittering prosperity for the nation, which had been deliberately aroused during the drive for peace. Had not the heavens shown their disapproval of the *monstreuse* Munster treaty, asked one author,[21] with the torrential rain that had fallen on Holland ever since? How ironic that many Dutchmen had supported the peace moves, anticipating cheaper food as a result of the reductions in the avidly consuming armies when, in fact, prices of basic foods had risen to unheard of heights. And what was the cause of the suffering of the poor? Was not the unprecedented cost of bread, butter, and cheese due to the lifting of the ban on grain exports to the South Netherlands and the cuts in 'convoy and license' money which

[19] Centen, 116–17, 126; Bang i, tables for 1647–51; Gutmann, 117–18.
[20] 'De Vrede verslint neemt wech wat de Oorloge heeft gegeven': see *De Na-Ween vande Vrede*, A3; see also *Vrymoedige Aenspraeck*, p. 11; *Hollandsche Mercurius*, 1650, p. 2.
[21] *De Na-Ween vande Vrede*, p. A2v.

together had so greatly stimulated the export of foodstuffs to Flanders and Brabant? 'Thus they have had abundance [since the peace] and we have had scarcity, indeed often food has been cheaper there than among us which all results from the abundance of food supplied there, from here, which in the war could not happen.'[22]

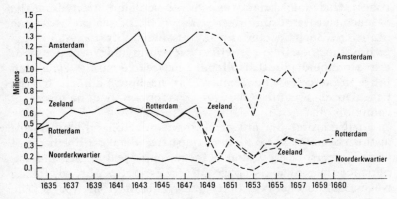

7 The 'Convoy and License' returns on all Dutch imports and exports collected by the Dutch admiralty colleges (1635–1660) in guilders. *Source*: Becht, table 1.

Not only was the land gripped by scarcity since the peace, it was pointed out, but trade and industry had 'markedly diminished'.[23] Once again, the breweries suffered, this time, apparently, particularly at Rotterdam. More seriously, the wholesale reductions in the fixed military garrisons which for decades had played an essential part in vitalizing the economy of the less developed eastern regions of the country, as well as of the Generality Lands, inevitably exerted a harshly depressive effect over wide areas.[24] These cuts took effect in

[22] Ibid., p. A3; Teelinck, *Vrijmoedige Aenspraeck*, 11.
[23] 'Sijn de Neeringen koopmanschappen alle Handt-wercken niet merckelijcken verachtet?', *De Na-Ween vande Vrede*, p. A3; *Hollandsche Mercurius*, 1650, p. 2.
[24] *De Na-Ween vande Vrede*, p. A3; Engelen, 10–13, 17–18.

1647-8. At Nijmegen, for instance, the removal of most of the troops, in 1648, dealt a paralyzing and long-remembered blow to the city's vitality and population. And in this respect, the entire east of the Republic can be said to have been adversely affected by the Spanish peace which drastically cut back what in a manner of speaking had been a form of subsidy to the east on the part of Holland. Moreover, as can be seen from graph 4, the peace undoubtedly did divert the transit trade of Zeeland and South Holland from along the Schelde and its tributaries to the Flemish sea-ports. As the States of Zeeland contended, this inevitably meant a long-term setback to the prosperity of Zeeland and to some extent also to that of South Holland. It appeared just as clear that the commerce of the Republic as a whole had lost by the peace as it was that that of Amsterdam had handsomely gained.

Furthermore, the industrial towns of Holland were swept at this time by a wave of anxiety, suffered a clear diversion of work to Flanders, Brabant, Liège, and Westphalia, and experienced a growing seepage of wool supplies abroad, falling wages, and generally deteriorating conditions for textile workers. It is true that Leiden's total output declined only slightly during the crisis years,[25] following the boom-cycle of the 1635-45 period, but it would be quite wrong to dismiss the claims of the *Na-Ween vande Vrede* and other contemporary pamphlets as to the damage dealt to the Dutch textile industry by the Spanish peace as merely politically motivated rhetoric. There was a sharp falling off in output of fine *lakens* which was now the most important sector, a collapse in the cheapest woollens, rashes, and fustians, caused by the post-1648 influx of cheap imports from Liège and Westphalia stimulated by the reduction in the Dutch tariffs, and, so it was said, severe difficulties were now experienced by the linen and bleaching industries at Haarlem.[26] In addition, Leiden manufacturers were now increasingly putting out spinning and other work to lower-paid

[25] Posthumus, *Leidsche Lakenindustrie* iii. 884, 930, 932.

[26] 'Die vande Laeckenneeringe der Vereenigde Nederlanden' (10 Aug. 1648) GA Leiden 2449; Res. Holl. 17, 28 Jan. and 18, 21 Dec. 1648, and 4 Mar. and 25 May 1651; de la Court, *Welvaren van Leiden*, 88.

workers, in the Meierij, particularly Tilburg, and in Spanish Brabant where costs were distinctly lower than in Holland. For all these reasons, there broke out in the years 1648-9 a rash of debates, both in the States of Holland and States General, over what was termed the 'diversion of the drapery industry out of these lands' at the instigation of the Haarlem and Leiden *vroedschappen*, pressed to act by the cloth guilds of those cities. Discontent was undoubtedly widespread at this time in Holland just as in the east and south of the country.

It was in this grim and sobre context that the States General voted, on 5 June 1649, to admit Philip IV's ambassador, Antoine Brun, to The Hague to take up his official duties.[27] The decision aroused widespread displeasure. Zeeland and Utrecht had voted against the resolution and continued to oppose Brun's admittance, refusing to send representatives to the modest state supper held to celebrate his arrival. On 26 June 1649 Brun delivered his first address before the States General, profusely asserting his master's desire for friendly relations and the wish of all his subjects to settle the remaining difficulties in Dutch–Spanish relations quickly. This address received a good deal of publicity and was published in Dutch translation[28], but much of the Dutch public seem to have regarded it as so much trickery. Antipeace pamphleteers, exploiting the mood, openly derided his words, maintaining that Spain still nourished the ambition of one day reconquering all the seven provinces, stamping the reformed faith under foot and subjecting free men again to the 'Spanish yoke'.[29] The treaty of Munster, like the 1609 truce, was frequently depicted as merely a sinister ploy with which to foment internal strife in the Republic. Brasset's acid comment — 'enfin le cheval de Troie est entre dans la Hollande'[30] — undoubtedly echoed the feelings of a good many Dutchmen about Brun's arrival.

[27] Wicquefort i. 589; Aitzema, *Hist.* vi. 724.
[28] Brun, *Oratie Gedaen door Monsievr D. Antonio de Brvn.*
[29] Teelinck, *Vrymoedige Aenspraeck*, p. 9; *Amsterdams Buer-Praetje*, A2[V]; *Lauweren-krans gevlochten*, fo. 13.
[30] *Archives* iv. 311.

While Brun was not the acutest of observers, he quickly and clearly grasped that Spain's real enemy in the Republic was neither the Stadholder nor any particular province, assembly, or institution, but the lower orders of society moved by a combination of economic frustration and religious prejudice. In February 1650 he advised the *Consejo de Estado* that most of the people disliked the peace, 'considering that there is less profit to be had now than during the war; thus it is essential to bribe the leading politicians lest they let themselves be moved by the preachers, *gente mecánica* (working people), and the military faction.'[31] Brasset likewise appreciated the significance of economic factors in the deepening political split in Holland, explaining the rift between Amsterdam and the 'bonnes villes', by which he meant Leiden, Haarlem, and the rest of the Holland opposition, 'à cause de la jalousie que est entre elles pour raison du commerce dans lequel chacune tasche de se bénéficier.'[32]

From July, through the rest of 1649, and the early months of 1650, Brun attended a series of audiences with the States General and conferred with a special committee of the assembly, set up during the autumn and headed by Adriaan Pauw, to handle the details of Dutch relations with the Spanish lands. Openly, Brun concentrated, apart from commercial matters, which figured large, on urging retraction or at least modification of the decree of expulsion of Catholic priests from the Generality Lands, on fighting for the Catholic church properties in the area, for the setting up of the *Chambre Mi-partie*, and for an interim solution for the Overmaas border dispute.[33] He also complained vigorously against unbridled 'pasquinades and libels' that appeared 'daily' attacking the king of Spain and his own person. Secretly, Brun urged Pauw, Knuyt, Andries Bicker, and the

---

[31] Muller, 172, citing Brun to Philip, 25 Feb. 1650; returning to this theme a month later, Brun wrote that 'es cosa cierta que el pueblo no gusta de la Paz imputandole toda la carestia que tiene particularmente de trigo sin querer considerar le esterilidad de los años pasados': Brun to Philip, 25 Mar. 1650. AGS Estado 2170.

[32] *Archives* iv. 361.

[33] Res. Holl. 14, 15, 21 July, 21 Dec. 1649, 8 Mar., 27 July 1650; Wicquefort i. 283-4; Wagenaar xii. 44.

baron van Obdam[34] as well as other Dutch politicians with whom he had or developed intimate links to consider the advantages of a 'close union' with Spain directed against France and particularly Portugal.[35] On all these issues except the Overmaas, progress was exceedingly slight. The dominant Holland faction evidently sympathized with Brun's request that the virulent anti-Spanish propaganda be restrained, and the province in fact submitted a draft-edict to the States General designed to ban 'pasquinades and libels' against all foreign kings and republics and their ministers, but the other provinces rejected it and the printed attacks in fact increased.[36]

An issue to which Brun gave particular attention, believing that its solution would do more than anything to reduce the opposition to the peace, was the compensation agreement that had been concluded with the House of Orange during the last weeks of Frederik Hendrik's life, in February 1647, though, as has been seen, the negotiations, through Knuyt, reached back long before this and during the later summer of 1646, from when the prince was taken to be openly supporting the peace process, it was widely rumoured in the Republic that the prince had agreed to accept from the Spanish monarch the Overkwartier (Geldern), together with the title of 'duke of Gelre'.[37] Under the eventual settlement which was incorporated into the terms of the treaty of Munster, Philip undertook to compensate Frederik Hendrik and his heirs for the family lands confiscated in the South Netherlands by Philip II, in particular by transferring to the House of Orange that portion of the barony of Bergen-op-Zoom which had remained in Spanish hands. The matter was long to remain controversial on the Dutch political scene for whilst Orangists habitually defended the arrangement as just

[34] Jacob van Wassenaer, baron van Obdam, distinguished cavalry officer at siege of Maastricht, inscribed in the Holland nobility in 1635, became governor of Heusden in 1651 and subsequently a distinguished admiral.

[35] Brun to Philip, 25 Mar. 1650. AGS Estado 2170; consultas, 4 June 1650, 25 Sept. 1650. AGS Estado 2072.

[36] Res. Holl. 13, 14 Jan. 1650; Brun to Philip, 10 July 1650. AGS Estado 2170.

[37] Van der Capellen ii. 147, 157, 183.

compensation for the wrongs Philip II had perpetrated against William the Silent, their opponents regarded it as a concealed bribe devised by Spain to secure the prince's co-operation in the peace process.[38] In any case, owing to legal complications arising from the refusal of the existing bene-factress to relinquish her title and lands, the original agree-ment was suspended and, during 1649-50, Spanish ministers sought to negotiate a new settlement compensating Prince Willem in cash and rents only, amounting to over 1½ million florins, which was certainly much less than the value of the original offer.[39] Brun tried repeatedly, during 1650, through Knuyt, to coax the young prince into accepting the new terms, but Willem steadfastly refused.[40]

The question of the settlement with the House of Orange worried Brun considerably more than Zeeland's indignation over the Flemish harbour tolls. The ambassador did note that trade was being diverted from Zeeland to Flanders as a conse-quence of the post-war changes, and reported to Madrid that Baltic cargoes for the South Netherlands were now being regularly shipped direct to Ostend, bypassing the Republic entirely. He was well aware of the resentment that this caused. 'Zeeland is becoming much poorer', he wrote, 'and has sent. . . [extraordinary] deputies here [The Hague] to declare that if Your Majesty does not agree to establish tolls equal to those that they maintain [on the Schelde], they would rather make war all on their own than remain as they are; but whilst I keep the other provinces well disposed, especially Holland, we need not fear their threats.'[41] Brun seems to have thought Zeeland so hostile as not to be worth any effort to placate. Certainly, ministers in Brussels were in no hurry to choke off Flanders's burgeoning new maritime trade for Zeeland's sake. Ostend was profiting visibly from Zeeland's distress.

Although Brun needed no reminding that, as he himself wrote, 'those of Amsterdam are our best friends, those who

[38] *Haeghs Hof-Praetje,* 19.
[39] *Corresp. d'Esp.* vi. 102-3; Wicquefort i. 341-3; Muller, 147.
[40] Brun to Philip, 8 Apr. 1650. AGS Estado 2170; consulta 23 July 1650. AGS Estado 2072.
[41] Brun to Philip, 25 Mar. 1650. AGS Estado 2170.

contributed most to the peace and who contribute most today to maintain it against the wishes of other towns',[42] he
was scrupulously careful, as the storm clouds of the 1650
political crisis gathered, neither to seem nor actually to take
sides. While the anti-peace pamphleteers had it that Brun
was brazenly partisan, working hand in hand with the corrupt
Amsterdam elite and the States of Holland, attending secret
meetings day and night at the residence of Burgomaster
Bicker,[43] in reality his secret efforts were directed more
towards cultivating his links with the prince's camp. He knew
that he could count on Amsterdam's friendship in any case.
The important thing in his eyes, since he regarded the prince's
power as increasingly formidable, was somehow to secure
Spain's interests with the opposition. In February 1650 he
reported to Madrid that he was in regular secret contact with
Willem himself, his mother, the Princess Amalia, and other
members of the prince's circle, that he believed he was
making steady progress in this direction and that 'every day I
see more clearly that he has very great power in these provinces'.[44] He undoubtedly maintained close links with
Knuyt, whose corrupt relationship with Spain he had arranged
at Munster, and with the princess who was notoriously
addicted to money and anxious not to lose the rents she
received under a separate clause of the 1647 settlement
from estates near Turnhout,[45] but he apparently greatly
exaggerated the influence of both of these personages. He
failed to make any impact on the prince's key advisors, the
younger Aerssen, Cornelis Musch and Count Willem Frederik,
stadholder of Friesland and Willem himself clearly remained
impervious to Brun's allurements.

While the anti-peace tracts accused Spain of sowing and
exploiting the discord among the provinces for its own ends,
in reality any thought of undermining of the stability of the
Republic was now far from the minds of Philip's ministers.
For as long as possible, the policy was to avoid taking sides
and to strive to improve relations with the *Prinsgezinden*. On
27 July 1650, just three days before Willem's dramatic

[42] Brun to G. de Torre, Cambrai, 27 Aug. 1649. AGS Estado 2070.
[43] *Lauweren-krans gevlochten*, fo. 16ᵛ.
[44] Muller, 172–3.   [45] Ibid., 147.

attempted coup against Amsterdam, the prince in person visited Brun, thanked him for his repeated compliments and solicitations as to his health and remarked, as if *en passant*, that his advisers were continually telling him that Brun was endeavouring to encourage Holland against him.[46] However ineffectively, Brun was certainly being truthful in protesting that such talk was sheer calumny. But with the progress of the dispute over Holland's proposed additional army cuts[47] and the deepening split in the Dutch body politic, Philip's ministers had to face the prospect of imminent civil war in the Republic accompanied by, or leading to, armed intervention by Zeeland and the inland provinces in the now defenceless rear of the Spanish Netherlands. Contemplating the outlook in August 1650, the *Consejo de Estado* concluded that Spain would have no choice but to side with Holland against the rest, but that Brun and the Archduke Leopold should wait until the last practicable moment before doing so.[48]

While Willem's attempted use of the army to surprise Amsterdam, on the morning of the 30 July 1650, failed, the dramatic effect of his clumsy coup, his arrest of various Holland politicians who had opposed him and the ejection of the Bickers from the Amsterdam *vroedschap*, stunned the Holland towns for the time being, leaving Willem virtual master of the Republic during the last three months of his short life. Brun's earlier assessment that, in the last resort, Holland was incapable of withstanding the coalition aligned against her, especially as the province itself was divided, proved accurate. During August the ambassador reported to Madrid that he saw scant likelihood of Holland retrieving her dominance in the foreseeable future, owing to the strength of Orangist feeling within the province and the reluctance of the Holland regents to risk losing their municipal and provincial offices.[49] During the brief ascendancy of the

[46] Brun to Philip, 28 July 1650. AGS EEH xxxii, fo. 46; Muller, 156.
[47] Willem was ready to settle for a standing army of 26,315 foot and 2,700 horse, but Holland insisted on a slightly lower figure; Rowen, 30.
[48] Consulta 16 Aug. 1650. AGS Estado 2072; *Corresp. d'Esp.* iv. 196; Poelhekke, *Geen Blyder*, 174.
[49] Muller, 178.

prince's party, Brun's whole attention was directed towards deflecting the new leadership from its plans to renew the war with Spain.

On 26 August, with one of his adherents, the Frisian deputy, Osinga, chairing the States General, Willem introduced, through him, a proposal directed against Spain which had originally been suggested to the prince by Mazarin in December 1648. It was proposed that the States General declare its refusal to countenance further Spanish inroads into France, offering to mediate a peace settlement between Spain and France and threatening to use force in favour of France if Spain refused to agree.[50] At the same time, Spain was to be required to fulfill its commitments to the House of Orange. 'Je ne désespère pas', Willem wrote to D'Estrades, 'que nous n'ayons bientost la guerre contre les Espagnolz',[51] but here he was undoubtedly too optimistic. Not only were the States of Holland still opposed to war with Spain, but so in varying degrees were the inland provinces and towns, despite the support of the latter for the prince's stance on military expenditure.[52] In this respect, little had changed since the spring of 1648. Only Zeeland pressed in earnest for a new Spanish war. At Holland's insistence, the initial proposal was amended to omit any explicit threat of force, changing its character from an ultimatum to a much milder form of pressure.[53] This diluted 'offer of mediation' was duly presented to Brun and Brasset respectively. Brun wrote on 2 September to Madrid for instructions on the main point and meanwhile redoubled his efforts, through Knuyt, to mollify the prince with regard to the financial settlement, though again without success.

However eager Philip may have been to extract himself from war with France during the early and mid 1640s, in 1650, with France paralysed by the Frondes and Spanish troops pushing the French back both in Flanders and Catalonia, Philip had no wish to comply with a demand which would have meant halting his armies at so advantageous a

[50] Aitzema vii. 165; Fruin, 221–2, 225–6; Kernkamp, *Willem II*, 164–5.
[51] *Archives* iv. 408–9.
[52] *Kernkamp, loc. cit.*
[53] Sec. Res. SG. 5 Sept. 1650. ARH SG 4565, fo. 33ᵛ.

moment. It was assumed in Madrid that the whole exercise was essentially Mazarin's work and that preventing further Spanish gains was its chief object. At the same time, neither king nor *Consejo* deemed it wise actually to reject the Dutch offer, thereby affronting the States General and playing into the hands of the Dutch war-party.[54] Accordingly, Brun was instructed to give no answer at all, but prevaricate assuring the States General that Spain sincerely desired peace with both France and the Republic. Meanwhile tension rose and there was mounting anxiety in the Spanish Netherlands lest the Dutch should attack. Within the Republic those politicians who had pressed hardest for peace during the Munster negotiations had ample cause for anxiety. Pauw confided to Brun that the Stadholder was on the point of initiating an enquiry to investigate the details of the relationship of the Dutch plenipotentiaries, at Munster, and other Dutch officials, with their Spanish counterparts, and in particular to explore the role of bribery. Pauw asked of the ambassador that henceforward he should not be mentioned in Spanish diplomatic correspondence 'with praise, but with much indifference'.[55] At Madrid and Brussels orders were issued that all documents referring to the Dutch politicians who had co-operated with Spain should be meticulously closeted. The outlook for the Dutch peace party appeared dismal in the extreme.

The sudden and totally unexpected death from smallpox of Prince Willem, on 6 November 1650, stunned the Republic and all Europe. His death precipitated one of the swiftest and most decisive power-shifts in Dutch history. Within days the States of Holland was asserting itself with renewed vigour, urging the other provinces to join in convening a common assembly of all the provincial states, or 'Great Assembly' as it became known, to secure the unity and efficient functioning of the state in the unprecedented situation which had now arisen, as well as to settle the outstanding issues relating to the army and other fundamental matters. Those who favoured preserving the peace with Spain

[54] Philip to Brun, 30 Nov. 1650. AGS EEH xxxii, fo. 170.
[55] Consulta 25 Nov. 1650. AGS Estado 2076.

were suddenly again at the helm and took charge of Dutch foreign policy. Holland, eventually followed by most of the other provinces, soon also took steps to eliminate the procedures by which, in the past, the Stadholder had influenced many appointments to provincial and municipal office. Though there was some opposition at first, ultimately Holland's ascendancy in the States General was assured.

From January to August 1651 Dutch politics revolved around the proceedings of the 'Great Assembly' at The Hague. The debates about the stadholdership and army matters were prolonged and at times acrimonious. Friesland, where Count Frederik Willem was Stadholder, argued that the Union of Utrecht required all the provinces to elect a Stadholder and that the natural choice for the five that were now Stadholderless was the deceased prince's newly born infant son, Willem III. There was considerable support for this view, but in the end Holland's desire to do without a Stadholder and reserve control of all appointments, civil and military, for the provinces, prevailed. At a stroke, the entire system of military patronage was transformed. Leading officers, including the foremost Dutch military figure of the early 1650s, Field-Marshal van Brederode (1599–1655) came to be closely tied to the provincial states and particularly those of Holland. This in turn, as the French ambassador noted in 1657, reinforced the traditionally anti-Orange, anti-popular, anti-French, crypto-Catholic, and pro-Spanish tendencies of the Dutch nobility.[56] In the view of the French, all but one or two of the Dutch nobles were pro-Spanish during the 1650s.

Although Brun was as jubilant at Willem's death as his French counterparts were dismayed and, although Pauw and his other associates in Holland had assured him, even before Willem's death, that Holland would do all in its power to cement relations with Spain,[57] the elimination of the Stadholder did not automatically dispel the strain from Dutch–Spanish relations, nor could this be expected in view of the varied causes of the continued tension. Apart from the unanswered mediation offer, which still stood, and, indeed, was

[56] De Thou to Mazarin, 14 June 1657. Archives v. 176.
[57] Brun to Philip, 22 Oct. 1650. AGS EEH xxxii, fo. 135.

renewed by the States General at the beginning of 1651,[58] numerous unsolved difficulties remained and there was still bitter resentment against Spain, particularly in Zeeland, but to some extent also elsewhere. In February 1651 the States General discussed whether to impose religious reformation in the Overmaas, as had been done in the Meierij and other Generality Lands in 1648; Holland blocked the proposal, pointing out that in the case of the Overmaas such action was explicitly forbidden under the peace treaty.[59] In March Holland pressed for the setting up of the long-delayed *Chambre Mi-partie*, as Brun had repeatedly requested, to solve the disputes over the Overmaas and Meierij, but the proposal was blocked by the other provinces. In April 1651, following renewed States General pressure for a reply to the mediation-offer and still in some doubt as to the position, the *Consejo* in Madrid again instructed the Archduke Leopold and Brun neither to accept nor to reject the Dutch offer, but to prevaricate, accepting it only at the last moment should the Republic move to the brink of declaring war on Spain.[60] Only gradually did the tension subside. In August 1651 there occurred a bizarre incident when the Conde de Oñate with 1,500 Neapolitan troops, being ferried in four vessels from Naples, arrived off Flushing expecting, though lacking permission from the Dutch authorities, to sail through, tranship, or march overland to Antwerp. The good burghers of Flushing rushed to arms and only with difficulty could the burgomasters prevent a tumult. Zeeland raised a storm in the States General, leading to fresh angry representations to Brun. Both Brun and the *Consejo* ruefully concluded that it would be best to keep Spanish troops well away from Dutch territory.[61]

ii ABORTIVE RAPPROCHEMENT, 1651–1661

During the spring and summer of 1651 the Spanish crown

---

[58] Poelhekke, *Geen Blijder*, 177.
[59] Res. Holl. 22 Feb. 1651.
[60] Philip to Leopold, 24 Apr. 1651. *Corresp. d'Esp.* iv. 255–6.
[61] Brun to Philip, 21 Aug. 1651. AGS EEH xxxiii, fo. 246; consulta 12 Nov. 1651. AGS Estado 2076.

resumed its diplomatic offensive to forge closer relations with the Dutch, meeting with increasing response on the Dutch side, at least from the States of Holland. In April the king reminded the Archduke Leopold to observe the articles of the peace with the utmost scrupulousness.[62] Soon after, following complaints from the States General that various administrative bodies in the Spanish Netherlands still styled the king 'Count of Holland and Zeeland', among his other titles, in their formal pronouncements, the Archduke was instructed that the use of such titles was to be meticulously avoided.[63] In April also Brun and the States General's committee for Spanish affairs reached agreement on means of solving the border demarcation disputes in Flanders, through a mixed commission which was to investigate the matter on the spot. The commission, the Dutch side of which was led by Amalis van Boeckhorst, heer van Wimmenum, a leading Holland noble who played an increasingly prominent role in Dutch–Spanish relations at this time, was quickly convened and made rapid progress, though there was some difficulty over demarcation around Sluis.[64] As Pauw had promised Brun the year before, Holland also now raised the question of the States General finally posting diplomatic representatives at Madrid and Brussels;[65] on 18 July Holland agreed to urge the States General to send an ambassador in Madrid and resident to Brussels, but, predictably the project was blocked by Zeeland and the inland provinces. Meanwhile Brun was secretly endeavouring to disrupt the Dutch–Portuguese talks over Brazil, which were then in progress at the Hague, with a view to exacerbating the animosity between Dutch and Portuguese.[66] He was also instructed by Philip to assure the States General's leadership that Spain would not agree to anything detrimental to the Republic should negotiations produce a settlement between Spain and France and that 'whenever they should be afraid of the French and wish to

---

[62] *Corresp. d'Esp.* iv. 253.

[63] Ibid. iv. 256–7.

[64] Res. Holl. 18 Apr., 6 May, 18 July 1651; Res. SG 26 Oct. 1651. ARH SG 12575–27.

[65] Res. Holl. 7, 18 July 1651.

[66] Brun to Philip, 22 June 1651. AGS EEH xxxiii, fo. 174.

secure themselves against them, entering into a league with
me, I shall respond and they shall see how far my intentions
are from the threats which the French use against them.'[67]

As the tension gradually subsided during 1651, Holland's
statesmen increasingly discarded their inhibitions about their
dealings with Spain, though they took good care to keep certain
matters secret. When the question of electing a new
Raadpensionaris of Holland to succeed Jacob Cats arose,
during September 1651, Brun informed the king that he was
actively supporting Pauw's candidacy, the latter being 'so
zealous for the Peace and the service of Your Majesty'.[68]
Upon his election, Pauw confided to Brun that he 'hoped to
clear within six months all the difficulties consequent upon
the peace treaty'. Knuyt likewise now felt able to renew his
claims on Spain. Brun recommended to the king that at least
30,000 guilders should be paid to him in view of the 'merit
of that man in having signed the peace, against the orders of
his province, which led to his being stripped of all his offices',
the Marqués de Castel-Rodrigo having promised him 60,000
guilders. Brun interceded also on behalf of Obdam, a leading
Holland nobleman who had likewise performed important
services for Spain during the Munster negotiations and was
one of the most active proponents of a pro-Spanish policy
in the Republic during 1651 and subsequently.[69] Obdam
asked nothing for himself but indicated his desire for a
prominent position in a nunnery, at Mons, for his Catholic
daughter, Elizabeth-Anne van Wassenaer, and this was duly
granted.

But despite Pauw's responsive attitude, the remaining
Dutch-Spanish disputes proved intractable and popular
antagonism to Spain, even in Holland, a formidable force.[70]
The dispute over the Overmaas had erupted anew, in August
1651, in clashes between Dutch and Spanish officials and
soldiery around Valkenburg and complaints from local

[67] Philip to Brun, 16 Aug. 1651. AGS EEH xxxiii, fo. 244.
[68] Consultas 12 Nov., 9 Dec. 1651. AGS Estado 2076; Haas, 70.
[69] Consulta 9 Dec. 1651, AGS Estado 2076; Brun to Philip, 1 May 1651.
AGS EEH xxxiii, fo. 110ᵛ.
[70] Brun to Philip, 31 Jan. 1652. AGS EEH xxxiv, fo. 22; Brun to Philip, 21
July 1652. AGS Estado 2079.

nobles and citizenry at the conduct of both sides;[71] the region continued to be very tense for several years. There was also repeated trouble involving soldiery from both sides on the extensive lands of the abbeys of Postel and Huybergen, on the edge of the Meierij, as well as bitter controversy over the status of Catholic religious practice throughout the Generality-Lands.[72] The extremely important issue of the Maas tolls likewise remained intractable, much to the discontent of the Maas-skippers and traders and the city of Dordrecht.[73] The latter issue together with the still highly controversial question of the Flemish harbour tolls was eventually submitted, with the agreement of both sides, to a second joint commission, of which Alexander van der Capellen was a member, which commenced deliberations at Mechelen during the autumn of 1652. The Spanish side continued to insist that under article fifteen of the peace treaty, the king was obliged to maintain imposts in the Flemish sea-ports only to the level of the Dutch 'convoy and license' money collected actually on the common border; according to this interpretation, the Flemish tolls could thus be much lower than the combined duty paid by foreign goods for the South Netherlands entering and leaving Dutch territory, as well as by South Netherlands products exported to other parts of Europe through the Republic, a situation which was detrimental to Rotterdam as well as to Zeeland. The Mechelen talks, having served only to increase the annoyance on both sides, were suspended without result in April 1653.[74] The one dispute which was successfully cleared was that concerning the Spanish king's financial settlement with the House of Orange, a matter over which the Holland leadership, with its decided lack of sympathy for the princely line, was little inclined to be difficult. Newly negotiated terms were submitted by Brun and approved by the States General in November 1651 and by the summer of 1653, 280,000

---

[71] Res. Holl. 9 Aug. 1651; Consulta 12 Nov. 1651. AGS Estado 2072; SG memorandum, 3 May 1653. ARH SG 7045.

[72] Brun to SG, 16 Jan. 1653. ARH SG 12, 575–27.

[73] Res. Holl. 27 Apr., 20 July, 22 Sept. 1651.

[74] SG's deputies to Leopold's deputies, Mechelen, 2 Jan., 24 Feb., 2 Mar. 1653. ARH SG 7045; *Corresp. d'Esp.* iv. 388.

guilders of a 500,000-guilder lump sum had been paid together with a first advance towards the 80,000-guilder annual
rent which formed the other part of the arrangement. Meanwhile agreement was reached in principle, but there was as
yet no actual convening of the *Chambre Mi-partie* which, in
Madrid and Brussels, was deemed to be a necessary token of
the permanency of the Peace.[75]

The period from late 1651 until early 1653, that of Adriaan
Pauw's second term as Holland's *Raadpensionaris*, when for
the first time tried friends of Spain controlled the policies of
the Republic, was also a time of continuing recovery for
Spain and its empire generally, but of deteriorating fortune
for the Dutch. During the late summer of 1652 Spanish arms
finally recovered both Barcelona and Dunkirk, much to the
distaste, as Brun informed Madrid, of a good many Dutchmen, always excepting the Catholic minority. Meanwhile the
Dutch suffered a series of setbacks in Brazil and became
dangerously entangled with the rising and increasingly
aggressive English Commonwealth of Cromwell. In May 1652
the first Anglo-Dutch war suddenly erupted with its temporarily ruinous effects on Dutch trade, industry, and fisheries. During the first months of the war, Pauw enquired of
Brun if there were any chance that the Spanish crown might
be interested in some form of Dutch–Spanish combination
against England, but this was the one type of alliance with
the Dutch that Philip was definitely not interested in.[76] Reviewing the situation in September 1652, the *Consejo* had no
doubt that a decisive shift in Europe's balance of power had
taken place and that England was now clearly stronger than
the Republic.[77] However, this did nothing to diminish the
Republic's eligibility as an ally for all other purposes in
Spanish eyes and particularly not Philip's impatience for a
further deterioration in the Republic's relations with Portugal.[78] Brun's proposals for an alliance against Portugal were
discussed first in secret by the States General's Spanish affairs

[75] Res. Holl. 1651, pp. 578–9. Consulta 19 Sept. 1652. AGS Estado 2079;
Corresp. d'Esp. iv. 398, 410–11.
[76] Brun to Philip, 21 July 1652. Consulta 14 Sept. 1652. AGS Estado 2079.
[77] Consulta 16 Feb. 1653, and Brun to Philip, 14 May 1653. AGS Estado
2081.
[78] Res. Holl. 3, 4 Dec. 1652.

committee and then at provincial level in the autumn of 1652.

In February 1653, at the king's request, the Conde de Peñaranda drew up a lengthy analysis of the general implications of the projected Spanish–Dutch offensive alliance against Portugal which was increasingly in the air at Madrid and then being considered by the Dutch. Peñaranda argued that joint conquest of the whole of Brazil by Spaniards and Dutch combined would probably suffice in itself to bring about the collapse of Portugal which was heavily dependent on its Brazilian trade and revenues. To make sure, however, a Spanish invasion by land would be much more certain of success if combined with a simultaneous Dutch blockade by sea. Although reconquest of Brazil would involve the ceding to the Dutch of all that the latter had held, as of 1641, as stipulated in the Peace, thus alienating an important territory from the 'bosom of the Church', Peñaranda urged his master to proceed 'without scruple', after consulting theologians for the sake of form. The principal danger, the Conde acknowledged, was the risk of antagonizing England with which the king was determined to remain at peace. If there lingered any prospect of an Anglo–Spanish understanding such would surely vanish the moment Philip signed an alliance with the Dutch. Even so, in Peñaranda's view, the king should give priority to seeking an alliance with the Dutch.

An alliance with the Dutch [he wrote] will be more advantageous, securer and easier to maintain on account of our territorial contiguity and interests. . .and if it is asked which is the stronger and more solid power, I would answer England under Parliament, but if it is asked which will be the better friendship with the greater advantages and reliability, I would always answer that with the Dutch.[79]

The King and *Consejo* as a whole tended to concur with Peñaranda's view even though one or two members were less emphatic in their taste for the Dutch.[80] The one major

[79] 'Parecer del Conde de Peñaranda sobre union con Olandeses', AGS Estado 2081 and EEH xxv, fos. 66–70: Peñaranda envisaged an 'amigable conformidad' between Dutch and Spaniards in their respective parts of Brazil 'como subcede el dia de oy en las del Pais Bajo'.

[80] Consulta 20 Feb. 1653. AGS Estado 2081; Philip to Brun, 27 Feb. 1653. AGS EEH xxv, fo. 55ᵛ.

dissenting voice was that of the Conde de Fuensaldaña who wrote from Antwerp, having read Peñaranda's discourse, that the policy advocated by the latter would be ruinous and would inevitably infuriate the English. If Spain had to ally with a Protestant power, he argued, it would be far more advantageous to combine with England against France than with the Republic against Portugal.[81] In March 1653, risking Cromwell's displeasure, Philip sent Brun formal authorization to negotiate terms with the Republic against Portugal.

But, for various reasons, the outcome was most unlikely to be the close alliance and friendship envisaged by Peñaranda. First there were the various lingering disputes which clouded the atmosphere between the two powers and the residual, but still considerable, popular resentment against Spain; this continued during the English war which, according to Brun, much of the Dutch populace and clergy, even in Holland, blamed on Spain.[82] Secondly, the death of Pauw, in February 1653, and the departure of Obdam from The Hague to succeed Tromp as commander of the Dutch navy against the English greatly hampered Brun's efforts by weakening the pro-Spanish group among Holland's chief policy-makers.[83] Johan de Witt, pensionary of Dordrecht, who was elected to succeed Pauw as *Raadpensionaris* and who, shortly after, together with Boeckhorst, came onto the States General's Spanish affairs committee, was, unlike his father at an earlier stage, distinctly wary of Spanish allurements. Johan's father, Jacob de Witt, had been promised 50,000 guilders by Peñaranda for his help in forcing through the treaty of Munster,[84] but while Jacob had certainly kept his part of the bargain, the money had not actually been paid to the De Witt family; it may be surmised that this fact played a part in the decidedly unresponsive attitude of both father and son at this time to Spanish interests. Brun was soon to be made aware of De Witt's coolness.

But in any case, Holland was fundamentally disinclined to

[81] Fuensaldaña to Philip, 16 May 1653. AGS Estado 2081.
[82] Brun to Philip, 21 July and 30 Oct. 1652. AGS EEH xxxiv, fos. 136ᵛ, 205.
[83] Brun to Philip, 30 Sept. 1653. AGS EEH xxv, fo. 192.
[84] Gamarra to Philip, 15 Feb. 1655. AGS EEH xxxviii, fo. 36.

embark on a course which would be bound to embroil the Republic with France, the arch-enemy of Spain and patron of Portugal, and would be apt to make more difficult a settlement of the Dutch conflict with England. Throughout the period of his ascendancy, De Witt showed a constant determination to avoid antagonizing the French crown, or at least to minimize friction with that power, and it is perhaps to this factor more than any other that one should attribute the failure of Spanish designs. As the discussion among the Dutch provinces and towns over the proposed Spanish alliance continued, the States General sent copies of the king's authorization to Brun to the provincial assemblies. The matter was discussed quite uninhibitedly on all sides, much to Brun's disgust, and there was certainly a good deal of interest, especially in ascertaining whether there was any prospect of widening the terms of the proposed alliance to secure some measure of Spanish aid against England.[85] But with the negative attitude of those at the helm the matter was allowed to drag on inconclusively for many months. Perhaps the most ironic and remarkable contradiction in the complex situation was that it was Zeeland, much more than Holland, which was anxious to come to the help of the West India Company, in Brazil, but precisely Zeeland among the provinces which remained most hostile to Spain, at this time, on account of the dispute over the Flemish harbour tolls.[86]

Brun's failure to make any impact with De Witt led during the final months before the ambassador's death, in January 1654, to a marked disillusionment on his part with the policies of Holland. Likewise the *Consejo* was disappointed and, as the political rift in the Republic widened once more during the course of the English war, began to think in terms of a *rapprochement* with the Orangist opposition which for all its anti-Spanish traditions was certainly keener to act against Portugal than De Witt and his adherents. Spanish thinking, during the opening phase of De Witt's dominance, was also drawn towards the Orangists on account of the latters' opposition to Holland's obvious determination to end the war

[85] Brun to Philip, 8 and 30 Sept. 1653. AGS EEH xxv, fos. 181, 192.
[86] Brun to Philip, 21 July 1652. EEH xxiv, fo. 136.

with England quickly, even on disadvantageous terms. For various reasons, principally that the conflict prevented either Protestant power assisting France or Portugal against Spain, Philip and his ministers had eagerly anticipated and were keen to prolong the Anglo-Dutch struggle and on this point Brun was instructed to work directly counter to De Witt's policy.[87] In February 1653 Brun informed Madrid that Holland was continuing its secret unilateral efforts to placate Cromwell, but that he was seeking to counteract these by sending the texts of Holland's secret resolutions, which he was able to obtain through bribery, to the Spanish ambassador in London for use in undermining the talks.[88] In the autumn of 1653 Brun advised the *Consejo* to speed the payments to the infant prince of Orange because the adherents of that House were fiercely opposing the proposed peace treaty, the terms of which they deemed unacceptable.[89]

The failure of Spanish policy in the Republic, during 1653, led to a pause, following Brun's death, in the Spanish pressure for an alliance which coincided with the period of bitter political dissension in the Republic known as the Exclusion Crisis (1654-5), Holland's attempt, at Cromwell's insistence, to debar the House of Orange for ever from the stadholdership and captaincy-general. Amid the defeat at English hands and inner turmoil, the Republic during the years 1654-5 was in no condition either to retaliate against the Portuguese who finally completed their conquest of Dutch Brazil during 1654, or to act in concert with any other power. Efforts continued, however, through the *Chambre Mi-partie* which had finally been constituted late in 1653 and commenced its deliberations at Mechelen in January 1654,[90] to clear away the remaining points of Dutch-Spanish contention. But months of laborious argument over the Overmaas, where Dutch troops had now occupied virtually all the disputed areas, and

[87] Consultas 11 Jan., 14 Sept. 1652. AGS Estado 2079.
[88] Brun to Philip, 18 Feb. 1653. AGS EEH xxxv. fo. 32; consulta, 16 Feb. 1654. AGS Estado 20883; the source of the information was presumably the same personage who passed Brun secrets relating to Dutch policy towards France; see Res. Holl. 23 May 1653.
[89] Consulta 16 Feb. 1654. AGS Estado 2083.
[90] Res. Holl. 2 Dec. 1653, 28 Jan., and 10 Mar. 1654.

Meierij yielded scant progress. The States General renewed its complaints to Brussels that Spain was violating the fifteenth article of the peace treaty by failing to raise the Flemish harbour tolls in line with those on the Schelde.[91] Among the Dutch, especially in Zeeland, strong resentment against Spain still lingered.

Not until February 1655 did Spain's second ambassador to the Republic, Esteban de Gamarra y Contreras, take up his post. In his first audience with the States General, on 17 February, he raised several issues relating to commerce and in the politest terms rejected the Dutch complaints concerning the Flemish harbour tolls.[92] The failure of the *Chambre Mi-partie*, meeting in its second year at Dordrecht, to find a solution to the Overmaas dispute, and the continuing dissatisfaction of leading Dutch politicians with Spain, caused consternation in Madrid and prompted renewed orders to Gamarra to try to find solutions and improve the atmosphere.[93] Gamarra tried to convey to Madrid the intricacies of the Exclusion Crisis and to gauge the strength of the rival factions. Groningen, he wrote, was deeply divided, Overijssel likewise, with Deventer and a minority of the Overijssel nobles backing De Witt, and Zwolle and Kampen, together with the majority of the nobles, being *Principistas*.[94] In Zeeland, he noted, Middelburg and Zierikzee backed De Witt, Tholen was split, and the rest Orangist. His overall assessment of the outlook for Spanish interests in the Republic was gloomy: 'owing to their particular interests, all those provinces, except Holland, desire to go to war with Your Majesty'.[95] To restrain the lingering animosity, Gamarra recommended that the payments owed to the House of Orange be paid more promptly than they had been.

Late in 1655 the States General partly as the result of pressure from Holland merchants finally resolved on establishing permanent diplomatic representation at Madrid and

---

[91] SG to Leopold, 3 Dec. 1654. ARH SG 7046; Aitzema viii. 469.
[92] Gamarra to SG, 17 Feb. 1655. ARH SG 4566.
[93] Consulta 28 Sept. 1655. AGS Estado 2085; *Corresp. d'Esp.* iv. 484, 501, 509; Haas, 98–127.
[94] Gamarra to Philip, 4 June 1655. AGS Estado 2085.
[95] Consulta 9 Sept. 1655. AGS Estado 2085.

Brussels, as Gamarra informed Madrid in November. Thomas Sasburg, a young Dordrecht regent and cousin of De Witt, was named as Dutch resident at Brussels.[96] After lengthy discussion as to the status and province of their representative at the Spanish court, the States General chose as Dutch resident the Utrecht noble, Baron Hendrik van Reede van Renswoude.[97] The baron held his first audience with Luis de Haro, Philip's principal minister, at Madrid on 31 May 1656. On 3 August Reede was received by the king personally and treated not merely courteously but with an affability and warmth which astonished him.[98] Besides Luis de Haro whom he deemed well intentioned, the baron noted that Velada and Peñaranda were especially zealous for close links with the Republic.

Meanwhile, during the early months of the Anglo-Spanish war which had broken out in 1655, Gamarra indicated to the Dutch leadership that Spain was now willing to form an alliance with the Republic not only against France or Portugal, but against England also.[99] In the short term Spanish ministers were pessimistic. They knew that the English expedition to the West Indies, repulsed from Santo Domingo, but successful in overrunning Jamaica, had aroused considerable misgivings, particularly at Amsterdam, where Dutch Caribbean trade, thriving since 1648, was esteemed increasingly highly. But they saw also that Holland was determined to abide by the treaty with Cromwell for reasons of 'its own particular interests'. In the longer term, Philip's advisers saw some hope in the opposition to this policy among the Orangist element and in the ceaseless Anglo-Dutch wrangling over shipping and commercial matters which seemed all too likely to intensify. In January 1656 Philip instructed his ambassador at The Hague to continue striving for a Dutch alliance 'as vigorously as possible',[1] spreading bribes liberally among the Dutch leadership, though it seems that owing to the plight of the royal finances in the Spanish Netherlands and the desperate

[96] Res. Holl. 23 Nov. 1655, 21 Mar. 1656; Rowen, 290.
[97] SG to Dutch consuls in Spain, 18 Apr. 1656. ARH SG 7048.
[98] Reede to SG, Madrid, 31 May, 9 Aug. 1656. ARH SG 7049.
[99] Leopold to Philip, 24 Nov. 1655. *Corresp. d'Esp.* iv.
[1] Philip to Gamarra, 23 Jan. 1656. AGS EEH xxxix, fo. 32.

need for money with which to check the French who, in the aftermath of the Frondes had now recovered their momentum, little or no money could be made available for this latter purpose. In March 1656 Gamarra was again instructed from Madrid to try every available means to obtain a Dutch–Spanish alliance against the English.[2] The Holland leadership and States General discussed the Spanish offer over a period of months, and it was certainly given serious consideration, but under De Witt's guidance the States General chose not to respond.[3] De Witt was undoubtedly anxious at the resumed French advances in the South Netherlands which he would have liked to have halted, but stuck to his view that the Republic's best hope of counteracting England and protecting its far-flung interests lay in cultivating closer links with France. Indeed during the spring and summer of 1656 the States General became preoccupied with a French scheme, which was taken up enthusiastically by De Witt, for a triple Anglo–French–English coalition designed to settle the differences between the powers and impose solutions for current problems in the Baltic, Germany, and elsewhere.[4] The proposal was probably a ruse of Mazarin's to derail Gamarra's efforts. Certainly, the French lost interest once the Dutch showed their determination not to join in any offensive action against Spain. Gamarra meanwhile obtained intelligence from his Dutch confidants that De Witt was in fact seriously pondering entry into an offensive alliance with France and England against Spain and became so alarmed that he circumvented the Holland leadership and sought to mobilize the Orangists and other provinces against De Witt's policy.[5] Thus in a secret States General session on the proposed Triple Alliance, Friesland formally protested that it would tolerate no step that would prejudice the treaty of Munster and peace with Spain.[6]

Mazarin's anger at Dutch refusal to co-operate with France

[2] Philip to Gamarra, 16 Mar. 1656. AGS EEH xxxix.
[3] Sec. Res. SG 7 Aug. 1656. ARH SG 4566, fos. 203^v–204^r.
[4] Res. SG 4 July 1656. ARH SG 4566, fo. 196^v; Gamarra to Philip, 13 July 1656. AGS EEH xxxix, fo. 197; Rowen, 275.
[5] Gamarra to Philip, 20 July 1656, and consulta, 21 Sept. 1656. AGS Estado 2089.
[6] Sec. Res. SG, 26 Oct. 1656. ARH SG 4566.

against Spain, or limit the now immense commercial and financial dealings between the Republic and the Spanish lands, together with growing friction over commercial matters, led, despite all De Witt's efforts, to a marked worsening in Franco–Dutch relations late in 1656 and during early 1657. Although Holland was in fact strictly neutral on the Franco–Spanish conflict, French diplomats were accustomed to characterize the province's stance as pro-Spanish, referring to the opposition towns, Haarlem and Leiden, as the 'villes d'inclination françoise'.[7] Among Holland politicians, Obdam particularly was identified as being 'espagnol dans le fond du coeur'. The activity of the Dutch fleet under De Ruyter, posted to the west Mediterranean, to protect Dutch merchant convoys sailing between Spain and Italy from French, English, and Algerian privateers, sparked a major crisis. When De Ruyter brought two French privateers into Barcelona, where they were confiscated by the Spaniards in February 1657, the French retaliated by temporarily embargoing all Dutch ships and goods in French ports. Philip and his advisers were greatly heartened. Orders were dispatched to Brussels and to Gamarra to do everything conceivable to inflame the Franco–Dutch quarrel and once again to offer the States General full military co-operation against France.[8] But during the summer of 1657 the crisis gradually died down. Neither Mazarin nor De Witt had any wish to pursue matters to the point of war.

The deterioration in Franco–Dutch relations coincided with a further worsening in relations between the Dutch and Portugal. Since the loss of the last Dutch foothold in Brazil in 1654, the Portuguese had offered neither restitution nor any satisfactory compensation. Several months before the decision taken during the summer of 1657 to send a powerful fleet to Lisbon to deliver a strongly worded ultimatum intended to extract a prompt offer of compensation, the Dutch leadership, much to the satisfaction of ministers in Madrid, enquired of Gamarra whether the king would still be interested

---

[7] *Archives* v. 164, 175.
[8] Philip to Gamarra, 25 May 1657, Gamarra to Philip, 30 June 1657. AGS EEH xl, fos. 122–4, 163.

in forming a Dutch–Spanish alliance against Portugal.[9] During
the winter and spring of 1657 the Amsterdam burgomasters
had already enquired of Madrid, through Gamarra, whether
in the event of the United Provinces being at war with
France, Spain would grant the Dutch access to the salt-pans
of Punta de Araya.[10] Indeed, the question of salt was certain to be urgent whether war broke out between the Republic
and France or Portugal, but the Dutch request at this juncture was clearly a roundabout way of preparing the ground
for a possible Dutch–Spanish alliance should the need arise.
De Witt's basic policy had not changed, but the dangerous
circumstances of 1657 had taught the Holland leadership the
value of an insurance policy that could be activated in case
of unavoidable necessity, despite the risk of angering Cromwell and Mazarin with such secret contacts. Gamarra was
told bluntly that the Republic could never afford to break
with France or Portugal unless Spain could guarantee access
to Punta de Araya. Although the *Consejo* in Madrid had
never before been brought to the point of having to consider
in detail granting access to Spain's American possessions to
another European power, Philip's ministers now jumped at
the opportunity that seemingly presented itself. The *Consejo
de Indias*'s objections were brushed aside and it was ordered
to draw up conditions on which the Dutch could be admitted to the Venezuelan salt-pans 'in case it should be
necessary to open the door to this'.[11]

De Witt was in a delicate position. Shortly after Amsterdam's approach to Gamarra, Cromwell challenged the Dutch
ambassador in London on the secret Dutch–Spanish contacts.
The latter who knew nothing about them wrote for instructions and was told to admit that these were in progress
but also to convey De Witt's personal assurances to Cromwell
that no Dutch–Spanish alliance would emerge.[12] The indispensable key to preserving Dutch liberty and commerce,
De Witt fervently maintained, was to improve relations with

[9] *Corresp. d'Esp.* iv. 576.
[10] Gamarra to Luis de Haro, 25 Jan. 1657, consulta 15 May 1657, AGS
Estado 2092.
[11] Consulta 2 June 1657. AGS Estado 2092.
[12] BGG, 333–4.

England and France. Gamarra meanwhile became increasingly frustrated by his lack of any positive relationship with De Witt. He was convinced that the *Raadpensionaris*'s frigid attitude towards Spain emanated from the king's failure to pay the promised 50,000 guilders to his father.[13] 'The non-fulfilment of this promise', wrote Gamarra, 'has been the cause that he [Jacob] and his son are so alienated from the interests of Your Majesty and have entered the faction supporting the Protector of England, who won them with gifts, and now they have also entered into the interests of France, the French ambassador having given them, I hear, estimable gifts.' Although these latter charges are probably groundless and the French resident himself attested to De Witt's 'désinteresse en son particulier', it remains likely that the Spanish failure to keep promise with his father had at least some bearing on De Witt's policy. After debating the question of the money owed to Jacob de Witt in November 1657, the *Consejo* belatedly resolved to pay the sum, the 50,000 guilders finally being dispatched from Madrid by letter of exchange in May 1658.[14]

The war that broke out between the Republic and Porgugal, in November 1657, was a somewhat desultory affair for which Holland, and particularly Amsterdam, displayed little zeal and to which French and English diplomats did their best to bring an early end.[15] However, Zeeland, Gelderland, Utrecht, and Groningen, though decidedly not Friesland, which refused to agree to the war at all, were more determined in their hostility to Portugal. So also was the East India Company, which now resumed its offensive against the Portuguese, in Ceylon. At Madrid, hopes rose that an alliance with the Republic would now at last be forthcoming, though the *Consejo* was disappointed to find, in March 1658, that Reede was empowered only to hear the details of any Spanish proposal, and settle the terms of access to Punta de Araya, but not actually to conclude an alliance.[16] What Spanish

[13] Gamarra to Philip, 12 Sept. 1657. AGS EEH xl, fo. 219.
[14] Philip to Gamarra, 27 Nov. 1657. AGS EEH xl, fo. 186; ibid. xli, fo. 42.
[15] Gamarra to Philip, 12 Apr. 1658. AGS EEH xli, fo. 35ᵛ.
[16] Philip to Gamarra, 22 Mar. 1658. AGS EEH xli, fos. 22-4.

ministers chiefly wanted was for the Dutch fleet to blockade Portugal from March to October for several years, thereby cutting off supplies to Portugal from northern Europe and disrupting the Brazil trade, thus facilitating the work of a Spanish army of invasion. Action of any kind in Brazil would be a welcome extra.

The Dutch leadership certainly had no intention, at any stage, of concluding a formal alliance with Spain, but they were eager to use the opportunity to increase contacts with Madrid and, in particular, to press for access to Punta de Araya, even without an alliance, on the ground that allowing the Dutch to obtain their salt there would considerably damage Portugal's European commerce and deprive the Portuguese crown of a major source of revenue.[17] The objective was to procure access to the Venezuelan pans for the duration of the war with Portugal without signing a formal alliance with Spain or agreeing on military co-operation.[18] Intricate negotiations between Reede and Spanish ministers took place at Madrid from August to October 1658.[19] Spain did not insist on a formal alliance but did insist as the price for so great a concession as access to Punta de Araya that the Dutch mount an annual blockade of Lisbon and central Portugal with at least thirty warships;[20] it was also made clear that access was to cease as soon as the Dutch–Portuguese conflict ended. These terms proved the sticking-point, for Holland had no intention of fighting Portugal in earnest, let alone facilitating Spanish reconquest of the country, which, in any case, France and England would refuse to accept, and when Reede at length declared that he was not empowered even to conclude this negotiation, the whole matter was remitted from Madrid to The Hague to be settled by Gamarra direct with the States General.[21] By early 1659,

[17] Sec. Res. SG. 25 Jan. 1658. ARH SG 12, 575–34.
[18] Sec. Res. SG. 8 June 1658. ARH SG 12, 575–34.
[19] Res. SG. 8 May, 8 June, 20 Nov. 1658, and Reede to SG, Madrid, 23 Oct. 1658. ARH SG 12, 575–34; consultas 4, 16 Aug., 1, 12, 19 Sept. 1658. AGS Estado 2091.
[20] Reede to SG, 30 Oct. 1658, ARH SG. 12, 575–34; consulta 22 Oct. 1658. AGS Estado 2091.
[21] Consulta 14 Nov. 1658. AGS Estado 2091; consulta 18 Jan. 1659. AGS Estado 2094.

however, Gamarra had come to realize that keen though the
Dutch leadership were for access to the Venezuelan salt-
pans, they would never agree to commit the Republic to a
naval blockade of Portugal.[22] As for an offensive or defensive
league between the Republic and Spain against England,
which Philip remained eager to secure,[23] the Dutch, Gamarra
reported, would never agree, neither would they break with
France, even if the king offered them free trade with all
his Indies.

Although the negotiations of 1658 failed to produce anything resembling military co-operation, enough was said regarding the common interests of the two powers in the New
World and in the Old to at least suggest the likelihood of co-
operation in the future. For all De Witt's fervent belief that
the Republic's prospects depended on achieving harmonious
relations with France and England, most Dutchmen, including De Witt, were uneasily aware that the aims of
Europe's two rising powers inevitably included the rich but
vulnerable commerce and possessions of Spain and the
Republic and that sooner or later the Dutch were likely to
be forced by circumstances into the willing arms of Spain.
The economic dealings between Holland the the hispanic
world had now burgeoned to such an extent that it was no
longer to be denied that these constituted a vital buttress of
the Republic's prosperity, second in importance only to the
Baltic trade itself. During the late 1650s, a time of prosperity and relatively cheap food, the old resentment and
desire for war with Spain, for so long evident in the Republic, gradually dissolved.[24] At the same time there was steady
progress on the lingering Dutch–Spanish disputes in the Low
Countries. In March 1658, after a decade of bitter argument,
Gamarra and the States General at last provisionally agreed
on a partition of the disputed Overmaas, though the Dutch
persisted in refusing to grant public practice of Catholicism
in their zones as long as Philip refused to concede the same
for the Protestants in his, and this the king flatly declined

[22] Gamarra to Philip, 6 Mar. 1659. AGS EEH xli, fo. 157.
[23] Philip to Gamarra, 27 July 1658. AGS EEH xli, fo. 59.
[24] *Archives* v. 164.

to do.[25] Under the partition, finalized and ratified in 1661-2, the town of 's-Hertogenrade reverted to Spain while those of Valkenburg and Dalhem fell to the States General; all three territories around the towns, however, were divided, resulting in a remarkable patchwork of jurisdictions.[26]

To confirm the improvement in political relations, round off the economic accords concluded since 1648, and proclaim to the world the partial *rapprochement* between the Republic and Spain, a step which the Dutch felt free to take once France and Spain had made peace under the treaty of the Pyrenees, signed in 1659, the States General resolved in the spring of 1660 to send a delegation of three extraordinary ambassadors to Madrid.[27] The latter landed at Laredo on 4 November 1660 and were received at court with full courtesy and notable warmth on 17 December, the envoys addressing the monarch in French, the diplomatic language of the Republic, the king raising his hat to them, replying in Castilian and German. In the subsequent talks the European political situation was reviewed, though most of the actual negotiation concerned commerce.[28] Various vestigial points were cleared up, the most significant outcome being Philip's agreement that with the French war ended there was no longer any need for such rigorous checking of ships and cargoes in Spanish ports, as had been practised since 1624, and therefore no longer any need for the *Almirantazgo*. By royal *cédula* of January 1661, the *Almirantazgo*, having been a central feature of Spanish life for nearly four decades was simply abolished.[29] The special and privileged position of the Dutch in Spanish trade was both confirmed and reinforced. The Dutch envoys returned home in the summer of 1661, Dutch opinion being well satisfied with the results of their mission.

[25] *Corresp. d'Esp.* iv. 596, 611, 619; *Groot Placaet-Boeck* ii. 2778/2848; Aitzema ix. 227.

[26] See Gutmann, 12; Haas, 158-259.

[27] Sec. Res. SG 27 Apr. 1660. ARH SG 4566, fo. 414.

[28] 'Verbael', ARH SG 8509; Aitzema ix, 1097-2000; Wagenaar xiii. 29.

[29] Cedula of Philip IV, 10 Jan. 1661. ARH SG 7055-i.

iii THE NEW ECONOMIC RELATIONSHIP

Despite the indisputable and evident decline of Spain during the early seventeenth century — the collapse of the manufacturing towns, the decay of agriculture, grievous loss of population, and the contraction of the Indies trade in the two decades to 1648 — the hispanic lands of the mid seventeenth century nevertheless formed a commercial network of vital and decisive importance to the whole European economy of the time. At the close, as at the beginning, of the Dutch–Spanish conflict, the commerce of the Spanish Indies was effectively channelled through Seville and its outports. The failure of the Dutch to breach the walls of the heavily controlled and taxed monopoly system had been amply demonstrated by the complete failure of the Dutch colonies of Curaçao and Guyana to develop any regular contraband business with either the Spanish American mainland or the Caribbean islands. From 1648, through the years to 1661, the west-Andalusian ports continued to be the main and virtually the only hub and entrepôt of the trade in Mexican and Peruvian silver and the other valuable products of the Spanish Indies — cochineal, indigo, dye-woods, tobaccos, and so forth. Equally, Europe's exports to Spanish America passed almost entirely via Spain. Thus impoverished, ruined, Castile paradoxically remained Europe's chief source of specie and most important market for imported manufactures of all kinds.

Furthermore, it is essential to appreciate that Spain's ruinous population loss was largely confined to the interior where both industry and agriculture had suffered so severely. Indeed, in the interior the treaty of Munster inaugurated the final phase of decline. By the early 1650s the 3,000 or so remaining textile workers at Segovia had been stripped of their market, their work, and even of their basic raw material as more and more of Castile's wool production was shipped to Holland in response to the rising prices for all kinds of Spanish wools on the Amsterdam exchange and as Spain was flooded with Flemish, Dutch and English woollens and linens brought in on Dutch ships.[30] But coastal Spain fared quite

[30] Ruiz Martin, 'Industria textil', 272; Ruiz Martin, 'Un testimonio', p. 9n; Le Flem, 535-6.

differently and, indeed, in the aftermath of Munster, enjoyed boom conditions.[31] Despite the decline of Spain's
population overall, there was a marked increase in population
in many coastal districts as the destitute and unemployed of
the interior drifted to the increasingly vibrant periphery.
Cadiz, Málaga, Alicante, and Bilbao all expanded rapidly
and vigorously in the years after Munster in the very same
years that the interior sank deepest into ruin. If the once
prosperous arable zones of the Duero valley and Toledo
were now largely abandoned and desolate, there was a boom
in coastal regions, most spectacularly around Málaga, in wine,
olive oil, raisins, almonds and other produce for export to
northern Europe. But this shift in the balance of agricultural
activity only served to increase Spanish dependence on imported basic foodstuffs. Population decline did not reduce
the level of demand for cheap grain and fish. At the same
time, the Spanish crown remained a leading purchaser of
munitions, naval stores, and Baltic timber and the most
dependent on foreign suppliers. In the years 1621–48 Spain
had, in effect, relied on English, Hanseatic, and latterly
Danish shipping, supplies, and skills for the servicing of virtually all their foreign and coast-to-coast trade. But even the
combined shipping of these powers could not be compared
with that of the Dutch as regards availability, capacity, or
cost. The plenipotentiaries who signed at Munster could
thus not help but be aware that they were transforming the
entire structure of world commerce.[32]

The efforts of the Dutch negotiators at Munster, late in
1646, to infiltrate Seville's monopoly of the Spanish American trade at least to the extent of procuring a role for the
West India Company in the slave trade to the Spanish
colonies, and for the East India Company in the lucrative
Philippines trade, had met with a blank refusal. Under the
treaty, the Dutch had had to accept their total exclusion
from the Spanish Indies, as had the English, under the treaty
of 1630. No sooner was the peace signed, however, than

---

[31] Dominguez Ortiz, *Sociedad española* i. 142–3.
[32] See the 'Poincten ende Articulen. . .in het tracteren van Vrede', 18 Nov.
1646. ARH SG 4856; Consulta, Junta de Estado, Zaragoza, 10 Sept. 1646. AGS
Estado 2255.

Dutch statesmen renewed their endeavours to secure entry to the Spanish American slave market as well as to the salt-pans of Punta de Araya.[33] In the summer of 1648 the Dutch plenipotentiaries at Munster put it to the Conde de Peña-randa, who had been made responsible by the king for liaising with the States General over all matters arising from the peace settlement, that during the Twelve Years Truce, the Dutch had enjoyed access to the salt-pans and that this had ceased only after the resumption of hostilities in 1621; with peace signed, they asked that the *status quo ante* at Punta de Araya be restored, pointing out that this would diminish Dutch and other traffic to the Portuguese salt-pans.[34] The *Consejo* at Madrid retorted that the Dutch had possessed an illegal, *de facto* access only and that permission to sail or trade anywhere in Castile's Indies had never been granted to foreigners or even to the king's non-Castilian subjects. To comply with the Dutch pressure, held the *Consejo*, would mean 'open commerce and the destruction of that of this realm with the Indies for the Dutch with their shipping and capacity to offer their wares on better terms will take most of what now goes from these realms and within a few years Seville's commerce will cease.'

After the arrival of Antoine Brun at The Hague in July 1649, the Amsterdam *vroedschap* took up with him the issues of both slaves and Venezuelan salt, on behalf of Robert Dommer, Willem Coninck, and other leading merchants. Amsterdam undertook that the blacks transported would not be fetched from the Portuguese territories, reminding Madrid that indigo, cochineal, tobacco, and pearl output in the Indies were now, since the secession of Portugal, in desperate need of slaves.[35] There were also offers to supply masts and other naval stores at cheap rates direct to Cartagena and Havana, but all these propositions were politely rejected. Adriaan Pauw personally took up the matter with Brun in November 1650, professing astonishment at the king's attitude, since safeguards could readily be devised to protect

---

[33] Menkman, 'Van de verovering', 166.

[34] Consultas, cons. de Indias, 1 Nov. 1648, 1 Feb. 1649. AGS Estado 2070.

[35] 'Papel que dieron los de Amsterdam', 9 Oct. 1649. AGS Estado 2070.

Seville's commerce, while the Dutch would by then already have been at war with Portugal were it not for their dependence, which he much regretted, on Portuguese salt.[36] The *Consejo* was sufficiently intrigued to refer the issue again to the *Consejo de Indias* but inevitably the reply was again negative.

But, while officially excluded, prospects for contraband activity on the part of the Dutch were obviously enhanced by the cessation of hostilities. Yet during the early years after the peace, relatively few reports reached the *Consejo de Indias* of attempted Dutch penetration, by comparison with the later 1650s and 1660s when a steady stream of such reports were received and the evidence from Curaçao confirms that there was no regular contraband trade until the late 1650s.[37] There was an apparently isolated case of Dutch ships trading on the Venezuelan coast in 1650. The seizure of a Dutch vessel attempting to trade in Santo Domingo in 1651 was a sufficiently isolated incident to warrant consideration by the *Consejo de Estado* as well as the *Consejo de Indias*.[38] Apparently not until August 1652 was there an attempt of any significance on the Colombian coast. On that occasion two Dutch ships loaded with slaves anchored for thirty days off the Rio de la Hacha, endeavouring to sell their cargo to Spanish colonists who were suffering from a severe shortage of black labour. The governor of the province issued a public order threatening with death any subject of the king who dealt with the Dutch. Even though the governor of Cartagena purposely kept his patrol vessels away from the scene to avoid an armed clash, the Dutch were eventually forced to sail off with nothing achieved. After discussing the problem, in January 1654, the *Consejo de Indias* laid down that in no case should royal officers and troops in the Indies actually open fire on the Dutch.[39] They were to concentrate on confiscation of contraband cargoes and severely punishing those

[36] Consulta 29 Nov. 1650. AGS Estado 2076; Consulta 3 Dec. 1650. AGS Estado 2072.
[37] Van Brakel, 49-50.
[38] Consultas 7 July, 7 Oct. 1651. AGS Estado 2076.
[39] Consulta, Junta de Indias, 31 Jan. 1654. AGI Audiencia de Santa Fe, leg. 215.

of the king's subjects who ventured to infringe the regulations. Peñaranda's Jewish agent, at Amsterdam, Lopo Ramírez, confirmed in 1649 that already huge quantities of contraband American bullion were reaching Amsterdam. He estimated the amount that arrived in that year at 3 million ducats, but that all this silver was being transferred to Holland from the Bay of Cadiz.[40]

As yet, lacking the contraband option, Dutch merchants who wished to tap the wealth of the hispanic world faced the unavoidable challenge of ousting the English, Hanseatics, and Danes from their entrenched position in the official carrying trade to and from Seville and its outports. Under the special commercial supplement to the peace treaty, signed at Munster on 4 February 1648, Philip had undertaken to re-admit the Dutch to his European territories on the same basis as other friendly nations; Spanish officials could no longer detain, confiscate, or otherwise interfere with Dutch cargoes except in the case of prohibited French and Portuguese goods and shipments of arms and munitions to enemies of Spain.[41] Under the treaty and its supplement, the Dutch were thus placed on the same footing as their competitors, but in practice it soon emerged that it was the Dutch who now enjoyed favoured status.[42] The *Almirantazgo* remained a formidable institution and besides its legitimate activities one which was prone to practise all manner of abuses against foreign merchants. But in the case of the Dutch, heavy pressure was exerted from Madrid to restrain its zeal. As a result of Dutch complaints, a member of the Council of Castile was sent to the Cantabrian ports during 1649 to release any Dutch ships being detained, to simplify and reduce the pressure of boarding and inspection procedures, to reduce the number of guards placed on foreign ships in Cantabrian ports to just one, and generally to ensure a courteous welcome to the Dutch.[43] In cases where it was

[40] Consulta 26 Dec. 1649. AGS Estado 2070; see also Consulta 16 Aug. 1650. AGS Estado 2072.

[41] Aitzema, *Hist.* vi. 493–4.

[42] Consulta, Junta, 3 May 1649. AGS Estado 4126; van den Hove to SG, Cadiz, 15 Mar. 1649. ARH SG 7042.

[43] Consulta, 18 Jan. 1649, and instructions to Martin Iniguez de Arnedo, AGS Estado 4126.

impossible to ascertain whether merchandise was originally
Dutch or Portuguese, as in the case of a Dutch shipment of
pepper and tobacco held by the *veedor de contrabando* of
Málaga in 1649 and several shipments of East India spices
detained in Cadiz, the *Consejo* laid down that the Dutch
were to be given the benefit of the doubt, surmising that
in any case it was unlikely that the Dutch should want to
deal in Portuguese supplies, since spice prices tended to be
much lower in Holland than at Lisbon.[44] In cases of friction
with the *Almirantazgo* at Cadiz, the Dutch consul, Jacome
van den Hove, generally found a willing ally in the *Consejo
de Estado*. Following the seizure, in Galicia in 1651, of a
Dutch ship loaded with arms and munitions in which two
prominent Dutch politicians, Pauw and Mathenes, reportedly
had shares, the local officials concerned were brusquely reminded that in the case of Dutch ships such incidents must
stop.[45]

The issue which generated most friction between *Almirantazgo* and Dutch skippers during the early years after the
peace and which prompted a co-ordinated campaign by the
Dutch consuls at Cadiz, Seville, and Málaga was the levying
of deposits which had been uniformly practised in the Andalusian ports on English and Hanseatic skippers to ensure that
they would not leave port until they had the *Almirantazgo*'s
permission to do so, and to ensure that they did not anchor
or loiter within 20 miles of the Bay of Cadiz, the latter being
intended to prevent the switching of unregistered silver from
the *flotas* in the approaches to the Bay.[46] The strong resistance of the Dutch skippers and consuls to this practice led to
its provisional suspension and the referring of the matter to
the *Consejo de Estado*. The *Consejo*, after considerable hesitation, eventually confirmed the suspension, in the spring of
1649, pending efforts via Peñaranda, who was now at Brussels,
to persuade the States General to acquiese in the system.[47]

[44] J. van den Hove to SG, 14, 29 Nov. 1648, and van de Hove to Consejo de
Guerra, 6 June 1649; consultas, 29 Mar., 24 Aug. 1650. AGS Estado 2670.

[45] Consulta 7 Sept. 1651. AGS Estado 1651.

[46] Van den Hove to SG, 15 Mar. 1649. ARH SG 7043; consultas, 11 May, 15
Jul. 1650. AGS Estado 2669.

[47] Van den Hove to SG, 2 May 1649. ARH SG 7042; consulta 11 May 1649.
AGS Estado 2669.

Peñaranda had no success, and eventually the crown issued a *cédula* to the governor of Cadiz in December 1651, to the effect that the system of deposits was to remain suspended.[48] The vendetta of the Dutch consuls in Spain against the *Almirantazgo* which resulted in a series of limited victories in the early years after the peace, a campaign vigorously backed by the States of Holland and Zeeland and the States General, was finally to end in total success with the abolition of the board by the Spanish crown in January 1661.

The suspension of deposits and weakening of the *Almirantazgo* clearly facilitated both Dutch participation in the official Indies trade and the working of what, by 1649, had become the chief method of transferring unregistered bullion to Amsterdam. The Spanish authorities received a series of reports from both Cadiz and Amsterdam as to precisely how the latter system functioned. On their departure from Cadiz, the *flotas* became accustomed to pause a few miles beyond the Bay where they took on unregistered and untaxed woollens, linens, and other goods from Dutch ships which waited in the area, often for many months, like off-shore shops.[49] On their return, the galleons delivered payment in the form of unregistered silver bars and ingots in the same manner. A subsidiary method, which also caused heavy seepage of silver and American dyestuffs, was the shipping of textiles illegally to the Canaries where a group of New Christian merchants were active at this time, and from where it was possible to pass goods to the outgoing *flotas* and receive unlisted silver on their return. Evidence abounds that the Canaries were a far more important loophole for contraband trade between northern Europe and the Spanish Indies, during the 1650s, than either the Dutch or English West Indies.[50] The difficulty of co-ordinating from Amsterdam with the unpredictable schedules of the *flotas* led to the piling up of great quantities of merchandise in large Dutch warehouses at Cadiz such as the one that belonged to the

[48] Philip to governor of Cadiz, 27 Dec. 1651. ARH SG 7043.
[49] Peñaranda to Philip, 4 Dec. 1649, Consulta 5 Feb. 1650. AGS Estado 2072; Consulta, Consejo de Indias, 19 Apr. 1652, Consulta 30 Apr. 1652. AGS Estado 2078.
[50] Brun to SG, 1 Feb. 1652. ARH SG 7044; Israel, 'Further Data', 14-15.

Dutch consul, Jacome van den Hove.[51] Dutch ships and seamen frequently lingered in the Bay of Cadiz for many months
on end.

The stream of bullion set flowing from Andalusia to Holl-
and in the immediate aftermath of the peace was regarded
by both Spanish officials and Dutch consuls as being largely
the inevitable consequence of the new relationship. With
hundreds of ships employed in bringing relatively bulky
wares such as grain, fish, timber, and naval stores, Dutch
businessmen met with constant difficulty in finding enough
goods to fill their ships for the return voyage. No more than
a fraction of the capacity involved was needed to shift
Spain's wool exports to Holland and Italy or the relatively
small quantities of colonial dyestuffs, iron ore, wine, olive
oil, and fruit. With the availability of Setúbal salt in the
Republic, there was little incentive to ship highly taxed Cadiz
salt, except briefly during the Dutch–Portuguese war of
1657-60.[52] Thus, unlike Dutch trade to the Baltic, Russia,
and the Far East which were all deficit financed and required
the transfer to those markets from Holland of large quantities
of silver, Spanish commerce offered the Republic a uniquely
favourable balance of trade.[53] The *corregidor* of Asturias
reported in 1650 that Dutch ships anchoring in that province's
harbours could find almost nothing to take in payment for
their salt and grain except silver.[54] The difficulty was just as
acute in Galicia and only marginally less so in the ports of
Valencia and Catalonia. The Dutch vessels crowding into
the Bay of Cadiz loaded chiefly with wool, olive oil, wine,
and occasionally, salt; but even so they often sailed off half
empty,[55] though the problem eased somewhat during the
1650s, as Andalusian agriculture became increasingly geared

[51] Van den Hove to SG, 24 July 1650. ARH SG 7043; I. van Swanenburg to
SG, Seville, 6 Aug. 1652. ARH SG 7044; Van den Hove to SG, 17 Jan. 1655.
ARH SG 7047-i; see also Barbour, 87.
[52] Van den Hove to SG, 1 Nov. 1648. ARH SG 7042; in 1659 even the agent
of the Portuguese crown at Amsterdam, the Jewish merchant Jeronino Nunes da
Costa, (Moses Curiel) was shipping Cadiz salt to Holland, GA Amsterdam NA
1539, p. 274.
[53] De la Court, *Interest van Holland*, 164; Barbour, 52.
[54] Consulta 2 Aug. 1650. AGS Estado 2670.
[55] Van den Hove to SG, 1 Nov. 1648. ARH SG 7042.

to producing for export via the Dutch. A substantial part of the Dutch traffic to and from Cadiz was directly linked with Italy. Many Dutch vessels, after loading at Cadiz, proceeded via Málaga or Alicante to Livorno, Genoa, and Venice carrying silver, dyestuffs, wool, and salt.[56] Much of this silver was for use by Dutch factors in Italy for financing the Levant trade which necessarily absorbed large quantities of bullion. To service Amsterdam's burgeoning trade with Andalusia a sizeable number of Dutch merchants settled in Cadiz and Málaga and appreciable subsidiary colonies formed at San Lúcar, Seville, and elsewhere.[57]

The advantages enjoyed by the Dutch in Spanish commerce, during the 1650s, soon led, as La Court noted with satisfaction,[58] to an undisputed dominance. Within a year or two of the peace, the English were completely ousted from their former pre-eminence in the 'Biskey trade' and the Dutch were shipping more than four times as much wool as they from the Spanish north coast.[59] During the Anglo–Spanish war of 1655–60, when English ships were excluded from Spanish ports, the Dutch ascendancy became almost total. In January 1658 the Dutch consul at Seville reported to the States General that all the foreign ships then anchored at Cadiz, San Lúcar, and Puerto de Santa Maria, apart from one or two from Hamburg, were Dutch.[60] Virtually the entire annual export of Spanish wool was carried by the Dutch either to the Low Countries or to Italy.[61] To an

[56] Van den Hove to SG, 17 Aug. 1653. ARH SG 7045; Barbour, 51.

[57] In 1656 the Dutch merchants, subjects of the States General, resident at Cadiz, and presided over by Jacome van den Hove were the following: Elias van Colen, Pieter de Leeuw, Vicente Zegers, Willem Suares, Jan Dormons, Maarten van den Hart, Francisco de Boys, Frederik Valkenier, Francisco Canson, Pieter Reyniers, Daniel Rundvleesch, Michiel Casal, Andries van Bellen, Estevan Tellyer, Willem Estendorp, Adriaen Dam, Pieter Schryver, Hendrik van Cockhorst, Pieter Poulle, A. van Sittert, Geronimo Peres, Pieter Colaert, Matheo Maarten, Daniel Sloyer, Fadrique Beuven, Jan Belniss, Jan de Wint, David Brandon, and Simon Engyacht, several of whom had relatives at Seville and elsewhere in Spain: see Dutch merchants resident at Cadiz to SG, 5 May and 19 Aug. 1656. ARH SG 7049.

[58] De la Court, *Interest van Holland*, 162; Diferee, 206.

[59] *A Brief Narration*, 1, 2, 9.

[60] H. van Deutecom to SG, 20 Jan. 1658. ARH SG 7052.

[61] *A Brief Narration*, 2, 9; Diferee, 209.

increasing extent, the capital and merchandise on the Indies run, even in some cases the ships and crews, were Dutch. But the safeguarding and advancement of so vital a commerce obviously required not only commercial expertise and shipping capacity but the constant vigilance of the States General, powerful naval backing, and a comprehensive system of consuls and sub-consuls to counteract both the machinations of foreign rivals in Spain and the pretensions of Spanish local officials. The network of Dutch consuls in the Spanish lands during the 1650s, as is shown on Table 9, assumed impressive proportions.[62]

The constant need to protect the burgeoning Dutch shipping in Spanish waters from Muslim pirates, French privateers, and, during the war of 1652–4, from the powerful English navy, led rapidly to a totally new pattern of deployment for the Dutch navy. Immediately after Van den Hove's arrival in Cadiz, in 1648, a Dutch naval squadron stayed in the Bay for some time having their hulls cleaned and taking on provisions.[63] From 1648 until late 1652 visits of Dutch naval squadrons continued but on an occasional basis only. However, on the outbreak of the English war, during the summer and autumn of 1652, a wave of panic with respect to Dutch shipping swept the Andalusian ports. Some silver was actually removed from Dutch ships that were already loaded and reloaded onto Hanseatic vessels.[64] From then on the States General maintained a powerful naval presence in Spanish waters more or less permanently. During 1653–4 confidence was restored by means of organizing Dutch merchant shipping both between Holland and Spain and between Spain and Italy in heavily escorted convoys, and these continued after the end of the English war. The Cadiz–Amsterdam convoy of June 1655, the second of that year, consisted of thirty ships; scarcely had these left than another score of Dutch vessels arrived in convoy from Málaga. On its return to

[62] According to Vincent Richard, secretary at the Spanish embassy at The Hague, there were in 1658 in all twenty-five Dutch consuls and sub-consuls in the Spanish lands: Richard to SG, 22 July 1658. ARH SG 7052-i.

[63] Van den Hove, 20 Sept. 1648. ARH SG 5543-ii.

[64] Swanenburg to SG, 6 Aug., Van den Hove to SG, 25 Sept. 1652. ARH SG 7044.

[65] Van den Hove to SG, 14 Oct. 1655. ARH SG 7047-ii.

TABLE 9 The Dutch consuls in the Spanish Lands during the 1650s

Consulship	Date Established	First Encumbent	Successor
Cadiz	August 1648	Jacome van de Hove	van den Hove continued until after 1661
Seville[a]	September 1648	Isaac van Swanenburg (1648–56)	Hendrik van Deutecom[b]
Málaga	November 1648	Maarten Symonsz. Hooghwoude (1648–54)	
Alicante	1649?	Jacome Vinck	Jacome Drielenburg ?
Bilbao and San Sebastián	1649?	Pieter Jan Oorschot	Oorschot continued until after 1661
Barcelona	1653	Mathieu Aerten de Piethoven	Jan Dommer[c]
Vigo	1656	Andries Aermouts of Flushing	?
Mallorca	?	Jan Andries Coural	Robert Pregent
Canaries	December 1649	Baltasar Polster	Hans Runtvleesch
Messina (Sicily)	January 1649	Abraham Casembrooth	Casembrooth continued until after 1661
Naples	1649?	Niccolo Waermont	?
Puglia	?	?	In 1657 this consulship was merged with that of Naples

a Under this consul came the sub-consulship of San Lúcar which, in the later 1650s, was held first by Filip Niccolai and then by Bernard Sterk, see Deutecom to SG, Seville, 10 May 1660. ARH SG 7054.
b Formerly Dutch consul at Le Havre, Res. Holl. 13 Jan. 1657.
c This consul was murdered in Barcelona in 1660.

Cadiz, in March 1656, the Spanish Peru fleet found anchored in the Bay, awaiting its arrival, besides a fleet of Dutch merchantmen, a powerful naval force under De Ruyter, part of which was assigned to escort the merchantmen back to Holland, part to escort another convoy to Málaga, Alicante, and Italy and part to maintain the Dutch naval presence in Spanish waters.[66] During the autumn of 1656 a second Dutch convoy was escorted from Cadiz to Amsterdam by a squadron under Cornelis Evertsen; scarcely had this fleet departed, than a convoy arrived in Cadiz from Zeeland. De Ruyter was back in Cadiz in January 1657; in July he was anchored at Alicante with sixteen warships. The Dutch navy in fact during the 1650s became almost as familiar a sight, particularly at Cadiz, San Lucar, Málaga, and Alicante, as the fleets of Dutch merchantmen.

Another important respect in which the States General asserted itself in defence of Holland's blossoming trade with the hispanic world was in its endeavours to protect the participation of Amsterdam's Sephardi Jews. During the 1650s the latter indisputably accounted for a relatively high proportion of all Dutch commerce with Spain, one estimate putting their share as high as 20 per cent, though in fact the data are too sporadic to be quantifiable.[67] What is clear from the Amsterdam freight-contracts is that much of the business with Cadiz, a large part of the wool importing from the Basque ports and Santander, an appreciable slice of the Málaga trade, and probably most of the illicit trade to the Canaries and through Navarre to Bayonne were in Jewish hands.[68] Some of this trade was by means of Dutch factors resident in Spain. For instance, Bernard Estendorp at Seville acted for, among others, at least three Amsterdam Jews — Manuel Toralta, Diego Enríquez, and Juan de Castro.[69] In the main, however, they dealt with Portuguese New Christian merchants resident at Madrid, Seville, and Málaga, personages who were often relatives and secret co-religionists. The latter

[66] Van den Hove to SG, 23 and 26 Mar. 1656. ARH SG 7048.
[67] Swetchinski, 165-6.
[68] Richard to Philip, The Hague, 3 Sept. 1658. AGS Estado 2091; Israel, 'Dutch Sephardim', 38-42, 57-61; Israel, 'Further data', 7-19.
[69] Israel, 'Dutch Sephardim', 59-60.

lacked the protection of the Dutch government and were highly vulnerable in particular to the attentions of the Inquisition.[70]

Although the question of the Jews had not arisen during the formal negotiations at Munster, in contrast to the 1632-3 peace talks, no sooner had Antoine Brun taken up his post at The Hague in 1649, than the Jews became a major issue in Dutch-Spanish relations and were to remain so until 1661. As a first step, in July 1649 the Amsterdam Sephardim arranged through the States of Holland for formal permission to be sought from the Spanish crown for Dutch Jews to trade, through factors, with Spain.[71] There was no response. In the following year the States General went much further, demanding freedom of movement for its Jewish subjects in the European lands of the king on precisely the same basis as other Dutch subjects under articles two, four, and eleven of the peace treaty.[72] Philip readily conceded that Dutch Jews should have full freedom to trade with his European lands, through factors Catholic or Protestant (in effect, he had already granted such freedom to the Jews of Hamburg and Denmark though not explicitly), but steadfastly refused to yield the right of access in person, on the grounds that the general expulsion from Spain, in 1492, and subsequent expulsions of the Jews from Sicily, Portugal, Naples, and Milan, took precedence among the fundamental laws of the Spanish Monarchy over the peace treaty.[73] Heavy pressure was brought to bear by the Amsterdam *vroedschap* via the States of Holland on the Spanish ambassador, but the king remained adamant.[74] As part of its general policy of cultivating good relations with the Dutch, however, the Spanish crown, after 1648, showed notable readiness to restrain the Inquisition from seizing or interfering with the goods and assets of Dutch Jews found in the hands of New Christian factors in Spain, even in the case of recent immigrants to

[70] Ibid., pp. 36-7, 41.
[71] Res. Holl. 27 July 1649; Silva Rosa, 84-5.
[72] Consulta 27 June 1650. AGS Estado 2072.
[73] Philip to Brun, 9 July 1650. AGS EEH xxxii, fo. 11; Aitzema *Hist.* vii. 178.
[74] Brun to Philip, 30 Sept. 1650. AGS EEH xxxii, fos. 118-20; Philip to Brun, 4 Dec. 1650. AGS Estado 2259.

Holland who were themselves former subjects of the king and fugitives from the Inquisition.[75] In 1656, for instance, after the seizure of the persons and warehouses of two New Christian Indies merchants at Seville, the Inquisition was compelled by the crown, following the intercession first of the Dutch consul, and subsequently of the States General, to restore all goods and assets belonging to Jews resident in Holland.

Despite repeated guarantees from the *Consejo* that the trade and assets of Dutch Jews in Spain would be protected and privileged on the same basis as that of other Dutch subjects friction constantly arose over the business dealings of the Jews who tended to specialize in types of transaction prohibited by the crown. The *Almirantazgo*, Spanish ambassador at The Hague, and, best informed of all, the Spanish consul at Amsterdam, Jacques Richard, were all quite convinced, and not without some reason (though they exaggerated) that the Jews were those chiefly responsible for the constant seepage of prohibited French and Portuguese merchandise into Spain and the Spanish Indies and the illicit transfer of silver from the Bay of Cadiz and the Canaries to Amsterdam.[76] It was with some vexation therefore that the crown responded to the determined attitude adopted by Amsterdam on behalf of the Jews whenever suspect cargoes or dealings involving Dutch Sephardim were intercepted by Spanish officials. A particularly dramatic exchange between The Hague and Madrid followed the bringing to San Sebastian in 1657, by an Irish privateer in Spanish service, of the ship, *The Pearl*, of uncertain provenance, carrying Jewish emigrants from Amsterdam to Barbados, over 1 million guilders' worth of goods and a bewildering mixture of English and Dutch papers.[77] On this, as on other occasions the States General reacted with great vigour on behalf of the Jewish community. When during the Anglo–Spanish war, the crown tried to tighten up procedures in the Spanish ports, in order

[75] SG to Swanenburg, 9 Dec. 1655. ARH SG 7047--i; consulta, 18 Oct. 1656. AGS Estado 2088.
[76] Gamarra to Philip, 31 Aug. 1656, AGS Estado 2089; consulta 22 Mar. 1657, AGS Estado 2092; consulta 1 Feb. 1661. AGS Estado 2198.
[77] Israel, 'Dutch Sephardim', 37-8.

to make effective the exclusion of English goods, the Spanish ambassador at The Hague predicted that the main opposition would come from the Amsterdam Jews.[78]

During the drive of the later 1650s by the Spanish authorities to regain some measure of control over Dutch commercial dealings in Spain, the crown sought to exploit the plausible argument that continuing percolation of English and French manufactures into the hispanic world, on Dutch ships, scarcely served the interests of the Republic any more than of Spain. In November 1655, following attempts to tighten procedures at Cadiz, Philip pressed the States General to agree to the setting up of a Spanish sub-consulate at Rotterdam to work in conjunction with Jacques Richard and to allow that in future all Dutch cargoes consigned to Spain should be covered by certificates attesting that the goods concerned were not of English, French, or Portuguese origin signed by the Spanish consular officials in Holland. In delivering this request, Gamarra laid heavy emphasis on the Dutch interest in excluding English and French manufactures, arguing that the Dutch 'ne peuvent tirer qu'un extreme proffit et utilité d'avoir seulles tout le commerce d'Espagne, sans que l'on y admette d'autres marchandises que celles qu'il constera y avoir esté fabriquées'.[79] Some Amsterdam merchants began voluntarily to co-operate with the new system of Spanish certificates 'pour ne se pas exposer', as Gamarra put it, 'aux fascheries qui sont à craincre pour ceux qui refuseront de s'y conformer',[80] but the States General, alerted by Amsterdam, refused to agree to making this obligatory or to the inconveniencing in any way of Dutch-owned cargoes which lacked Richard's certificates. Obtaining no answer to his first request, Gamarra repeatedly raised the matter in subsequent years but met with nothing but obstruction even to the setting up of the sub-consulate at Rotterdam.[81] Finally, in December 1660 the States General

[78] Gamarra to Philip, 31 Aug. 1656. AGS Estado 2089.

[79] Gamarra to SG, 17 Nov. 1655. ARH SG 7047-ii.

[80] Gamarra to SG, 6 May 1656. ARH SG 7048; Reede to SG, 24 Jan. 1657. ARH SG 7050.

[81] Gamarra to SG, 14 Nov. 1657. ARH SG 7051; Gamarra to SG, 1 May 1658. ARH SG 7052-i.

emphatically rejected the system of certificates being operated by Richard as being in violation, as indeed it was, of the
1650 Dutch–Spanish commercial treaty.[82] The Dutch extraordinary ambassadors at Madrid who had already been instructed to support the interests of the Dutch Jews in Spain
with all vigour,[83] were told to impress this rejection force-
fully on His Catholic Majesty.

Though doubtless unintended, there was much irony in
Gamarra's professed concern for the interests of Dutch
industry both in view of the role that Holland's manufacturing
interest had played in the past in obstructing efforts to forge
closer Dutch–Spanish relations and on account of the at least
partially adverse impact of the peace settlement on Holland's
industrial performance. If the economic benefits of the peace
for Amsterdam were undeniable, it cannot be said with anything like the same certainty that they were as positive for
either the manufacturing towns or other sections of the
country. Indeed, it may be said, without exaggeration, that
Amsterdam's success in the hispanic world was bought at a
price for most other parts of the country, creating a situation
with ominous implications for the future.

In the first place, the treaty of Munster inevitably involved
abolition of the existing Dutch tariff list which was geared to
war with Spain, to collecting large revenues for naval expenditure, and to penalizing goods entering the Republic from
the Spanish Netherlands, as well as restricting exports by
river and overland. The quest for agreement on a new peace-
time list was the principal preoccupation of the States
General and provincial assemblies during the summer and
autumn of 1648. In Holland, Dordrecht took the lead in
pressing for early reductions in the customs duties, as well
as for dissolving the bulk of the large and costly river gun-
boat force which had been maintained by the Republic
since 1621.[84] Amsterdam and Rotterdam were likewise eager
for tariff reductions, but rather than urge a return to the very
low 1609 list, as desired by Middelburg and Flushing, preferred

---

[82] Res. SG, 18 Dec. 1660. ARH SG 8509, fo. 48ᵛ.
[83] ARH SG 8509, fos. 9ᵛ–10ʳ.
[84] Res. Holl. 26, 29 June, 7 July 1648; see also 'Voorslach', 26 Sept. 1648.
GA Dordrecht 115. no. 336. Res. Holl. 26, 29 June, 7 July 1648.

to compromise with the inland towns, partly to minimize friction and partly because they were unwilling to see the navy almost completely dissolved, thus stripping Dutch merchantmen in the Mediterranean, a high risk area, even in peace time, of naval protection. The States of Holland, therefore, eventually agreed to establish provisionally the so-called second and third columns of the published 1625 list, thus removing the heavy *licenten*, and considerably reducing the imposts, but not to so low a level as had prevailed in 1609. Leiden, where the burgomasters consulted local businessmen and the drapery industry, and where there was intense interest in the issue, concurred in the decision, though with reservations regarding certain specific commodities, such as exports of Spanish wool which the *vroedschap* would have wished to restrict with a very heavy duty.[85] Despite fierce opposition from the States of Zeeland, which urged adoption of the 1609 list, Holland's solution was adopted, on a provisional basis, in October 1648.[86] After the constitutional crisis of 1650 the whole matter was reconsidered in the spring of 1651 and a permanent peace list was finally drawn up and published in April 1651.[87] As can be seen from Table 10, the loss of protection suffered by Dutch manufacturing, with regard both to imports of foreign manufactures and to exports of raw materials, was quite drastic. For example, the duty on Flanders's most successful industrial product, linen, was more than halved and that on exports of Spanish wool from the Republic reduced by more than three-quarters.

The overall impact of these tariff reductions was greatly increased by the general upsurge of industrial activity, from 1648, around the borders of the Republic. It is true that as a consequence of the continuing Franco–Spanish conflict, production of *says* and other fabrics at Lille, and particularly at Hondschoote, declined steadily after 1640.[88] But much of

[85] GA Leiden Sec. Arch. 450. vroed. res. 5, 7 Oct. 1648.

[86] Res. Hol. 3, 10 Oct. 1648; Res. Col. Middelburg, 9 Nov. 1648. ARH Admiraliteiten 2467; 'Journalen Willem II', 470, 471, 473; Aitzema, *Hist.* vi. 565; At. Amsterdam to SG, 16 Feb. 1651. GA Dordrecht 115, no. 336.

[87] *Groot Placaet-Boeck* i. cols. 2488-555.

[88] Coornaert, 57.

TABLE 10 The Dutch Tariff Reductions of 1648–51 on selected industrial imports and raw material exports*

Item	Duty under the 1621–48 War-List		October 1648		April 1651	
	In	Out	In	Out	In	Out
Hondschoote-Brugge *says*	1–11	–	1–0	–	1–0	–
Flemish linens	1–2½	–	0–6	–	0–12	–
Munster–Osnabruck *lakens*	1–5	–	0–4	–	0–4	–
English unfinished *lakens*	free		free		1–10	–
English *bays*	1–17½		0–6		0–6	–
German wool (100 lb.)	–	2–12	–	1–2	–	0–6
Spanish wool (100 lb.)	–	2–12	–	0–15	–	0–12
Baltic flax (100 lb.)	–	2–10	–	0–10	–	0–10

*Duty given in guilders and stuivers

this loss was made good by expanded output at various places, notably at Brugge, a town to which many Hondschoote weavers moved to escape the disruptions caused by the French. Moreover, output of linens at Ghent, Oudenaarde, and Kortrijk continued to grow.[89] Still more damaging to Haarlem, however, was the re-routing of Flemish linen exports from 1648. Between the closing of the French border to Flemish products in 1635 and the end of the Spanish war, Ghent linens, the bulk of which were destined for Spain and the Spanish Indies, had been exported almost entirely in English ships, via Dover. But from 1648 the English ceased handling Flemish linens and while some of the output was conveyed direct from Ostend to Spain, in Dutch ships, much of it entered by river and canal across Zeeland onto the Dutch market.[90] While much, or most, of this linen was forwarded to Amsterdam dealers for reshipment to Spain, it now worked in direct competition to the Haarlem product forcing down prices, profits and wages. Once again, Amsterdam profited from the industrial towns' distress.

But more ominous for the woollen industries of Leiden, Delft, and Gouda than the continuing industrial vitality of the Spanish Netherlands, was the threat from neighbouring lands further east. Until 1648 high tariffs and the ceaseless turmoil of war had held decisively in check industrial growth

[89] Bastin, 136; Everaert, 45–9.
[90] The Flemish linens were shipped to Amsterdam along the *binnenstromen* via Sas van Gent: see Bastin, 136, 145.

in Westphalia, Liège, and the Overmaas districts which soon proved to be exceptionally favoured as centres of textile as well as metal production. Connected by a prolific river traffic with Holland's ports, these regions could procure foreign wools and export their output once the tariffs were down, almost as cheaply as the Holland textile towns, and to these facilities and the fast-flowing streams feeding the Maas and abundant supplies of fuller's earth they added wages, rents, and taxes which were a mere fraction of those pertaining in Holland.[91] Production of *rashes* at Verviers and neighbouring towns, the main factor in the destruction of Leiden's *rash* industry,[92] already something of a threat before 1648, overwhelmed that of Holland during the decade after the peace. The upsurge of cloth production in and around Munster, Osnabrück, Jülich, and Dalhem was even more markedly a phenomenon of the post-Munster decade. When, in 1663, the States of Holland, admiralty colleges and States General received and studied detailed reports on the ills of the Dutch textile industry, in response to a rising crescendo of complaints, almost all the main cloth guilds blamed their difficulties principally on foreign competition. As in the past, English rivalry was a key factor and was keenly resented on account of the English policy of excluding Dutch fabrics from British and Irish markets. But the new element, and the one chiefly responsible for undermining the vulnerable branches of Holland's cloth industry, was the sudden, explosive growth on the Republic's eastern borders.[93] With the obstacles to imports of foreign cloth removed, the inevitable result, during the decade following the treaty of Munster, was an uninterrupted and inexorable drift downwards in the price of almost every kind of fabric, including that of the finest quality woollens.[94] The market was patently saturated and while Amsterdam profited from this, the profits and wages of industrial Holland were mercilessly squeezed.

[91] Huet, 82; Posthumus, 'De industrieele concurrentie', 372–8; Harsin, 84–5.
[92] De la Court, *Welvaren van Leiden*, 88.
[93] 'Adviezen uit het jaar 1663', 11, 13–14, 26, 29; 'Vertooch op't poinct van de manifacturen', *Bronnen textielnij* v. 40–3.
[94] Ibid., pp. 42–3; Posthumus, *An Inquiry* ii. 217–18, 324–5, 328–9, 334, 336.

But despite its alarming predicament, the Dutch cloth industry was not done for yet. Unlike Segovia and Toledo, which totally collapsed in the post-Munster era under the suddenly increased influx of foreign manufactures, Leiden succeeded in adapting to the new circumstances with remarkable success and indeed was to retain considerable vitality until the beginning of the eighteenth century. For it was solely in the cheaper branches, based on home-produced and German wools and relying chiefly on sales in the home market, that the handicap of high labour costs proved insurmountable. Undermined by Verviers, Leiden's output of *rashes* fell from over 8,000 yearly in 1648 to little more than 3,000 yearly by 1660.[95] Manufacture at Leiden of cheap *says* for the home market almost completely collapsed.[96] Production of Leiden fustians fell from 13,000 yearly in 1648 to less than 7,000 by 1660.[97] Output of *say*-fustians at Gouda, amounting to 2,500 pieces in 1648, had virtually ceased by 1660.[98] Among medium-quality woollens, such as *bays*, where English competition was the main threat, some difficulty was certainly encountered,[99] but production nevertheless held up at a fairly constant level, and during the years 1655–60, when English *bays* were excluded from Spain and Spanish America, *bay*-production was stepped up at various towns in Holland and Leiden's *bay*-output soared as never before, though it declined again as soon as England and Spain made peace.[1]

In the field of fine cloth woven from expensive Spanish and Turkish wools where high labour costs, taxation, and rents counted for relatively less in determining the overall competitiveness of the finished product, the picture was entirely different.[2] Leiden soon recovered from the slump of 1647–9 and not only regained, but slightly exceeded, its

[95] *Bronnen textielnij.* v. 42; Posthumus, *Leidsche La lenindustrie* iii. 930.
[96] *Bronnen textielnij.* v. 42.
[97] Posthumus, *Leidsche Lakenindustrie* iii. 930.
[98] Gezelschap, 146–7.
[99] *Bronnen textielnij.* v. 41.
[1] Reede to SG. Madrid, 29 Aug. 1657. ARH SG 7051; Philip to Gamarra, 31 Aug. 1657. AGS EEH xl, fo. 99; Posthumus, *Leidsche Lakenindustrie* iii. 930.
[2] Ibid.; Wilson, 216.

former output, maintaining production at close to 20,000 cloths annually during the years 1653–60. Moreover, output of a new fabric, the *greinen*, a blend of costly wools, expanded rapidly during these years. Thus evidently Amsterdam's newly assumed preponderance in the international trade in Spanish wools worked in considerable measure as a palliative mitigating the pressures and disruption caused to the Dutch textile industry by the Spanish peace. Prices for Spanish wools on the Amsterdam exchange tended to rise in the 1650s in line with the mounting demand in the international market,[3] but undoubtedly this key industrial material remained cheaper in Holland than elsewhere in northern Europe. According to an English estimate, of 1667, no less than 22,000 of a total of 40,000 sacks of wool exported each year from Spain were shipped to the Low Countries, as opposed to less than one third of this amount shipped to England.[4]

Even in the crucial instance of Spanish wools, however, it would be inexact to say that the interests of Amsterdam and the manufacturing towns tended to coincide after 1648. In September 1648 the *laeckendrapiers* of Leiden and Delft had jointly pressed for a heavy tariff of 3 guilders per 100 lb. on all types of Spanish wool re-exported from the Republic in order to discourage re-exports and lower the price of the commodity in Holland. This appeal was overruled by the mercantile interest and the actual tariff imposed under the 1648 and 1651 lists amounted to less than a quarter of that they had demanded.[5] Subsequent appeals for a heavier duty on re-exports of Spanish wool were similarly ignored.[6] Amsterdam insisted on purveying Spanish, as indeed German and all imported wools, not just to Holland's industrial towns but to their competitors likewise. Thus while the main thrust of foreign competition came to be felt in the cheaper branches, something of the intensified pressure,

---

[3] Posthumus, *An Inquiry* ii. 266, 268; however, as a result of the return of Dutch shipping to Andalusia, prices for Guatemalan indigo and Mexican cochineal at Amsterdam fell very considerably after 1648.

[4] Godolphin 106–9.

[5] GA Leiden Sec. Arch. 450, fo. 320. vroed. res. 7 Oct. 1648; *Bronnen textieln.* iv. 481.

[6] 'Adviezen uit' het jaar 1663', p. 13.

especially from Tilburg, Eindhoven, Aachen, Eupen, Jülich, Verviers, and Dalhem, was felt by Holland's manufacturers of fine cloth also.[7] Scarcely any Spanish wool had been used in these areas, it seems, before 1648, but following the lowering of tariffs, the *fabrikanten* of these localities had begun to compete with their counterparts in Holland for the supplies reaching Amsterdam, pushing up the price of the raw material and forcing down that of the finished product all to Amsterdam's profit and Leiden's loss.

If Haarlem, Leiden, and Gouda were at least partly right in their predictions of adverse internal consequences from the Spanish peace, the *vroedschappen* of Middelburg and Flushing were entirely vindicated with regard to their apprehensions. With mounting bitterness, the Zeelanders witnessed their prosperity wane as much of their wartime transit trade to Antwerp, Brugge, and Ghent was diverted to Ostend, Nieuwpoort, and Blankenberge. It is true that the picture was not wholly bleak. The trade of both Antwerp and Ghent certainly expanded during the 1650s.[8] After 1648 Ghent linens were customarily shipped to Amsterdam along the *binnenstromen* via Zeeland. Re-exports of grain from the Republic to the Spanish Netherlands, forbidden until 1647, evidently formed an important element in Zeeland's remaining transit trade with the South Netherlands after the peace.[9] But over all, as emerges from Graph 7, it is undeniable that Zeeland's economy suffered severely from the transition to peace with Spain.

Ironically, the interests of Zeeland and the Holland manufacturing towns which had for so long converged in war, diverged sharply in peace. In 1648 Zeeland had pressed for still lower tariffs than those than Holland had settled for and in 1651, despairing of the States General's efforts to persuade the Spanish crown to raise the imposts in the Flemish seaports, Zeeland resumed its campaign for lower tariffs on the part of the Republic, urging readoption of the 1609 list.[10]

[7] 'Alsoo de Laeckendrapiers van Tilburch GA Leiden. Sec. Arch. 2449.

[8] Baetens, *Antwerpens welvaart* i. 321, 323–4.

[9] See the lists of licences for shipping grain through Zeeland to Flanders in 1648 in ARH Admiraliteiten 2466, 2467.

[10] Res. Holl. 29 Sept. 1650, 5 Jan. 1651.

And other interests besides Zeeland's contributed to the campaign. It was claimed that Friesland and Groningen would also gain from a further lowering in tariffs as this would enable those provinces to divert more of the traffic to and from Westphalia, from Emden and the Ems, through their own territory. It was argued that the Holland maritime towns would also benefit, since much of the commerce with central and southern Germany, from the Peninsula, France, and England, passed via Hamburg and the Elbe only because Hamburg's imposts were lower than the Republic's. Thus, it can be said that in the States General, the position of the Holland manufacturing towns was even weaker than in the States of Holland. In a sense, the industrial interest now relied on Amsterdam to shield it from the pressure for further tariff reductions. The 1651 tariff list was in this way essentially a compromise between the two main groupings in Holland. The decisive argument used against Zeeland in 1651 by the Amsterdam admiralty college was that lower customs duties would inevitably prompt a still greater influx of manufactures from Flanders and Brabant where, it was argued once again, wages and costs were much lower than in the Republic so that Holland's industries would inevitably suffer further and that ultimately this would be disadvantageous for the commerce of Amsterdam also.[11]

[11] At. Amsterdam to SG, 5 Jan. and 16 Feb. 1651. GA Dordrecht section 115, no. 336.

Chapter VIII

Epilogue: The 1660s

The complex and far-ranging impact of the treaty of Munster on the subsequent development of both the Dutch Republic and the hispanic world to a considerable extent justified both the hopes and the fears which had, for so long, fed the deliberations, dissension, and doubts on both sides over whether or not to make peace and how subsequently to shape the Dutch–Spanish relationship. These conflicting expectations had in turn derived from a whole half-century of bitter debate and struggle. There is, in fact, a remarkable degree of continuity in the long and hard-fought controversies which had continued on either side almost without interruption since the deliberations of 1606-9. Certain core issues and themes — Dutch pressure on the Spanish Indies, the concentration of Spain's military might in the South Netherlands, the industrial rivalry between Holland and the southern provinces, and the incompatible commercial interests of different regions of both Spain and the Republic — figured prominently throughout, though this is not to say that a variety of other political as well as religious pressures did not also influence the course of events sporadically. But the central themes, a mélange of quests for power and especially profit, by and large remained constant. Politics and economics merged at every point.

But how, more precisely, should one characterize the Dutch–Spanish struggle from 1606, and assess its general significance? Clearly, it was not in any sense a war of religion. While, during the first half of the seventeenth century, it was still usual, in Europe, to adorn political and economic objectives with tokens of religious zeal, increasingly this was so only for the sake of form. On the Spanish side, resounding pronouncements on behalf of Catholicism and specific demands on behalf of the Dutch Catholics, were repeatedly

435

made, not least by Olivares, but invariably these can be shown to have been peripheral to the real concerns of the Spanish crown. On the Dutch side, it is true, religious pressures occasionally amounted to a little more than mere façade, notably during the deliberations of 1606-9, 1629-30 and 1648-51, but even so what is chiefly striking is how extremely limited the influence of religious arguments and of the Dutch Calvinist clergy remained. Inevitably, the international balance of power, the drive for hegemony of the Habsburgs and the resistance offered by their opponents, played an important part, certainly more so than religion. And yet, again, such considerations, especially on the Dutch side, mostly counted for much less than one might expect. There is very little to suggest that the towns and provinces of the Republic were ever principally swayed in their decisions for and against a Spanish peace, or for or against war, by strategic or international arguments. On the Spanish side, weighing up the European balance tended to play a greater role, especially after Olivares's downfall, when the Spanish crown can be said to have deliberately sacrificed various colonial and economic interests to the Dutch for the sake of strengthening its hand against France. And yet, for most of the struggle, even when it was patently obvious that the war was undermining Spain's ability to withstand the resurgence in French power or intervene effectively in Germany, the Spanish leadership insisted that the colonial and economic interests at stake must take precedence over strategic considerations.

The conflict was by no means totally an economic struggle but, except perhaps in the case of Spanish policy after 1640, colonial and economic factors usually figured larger than any others. But by no means was the struggle a straightforward clash between two rival, national sets of interests, one Dutch, one Spanish. The picture was complicated throughout by a further underlying clash of economic interest within each rival camp. Indeed the deep-seated tensions on either side revealed by the Dutch-Spanish struggle after 1606 strongly suggest that the conflict affected the development of both societies in a mixture of both beneficial and adverse ways. On the Dutch side, nobility, bourgeoisie, peasantry, and artisans were all thoroughly split over the issue. On the Spanish side, one can make a better case for the role of a particular class, namely the Castilian nobility, which, at any rate until the late 1620s, can be said to have backed the war for reasons which do smack of class interest. After 1629, however, even this meagre element of class motivation is no longer discernible. By and large, the conflicting economic factions cut right across class and were generally determined chiefly by locality and whether the groups concerned were active in trade, industry, bureaucracy, or the army.

The Dutch economy, the most advanced in Europe at this time, was also, in many ways, one of the most vulnerable. While it is true that the period of Dutch economic greatness continued well into the late seventeenth century, the treaty of Munster which marked the defeat of one of the rival Dutch factions directly contributed to the growing lack of balance that characterized the last phase of Holland's golden age: the continuing vitality and dynamism of Amsterdam at the expense of other sectors, notably the industrial towns, South Holland and Zeeland.[1] This increasingly ominous trend doubtless arose from a variety of causes, but by no means all of these lay within the structure of the economy itself. The pace and extent of this development also owed much to factors such as the changes in the Republic's tariff policy, the maintenance of the Schelde restrictions in the post-1648 circumstances and the commercial concessions obtained from Spain in 1648, 1650, and 1661, all part of the political outcome of the Dutch–Spanish struggle. The future direction of Dutch economic life, in other words, can be said to have been determined by the interaction of structure with a specific sequence of political events.

In the case of Spain, the significance of the war and its political aftermath was certainly no less fundamental and points to a specific, and in some respects, perhaps, novel interpretation of the process which historians term the 'decline of Spain'. Not only is it evident that a severe contraction in the industrial and agricultural base of Castile took

---

[1] 'Amsterdam drew to itself', as Jan de Vries has expressed it, 'much of the activity that had previously been carried out throughout the urban system': De Vries, 'Barges and Capitalism', 354.

place, but that this collapse occurred within a relatively short space of time. Again, the process was caused less by any fundamental structural trends within Spain than by the interaction between the internal structure and Spain's changing political relationship with the other west European powers, particularly the Dutch Republic. The underlying weaknesses which historians have traditionally seen as being at the root of Spain's decline — the unfavourable balance of trade, uncompetitive industries, vulnerable agriculture, and heavy taxation — are in themselves largely irrelevant to the timing and extent of Spain's decline. All these weaknesses are as evident in the Spain of the fifteenth and sixteenth as of the seventeenth century.[2] These shortcomings did not prevent the sustained expansion of the Spanish economy in the sixteenth century any more than they were, in themselves, the causes of decline in the seventeenth. The collapse was the consequence of potentially vulnerable industries and agriculture being suddenly exposed to a massive influx of north-European industrial and agricultural products which, for a combination of reasons, did not happen before 1600. The most important factors which cushioned the Spanish economy from such penetration during the second half of the sixteenth were the Low Countries disturbances which disrupted industrial activity in Flanders, the French Wars of Religion which reduced the industrial output of northern France and the long war between Spain and England, ending in 1604. However, the first full blast of foreign competition, precipitated by Lerma's peace policy, and in particular, by the signing of the Twelve Years Truce, however devastating did not long continue. The decline of Spain was thus temporarily arrested, in 1621 precisely, with the huge reduction in foreign imports and the fall in raw material exports caused by the resumption of the Dutch–Spanish struggle. The real process of collapse only continued from the late 1640s onwards, following the signing of the treaty of Munster and the renewed heavy influx of foreign merchandise and exports of wool.

Interpreting the 'decline of Spain' in this way, as the

[2] Larraz., 71–5.

impact of the changing relationship with the Dutch on Spain's domestic economy, provides us with insights into what would otherwise be certain highly perplexing features of Spanish economic life during the period of decline. For while the towns, industries, and agriculture of the interior decayed, Spain's foreign trade, at least within Europe, undoubtedly expanded and that with the Indies recovered much of its former buoyancy after 1648. The country's wool exports, except for the temporary reversal during the 1620s, appear to have grown during the period of decline by about one-third, from well under 30,000 to over 40,000 sacks yearly between 1610 and the 1660s.[3] Exports of Spain's agricultural cash crops — wines, olive oil, raisins, and other fruit — essentially the produce of the southern maritime zone, likewise expanded vigorously. Despite the overall decline in Spain's population, coastal cities which throve on foreign trade, particularly San Lúcar, Cadiz Málaga, Alicante, and the Basque ports flourished, in some cases as never before.[4] Meanwhile, towns of the interior, such as Toledo, Valladolid, Segovia, and many more, lost more than half of their population and whole villages were abandoned.[5]

During the 1660s the destinies of Spain and the United Provinces continued to be intimately linked. As in the 1650s, the Dutch dominated key sectors of Spanish trade, particularly the movement within Europe of American silver, indigo, and cochineal, and Castilian wools, but, following the Peace of the Pyrenees in 1659, it would seem that the French rapidly ousted the English from second place and eventually surpassed the Dutch themselves in some sectors, notably in volume of manufactures exported to Spain.[6] The growth of Franco-Dutch rivalry in Spain was paralleled by a steady worsening of relations between France and the Republic in almost every economic and political sphere. At the same time, the disparity between French and Spanish military power increased and Spain's European empire was seen to be increasingly vulnerable to the ambitions of Louis XIV. More

---

[3] Godolphin, 106–9; Israel, 'Spanish Wool Exports', 195, 207.
[4] Dominguez Ortiz, *La Sociedad espanola* i. 142–6.
[5] Larraz, 94–5.   [6] Kamen, 117, 120.

than ever it seemed vital to Dutch politicians that the Spanish Netherlands should be preserved as a buffer against an expansionist France and that Spain should not be utterly overwhelmed. But equally, it seemed essential to the Republic's well-being that it should at all costs avoid being caught in any war with France. This was the essence of the Dutch dilemma of the 1660s and ultimately, perhaps, one that was insoluble.

In its political relations with Spain, the States General consistently refused to go beyond the point reached with the extraordinary embassy of 1661. In that year, moderately cordial Dutch–Spanish relations were established and the Republic secured sweeping economic gains, notably abolition of the *Almirantazgo* and an end to Spanish attempts to recover a measure of administrative control over Dutch trade with the hispanic lands. Subsequently, the Dutch remained eager to cultivate close economic links, and in this connection agreed to a measure of naval co-operation in both the Mediterranean and the Atlantic. But always the States General refused to enter into any form of military co-operation on land. As we know, De Witt was deeply concerned throughout the 1660s by the problem of the Spanish Netherlands. He was as convinced as any member of the Dutch political élite that no more dangerous threat to the Republic could arise than that Brabant and Flanders should fall into French hands. And yet he remained exceedingly reluctant to consider any kind of pact with Spain as a means of preventing such an outcome. Evidently, he preferred to contemplate either an amicable Franco–Dutch partition agreement which would leave the bulk of Brabant and Flanders in the hands of the Republic, or the transfer of the southern provinces to Austrian rule, or else allowing the provinces to achieve self-rule.[7] During Louis XIV's unprovoked aggression against the Spanish Netherlands in the War of Devolution of 1667–8, Spanish ministers were astonished by De Witt's icy, unyielding attitude towards the Spanish crown.[8] Rather than approach Spain, he preferred to deal with England, Sweden,

---

[7] Rowen, 474–7.
[8] Consultas 16 Sept., 1 and 27 Oct. 1667. AGS Estado 2203.

and various German states in order to pressure Louis into halting his invasion and, indeed, exerted heavy pressure on Madrid to cede to France the localities that Louis had already seized as the price of peace.

And yet, even before the débâcle of 1672 which finally forced the Dutch into an alliance with Spain, De Witt's determination to placate France and avoid the embrace of Spain by no means met with universal acceptance in the Republic. There were those, not least in Amsterdam, who would have preferred a pro-Spanish policy, seeing this, in the circumstances, as the natural direction for the Republic to take. Spain was determined to retain the South Netherlands as the principal *plaza de armas* of the Spanish Monarchy but fully accepted the integrity of the Dutch state, was reconciled to leaving the Schelde restrictions in force, condemning Antwerp to continued eclipse, and was dependent on the Republic for a variety of financial and commercial services. Holland's commercial links with Spain and its empire were now undeniably of vital importance to the Dutch economy. England, of course, would potentially have been a more powerful ally than Spain, but, from the Dutch point of view, much less reliable and more dangerous. But De Witt's aversion to a Spanish alliance was certainly much more than merely a personal whim or idiosyncrasy. It may be that old attitudes lingered on and that there were those in the Republic who remained fixed in a mental posture, moulded by decades of struggle, who just could not accept Spain as a friend and ally. What is certain is that there were various parts of the Republic, the manufacturing towns, South Holland and Zeeland being not the least of these which had good reason to regret the effects on local life of the ending of the struggle with Spain and its empire. Thus, in a sense, the old opposition to the Spanish peace, with its various economic motivations, persisted even into the 1660s.

Bibliography

PRIMARY PRINTED SOURCES CITED IN THE TEXT

Actas de las Cortes de Castilla (ACC) vols. i–lx thus far (Madrid, from 1861).

Actes des Etats-Généraux de 1632, 2 vols. ed. L. P. Gachard (Brussels, 1853–66).

'Adviezen uit het jaar 1663 betreffende den toestand en de bevordering der textielnijverheid in Holland' ed. N. W. Posthumus, *BMGH* xxxvii (1916), 1–60.

Aen-merckinge op de Propositie vanden Ambassadeur Peckius, (Amsterdam, 1621), Kn. 3196.

Aenwysinge datmen van de Oost en West-Indische Compagnien een Compagnie dient te maecken (The Hague, 1644), Kn. 5177.

AERSSEN, FRANÇOIS VAN, *Noodtwendigh ende Levendigh Discours van eenige getrouwe Patriotten ende Liefhebberen onses Vaderlandts; over onsen droevigen ende periculeusen Staet* (n. p. 1618) (Kn. 2610).

——, *Practycke van den Spaenschen Raedt* (n. p. 1618) (Kn. 2618).

AITZEMA, LIEUWE VAN, *Historie of verhael van saken van staet en oorlogh in, ende ontrent de Vereenigde Nederlanden*, 14 vols. (The Hague, 1667–71).

——, *Verhael van de Nederlantsche Vreedehandeling*, 2 vols. (The Hague, 1650).

Alder-Ghedenckwaerdichste Oorloghs-Memorien van het groot Wonder-Iaer, Anno 1622, De (Leiden, 1623), Kn. 3401.

Amsterdams Buer-Praetje (Amsterdam, 1650).

Antecedentes de política económica en el Rio de la Plata, documents ed. R. Levillier, 2 vols. (Madrid, 1915).

Antwoordt op sekeren Brief Evlaly vervattende de redenen waerom datmen met den vyandt in gheen conferentie behoort te treden (n. p. 1629), Kn. 3915.

Antwoordt op 't Mvnsters Praetie (Dordrecht, 1646), Kn. 5296.

Archives ou correspondance inédite de la Maison d'Orange-Nassau, ed. G. Groen van Prinsterer, 2nd ser. (5 vols. Utrecht, 1857–61).

AUBERY DU MAURIER, B, 'Rapport van den ambassadeur Aubéry du Maurier na zijn terugkeeer uit Holland in 1624', *BMHG* ii (1879).

Avisos muy verdaderos que ha traydo el vltimo correo extraordinario de Flandes (Madrid, 1624).

BARLAEUS, CASPAR, *Brasilianische Geschichte, Den Achtjähriger in selbigen Landen geführeter Regierung seiner fürstlichen Gnaden Hern Johan Moritz fürstens zu Nassau*, (Cleves, 1659).

——, *Oratie over de Zee-Strydt, met de Spaensche vloodt in Duyns* (Amsterdam, 1639), Kn. 4628.

Basuyne des Oorloghs ofte Waerschouwinghe aen de Vereenichde Nederlanden dat de selvige in den Oorloge met den Coningh van Spaengien moeten continueren (np. 1625), Kn. 3608.

BAUDIUS, DOMENICUS, *Van 'T Bestant des Nederlantschen Oorlogs* (Amsterdam, 1616).

BENTIVOGLIO, CARDINAL, *Las Guerras de Flandes . . . hasta la conclusion de la Tregua de doze años* (Antwerp, 1687).

Bergues sur le Soom Assiégée le 18 de Juillet 1622 et Dessassiegée le 3 d'Octobre ensuivant selon la Description faite par les trois pasteurs d'Eglise d'Icelle, ed. C.A. Campan, (Brussels, 1867).

Breve y Ajustada Relacion de lo svcedido en España, Flandes, Alemania . . . etc. (Seville, 1639).

Breve y verdadera relacion de como por parte de su Magestad Catolica. . .se gano el Fuerte llamado de Eschenk (Seville, 1635).

Brief Narration of the Present Estate of the Bilbao Trade, A (n. p., n. d.) (London? 1650?).

Briefwisseling van Constantijn Huygens (1608-1687), ed. J.A. Worp, 6 vols. (The Hague, 1911–17).

'Brieven over het beleg van 's-Hertogenbosch in het jaar 1629', ed. J.S. van Veen, *BMHG* xxvi (1915), 1–38.

Briefwisseling van Hugo Grotius, thus far 10 vols. (The Hague, 1928–).

Brieven van Lionello en Suraino uit Den Haag aan Doge en Senaat van Venetiën 1616-1618. Werken van het Historisch Genootschap, no. 37 (Utrecht, 1873).

Brieven van Nicolaes van Reigersberch aan Hugo de Groot, Werken van het *Historisch Genootschap* ser. iii, no. 15 (Amsterdam, 1901).

'Brieven van Samuel Blommaert aan den zweedschen rijkskanselier Axel Oxenstierna, 1635-1641', *BMHG* xxviii (1908), 3–16.

Bronnen tot de geschiedenis der wisselbanken (Amsterdam, Middelburg, Delft, Rotterdam), vol. 1 ed. J.G. van Dillen. RGP gr. ser. 59 (The Hague, 1925).

Bronnen tot de geschiedenis van de Leidsche textielnijverheid, 6 vols. ed. N.W. Posthumus (The Hague, 1910–22).

BRUN, ANTOINE, *Oratie Gedaen door Monsieur D. Antonio de Brvn, Ordinaris Ambassadeur van den Koningh van Spangien. . .den 26 Iunius, Anno 1649* (n. p., 1649), Kn. 6457.

——, *Vertoogh van Antoine de Brun, Raedt ende Ambassadeur van sijne Majesteyt van Spagnien tot bevordering der aengevangen Vredehandelinge tot Munster* (Dordrecht, 1647), Kn. 5448.

CABRERA DE CORDOBA, LUIS DE., *Relaciones de las cosas sucedidas en la corte de España desde 1599 hasta 1614* (Madrid, 1857).

CAPELLEN, ALEXANDER VAN DER, *Gedenkschriften*, 2 vols. (Utrecht, 1777-8).

Capita Selecta Veneto-Belgica, ed. J.J. Poelhekke 1, 1629–31. *Studiën van het Nederlands Historisch Instituut te Rome* (The Hague, 1964).

CASONI, FILIPPO, *Vita del Marchese Ambrogio Spinola. L'Espvgnator delle Piazze* (Genoa, 1691).

Catálogo de las cartas y peticiones del cabildo de San Juan Bautista de Puerto Rico en el Archivo General de Indias (Siglos XVI–XVII), ed. J. J. Real Diaz (San Juan, 1968).

Catálogo de los documentos relativos a los Islas Filipinas existentes en el Archivo de Indias de Sevilla, ed. P. Torres y Lanzas and P. Pastells, 9 vols. (Barcelona, 1925–36).

Cavsas por donde crecio el comercio de Olanda, y se hizo vn monipolio vniversal (n. p. n. d.) [Madrid? *c.* 1645].

CESPEDES Y MENESES, GONZALO DE, *Primera Parte de la Historia de D. Felippe el IIII, Rey de las Españas* (Lisbon, 1631).

CHIFFLET, PHILIPPE, *Le Diaire de Philippe Chifflet. L'Infante Isabelle gouvernante des Pays-Bas à Dvnkerque* (Aug.–Nov. 1625) (Dunkirk, 1926).

Comercio Impedido. Primera Prosposicion, si es util a la Monarchia de España el comercio abierto con Francia y Olanda (by Juan de la Porsa? (Madrid, 1640).

COMMELIN, ISAAK, *Frederik Hendrik van Nassauw, Prince van Orangien, zyn leven en bedrijf* (Amsterdam, 1651).

Compaignon vanden verre-sienden Waerschouwer, thoonende met veele redenen waerom tot bevestinghe vanden staet van dese Landen, den Oorlogh veel dienstiger is dan den Treves, Den (The Hague, 1621), Kn. 3204.

Collección de documentos inéditos para la historia de España (CODOIN) 113 vols. (Madrid, 1842–95).

Consideratien ende redenen der E. Heeren Bewind-hebbers vande Geoctrojeerde West-Indische Compagnie. . .nopende de tegenwoordige deliberatie over den Treves met den Coning van Hispanien (Haarlem, 1629), Kn. 3909.

Consideratien op den Treves ende op het gheen dat by occasie van den Treves in deliberatie ghenomen wordt.

'Considérations d'Estat sur le Traicté de la Paix avec les serenissimes Archiducz d'Austriche' (1607), *Collection de Mémoirs relatifs à l'Histoire de Belgique* xxxii (Brussels, 1869; Kraus repr., 1977).

Copie van een Discours tusschen een Hollander ende een Zeeuw (n. p. 1608), Kn. 1454.

Copie van requesten van de goede gehoorsame Burgeren ende Gemeente deser Stede Amstelredamme (Amsterdam? 1628), Kn. 3813.

Corps universel diplomatique du droit des gens, ed. J. Dumont (8 vols. Amsterdam–The Hague, 1726–31).

Correspondance authentique de Godefroy d'Estrades, ed. A. de Saint Léger and L. Lemaire (Paris, 1924).

Correspondance de la Cour d'Espagne sur les affaires des Pays-Bas au XVIIe siècle, ed. H. Lonchay, J. Cuvelier, and J. Lefèvre (6 vols. Brussels, 1923–37).

Correspondance de Richard Pauli Stravius (1634-1642), ed. W. Brulez, *Analecta Vaticano-Belgica*, 2nd ser. no. X (Brussels–Rome, 1966).

Correspondance du Nonce Fabio de Lagonissa, Archevêque de Conza (1627-1634), ed. L. van Meerbeeck, *Analecta Vaticano-Belgica*, 2nd ser. no. XI. (Brussels–Rome, 1966).

Correspondance de Giovanni Guidi del Bagno (1621-1627), ed. B. de Meester, *Analecta Vaticano-Belgica* 2nd ser. vi (Brussels, 1936-8).

'Correspondencia de D. Jerónimo de Silva con Felipe III y otros sobre las Islas Molucas (1612-1617)', *CODOIN* lii, pp. 1-439.

Correspondencia de la Ciudad de Buenos Aires con los reyes de España, ed. R. R. Levillier, 2 vols. (Buenos Aires, 1915-18).

Correspondencia de la Infanta Archiduquesa Doña Isabel Clara Eugenia de Austria con el duque de Lerma y otros personajes, ed. A. Rodríguez Villa (Madrid, 1906).

'Correspondencia del Archiduque Alberto con D. Francisco de Sandoval y Rojas, marqués de Denia (1598-1611)': i, *CODOIN* xlii. 276-572 and ii, *CODOIN* xliii. 5-220.

Correspondencia diplomática de Francisco de Sousa Coutinho durante a sua embaixada em Holanda, 3 vols. (Coimbra, 1920-55).

Correspondencia diplomática de los plenipotenciarios españoles en el Congreso de Munster (1643-1648), 3 vols., *CODOIN* lxxxii-lxxxiv.

Correspondencia oficial de don Diego Sarmiento de Acuña, conde de Gondomar, 4 vols., *Documentos inéditos para la historia de España* i-iv (Madrid, 1936-45).

Cort verhael dienende tot justificatie vande schutters der stede Leyden (n. p. 1617).

Cort ende Klaer Contra-Discours, Over den Nederlantschen Treves (n. p. 1617) (Kn. 2457).

Cosas notables svcedidas en las costas de la civdad de Lima, en las Indias (Seville, 1625?).

COURT, PIETER DE LA, *Het interest van Holland, ofte grond van Hollands welvaren* (Amsterdam, 1662).

——, *Het welvaren van Leiden: Ms van het jaar 1659*, ed. F. Driessen (The Hague, 1911).

Dagh-Register gehouden int Casteel Batavia vant passerende daer ter plaetse als over geheel Nederlandts India, 1624-1682, 18 vols. (The Hague, 1896-1919).

DECA, LOPE DE, *Govierno Polytico de Agricultura* (Madrid, 1618).

Discours aengaende Treves of Vrede met de Infante ofte Koning van Hispanien (Haarlem, 1629), Kn. 3919.

Discours op den swermenden Treves (Middelburg, 1609), Kn. 1576.

Discovrs overden Nederlandschen Vrede-handel ghestelt door een liefhebber des Vaderlandts (Leeuwarden, 1629), Kn. 3917.

Discurso sobre la importancia de la Guerra maritima, o medio de abaxar el altivez de los Holandeses (Antwerp? 1643).

Druckers Belydenisse, Des, (n. p. 1648) (Kn. 5765).

'Een merkwaardig annvalsplan gericht tegen visscherij en handel der vereenigde Nederlanden in de eerste helft der 17de eeuw', ed. P. J. Block, *BMHG* xix (1898).

Efetos de las Armas Españoles del rey Catolico nuestro señor, en Flandes...deste año de 1638 (Madrid, 1638).

Elementos para a historia do município de Lisboa, ed. E. Freire de Oliveira, 19 vols. (Lisbon, 1882–1943).

Entrada qve el exercito de sv Magestad en Flandes, Hiso en Olanda, en la tierra de equellos Rebeldes, (Seville, 1624).

Famoso Vitoria que ha tenido el señor Infante Cardenal contra el exercito de Olanda, en el sitio de la Ciudad de Gueldres (Seville, 1638).

FERNANDEZ NAVARRETE, PEDRO, *Discvrsos Politicos* (Barcelona, 1621).

FOCKENS, JACOB, *Adoni-Beseck of Lex Talionis, dat is Rechtvaerdige straffe Godts over den Tyrannen* (Delft, 1629), Kn. 3922.

Gazette van Antwerpen. Irregular newsheet (Antwerp, 1619–22).

Gedenkstukken van Johan van Oldenbarnevelt en zijn tijd, vols. 2 and 3, 1593–1609 ed. M. L. van Deventer (The Hague, 1862–5).

Generale Missiven van gouverneurs-generaal en raden aan Heren XVII der Vereenigde Oostindische Compagnie 1 (1610–38) ed. W. P. Coolhaas (The Hague, 1960).

Ghelichte Munstersche Mom-Aensicht, Ofte de Spaensche Eclipse in zijne Nederlanden, Het, (n. p. 1646), Kn. 5326.

Groot Placaet-Boeck, onhoudende de placaten ende ordonnantien vande Hoogh Mog: Heeren Staten Generaal der Vereenighde Nederlanden, vols. i–iii (The Hague, 1658–83).

Groot Utrechts Placaetboek, 3 vols. (Utrecht, 1729).

GROTIUS, HUGO, *Annales et Historiae de Rebus Belgicis* (Amsterdam, 1657).

Haeghs Hof-Praetje, Ofte 't samen-spraeck tusschen een Hagenaer, Amsterdammer, ende Leyenaer op ende tegens de valsche calumnien ende versiende leugenen van Pieter la Court (Leiden, 1662), Kn. 8654.

Historia del Marques Virgilio Malvezzi, in *Memorias para la historia de Don Felipe III Rey de España*, ed. Juan Yañez (Madrid, 1723).

HOEVEN, EMANUEL VAN DER, *Leeven en Dood der Doorlugtige Heeren Gebroeders Cornelis de Witt...en Johan de Witt* (Amsterdam, 1705).

Hollandsche Mercurius, 41 vols. (Haarlem, 1650–91).

Hollandsche Sybille (Amsterdam, 1646), Kn. 5304.

Ivstificatie van de procedueren by schout, burghermeesteren ende regeerders der Stadt Haerlem gehouden aenden Jare XCIc ende zeventhien (Haarlem, 1618), Kn. 2554.

JEANNIN, PIERRE, *Les Négociations de Monsieur le President Jeannin*, 2 vols. (Amsterdam, 1695).

Journalen van de gedenckwaerdige reijsen van Willem Ijsbrantsz. Bontekoe, ed. G.J. Hoogewerff (The Hague, 1952).

'Journalen van den Stadhouder Willem II uit de jaren 1641-50', *BMHG* xxvii (1906).

Junta de Reformación, La, documents ed. Angel González Palencia (Valladolid, 1932).

Klare Aenwijsinge Dat de Vereenigde Nederlanden gheen Treves met den vijandt dienen te maecken (The Hague, 1630), Kn. 4014.

'Koopmansadviezen aangaande het plan tot oprichting eener Compagnie van Assurantie' (1629-35) ed. P. J. Block *BMHG* xxi (1900), 1-160.

Korte Onderrichtinghe ende vermaeninge aen all liefhebbers des Vaderlants om liberalijcken te teeckenen inde West-Indische Compagnie (Leiden, 1622) Kn. 3363.

Kroniek van het Historische Genootschap Gevestigd te Utrecht, 31 vols., (Utrecht, 1846-75).

LAET, JOHANNES DE, *Iaerlyck Verhael van de Verrichtinghen der Geoctroyeerde West-Indische Compagnie* (1644), ed. S. P. L'Honoré Naber, 4 vols. (The Hague, 1931-7).

Lauweren-krans gevlochten voor Sijn Hoocheyt, Wilhelm, de Heer Prince van Oranjen (n. p. 1650) Kn. 6851.

Letters from and to Sir Dudley Carleton, Knt. During his Embassy in Holland, from January 1616 to Dec. 1620, 2nd edn. (London, 1775).

Letters of Peter Paul Rubens, The, trans. and ed. Ruth Saunders Magurn (Harvard, 1955).

Levendich Discours vant ghemeyne lants welvaert voor desen de Oost ende nu oock de West-Indische generale Compaignie aenghevanghen seer notabel om te lesen (Amsterdam, 1622), Kn. 3362.

LISON Y BIEDMA, M., *Discursos y Apuntamientos en que se trata materias importantes del govierno de la Monarchia* (n. p. n. d. *c*. 1626).

LOIS, S., *Cronycke ofte Korte Beschryvinge der Stad Rotterdam* (The Hague-Delft, 1746).

LUNA Y MORA, DIEGO DE, 'Relación de la campaña del año de 1635', *CODOIN* lxxv.

Magasyn van meyneedige ontucht (n. p. 1647) Kn. 5593.

MALVEZZI, VIRGILIO, *Historia de los premeros años del reinado de Felipe IV*, ed. D. L. Shaw (London, 1968).

MEERBEECK, ADRIANUS VAN, *Chroniecke vande Gantsche Werelt, ende sonderlinghe vande seventhien Nederlanden* (Antwerp, 1620).

Mémoires de Frédéric Henri Prince d'Orange (Amsterdam, 1733).

Memorial Histórico Español: colección de documentos opúsculos y antiquedades, 49 vols. (Madrid, 1851-1948).

Memoriales y cartas del conde duque de Olivares: 1, ed. J.H. Elliott and J. F. de la Peña (Madrid, 1978).

METEREN, EMANUEL VAN, *Historie van de Oorlogen en Geschiedenissen der Nederlanderen, en der zelver naburen*, 10 vols. (Gorinchem, 1748-63).

MIJLE, CORNELIS VAN DER, *Ontdeckinge vande valsche Spaensche Jesuijtische practijcke: Ghebruyckt jeghens eenige vande beste patriotten, ende ghetrouste Dienaren van 't Landt* (The Hague, 1618), Kn. 2632.

Missive daer in kortelijk ende grondigh werdt vertoont hoe veel de

*vereenighde Nederlanden ghelegen is aen de Oost ende West-Indische
　Navigatie* (Arnhem, 1621), Kn. 3237.
*Missive Inhoudende den Aerdt vanden Treves tusschen den Koninck
　van Spaengien ende de Gheunieerde Provincien* (n. p. 1630), Kn.
　4023.
Missive uyt Middelburgh aen sijn vrient in Hollandt (Middelburg, 1647),
　Kn. 5496.
MONCADA, SANCHO DE, *Restauración política de España* (Madrid,
　1619).
MONTANUS, ARNOLDUS, *'T vermeerderde Leven en Bedryf van
　Frederik Hendrik, prinse van Oranjen.* (Amsterdam, 1653).
Montstopping aende Vrede-haters (Leiden, 1647), Kn. 5514.
Munsters Praetje. Deliberant dum fingere nesciunt (Deventer, 1646),
　Kn. 5290.
*De Na-Ween vande Vrede. Ofte Ontdeckinge van de kommerlijcke
　ghelegentheyt onses lieven Vaderlants,* (n. p. 1650), Kn. 6756.
Nederlanders op de West-Indische eilanden, De, documents ed. J.H.
　J. Hamelberg, 2 vols. (Amsterdam, 1901–3).
*Nederlandsche Zeevaarders op de Eilanden in de Caraibische Zee en
　aan de Kust van Colombia en Venezuela (1621–1648)* 2 vols., ed.
　I. A. Wright.
*Nederlants Beroerde Ingewanden over de laetste tijdinge van de Mun-
　stersche Vrede handelinge* (n. p. 1647), Kn. 5519.
*Negociación secreta que de orden de Felipe IV llevó a Flandés Francisco
　de Galarreta para hacer la paz con holandeses, CODOIN* lix (Madrid,
　1873), 205–413.
Négociations secrètes touchant la Paix de Munster et d'Osnabrug, ed.
　Jean Le Clerc, 4 vols. (The Hague, 1725).
*Niederländische Akten und Urkunden zur Geschichte der Hanse und
　zur deutschen Seegeschichte,* ed. H. Häpke, 2 vols. (Munich–Leipzig,
　1913–23).
*Nieuwe Lijste van 't Recht vande Licenten datmen voortaan betalen sal
　voor alle toeghelaten ende ghepermitteerde waeren ende coopman-
　schappen* (Antwerp, April 1629).
Notulen der Staten van Zeeland. (Middelburg n. d.).
Oogen-Salve, Voor de Blinde Hollanders (Rotterdam, 1650), Kn. 6852.
*Ordinantie ons Heeren des Conincx, Inhoudende verbodt vanden Coop-
　handel mette gherebelleerde provintien* (Brussels, July 1625).
*Original Unpublished Papers illustrative of the Life of Sir Peter Paul
　Rubens as an artist and a diplomatist, preserved in H.M. State Paper
　Office,* ed. W.N. Sainsbury (London, 1859).
PALAFOX, JUAN DE, 'Informe del Ilmo. señor Don Juan de Palafox
　. . .al conde de Salvatierra, virrey de esta Nueva España' (1642),
　Documentos inéditos o muy raros para la historia de México, ed.
　G. Garcia, vol. vii (Mexico City, 1906).
*Particuliere Artyckelen rakende de schipvaert en Coophandel in ghe-
　volgh vanden Peys* (n. p. 1648).
Piet Heyn en de zilvervloot. Bescheiden uit Nederlandsche en Spaansche

archieven bijeenverzameld, edd. S.P. L'Honoré Naber and I.A. Wright (Utrecht, 1928).

PISE, JOSEPHE DE LA, *Tableau de l'histoire des princes et principauté d'Orange* (The Hague, 1639).

Politiicq Discovrs, over den welstandt van dese vereenichde Provintien nu wederomme met haren vyandt ghetreden zijnde in openbare Oorloghe (n. p. 1622), Kn. 3358.

Provisionele Ordre ende Reglement waer nae de schippers die met hunne schepen van dese Stadt Hoorn, naer West-Indien oft eenige Eylanden daer omtrent om Sout te laden sullen willen varen (Hoorn, 1622).

PUTEANUS, ERIC, *Des Oorlogs ende Vredes Waeg-schale, waer inne den Treves door koninkliijcke aen-leydinge tuschen de koninklijcke ende Vereenigde Provincien in handelinge zijnde wert over-wogen* (The Hague, 1633), Kn. 4304.

Quellen und Forschungen zur Bremischen Handelsgeschichte ii, *Bremen und die Niederlande*, ed. L. Beutin (Weimar, 1939).

Auerela Pacis, dat is Vreden-clacht, Aende Vereenichde Nederlanden (Leeuwarden, 1612), Kn. 1991.

QUEVEDO Y VILLEGAS, FRANCISCO DE, *Obras completas* i, *Obras en prosa*, ed. F. Buendía (Madrid, 1966).

Reden van dat de West-Indische Compagnie oft Handelinge niet alleen profijtelijck maer oock noodtsaeckelijck is tot behoudenisse van onsen Staet. (n. p. 1636).

Redenen waeromme dat de V. Nederlanden, geensints eenighe Vrede met den koningh van Spaignen konnen, mogen, noch behooren te maecken (The Hague, 1630) Kn. 4013.

Relacion cierta del famoso vitoria que tuvo el Capitan Benito Arias Montano, sobrino del doctissimo Arias Montano. . .contra los enemigos Olãdeses (Seville, 1634).

Relacion del Rencuentro qve ha tenido Don Juan Faxardo de Guevara . . .capitan general de la armada real de la guardia del Estrecho de Gibraltar, con ochenta navios de Olanda (Seville, 1622).

Relacion en que se da aviso de como los Olandeses que escaparon de la Rota de los Portugueses de Macan, fueron a la Provincia de Foquin (Seville, 1629).

Relacion verdadera de las Treguas y Paces qve el principe de Orange y las Islas reveladas de Olanda y Gelanda tratan con la señora Infanta doña Ysabel (Seville, 1625).

Relacion verdadera y nueva, de la Victoria que an tenido las Naos de la señora Infanta de Flãdes que estã en Vnquerque (Seville, 1632).

Relazioni veneziane. Venetiaanse berichten over de Vereenigde Nederlanden van 1600–1795, ed. P.J. Blok (The Hague, 1909), RGP no. 7.

Resolutie bij de Heeren Raeden ende Vroetschappen der Stadt Haarlem ghenomen op seeckere Missive aen haerlieden ghesonden van de E. Groot Mogende Heeren Staten van Hollandt. . .nopende 't stuck vanden Treves (Haarlem, 1630) Kn. 4009.

ROCO DE CAMPFRIO, JUAN, *España en Flandes (1595–1608)*, ed. P. Rubio Merino (Madrid, 1973).

450 *Bibliography*

RUYTERS, DIERICK, *Toortse der zeevaert*, ed. S. P. L'Honoré-Naber (The Hague, 1913).

SCHREVELIUS, T., *Harlemias, of Eerste Stchting der Stad Haarlem; haer Toenemen en Vergroten; etc.* (Haarlem, 1754).

Schuyt-praetgens, Op de vaert naer Amsterdam, tusschen een Lantman, een Hovelinck, een Borger, ende Schipper (n. p. 1608) Kn. 1450.

Sir Dudley Carleton's State Papers, during his Embassy at The Hague A.D. 1627, ed. T. Phillipps (London, 1841).

Sources inédites de l'histoire du Maroc, ed. H. de Castries et al., several series (Paris, 1921–56).

Suchtich en Trouwhertich Discours, over dese tegenwoordige gestalte des Lants in bedenckinge van onderhandelinge zijnde met den Coninck van Spaengien (n. p. 1646), Kn. 5312.

Tafels van de Resolutieboeken der Staten van Vlaanderen (1580–1656), 2 vols. (Brussels, 1936–41).

TEELINCK, MAXIMILIAN, *Vrijmoedige Aenspraeck Aen sijn Hoogheyt de Heer Prince van Orangien* (Middelburg, 1650), Kn. 6857.

THURLOE, JOHN, *A Collection of State Papers of John Thurloe*, 7 vols. (London, 1742).

Tuba Pacis, Ofte Baskijne des Vredes tegen het Suchtig en Trouhertig Discours van E. P. (n. p. 1647), Kn. 5503.

USSELINCX, WILLEM, *Discours by forme van Remonstrantye: vervatende de Nootsaeckelickheydt vande Oost-Indische Navigatie* (1608), Kn. 1428.

——, *Grondich Discours over desen aen-staenden Vrede-handel* (n. p. 1608), Kn. 1439.

——, *Naerder Bedenckingen over de zee-vaerdt, Coophandel ende Neeringhe als mede de versekeringhe vanden staet deser vereenichde Landen inde teghenwoordighe vrede-handeling met den Coninck van Spangien* (n. p. 1608), Kn. 1441.

——, *Waerschouwinghe over den Treves met den Coninck van Spaengien aen alle goede Patriotten ghedaen met ghewichtige redenen* (Flushing 1630), Kn. 4016.

VEENENDAAL, A.J. (ed.), *Johan van Oldenbarnevelt. Bescheiden betreffende zijn staatkundig beleid en zijn familie (1602–1620)*, 2 vols. RGP 108, 121 (The Hague, 1962, 1967).

VELIUS, THEODORUS, *Chroniik van Hoorn. . .tot op den jare 1630*, (Hoorn, 1648).

Verdadera relacion en la qval se refiere. . .todo lo que ha sucedido en los estados de Flandes (Seville, 1631).

Verscheyde stvcken raeckende de vrede-handelinge noyt voor desen gedruckt (n. p. 1647), Kn. 5479.

VINCART, JEAN-ANTOINE, *Les Relations militaires des années 1634 et 1635*, ed. M. Huisman et al. (Brussels, 1958).

——, *Les Relations militaires des années 1644 et 1646*, ed. P. Henrard (Brussels, 1869).

—— *Relatión de la campaña de 1636, CODOIN* lix, p. 1–111.

——, *Relación de los progresos de las armas de S.M.. . .del ano 1642, CODOIN* lix. 113–204.

——, *Relación de los sucesos. . .de la camapaña de 1637, CODOIN* xcix. 1-77.

Vitoria famosa qve a tenido el exercito de el rey nuestro señor sobre las Islas reveladas de Olanda (Seville, 1629).

Voortganck vande West-Indische Compaignie (Amsterdam 1623), Kn. 3426.

Vrede-vaen voor alle Liefhebbers vant Vaderlant aen de Edele Mogh. Heeren Staten van Hollant ende West-Vrieslant (n. p. 1627,), Kn. 3763.

Vrymoedich Discovrs op de tegenwoordighe handelingh van Treves (n. p. 1633), Kn. 4301.

WALEN, JOHAN, *Magasyn van meyneedige ontucht ende Bastard Spaensche Moedt-wil* (n. p. 1647), Kn. 5593.

WASSENAER, NICHOLAS VAN, *Historisch Verhael aldaer ghedencwerdichste geschiedenisse, die hier en daer. . .van den beginne des jaers 1621 voorgevallen syn*, 21 vols. (Amsterdam 1622-32).

WICQUEFORT, ABRAHAM De, *Histoire des Provinces-Unies des Pais-Bas*, 4 vols. (Amsterdam 1861-4).

YAÑEZ, JUAN ISIDRO, *Memorias para la Historia de Don Felipe III rey de España* (Madrid, 1723).

SECONDARY SOURCES CITED

ACQUOY, J., *Deventer's participatie in de West-Indische Compagnie* (Deventer, 1922).

ALCALA-ZAMORA Y QUEIPO DE LLANO, *España, Flandés y el Mar del Norte (1618-39)* (Barcelona, 1975).

ARCILA FARIAS, EDUARDO, *Comercio entre Venezuela y México en los siglos XVII y XVIII* (Mexico City, 1950).

BAETENS, R., *De Nazomer van Antwerpens Welvaert*, 2 vols. (Brussels, 1976).

——, 'The organization and effects of Flemish Privateering in the seventeenth century', *Acta Historiae Neerlandicae* ix (1976), 48-75.

BARENDRECHT, S., *François van Aerssen. Diplomaat aen het Franse hof (1598-1613)* (Leiden, 1965).

BAKEWELL, P.J., *Silver Mining and Society in Colonial Mexico. Zacatecas, 1546-1700* (Cambridge, 1971).

BANG, NINA ELLINGER, *Tabeller over skibsfart og varetransport gennem Øresund, 1497-1660*, 2 parts (Copenhagen, 1906-33).

BARBOUR, V., *Capitalism in Amsterdam in the Seventeenth Century* (1950) (Ann Arbor, 1976).

BARROS ARANA, DIEGO, *Historia general de Chile*, 6 vols. (Santiago, 1884-1902).

BASTIN, J., 'De Gentse lijnwaadmarkt en linnenhandel in de xviie eeuw', *Handelingen der Maatschappij voor Geschiedenis en Oudheidkunde te Gent* xxi (1967), 131-62.

BECHT, H.E., *Statistische gegevens betreffende den handelsomzet van de Republiek der Vereenigde Nederlanden gedurende de 17 de eeuw* (The Hague, 1923).

BERING, LIISBERG, *Danmarks Søfart of Søhandel. Fra de Aeldste tider til vore dage*, 2 vols. (Copenhagen, 1919).

BIJLSMA, R., 'Rotterdams Amerikavaart in de eerste helft der zeventiende eeuw', *BVGO* lv (1915), 97–142.

BINDOFF, S.T., *The Scheldt Question to 1839* (London, 1945).

BLUSSE, LEONARD, 'The Dutch Occupation of the Pescadores (1622–1624)', *Transactions of the International Conference of Orientalists in Japan* XVIII (1975), pp. 29–44.

BOER, DE M.G., *Die Friedensunterhandlungen zwischen Spanien und den Niederlanden in den Jahren 1632 und 1633* (Groningen, 1898).

——, 'De hervatting der vijandelijkheden na het twaalfjarig bestand', *TvG* xxxv (1920), pp. 34–49.

——, 'Nogmaals de benoeming van Maarten Harpertsz Tromp tot Luitenant-Admiraal en wat er aan voorafging', *TvG* lv (1940), 337–46.

——, *Het Proefjaar van Maarten Harpertsz. Tromp (1637-9)* (Amsterdam, 1946).

——, *Tromp en de Armada van 1639* (Amsterdam, 1941).

——, *Tromp en de Duinkerkers* (Amsterdam, 1949).

——, 'De verovering der zilvervloot', *TvG* xxxi (1916), 1–16.

BOGUCKA, M., 'Amsterdam and the Baltic in the first half of the seventeenth century', *Econom. Hist. Rev.* 2nd ser., xxvi (1973), 433–47.

BOOY, A. DE, *De derde reis van de VOC naar Oost-Indië onder het beleid van Admiraal Paulus van Caerden uitgezeild in 1606*, 2 vols. (The Hague, 1968–70).

BORDES, P. DE, *De verdediging van Nederland in 1629* (Utrecht, 1856).

BOXER, C.R., *The Dutch in Brazil, 1624-54* (1957, repr. Hamden, Conn., 1973).

——, *Jan Compagnie in War and Peace, 1602-1799* (Hong Kong–Singapore, 1979).

——, *The Journal of Maarten Harpertszoon Tromp. Anno 1639* Cambridge, 1930).

——, 'War and Trade in the Indian Ocean and South China Sea, 1600–1650', *The Great Circle. Journal of the Australian Association for Maritime History*, 1. 3–17.

——, *Salvador de Sá and the Struggle for Brazil and Angola, 1602-1686* (London, 1952).

BRADING, D.A., and CROSS, H.E., 'Colonial Silver Mining: Mexico and Peru', *Hispanic American Historical Review* lii (1972), 545–79.

BRAKEL, S. VAN, 'Bescheiden over den slavenhandel der West-Indische Compagnie', *Economisch-Historisch Jaarboek* iv (1918), 47–83.

BRAND, P.J., *De Geschiedenis van Hulst* (Hulst, 1972).

BRIGHTWELL, P.J., 'The Spanish System and the Twelve Years Truce', *English Historical Review* lxxxix (1974), 270–92.

——, 'The Spanish Origins of the Thirty Years War', *European Studies Review* ix (1979), 409–31.

BRONNER, F., 'La unión de las armas en el Peru. Aspectos político-

legales', *Anuario de Estudios Americanos* xxiv (1967), 1133–73.
BRUIJN, J. R., 'Scheepvaart in de Noordelijke Nederlanden, 1580–1650', *Algemene Geschiedenis der Nederlanden* vii (1980), 137–55.
CABRAL DE MELLO, EVALDO, *Olinda restaurada. Guerra e açúcar no Nordeste, 1630-1654* (Sao Paulo, 1975).
CANABRAVA, A. P., *O comércio português no Rio da Prata (1580–1640) (São Paulo, 1944).*
CARDOT, CARLOS FELICE, 'Algunos acciones de los holandeses en el region del Oriente de Venezuela', *Boletín de la Academia Nacional de la Historia* (Caracas) xlv (1962), 349–72.
CASEY, JAMES, *The Kingdom of Valencia in the Seventeenth Century* (Cambridge, 1979).
CASTILLO PINTADO, ALVARO, *Tráfico marítimo y comercio de importación en Valencia a comienzos del siglo xvii* (Madrid, 1967).
CENTEN, SEBASTIAAN, *Vervolg der Historie van de vermaarde zee-en koop-stad Enkhuizen* (Hoorn, 1747).
CHAUNU, PIERRE and HUGUETTE, *Séville et l'Atlantique, 1504–1650*, 9 vols. in 12 (Paris, 1955–60).
CHRISTENSEN, A. G., *Dutch Trade to the Baltic about 1600* (Copenhagen–The Hague, 1941).
CHUDOBA, BOHDAN, *Spain and the Empire, 1519-1643* (Chicago, 1952).
COLENBRANDER, H. T., *Jan Pietersz. Coen. Levensbeschrijving* (The Hague, 1934).
—, *Koloniale Geschiedenis*, 3 vols. (The Hague, 1925–6).
COLMEIRO, MANUEL, *Historia de la economía política en España*, 2 vols. (Madrid, 1863).
COOLHAAS, W. Ph., 'De verenigde Oostindische Compagnie', *Algemene Geschiedenis der Nederlanden* vi (Utrecht, 1953), 147–82.
COORNAERT, EMILE, *Un Centre industriel d'autrefois. La draperie-sayetterie d'Hondschoote* (Paris, 1930).
CUVELIER, J., 'La correspondance secrète de l'Infante Isabelle (1621–33)', *Bulletin de l'Institut historique belge de Rome* iv (Rome–Brussels, 1924).
—, 'Les négociations de Roosendael (1627–1630); *Mélanges d'histoire offers à Henri Pirenne*, 2 vols. (Brussels, 1926) i. 73–80.
DANVILA, MANUEL, 'Nuevos datos para escribir la historia de las Cortes de Castilla en el reinado de Felipe IV', *Boletín de la Real Academia de la Historia*, xv (1889), 385–433, 497–542.
DELPLANCHE, R., *Un Légiste anversois au service de l'Espagne. Pierre Roose, chef-président du Conseil-Privé des Pays-Bas (1583–1673)* (Brussels, 1945).
DENUCE, J., 'Koningin Christina van Zweden te Antwerpen in 1654 en Don Garcia de Yllan', *Antwerpsch Archievenblad*, 2nd ser. 11 (1927), 31–4.
DEURSEN, A. TH. VAN, *Het kopergeld van de Gouden Eeuw*, 3 vols. thus far (Amsterdam–Assen, 1978).
DEYON, P., 'Variations de la production textile au 16e et 17e siècles', *Annales. E.S.C.* xviii (1963).

454 *Bibliography*

——, and LOTTIN, A., 'Evolution de la production textile à Lille au xvie et xviie siècles', *Revue du Nord* xlix (1967), 23–24.

DICKMANN, FRITZ, *Der Westfälische Frieden* (Munster, 1959).

DIFEREE, H. C., *De geschiedenis van den Nederlandschen handel tot den val der Republiek* (Amsterdam, 1908).

DILLEN, J. G. van, 'Effectenkoersen aan de Amsterdamsche beurs', *Economisch-Historisch Jaarboek* xvii (1931), 1–46.

——, 'Leiden als industriestad tijdens de Republiek', *TvG* lix (1946), 25–51.

——, 'De opstand en het Amerikaanse zilver', *TvG* lxxiii (1960), 25–38.

——, *Het oudste aandeelhoudersregister van de kamer Amsterdam der Oost-Indische Compagnie*, (The Hague, 1958).

——, 'Vreemdelingen te Amsterdam in de eerste helft der 17de eeuw: I, De Portugeesche Joden', *TvG* i (1935), 4–35.

——, 'De West-Indische Compagnie, het Calvinisme en de politiek', *TvG* lxxiv (1961), 145–71.

DISNEY, A. R., *Twilight of the Pepper Empire. Portuguese Trade in southwest India in the early seventeenth century* (Harvard, 1978).

DOLLINGER, PHILIPPE, *The German Hansa*, trans. and ed. D. S. Ault and S. H. Steinberg, (London, 1970).

DOMINGUEZ ORTIZ, ANTONIO, 'Guerra económica y comercio extranjero en el reinado de Felipe IV', *Hispania* xxiii (1963), 71–113.

——, 'Los extranjeros en la vida española durante el siglo xvii', *Estudios de Historia Social de España* iv, ii (1960), 293–426.

——, 'Instituciones políticas y grupos sociales en Castilla durante el siglo xvii', *Annuario dell'Istituto Storico Italiano per l'età moderna e contemporanea* xxix–xxx (1977–8), 115–138.

——, *Alteraciones andaluzas* (Madrid, 1973).

——, *Política y hacienda de Felipe IV* (Madrid, 1960).

——, *La sociedad española en el siglo xvii*, i (Madrid, 1963).

EDMUNDSON, G., 'The Dutch on the Amazon and Negro in the Seventeenth Century', *English Historical Review* xviii (1903), 642–63; xix (1904), 1–25.

ELIAS, H. J., 'Le Renouvellement de la trêve de douze ans entre l'Espagne et les Provinces-Unies. La mission de Chancelier Pecquieu à La Haye (1621)', *Hommage à Dom Ursmer Berlière* (Brussels, 1931), 105–16.

——, 'Het oordeel van een tidgenoot over de hernieuwing van het twaalfjarig bestand (1621)', *Annales de la Societé d'Emulation de Bruges* lxviii (1925), 84–104.

ELIAS, J. E. *De vlootbouw in Nederland, 1596–1655* (Amsterdam, 1933).

——, *Het voorspel van den eersten Engelschen Oorlog*, 2 vols. (The Hague, 1920).

——, *De vroedschap van Amsterdam, 1578–1795*, 2 vols. (Haarlem, 1903–5).

ELLIOTT, J. H., 'América y el problema de la decadencia española', *Anuario de Estudios Americanos* xxviii (1971), 1–23.

——, *El Conde-Duque de Olivares y la herencia de Felipe II* (Valladolid, 1977).

——, *The Revolt of the Catalans. A Study in the Decline of Spain (1598-1640)* (Cambridge, 1963).

ENGELEN, T. L. M., 'Nijmegen in de Zeventiende eeuw.', *Nijmeegse Studiën* VII (Nijmegen, 1978).

EVERAERT, J., 'L'exportation textile des Pays-Bas méridionaux vers le monde hispano-colonial (cr. 1650-1700)', *IISEA* ii. 45-9.

FAULCONNIER, P., *Description historique de Dunquerque, ville maritime et port de mer tres fameux dans la Flandre occidentale*, 2 vols. (Bruges, 1735).

FEIJST, G. VAN DER, *Geschiedenis van Schiedam* (Schiedam, 1975).

FERNANDEZ DURO, CESAREO, *Armada española desde la unión de los reinos de Castilla y de León*, 9 vols. (Madrid, 1895-1903).

FONTANA LAZARO, JOSE, 'Sobre el comercio exterior de Barcelona en la segunda mitad del siglo xvii', *Estudios de Historia Moderna* v (1955), 199-219.

FRUIN, R., 'De bemiddeling tusschen de kronen van Frankrijk en van Spanje door de Staten der vereenigde Nederlanden in 1650 aangeboden', *BVGO* 3rd. ser. x (1897), 197-234.

FUENTES, JULIO, *El Conde de Fuentes y su tiempo* (Madrid, 1908).

GACHARD, L. P., *Histoire politique et diplomatique de Pierre-Paul Rubens* (Brussels, 1877).

GERHARD, P., *Pirates on the West Coast of New Spain, 1575-1742* (Glendale, Calif. 1960).

Geschiedenis van Breda ii, *Aspecten van de stedelijke historie, 1568-1795*, ed. F. A. Brekelmans *et al.* (Schiedam, 1977).

GEYL, PIETER, *Christoforo Suriano. Resident van den serenissime Republiek van Venetië in Den Haag, 1616-1623* (The Hague, 1913).

——, 'Een verzuimde kans: Noord en Zuid in 1632', *Kernproblemen van onze geschiedenis* (Utrecht, 1937).

——, *Geschiedenis van de Nederlandse Stam*, 3 vols. (Amsterdam–Antwerp, 1948-9).

GEZELSCHAP, E., 'De lakennijverheid, 1331-1778', in *Gouda. Zeven Eeuwen Stad. Hoofdstukken uit de geschiedenis van Gouda* (Gouda, 1972).

GIELENS, A., 'Onderhandelingen met Zeeland over de opening der Schelde (1612-1613), *Antwerpsch Archievenblad*, 2nd ser. vi (1931), 194-221.

GIRARD, A., *Le Commerce français à Séville et Cadiz au temps des Habsbourg (Bordeaux-Paris, 1932)*.

GLAMANN, K., *Dutch-Asiatic Trade, 1620-1740* (Copenhagen-The Hague, 1958).

GODOLPHIN, SIR WILLIAM, *Hispania Illustrata, or, The Maxims of the Spanish from the year 1667 to the year 1678* (London, 1703).

GOONEWARDENA, K. W., *The Foundation of Dutch Power in Ceylon (1638-1658)* (Djambatan-Amsterdam, 1958).

GOSLINGA, CORNELIS, *The Dutch in the Caribbean and on the Wilde Coast, 1580-1680)* (Assen, 1971).

GOULD, J. D., 'The Trade Depression of the early 1620s', *Economic History Review*, 2nd ser., vii. 81-9.

GRAAF, H. J. de, *De Regering van Sultan Agung van Mataram, 1613-1645* (The Hague, 1958).

GRAEFE, F., *De Kapiteinsjaren van Maerten Harpertszoon Tromp* (Amsterdam, 1938).

——, 'Vizeadmiral Marinus Hollare und die Blockade der fländrischen Küste', *BVGO* ser. viii, no. 2, pp. 171-210.

GRENDI, E., 'I Nordici e il traffico del porto di Genova, 1590-1665', *Rivista Storica Italiana* lxxxiii (1971), 28-55.

GROENEVELDT, W. P., *De Nederlanders in China*, vol. 1 (The Hague, 1898).

GROENVELD, SIMON, *De Prins voor Amsterdam* (Bussum, 1967).

GROOT, A. H. de, *The Ottoman Empire and the Dutch Republic. A History of the Earliest Diplomatic Relations, 1610-1630* (Leiden-Istanbul, 1978).

GUTMANN, M. P., *War and Rural Life in the Early Modern Low Countries* (Princeton, 1980).

HAAN, HANS de, *Moedernegotie en grote vaart. Een studie over de expansie van het hollandse handelskapitaal in de 16de en 17de eeuw* (Amsterdam, 1977).

HAAS, J. A. K., *De Verdeling van de landen van Overmaas, 1644-1662* (Assen, 1978).

HAGEDORN, B., *Ostfrieslands Handel und Schiffahrt vom Ausgang des 16. Jahrhunderts bis zum Westfälischen Frieden (1580-1648)* (Berlin, 1912).

HALLEMA, A., 'Friesland en de voormalige compagnieën voor den handel op oost en west', *West Indische Gids* xv (1933), 81-96.

HAMEL, J.A. van, *De Eendracht van het land, 1641* (Amsterdam, 1945).

HARSIN, PAUL, 'Etudes sur l'histoire économique de la principauté de Liège, particulièrement au xviie siècle', *Bulletin de l'Institut Archéologique Liégeois* lii (1928), 100-61.

HARTSINCK, J. J., *Beschryving van Guiana, of de Wilde Kust in Zuid-America*, 2 vols. (Amsterdam, 1770).

HEURN, JOHAN HENDRIK VAN, *Historie der stad en Meyerye van 's Hertogenbosch, 4 vols. (Utrecht, 1776-8)*.

HIRSCHAUER, CHARLES, *Les Etats d'Artois de leurs origines à l'occupation française*, 2 vols. (Paris-Brussels, 1923).

HOBOKEN, W. J. van, 'The Dutch West India Company; the Political Background of its Rise and Decline', in *Britain and the Netherlands* 1, ed. J. S. Bromley and E. H. Kossmann (London, 1960), 41-61.

HOOGSTRATEN, F. J. K. van, *Proeve eener geschiedenis der Chambre Mi-Partie in de tweede helft der xviide eeuw te Mechelen en Dordrecht gevestigd* (Utrecht, 1860).

HUBERT, E., *Les Pays-Bas espagnols et la République des Provinces-Unies depuis la paix de Munster jusqu'au traité d'Utrecht (1648-1713)* (Brussels, 1907).

HUET, P. D., *Mémoirs sur le commerce des hollandais* (Paris, 1658).

ISRAEL, JONATHAN I., 'A Conflict of Empires: Spain and the Netherlands, 1618–48', *Past and Present* 76 (Aug. 1977), 34–74.
——, 'The Holland towns and the Dutch-Spanish conflict, 1621–48', *BMGN* 94 (1979), 41–69.
——, 'The Jews of Spanish North Africa, 1600–1669', *Transactions of the Jewish Historical Society of England* xxvi (1979), 71–86.
——, 'Mexico and the 'General Crisis' of the Seventeenth Century', *Past and Present* 63 (May 1974), 33–57.
——, *Race, Class and Politics in Colonial Mexico, 1610–1670* (Oxford, 1975).
——, 'Spain and the Dutch Sephardim, 1609–60', *SRA* xii (1978), 1–61.
——, Some further data on the Amsterdam Sephardim and their trade with Spain during the 1650s', *SRA* xiv (1980), 7–19.
——, 'Spanish Wool Exports and the European Economy, 1610–40', *Economic History Review*, 2nd ser. xxxiii (1980), 193–211.
——, 'The States General and the strategic regulation of the Dutch river trade, 1621–36', *BMGN* 95 (1980), 461–91.
JOHNSON, O. A., 'Les Relations commerciales entre la Norvège et l'Espagne dans les temps modernes', *Revue Historique* clxv (1930), 77–82.
JONGE, J. C. de, *Het Nederlandsche Zeewezen* 5 vols. (Haarlem, 1858–62).
——, *Nederland en Venetië* (The Hague, 1852).
——, *Levensbeschrijving van Johan en Cornelis Evertsen* (The Hague, 1820).
JONGE, J. K. J. de, *De Oorsprong van Nederland's bezittingen op de kust van Guinea* (The Hague, 1871).
JÜRGENS, A., *Zur Schleswig-Holsteinischen Handelsgeschichte der 16. und 17. Jahrhundert* (Berlin, 1914).
KAMEN, HENRY, *Spain in the Later Seventeenth Century, 1665–1700* (London, 1980).
KELLENBENZ, H., *Sephardim an der unteren Elbe* (Wiesbaden, 1958).
——, 'Spanien, die nördlichen Niederlande und der skandinavisch-baltische Raum in der Weltwirtschaft und Politik um 1600', *Vierteljahrschrift für Sozial- und Wirtschaftgeschichte* xli (1954), 289–332.
——, *Unternehmerkrafte im Hamburger Portugal und Spanienhandel, 1590–1625* (Hamburg, 1954).
KEMP, C. M. van der, *Maurits van Nassau. Prins van Oranje in zyn leven, waardigheden en verdiensten*, 4 vols. (Rotterdam, 1843).
KEPLER, J. S., *The Exchange of Christendom. The international Entrepot at Dover, 1622–51* (Leicester, 1976).
KERNKAMP, G. W. *Prins Willem II* (Amsterdam, 1943).
KERNKAMP, J. H., *De Handel op den vijand, 1572–1609*, 2 vols. (Utrecht, 1931–4).
——, *De Economische artikelen inzake Europa van het Munsterse vredesverdrag* (Amsterdam, 1951).
KESLER, C. K., 'Tobago. Een vergeten Nederlandsche kolonie', *West Indische Gids* x (1928), 527–34.

KESSEL, JURGEN, *Spanien und die geistlichen Kurstaaten am Rhein während der Regierungszeit der Infantin Isabella* (1621–33) (Frankfurt, 1979).

KLAVEREN, J. van, *Europäische Wirtschaftgeschichte Spaniens im 16. und 17. Jahrhundert* (Stuttgart, 1960).

KLOMPMAKER, H., 'Handel, geld- en bankwezen in de Noordelijke Nederlanden, 1580-1650', *Algemene Geschiedenis der Nederlanden* vii (1980), 98-127.

KNUTTEL, W. P. C., *Catalogus van de pamfletten-verzameling berustende in de Koninklijke Bibliotheek*, 9 vols. (The Hague, 1889-1920).

KRANENBURG, H. A. H., *De Zeevisscherij van Holland in den tijd der Republiek* (Amsterdam, 1946).

LABAYRU Y GOICOECHEA, E. de, *Historia general del señorío de Bizcaya*, 6 vols. (Bilbao–Madrid, 1895-1903).

LARRAZ, JOSE, *La época del mercantilismo en Castilla (1500-1700)* 2nd edn. (Madrid, 1943).

LEFEVRE, J., 'L'intervention du duc de Lerme dans les affaires des Pays-Bas (1598-1618)', *Revue Belge de Philologie et d'Histoire* xviii (1939), 463-85.

——, *Spinola et la Belgique (1601-1627)* (Brussels, 1947).

LE FLEM, J. P., 'Vraies et fausses splendeurs de l'industrie textile ségovienne (vers 1460-vers 1650), *IISEA* ii. 525-36.

LEMAN, A., 'Urbain VIII et les origines du Congrès de Cologne de 1636', *Revue d'Historie Ecclésiastique* xix (1923), 370-81.

LOHMANN, VILLENA, G., *Las defensas militares de Lima y Callao* (Seville, 1964).

LUZAC, E., *Hollands rijkdom*, 4 vols. (Leiden, 1780).

MACLEOD, M. J., *Spanish Central America. A socio-economic history, 1520-1720* (Berkeley–Los Angeles, 1973).

MAC LEOD, N., *De Oost-Indische Compagnie als zeemogendheid in Azië*, 2 vols. (Rijswijk, 1927).

MALO, H., *Les Corsaires dunquerquois et Jean Bart*, 2 vols. (Paris, 1913-14).

MEILINK-ROELOFSZ, M. A. P., *Asian Trade and European Influence in the Indonesian Archipelago between 1500 and about 1630* (The Hague, 1962).

MENKMAN, W. R., *De Nederlanders in het Caraïbische zeegebied waarin vervat de geschiedenis der Nederlandsche Antillen* (Amsterdam, 1942).

——, 'Van de verovering van Curaçao tot de vrede van Munster', *West Indische Gids* xviii (1935), 65-115.

——, *De West-Indische Compagnie* (Amsterdam, 1947).

MESSOW, HANS-CHRISTOPH, *Die Hansastädte und die Habsburgische Ostseepolitik im 30 jährigen Kriege (1637-8)* (Berlin, 1935).

MULLER, P. L., 'Spanje en de partijen in Nederland in 1650. Uit de correspondentie van Antoine Brun', *BVGO* n. s. vii (1872), 136-83.

NETSCHER, P. M., *Geschiedenis van de kolonien Essequibo, Demerary en Berbice van de vestiging der Nederlanders aldaar tot op onzen tijd* (The Hague, 1888).

NETTESHEIM, FRIEDRICH, *Geschichte der Stadt und des Amtes Geldern* (1863; repr. Geldern, 1963).

NUYENS, W. J. F., *De Nederlandsche Republiek gedurende het twaalf-jarig bestand 1598-1625*, 2 vols. (Amsterdam, 1905).

OLECHNOWITZ, K. F., *Der Schiffbau der Hansischen Spätzeit. Eine Untersuchung zur Sozial- und Wirtschaftgeschichte der Hanse* (Weimar, 1960).

OPSTALL, M. E. van, *De Reis van de vloot van Pieter Willemsz. Verhoeff naar Azië, 1607-12*, 2 vols. (The Hague, 1972).

OUVRE, H., *Aubéry du Maurier. Etude sur l'histoire de la France et de la Hollande, 1566-1636* (Paris, 1853).

PALACIO ATARD, VICENTE, *Derrota, agotamiento, decadencia en la España del siglo XVII*, 2nd edn. (Madrid, 1956).

PALMER, G. A., *Slaves of the White God. Blacks in Mexico, 1570-1650* (Cambridge, Mass., 1976).

PANGE, JEAN de, *Charnacé et l'alliance Franco-Hollandaise (1633-1637)* (Paris, 1905).

PARKER, GEOFFREY, *The Army of Flanders and the Spanish Road, 1567-1659*, 2nd edn. (Cambridge, 1975).

—, *The Dutch Revolt* (London, 1977).

—, *Europe in Crisis, 1592-1648* (London, 1980).

—, *Spain and the Netherlands, 1559-1659* (London, 1979).

PATER, J. C. H. de, *Maurits en Oldenbarnevelt in den strijd om het Twaalf-jarig Bestand* (Amsterdam, 1940).

PEREZ DE TUDELA Y BUESO, *Sobre la defensa hispana del Brasil contra los holandeses (1624-1640)* (Madrid, 1974).

POELHEKKE, J. J., *Geen Blijder Maer in Tachtigh Jaer. Verspreide Studiën over de Crisisperiode, 1648-1651* (Zutphen, 1973).

—, *Frederik Hendrik. Prins van Oranje* (Zutphen, 1978).

—, *De Vrede van Munster* (The Hague, 1948).

—, *'t Uytgaen van den Treves. Spanje en de Nederlanden in 1621* (Groningen 1960).

POHL, HANS, *Die Portugiesen in Antwerpen (1567-1648). Zur Geschichte einer Minderheit* (Wiesbaden, 1977).

—, 'Die Zuckereinfuhr nach Antwerpen durch portugiesische Kaufleute während der 80 jährigen Krieges, *Jahrbuch für Staat, Wirtschaft und Gesselschaft Lateinamerikas* iv. 348-373.

PÓLLENTIER, F., *De Admiraliteit en de oorlog ter zee onder de Aartshertogen (1596-1609)* (Brussels, 1972).

POSTHUMUS, N. W., *De Geschiedenis van de Leidsche Lakenindustrie*, 3 vols. (The Hague, 1908-39).

—, *An Inquiry Into The History of Prices in Holland*, 2 vols. (Leiden, 1946-64).

—, 'De industriëele concurrentie tusschen Noord- en Zuid- Nederlandsche nijverheidscentra in de XVIIe ende XVIIIe eeuw, *Mélanges d'histoire offerts à Henri Pirenne* (Brussels, 1926) i.

RAA, F. J. G. TEN, and F. de BAS, *Het Staatsche Leger, 1568-1795*, 11 vols. (Breda-The Hague).

RATELBAND, K., *De Westafrikaanse Reis van Piet Heyn, 1624-5* (The Hague, 1962).

RAU, VIRGINIA, *A exploraçao e o comércio do sal de Setúbal* 1 (Lisbon 1951).

—, 'Subsidios para o estudo de movimiento dos portos de Faro e Lisboa durante o século XVII., *Academia Portuguesa de Historia Anais*, 2nd ser. v (Lisbon, 1954).

RAYCHAUDHURI, T. *Jan Company in Coromandel, 1605-1690* (The Hague, 1962).

RENIER, G. J., *The Dutch Nation: An Historical Study* (London, 1944).

RESTREPO TIRADO, ERNESTO, *Historia de la provincia de Santa Marta* (Bogotá, 1975).

RODENAS VILAR, RAFAEL, 'Un gran proyecto anti-holandes en tiempo de Felipe IV: la destrucción del comercio rebelde en Europa, *Hispania* xxii (1962).

RODRIGUEZ VICENTE, MARIA ENCARNACION, *El Tribunal del consulado de Lima* (Madrid, 1904).

RODRIGUEZ VILLA, ANTONIO, *Ambrosio Spínola. Primer marqués de los Balbases* (Madrid, 1905).

ROGIER, L. J. *Geschiedenis van het katholicisme in Noord-Nederland in de 16e en 17e eeuw* (2 vols. Amsterdam, 1945-6).

ROWEN, H. H., *John de Witt. Grand Pensionary of Holland, 1625-1672* (Princeton, 1978).

RUIZ MARTIN, FELIPE, 'La empresa capitalista en la industria textil castellana durante los siglos XVI y XVII', *Third International Conference of Economic History, Munich 1965*, 5 vols. (Paris-The Hague, 1968-74) v.

—, 'Un testimonio literario sobre las manifacturas de paños en Segovia por 1625', *Homenaje al Profesor Alarcos*.

SABBE, MAURITS, *Brabant in 't verweer. Bijdrage tot de studie der zuidnederlandsche strijdliteratuur in de eerste helft der 17de eeuw* (Antwerp, 1933).

SABBE, G., *De belgische vlasnijverheid, 1: De zuidnederlandsche vlasnijverheid tot het verdrag van Utrecht* (Bruges, 1943).

SCHNEELOCH, N. H., 'Die Bewindhebber der Westindischen Compagnie in der Kamer Amsterdam, 1674-1700', *Economisch en Sociaal Historisch Jaarboek* xxxvi (1973).

SCHREINER, J., 'Die Niederländer und die Norwegische Holzausfuhr im 17. Jahrhundert', *TvG* slix (1934), 303-28.

SCHURZ, W. L., *The Manila Galleon* (New York, 1939).

SICKENGA, F. W., *Bijdagen tot de geschiedenis der belastingen in Nederland* (Leiden, 1864).

SILVA ROSA, J. S. da, *Geschiedenis der Portugeesche joden te Amsterdam, 1593-1925* (Amsterdam, 1925).

SNAPPER, F., *Oorlogsinvloeden op de overzeese handel van Holland, 1551-1719* (Amsterdam, 1959).

STEENSGAARD, NIELS, *Carracks, Caravans and Companies: the structural crisis in the European Asian trade in the early seventeenth century* (Copenhagen, 1973).

STOLS, EDDY, 'Handel, geld- en bankwezen in de Zuidelijke Nederlanden, 1580-1650', *Algemene Geschiedenis der Nederlanden*, vii (1980), 128-36.

——, *De Spaanse Brabanders of de handelsbetrekkingen der zuidelijke Nederlanden met de Iberische wereld, 1598-1648* (Brussels, 1971).

STRADLING, R. A., 'The Spanish Dunkirkers, 1621-48: a record of plunder and destruction', *TvG* xciii (1980), 541-58.

——, 'A Spanish statesman of appeasement: Medina de las Torres and Spanish policy, 1639-1670', *Historical Journal* xix (1976), 1-31.

STRAUB, EBERHARD, *Pax et Imperium. Spaniens Kampf um seine Friedensordnung in Europa zwischen 1617 und 1635* (Paderborn, 1980).

SUPPLE, B. E., *Commercial Crisis and Change in England, 1600-1642* (Cambridge, 1959).

SWART, K. W., 'The Black Legend during the Eighty Years War', in *Britain and the Netherlands* v (1975), ed. J. S. Bromley and E. H. Kossmann, 36-57.

SWETSCHINSKI, D. M., 'The Spanish Consul and the Jews of Amsterdam', *Texts and Responses: Studies presented to Nahum N. Glatzer* (Leiden, 1975), 158-72.

TERPSTRA, HEERT, *De Nederlanders in Voor-Indië* (Amsterdam, 1947).

TEX, JAN DEN, *Oldenbarnevelt*, 5 vols., (Haarlem-Groningen, 1960-72).

TREVOR-ROPER, H. R., 'Spain and Europe, 1598-1621', *New Cambridge Modern History* iv (1970), 260-82.

TRUCHIS DE VARENNES, A. de, *Antoine Brun (1599-1654). Un diplomate franc-comtois au xviie siècle* (Besançon, 1932).

UNGER, R. W., 'Dutch Herring, Technology, and International Trade in the Seventeenth Century', *Journal of Economic History* xl (1980), 253-79.

VALENTIJN, FRANCOIS, *Oud en Nieuw Oost-Indiën*, ed. S. Keijzer, 3 vols. (Amsterdam, 1760).

VAZQUEZ DE PRADA, VALENTIN, 'La Industria lanera en Barcelona (s. xvi-xviii)' *IISEA* ii. 553-65.

VILA VILAR, ENRIQUETA, *Historia de Puerto Rico (1600-1650)* (Seville, 1974).

VILLARI, ROSARIO, *La rivolta antispagnola a Napoli. Le origini (1585-1647)* (Rome-Bari, 1976).

VOETEN, P., 'Antwerpens handel over Duinkerken tijdens het twaalfjarig Bestand', *Bijdragen tot de Geschiedenis inzonderheid van het oude hertogdom Brabant* xxxix (1956), 67-78.

——, 'Antwerpse reacties op het Twaalfjarig Bestand', *Bijdragen tot de Geschiedenis. . .Brabant* xli (1958), 202-39.

VOGEL, W., 'Beiträge zum Statistik der deutschen Seeschiffahrt im 17. und 18. Jahrhundert', *Hansische Geschichtsblätter* liii (1928), 110-52.

VOORBEIJTEL CANNENBURG, W., *De reis om de wereld van de Nassausche vloot, 1623-1626* (The Hague, 1964).

VREEDE, G. W., *Inleiding tot eene geschiedenis der Nederlandsche diplomatie*, 6 vols. (Utrecht, 1856-65).

VRIES, JAN de, *The Dutch Rural Economy in the Golden Age, 1500-1700* (Yale, 1974).

——, 'An Inquiry into the Behaviour of Wages in the Dutch Republic and the Southern Netherlands, 1580-1800', *Acta Historiae Neerlandicae* x (1978), 79-97.

——, 'Barges and capitalism. Passenger transportation in the Dutch economy, 1632-1839', *Bijdragen Landbouw Hogeschool*, Wageningen: Afdeling Agrarische Geschiedenis, publication no. xxi (Wageningen, 1978).

WADDINGTON, A., *La République des Provinces-Unies, la France, et les Pays-Bas espagnols, 1630-1650*, 2 vols. (Lyons, 1895-7).

WAGENAAR, JAN, *Vaderlandsche Historie, vervattende de geschiedenissen der nu Vereenigde Nederlanden*, 21 vols. (Amsterdam, 1752-9).

——, *Amsterdam in zijne opkomst, aanwas, geschiedenissen, etc.*, 3 vols. (Amsterdam, 1760).

WATJEN, H., *Die Niederländer im Mittelmeergebiet zur Zeit ihrer höchsten Machtstellung* (Berlin, 1909).

——, 'Zur Statistik der Holländischen Heringfischerei im 17. und 18. Jahrhundert', *Hansische Geschichtsblätter* xvi (1910), 129-85.

WEISSER, M., 'The Decline of Castile revisited: The Case of Toledo' *Journal of Eur. Econ. Hist.* ii (1973), 614-31.

WESTERMANN, 'Statistische gegevens over den handel van Amsterdam in de zeventiende eeuw' *TvG* lxi (1948), 3-30.

WILSON, CHARLES, 'Cloth Production and International Competition in the Seventeenth Century' *Econom. Hist. Rev.* 2nd ser. xiii (1960), 209-21.

WINKEL-RAUWS, H. *Nederlandsch-Engelsche Samenwerking in de Spaansche wateren, 1625-1627*, (Amsterdam, 1947).

WINTER, P. J. van, *De Westindische Compagnie ter Kamer Stad en Lande* (The Hague, 1978).

WITTMAN, TIBOR, *Estudios económicos de Hispanoamerica Colonial* (Budapest, 1979).

WIZNITZER, A., *Jews in Colonial Brazil* (New York, 1960).

WORP, J. A., 'Vredesonderhandelingen in 1638 gevoerd' *BVGO* ser. 3, viii. 421-4.

WOUDE, A. M. van der, *Het Noorderkwartier. Een regionaal historisch onderzoek in de demografische en economische geschiedenis van westelijk Nederland*, 3 vols. (Wageninger, 1972).

WRIGHT, I. A., *Historia documentada de San Cristóbal de la Habana en la primera mitad del siglo XVII* (Havana, 1930).
——, *Santiago de Cuba and its District (1607–1640)* (Madrid, 1918).

Index